Volume 2: Implementations

TUTORIAL: Object-Oriented Computing

Gerald E. Peterson

IEEE Computer Society Press   The Institute of Electrical and Electronics Engineers, Inc.

Published by the
IEEE Computer Society Press
10662 Los Vaqueros Circle
PO Box 3014
Los Alamitos, CA 90720-1264

IEEE Computer Society Press Order Number 822
Library of Congress Number 87-80433
IEEE Catalog Number EH0264-2
ISBN 0-8186-0822-6 (paper)
ISBN 0-8186-4822-8 (microfiche)

Additional copies can be ordered from

IEEE Computer Society Press
Customer Service Center
10662 Los Vaqueros Circle
PO Box 3014
Los Alamitos, CA 90720-1264

IEEE Service Center
445 Hoes Lane
PO Box 1331
Piscataway, NJ 08855-1331

IEEE Computer Society
13, avenue de l'Aquilon
B-1200 Brussels
BELGIUM

IEEE Computer Society
Ooshima Building
2-19-1 Minami-Aoyama
Minato-ku, Tokyo 107
JAPAN

Cover designed by Jack I. Ballestero

 THE INSTITUTE OF ELECTRICAL AND ELECTRONICS ENGINEERS, INC.

Preface

Object-oriented computing is a style of computing in which data and associated procedures are encapsulated to form an *object*. An object is a useful computing entity existing at a higher level than procedures or data structures.

Object-oriented computing has gained considerable interest in the last few years. This interest is being fanned by the U. S. Department of Defense's push of Ada, a common (partially) object-oriented language.

This tutorial should be of interest to that group of computer professionals who have heard the term "object-oriented," know it is important, and want to obtain a more substantial understanding of the concept. This group includes
- software engineers
- AI professionals
- professors and students of programming language and computer architecture courses
- those who are building or proposing new computer languages or architectures

Most of the papers are at the level of the practicing computer engineer. Some papers, especially those in Chapters 1 and 2 of Volume 1, are accessible to the computer-knowledgeable layman.

All aspects of object-oriented computing are considered, including object-oriented languages, object-oriented design and development, examples of object-oriented programming, object-oriented databases, and object-oriented computer architectures.

Volume 1 presents the basic concepts of object-oriented programming and describes several object-oriented languages.

An overview of the fundamental ideas of object-oriented programming is given in Chapter 1.

Smalltalk is a language based entirely on the use of objects. Everything in the language, including integers, is an object. A great deal of knowledge about object-oriented computing can be obtained by studying Smalltalk. Chapter 2 is devoted exclusively to this language.

Other languages are supportive of the object philosophy. These languages include Ada, in which objects can be created as packages; Modula-2, in which objects are created as modules; and some dialects of Lisp. The manner in which the object-oriented philosophy can be incorported in these languages is considered in Chapters 3 and 4.

Volume 2 is devoted to the manner in which programs are implemented using object-oriented methods, and the manner in which object-oriented languages are themselves implemented.

It has been found that many problems decompose naturally into objects and messages that pass between them. Object-oriented development is the process of decomposing a problem into objects and messages and maintaining these structures in the implementation. Object-oriented development techniques and examples of their use are presented in Chapter 1.

Much insight into the nature of object-oriented programming can be obtained by studying examples where it was successfully put to use. Several examples of object-oriented programming are considered in Chapter 2.

The biggest problem with languages that fully support the object-oriented philosophy is efficient implementation. On a dedicated processor costing in the neighborhood of $100K, Smalltalk runs satisfactorily. On less expensive machines, however, Smalltalk implementations have been too slow to be practical for large programs. Chapter 3 contains many ideas about how to overcome this problem.

Several important concepts and issues that did not fit in other chapters are considered in Chapter 4.

Object-oriented computer architectures have also been addressing, which have guided these implementations. Several examples of object-based architectures are described in Chapter 6. These include the Intel iAPX 432 and the IBM System/38.

Gerald E. Peterson

Acknowledgments

The author wishes to thank the McDonnell Douglas Astronautics and Aerospace Information Services Companies for providing a pleasant climate in which this work could be undertaken. This tutorial resulted from studies which were undertaken in order to improve the manner in which software is developed at McDonnell Douglas Corporation.

Table of Contents

Chapter 1: Object-Oriented Design

Object-oriented design is the process of decomposing a program into objects and establishing the relations between them. Ideally, object-oriented design would be part of a software development process in which an object-oriented philosophy was used in every life-cycle phase. However, little is known about object-oriented requirements creation or object-oriented testing. Thus, we are content to focus our attention on only two phases of the life-cycle: implementation and design. All of Volume 1 and Chapter 2 of this volume are concerned with the implementation phase. Design is covered here.

Object-oriented design is neither a functional nor a data decomposition process. Instead, it seeks to identify those objects in the real world that must be manipulated to effect a solution to the user's problem. Then, these real world objects are simulated in the computer with corresponding software objects that mirror their behavior.

This design philosophy views all programs as simulations of some external process that humans could perform if they were fast enough. The program is simply the image in the computer of the process in the outside world.

For example, suppose an index of a book has to be made. In doing this by hand we would examine each word, associate it with its page number, and add this association to an intermediate form of the index. This intermediate form would be kept in some kind of random access structure, perhaps a card file. After all words had been added to the intermediate file, the index would be typed in alphabetical order.

The objects being manipulated in this process are the book, the intermediate form, and the final index. In creating a computer solution to the problem, corresponding objects would be created in the program. (See Figure 1.) The book would be a text file together with a procedure for accessing the next word and its page number. The intermediate form would be a set of associations, that is, a dictionary, together with the operations of adding a new association and creating a text file with the associations in alphabetical order. The final index would be this text file.

An overriding concern when creating software designs is the identity of the implementation language. For object-oriented designs it is helpful if the implementation language supports object-oriented features. We consider here the trade offs between using Ada and Smalltalk as the implementation language.

Smalltalk is more object-oriented than Ada primarily because Smalltalk supports an inheritance mechanism, but Ada does not. However, Ada has a strong typing mechanism that is lacking in Smalltalk. Ada's strength is safety; Smalltalk's is flexibility. For certain systems, safety is more important that flexibility. Thus, even when using an object-oriented design methodology, for which Smalltalk provides a better matching target language, Ada may be the implementation language of choice. Grady Booch's point of view is that object-oriented design followed by an Ada implementation is a very powerful combination.

Booch's paper, ''Object-Oriented Development,'' describes an approach to object-oriented design that begins with a data flow diagram, decomposes it into objects, finds the dependencies between objects, and maps the design to an Ada program with each object becoming a package. Booch uses an important graphical notation for Ada objects, now called a *Booch-gram*, which is helpful in visualizing the structure of the entire system and in realizing the Ada implementation. More information can be found in Booch's *Software Engineering with Ada,* which is described in Additional References.

Ed Seidewitz and Mike Stark, in ''Towards a General Object-Oriented Software Development Methodology,'' describe a diagramming technique called an *object diagram* for object-oriented design, which is similar to Booch-grams, but is simpler and independent of any programming language. Each object is a node of a graph, and if object A uses any resources of object B, then there is an arrow from A to B. In addition to the graph, for each object there is an *object description*, which is a list of the operations the object provides and for each outgoing arrow, the operations it uses.

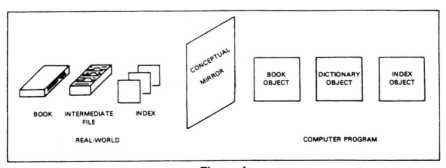

Figure 1

Seidewitz and Stark then describe how to obtain an object-oriented design in the form of an object diagram from a data flow diagram. The key problem is to identify the objects. Once the top-level design is complete, each top-level object may be decomposed into sub-objects. Then each object is implemented in the target language. The methodology appears to be simple and effective.

Richard F. Sincovec and Richard S. Wiener in "Modular Software Construction and Object-Oriented Design Using Ada," present principles and methods similar to those in the previous two papers. They apply their method to a specific problem: that of finding the youngest common ancestor connecting two arbitrary nodes in a binary tree. In presenting the solution, they introduce a modular design chart, which is the most interesting aspect of the paper. Like Booch-grams and object diagrams, each object is represented by a rectangle. Within each object, the types and operations that make up its interface to the outside world are listed. The dependencies, however, are somewhat more specific than in object diagrams or Booch-grams. Each operator or data type is shown connected to those other objects that make use of it in their processing. This connection is shown going through what the authors call a *software bus*. The modular design chart is in essence a combination of the object diagram and the object descriptions of Seidewitz and Stark.

The manner of representing a software design is a very important part of any design methodology. The first three papers have different but similar graphical representations of an object-oriented design. In comparing these, we see that object diagrams are the most general, showing only the objects and dependencies between full objects. Booch-grams show these and also an icon for each procedure or type provided by the object. Modular design charts contain the most information. They show, in addition, the names of the operations or types provided by each object and the dependencies that objects have on the parts of other objects. It is not clear which of these is the most valuable; what is clear is that a graphical representation of an object-oriented design is very helpful and, at the very least, an object diagram should be provided to help anyone who is studying the design.

"Reusability: The Case for Object-Oriented Design," by Bertrand Meyer, is based on the thesis that "object-oriented design is the most promising technique now known for attaining the goal of reusability." Meyer describes why creating reusable software components has been difficult in the past. The problem is that although two software elements may be based on the same algorithm, there is too much variation in details. This could be overcome if it were possible to program at a high enough level of abstraction. Approaches to overcoming the problem include modular languages, overloading of operators, and generic routines. However, Meyer found that none of these approaches really solves the problem. The idea that does work is object-oriented programming in a language that supports inheritance. This is illustrated by using an interactive program that provides full-screen panels for user guidance at each stage of processing.

The kernel of the idea of using inheritance to create reusable software will be illustrated with a small example taken from Smalltalk/V. In Smalltalk, one of the primary class hierarchies is that of *Collection*. In fact, Collection is a subclass of Object and some of the subclasses of Collection are

   Bag
   Indexed Collection
      FixedSize Collection
        Array
        Bitmap
        ByteArray
        String
      Ordered Collection
        SortedCollection
  Set
    Dictionary
      Identity Dictionary
    SymbolSet

in which indentation represents subclassing. Now, what can be programmed in class Collection that could be useful in all of these subclasses? Suppose that an *Add* method, which adds an element to a collection, is available in every subclass, and suppose that a *Do* method, which iterates over every element in the collection, is also available in every subclass. Further, suppose that *Add* has the same syntax in each of the subclasses, and *Do* has the same syntax in each of the subclasses. Then, if A and B are both Collections, a method *A AddAll B, which adds every element of B to A,* can be defined by using *Do* to iterate over the elements of *B*. As each is processed, *Add* is used to add it to *A*. *AddAll* will be inherited by every subclass of Collection and will work without modification for all of the subclasses.

Another way to promote reusability is to create software components that are easy to mold into something new. The idea is to design in such a way that any changes will be localized in a single module. The problem with this approach is in knowing in advance which things in a system will change. Some possible changes may be clear (e.g., new hardware is known to be coming), but other changes will certainly come as surprises. The object point of view helps to overcome this problem. The software mirrors some physical process dealing with tangible objects, and changes are likely to be to the individual objects. This means that changes in the software are likely to be confined to single modules that implement the objects. Thus, object-oriented design has automatically caused a module decomposition that will foster reusability.

The final paper, "Object-Oriented Design and Ballistics Software," by Mark Temte, is included because it contains a more realistic example of object-oriented design. The example is that of calculating ballistics for various weapons and shells. Four objects, each containing several operations, are created in the top level of the decomposition. Then Temte illustrates how to iterate the object-oriented design process to lower levels of the decomposition. One path is taken to the lowest level of decomposition, and the objects created along the way are described and diagrammed with Booch-grams.

Additional References

G. Booch, *Software Engineering with Ada*, 2nd edition, Benjamin/Cummings, Menlo Park, Calif., 1986.

This book contains a description of the Ada language and principles of software engineering that mesh well with Ada programming. It explains an object-oriented development methodology and presents five completely worked-out examples including the Ada programs that result.

G. Booch, *Software Components with Ada: Structures, Tools, and Subsystems*, Benjamin/Cummings, Menlo Park, Calif., 1987.

Contains the definitions of many abstract data types and their concrete realizations as Ada objects. It includes implementations of stacks, lists, strings, queues, dequeues, rings, maps, sets, bags, trees, graphs, filters, pipes, sorting, and searching.

EVB Software Engineering, Inc., *Object Oriented Design Handbook*, Benjamin/ Cummings, Menlo Park, Calif., 1987.

This is a very detailed explanation of object-oriented design as espoused by Booch.

D.L. Parnas, "On the Criteria to Be Used in Decomposing Systems into Modules," *Communications of the ACM*, Volume 15, Number 12, December 1972, pages 1053-1058.

An extremely insightful paper in which the idea of information hiding was first presented. Many concepts relating to object-oriented programming are evident here.

R.J. Abbott, "Program Design by Informal English Descriptions," *Communications of the ACM*, Volume 26, Number 11, November 1983, pages 882-894.

A seminal paper in which key ideas related to object-oriented design were first described. Abbott's idea of using the nouns of an informal description as possible objects and the verbs as possible operations is carefully explained by using examples.

J. Hemenway, "Object-Oriented Design Manages Software Complexity," *EDN*, August 19, 1981, pages 141-146.

W. Cunningham and K. Beck, "A Diagram for Object-Oriented Programs," *OOPSLA '86, SIGPLAN Notices*, ACM, Inc., New York, New York, Volume 21, Number 11, November 1986, pages 361-367.

Describes a diagramming technique for object-oriented design similar to Sincovec and Wiener's modular design chart.

I. Jacobson, "Language Support for Changeable Large Real Time Systems," *OOPSLA '86, SIGPLAN Notices*, ACM, Inc., New York, New York, Volume 21, Number 11, November 1986, pages 377-384.

Describes a set of concepts used for modeling large real time systems at Ericsson Telecom.

Object-Oriented Development

GRADY BOOCH, MEMBER, IEEE

Abstract—Object-oriented development is a partial-lifecycle software development method in which the decomposition of a system is based upon the concept of an object. This method is fundamentally different from traditional functional approaches to design and serves to help manage the complexity of massive software-intensive systems. The paper examines the process of object-oriented development as well as the influences upon this approach from advances in abstraction mechanisms, programming languages, and hardware. The concept of an object is central to object-oriented development and so the properties of an object are discussed in detail. The paper concludes with an examination of the mapping of object-oriented techniques to Ada® using a design case study

Index Terms—Abstract data type, Ada, object, object-oriented development, software development method.

I. INTRODUCTION

RENTSCH predicts that "object-oriented programming will be in the 1980's what structured programming was in the 1970's" [1]. Simply stated, *object-oriented development* is an approach to software design in which the decomposition of a system is based upon the concept of an object. An *object* is an entity whose behavior is characterized by the actions that it suffers and that it requires of other objects.

Object-oriented development is fundamentally different from traditional functional methods, for which the primary criteria for decomposition is that each module in the system represents a major step in the overall process. The differences between these approaches becomes clear if we consider the class of languages for which they are best suited.

The proper use of languages like Ada and Smalltalk requires a different approach to design than the approach one typically takes with languages such as Fortran, Cobol, C, and even Pascal. Well-structured systems developed with these older languages tend to consist of collections of subprograms (or their equivalent), mainly because that is structurally the only major building block available. Thus, these languages are best suited to functional decomposition techniques, which concentrate upon the algorithmic abstractions. But as Guttag observes, "unfortunately, the nature of the abstractions that may be conveniently achieved through the use of subroutines is limited. Subroutines, while well suited to the description of abstract events (operations), are not particularly well suited to the

Manuscript received June 17, 1985.
The author is with Rational, Mountain View, CA 94043.
IEEE Log Number 8405735.
®Ada is a registered trademark of the U.S. Department of Defense (Ada Joint Program Office).

description of abstract objects. This is a serious drawback" [2].

Languages like Ada also provide the subprogram as an elementary building block. However, Ada additionally offers the package and task as major structural elements. The package gives us a facility for extending the language by creating new objects and classes of objects, and the task gives us a means to naturally express concurrent objects and activities. We can further extend the expressive power of both subprograms and packages by making them generic. Together, these facilities help us to better build abstractions of the problem space by permitting a more balanced treatment between the nouns (objects) and verbs (operations) that exist in our model of reality.

Of course, one can certainly develop Ada systems with the same methods as for these more traditional languages, but that approach neither exploits the power of Ada nor helps to manage the complexity of the problem space.

In general, functional development methods suffer from several fundamental limitations. Such methods
• do not effectively address data abstraction and information hiding;
• are generally inadequate for problem domains with natural concurrency;
• are often not responsive to changes in the problem space.
With an object-oriented approach, we strive to mitigate these problems.

Before we get too detailed, let us consider alternate designs for a simple real-time system using functional and object-oriented techniques.

A cruise-control system exists to maintain the speed of a car, even over varying terrain [3]. In Fig. 1 we see the block diagram of the hardware for such a system. There are several inputs:

• System on/off	If on, denotes that the cruise-control system should maintain the car speed.
• Engine on/off	If on, denotes that the car engine is turned on; the cruise-control system is only active if the engine is on.
• Pulses from wheel	A pulse is sent for every revolution of the wheel.
• Accelerator	Indication of how far the accelerator has been

Reprinted from *IEEE Transactions on Software Engineering*, Volume SE-12, Number 2, February 1986, pages 211-221. Copyright © 1986 by The Institute of Electrical and Electronics Engineers, Inc.

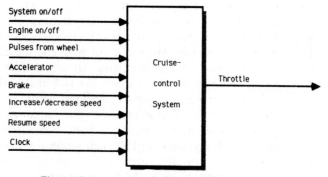

Fig. 1. Cruise-control system hardware block diagram.

- **Brake** — On when the brake is pressed; the cruise-control system temporarily reverts to manual control if the brake is pressed.

- **Increase/Decrease Speed** — Increase or decrease the maintained speed; only applicable if the cruise-control system is on.

- **Resume** — Resume the last maintained speed; only applicable if the cruise-control system is on.

- **Clock** — Timing pulse every millisecond.

There is one output from the system:

- **Throttle** — Digital value for the engine throttle setting.

How might we approach the design of the software for the cruise control system? Using either functional or object-oriented approaches, we might start by creating a data flow diagram of the system, to capture our model of the problem space. In Fig. 2, we have provided such a diagram, using the notation by Gane and Sarson [4].

With a functional method, we would continue our design by creating a structure chart. In Fig. 3, we have used the techniques of Yourdon and Constantine [5] to decompose the system into modules that denote the major functions in the overall process.

With an object-oriented approach, we proceed in an entirely different manner. Rather than factoring our system into modules that denote operations, we instead structure our system around the objects that exist in our model of reality. By extracting the objects from the data flow diagram, we generate the structure seen in Fig. 4. We will more fully explain the process and the meaning of the symbols used in the figure later. For the moment, simply recognize that the amorphous blobs denote objects and the directed lines denote dependencies among the objects.

Immediately, we can see that the object-oriented decomposition closely matches our model of reality. On the other hand, the functional decomposition is only achieved through a transformation of the problem space. This latter design is heavily influenced by the nature of the subpro-

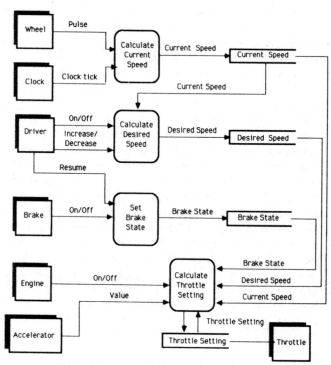

Fig. 2. Cruise-control system data flow diagram.

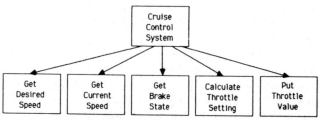

Fig. 3. Functional decomposition.

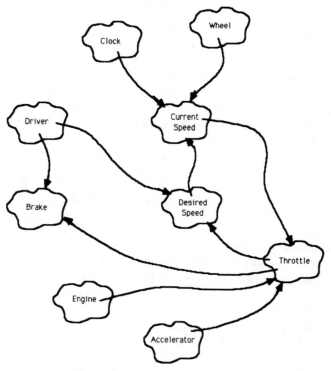

Fig. 4. Object-oriented decomposition.

6

gram and so emphasizes only the algorithmic abstractions that exist. Hence, we can conclude that a functional decomposition is imperative in nature: it concentrates upon the major actions of a system and is silent on the issue of the agents that perform or suffer these actions.

The advantages of the object-oriented decomposition are also evident when we consider the effect of change (and change will happen to any useful piece of software). One side-effect of the functional decomposition is that all interesting data end up being global to the entire system, so that any change in representation tends to affect all subordinate modules. Alternately, in the object-oriented approach, the effect of changing the representation of an object tends to be much more localized. For example, suppose that we originally chose to represent car speed as an integer value denoting the number of wheel revolutions per some time unit (which would not be an unreasonable design decision). Suppose that we are now told to add a digital display that indicates the current speed in miles per hour. In the functional decomposition, we might be forced to modify every part of the system that deals with the representation of speed, as well as to add another major module at the highest level of the system to manage the display. However, in the object-oriented decomposition, such a change directly affects only two objects (current speed and desired speed) and would require the addition of one more object (the display) that directly parallels our modification of reality.

Regarding an even more fundamental change, suppose that we chose to implement our cruise-control system using two microcomputers, one for managing the current and desired speeds and the second to manage the throttle. To map the functional decomposition to this target architecture requires that we split the system design at the highest level. For the object-oriented approach, we need make no modification at this level of the design to take advantage of the physical concurrency.

II. Object-Oriented Development

Let us examine the process of object-oriented development more closely. Since we are dealing with a philosophy of design, we should first recognize the fundamental criteria for decomposing a system using object-oriented techniques:

Each module in the system denotes an object or class of objects from the problem space.

Abstraction and information hiding form the foundation of all object-oriented development [6], [7]. As Shaw reports, "an abstraction is a simplified description, or specification, of a system that emphasizes some of the system's details or properties while suppressing others" [8]. Information hiding, as first promoted by Parnas, goes on to suggest that we should decompose systems based upon the principle of hiding design decisions about our abstractions [9].

Abstraction and information hiding are actually quite natural activities. We employ abstraction daily and tend to develop models of reality by identifying the objects and

operations that exist at each level of interaction. Thus, when driving a car, we consider the accelerator, gauges, steering wheel, and brake (among other objects) as well as the operations we can perform upon them and the effect of those operations. When repairing an automobile engine, we consider objects at a lower level of abstraction, such as the fuel pump, carburetor, and distributor.

Similarly, a program that implements a model of reality (as all of them should) may be viewed as a set of objects that interact with one another. We will study the precise nature of objects in the following section, but next, let us examine how object-oriented development proceeds. The major steps in this method are as follows:

• Identify the objects and their attributes.
• Identify the operations suffered by and required of each object.
• Establish the visibility of each object in relation to other objects.
• Establish the interface of each object.
• Implement each object.

These steps are evolved from an approach first proposed by Abbott [10].

The first step, *identify the objects and their attributes*, involves the recognition of the major actors, agents, and servers in the problem space plus their role in our model of reality. In the cruise-control system we identified concrete objects such as the accelerator, throttle, and engine and abstract objects such as speed. Typically, the objects we identify in this step derive from the nouns we use in describing the problem space. We may also find that there are several objects of interest that are similar. In such a situation, we should establish a class of objects of which there are many instances. For example in a multiple-window user interface, we may identify distinct windows (such as a help window, message window, and command window) that share similar characteristics; each object may be considered an instance of some window class.

The next step, *identify the operations suffered by and required of each object*, serves to characterize the behavior of each object or class of objects. Here, we establish the static semantics of the object by determining the operations that may be meaningfully performed on the object or by the object. It is also at this time that we establish the dynamic behavior of each object by identifying the constraints upon time or space that must be observed. For example, we might specify that there is a time ordering of operations that must be followed. In the case of the multiple-window system, we should permit the operations of open, close, move, and size upon a window object and require that the window be open before any other operation be performed. Similarly, we may constrain the maximum and minimum size of a particular window.

Clearly, the operations suffered by an object define the activity of an object when acted upon by other objects. Why must we also concern ourselves with the operations required of an object? The answer is that identifying such operations lets us decouple objects from one another. For example, in the multiple-window system we might assume the existence of some terminal object and require the operations of Move__Cursor and Put. As we will see later, languages such as Ada provide a generic mechanism that can express these requirements. The result is that we can derive objects that are inherently reusable because they are not dependent upon any specific objects, but rather depend only upon other classes of objects.

In the third step, to *establish visibility of each object in relation to other objects*, we identify the static dependencies among objects and classes of objects (in other words, what objects see and are seen by a given object). The purpose of this step is to capture the topology of objects from our model of reality.

Next, to *establish the interface of each object*, we produce a module specification, using some suitable notation (in our case, Ada). This captures the static semantics of each object or class of objects that we established in a previous step. This specification also serves as a contract between the clients of an object and the object itself. Put another way, the interface forms the boundary between the outside view and the inside view of an object.

The fifth and final step, *implement each object*, involves choosing a suitable representation for each object or class of objects and implementing the interface from the previous step. This may involve either decomposition or composition. Occasionally an object will be found to consist of several subordinate objects and in this case we repeat our method to further decompose the object. More often, an object will be implemented by composition; the object is implemented by building on top of existing lower-level objects or classes of objects. As a system is prototyped, the developer may chose to defer the implementation of all objects until some later time and just rely upon the specification of the objects (with suitably stubbed implementations) to experiment with the architecture and behavior of a system. Similarly, the developer may chose to try several alternate representations over the life of the object, in order to experiment with the behavior of various implementations.

We must point out that object-oriented development is a partial-lifecycle method; it focuses upon the design and implementation stages of software development. As Abbott observes, "although the steps we follow in formalizing the strategy may appear mechanical, it is not an automatic procedure. . . [it] requires a great deal of real world knowledge and intuitive understanding of the problem" [11]. It is therefore necessary to couple object-oriented development with appropriate requirements and analysis methods in order to help create our model of reality. We have found Jackson Structured Development (JSD) to be a promising match [12] and recently, there has been interest in maping requirements analysis techniques such as SREM to object-oriented development [13].

Systems designed in an object-oriented manner tend to exhibit characteristics quite different than those designed with more tranditional functional approaches. As Fig. 5 illustrates, large object-oriented systems tend to be built in layers of abstraction, where each layer denotes a collection of objects and classes of objects with restricted vis-

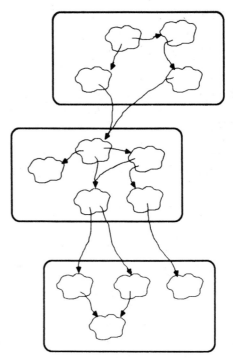

Fig. 5. Canonical structure of large object-oriented systems.

ibility to other layers; we call such a collection of objects a *subsytem*. Furthermore, the components that form a subsystem tend to be structurally flat (like we saw in Fig. 4), rather than being stricly hierarchical and deeply nested.

It is also the case that the global flow of control in an object-oriented system is quite different from that of a functionally decomposed system. In the latter case, there tends to be a single thread of control that follows the hierarchical lines of decomposition. In the case of an object-oriented system, because objects may be independent and autonomous, we typically cannot identify a central thread of control. Rather, there may be many threads active simultaneously throughout a system. This model is actually not a bad one, for it more often reflects our abstraction of reality. We should add that the subprogram call profile of an object-oriented system typically exhibits deeply nested calls; the implementation of an object operation most often involves invoking operations upon other objects.

There are many benefits to be derived from an object-oriented approach. As Buzzard notes, "there are two major goals in developing object-based software. The first is to reduce the total life-cycle software cost by increasing programmer productivity and reducing maintenance costs. The second goal is to implement software systems that resist both accidental and malicious corruption attempts" [14]. Giving empirical evidence that supports these points, a study by Boehm-Davis notes that "the completeness, complexity, and design time data would seem to suggest that there is an advantage to generating program solutions using. . .object-oriented methods" [15]. Regarding the maintainability of object-oriented systems, Meyer observers that "apart from its elegance, such modular, object-oriented programming yields software products on which modifications and extensions are much easier to perform than with programs structured in a more conventional, procedure-oriented fashion" [16]. In general, understandability and maintainability are enhanced due to the fact that objects and their related operations are localized.

Perhaps the most important benefit of developing systems using object-oriented techniques is that this approach gives us a mechanism to formalize our model of reality. As Borgida notes, "the chief advantage of object-oriented frameworks is that they make possible a direct and natural correspondence between the world and its model" [17]. This even applies to problems containing natural concurrency, for as the Boehm-Davis study reports, "the object-oriented method seemed to produce better solutions for [a problem] which involved real-time processing" [18].

III. The Properties of an Object

The notion of an object plays the central role in object-oriented systems, but actually, the concept is not a new one. Indeed, as MacLenna reports, "programming is object-oriented mathematics" [19]. Lately, we have observed a confluence of object-oriented work from many elements of computer science. Levy suggests that the following events have influenced object-oriented development [20]:
• advances in computer architecture, including capability systems and hardware support for operating systems concepts;
• advances in programming languages, as demonstrated in Simula, Pascal, Smalltalk, CLU, and Ada;
• advances in programming method, including modularization and information hiding and monitors.
We would add to this list the work on abstraction mechanisms by various researchers.

Perhaps the first person to formally identify the importance of composing systems in levels of abstraction was Dijkstra [21]. Parnas later introduced the concept of information hiding [9] which, as we will discuss later, is central to the nature of an object. In the 1970's, a number of researchers, most notably Liskov, Guttag, and Shaw, pioneered the development of abstract data type mechanisms [22]–[24]. The late 1970's and early 1980's also saw the application of a number of software development methods (such as JSD) that were declarative rather than imperative in nature.

The greatest influence upon object-oriented development derives from a small number of programming languages. SIMULA 67 first introduced the class as a language mechanism for encapsulating data, but, as Rentsch reports, "the Smalltalk programming system carried the object-oriented paradigm to a smoother model." Indeed, "the explicit awareness of the idea, including the term object-oriented, came from the Smalltalk effort" [1]. Other object-oriented languages such as Ada and Clascal followed the more tranditional path of SIMULA, but in the early 1980's we also saw a number of languages merge the concepts of Lisp and Smalltalk; thus evolved languages such as Flavors and LOOPS. It is also clear that Lisp alone may be effectively used to apply object-oriented techniques [25]. More recently, there has been work to add Smalltalk constructs to C, resulting in a language named Objective-C [26]. Languages such as Smalltalk have collectively been called actor languages, since they emphasize the role of entities as actors, agents, and servers in the structure of the real world [27].

Interestingly, the concept of an object has precedence in hardware. Work with tagged architectures and capability-based systems has led to a number of implementations that we can classify as object-oriented. For example, Myers reports on two object-oriented architectures, SWARD and the Intel 432 [28]. The IBM System 38 is also regarded as an object-oriented architecture [29].

Every source we have introduced presents a slightly different view of object-oriented systems, but from this background we can extract the common properties of the concept. Thus, we may define an object as an entity that:
• has state;
• is characterized by the actions that it suffers and that it requires of other objects;
• is an instance of some (possibly anonymous) class;
• is denoted by a name;
• has restricted visibility of and by other objects;
• may be viewed either by its specification or by its implementation.
The first and second points are the most important: an object is something that exists in time and space and may be affected by the activity of other objects. The state of an object denotes its value plus the objects denoted by this value. For example, thinking back to the multiple-window system we discussed in the first section, the state of a window might include its size as well as the image displayed in the window (which is also an object). Because of the existence of state, objects are not input/output mappings as are procedures or functions. For this reason, we distinguish objects from mere processes, which are input/output mappings.

From Smalltalk, we get the notion of a method, which denotes the response by an object to a message from another object. The activity of one method may pass messages that invoke the methods of other objects. Abstract data types deal with operations is a related way. Liskov suggests that such operations be divided "into two groups: those which do not cause a state change but allow some processes. Whereas a aspect of the state to be observed…and those which cause a change of state" [30]. In practice, we have encountered one other useful class of operations, the iterator, which permits us to visit all subcomponents of an object. The concept of an iterator was formalized in the language Alphard [31]. For example, given an instance of a terminal screen, we may wish to visit all the windows visible on the screen.

Together, we may classify these operations as follows:
• *Constructor:* An operation that alters the state of an object.

- *Selector:* An operation that evaluates the current object state.
- *Iterator:* An operation that permits all parts of an object to be visited.

To enhance the reusability of an object or class of objects, these operations should be primitive. A primitive operation is one that may be implemented efficiently only if it has access to the underlying representation of the object. In this sense, the specification of an object or class of objects should define "the object, the whole object, and nothing but the object."

We may classify an object as an actor, agent, or server, depending upon how it relates to surrounding objects. An actor object is one that suffers no operations but only operates upon other objects. At the other extreme, a server is one that only suffers operations but may not operate upon other objects. An agent is an object that serves to perform some operation on the behalf of another object and in turn may operate upon another object.

Another important characteristic of objects is that each object is a unique instance of some class. Put another way, a class denotes a set of similar but unique objects. A class serves to factor the common properties of a set of objects and specify the behavior of all instances. For example, we may have a class named Window from which we create several instances, or objects. It is important to distinguish between an object and its class: operations are defined for the class, but operations only have an effect upon the object.

Of course, and this gets a little complicated, one can treat a class as an object (forming a *metaclass*), with operations such as creating an instance of the class. This strange loop in the definition is not only academically interesting, but also permits some very elegant programs.

The term *class* comes from SIMULA 67 and Smalltalk; in other languages, we speak of the *type* of an object. Also from Smalltalk, we get the concept of inheritance, which permits a hierarchy of classes. In this sense, all objects are an instance of a class, which is a sublclass of another class (and so on). For example, given an object, its class may be Text__Window, which is in turn a subclass of the more general class Window. An object is said to inherit the methods of this chain of classes. Thus, all objects of the class Text__Window have the same operations as defined by the class Window (and we may also add operations, modify existing operations, and hide operations from the superclass).

Now, and this is an area of much emotional debate, we suggest that inheritance is an important, but not necessary, concept. On a continuum of "object-orientedness," development without inheritance still constitutes object-oriented development. On the other hand, object-oriented development is more than just programming with abstract data types, although abstract data types certainly serve as an important influence; indeed, we can characterize the behavior of most objects using the mechanisms of abstract data types. Whereas development with abstract data types tends to deal with passive objects (that is, *agents* and *servers*), object-oriented development also concerns itself with objects that act without stimulus from other objects (we call such objects *actors*). Another difference between programming with abstract data types and object-oriented development is that, in both cases, we concern ourselves with the operations suffered by an object, but in the latter case, we also concern ourselves with the operations that an object requires of other objects. As we have mentioned, the purpose of this view is to decouple the dependencies of objects, especially when coupled with a language mechanism such as Ada generic units.

Another way to view the relationship between object-oriented development and programming with abstract data types is that object-oriented development builds on the concepts of the latter, but also serves as a method that exposes the interesting objects and classes of objects from our abstraction of reality.

In some cases, the class of an object may be anonymous. Here, the object does have a class but its class is not visible. The implication is that there may be only one object of the class (since there is no class name from which instances may be declared). Practically, we implement such objects as abstract state machines instead of instances of a class.

Another important consideration of any object-oriented system is the treatment of names. The rule is simple: objects are unique instances of a class, and names only serve to denote objects. As Liskov observes, "variables are just the names used in a program to refer to objects" [32]. Thus, an object may be denoted by one name (the typical case) or by several names. In the latter situation, we have an alias such that operation upon an object through one name has the side-effect of altering the object denoted by all the aliases. For example, we may have several variables in our window system that denote the same window object; operating upon an object through one name (such as destroying the window) has the effect of altering the object denoted by all other names. This one object/many name paradigm is a natural consequence of the notion of an object, but depending upon the manner of support offered by the underlying language, is the source of many logical errors. The key concept to remember is that supplying a name to an constructor does not necessarily alter the value of the name, but instead, alters the object denoted by the name.

The names of objects should have a restricted scope. Thus, in designing a system, we concern ourselves with what objects see and are seen by another object or class of objects. This in fact is the purpose of one of the steps in our method, that of establishing the visibility among objects. In the worst case, all objects can see one another, and so there is the potential of unrestricted action. It is better that we restrict the visibility among objects, so as to limit the number of objects we must deal with to understand any part of the system and also to limit the scope of change.

Finally, every object has two parts, and so may be viewed from two different ways: there is an outside view and an inside view. Whereas the outside view of an object serves to capture the abstract behavior of the object, the inside view indicates how that behavior is implemented. Thus, by seeing only the outside view, one object can interact with another without knowing how the other is represented or implemented. When designing a system, we first concern ourselves with the outside view.

The outside view of an object or class of objects is its specification. The specification captures all of the static and (as much as possible) dynamic semantics of the object. In the specification of a class of objects, we export a number of things to the rest of the system, including the name of the class and the operations defined for objects of the class. Ideally, our implementation language enforces this specification, and prevents us from violating the properties of the specification.

Whereas the outside view of an object is that which is visible to other objects, the inside view is the implementation and so is hidden from the outside. In the body of an object or object class, we must chose one of many possible representations that implements the behavior of the specification. Again, if the language permits it, we may replace the implementation of an object or class of objects without any other part of the system being affected. The benefits of this facility should be clear: not only does this enforce our abstractions and hence help manage the complexity of the problem space, but by localizing the design decisions made about an object, we reduce the scope of change upon the system.

IV. Ada and Object-Oriented Development

Clearly, some languages are better suited than others to the application of object-oriented development; the major issue is how well a particular language can embody and enforce the properties of an object. Smalltalk and its immediate relatives provide the best match with these concepts, but it is also the case that languages such as Ada may be applied in an object-oriented fashion. Specifically, in Ada:
• Classes of objects are denoted by packages that export private or limited private types.
• Objects are denoted by instances of private or limited private types or as packages that serve as abstract state machines.
• Object state resides either with a declared object (for instances of private or limited private types) or in the body of a package (in the case of an abstract state machine).
• Operations are implemented as subprograms exported from a package specification; generic formal subprogram parameters serve to specify the operations required by an object.
• Variables serve as names of objects; aliases are permitted for an object.
• Visibility is statically defined through unit context clauses.

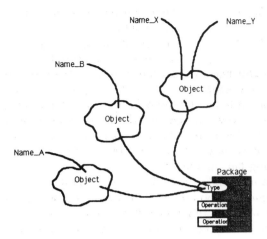

Fig. 6. Names, objects, and classes.

• Separate compilation of package specification and body support the two views of an object.
• Tasks and task types may be used to denote actor objects and classes of objects.

Fig. 6 illustrates the interaction of these points.

It is also the case that we can provide a form of inheritance using derived types. Thus, we could define a class of objects in a package that exports a nonprivate type, and then build on top of this class by deriving from the first type. The derivation inherits all the operations from the parent type. Because we have used an unencapsulated type (a type that is not private or limited private), we may add new operations, replace existing operations, and hide operations from the parent class. However, we must realize that there is a tradeoff between safety and flexibility. By using an unencapsulated type, we avoid much of the protection offered by Ada's strong typing mechanism. Smalltalk favors the side of flexibility; we prefer the safety offered by Ada, especially when applied to massive software-intensive systems.

Earlier, we used a few simple symbols to represent the design of the cruise-control system. It should come as no surprise that some people can grasp the essence of a design just by reading package specifications, while others are more effective if they are first given a graphical representation of the system architecture; we fall into the latter category. Since neither structure charts nor data flow diagrams capture the interesting properties of an object, we offer the set of symbols in Fig. 7, evolved from our earlier work [33]. We have found them to be an effective design notation that also serve to directly map from data flow diagrams to Ada implementations.

As Fig. 7 represents, these symbols are connected by directed lines. If we draw a line from object A to object B, this denotes that A depends upon the resources of B in some way. In the case of Ada units, we must make a distinction regarding the parts of a unit that exhibit these dependencies. For example, if the specification of package X depends upon Y, we start the directed line from the colorless part of the symbol for X; if the body of X depends

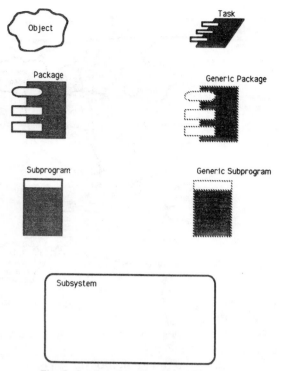

Fig. 7. Symbols for object-oriented design.

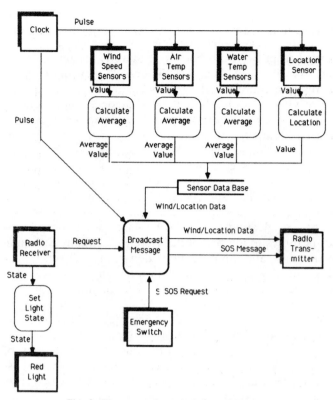

Fig. 8. Host at sea buoy data flow diagram.

upon Y, we start the directed line from the shaded part of X.

V. DESIGN CASE STUDY

Let us apply the object-oriented method to one more problem, adapted from the study of Boehm-Davis [15].

There exists a collection of free-floating buoys that provide navigation and weather data to air and ship traffic at sea. The buoys collect air and water temperature, wind speed, and location data through a variety of sensors. Each buoy may have a different number of wind and temperature sensors and may be modified to support other types of sensors in the future. Each buoy is also equipped with a radio transmitter (to broadcast weather and location information as well as an SOS message) and a radio receiver (to receive requests from passing vessels). Some buoys are equipped with a red light, which may be activated by a passing vessel during sea-search operations. If a sailor is able to reach the buoy, he or she may flip a switch on the side of the buoy to initiate an SOS broadcast. Software for each buoy must:

• maintain current wind, temperature, and location information; wind speed readings are taken every 30 seconds, temperature readings every 10 seconds and location every 10 seconds; wind and temperature values are kept as a running average.

• broadcast current wind, temperature, and location information every 60 seconds.

• broadcast wind, temperature, and location information from the past 24 hours in response to requests from passing vessels; this takes priority over the periodic broadcast.

• activate or deactivate the red light based upon a request from a passing vessel.

• continuously broadcast an SOS signal after a sailor engages the emergency switch; this signal takes priority over all other broadcasts and continues until reset by a passing vessel.

To formalize our model of reality, we begin by devising a data flow diagram for this system, as illustrated in Fig. 8. The design proceeds by first identifying the objects and their attributes. Drawing from this level of the data flow diagram, we include all sources and destinations of data as well as all data stores. In general, data flows have a transitory state; we will typically not treat them as objects, but rather just as instances of a simple type. Additionally, wherever there is a major process that transforms a data flow, we will allocate that process to an object that serves as the agent for that action. Thus, our objects of interest at this level of decomposition include the following:

• Clock	Provides the stimulus for periodic actions.
• Wind Speed Sensors	Maintains a running average of wind speed.
• Air Temperature Sensors	Maintains a running average of air temperature.
• Water Temperature Sensors	Maintains a running average of water temperature.

- Location Sensor — Maintains the current buoy location.
- Sensor Database — Serves to store weather and location history.
- Radio Receiver — Provides a channel for requests from passing vessels.
- Radio Transmitter — Provides a channel for broadcast of weather and location reports as well as SOS messages.
- Emergency Switch — Provides the stimulus for the SOS signal.
- Red Light — Controls the activity of the emergency light.
- Message Switch — Serves to generate and arbitrate various broadcast messages.

Next, we consider the operations suffered by and required of each object. We will take a first cut by simply listing the operations that characterize fundamental behavior. First, we identify the operations suffered by each object from within the system; these operations roughly parallel the state change caused by a data flow into an object:

- Clock — None
- Wind Speed Sensors — Take Sample
- Air Temperature Sensors — Take Sample
- Water Temperature Sensors — Take Sample
- Location Sensor — Take Sample
- Sensor Database — Put Value / Get Value
- Radio Receiver — None
- Radio Transmitter — Broadcast Weather/Location Report / Broadcast SOS
- Emergency Switch — None
- Red Light — Set State
- Message Switch — Request History Report / Request Periodic Report / Request SOS

Notice that for the Sensor Database, we have the operation Get Value which seems to go against the data flow implied by all other operations. In practice, we will encounter some objects that are passive in nature, especially those that denote data stores. Whereas Get Value does not change the state of the object, it returns a value of the state of the object. Since a passive object such as the Sensor Database cannot know when a value is needed, we must supply this operation to permit the state to be retrieved by another object.

Second, we must identify the operations required of each

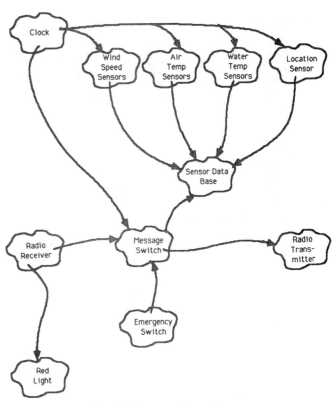

Fig. 9. Host at sea buoy objects.

object; these operations roughly parallel the action of a data flow from an object:

- Clock — Force Sample / Force Periodic Report
- Wind Speed Sensors — Put Value
- Air Temperature Sensors — Put Value
- Water Temperature Sensors — Put Value
- Location Sensor — Put Value
- Sensor Database — None
- Radio Receiver — Force History Report / Set Light State
- Radio Transmitter — None
- Emergency Switch — Force SOS
- Red Light — None
- Message Switch — Send Weather/Location Report / Send SOS

Notice that we have a balance between the operations suffered by and required of all objects. For each operation suffered by an object, we have some other object or set of objects that requires that action.

This analysis leads us directly to the next two steps, establishing the visibility of each object in relation to other objects and its interface. Using the symbols we introduced earlier, we may start by indicating the dependencies among objects, as denoted in Fig. 9. In general, the dependencies follow the direction of the operations required of each object.

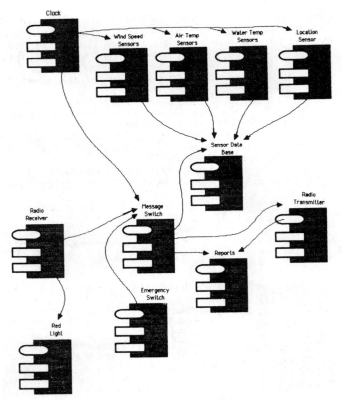

Fig. 10. Host at sea buoy objects.

In the previous section, we noted the correspondence between Ada units and objects. Hence, we may transform the design in Fig. 9 to an Ada representation. This transformation is simple: we denote each object or class of objects as a package, and for all but the most primitive data flows, we also provide a package that exports the type of the data flow, made visible to both the source and the destination of the flow. Fig. 10 illustrates this design after the transformation. Notice that there is a one-to-one correspondence between the objects in Fig. 9 with the packages in Fig. 10. We have only introduced one new package, Reports, which provides types that denote messages broadcast from the system.

Continuing our object-oriented development, we would next write the Ada specification for every package and then implement each unit. For example, we might write the specification of the Air Temperature Sensors as:

```
generic
    type Value is digits < >;
    with procedure Put__Value (The__Value: in Value);
package Air__Temperature__Sensors is

    type Sensor is limited private;

    procedure Take__Sample (The__Sensor: in out
        Sensor);

private
    type Sensor is . . .
end Air__Temperature__Sensors;
```

In this package, we export a limited private type (so as

to provide a class of sensors) as well as one operation (Take__Sample). We also import one operation (Put__Value), that each sensor requires of the Sensor Database.

There are some interesting generalities we can draw from the design in Fig. 10. Notice that each package that denotes a sensor has the same set of dependencies and roughly the same set of operations that characterize its behavior. Therefore, it would be possible for us to factor out the similarities among these objects, produce one generic Sensor package and then treat each sensor object as an instance of this component. Furthermore, if we already have a simple data base package, we might adapt it to provide the Sensor Database instead of creating a new one for this application. Finally, if we are careful, we could write the Radio Transmitter and Radio Receiver packages such that they could be applied in other problems that use similar equipment.

In all these cases, we have identified the need for a reusable software component. Indeed, we find that there is a basic relationship between reusable software components and object-oriented development:

Reusable software components tend to be objects or classes of objects.

Given a rich set of reusable software components, our implementation would thus proceed via *composition* of these parts, rather than further *decomposition*.

VI. CONCLUSION

We must remember that object-oriented development requires certain facilities of the implementation language. In particular, we must have some mechanism to build new classes of objects (and ideally, a typing mechanism that serves to enforce our abstractions). It is also the case that object-oriented development is only a partial-lifecycle method and so must be coupled with compatible requirements and specification methods. We believe that object-oriented development is amenable to automated support; further research is necessary to consider the nature of such tools.

Perhaps the greatest strength of an object-oriented approach to development is that it offers a mechanism that captures a model of the real world. This leads to improved maintainability and understandability of systems whose complexity exceeds the intellectual capacity of a single developer or a team of developers.

REFERENCES

[1] T. Rentsch, "Object-oriented programming." *SIGPLAN Notices*, vol. 17, no. 9, p. 51, Sept. 1982.
[2] J. Guttag, E. Horowitz, and D. Musser, *The Design of Data Type Specification* (Current Trends in Programming Methodology, Vol. 4). Englewood Cliffs, NJ: Prentice-Hall, 1978, p. 200.
[3] Adapted from an exercise provided by P. Ward at the Rocky Mountain Institute for Software Engineering, Aspen, CO, 1984.
[4] C. Gane and T. Sarson, *Structured Systems Analysis: Tools and Techniques.* Englewood Cliffs, NJ: Prentice-Hall, 1979.
[5] E. Yourdon and L. Constantine, *Structured Design.* Englewood Cliffs, NJ: Prentice-Hall, 1979.

[6] H. Levy, *Capability-Based Computer Systems*. Bedford, MA: Digital Press, 1984, p. 13.

[7] G. Curry and R. Ayers, "Experience with traits in the Xerox Star workstation," in *Proc. Workshop Reusability in Program.*, ITT Programming, Stratford, CT, 1983, p. 83.

[8] M. Shaw, "Abstraction techniques in modern programming languages," *IEEE Software*, vol. 1, no. 4, p. 10, Oct. 1984.

[9] D. L. Parnas, "On the criteria to be used in decomposing systems into modules," *Commun. ACM*, Dec. 1972.

[10] R. Abbott, "Report on teaching Ada," Science Applications, Inc., Rep. SAI-81-312WA, Dec. 1980.

[11] ——, "Program design by informal English descriptions," *Commun. ACM*, vol. 26, no. 11, p. 884, Nov. 1983.

[12] M. Jackson, *System Development*. Englewood Cliffs, NJ: Prentice-Hall, 1983.

[13] M. Alford, "SREM at the age of eight: The distributed computing design system," *Computer*, vol. 18, no. 4, Apr. 1985.

[14] G. Buzzard and T. Mudge, "Object-based computing and the Ada programming language," *Computer*, vol. 18, no. 3, p. 12, 1985.

[15] D. Boehm-Davis and L. Ross, "Approaches to structuring the software development process," General Elec. Co., Rep. GEC/DIS/TR-84-B1V-1, Oct. 1984, p. 13.

[16] B. Meyer, "Towards a two-dimensional programming environment," in *Readings in Artificial Intelligence*. Palo Alto, CA: Tioga, 1981, p. 178.

[17] A. Borgida, S. Greenspan and J. Mylopoulos, "Knowledge representation as the basis for requirements specification," *Computer*, vol. 18, no. 4, p. 85, Apr. 1985.

[18] D. Boehm-Davis and L. Ross, "Approaches to structuring the software development process," General Elec. Co., Rep. GEC/DIS/TR-84-B1V-1, Oct. 1984, p. 14.

[19] B. MacLennan, "Values and objects in programming languages," *SIGPLAN Notices*, vol. 17, no. 12, p. 75, Dec. 1982.

[20] H. Levy, *Capability-Based Computer Systems*. Bedford, MA: Digital Press, 1984, p. 13.

[21] B. Liskov, "A design method for reliable software systems," in *Proc. Fall Joint Comput. Conf.*, AFIPS, 1972, p. 67.

[22] B. Liskov and S. Zilles, "Specification techniques for data abstractions," *IEEE Trans. Software Eng.*, vol. SE-1, Mar. 1975.

[23] J. Guttag, E. Horowitz, and D. Musser, *The Design of Data Type Specification* (Current Trends in Programming Methodology, Vol. 4). Englewood Cliffs, NJ: Prentice-Hall, 1978.

[24] M. Shaw, "Abstraction techniques in modern programming languages," *IEEE Software*, vol. 1, no. 4, Oct. 1984.

[25] A. Abelson, G. Sussman, and J. Sussman, *Structure and Interpretation of Computer Programs*. Cambridge, MA: M.I.T. Press, 1985.

[26] B. Cox, "Message/object programming: An evolutionary change in programming technology," *IEEE Software*, vol. 1, no. 1, Jan. 1984.

[27] "A symposium on actor languages," *Creative Comput.*, Oct. 1980.

[28] G. Myers, *Advances in Computer Architecture*. New York: Wiley, 1982.

[29] H. Deitel, *An Introduction to Operating Systems*. Reading, MA: Addison-Wesley, 1983, p. 456.

[30] B. Liskov and S. Zilles, *An Introduction to Formal Specifications of Data Abstractions* (Current Trends in Programming Methodology, Vol. 1). Englewood Cliffs, NJ: Prentice-Hall, 1977, p. 8.

[31] M. Shaw, W. Wulf, and R. London, "Abstraction and verification in Alphard: Iteration and generators," in *Alphard: Form and Content*. New York: Springer-Verlag, 1981.

[32] B. Liskov, R. Atkinson, T. Bloom, E. Moss, J. Schaffert, R. Schiefler, and A. Snyder, *CLU Reference Manual*. New York: Sprinter-Verlag, 1981, p. 8.

[33] E. G. Booch, "Describing software design in Ada," *SIGPLAN Notices*, Sept. 1981.

Grady Booch (M'82) received the B.S. degree from the United States Air Force Academy, Colorado Springs, CO, in 1977 and the M.S.E.E. degree from the University of California at Santa Barbara in 1979.

He is Director of Software Engineering Projects at Rational, Inc. He has been actively involved in Ada research, implementation, and education since 1979. He has lectured on Ada and software development methods across the United States and in Europe, and has published over 30 technical articles. In addition, he has written *Software Engineering with Ada* (Benjamin/Cummings), and is currently working on another book dealing with reusable software components. He also is author of the column "Dear Ada" which appears regularly in *Ada Letters*. Previously, he was a faculty member in the Department of Computer Science at the United States Air Force Academy. In his other assignments, prior to leaving the Air Force in 1982, he was a project director and project engineer for several large real-time software developments for space and missile systems.

Mr. Booch is a member of the Association for Computing Machinery and the American Association for Artificial Intelligence. In 1983, he was given an award, for distinguished service to the Ada program, from the Undersecretary of Defense.

TOWARDS A GENERAL OBJECT-ORIENTED
SOFTWARE DEVELOPMENT METHODOLOGY

Ed Seidewitz / Code 554
Mike Stark / Code 552
Goddard Space Flight Center
Greenbelt, MD 20771

1. INTRODUCTION

An object is an abstract software model of a problem domain
entity. Objects are packages of both data and operations on
that data [Goldberg 83, Booch 83]. The Ada (tm) package
construct is representative of this general notion of an object.
Object-oriented design is the technique of using objects as the
basic unit of modularity in system design. The Software
Engineering Laboratory at the Goddard Space Flight Center is
currently involved in a pilot project to develop a flight
dynamics simulator in Ada (approximately 40,000 statements)
using object-oriented methods. Several authors have applied
object-oriented concepts to Ada (e.g., [Booch 83, Cherry 85b]).
In our experience we have found these methodologies limited
[Nelson 86]. As a result we have synthesized a more general
approach which allows a designer to apply powerful,
object-oriented principles to a wide range of applications and
at all stages of design. The present paper provides an overview
of our approach. Further, we also consider how object-oriented
design fits into the overall software life-cycle.

2. OBJECTS AND OBJECT DIAGRAMS

We can model a procedure as a mathematical function. That
is, given a certain set of inputs (arguments and global data), a
procedure always produces the same set of outputs (results and
global updates). A procedure, for example, cannot directly
model an address book, because an address book has memory (a set
of addresses) which can be accessed and updated. Normally, the
solution to this is to place such memory in global variables.

Figure 1 gives a representation of the above situation.
This diagram uses a notation similar to [Yourdon 79] to show
both data and control flow. The arrow from CALLER to PROCEDURE
indicates that CALLER transfers control to PROCEDURE. Note that
there is an implicit return of control when PROCEDURE finishes.
The smaller arrows in figure 1 show the data flows, which may go
in either direction along the control arrow. Also, figure 1
includes an explicit symbol for the GLOBAL DATA. Control arrows
directed towards this symbol denote data access, even though
control never really flows into the data, of course. This
convention indicates that the data is always passive and never
initiates any action.

Reprinted from *Proceedings of the First International Conference on Ada
Programming Language Applications for the NASA Space Station*, 1986, pages
D.4.6.1-D.4.6.14. U.S. Government work not protected by U.S. copyright.   16

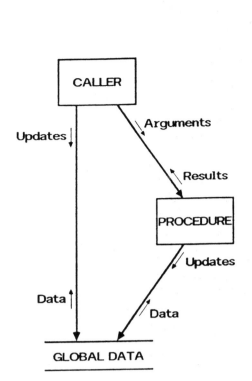

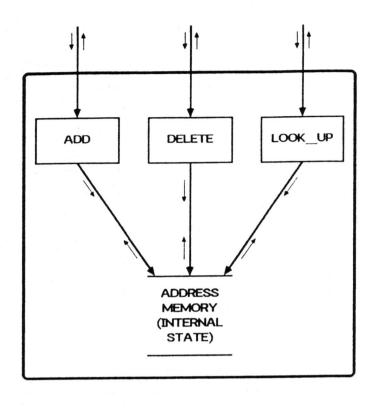

FIGURE 1 A procedure call   FIGURE 2 An ADDRESS BOOK object

The use of global storage leaves data open to illicit modification. To avoid this, an object packages some memory together with all allowable operations on it. We can model an object as a mathematical "state machine" with some internal state which can be accessed and modified by a limited number of mathematical functions. We thus implement an object as a packaged set of procedures and internal data, as shown in figure 2. For an address book object, the internal memory would be a set of addresses, and the allowable operations would be accessing an address by name, adding an address, etc. Unlike a procedure, the same arguments to an object operation may produce different results at different times, depending on the hidden internal state. We will diagram an object showing only its operational connections to other objects, as in the object diagram of figure 3 [Seidewitz 85a].

When there are several control paths on a complicated object diagram, it rapidly becomes cumbersome to show data flows or all individual procedure control flows. Therefore, an arrow between objects on an object diagram indicates that one object invokes one or more of the operations provided by another object and is not marked with data flow arrows. Object descriptions for each object on a diagram provide details of the data flow. An object description includes a list of all operations provided by an object and, for each arrow leaving the object, a list of operations used from another object. For example, the object description for DATE BOOK from figure 3 is:

```
    Provides:
      Next_Appointment () NAME + ADDRESS
      Get_Appointment (DATE + TIME) NAME + ADDRESS
      Make_Appointment (DATE + TIME + NAME)
      Cancel_Appointment (DATE + TIME)

    Uses:

      ADDRESS BOOK
        Look_Up

      CLOCK
        Get_Date
        Get_Time
```

Data in parentheses are arguments which flow <u>along</u> the control arrow, while unparenthesized data are results which are returned.

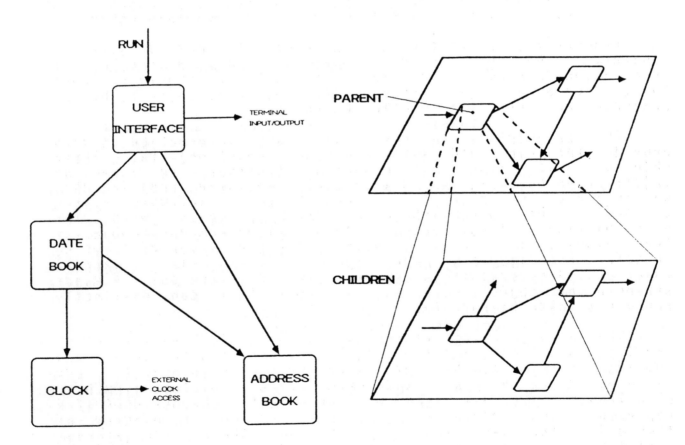

FIGURE 3 A simple schedule organizer   FIGURE 4 Parent-child hierarchy

3. OBJECT-ORIENTED DESIGN

The intent of an object is to represent a problem domain entity. The concept of abstraction deals with how an object presents this representation to other objects [Dijkstra 68, Liskov 74, Booch 83]. There is a spectrum of abstraction, from objects which closely model problem domain entities to objects which really have no reason for existence. The following are some points in this scale:

Best   Entity Abstraction - An object represents a useful model of a problem domain entity.

Action Abstraction - An object provides a generalized set of operations which all perform the same kind of function.

Virtual Machine Abstraction - An object groups together operations which are all used by some superior level of control or all use some junior level set of operations.

Worst   Coincidental "Abstraction" - An object packages a set of operations which have no relation to each other.

The stronger the abstraction of an object, the more details are suppressed by the abstract concept. The principle of information hiding states that such details should be kept secret from other objects [Parnas 72, Booch 83], so as to better preserve the abstraction modeled by the object.

The principles of abstraction and information hiding provide the main guides for creating "good" objects. These objects must then be connected together to form an object-oriented design [Seidewitz 85b]. Following [Rajlich 85], we consider two orthogonal hierarchies in software system designs. The parent-child hierarchy deals with the decomposition of larger objects into smaller component objects. The seniority hierarchy deals with the organization of a set of objects into "layers". Each layer defines a virtual machine which provides services to senior layers [Dijkstra 68]. A major strength of object diagrams is that they can distinctly represent these hierarchies.

The parent-child hierarchy is directly expressed by leveling object diagrams (see figure 4). At its top level, any complete system may be represented by a single object. For example, figure 5 shows a diagram of the complete SCHEDULE ORGANIZER of the last section. The object SCHEDULE ORGANIZER represents the "parent" of the complete object diagram of figure 3. The boxes labeled "USER" and "CLOCK" are external entities, objects which are not included in the system, but which communicates with the top level system object. Note the arrow labeled "RUN". By convention, RUN is the operation used to initially invoke the entire system.

19

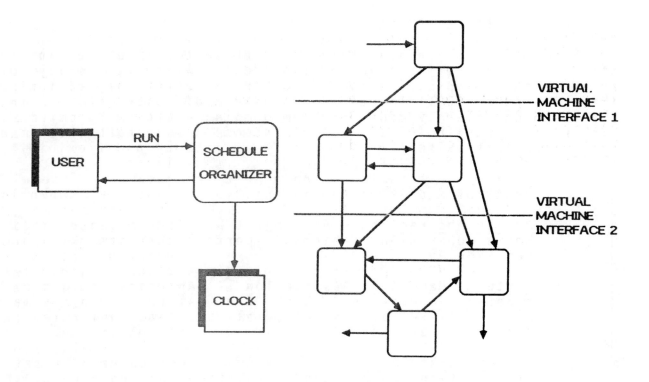

FIGURE 5 External Entities Diagram

FIGURE 6 Seniority hierarchy

Figure 3 is the <u>decomposition</u> of the SCHEDULE ORGANIZER of figure 5. Beginning at the system level, each object can be refined in this way into a lower level object diagram. The result is a leveled set of object diagrams which completely describe the structure of a system. At the lowest level, objects are completely decomposed into <u>primitive objects</u>, procedures and internal state data stores, resulting in diagrams similar to figure 2.

The seniority hierarchy is expressed by the topology of connections on a single object diagram (see figure 6). Any layer in a seniority hierarchy can call on any operation in junior layers, but <u>never</u> any operation in a senior layer. Thus, all cyclic relationships between objects must be contained within a virtual machine layer. Object diagrams are drawn with the seniority hierarchy shown vertically. Each senior object can be designed as if the operations provided by junior layers were "primitive operations" in an extended language. Each virtual machine layer will generally contain several objects, each designed according to the principles of abstraction and information hiding.

The main advantage of a seniority hierarchy is that it reduces the coupling between objects. This is because all objects in one virtual machine layer need to know nothing about senior layers. Further, the centralization of the procedural and data flow control in senior objects can make a system easier to understand and modify. However, this very centralization can cause a messy bottleneck. In such cases, the complexity of senior levels can be traded off against the coupling of junior levels. The important point is that the strength of the seniority hierarchy in a design can be chosen from a spectrum of possibilities, with the best design generally lying between the extremes. This gives the designer great power and flexibility in adapting system designs to specific applications.

In the simple automated plant simulation system shown in figure 7, the junior level components do not interact directly. This design is somewhat like an object-oriented version of the structured designs of [Yourdon 79]. We can remove the data flow control from the senior object and let the junior objects pass data directly between themselves, using operations within the virtual machine layer (see figure 8). The senior object has been reduced to simply activating various operations in the virtual machine layer, with very little data flow. We can even remove the senior object completely by distributing control among the junior level objects (see figure 9). The splitting of the RUN control arrow in figure 11 means that the three objects are activated simultaneously and that they run concurrently. The seniority hierarchy has collapsed, leaving a homologous or non-hierarchical design [Yourdon 79] (no seniority hierarchy, that is; the parent-child hierarchy still remains). A design which is homologous at all decomposition levels is very similar to what would be produced by the PAMELA (tm) methodology of [Cherry 85a, Cherry 85b].

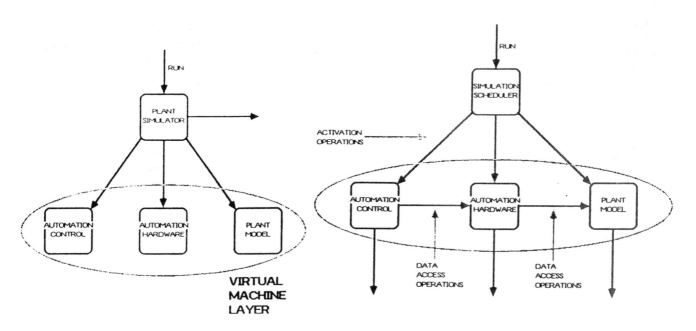

FIGURE 7 A simple plant automation simulation system

FIGURE 8 plant simulator with junior-level connections

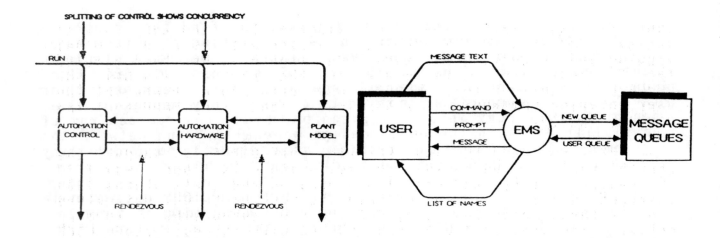

FIGURE 10 EMS context diagram

FIGURE 9 Plant simulator, homologous design

4.   OBJECT-ORIENTED LIFE CYCLE

Object diagrams and the object-oriented design concepts discussed above can be used as part of an object-oriented life cycle. To do this, we must show that a specification can be translated into object diagrams, and that object diagrams map readily into Ada. We use structured analysis for developing the specification [DeMarco 79]. The data flow diagrams of a structured specification provide a leveled, graphical notation containing the information needed to represent abstract entities, but in a form emphasizing data flow and data transformation.

Abstraction analysis is the process of making a transition from a structured specification to an object-oriented design [Stark 86]. We will use a simplified version of an Electronic Message System (EMS) as an example of abstraction analysis. Figure 10 is the context diagram for EMS, and Figure 11 is the level 0 data flow diagram. EMS must allow the user to send, read, and respond to messages, to obtain a directory of valid users to which messages can be sent, and to add and delete users from that directory.

The first step of abstraction analysis is to find a central entity. This is the entity that represents the best abstraction for what the system does or models. The central entity is identified in a similar way to transform analysis [Yourdon 79], but instead of searching for where incoming and outgoing data flows are most abstract we look for a set of processes and data stores that are most abstract. It may sometimes be necessary to

22

look at lower level data flow diagrams to find the central
entity. EMS is a system serving a person sitting at a terminal
sending and receiving messages. On figure 11 we have circled
the "current user" data store and the process 1.0 GET EMS
COMMAND. Together this process and data store represent the
user entering commands at a terminal. Thus they represent the
central entity.

Next, we need to find entities that directly support the
central entity. We do this by following data flows away from
the central entity and grouping processes and data stores into
abstract entities. In our example the USER DIRECTORY data store
and the three processes (2.0, 4.0 and 5.0) supporting it form an
entity. The process 3.0 ACCESS QUEUES with the data store USER
QUEUE INDEX also form an entity. All these entities are circled
and labeled on figure 11. We continue to follow the data flows
and to identify entities until all the processes and data stores
are associated with an entity.

Figure 12 is the entity graph for EMS. Squares represent
entities, lines with arrows represent flow of control from one
entity to another, and lines with no arrowhead represent
interactions where flow of control is not yet determined. A
"most senior" entity is placed into the design to give an
initial flow of control. In the EMS example, entity EMS is this
most senior object, and we have the USER INTERFACE entity
"controlling" the external entity USER. This flow of control

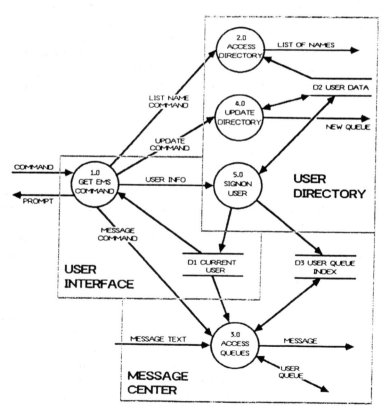

FIGURE 11 EMS level O data flow diagram

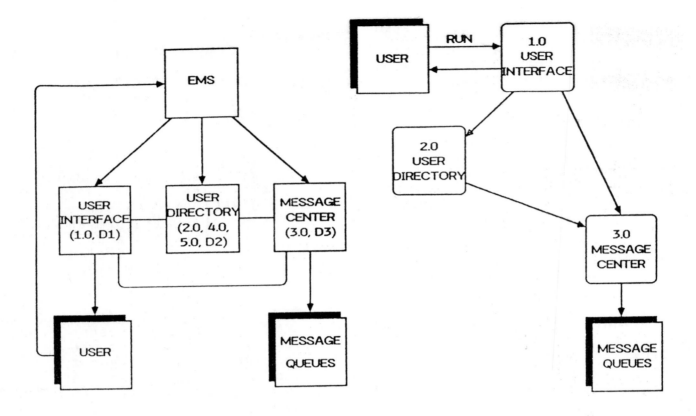

FIGURE 12 EMS entity graph   FIGURE 13 EMS object diagram

into USER will ultimately be implemented as read and write operations. Note also that the USER entity controls EMS. This flow of control represents the user invoking the EMS system. After this invocation control resides with EMS until the system is exited. All other potential interfaces are shown by lines with no arrows. The numbers inside the squares represent the processes and the data stores contained in the entity. This provides traceability from requirements to design.

The entity graph is the starting point for object identification. It shows entities with the highest abstraction possible and also shows all the possible interconnections between the entities. Since we are trying to balance design complexity, object abstraction, and control hierarchy, we will alter the entity graph to form the final object diagram. In EMS the entities are easily mapped into objects. The entities USER, USER INTERFACE, and EMS form a cyclic graph and therefore are on the same virtual machine level. We cannot combine an external entity into an object, but combining EMS and USER INTERFACE yields a single object that is senior to USER DIRECTORY and MESSAGE CENTER. Combining the two junior objects would simplify the design, but at the expense of abstraction, as the message passing mechanisms have little to do with the directory. We have also chosen to make USER DIRECTORY senior to MESSAGE CENTER, since the data flows are from USER DIRECTORY into data stores contained by MESSAGE CENTER. Figure 13 shows the resulting object diagram.

Needless to say, identifying objects is not always this simple. Usually there is a trade-off made between level of abstraction and design complexity, or a balancing of these two considerations and the virtual machine hierarchy. When these situations occur it is still the designer's judgement that must determine which side of the trade-off matters more for the application being designed.

Once the object diagrams are drawn we can identify the operations provided and used by each object. In the case of 2.0 USER DIRECTORY the operations are identified by examining the primitive processes contained within processes 2.0, 4.0 and 5.0 on figure 11. The data exchanged are identified by looking at data flows crossing the object boundaries, with the detailed information about the data being found in the data dictionary. The object description is produced by matching the operations and the data. The description generated for 2.0 USER DIRECTORY is as follows:

```
Provides:
   List_Names () LIST_OF_NAMES
   Add_User (USER_NAME + PASSWORD)
   Delete_User (USER_NAME)
   Signon (USER_NAME + PASSWORD) VALIDITY_FLAG

Uses:
   3.0 MESSAGE QUEUES
      Reset_Queue
      Create_New_Queue
```

Using the subset data flow diagram of processes and data stores that an object contains, the process of object identification can be repeated to produce a child object diagram. The only difference is that entities are identified based on how they support the object's operations, not by finding a central entity. This process is used until the lowest level of data flow diagrams is exhausted.

The transition from an object diagram to Ada is straightforward. The relationship between object diagram notations and Ada language features is:

Object Diagram	Ada Construct
Object	Package
Procedure	Subprogram
State	Package or task variables
Arrow	Procedure/function/entry call
Actor	Entries/Accepts
	(not covered in this paper)

Package specifications are derived from the list of operations provided by an object. For the EMS USER DIRECTORY object the package specification is:

```ada
package User_Directory is

   subtype USER_NAME is STRING(1..20);
   subtype PASSWORD is STRING(1..6);
   type LIST_OF_NAMES is array (POSITIVE range <>) of USER_NAME;

   procedure Signon (User: in USER_NAME; PW : in PASSWORD;
      Valid_User : out Boolean);
   procedure Add_User (U: in USER_NAME; PW : in PASSWORD);
   procedure Delete_User (U: in USER_NAME);
   function List_Names return LIST_OF_NAMES;

end User_Directory;
```

The package specifications derived from the level 0 object diagram are placed in the declarative part of the top level Ada procedure as follows:

```ada
procedure EMS is
   package User_Interface is
      procedure Start;
      ...
   end User_Interface;

   package User_Directory is
      ...
   end User_Directory;

   package Message_Queues is
      ...
   end Message_Queues;

   package body User_Interface is separate;
   package body User_Directory is separate;
   package body Message_Queues is separate;

begin
   User_Interface.Start;
end EMS;
```

For lower level object diagrams the mapping is similar, with package specifications being nested in the package body of the parent object. States are mapped into package body variables. This direct mapping produces a highly nested program structure. To implement the same object diagram with library units would require the addition of a package to contain data types used by two or more objects. This added package would serve as a global data dictionary.

The process of transforming object diagrams to Ada is followed down all the child object diagrams until we are at the level of implementing individual subprograms. If the mapping is done without explicitly creating library units the lowest level subprograms will all be implemented as subunits, rather than by embedding the code in package bodies.

5. EVALUATION OF THE METHODOLOGY

To measure how well abstraction analysis works as a methodology we must first define our criteria for a good methodology. We will use Barry Boehm's "Seven Principles of Software Engineering" [Boehm 76] as a basis of comparison. These principles are:

Manage using a sequential life cycle plan
Maintain disciplined product control
Perform continuous validation
Use enhanced top down structured design
Maintain clear accountability for results
Use better and fewer people
Maintain a commitment to improve the process

Abstraction analysis supports all these principles. The life cycle plan is supported by providing the abstraction analysis method for producing object diagrams, which are in turn mappable into Ada. This also provides a means of disciplined product control by tracing how Ada software implements an object oriented design, and also tracing how the design meets the specification. This traceability allows a manager to see that software meets its specification, and allows maintenance of specifications, design, and software to be consistent. Grady Booch's [Booch 83] work influenced our methodology, but did not provide a sufficient means of specifying large systems. Another drawback is that Booch does not define a formal mapping from a specification to a design.

The graphic notation supports a top down approach to software development. The leveling of both dataflow diagrams and of object diagrams allows the designer to start at a high level and work top-down to a design solution. The use of graphics also supports continuous validation by making design walkthroughs and iterative changes easier tasks to perform. Both Booch and Cherry [Cherry 85b] use graphics, but Booch's notation was not designed for large applications, and Cherry's methodology stops graphing after all the concurrent objects have been identified. The graphics used by structured analysis [DeMarco 79] provide the best analogy to how graphics are used in the object diagram notation.

The life cycle model we have defined also supports the remaining three principles. Objects are defined in the design phase and implemented as separate Ada compilation units. Tools such as unit development folders can be used to maintain accountability for completion of the design, implementation, and testing of objects. It is hoped that the object-oriented approach and the use of Ada will enhance both productivity and software reliability. This assertion will be tested by measuring the outcome of the pilot project in the Software Engineering Laboratory at Goddard Space Flight Center. The success of this methodology would allow better and fewer people to concentrate more effort on producing a good design.

Finally, we are certainly <u>committed to improving the</u> <u>process</u>. The object diagram notation and abstraction analysis have already seen much change since the initial versions were defined. Further refinement will be to define criteria for using parallelism, criteria for choosing between library units and the nested approach defined above, and to generate object-oriented approaches to software specifications and software testing.

6. CONCLUSION

Object diagrams have been used to design a 5000 statement team trainging exercise and to design the entire dynamics simulator. They are also being used to design another 50,000 statement Ada system and a personnal computer based system that will be written in Modula II. Our design methodology evolved out of these experiences as well as the limitations of other methods we studied. Object diagrams, abstraction analysis and associated principles provide a unified framework which encompasses concepts from [Yourdon 79], [Booch 83] and [Cherry 85b]. This general object-oriented approach handles high level system design, possibly with concurrency, through object-oriented decomposition down to a completely functional level. We are currently studying how object-oriented concepts can be used in other phases of the software life-cycle, such as specification and testing. When complete, this synthesis should produce a truly general object-oriented <u>development</u> methodology.

TRADEMARKS

Ada is a trademark of the US Government (Ada Joint Program Office).

PAMELA is a trademark of George W. Cherry.

REFERENCES

[Boehm 76]   Boehm, Barry W. "Seven Basic Principles of Software Engineering," NASA/GSFC Engineering Colloquium, 1976.

[Booch 83]   Grady Booch. <u>Software Engineering with Ada</u>, Benjamin/Cummings, 1983.

[Cherry 85a]   George W. Cherry. <u>PAMELA: Process Abstraction Method for Embedded Large Applications</u>, Course notes, Thought**Tools, January 1985.

[Cherry 85b]   George W. Cherry and Grad S. Crawford. <u>The PAMELA (tm) Methodology</u>, November 1985.

[DeMarco 79]   Tom DeMarco. <u>Structured Analysis and System Specification</u>, Prentice-Hall, 1979.

[Dijkstra 68]   Edsgar W. Dijkstra. "The Structure of the 'THE' Multiprogramming System," <u>Communications of the ACM</u>, May 1968.

[Goldberg 83]   Adele Goldberg and David Robison. <u>Smalltalk 80: The Language and Its Implementation</u>. Addison-Wesley, 1983.

[Liskov 74]   Barbara H. Liskov and S. N. Zilles. "Programming with Abstract Data Types," Proc. of the ACM Symp. on Very High Level Languages, <u>SIGPLAN Notices</u>, April 1974.

[Nelson 86]   Robert W. Nelson. "NASA Ada Experiment -- Attitude Dynamic Simulator," <u>Proc. of the Washington Ada Symposium</u>, March, 1986.

[Parnas 72]   David L. Parnas. "On the Criteria to be Used in Decomposing Systems into Modules," <u>Communications of the ACM</u>, December 1972.

[Rajlich 85]   Vaclav Rajlich. "Paradigms for Design and Implementation in Ada," <u>Communications of the ACM</u>, July 1985.

[Seidewitz 85a] Ed Seidewitz. <u>Object Diagrams</u>, unpublished GSFC report, May 1985.

[Seidewitz 85b] Ed Seidewitz. <u>Some Principles of Object Oriented Design</u>, unpublished GSFC report, August 1985.

[Stark 86]   Mike Stark. <u>Abstraction Analysis: From Structured Specification to Object-Oriented Design</u>, unpublished GSFC report, April 1986.

[Yourdon 79]   Edward Yourdon and Larry L. Constantine. <u>Structured Design: Fundamentals of a Discipline of Computer Program and Systems Design</u>, Prentice-Hall, 1979.

Modular Software Construction and Object-Oriented Design Using Ada

by
Richard F. Sincovec
and
Richard S. Wiener

Department of Computer Science
University of Colorado at Colorado Springs

*A methodology for modular software construction
and object-oriented software design*

Introduction. This paper describes a software development methodology which we refer to as modular software construction and object-oriented design. This powerful and modern approach to software development has recently gained tremendous currency with the advent of software engineering languages such as Ada and Modula-2. In this paper, we focus on the use of Ada in conjunction with this methodology.

All software design involves a process of abstraction. Objects and operations found in the problem-domain or real-world domain must be translated into corresponding objects and operations in the problem-solving domain, namely the software system.

In the early days of software development, circa 1940s and 1950s, when programs were hand-wired on a particular machine, the software design process involved a transformation from the problem-domain to the 0's and 1's of the particular machine being programmed. Very little abstraction was possible.

In the late 1950s and early 1960s, when the first widely used high-level languages like FORTRAN, ALGOL and COBOL came into existence, the first significant jump in software abstraction took place. Now the objects and operations found in the problem-domain could be represented in terms of the predefined data and control structures present in these early high-level languages. A list of numbers, a problem-domain entity, could, for example, be represented in FORTRAN as an array of floating point numbers. Two lists of related numbers (e.g. social security number and annual income) could, for example, be represented as two related arrays, with the array index the common factor linking the two arrays.

Several generations of programmers have learned to translate and abstract the entities of the real-world problem they are solving into the basic building blocks (the data and control structures) of the high-level language being used. In the 1970s, languages like Pascal introduced a richer variety of basic data and control structure building blocks that software developers could use to represent the problem-domain. The set structure, the record structure, the pointer type, the repeat and while loops, the case, and if-then-else control structures, are examples of the additional building blocks made available to software developers using Pascal.

Even with the additional Pascal-like constructs introduced in many languages during the 1970s, the fundamental approach to software design remained the same; map the entities of the real-world problem to the structures available in the high-level language. Software design continued to be preoccupied with representational details for data and control structures.

The reliability and maintainability of software may be compromised when the software design is centered on a particular scheme for representing objects. If the representational details must be altered to suit a new environment (e.g. a new computer or operating system), then, most often, the fall-out effects on the software system are profound. Quite often it is cheaper and more reliable to rebuild the entire software system from scratch than to modify the existing system. All of this because of the strong dependence of the software system on the representational scheme used for the major data types.

Modular software construction and object–oriented design supports the second major jump in abstraction that is possible in the software development process. No longer is it necessary for the system designer to map the problem–domain to the predefined data and control structures present in the implementation language. Instead, the designer may create his or her own abstract data types and functional abstractions and map the real–world domain to these programmer–created abstractions. This mapping, incidently, may be much more natural because of the virtually unlimited range of abstract types that can be invented by the software designer. Furthermore, the software design becomes decoupled from the representational details of the data objects used in the system. These representational details may be changed many times without any fall–out effects being induced in the overall software system.

Is this magic? No! The secret is to be found in modular software construction and object abstraction--object–oriented design. The term object–oriented design is used by Booch (reference 1). We will describe this methodology in the next section.

The Ada package with its private types and the complete separation between the specification and implementation of these modules makes modular software construction and object–oriented design a reality. See Wiener and Sincovec (reference 2) for an introduction to Ada packages.

One of the principle goals of this article is to make a case for this approach to software development. We also introduce what we believe to be a powerful design aid, the modular design chart. We present a small case study that uses this methodology of modular and object–oriented design. Several case studies using this approach to software development are presented in the recent book by Wiener and Sincovec (reference 3).

Modular Software Construction. The ability to perform the separate compilation of package specifications and package bodies provides the power necessary to do modular software construction in Ada and to use Ada as a program design language (PDL). The architecture of the system and interfaces may be specified and compiled before the detailed design commences. The compiler enforces these interfaces during the development and implementation of each module.

Object–oriented modular design uses as a centerpiece the modular design chart introduced in reference 3. The modular design chart serves as a graphical tool for designing the architecture of a software system. In Table 1, we present the steps that comprise object–oriented modular design.

Table 1
Object–Oriented and
Modular Software Construction

1. Define an informal strategy for the problem solution.
2. Identify objects and their attributes used in the informal strategy. Objects are the nouns of the informal strategy.
3. Identify operations on the objects used in the informal strategy. Operations are the verbs of the informal strategy.
4. Define the software system architecture using one or more modular design charts.
5. Create a compilable modular design listing in Ada that in-

cludes the initial version of the main driver program.
6. Develop the implementation details for each module. .

In step 5, the compiler performs high–level integration testing by checking all package and module interfaces for correctness. In step 6, additional software components (data types, procedures, etc.) may need to be created in some of the packages or modules to support the implementation portion of the system. Some of the steps in Table 1 may need to be iterated as the software construction progresses.

A Case Study. We now illustrate the process of modular and object–oriented design and the use of modular design charts with an example. We begin with the following brief description and informal strategy for the system.

The Problem. We wish to find the youngest, common ancestor connecting two arbitrary nodes in a binary tree. The interested reader may wish to consult a book such as Tenenbaum and Augenstein (reference 4) for additional information on binary trees. The software system must allow the user to do the following:
1) Construct a binary tree with integer values for each node.
2) Input the integer values for the two descendant nodes.
3) Determine and output the node in the tree that is the youngest, common ancestor of the two descendant nodes.
4) An error message should be provided if the user attempts to input descendant node(s) that do not exist in the tree.

Informal Strategy For Solution.
1) Build a binary search tree (the type of tree is not important).
2) Locate the position of the two tree nodes that correspond to the integer values that the user inputs. If at least one of the values is not in the tree, then print an error message and halt.
3) Compute the levels for each of the two descendant nodes.
4) If the levels are not the same, move up from child to parent, starting at the lower descendant node, to a node whose level is the same as the higher descendant node.
5) With both nodes now at the same level, move up from child to parent along the two branches until convergence to the same node (equality) occurs.
6) Output the value of this final node.

We illustrate this informal strategy in Figure 1. For the purposes of illustration, let us assume that descendant node 1 is 125, and descendant node 2 is 500. Node 500 is at level 4, if we assume the root node to be at level 0. Node 125 is at level 3.

According to the informal strategy, we move up the tree starting at node 500 until we reach level 3. This takes us to node 400. From nodes 125 and 400, we move up each of the branches to nodes 150 and 300. Then we move up again to node 200 where convergence occurs. We output the resulting youngest, common ancestor, namely node 200.

If two legal nodes are input as the descendant nodes, then a solution is guaranteed. In the worst case, the root node will be a youngest, common ancestor of two descendant nodes.

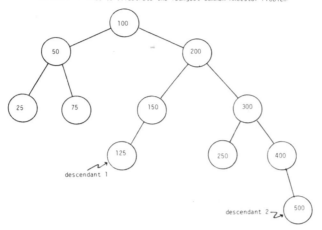

Figure 1 - Tree to Illustrate the Youngest-Common-Ancestor Problem

We must now find a software solution to the above problem. From the informal problem solution it is evident that we have identified the abstract object, tree, and several important operations on this object. Specifically, the following entities have been identified:

Abstract Objects Used in Informal Strategy

Tree (Binary Search Tree)

Operations on Abstract Objects

Build Tree
Locate Position
Compute Level
Move Up
Is Null
Equal Value

Our design will use an abstract data type called a tree. We will assume that an Ada package that defines the abstract data type tree and some associated general tree operations is available for our use. Further, we assume that the implementation details and, in particular, the data structure for the abstract data type tree are hidden and inaccessible. We assume that the tree package specification is available.

We must design the system independent of the representational details of the tree abstract data type. There is a price that must be paid for this. The primitive operations normally available for tree manipulations when the representational details are given are no longer accessible. Since the Ada package that we are given hides the tree structure, then, for example, we cannot access the left child or right child of a given node directly. The Ada package specification must explicitly make these operations available for our use. Similarly, we cannot assign one node to another or determine whether a tree is empty unless these operations are defined in the Ada package. In short, the Ada tree package must support the tree data abstraction with functional abstractions (i.e. a set of procedures and functions that perform the usual and necessary tree operations).

If specific tree operations are required in the design of the software system that are not supplied in the Ada tree

package, then we must define these operations separately. In particular, another package defining the required specialized tree operations for the problem may be created. However, since the data structure used for the type tree is hidden, we must be able to create these additional operations by using only those operations that are available to us in the general Ada tree package.

The overhead of supporting the tree abstraction with general tree manipulation procedures is well worth it. If, in the future, the hidden representational details of the tree structure and the procedures that operate on the tree in the Ada tree package are changed, the software system(s) that use the tree modules will not have to be changed at all. They may not even need to be recompiled. Only the module body that contains the implementation details of the Ada tree package and its supporting procedures would have to be changed. This kind of localized maintenance is difficult to achieve using older methods of software design.

The Modular Design Chart. We now introduce a design tool which we call the modular design chart. This chart provides a graphical overview of the software system architecture. It represents the modular decomposition of the system into its component modules. Each package specification is represented by a box. The exportable software components including constants, types, objects, subprograms (functions and procedures) are listed in the box. In addition, the package bodies are also represented by boxes. A software bus provides the logical interconnection between the modules that makeup the software system. The interdependencies that exist among the modules are made evident in the modular design chart. Finally, the main driver program with its connection to the system is shown.

The modular design chart is a useful design aid for representing the architecture of a software system. Such a design chart clearly indicates the resources available in each module or package, the interface connections of the module to the software outside of the module, and the interconnection of the modules that comprise the design.

Complex systems may be partitioned into many different sets of modules. Indeed, the main challenge of modular software design is determining the most sensible decomposition of the software system. This creative process of problem decomposition may be performed using the modular design chart as an aid.

We display the first modular design chart for the youngest-common-ancestor problem in Figure 2. We have partitioned the system into two main modules, GENERAL_TREE_OPS and SPECIALIZED_TREE_OPS.

The first module (package), GENERAL_TREE_OPS, contains a set of basic tree manipulations that are available to us in the supplied Ada tree package. We have not listed all the operations available in the given Ada tree package but only those that are required for this level of the design. The operations contained in GENERAL_TREE_OPS were specified by the designers of this package so that they might prove useful in other applications involving trees.

The specialized tree operations (Build Tree, Locate Position, Compute Level, and Move Up) that we previously identified in the informal strategy are not available in the supplied GENERAL_TREE_OPS package because they do not represent commonly used operations associated with tree manipulations.

Journal of Pascal, Ada & Modula-2 Mar/Apr '84

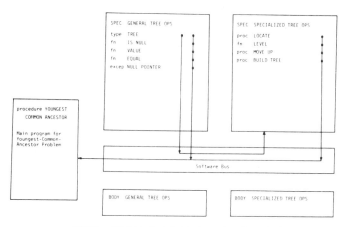

Figure 2 - First Modular Design Chart for Youngest-Common-Ancestor Problem

```
      procedure LOCATE (T : TREE;   INFO : INTEGER;   S : in out TREE);
         -- This procedure returns a pointer S to the node with
         -- value INFO.

      function LEVEL (T,S : TREE) return INTEGER;
         -- This function returns the level within tree T of a node
         -- S.  The root node is defined to have level zero.

      procedure MOVE_UP (T : in TREE;   S : in out TREE);
         -- This procedure replaces node S by its parent in tree T.

      procedure BUILD_TREE (T : in out TREE);
         -- This procedure takes input from the user and constructs
         -- a search tree.

   end SPECIALIZED_TREE_OPS;
------------------------------------------------------------------

   with GENERAL_TREE_OPS, SPECIALIZED_TREE_OPS, TEXT_IO;
   use  GENERAL_TREE_OPS, SPECIALIZED_TREE_OPS, TEXT_IO;

      --From GENERAL_TREE_OPS
      --        import type TREE,
      --        import functions IS_NULL, EQUAL, VALUE,
      --        import exception NULL_POINTER.

      --From SPECIALIZED_TREE_OPS
      --        import function LEVEL,
      --        import procedures LOCATE, MOVE_UP, BUILD_TREE.

      --From TEXT_IO
      --        import put_line, put, get, new_line.

   procedure YOUNGEST_COMMON_ANCESTOR is

      T, N1, N2         : TREE;
      LEVEL1, LEVEL2 : INTEGER;
      VALUE1, VALUE2 : INTEGER;

   begin  --YOUNGEST_COMMON_ANCESTOR
      BUILD_TREE( T );
      new_line;
      put_line ("Compute the youngest common ancestor of two nodes.");
      put ("Enter the value of the first node: ");
      get ( VALUE1 );
      LOCATE( T, VALUE1, N1 );
      put ("Enter the value of the second node: ");
      get ( VALUE2 );
      LOCATE( T, VALUE2, N2 );
      if ( IS_NULL( N1 ) or IS_NULL( N2 ) ) then
         new_line;
         put_line ("At least one of the values is not in the tree.");
         put_line ("Cannot continue processing.");
      else
         LEVEL1 := LEVEL( T, N1 );
         LEVEL2 := LEVEL( T, N2 );
         while LEVEL1 > LEVEL2 loop
            MOVE_UP( T, N1 );
            LEVEL1 := LEVEL1 -1;
         end loop;
         while LEVEL2 > LEVEL1 loop
            MOVE_UP( T, N2 );
            LEVEL2 := LEVEL2 - 1;
         end loop;
         --N1 and N1 are now at the same level.
         while not EQUAL( N1, N2 ) loop
            MOVE_UP( T, N1 );
            MOVE_UP( T, N2 );
         end loop;
         new_line;
         put ("The youngest common ancestor is ");
         put ( VALUE( N1 ) );
      end if;
   exception
      when NULL_POINTER =>
         put ("Cannot return the value of a null pointer.");
   end YOUNGEST_COMMON_ANCESTOR;
```

The second package, SPECIALIZED__TREE__OPS, contains the more specialized operations (abstractions) BUILD__TREE, LOCATE, LEVEL, and MOVE__UP, that are required to develop the software system for the youngest-common-ancestor problem. SPECIALIZED__TREE__OPS imports the abstract tree type from the first module.

Finally, the modular design chart displays the main program module which must import operations from each of the two system modules. We have chosen not to display standard system library modules such as TEXT__IO and STANDARD even though we import procedures f.om these modules.

Corresponding to the modular design chart given in Figure 2, is a modular design listing. This listing is given below. We have included a partial package specification for the GENERAL__TREE__OPS package (this package specification must be supplied with the package software). The dashed lines are used to indicate separately compiled units.

```
Modular Design Listing
----------------------

package GENERAL_TREE_OPS is

   type TREE is limited private;

   function IS_NULL (T : TREE) return BOOLEAN;
      -- This function returns the value TRUE if the tree
      -- pointer T is NULL and FALSE otherwise.

   function VALUE (T : TREE) return INTEGER;
      -- This function returns the value of node T.

   function EQUAL (T,S : TREE) return BOOLEAN;
      -- This function returns TRUE if T and S are equal,
      -- FALSE otherwise.

   NULL_POINTER : exception;
      -- This exeception is raised if VALUE is called with
      -- a null pointer.

private
   type NODE;
   type TREE is access NODE;
   type NODE is
      record
         VAL   : INTEGER;
         LEFT  : TREE;
         RIGHT : TREE;
      end record;

end GENERAL_TREE_OPS;

with GENERAL_TREE_OPS;  use GENERAL_TREE_OPS;

package SPECIALIZED_TREE_OPS  is

   -- From GENERAL_TREE_OPS
   --       import type TREE,
```

You may note how the main program reads almost like the informal problem solution. This is true because of the high level of abstraction employed in the design process.

The Ada specification for GENERAL__TREE__OPS contains a private part that indicates to the compiler the data structure for the abstract object TREE. The user of this package (i.e. the software developer) cannot access this data structure directly thus forcing true data abstraction and information hiding to be part of the system design.

The modular design listing may be compiled. This assures us of correct high-level system integration early in the design process. We have built the frame of our software system at the design level with the modular design chart and associated modular design listing as the foundation for the design. This approach to software design uses Ada as a program design language.

As we begin to implement the system (i.e. construct the package bodies), we expect that additional components will have to be added to some or all of the package specifications because additional tree manipulations such as finding the left and right offspring of a given node may have to be performed at the implementation level. Ordinarily, these low-level operations would be performed directly in terms of the data structure defined for the tree. Here, using object-oriented design, additional functional abstractions must be created in order that the implementation may proceed smoothly. Thus the design must be iterated as the implementation evolves.

A package that defines an abstract data type for general purpose use (such as a tree) must provide functional abstractions (subprogram specifications) for the numerous low-level operations that must be performed on the abstract data type so that the user of such a package, the software developer, can implement specific application-dependent operations. If the designers of the abstract data type package fail to do this, then the package may be useless in many applications unless the software developer can request of the original package designers (those who have the source code for the package body) that they add the required additional operations to the original package. This mode of operation may be feasible on large in-house software development projects but is probably close to impossible for widely distributed Ada software packages.

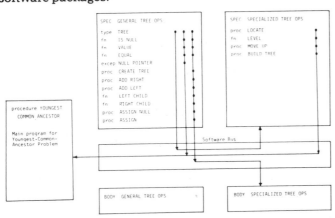

Figure 3 - Final Modular Design Chart for Youngest-Common-Ancestor Problem

To illustrate this, we display the modular design chart for the final software system in Figure 3. Note the additional components of GENERAL__TREE__OPS that were required to support the implementation of the system. If all of these additional operations were not defined in the original Ada tree package supplied to us, then we would have to implement the required operations in our specialized tree operations package in order to complete the software system. This might be impossible because the implementation of some of the important low-level tree operations require access to the implementation details of the tree data structure itself. Only the GENERAL__TREE__OPS package body has access to these details. It is therefore very important that the designers of the general purpose Ada tree package define those tree operations that will enable us to develop our specialized

operations without knowledge of the data structure used to implement the abstract data type tree.

The Finished Software System. We now display the complete software system for the youngest-common-ancestor problem.

```
5.0  The Finished Software System

      We now display the complete software system for the
youngest common ancestor problem.

package GENERAL_TREE_OPS is

   type TREE is limited private;

   procedure CREATE_TREE (T : in out TREE; INFO : in INTEGER);
      -- This procedure returns the root node for a new tree.

   procedure ADD_RIGHT (T : in out TREE;  INFO : in INTEGER);
      -- This procedure adds a right child containing INFO to
      -- the node T.

   procedure ADD_LEFT (T : in out TREE;  INFO : in INTEGER);
      -- This procedure adds a left child containing INFO to
      -- the node T.

   function IS_NULL (T : TREE) return BOOLEAN;
      -- This function returns the value TRUE if the tree
      -- pointer T is NULL and FALSE otherwise.

   function LEFT_CHILD (T : TREE) return TREE;
      -- This function returns the left child of node T.

   function RIGHT_CHILD (T : TREE) return TREE;
      -- This function returns the right child of node T.

   function VALUE (T : TREE) return INTEGER;
      -- This function returns the value of node T.

   procedure ASSIGN_NULL (T : in out TREE);
      -- This procedure assigns the pointer T to NULL.

   function EQUAL (T,S : TREE) return BOOLEAN;
      -- This function returns TRUE if T and S are equal,
      -- FALSE otherwise.

   procedure ASSIGN (T : in TREE; S : in out TREE);
      -- This procedure assigns S to have the same value as T.

   NULL_POINTER : exception;
      -- This exception is raised if VALUE is called with
      -- a null pointer.

private
   type NODE;
   type TREE is access NODE;
   type NODE is
      record
         VAL   : INTEGER;
         LEFT  : TREE;
         RIGHT : TREE;
      end record;

end GENERAL_TREE_OPS;
-------------------------------------------------------------------

with GENERAL_TREE_OPS;  use GENERAL_TREE_OPS;

package SPECIALIZED_TREE_OPS  is

      -- From GENERAL_TREE_OPS
      --
      --       import type TREE,
      --       import procedures ADD_RIGHT, ADD_LEFT.

   procedure LOCATE (T : TREE;  INFO : INTEGER;  S : in out TREE);
      -- This procedure returns a pointer S to the node with
      -- value INFO.

   function LEVEL (T,S : TREE) return INTEGER;
      -- This function returns the level within tree T of a node
      -- S.  The root node is defined to have level zero.

   procedure MOVE_UP (T : in TREE;  S : in out TREE);
      -- This procedure replaces node S by its parent in tree T.

   procedure BUILD_TREE (T : in out TREE);
      -- This procedure takes input from the user and constructs
      -- a search tree.

end SPECIALIZED_TREE_OPS;
-------------------------------------------------------------------

with GENERAL_TREE_OPS, SPECIALIZED_TREE_OPS, TEXT_IO;
use  GENERAL_TREE_OPS, SPECIALIZED_TREE_OPS, TEXT_IO;

   --From GENERAL_TREE_OPS
   --       import type TREE,
   --       import functions IS_NULL, EQUAL, VALUE,
   --       import procedures CREATE_TREE, ADD_NODE,
   --       import exception  NULL_POINTER.
```

```
    --From SPECIALIZED_TREE_OPS
    --      import function LEVEL,
    --      import procedures LOCATE, MOVE_UP, BUILD_TREE.

    --From TEXT_IO
    --      import put_line, put, get, new_line.

procedure YOUNGEST_COMMON_ANCESTOR is

    T, N1, N2       : TREE;
    LEVEL1, LEVEL2 : INTEGER;
    VALUE1, VALUE2 : INTEGER;

  begin  --YOUNGEST_COMMON_ANCESTOR
    BUILD_TREE( T );
    new_line;
    put_line ("We compute the youngest common ancestor of two nodes.");
    put ("Enter the value of the first node: ");
    get ( VALUE1 );
    LOCATE( T, VALUE1, N1 );
    put ("Enter the value of the second node: ");
    get ( VALUE2 );
    LOCATE( T, VALUE2, N2 );
    if ( IS_NULL( N1 ) or IS_NULL( N2 ) ) then
       new_line;
       put_line ("At least one of the values is not in the tree.");
       put_line ("Cannot continue processing.");
    else
       LEVEL1 := LEVEL( T, N1 );
       LEVEL2 := LEVEL( T, N2 );
       while LEVEL1 > LEVEL2 loop
          MOVE_UP( T, N1 );
          LEVEL1 := LEVEL1 -1;
       end loop;
       while LEVEL2 > LEVEL1 loop
          MOVE_UP( T, N2 );
          LEVEL2 := LEVEL2 - 1;
       end loop;
       --N1 and N1 are now at the same level.
       while not EQUAL( N1, N2 ) loop
          MOVE_UP( T, N1 );
          MOVE_UP( T, N2 );
       end loop;
       new_line;
       put ("The youngest common ancestor is ");
       put ( VALUE( N1 ) );
    end if;
  exception
    when NULL_POINTER =>
       put ("Cannot return the value of a null pointer.");
end YOUNGEST_COMMON_ANCESTOR;
----------------------------------------------------------------

package body GENERAL_TREE_OPS is

    procedure CREATE_TREE( T : in out TREE;  INFO : in INTEGER) is
    begin
       T := new NODE;
       T.VAL := INFO;
    end CREATE_TREE;

    procedure ADD_RIGHT( T : in out TREE;  INFO : in INTEGER) is
       P : TREE;
    begin
       CREATE_TREE( P, INFO );
       T.RIGHT := P;
    end ADD_RIGHT;

    procedure ADD_LEFT( T : in out TREE; INFO : in INTEGER) is
       P : TREE;
    begin
       CREATE_TREE(P, INFO );
       T.LEFT := P;
    end ADD_LEFT;

    function IS_NULL( T : TREE) return BOOLEAN is
    begin
       if T = null then
          return TRUE;
       else
          return FALSE;

       end if;
    end IS_NULL;

    function LEFT_CHILD( T : TREE) return TREE is
    begin
       return T.LEFT;
    end LEFT_CHILD;

    function RIGHT_CHILD( T : TREE) return TREE is
    begin
       return T.RIGHT;
    end RIGHT_CHILD;

    function VALUE( T : TREE) return TREE is
    begin
       if T /= null then
          return T.VAL;
       else
          raise NULL_POINTER;
       end if;
    end VALUE;

    procedure ASSIGN_NULL( T : in out TREE) is
    begin
       T := null;
    end ASSIGN_NULL;
```

```
    function EQUAL( T,S : TREE) return BOOLEAN is
    begin
       if T = S then
          return TRUE;
       else
          return FALSE;
       end if;
    end EQUAL;

    procedure ASSIGN( T : in TREE; S : in out TREE) is
    begin
       S := T;
    end ASSIGN;

end GENERAL_TREE_OPS;
----------------------------------------------------------------

with GENERAL_TREE_OPS, TEXT_IO;
use  GENERAL_TREE_OPS, TEXT_IO;

package body SPECIALIZED_TREE_OPS is

    --From GENERAL_TREE_OPS
    --      import type TREE,
    --      import functions IS_NULL, LEFT_CHILD, RIGHT_CHILD,
    --                ADD_RIGHT, ADD_LEFT, EQUAL, VALUE,
    --      import procedures CREATE_TREE, ASSIGN_NULL, ASSIGN.

    --From TEXT_IO

           import put, get, put_line, new_line.

    procedure LOCATE (T : TREE; INFO : INTEGER; S : in out TREE) is

       procedure L( T : TREE; S : in out TREE) is
       begin
          if not IS_NULL( T ) then
             L( LEFT_CHILD( T ), S );
             if VALUE( T ) = INFO then
                ASSIGN( T, S );
             end if;
             L( RIGHT_CHILD( T ), S);
          end if;
       end L;

    begin  --LOCATE
       ASSIGN_NULL( S );
       L( T, S );
    end LOCATE;

    function LEVEL (T, S : TREE) return INTEGER is

       FOUND : BOOLEAN;
       COUNT : INTEGER;

       procedure L( T, S : TREE;  COUNT : in out INTEGER) is
       begin
          if not IS_NULL( T ) then
             if ( not FOUND ) and
                not (IS_NULL( LEFT_CHILD( T ) ) and
                     IS_NULL( RIGHT_CHILD( T ) ) )
             then
                COUNT := COUNT + 1;
             end if;
             L( LEFT_CHILD( T ), S, COUNT );
             L( RIGHT_CHILD( T ), S, COUNT );
             if ( not FOUND ) and
                not (IS_NULL( LEFT_CHILD( T ) ) and
                     IS_NULL( RIGHT_CHILD( T ) ) )
             then
                COUNT := COUNT + 1;
             end if;
             if EQUAL( T, S ) then
                FOUND := TRUE;
             end if;
          end if;
       end L;

    begin  --LEVEL
       FOUND := FALSE;
       COUNT := 0;
       if EQUAL( S, T ) then
          return 0
       else
          L( T, S, COUNT );

          return COUNT;
       end if;
    end LEVEL;

    procedure MOVE_UP( T : in TREE;  S : in out TREE) is
    begin
       if not EQUAL( T, S ) then
          if not IS_NULL( T ) then
             if EQUAL( LEFT_CHILD( T ), S ) or
                EQUAL( RIGHT_CHILD( T ), S )
             then
                ASSIGN( T, S );
             end if;
             MOVE_UP( LEFT_CHILD( T ), S );
             MOVE_UP( RIGHT_CHILD( T ), S );
          end if;
       end if;
    end MOVE_UP;

    procedure BUILD_TREE( T : in out TREE) is

       I : INTEGER;
```

35

```
procedure ADD_NODE( T : in out TREE;   INFO : in INTEGER) is
   P,Q : TREE;
begin
   ASSIGN( T, Q );
   while not IS_NULL( Q )
      loop
         ASSIGN( Q, P );
         if INFO < VALUE( P ) then
            ASSIGN( LEFT_CHILD( P ), Q );
         else
            ASSIGN( RIGHT_CHILD( P ), Q );
         end if;
      end loop;
   if INFO < VALUE( P ) then
      ADD_LEFT( P, INFO );
   else
      ADD_RIGHT( P, INFO );
   end if;
end ADD_NODE;

begin  --BUILD_TREE
   put ("Enter the first node of the search tree: ");
   get ( I );
   CREATE_TREE( T, I );
   new_line;
   put_line ("Enter the sequence of values for the search tree");
   put_line ("Use - 1 as a terminator to end the sequence");
   new_line;
   loop
      put ("Enter a node in the tree: ");
      get ( I );
      exit when I = - 1;
      ADD_NODE( T, I );
      end loop;
   end BUILD_TREE;

   .

end SPECIALIZED_TREE_OPS;
```

References

1. Booch, G., *Software Engineering with Ada*, Benjamin/ Cummings, 1983.
2. Wiener, R. and R. Sincovec, *Programming in Ada*, John Wiley, 1983.
3. Wiener, R.S. and R.F. Sincovec, *Software Engineering with Modula-2 and Ada*, John Wiley, 1984.
4. Tenenbaum, A.M. and M.J. Augenstein, *Data Structures Using Pascal*, Prentice-Hall, 1981.

"Neither ever quite the same, nor ever quite another"

Reusability: The Case for Object-Oriented Design

Bertrand Meyer, Interactive Software Engineering

Simply being more organized will not make the reuse problem go away. The issues are technical, not managerial. The answers lie in object-oriented design.

"Why isn't software more like hardware? Why must every new development start from scratch? There should be catalogs of software modules, as there are catalogs of VLSI devices: When we build a new system, we should be ordering components from these catalogs and combining them, rather that reinventing the wheel every time. We would write less software, and perhaps do a better job at that which we do develop. Then wouldn't the problems everyone laments — the high costs, the overruns, the lack of reliability — just go away? Why isn't it so?"

If you are a software developer or manager you have probably heard such remarks before. Perhaps you have uttered them yourself.

The repetitive nature of computer programming is indeed striking. Over and over again, programmers weave a number of basic patterns: sorting, searching, reading, writing, comparing, traversing, allocating, synchronizing. . . Experienced programmers know well the feeling of *déjà vu* that is so characteristic of their trade.

Attempts have been made to measure this phenomenon; one estimate is that less than 15 percent of new code serves an original purpose.[1]

A way to assess this situation less quantitatively but perhaps closer to home is to answer the following question honestly, again assuming you develop software or direct people who do. Consider the problem of table searching: An element of some kind, say x, is given with a set of similar elements, t; the program is to determine if x appears in t. The question is: How many times in the last six months did you or people working for you write some program fragment for table searching?

Reprinted from *IEEE Software*, March 1987, pages 50-64. Copyright © 1987 by The Institute of Electrical and Electronics Engineers, Inc.

Chances are the answer will be one or more. But what is really remarkable is that, most likely, the fragment or fragments will have been written at the lowest reasonable level of abstraction — as code instead of by calling existing routines.

Yet table searching is one of the best researched areas of computer science. Excellent books describe the fundamental algorithms — it would seem nobody should need to code a searching algorithm in standard cases anymore. After all, electronic engineers don't design standard inverters, they buy them.

This article addresses this fundamental goal of software engineering, reusability, and a companion requirement, extendibility (the ease with which software can be modified to reflect changes in specifications). Progress in one of these areas usually advances the aims of the other as well, so when we discuss reusability, we will be adding *in petto*, ". . .and extendibility."

Our main thesis is that object-oriented design is the most promising technique now known for attaining the goals of extendability and reusability.

Ni tout à fait la même. . .

Why isn't reuse more common? Some of the reasons are nontechnical:

• Economic incentives tend to work against reusability. If you, as a contractor, deliver software that is too general and too reusable, you won't get the next job — your client won't need a next job!

• The famous not-invented-here complex also works against reusability.

• Reusable software must be retrievable, which means we need libraries of reusable modules and good database searching tools so client programmers can find appropriate modules easily. (Some terminology: A client of a module *M* is any module relying on *M*; a client programmer is a person who writes a client module; an implementer of *M* is the programmer who writes *M*.)

In the US, the STARS project is an effort that aims, among other things, to overcome such obstacles.

Tip of the iceberg. In my opinion, these issues are only the tip of the iceberg; the main roadblocks are technical. Reuse is limited because designing reusable software is hard. This article elaborates on what makes it so hard and should dispel any naive hope that software problems would just go away if we were more organized in filing program units.

Let's take a closer look at the repetitive nature of software development. Programmers do tend to do the same kinds of things time and time again, but they are not *exactly* the same things. If they were, the solution would be easy, at least on paper; but in practice, so many details may change as to render moot any simple-minded attempt at capturing commonality.

Such is the software engineer's plight: time and time again composing a new variation that elaborates on the same basic themes: "neither ever quite the same, nor ever quite another. . ."*

Take table searching again. True, the general form of the code is going to look the same each time: Start at some position in the table *t*; explore the table from that position, checking if the element found at the current position is the one being sought; if not, move to another position. The process terminates either when the element has been found or when all positions of interest in the table have been unsucessfully probed.

This paradigm applies to all standard cases of data representation (unsorted or sorted array, unsorted or sorted linked list, sequential file, binary tree, B-tree, hash table, etc.). It may be expressed more precisely as a program schema:

```
Search(x : ELEMENT, t :
TABLE_OF_ELEMENT)
return boolean is
    --Look for element x in table t
  pos: POSITION
begin
  pos:= INITIAL_POSITION (x,t);
  while not EXHAUSTED (pos,t)
  and then not FOUND (pos,x,t) do
    pos := NEXT (pos,x,t);
  end;
```

---

* *Et qui n'est chaque fois ni tout à fait la même. Ni tout à fait une autre. . .: And [she] who from one [dream] to the next is neither ever quite the same, nor ever quite another. . . — Gérard de Nerval.*

```
    return not EXHAUSTED (pos,t)
end -- Search
```

Too many variants. The difficulty in coming up with a general software element for searching is apparent: Even though the pattern is fixed, the amount of variable information is considerable. Details that may change include the type of table elements (ELEMENT), how the initial position is selected (INITIAL_POSITION), how the algorithm proceeds from one position to the next (NEXT), and all the types and routines in uppercase, which will admit a different refinement for each variant of the algorithm.

Not only is it hard to implement a general-purpose searching module, it is almost as hard to *specify* such a module so that client modules could rely on it without knowing the implementation.

Beyond the basic problem of factoring out the parts that are common to all implementations of table searching, an even tougher challenge is to capture the commonality within some conceptual subset. For example, an implementation using sequential search in arrays is very similar to one based on sequential linked lists; the code will differ only by small (yet crucial) details, shown in Table 1.

Within each group of implementations (all sequential tables, for example), there are similarities. If we really want to write carefully organized libraries of reusable software elements, we must be able to use commonalities at all levels of abstraction.

All these issues are purely technical; solving all the managerial and economical obstacles to reusability that one hears about in executives' meetings will not help a bit here.

Routines

Work on reusability has followed several approaches (see the box on p. 54). The classical technique is to build libraries of routines (we use the word "routine" to cover what is variously called procedure, function, subroutine, or subprogram). Each routine in the library implements a well-defined operation. This approach has been quite successful in scientific computation — excellent libraries exist for numerical applications.

Table 1.
Implementation variants for sequential search.

	Sequential array	Linked list	Sequential file
Start search at first position	$i := 1$	$l := first$	rewind
Move to next position	$i := l + 1$	$l := l.next$	read
Test for table exhausted	$i >$ size	$l =$ null	end_ of_ file

Indeed, the routine-library approach seems to work well in areas where a set of individual problems can be identified, provided the following limitations hold:

• Every instance of each problem should be identifiable with a small set of parameters.

• The individual problems should be clearly distinct. Any significant commonality that might exist cannot be put to good use, except by reusing some of the design.

• No complex data structures should be involved because they would have to be distributed among the routines and the conceptual autonomy of modules would be lost.

The table-searching example may be used to show the limitations of this approach. We can either write a single routine or a set of routines, each corresponding to a specific case.

A single routine will have many parameters and will probably be structured like a gigantic set of case instructions. Its complexity and inefficiency will make it unusable. Worse, the addition of any new case will mean modification and recompilation of the whole routine.

A set of routines will be large and contain many routines that look very similar (like the searching routines for sequential arrays and sequential linked lists). But there is no simple way for the implementers to use this similarity. Client programmers will have to find their way through a maze of routines.

Modular languages

Languages like Modula-2 and Ada offer a first step toward a solution. These languages use the notion of module (the Ada term is package), providing a higher level structuring facility than the routine. A module may contain more than one routine, together with declarations of types, constants, and variables. A module may thus be devoted to an entire data structure and its associated operations.

This approach is rooted in the theory of data abstraction, but its basic concepts may be illustrated simply with our table-searching example.

A table-searching routine isn't worth very much by itself; it must be complemented by routines that create and delete tables and insert and delete elements, all governed by a certain representation of the table, given by a type declaration. These routines and the type declaration are closely connected logically, so they might as well be part of the same syntactic unit. Such units are basically what modular languages offer.

This is a significant improvement: We can now keep under one roof a set of related routines that pertain to a specific implementation of a data abstraction. For example, the module for a binary search tree of integers (INT_BINARY_TREE) will contain the declaration of a type intbintree and routines Create, Search, Insert, and so on. The client code might look like:

```
x : integer; b : boolean; p :
INT_BINARY_TREE.intbintree;
INT_BINARY_TREE.Create (t);
INT_BINARY_TREE.Insert (x,b) ;
b := INT_BINARY_TREE.Search(x,p)
```

(Here I use the Ada dot notation: $A.f$ means "feature f, such as a type or routine, from module A." In Ada and other languages, simpler notations are available when a client repeatedly uses features from a given module.)

For reusability, these techniques are useful but limited. They are useful because encapsulating groups of related features helps implementers (in gathering features) as well as clients (in retrieving features), and all of this favors reusability. But they

are limited because they do not reduce significantly the amount of software that needs to be written. Specifically, they don't offer any new clue as to how to capture common features.

Overloading and genericity

A further improvement is overloading, as provided in Algol 68 and Ada. Overloading means attaching more than one meaning to a name, such as the name of an operation.

For example, when different representations of tables are each defined by a separate type declaration, you would use overloading to give the same name, say Search, to all associated search procedures. In this way, a search operation will always be invoked as $b := $ Search (x,t), regardless of the implementation chosen for t and the type of table elements.

Overloading works well in a strictly typed language where the compiler has enough type information about x and t to choose the right version of search.

A companion technique is genericity, provided in Ada and Clu. Genericity allows a module to be defined with generic parameters that represent types. Instances of the module are then produced by supplying different types as actual parameters. This is a definite aid to reusability because just one generic module is defined, instead of a group of modules that differ only in the types of objects they manipulate.

For example, instead of having an INT_BINARY_TREE module, a REAL_BINARY_TREE module, and so on, you could define a single generic BINARY_TREE [T] module. Any actual type (INTEGER, REAL, etc.) could correspond to the formal generic parameter T. The search routine can be defined in the generic module to act on an argument x of type T. Then every instance of the module automatically has its own version of search.

In summary, overloading and genericity each offer something toward reuse:

• with overloading, the client programmer may write the same code when using different implementations of the same data

abstraction, as provided by different modules;

• with genericity, the implementer may write a single module for all instances of the same implementation of a data abstraction, applied to various types of objects.

These techniques are interesting advancements in reusability. But they do not go far enough. Roughly speaking, they do not provide enough flexibility and they force programmers to decide too much too soon.

Not enough flexibility. They are not flexible enough because they cannot capture fine grains of commonality between groups of implementations of the same general data abstraction. This is because there are only two levels of modules: generic modules, which are parameterized and thus open to variation, but not directly usable; and fully instantiated modules, which are directly usable but not open to refinement. Thus we cannot describe a complex hierarchy of representations that have different levels of parameterizations.

Too much too soon. Neither technique allows a client to use various implementations of a data abstraction (say the table) without knowing which implementation is used in each instance.

On one hand, each generic module refers to a single, explicitly specified instance of that module. Overloading, on the other hand, is essentially a syntactic facility that relieves the programmer of having to invent names for different implementations; the burden is placed on the compiler instead. Nevertheless, each invocation of an overloaded operation name, say Search(x,t), refers to a specific version of the operation — and both the client programmer and compiler know which version that is.

Client programmers do not actually need to know how each version is implemented, since Ada and Modula-2 modules are used by clients through an interface that lists the available routines, independent of their implementation. But they do need to decide explicitly which version is used. For example, if your modules use various kinds of tables, you don't have to know how to implement hash tables, indexed sequential files, and the like — but you must say which representation you want each time you use a table operation.

True representation-independence only happens when a client can write the invocation Search(x,t) and mean, "look for x in t using the appropriate algorithm for whatever kind of table and element x and t happen to be at the time the invocation is executed."

This degree of flexibility, essential for the construction of reusable software elements, can only be achieved with object-oriented design.

Object-oriented design

This fashionable term has been somewhat overused in recent years. The definition used here is fairly dogmatic. Object-oriented design is viewed as a *software decomposition technique*. An overview of some object-oriented languages is given in the box on p. 59.

Object-oriented design may be defined as a technique which, unlike classical (functional) design, bases the modular decomposition of a software system on the classes of objects the system manipulates, not on the functions the system performs. Classical approaches like functional top-down design (even, to a large extent, dataflow analysis methods) require designers to first ask what the system does. Object-oriented design avoids such questions as long as possible, in fact until the system actually is run. Why?

The top-down functional approach is probably adequate if the program you are writing solves a fixed problem once and for all. But the picture changes when you take a long-term view, for what the system will do in its first release is probably going to be a little different from what you think it will do at requirements time, and *very* different from what it will do five years later, if it survives that long.

However, the categories of objects on which the system acts will probably be more or less the same. An operating system will always work on devices, memories, processing units, communication channels, and so on; a document processing system will always work on documents, chapters, sections, paragraphs, and so on.

Thus it is wiser in the long term to rely on categories of objects as a basis for decomposition, but (and this is an important but) only if these categories are viewed at a sufficiently high level of abstraction. This is where abstract data types come in.*

Abstract data types

If we use the physical structure of objects as the basis for decomposition, we won't go very far toward protecting our software's structure against requirement changes. In fact, we will probably be worse off than we would be with functional design. A study by Lientz and Swanson,[3] quoted by Boehm,[4] shows that 17.5 percent of the cost of software maintenance stems from changes in programs that reflect changes in data formats. This emphasizes the need to separate the programs from the physical structure of the objects they handle.

Abstract data types provide a remarkable solution to this problem. An abstract data type describes a class of objects through the external properties of these objects instead of their computer representation. More precisely, an abstract data type is a class of objects characterized by the operations available on them and the abstract properties of these operations.

It turns out that abstract data types, which provide an excellent basis for software specification, are also useful at the design and implementation stage. In fact, they are essential to the object-oriented approach, and enable us to refine the definition of object-oriented design: Object-oriented design is the construction of software systems as structured collections of abstract data-type implementations.

An important aspect of the object-oriented method is that it actually identifies modules with implementations of

---

* One other design method that does emphasize the motto "look at the data before you look at the functions" is Jackson's method.[2] However, a comparative analysis of Jackson's method and object-oriented design falls beyond the scope of this article.

abstract data types. It is not only that modules *comprise* these implementations (as in Ada and Modula-2, and in Fortran-77, thanks to multiple-entry subroutines); a single program structure *is* both a module and a type. Such a dual-purpose structure was dubbed a "class" by the creators of the pioneer object-oriented language, Simula 67.

Two words should be emphasized in the above definition. The first is "implementation": A module of an object-oriented program is not an abstract data type, but one implementation of an abstract data type. However, the details of the implementation are not normally available to the rest of the world, which only sees the official specification of the abstract data type.

The second is "structured." Collections of classes may indeed be structured using two different relations: client and inheritance. Figure 1 illustrates these two relations. The client relation is represented by horizontal double arrows; inheritance by a single, vertical arrow.

Class A is said to be a client of B if A contains a declaration of the form *bb: B*. (In this and all other object-oriented examples, I use the notations and terminology of the object-oriented language Eiffel. See the box on p. 60 for more about Eiffel.)

In this case, A may manipulate *bb* only through the features defined in the specification of B. Features comprise both attributes (data items associated with objects of type B) and routines (operations for accessing or changing these objects). In Eiffel, features are applied through dot notation, as in $bb.x$, $bb.f (u, w, x)$.

As an example, consider a client class X of class BINARY_SEARCH_TREE that implements a specific form of tables. Client X may contain elements of the form:

```
bb:BINARY_SEARCH_TREE;
    -- declare bb as binary search tree
bb.Create;
    -- allocate table (routine call)
bb.insert (x);
    -- insert x into bb (routine call)
y:= bb.size ;
    -- (attribute access)
```

The second relation between classes, inheritance, is fundamental to true object-oriented languages. For example, our BINARY_SEARCH_TREE class may be defined as an heir (possibly indirect) to a class TABLE that describes the general properties of tables, independent of the representation.

A class C defined as an heir to a class A has all the features of A, to which it may add its own. Descendants of a class include its heirs, the heirs of its heirs, and so on. The relationship between C and A may be defined from the viewpoint of both the module and the type.

From the module perspective, inheritance allows the programmer to take an existing world (class A) and plunge it as a whole into a new world, C, which will inherit all its properties and add its own. In *multiple* inheritance, as present in Eiffel, more than one world may be used to define a new one.

From the type perspective, C is considered a special case of A: Any object of type C may also be interpreted as an object of type A. In particular, a variable of type A may be assigned an object of type C, although the reverse is not true, at least in a statically typed language like Eiffel. This

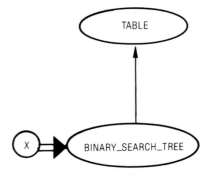

Figure 1. The client and inheritance relations in abstract data types. The client is represented by a horizontal double arrow; inheritance by a single, vertical arrow.

also holds in the case of multiple inheritance, as Figure 2 shows. This property is extremely important because it allows program entities to take different forms at runtime. The relation between *C* and *A* is an instance of the so-called Is-a relation (every lily *is a* flower; every binary search tree *is a* table).

The powerful combination of object-oriented design and these two relations — client and inheritance — is a key element in achieving extendibility and reusability.

An illustrative example

A new example, a full-screen entry system, will help contrast the object-oriented approach with classical functional decomposition. The example, a common data processing problem, should be interesting on its own: The problem is to write an interactive application that guides the user with full-screen panels at each stage.

The problem. Interactive sessions for such systems go through a series of states, each with a well-defined general pattern: A panel is displayed with questions for the user; the user supplies the required answer; the answer is checked for consistency (questions are asked until an acceptable answer is supplied); and the answer is processed somehow (a database is updated, for example). Part of the user's answer is a choice of the next steps; the system translates the user's choice into a transition to another state, and the same process is applied in the new state.

Figure 3 shows a panel for an imaginary airline reservation system. The screen shown is toward the end of a step; the user's answers are in italics.

The process begins in some initial state and ends whenever any among a set of final states is reached. A transition graph, like that in Figure 4, shows the overall structure of a session — the possible states and the transitions between them. The edges of the graph are labeled by numbers that correspond to the user's possible choices for the next step.

Our mission is to come up with a design and implementation for such applications that have as much generality and flexibility as possible.

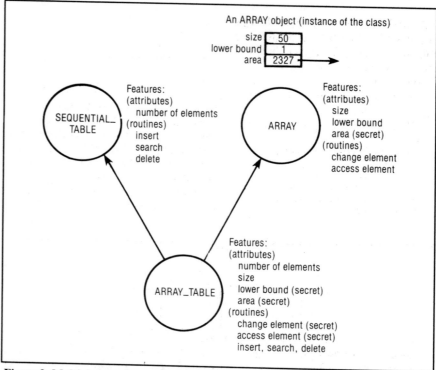

Figure 2. Multiple inheritance. In Eiffel, more than one world can be used to define a new world, which will inherit all the properies and add its own.

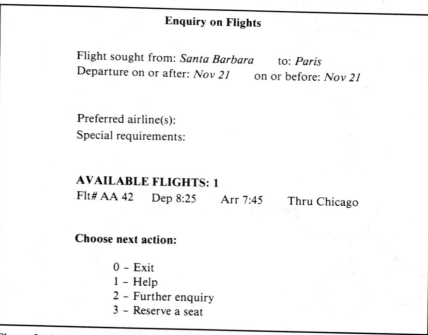

Figure 3. A panel for an interactive airline reservation system. The screen shown is toward the end of a step; the user's answers are in italics.

A simple-minded solution. We'll begin with a straightforward, unsophisticated program scheme. This version is made of a number of blocks, one for each state of the system: $B_{Enquiry}$, $B_{Reservation}$, $B_{Cancellation}$, and so on. A typical block looks like:

```
B_Enquiry:
    output "enquiry on flights" panel;
    repeat
        read user's answers and choice C for
        next step ;
        if error in answer then
        output appropriate message
    end until not error in answer end;
    process answer;
```

```
case C in
    C_0:goto Exit,
    C_1:goto B_help,
    C_2:goto B_Reservation,
    ...
end
```

(And similarly for each state.)

This structure will do the job, but of course there is much to criticize. The numerous goto instructions give it that famous spaghetti bowl look. This may be viewed as a cosmetic issue, solved by restructuring the program to eliminate jumps. But that would miss the point.

The problem is deeper. This program is bad not just because it has a lot of explicit branch instructions, but because the physical form of the problem has been wired into it. The branching structure of the program reflects exactly the transition structure of the graph in Figure 4.

This it terrible from a reusability and extendability standpoint. In real-world data-entry systems, the graph of Figure 4 might be quite complex — one study mentions examples with 300 different states.[5]

It is highly unlikely that the transition structure of such a system will be right the first time it is designed. Even after the first version is working, users will inevitably request new transitions, shortcuts, or help states. The prospect of modifying the whole program structure (not just program elements — the overall organization) for any one change is horrendous.

To improve on this solution we must separate the graph structure from the traversal algorithm. This seems appropriate because the structure depends on the particular interactive application (airline reservation), while its traversal is generic. As a side benefit, a functional decomposition will also remove the heretical gotos.

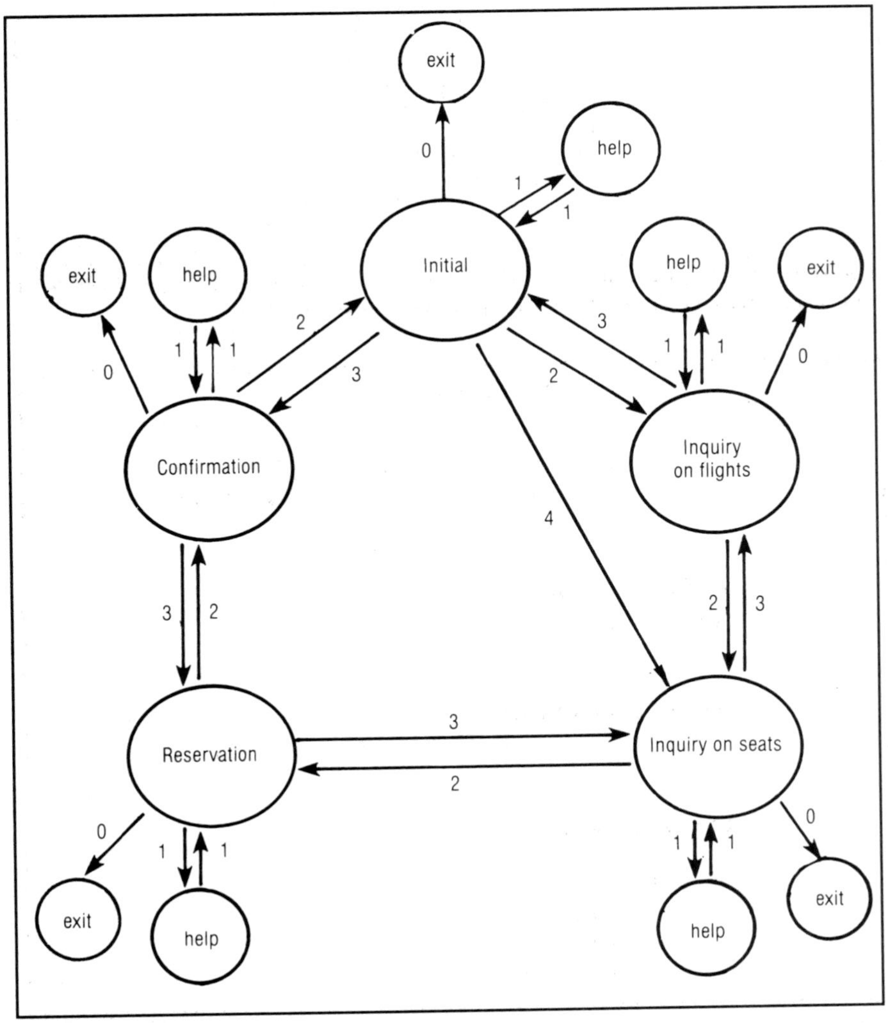

A procedural, "top-down" solution. We may encapsulate the graph structure in a two-argument function, Transition, such that Transition(s,c) is the state obtained when the user chooses c on leaving state s.

We use the word "function" in a mathematical sense: Transition may be represented either by a function in the programming sense (a routine that returns a value) or by a data structure, such as an array. The first solution may be preferable for readability because the transitions will appear in the program code itself. The second is better for flexibility because it is easier to change a data structure than a program. We can afford to postpone this decision.

The function transition is not sufficient to describe the transition graph. We must also define the state, initial, that begins the traversal and a Boolean-valued function is-final(s) that determines when a state is final. Initial and final states are treated dissymmetrically; while it is reasonable to

Figure 4. A state transition graph for an interactive application. The edges of the graph are labeled by numbers that correspond to the user's possible choices for the next step.

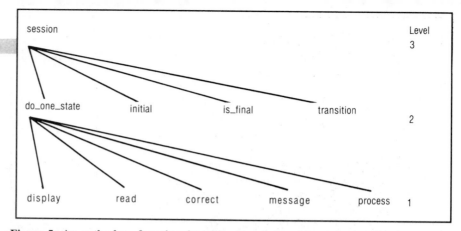

Figure 5. An orthodox, functional architecture for an interactive application. The "top," or main program, is the routine Session.

expect the dialog to always begin in the same state, we cannot expect it to always end in the same state.

Figure 5 shows the orthodox, functional architecture derived from this solution. As the top-down method teaches, this system has a "top," or main program. What else could it be but the routine that describes how to execute a complete interactive session?

This routine may be written to emphasize application-independence. Assume that a suitable representation is found for states (type STATE) and for the user's choice after each state (CHOICE):

```
session is
    -- execute a complete session of
    -- the interactive system
    current: STATE ; next: CHOICE
begin
    current := initial ;
    repeat
        do_one_state (current, next) ;
        -- the value of next is returned by routine
        -- do_one_state
        current := transition (current, next)
    until is_final (current) end
end -- session
```

This procedure does not show direct dependency upon any interactive application. To describe such an application, we must provide three of the elements on level two in Figure 5: a transition function (routine or data structure), an initial state, and an is_final predicate.

To complete the design, we refine the do_one_state routine, which describes the actions to be performed in each state. The body of this routine is essentially an abstracted form of the blocks in our spaghetti version:

```
do_one_state (in s : STATE ; out c : CHOICE) is
    --execute the actions associated with
    --state s,
    --returning into c the user's choice
    --for the next state
    a: ANSWER ; ok: BOOLEAN ;
begin
    repeat
        display(s) ; read(s,a) ;
        ok := correct(s,a) ;
        if not ok then message(s,a) end
    until ok end ;
    process (s,a) ; c := next_choice (a)
end -- do_one_state
```

For the remaining routines, we can only give a specification, because the implementations depend on the details of the appli-

cation and its various states: display(s) outputs the panel associated with state s; read(s,a) reads the user's answer to state s into a; correct(s,a) returns true if and only if a is an acceptable answer; if it is, process(s,a) processes answer a; if it isn't, message(s,a) outputs the relevant error message.

Type ANSWER is left unspecified. A value of this type, say a, globally represents the input entered by the user in a given state, including the user's choice of the next step, next_choice(a).

Data transmission. Is this solution satisfactory? Not from the standpoint of reusability.

True, we did separate what is generic and what is specific to a particular application, but this does not buy much flexibility. The main problem is the system's data transmission structure. Consider the functionalities (types of arguments and results) of the routines:

```
do_one_state: (in s: STATE ; out c: CHOICE)
display: (in s: STATE)
read: (in s: STATE ; out a: ANSWER)
correct: (in s: STATE ; a: ANSWER):
BOOLEAN
message: (in s: STATE, a: ANSWER)
process: (in s: STATE, a: ANSWER)
```

All these routines share the state s as a parameter, coming from the top module Session (where it is known as Current). The flow of data, illustrated in Figure 6, shows that (as a conservative economist might say) there's far too much state intervention. As a result, all the above routines must perform some form of case discrimination on s:

```
case s of
    State_1:....,
    ..................,
    State_n:....,
end
```

This implies long, complex code (a problem which could be solved with further decomposition) and (more annoying) it means that every routine must deal with, and thus know about, all possible states of the application. This makes it very difficult to implement extensions. Adding a new state, for example, entails modifications throughout. Such a situation is all too common in software development. System evolution becomes a nightmare as simple changes touch off a complex chain reaction in the system.

The situation is even worse than it appears. It would seem desirable to profit from the similar aspects of these types of interactive applications by storing the common parts in library routines. But this is unrealistic in the solution above: On top of the explicit parameters, all routines have an implicit one — the application itself, airline reservations.

A general-purpose version of display, for example, should know about all states of all possible applications in a given environment! The function transition should contain the transition graph for all applications. This is clearly impossible.

The law of inversion. What is wrong? Figure 6 exposes the flaw: there is too much data transmission in the software architecture. The remedy, which leads directly to object-oriented design, may be expressed by the following law: If there is too much data transmission in your routines, then put your routines into your data.

Instead of building modules around operations (session, do_one_state) and distributing data structures between the resulting routines, object-oriented design does the reverse. It uses the most important data structures as the basis for modularization and attaches each routine to the data structure to which it applies most closely.

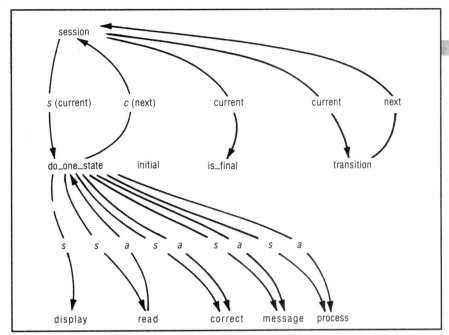

Figure 6. Data transmission in the architecture derived from with the top-down approach.

This law of inversion is the key to turning a functional decomposition into an object-oriented design: reverse the viewpoint and attach the routines to the data structures. To programmers trained in functional approaches, this is as revolutionary as making the Sun orbit Earth.

Of course, it's best to design in an object-oriented fashion from the beginning. However, the process of moving from a functional decomposition to an object-oriented structure is itself interesting. How do we find the most important data structures, around which modules are to be built?

Data transmission provides a clue. The data structures that are constantly transmitted between routines must be important, mustn't they?

Here the first candidate is obvious, the state (current, s). So our object-oriented solution will include a class STATE to implement the corresponding abstract data type. Among the features of a state are the five routines of level one in Figure 5 that describe the operations performed in a state (display, read, message, correct, and process), and the routine do_one_state without the state parameter.

In Eiffel notation, the class STATE may be written:

```
class STATE export
    next_choice, display, read, correct,
    message, process, do_one_state
feature
    user_answer: ANSWER ;
    next_choice: INTEGER ;
    do_one_state is
        do
            ...body of the routine...
```

```
        end;
    display is ... ;
    read is... ;
    correct: BOOLEAN is... ;
    message: is... ;
    process is... ;
end -- class STATE
```

The features of the class include two attributes, next_choice and user_answer, and six routines. Routines are divided into functions, which return a result (like correct, which returns a Boolean value) and procedures, which don't.

The export clause is used for information hiding: In a client class containing a declaration *s:* STATE, a feature application *s.f* is only correct if *f* is one of the features listed in the clause. Here all features are exported, except for user_answer, which is accessible by STATE routines but not by the outside world. A nonexported feature is said to be secret. As before, we assume that type ANSWER is declared elsewhere, now as a class. Values that represent exit choices are coded as integers.

Unlike its counterpart in a functional decomposition, each routine has no explicit STATE parameter. The state to which routines apply reappears in calls made by clients:

```
s: STATE; b:BOOLEAN;
choicecode: INTEGER;
s.do_one_state ; s.read ;
b := s.correct ;
choicecode := s.next_choice;
etc.
```

We have also replaced the ANSWER parameter in level-one routines with the secret

attribute user_answer. Information hiding is the motive — client code doesn't need to look at answers except through the interface provided by the exported features.

Inheritance and deferred features. There's a problem, however. How can we write the class STATE without knowing the properties of a specific state? Routine do_one_state and attribute next_choice are the same for all states, but display is not.

Inheritance is the key to this problem. At the STATE level we know (1) all details of routine do_one_state, (2) the attribute next_choice; (3) the fact that routines like display must exist and (4) what their functionalities are.

So we write the class and define these partially known routines as *deferred*. This means that, while any actual state must have them, their details are postponed to descendant classes that describe specific states. (The notion of deferred routines come from Simula 67, where they are called "virtual.") Thus the class is written:

```
class STATE export
    next_choice, display, read, correct,
    message, process, do_one_state

feature
    user_answer: ANSWER ;
        -- secret attribute
    next_choice: INTEGER ;

    do_one_state is
        -- execute the actions associated
        -- with the current state
        -- and assign to next_choice the
        -- user's choice for the next state
    local
        ok: BOOLEAN
    do
        from
            ok:= false
        until
            ok
        loop
            display ; read ; ok := correct ;
            if not ok then
                message
            end
        end ; -- loop
        process
    ensure
        correct
    end; -- do_one_state

display is
    -- display the panel associated
    -- with current state
```

```
deferred
end ; -- display
read is
   -- return the user's answer
   -- into user_answer
   -- and the user's next choice
   -- into next_choice
   deferred
   end ; -- read

correct: BOOLEAN is
   -- return true if and only if
   -- user_answer is
   -- a correct answer
   deferred
   end; -- correct

message is
   -- output the error message
   -- associated with user_answer
   require
      not correct
   deferred
   end ; -- message

process is
   -- process user_answer
   require
      correct
   deferred
   end -- process
end -- class STATE
```

Note the syntax of the Eiffel loop, with initialization in the from clause and the exit test in the until clause. This is equivalent to a while loop, with an exit test rather than a continuation test.

Also note the require clauses that appear at the beginning of routines message and process. These clauses introduce preconditions that must be obeyed whenever a routine is called. Similarly, a postcondition, introduced by the keyword ensure, may be associated with a routine. Preconditions and postconditions express the precise effect of a routine. They can also be monitored at runtime for debugging and control.

The class just described does not by itself describe any actual states — it expresses the pattern common to all states. Specific states are defined by descendants of STATE. It is incumbent on these descendants to provide actual implementations of the deferred routines, such as:

```
class ENQUIRY_ON_FLIGHTS export....
inherit
   STATE
feature
   display is
      do
         ...specific display procedure...
      end ;
   ...and similarly for read, correct,
   message, and process...
end -- class ENQUIRY_ON_FLIGHTS
```

Several important comments are in order:

• We have succeeded in separating — at the exact grain of detail required — the elements common to all states from those specific to individual states. Common elements are concentrated in STATE and need not be redeclared in descendants of STATE like ENQUIRY_ON_FLIGHTS.

• If *s* is an object of type STATE and *d* an object of type DS, where DS is a descendant of STATE, the assignment *s* := *d* is permitted and *d* is acceptable whenever an element of type STATE is required. For example, the array Transition introduced below to represent the transition graph of an application may be declared of type STATE and filled with elements of descendant types.

• This goes beyond Ada-style separation of interface and implementation. First, an Ada interface may contain only bodiless routines; it corresponds to a class where all routines are deferred. In Eiffel, however, you may freely combine nondeferred and deferred routines in the same class. Even more important, Eiffel allows any number of descendant types of STATE to coexist in the same application, whereas Ada allows at most one implementation per interface. This openness of classes (a class may always be extended by new descendants) is a fundamental advantage of object-oriented languages over the closed modules of such languages as Ada and Modula-2.

• The presence of preconditions and postconditions in Eiffel maintains the conceptual integrity of a system. Just as a deferred routine must be defined in descendant classes, so must we define the constraints such a definition must observe. This is why a precondition and postcondition may be associated with a routine even in a deferred declaration. These conditions are then binding on any actual definition of the routine in a descendant of the original class. The technique is paramount in

---

Object-oriented languages.

Other languages implement the concept of object-oriented programming with inheritance and would allow solutions to our airline reservation system example, in a manner similar to the one given here in Eiffel.

These include Simula, the father of all object-oriented language, object-oriented expressions of C such as Objective C and C++, and an extension of Pascal, Object Pascal. These four languages, however, support only single inheritance. Other object-oriented languages include Smalltalk and extensions of Lisp such as Loops, Flavors, and Ceyx. The Clu language shares some of the properties of these languages, but does not offer inheritance.

In recent years, many languages have been added to the above list, mostly for exploratory programming and artificial intelligence purposes.

Bibliography
Birstwistle, G., et al., *Simula Begin*, Studentlitteratur and Auerbach Publishers, Berlin, 1973.
Bobrow, D.G, and M.J. Sefik, "Loops: An Object-Oriented Programming System for Interlisp," Xerox PARC, Palo Alto, Calif., 1982.
Booch, G., "Object-Oriented Software Development," *IEEE Trans. Software Eng.*, Feb. 1986, pp. 211-221.
Cannon, J.I., "Flavors," MIT Artificial Intelligence Lab, Cambridge, Mass., 1980.
Cox, B., *Object-Oriented Programming: An Evolutionary Approach*, Addison-Wesley, Reading, Mass., 1986.
Goldberg, A., and D. Robson, *Smalltalk-80: The Language and Its Implementation*, Addison-Wesley, Reading, Mass., 1983.
Hulot J.-H., "Ceyx, Version 15: 1 — Une Initiation," Tech. Report 44, INRIA, Paris, 1984.
Liskov, et al., *Clu Reference Manual*, Springer Verlag, Berlin-New York, 1981.
Stroustrup, B., *The C++ Programming Language*, Addison-Wesely, Menlo Park, Calif., 1986.
Tesler, L., "Object Pascal Report," *Structured Language World*, 1985.

More on Eiffel

The Eiffel language is part of an environment developed by the author and his colleagues at Interactive Software Engineering. It is accompanied by a design method, a library, and a set of supporting tools. It promotes reusability, extendibility, and software construction by a combination of flexible modules.

The Eiffel library provides the basic building blocks: a set of classes implementing some of the most important data structures and associated operations.

Inheritance plays a central role in this approach. The language supports multiple inheritance, used heavily in the basic library; we have found single inheritance to be insufficient. (Repeated inheritance, not described here, is also supported.) The use of inheritance is made safe and practical with renaming and redefinition techniques. Type parameterization (genericity) is also available.

Inheritance and genericity are powerful techniques for building reusable, extendable software. Their very power entails a risk of misuse. To enhance correctness and reliability, Eiffel includes primitives for systematic software construction: class and loop invariants, and routine preconditions and postconditions, all of which describe semantic constraints imposed on classes and their features.

These constraints (which may be monitored at runtime to help in debugging) must be obeyed by any redefinition of the features in descendant classes, thus preserving the semantic consistency of descendants and helping to control the scope of the inheriance mechanism.

Eiffel is a typed language, where all type checking may be done statically. The language and method are intended for the development of sizable software systems; thus the implementation, which uses C as an intermediate language, emphasizes efficiency. Access to any feature of an object (as in *a.f*) always takes constant time, despite the possiblities for overloading provided by multiple inheritance, renaming, redefinition and genericity (which imply that the version of *f* to be applied depends on the runtime form of *a*). Also, the code for a routine is not duplicated in classes which inherit the routine, even in the presence of multiple inheritance and genericity.

Because the emphasis is on the incremental development of large systems, the Eiffel translator supports separate compilation, class by class. Automatic configuration management is provided, so that each needed module is always used in an up-to-date version (necessary recompilations, and these only, being automatically triggered by the system). The implementation includes a set of supporting tools, in particular for automatic memory management, execution tracing, symbolic debugging, and documentation. The implementation is currently available on Unix systems.

The language and method are described in "Eiffel: A Language and Environment for Software Engineering," to appear in the Journal of Systems and Software, and "Eiffel: Programming for Reusability and Extendibility," SIGPlan Notices, 1987.

using Eiffel as design language: A design module will be written as a class with deferred routines, whose effects are characterized by pre- and postconditions.

A complete system. The final step in our example is to adapt the routine that was at the top of the functional decomposition: session. But we should be a little wiser by now.

The top of the top-down method is mythical. Most real systems have no such thing, especially if the top is meant to be a routine — *the* function of the system. Large software systems perform many functions, all equally important. Again, the abstract data type approach is more appropriate because it considers the system as an abstract entity capable of rendering many services.

In this case the obvious candidate is the notion of application: a specific interactive system like the airline reservation system.

It makes sense to associate with this concept a full-fledged abstract data type that will yield a class, say INTERACTIVE_APPLICATION, at the design and implementation stages. For, although INTERACTIVE_APPLICATION will include as one of its features the routine session describing the execution of an applicaton, there are other things we may want to do with an application, all of which may be added incrementally to class APPLICATION.

By renouncing the notion of "main program" and seeing session as just one feature of the class INTERACTIVE_APPLICATION, we have added considerable flexibility.

The class is given in Figure 7. Its principal features include the remaining elements at levels two and three in Figure 5. The following implementations decisions have been made:

• The transition function is represented by a two-dimensional array, Transition, of size $n \times m$, where n is the number of states

and m the number of possible exit choices.

• States are numbered 1 to n. An auxiliary, one-dimensional array, associated_state, yields the state corresponding to any integer.

• The number of the initial state is set by the routine Choose_initial and kept in the attribute Initial_number. The convention for final states is a transition to pseudostate 0; normal states have positive numbers.

The class includes a Create procedure that will be executed on object initialization. As in most object-oriented languages, objects are created dynamically. If a is declared of type C, the instruction a.Create creates an object of type C and associates it with a.

The Create procedure and its parameters makes it possible to execute specific initialization actions on creation, instead of initializing the new object with standard default values.

The procedure Create of class INTERACTIVE_APPLICATION itself uses the Create procedures of library classes ARRAY and ARRAY2, which allocate arrays dynamically within the bounds given as parameters. For example, a two-dimensional array may be created by a.Create (1,25, 1,10).

Classes ARRAY and ARRAY2 also include features Entry and Enter for array access and modification. Other features of an array are its bounds, upper and lower for a one-dimensional array, and so on.

These classes are declared as ARRAY[T] and ARRAY2[T], an example of Eiffel classes with generic parameters, in this case the type of array elements. Many fundamental classes in the Eiffel library (lists, trees, stacks) are generic. With Eiffel a programmer can combine genericity with inheritance in a type-safe manner.[6]

Class INTERACTIVE_APPLICATION uses Eiffel assertions, an aspect of the language designed to emphasize correctness and reliability. Assertions express formal properties of program elements. They may appear in preconditions and postconditions, the loop invariants, and the class invariants.

Such constructs are used primarily to ensure correct program designs and to document the correctness of arguments, but they may also be used as checks at runtime. More profoundly, assertions (especially pre- and postconditions and class invariants) bring the formal properties of abstract data types back into classes.

An interactive application will be represented by an entity, air_reservation, declared of type INTERACTIVE_APPLICATION and initialized by

    air_reservation.Create (number_of_states,
    number_of_possible_choices)

The states of the application must be defined separately as entities, declared of descendants STATE, and created. Each state s is assigned a number i:

    air_reservation.enter_state(s,i)

One state, i_0, is chosen as the initial:

    air_reservation.choose_initial(i_0)

Each successive transition (from state number sn to state number tn, with label l) is entered by:

    air_reservation.enter_transition(sn,tn,l)

This includes exits, for which tn is 0. The application may now be executed by air_reservation.session.

The same routines can by used during system evolution to add a new state, a new transition, and so on. The class may be extended, of course (either by itself or through descendants).

Multiple inheritance. This example exposes many of the principles in Eiffel, except the concept of multiple inheritance. A previous article on the same example[7,8] relied on Simula 67, which supports only single inheritance. Multiple inheritance is another concept that is essential to a practical use of object-oriented design and programming.

Multiple inheritance makes it possible to define a class as heir to more than one other class, thus combining the features of several previously defined environments. Multiple inheritance would be essential, for example, to implement a satisfactory solution to the table-management problem, detailed in the box on p. 62.

```
classINTERACTIVE_APPLICATION export
   session, first_number, enter_state,
   choose_initial, enter_transition, ...
feature
   transition: ARRAY2 [STATE] ; associated_state: ARRAY [STATE] ;
   -- secret attributes
   first_number; INTEGER ;
   Create (n,m:INTEGER) is
   -- allocate application with n states and m possible choices
      do
         transition.Create (1,n,1,m) ;
         associated_state.Create (1,n)
      end; -- Create

   session is -- execute application
      local
         st: STATE ; st_number: INTEGER ;
      do
         from
            st_number:=first_number ;
         invariant
            0 ≤ next; next ≤ n
         until st_number = 0 loop
            st:=associated_state.entry(st_number) ;
            st.do_one_state ;
            st_number:=transition.entry(st_number, st.next_choice)
         end -- loop
      end; -- session

   enter_state (s: STATE ; number: INTEGER) is
   -- enter state s with index number
      require
         1 ≤ number;
         number ≤ associated_state.upper
      do
         associated_state.enter (number,s)
      end; -- enter_state

   choose_initial (number: INTEGER) is
   -- define state number number as the initial state
      require
         1 ≤ number;
         number ≤ associated_state.upper
      do
         first_number:=number
      end; -- choose_initial
   enter_transition (source: INTEGER ; target:INTEGER ; label: INTEGER) is
   -- enter transition labeled ''label'' from state number source
   -- to state number target
      require
         1 ≤ source; source ≤ associated_state.upper ;
         0 ≤ target; target ≤ associated_state upper ;
         1 ≤ label; label ≤ transition.upper2 ;
      do
         transition.enter (source, label, target)
      end -- enter_transistion

...other features...

invariant
   0 ≤ st_number ; st_number ≤ n ;
   transition.upper1 = associated_state.upper ;
end -- class INTERACTIVE_APPLICATION
```

Figure 7. The class INTERACTIVE_APPLICATION.

A table-searching module

It is impossible to give, in one article, a satisfactory solution to the problem of designing a general-purpose table-searching module. But we can outline how Eiffel would be applied to that case.

First, it is obvious that we are talking not about a table-searching module, but about a module for table management. In fact, we're talking just about the table as an abstract data type with operations such as search, insert, delete, and so on.

As with STATE, the most general notion of table will be represented by a class with deferred routines. The various kinds of tables are descendants of this class. To obtain them, an in-depth analysis of the notion of table and its possible implementations is required. Such an analysis and the associated design and implementation effort are a considerable endeavor, especially as you realize that there is not a single notion of table, but a network of related notions.

The inheritance mechanism can help express the structure of this network and capture differences and similarities at the exact grain of detail required. For example, we may have a descendant of TABLE, SEQUENTIAL_TABLE, that covers tables stored sequentially in arrays, linked lists, or files, with a version of the function search (x):

```
from
    restart
until
    off_limits or else current_value = x
invariant
    -- x does not appear in the table before current postion
loop
    move_forth
end ;
if off_limits ...(etc.)
```

The structure is similar to that of STATE, where the essential routine do_one_state was not deferred, but was expressed in terms of other deferred routines. In this case, search is not deferred but uses deferred routines for which the descendants of TABLE must provide implementations.

What's remarkable is that an entity t declared of type TABLE may dynamically refer to an object of any descendant type of TABLE; however the call t.search(x) may be written without any knowledge of what kind of table implementation t will actually be at runtime.

This approach captures — at the exact grain of detail required — the commonality within a family of implementations of the same data abstractions. A family will consist of a header class (SEQUENTIAL_TABLE) and specific descendants (ARRAY_TABLE).

The inheritance graph may span more than one level. Features common to all members of the family (like Search for sequential tables) are concentrated at the header level and shared; features unique to various members are deferred in the header and expanded on in the individual members. The diagram below illustrates this inheritance structure.

Both genericity and multiple inheritance are essential to this problem's solution: All table classes take the type of table elements as a generic parameter, and several will combine two or more parent classes (BINARY_SEARCH_TREE from both BINARY_TREE and TABLE).

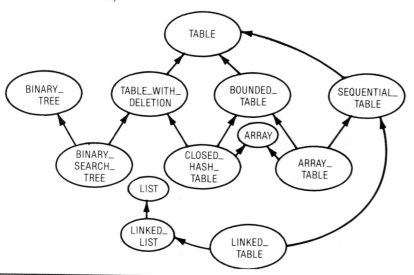

Even in the previous example, multiple inheritance is not far away — if we had defined a data abstraction WINDOW to describe screen panels, some descendants of STATE might inherit from this class, too.

In lieu of conclusion

This article has promoted the view that, if one accepts that reusability is essential to better software quality, the object-oriented approach — defined as the construction of software systems as structured collections of abstract data type implementations — provides a promising set of solutions.

One epithet this approach certainly does not deserve is "top-down." It is puzzling to see this adjective used almost universally as a synonym for "good." Top-down design may be an effective method for developing individual algorithms and routines. But applying it at the system level is inappropriate unless the system can be characterized by a single, frozen, top-level function, a case that is rare in practice.

> **One epithet this approach certainly does not deserve is "top-down."**

More importantly, top-down design goes against the key factor of software reusability because it promotes one-of-a-kind developments, rather than general-pupose, combinable software elements.

It is surprising to see top-down design built in as an essential requirement in the US Dept. of Defense directive MIL-STD-2167, which by the sheer power of its sponsor is bound to have a serious (and, we fear, negative) influence for years to come.

Of course, the bottom-up method promoted here does not mean that system design should start at the lowest possible level. What it implies is construction of systems by reusing and combining existing software. This is a bootstrapping approach in which software elements are progressively combined into more and more ambitious systems.

As a consequence of this approach, there is no notion of main program in Eiffel. Classes are meant to be developed separately. Integrating those classes into an Eiffel "system" is the last, and least binding, decision.

A system is a set of classes with one distinguishing element, the root. The only role of the root is to initiate the execution of the system (by creating an object of the root type and executing its create procedure). A system has no existence as Eiffel construct; it is simply a particular assembly of classes.

Such an approach is viable only if there are adequate facilities to produce flexible software elements and combine them effectively. The concepts of object-oriented design with multiple inheritance and genericity provide such facilities.

Object-oriented design means more than just putting data types into modules; the inheritance concept is essential. This requires an object-oriented language. As structured programming showed a few years ago, you can attempt to implement new methodological concepts without a language that directly supports them — but it will never be quite as good as the real thing: using the right language to implement the right concepts.

Another aspect of the approach promoted here is that it tends to blur the distinction between design and implementation. While this distinction may be unavoidable today, it is undesirable because it tends to introduce an artificial discontinuity in software construction.

Design and implementation are essentially the same activity: constructing software to satisfy a certain specification. The only difference is the level of abstraction — during design certain details may be left unspecified, but in an implementation everything should be expressed in full. However, the process of filling in the details should be continuous, from system architecture to working program. Language constructs such as deferred features are particularly helpful in this process. Software development is made much smoother when you use a language that encompasses the traditional area of design and implementation, but that is no more difficult to master than conventional programming languages. Such is the aim of Eiffel.

We do not propose, however, to remove the boundary between design and implementation, on the one hand, and system specification on the other. These activities are of a different nature: specification states problems, design and implementation solve them. (A companion effort, the specification method M,[9] applies similar concepts to formal, nonexecutable specifications.)

One more fundamental theme has been guiding this discussion: the idea that today the essential problems of software engineering are *technical* problems.

Not everybody agrees. There is a large and influential school of thought that sees management, organization, and economic issues as the biggest obstacles to progress in software development. Programming aspects, in this view, are less important. This view is evidenced in many discussions of reusability that consider technical issues, such as the choice of programming language, as less important for reusability than such things as an easily accessible database of components.

As evidence of the limitations of the "managerial" approach to reusability, consider the relations that exist between these components, such as specialization (a hash table is a specialized table, a B-tree is a specialized tree). If an object-oriented language is used, they can be expressed directly by inheritance and recorded within the components themselves. But if the language does not provide direct support for expressing this relation, the information must be entered explicitly into the database, separate from the components.

Give your poor, your huddled projects a decent technical environment in the first place. Then worry about whether you are managing them properly.

This immediately raises some difficult issues: how to provide an adequate user interface, check the consistency of the relation information, and maintain the integrity of this information as components are updated. Advanced project-management techniques are required to solve these issues. This is a typical example of an organizational solution to a technical problem, with the resulting complexity and loss of effectiveness.

Overemphasis on management issues is premature. While it is indeed true that many software projects are plagued with management problems, focusing on these problems first confuses the symptom with cause. It's like expecting better hospital management to solve the public hygiene problem 10 years before Pasteur came along!

Give your poor, your huddled projects a decent technical environment in the first place. *Then* worry about whether you are managing them properly. □

Acknowledgments
The comments and suggestions made by the referees, those who agreed with the article's thesis and those who didn't, were much appreciated. The influence of Simula 67, the first object-oriented language and still one of the best, is gratefully acknowledged.

References

1. T.C. Jones, "Reusability in Programming: A Survey of the State of the Art," *IEEE Trans. Software Eng.* Sept. 1984, pp. 488-494.

2. M.A. Jackson, *System Development*, Prentice-Hall, Englewood Cliffs, N.J., 1983.

3. B.P. Lientz and E.B. Swanson, "Software Maintenance: A User/Management Tug of War," *Data Management*, April 1979, pp. 26-30.

4. B.W. Boehm, "Software Engineering — As It Is," *Proc. Fourth Int'l Conf. Software Eng.*, CS Press, Los Alamitos, Calif., Sept. 1979, pp. 11-21.

5. B. Dwyer, "A User-Friendly Algorithm," *Comm. ACM*, Sept. 1981, pp. 556-561.

6. B. Meyer, "Genericity versus Inheritance," *Proc. ACM Conf. Object-Oriented Programming Syst, Languages, and Applications*, ACM, New York, pp. 391-405 (revised version to appear in *J. Pascal, Ada, and Modula-2*).

7. B. Meyer, "Vers un Environnement Conversationnel à Deux Dimensions," *Journées BIGRE*, Grenoble, France, Jan. 1982, pp. 27-39.

8. B. Meyer, "Towards a Two-Dimensional Programming Environment," *Proc. 1982 European Conf. Integrated Computer Syst.*, P. Degano and R. Sandewall, eds., North Holland, Amsterdam, 1983, pp. 167-179.

9. B. Meyer, "M: A System Description Method," Tech. Report TRCS 85-15, Computer Science Dept., University of California, Santa Barbara, May 1985.

Bertrand Meyer is president of Interactive Software Engineering, Inc., a Santa Barbara, California, company specializing in tools and education for improving software quality. The Eiffel environment is one of Interactive's products.

From 1983 to 1986, he was a visiting associate professor at the University of California, Santa Barbara. Previously, he was division head at Electricité de France. He is a member of AFCET, the Computer Society of the IEEE, and ACM. He has engineering degrees from Polytechnique and Suptélécom, an MS from Stanford University, and the Dr. Sc. from the University of Nancy, France.

OBJECT-ORIENTED DESIGN AND BALLISTICS SOFTWARE

by Mark Temte*

Indiana University – Purdue University at Fort Wayne
Fort Wayne, Indiana 46805

ABSTRACT

The object-oriented design methodology is applied to the problem of designing ballistics software. This problem is sufficiently large and complex that the methodology must be iterated at successively lower levels of abstraction. The manner in which the design unfolds is illustrated.

INTRODUCTION

The intent of this article is to present the application of object-oriented design (OOD) methodology to the development of ballistics software. This methodology is becoming well known in the Ada** community. However, most of the illustrations of OOD found in the literature involve relatively small applications which do not require top-down iteration of the methodology to successively lower levels of abstraction. Ballistics software is more representative of actual large applications and is sufficiently complex to require this iteration.

The need to perform ballistics calculations contributed to the early development of computing machinery. Indeed, the Ballistic Research Laboratory of the Aberdeen Proving Grounds funded a project that led to the construction of the ENIAC machine at the University of Pennsylvania in the 1940's. More portable computers are currently replacing the manual firing tables used by field artillery units with automatic ballistics calculations that are both rapid and accurate.

Although Magnavox has had a fairly long history of ballistic software development, work in Ada began in 1983 with the design and implementation of a prototype ballistics system. At that time, a proposal effort was underway in connection with the Advanced Field Artillery Tactical Data System (AFATDS) for the Army, of which ballistics software is one component. The intent of implementing the prototype system was not only to serve as a demonstration to the proposal evaluation team, but also to begin the move of ballistics software from FORTRAN to Ada. As this software matured, it had become increasingly difficult to maintain and transport. The move was to include the establishment of a Ballistics Software Development and Test Facility, whose purposes were to produce reliable ballistic

---

* The author serves as a consultant to the Magnavox Electronic Systems Co., Fort Wayne, Indiana.
** Ada is a registered trademark of the U. S. Government, Ada Joint Program Office.

Reprinted with permission from *ACM Ada Letters*, Volume 4, Number 3, November/December 1984, pages 25-36. Copyright © 1984 by Mark Temte.

trajectory simulations for the full spectrum of field artillery, consist of subsystems that could be used to rapidly and accurately build various application systems, be portable to a variety of processors, and be modifiable.

Development of the prototype system was hindered somewhat by lack of an Ada compiler, since the TeleSoft-Ada* compiler being used supported only a subset of Ada at that time. Nonetheless, it resulted in a successful demonstration and provided practical experience in using both Ada and the object-oriented design methodology. This experience is currently being applied to the design of the Development and Test Facility using full Ada and to the AFATDS contract, which was awarded to Magnavox in May. It may be of interest to the Ada community that the AFATDS software effort is expected to involve around 300_000 lines of code and, at this writing, represents the largest DoD system being implemented in Ada. The primary design methodology will be OOD.

In this article, a summary of the ballistics problem is followed by an application of OOD to this problem at the highest level of abstraction. Then, iteration of OOD is illustrated by following one path from this level downward. Finally, some observations are presented on how Ada supports OOD and ballistics software.

BALLISTICS SOFTWARE OVERVIEW

As used here, the term ballistics software refers to computer programs that perform calculations related to artillery and mortar shells. We identify three types of high-level calculations. Operations that use numerical integration to determine the path of a shell are said to "fly" the shell. Operations that yield aiming instructions "aim" the cannon or mortar. Finally, operations that determine an optimum charge of powder "select" the charge.

These actions form a hierarchy. The basic action is that of flying a shell. Aiming a cannon consists of successively alternating better guesses of the cannon's angular quadrant elevation and azimuth with numerical test flights until sufficiently accurate aiming instructions are determined. Similarly, selecting an optimum charge consists of selecting an approximate initial charge according to certain criteria and calculating aiming instructions if possible. If the selected charge does not yield a solution to the aiming problem, then a new charge is selected and the process iterated until an appropriate charge is determined.

It is worthwhile to note that shells "fly" in a number of distinct ways: rocket assisted shells contain rocket motors that engage several seconds after firing; illumination rounds fly with a parachute; some shells have trajectories which consist of two ballistically distinct parts; another has wings that deploy during a laser-guided glide phase. Although most shells are spin-stabilized and are subject to gyroscopic effects, some are not.

----

* TeleSoft-Ada is a registered trademark of TeleSoft, Inc.

Although one might expect that ballistics software is primarily numerical in nature and naturally admits the traditional "functional" decomposition, the bulk of the effort expended in implementing a reasonably complete ballistics software system is actually associated with managing objects. Such a system typically involves nearly 25 weapons (cannons and mortars) divided among six calibers, 60 distinct shells, 50 fuzes, and 30 powder models. Many items in this inventory have special characteristics, hold specific relationships with other items, or carry restrictions on usage. Because of this, an "object-oriented" strategy is more appropriate.

For each weapon/shell combination, modern ballistics software relies upon a large base of empirically determined information to fly a shell. This data, known as fire control input (FCI) data, has been determined for supported shells by the Ballistics Research Laboratory (BRL) and is used in connection with BRL's standard ballistic model and associated methodology. In addition to FCI data, BRL's ballistic model also requires a "met message" consisting of atmospheric information at up to 27 selected altitudes. At each altitude, this includes wind speed and direction together with barometric pressure and air temperature.

In order to initiate ballistic calculations (to fly, aim, or select), a user must first provide a number of inputs. These can be grouped into three areas: materiel (weapon, shell, fuze, etc.), environment (met message, powder temperature, latitude, etc.), and inputs specific to the type of calculations desired. To fly a shell, for example, the quadrant elevation and azimuth of the cannon must be specified. To aim the cannon, however, gun and target coordinates must be provided instead. The actual situation is somewhat more complicated than this indicates due to special options and requirements for individual shells. Furthermore, only appropriate combinations of inputs may be accepted. A modern ballistics system must operate within these confines automatically.

In order to achieve reliability and maintainability at a reasonable cost, a ballistics system needs a design that abstracts the ballistics environment and an implementation language in which this design can take form. The object-oriented design methodology is well-suited to such a design and, moreover, maps naturally to Ada packages. Ada, on the other hand, not only can represent the objects that OOD establishes but also provides the means to enforce the abstractions.

OBJECT-ORIENTED DESIGN

It is not the intent of this article to describe the object-oriented design (OOD) method. However, a brief overview is in order. The goal of OOD is to produce a solution in the environment of programming language objects and operations that parallels the problem in the environment of real-world objects and operations.

At any particular level of abstraction, the basic OOD method* is comprised of the following steps:

1. define the problem
2. develop an informal strategy in the problem environment
3. formalize the strategy by
   a. identifying the objects and their attributes
   b. identifying the operations on these objects
   c. establishing the interfaces among the objects and operations
   d. implementing the operations

Implementation of an operation may require that this methodology be recursively applied at the next lower level of abstraction. This occurs when the operation cannot be immediately implemented using existing facilities. Note that the starting point of OOD iteration is implementation of an operation. Eventually a type of top-down design solution is obtained, although the design will not necessarily be the traditional functional decomposition.

The identification of objects and operations often involves considerable local iteration between the development of the informal strategy and the formalization of that strategy until sufficient understanding of the original problem is obtained. It has been the author's personal experience that, when a design does not appear to formalize nicely, the difficulty usually can be traced to an informal strategy that does not adequately capture the real-world situation. Often this is because something was left out. However, some implementation consideration may also be present that is inappropriate.

Object-oriented design should not be viewed as a panacea but rather as a way of organizing a complex activity in terms of basic components. Although it is readily learned, mastery requires some experience. It often takes effort to break the habit of always decomposing a problem functionally. (This was so with ballistics software where the basic algorithms are functional in nature and a FORTRAN implementation already existed.) A real understanding of the original problem is, of course, still needed. Nonetheless, the guidance offered by the well-defined OOD methodology can produce a superior design that can then be implemented in a minimum amount of time. The object-oriented approach should produce, in addition, a solution that is modifiable, since it parallels the problem.

It is worthwhile to observe that one tool to use to gain understanding of the original problem is to generalize it to a higher level of abstraction. In generalizing a problem, the designer is forced to eliminate some of the implementation-specific considerations that needlessly complicate the design at the original level of abstraction. Problem generalization occurred naturally at Magnavox with the ballistics software problem since this software is viewed as a component of larger systems.

----

* G. Booch, "Object-Oriented Design," Ada Letters, Vol. 1, No. 3 (March/April 1982), pp. 64-76.

The generalization focused on an appropriate interface. In an interactive system, ballistics software should prompt the user for information when necessary. In an automated testing system, on the other hand, the software must accept a sequence of stored ballistic problems fed from a queue. The interactive system viewpoint is desirable since it tends to localize the data gathering aspect of an operation with the operation.

Both of these viewpoints, however, are quite similar. Prompting a user for an item of information is not essentially different from requesting the item from a database inquiry system which had been previously loaded with all the input data needed for a ballistics problem. Using Ada, a package can be included with each intended application to provide the necessary services. Once these viewpoints had been reconciled, the design of the ballistics system not only became more adaptable but also simpler.

Statement of the Problem

Design a general purpose ballistic calculator for all weapons and shells supported by BRL.

What is wanted is an Ada system that abstracts the facilities of the ballistic calculator indicated above. Given a ballistic problem, the calculator is to produce the corresponding solution. However, to be general purpose, the calculator is to operate in three distinct modes: FLY, AIM, and SELECT. These correspond to the three interrelated classes of ballistic problems that it must solve. At this level of the design, we are primarily interested in determining which of the problems is to be solved and in marshalling the resources necessary to provide the solution.

Informal Strategy

The following paragraph represents an informal strategy for solving the problem at this level of abstraction. Nouns are underlined and verbs are in boldface. The objective is to capture objects, operations, and the situation that ties them together. Even though the strategy is quite functional (in keeping with the nature of the problem), it still leads to a design that centers about objects.

The ballistics calculator operates in three modes. It prompts the user for the desired weapon and shell, for meteorological data, and for the mode in which to operate. In the first mode, the ballistics calculator determines the impact point of the shell from the aiming orders of the weapon. In the second mode, the ballistics calculator converges on aiming orders of the weapon for a given target. To do this, it alternately estimates aiming orders and determines the resulting impact points. In the third mode, the ballistics calculator selects an optimum powder charge for a given target. To do this, it chooses powder charges until it can converge on aiming orders. In each mode, the result is displayed to the user.

Identify Objects and Their Attributes

The objects which are part of the solution space are listed below together with an Ada identifier and an attribute.

OBJECT	IDENTIFIER	ATTRIBUTE
ballistic calc.	BALLISTIC_CALCULATOR	the Ada system
materiel	MATERIEL	includes weapon and shell
met. data	ENVIRONMENT	also includes latitude, etc.
mode	MODE	FLY, AIM, SELECT
target	TARGET_POSITION	given
impact point	TERMINAL_STATE	result in first mode
aiming orders	GUN_ORDERS	result in second mode
powder charge	SELECTED_CHARGE	result in third mode

Identify the Operations

Each operation in the solution space is listed together with the object upon which it acts and an Ada identifier.

OPERATION	OBJECT	IDENTIFIER
prompt for materiel	MATERIEL	PROMPT_FOR_MATERIEL
prompt for met data	ENVIRONMENT	PROMPT_FOR_ENVIRONMENT
prompt for mode	MODE	PROMPT_FOR_MODE
determine	TERMINAL_STATE	FLY_SHELL
converge	GUN_ORDERS	AIM_WEAPON
estimate	GUN_ORDERS	ESTIMATE
select	SELECTED_CHARGE	SELECT_CHARGE
choose	SELECTED_CHARGE	CHOOSE
display first mode	TERMINAL_STATE	DISPLAY_TERMINAL_STATE
display second mode	GUN_ORDERS	DISPLAY_GUN_ORDERS
display third mode	SELECTED_CHARGE	DISPLAY_CHARGE

Establish the Interfaces

An analysis of this situation led to four packages: PROMPT, FLY, AIM, and SELECT. PROMPT serves to consolidate type definitions MATERIEL_TYPE, ENVIRONMENT_TYPE, and MODE_TYPE together with prompting actions which act upon objects of these types. These actions were renamed PROMPT.FOR_MATERIEL, PROMPT.FOR_ENVIRONMENT, and PROMPT.FOR_MODE. Depending on the mode, prompts for other items (such as TARGET_POSITION) are needed and the operations for these were naturally included in PROMPT as the design evolved. The last three packages each abstract one of the modes in which the ballistic calculator is to operate.

The package SELECT exports the type SELECTED_CHARGE_TYPE, the operation SELECT.CHARGE previously identified, and the operation SELECT.ANGLE, which certain mortars require instead. The distinction in the two cases is accommodated by making SELECTED_CHARGE_TYPE a variant record. The operation DISPLAY_CHARGE is also exported. The operation CHOOSE is not made visible in the package specification since it is part of the implementation of SELECT.CHARGE.

Package AIM contains operations AIM.WEAPON and AIM.MORTAR, which act in a similar manner on objects of GUN_ORDER_TYPE. These are exported together with the operation DISPLAY_GUN_ORDERS. Again, the operation ESTIMATE is not made visible since it is part of the implementation of WEAPON.

Finally, FLY exports the operations FLY.SHELL and DISPLAY_TERMINAL_STATE, which operate on objects of TERMINAL_STATE_TYPE. The complete implementation of FLY.SHELL is quite involved since the various shells fly in nine distinct ways. However, at this level of abstraction, implementation consists of determining the unique manner in which the designated shell flies and then invoking the appropriate resources. As we shall see, these resources will be available in packages identified in the next level.

The informal strategy not only indicated objects and operations but also the relations among these. For example, AIM needs FLY in order to converge on aiming orders and SELECT needs AIM to select an optimum powder charge. These interface considerations are represented below using the symbols that are being referred to as "Booch-O-Grams."

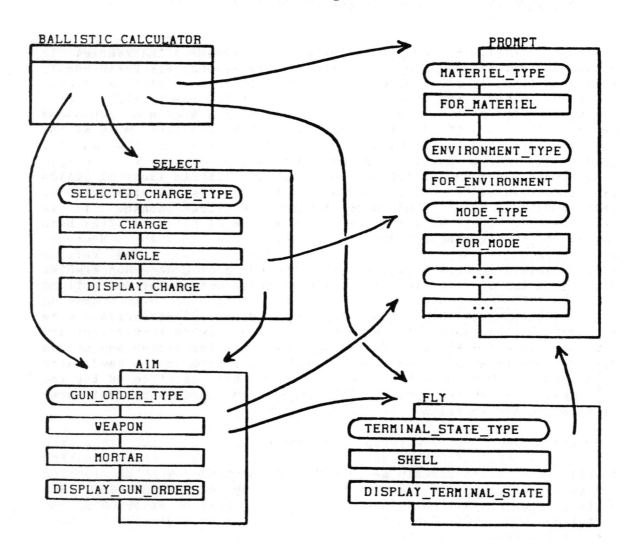

ITERATION OF OOD AT LOWER LEVELS

To illustrate the result of applying the OOD strategy repeatedly at successively lower levels of abstraction, we will follow one path of decomposition down to its lowest level. At each level, objects and operations are listed and then one operation (identified by @) is chosen for refinement at the next lower level. The starting point will be the operation FLY.SHELL.

Fly.Shell

The visible interface of this procedure is

```
procedure FLY.SHELL
  (
  MATERIEL          : in      PROMPT.MATERIEL_TYPE;
  ENVIRONMENT       : in      PROMPT.ENVIRONMENT_TYPE;
  CHARGE            : in      PROMPT.CHARGE_TYPE;
  ORIENTATION       : in      PROMPT.ORIENTATION_TYPE;
  TERMINATION_CRIT  : in      PROMPT.TERMINATION_CRIT_TYPE;
  TERMINAL_STATE    :     out TERMINAL_STATE_TYPE
  );
```

As was mentioned above, this operation determines the manner in which the shell flies and then invokes the appropriate resources to simulate this flight. Recall, however, that to "fly" a shell, ballistics software requires fire control input (FCI) data. Typically, this data yields seven aerodynamic coefficients expressed as functions of Mach number, various system constants (such as the rifling of the cannon and axial moment of inertia of the shell), applicable powder models and an enumeration of available charges within each model, eight charge dependent coefficients (most of which are functions of other inputs such as the cannon barrel orientation), and information whose nature depends upon the fuze chosen. It is desirable to store only one copy of each item of FCI data, from both the memory utilization and the maintenance points of view. However, since many items of data are shared among the various weapon/shell/fuze configurations, this necessitates a somewhat complex mapping of the appropriate data to the selected configuration.

Implementation of this mapping is straightforward with hierarchical packages of FCI data, selected component notation, and access objects (pointers). Within each caliber, the chosen weapon and shell index an array of records containing pointers to the associated data objects. Once a flexible name-space has been established for the FCI data, it is easy to establish these pointers. Additional local objects and the operations are listed below.

objects	operations	
ATMOSPHERE	INITIALIZE_ATMOSPHERE	@ TRACK.COMMON_SHELL
FCI_DATA	INITIALIZE_CANNON	TRACK.ROCKET_ASSISTED_SHELL
SHELL CANNON	INITIALIZE_SHELL	TRACK.ILLUMINATION_SHELL
FUZE_SETTING	SET_FUZE	etc.

INITIALIZE_ATMOSPHERE transforms the MET_MESSAGE in the ENVIRONMENT from its external coordinates to the internal azimuth based coordinates of the object ATMOSPHERE. A package MET was defined for the associated type definitions, for INITIALIZE_ATMOSPHERE, and for a procedure GET_MET_DATA which was identified at a lower level.

The object SHELL carries various FLIGHT_CONSTANTS, the AERO_DATA from the FCI_DATA, the TERMINATION_CRITerion, and a STATE. The STATE of the SHELL consists of POSITION, VELOCITY, ACCELERATION, SPIN, SPIN_ACCELERATION, and TIME_FROM_LAUNCH. INITIALIZE_SHELL initializes the SHELL by computing the FLIGHT_CONSTANTS which result from the orientation of the cannon and the muzzle VELOCITY and SPIN which result from the action of the cannon. Each of the nine procedures which may be invoked to fly a shell calculate the final POSITION, the TIME_OF_FLIGHT, an ERROR_MSG, etc. The SHELL object with all these operations was abstracted in another package TRACK.

The object CANNON abstracts the properties of a cannon or mortar and is initialized by INITIALIZE_CANNON. These are contained in a third package, WEAPON, along with procedures MUZZLE_VELOCITY and INITIAL_SPIN needed by INITIALIZE_SHELL. A fourth package FUZE contains functions which calculate the FUZE_SETTING for the particular fuze carried by the SHELL.

The TERMINAL_STATE which is acted upon by FLY.SHELL consists of the outputs of the procedures that fly the shell together with the FUZE_SETTING. The resources we have identified are sufficient for the implementation of the operation.

Track.Common_Shell

This procedure numerically integrates the equations of motion for the simplest kind of artillery shell. Implementation should be hidden since there are a number of integration methodologies possible. For the Magnavox implementation, strict adherence to BRL's published methodology was chosen because this facilitated implementation of certain features of special shells and because of the importance of validating the implementation against BRL's test data. Indeed, the real-world being abstracted in this case is the BRL model.

The BRL integration method is a self-starting predictor-corrector method and is straightforward to implement. It consists of following the flight of the SHELL as it interacts with the ATMOSPHERE over a number of time steps while CHECK_FOR_LAST_STEP monitors the progress. The objects and operations are:

objects	operations
SHELL	TIME_STEP.COMMON_SIZE
ACCELERATION	@ EVALUATE.ACCELERATION
TIME_STEP_SIZE	PREDICT_SHELL_STATE
ATMOSPHERE	CORRECT_SHELL_STATE
SAVED_STATE	REINITIALIZE_SHELL
	CHECK_FOR_LAST_STEP

Since the nine procedures that fly shells share related operations, new packages are desirable. One package named TIME_STEP contains TIME_STEP.SIZE_TYPE, the function TIME_STEP.COMMON_SIZE and other functions that obtain the size of the next time step for the other shell types. Another package EVALUATE contains ACCELERATION_TYPE, the procedure EVALUATE.ACCELERATION, and several other procedures that evaluate accelerations for mortars and the more exotic shells. CHECK_FOR_LAST_STEP and SAVED_STATE are simply local to TRACK.COMMON_SHELL. The remaining three procedures act upon SHELLs and are included in package TRACK. They are used by all nine procedures but need not be made visible outside the package.

Evaluate.Acceleration

This procedure evaluates the "equations of motion" and captures the BRL ballistic model. The operations use the information in all objects except ACCELERATION in order to accumulate the ACCELERATION. Although there are quite a number of objects and operations here, they are mutually interdependent and should be associated at this level of abstraction.

A type definition for FLIGHT_CONSTANTS is imported from a package defined in connection with the implementation of the operation INITIALIZE_SHELL encountered earlier. Type definitions for AERO.DATA_TYPE and the seven aerodynamic coefficients are contained in a new package AERO together with the operation GET_SEVEN_COEFS. This package also contains related operations needed by other procedures that evaluate accelerations. The procedure GET_MET_DATA and type MET_DATA_TYPE come from the package MET mentioned earlier. The remaining nine operations are grouped in another new package, MODEL, together with other similar operations and related type definitions.

objects		operations	
ACCELERATION	MET_DATA	GET_SEVEN_COEFS	GET_MET_DATA
AERO.DATA	MACH_NUMBER	GET_VELOCITY_IN_AIR	GET_MACH_NUM
seven aero coefs	YAW_VECTOR	GET_CORIOLIS_ACCEL	GET_MAGNUS
VELOCITY_IN_AIR	DRAG_ACCEL	@ GET_YAW_OF_REPOSE	
CORIOLIS_ACCEL	LIFT_ACCEL	GET_LIFT_AND_YAW_LIFT	
MAGNUS_ACCEL	SPIN_ACCEL	GET_AXIAL_SPIN_ACCEL	
FLIGHT_CONSTANTS	GRAV_ACCEL	GET_DRAG_AND_YAW_DRAG	
CURRENT_STATE	ATMOSPHERE	GET_GRAVITY_AT_ALTITUDE	

Get.Yaw_of_Repose

Implementation is immediate in the presence of a package of utilities, VECTOR, containing the needed vector operations.

objects		operations
YAW_VECTOR	OVERTURNING_MOMENT	VECTOR.CROSS_PRODUCT
VELOCITY_IN_AIR	(an aero coefficient)	VECTOR.SCALAR_PRODUCT
ACCEL_VECTOR	AXIAL_MOMENT	multiplication
SPIN CALIBER	AIR_DENSITY	division

At this point, we are at the lowest level along the chosen path of decomposition. Booch-O-Grams representing this path are shown below.

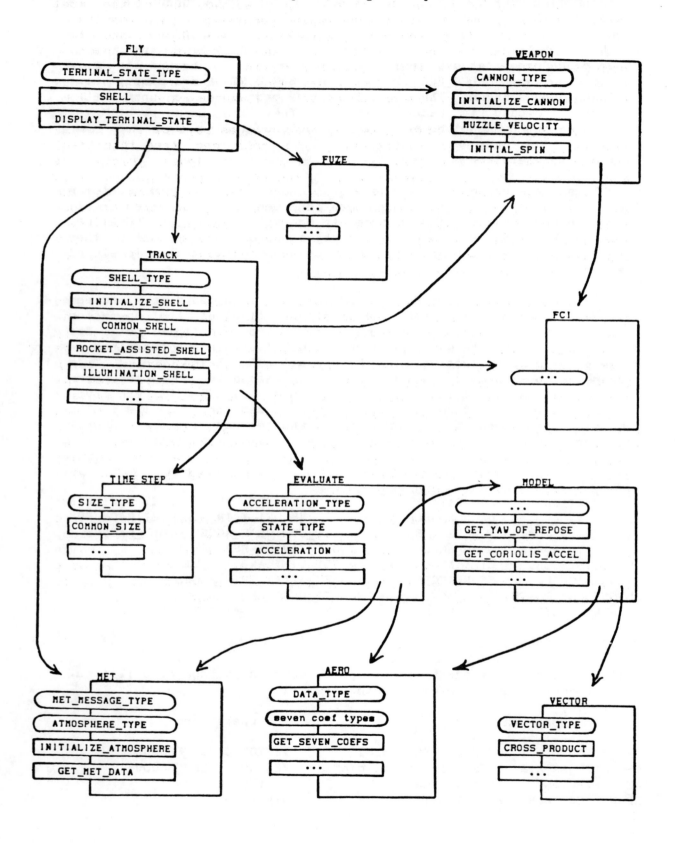

OBSERVATIONS ON ADA AND OOD

In applying OOD to the design of a large system, one of the most useful features of Ada is its packaging mechanism. This results in part from the ability of Ada packages to encapsulate objects and then enforce the abstraction. In the ballistics software system (and presumably in any system that requires iteration of OOD at several levels of abstraction), it results also because Ada packages provide an environment in which system resources can take root and grow.

By explicitly identifying system resources as part of the design process, the packages implementing the resources tend to attract related operations as they are discovered at lower levels of abstraction. Had we followed other paths of decomposition, we would not only have obtained other packages but also additions to the packages identified along the chosen path. Of course, top-down application of OOD makes bottom-up use of previously identified resources. This not only provides a genuine contribution to system organization but also saves lines of code and enhances maintainability by helping to identify common functions.

For ballistics software, several other features of Ada were found to be especially helpful. The exception handling feature eased the chore of identifying and recovering from errors with an orderly mechanism. The INLINE pragma freed the structure of the source code from considerations of overhead associated with procedural calls within the integration loop. The Ada enumeration type facilitated the definition and use of the inventory of ballistics materiel. Variant records and unconstrained arrays were found to adapt well to the variety inherent in ballistics data and methodology. Generic program units were found to be less useful. Tasking was not used in the design but could become a consideration in the future for battery calculations; the Node Computer Unit being developed for AFATDS will contain four Motorola 68020 processors.

It is to be emphasized, however, that language features alone are sufficient only to combat individual implementation difficulties. What is also needed in a large and complex system is a design methodology that promotes the cooperative application of language features in an orderly and systematic way. OOD was found to provide this methodology in the ballistics software environment.

Chapter 2: Examples of Object-Oriented Programming

The popularity of object-oriented methods for creating software is quickly growing as the advantages of the approach are recognized. In this chapter we illustrate this by presenting descriptions of several large projects that used object-oriented programming. Since a wide variety of projects have now been implemented by using the object-oriented approach and have benefited thereby, it is possible to conclude that an object-orientation can be useful for all kinds of programs.

Larry Tesler interviewed four people who were involved in large object-oriented computing projects and described their experiences in "Programming Experiences." The four projects were a windowing and menu system using C++, a system for shipboard navigation that used the MacApp framework, a CAD system on Sun workstations using Objective-C, and a knowledge-based system on an IBM PC using Methods, a dialect of Smalltalk. Each of the systems in this diverse variety benefited from the object-oriented approach. One clear benefit was shorter development times and this appears to be largely owing to the inheritance mechanism of object-oriented languages.

Kurt J. Schmucker, in "MacApp: An Application Framework," describes MacApp, an application framework for Macintosh programs. MacApp contains the generic features of a windowing and menu system and is structured as a class hierarchy with 30 classes and over 450 methods. The developer completes an application primarily by adding additional classes to the framework. These classes would be mainly for the purpose of supplying the contents of the windows and menus. If additional flexibility is needed, the developer can attain it by redefining some of MacApp's classes or methods. Schmucker used MacApp to create a program that draws a mouse. This took only 87 new lines of source code, but it is a full windowing system application that works on all Macs and interfaces correctly to several peripherals. It is estimated that MacApp can reduce both development time and the amount of source code by a factor of four or five.

Norman Meyrowitz, in "Intermedia: The Architecture and Construction of an Object-Oriented Hypermedia System and Application Framework," describes a large object-oriented application that is underway at Brown University. Intermedia runs on an IBM PC RT computer with the Unix 4.2 operating system, the Ingres data base system, and the MacApp applications framework. MacApp had to be ported from the Macintosh. Intermedia is supposed to allow its users to access media such as text and graphics from a wide variety of sources and manipulate it in various ways. The work proceeded by modifying many of MacApp's classes and creating the additional ones needed. The final product contained 219 classes, 1411 methods and 75,000 lines of source code. The technical goals of the project—extensibility, reusability, consistency, understandability, and modularity—were met primarily because an object orientation was chosen. The conclusion drawn from work on this project is "object-oriented techniques were vitally important to the user interface, the design, the architecture, the programmer interface, and the implementation of the Intermedia system."

The paper, "A Smalltalk System for Algebraic Manipulation," by S. Kamal Abdali, Guy W. Cherry, and Neil Soiffer describes an algebra system, *Views*, which is implemented in Smalltalk. Early algebraic systems, such as Macsyma, have become difficult to extend and maintain because of their procedure orientation. Views is attempting to remedy this by utilizing an object-oriented architecture. The paper does not describe the facilities of the system but describes three features: *parameterized classes, categories,* and *views*, which Abdali et al. found useful in the implementation and are proposing as extensions to object-oriented languages. What follows briefly describes these ideas.

The classes in Views correspond to standard mathematical structures such as groups, rings, and fields. Abdali et al. found that it would be useful at run-time to be able to create subclasses of an existing "parameterized" class by instantiating the parameters. For example, if *IntegersModn* is a class with parameter n, then it is useful to instantiate n to 5 to create the subclass *IntegersMod5*.

The set of integers may be viewed as a multiplicative semigroup or as an additive semigroup. The authors define a *category* to be a structure like a semigroup which has certain operators and axioms about the operators, and they define a *view* to be an assignment of specific operations on a specific set to the operators of the category. For example, if multiplication of integers is assigned to the semigroup operator, then the integers are being *viewed as as a multiplicative semigroup*; if addition is assigned to the semigroup operator, they are being *viewed as an additive semigroup*. This idea turns out to be a generalization of the inheritance concept. Several examples of the utility of categories and views are shown and a description of how to implement them in Smalltalk is given.

In their paper, "Objects, Icons, and Software-ICs," Brad Cox and Bill Hunt describe how to create iconic user interfaces by using object-oriented methods in Objective-C. With an *iconic* user interface, users see a pictorial representation of available resources on the screen and respond by using a mouse. The programming method is to create specialized subclasses of the generic class *View*. The inheritance hierarchy diagram in Figure 3 of this paper is valuable for helping a beginner obtain insight into the manner in which object-oriented programming works. Over four-fifths of the code consists of generic classes: tools with which to build applications (i.e., *software ICs*). Only one-fifth is specific to the particular application at hand. A general rule can be inferred from the example: *Abstract as much code as possible into useful generic classes.* This allows most of the work to be developed in advance and reused off-the-shelf as generic software-ICs. This example also illustrates the use of object-oriented programming in an area where complexity may have overwhelmed previous attempts.

The paper by James H. Alexander and Michael J. Freiling, "Smalltalk-80 Aids Troubleshooting System Development," describes how an expert system was built in Smalltalk. In particular, it describes how the object-orientation and other related features in the language facilitated the construction of the expert system. Smalltalk allowed the developers to build the system quickly and easily and to construct and modify program structures as the understanding of other requirements changed.

Additional References

J. Jacky and I. Kalet, "An Object-Oriented Approach to a Large Scientific Application," *OOPSLA '86, SIGPLAN Notices*, ACM, Inc., New York, New York, Volume 21, Number 11, November 1986, pages 368-376.

This paper describes an object-oriented design for a simulation of radiation therapy treatments for cancer. The main features of object-oriented languages, objects, inheritance, message passing, and windows are implemented in standard Pascal.

T.A. Cargill, "Pi: A Case Study in Object-Oriented Programming," *OOPSLA '86, SIGPLAN Notices*, ACM, Inc., New York, New York, Volume 21, Number 11, November 1986, pages 350-360.

Cargill describes how a debugger was written in C++.

J. Bonar, R. Cunningham, and J. Schultz, "An Object-Oriented Architecture for Intelligent Tutoring Systems," *OOPSLA '86, SIGPLAN Notices*, ACM, Inc., New York, New York, Volume 21, Number 11, November 1986, pages 269-276.

M. Rettig, "Using Smalltalk to Implement Frames," AI Expert, Volume 2, Number 1, January 1987, pages 15-18.

L.N. Garrett and K.E. Smith, "Building a Timeline Editor from Prefab Parts: The Architecture of an Object-Oriented Application," *OOPSLA '86, SIGPLAN Notices*, ACM, Inc., New York, New York, Volume 21, Number 11, November 1986, pages 202-213.

M.S. Miller, H. Cunningham, C. Lee and S.R. Vegdahl, "The Application Accelerator Illustration System," *OOPSLA '86, SIGPLAN Notices*, ACM, Inc., New York, New York, Volume 21, Number 11, November 1986, pages 294-302.

R.G. Smith, R. Dinitz, and P. Barth, "Impulse-86: A Substrate for Object-Oriented Interface Design," *OOPSLA '86, SIGPLAN Notices*, ACM, Inc., New York, New York, Volume 21, Number 11, November 1986, pages 167-176.

S. Bhaskar, J.K. Peckol and J.L. Beug, "Virtual Instruments: Object-Oriented Program Synthesis," *OOPSLA '86, SIGPLAN Notices*, ACM, Inc., New York, New York, Volume 21, Number 11, November 1986, pages 303-314.

Describes the construction in Smalltalk of an experimental programming environment for developing electronic test and measurement applications software.

PROGRAMMING EXPERIENCES

BY LARRY TESLER

*Programmers using object-oriented languages
say the benefits make the learning worthwhile*

WHAT IS IT LIKE to write a program in an object-oriented language? I posed that question to several people who program in Objective-C, C++, Object Pascal, and Smalltalk, hoping to gain insight into how different programmers think about object-oriented design. Their experiences had more in common than you might expect.

I asked each person to describe his project and discuss how object-oriented programming affected its progress. Their recollections tended to support oft-heard claims that object-oriented languages can be a boon to large programming projects. The software development benefits stem from three properties of object-oriented programs: object-based modular structure, data abstraction, and the ability to share code through inheritance.

The term *modularity* refers to the factoring of a large program into units that can be modified independently. In an object-oriented system, every module is an object, that is, a data structure that contains the procedures that operate upon it. Object-oriented design is the process of identifying objects that constitute a useful model

of the problem at hand. In the early stages of designing a program, the need to partition the problem into objects stimulates the designers to identify its principal constituents and to specify their behavior and interaction.

Data abstraction is the process of hiding a data structure behind a set of procedures through which access to the data is forced. In this way, the "concrete" representation chosen by the programmer is replaced by an "abstract" catalog of available operations. The advantage of data abstraction is that at any time the programmer can change representations without having to change other programs that relate to the operations. Data abstraction is a natural concomitant of object-oriented programming because each object contains not only its data structure but also the procedures that operate upon it. These procedures, often called methods, are usually the only aspects of the object accessible to other objects.

All object-oriented languages can share code through *inheritance*; that is, object-oriented languages provide the ability to define one type of object as a variation of an existing type. The

new object type is called a *subclass* of the old, and the old type a *superclass* of the new type. Objects in the subclass inherit all the properties of the superclass, including the implementations of methods. The subclass can define additional methods and redefine old methods by providing so-called *overrides*. By using inheritance during the development of an object-oriented program, code can be shared among similar objects. Later, certain kinds of enhancements can be made simply by creating new object types as variations of existing ones.

A WINDOWING SYSTEM
The first person I interviewed was Gary Walker, Manager of Primary Interaction Development in the Distributed Systems Group at Burroughs Corporation in Boulder, Colorado. He and his group of nine programmers were assigned the task of implement-

Larry Tesler, currently Manager of Advanced Development at Apple Computer, previously managed the development of Lisa applications, the Lisa Toolkit, and MacApp. He can be contacted at Apple Computer, 20525 Mariani Ave., Dept. 5770, Cupertino, CA 95014.

ing a general windowing environment, featuring menus, check boxes, buttons, and the other trappings of a see-and-point user interface. After conducting a comparative study of the available object-oriented languages, his group chose C++, an object-oriented extension of C inspired by Simula-67 and developed by Bjarne Stroustrup at Bell Laboratories in Murray Hill, New Jersey. Only object-oriented languages were considered for the project. "In a windowing system," Walker explained, "you want to instantiate objects for windows, each with its own private data. By defining separate types of windows as different classes, they can inherit common characteristics and still possess their own special properties."

Walker found data abstraction to be the most significant advantage of using C++. Smalltalk and some other object-oriented languages force data abstraction upon the programmer by hiding the internal structure of one object from other objects. For example, to move a chess piece, a Smalltalk program must invoke a method such as move_to, passing the destination square as a parameter. It cannot use an assignment statement to modify the data structure describing the chess piece's position. The advantage of the restriction is that both the representation of chess pieces and the implementation of move_to can be changed without having to alter the code in other objects that access them.

Unlike Smalltalk, Object Pascal and C++ allow objects to access part or all of the internal data of other objects. However, many textbooks warn against direct data access except when performance considerations are paramount. Walker's group found through experience with C++ that interobject direct data access is usually a detriment to modularity. "If you want to get at somebody else's variables," he said, "you should go through access functions [methods]."

Another property of object-oriented programs that benefited the windowing system project is modular structure. It gave the designers the ability to create what Walker calls "isolated

worlds of data and functions."

Walker also suggested a more pragmatic advantage of modularity based on objects: cutting down on the number of global variables in the program. The advantage of avoiding global variables in an interactive system is that multiple instances of each object can easily be created. It would be quite difficult to support multiple windows if the data describing a window resided in global variables. According to Walker, if you follow the advice of many software engineering books and avoid global variables, you usually end up passing too many parameters to functions. With C++, Walker explained, data can be "private" to an object, and all functions of that object can access its data without passing parameters.

Having heard Walker mention inheritance as a key factor in his choice of the object-oriented paradigm, I asked him for an example of its use in the windowing system. He cited the class Menu, a data abstraction with several subclasses, including Vertical-Menu, RadioButtons, and Check-Boxes. The system displays each type of menu a different way, and the user interacts with each a bit differently. But all serve the same basic purpose: They give the user choices, and they report the user's choice to the object in the application program.

Some methods of Menu are inherited by the subclasses without modification, while others are overridden by special implementations in each subclass. An example of an inherited method is selectionTitle, which returns the string containing the user's menu choice. The implementation of selectionTitle is shared by Menu and all its subclasses. An example of an overridden method is prompt, a function whose arguments are the text strings that represent the choices available in the menu. For example, my_menu.prompt("sherbert","cheese cake", "torte") specifies the choices in a dessert menu. Each subclass of Menu implements its own version of prompt. The version in the class VerticalMenu displays a list of the strings in a style similar to Macintosh pull-down menus, while the version in the class CheckBoxes displays the strings

side by side with a check box beside each one, similar to Macintosh dialogs.

The variable my_menu is declared to be of the type Menu, but at different times during execution its value may refer to objects of different subclasses of Menu. Whenever the my_menu.prompt is executed, it will invoke the version of prompt associated with the class of the object that is currently referred to by my_menu. This is one of several cases where Walker's group found a use for the so-called polymorphic property of objects. Polymorphism refers to the ability of one procedure call to invoke different procedures at run time depending on the type of one of its parameters. In object-oriented languages, polymorphism is achieved by letting different classes implement methods that have the same name and formal parameters but different implementations.

The ability of subclasses to inherit from superclasses can also simplify the maintenance of large object-oriented programs. The Burroughs team found that by making a change to the superclass, in effect they changed all the subclasses at once, and if they made changes to one of the subclasses to get distinctions they wanted, the code in the superclass and the other subclasses remained safe.

Walker's group was not alone in that finding. I heard similar claims from Seth Snyder and Dale Peterson of Recording Studio Equipment Company based in Miami, Florida, who used an object-oriented language to implement an integrated application that controls a spectrum analyzer while managing time billing for a recording studio. According to Snyder and Peterson, when new features had to be added to their program, they were able to add them reliably, without any risk of affecting the performance of features they had implemented earlier.

A SHIPBOARD NAVIGATION SYSTEM

Carl Nelson, a computer consultant in Seattle, Washington, was approached by a group of investors for his assistance in building a computer-assisted navigation system. The envisioned system, to be installed on boats in coastal waters, would consist of a Macintosh connected to a loran. A loran collects data on a ship's position from a radio receiver tuned to three or more land-based transmitters. Using a combination of triangulation and dead reckoning, it displays the ship's position and bearing on a simple (one- to three-line) display. The captain can key in the latitude and longitude of points along the desired course, and thereafter the loran will display the current heading and the distance to the next point in the course. If connected to an autopilot, the loran can command it to steer the vessel along the planned route.

The clients told Nelson that even though the loran and autopilot are mainstays of navigation for many boat owners, the equipment can be tedious and time-consuming to use. The digital information on the display does not relate to a position on a navigational chart at first glance. A "what you see is where you are" system—one that displays the chart on the screen with the present course lines superimposed on the image—was needed. Such a system would allow a navigator to plan a course on the chart with a mouse and then would transmit the coordinates electronically to the loran. The system would save time, increase accuracy, and avoid problems that arise when incorrect coordinates are entered.

The entrepreneurs used a Thunderscan digitizer to transfer images of nautical charts into MacPaint files, and they wrote a utility program to convert those files to a format usable by the application. One of the investors already had a Macintosh connected to the loran on his boat and recorded the telemetry of one day's voyage on a floppy disk. That disk enabled Nelson to test his program in the comfort of his office. For testing, Nelson used two computers. The main computer displayed the chart and allowed the course to be specified with a mouse. The other Macintosh served as a loran simulator, playing back the recorded telemetry through one of its serial ports to the main computer.

All that was left was to program the application and the simulator. Because he had only four months from project start to public demonstration, Nelson needed a software development environment that enabled rapid prototype development and implementation. He chose MacApp, an object-oriented software framework for the Macintosh (see "MacApp: An Application Framework" on page 189), and Object Pascal, the only language available then (mid-1985) that could be used with MacApp.

To understand MacApp, you must be familiar with certain standard concepts underlying Macintosh applications, including the concepts of document, view, window, and command. A document in the Macintosh corresponds roughly to a file in a traditional computer. The programmer must design a file format for storing it on disk and a data structure for storing it in memory. The programmer must also provide one or more ways to represent the document visually on the display and on the printed page.

Each different visual representation is called a view. For example, an array of floating-point numbers can be viewed as a tabular column of text containing digits and decimal points, or as a pie chart with shaded wedges of varying size. The size of a view often exceeds the size of the screen, but you can see portions of it through a window that you can scroll and resize. Using the mouse and the keyboard, you can issue commands that change the document. The changes are reflected in all views of that document that are presently displayed.

MacApp defines the abstract classes Document, View, Window, and Command, corresponding to the above concepts. A class includes a set of methods that define what the class can do. For example, a document can open and save, a view can draw and print, a window can resize and move, and a command can do and undo. To use MacApp, you must structure the application in a modular fashion in terms of these objects. Once that is done, the application can inherit an extensive library of user-interface and error-handling facilities.

According to Nelson, the framework provided by MacApp gave him a structure to plug things into. As he studied the navigation problem, he asked himself, "What do I have in this application that maps onto objects supplied by MacApp?" After identifying all the concepts that mapped easily into MacApp objects, he found that the whole user interface was accounted for. The only code that remained to be designed was that which manipulated internal data structures unrelated to the user interface.

In the navigation application, the most important subclass of the class View was easy to identify: a digitized chart with latitude and longitude lines. The window in which that view was displayed was a little harder to design, because it had to provide nonstandard controls for scrolling around a spherical world. The command objects were easily determined by enumerating the commands available in the user interface, such as place marker and show navigation info. The choice of document objects was not so clear-cut.

A document in MacApp is an object that manages the principal data structures of an application both in RAM and in file storage. In Nelson's application, several different files are employed, including the digitized nautical chart image with added annotations, and a trip file, which consists mainly of the trail of coordinates recorded during a specific voyage. Nelson had to decide whether the document object of his application should be of the class NauticalChart or of the class Trip, or whether his application should support both kinds of documents. He based his decision on an analysis of the operations associated with each type of object. For example, he wanted the client to be able to save the history of a trip in a file and then reopen that file by clicking an icon in the Macintosh Finder. But he also wanted the client to be able to open a chart file to review the annotations that had been made on the chart. He concluded that both the trip and the chart are appropriate document objects, and his ap-

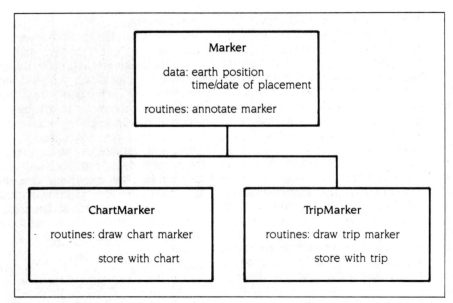

Figure 1: *An example of class hierarchy.*

plication defines both as subclasses of **Document**.

The chart file consisted of a digitized image plus markers indicating significant locations such as reefs and buoys. Once the program was running, Nelson and his client realized that not all markers should be associated with the chart file. It made sense for a marker labeled "lighthouse" to be stored with the chart, but a marker labeled "caught 30 lb salmon" really belonged with the trip. Nelson decided to divide all markers into two subclasses of the object class **Marker**, namely, **TripMarker** and **ChartMarker**. He analyzed what the two kinds of markers had in common—for example, the display algorithm and the routines to edit an annotation—and implemented that common behavior in the superclass **Marker**, from which the subclasses could inherit it. He also determined what differentiated them—for example, the shape of the displayed icon and the file used for storage—and implemented that special behavior as overrides in the subclasses. Nelson called the differentiation process "pushing down the details" from superclass to subclass (see figure 1).

A CAD SYSTEM

At Artecon Inc. in Carlsbad, California, a group of 20 programmers led

by Dana Kammersgard used an object-oriented language on Sun-2 and Sun-3 workstations in the development of ArteMate, an integrated CAD and office automation system. To make the system as portable as possible, Kammersgard's graphics group coded their routines according to an industry standard called GKS (Graphical Kernel System). GKS provides a way to construct images by transforming and combining primitive forms such as lines, polygons, curves, and ellipsoids. The standard specifies a device-independent set of procedure calls, leaving to each implementation the task of interpreting those calls in a manner appropriate to the available output devices.

According to Kammersgard, his team wanted the CAD portion of Arte-Mate to display two-dimensional and three-dimensional graphics on a wide variety of plotters and screens. To obtain that flexibility, an object-oriented approach seemed best. The language they chose for their implementation was Objective-C, developed by Productivity Products International of Sandy Hook, Connecticut, and available on a variety of computers and operating systems.

The first question Kammersgard's group addressed was how to organize the code for a number of graphics devices, including the CalComp 1043

and 1044 and the HP 758X models, in such a way that it could perform both input and output to a number of black-and-white and color display systems, including the Sun Color Graphics Processor and the IBM 5080. The programmers decided that each type of device should be represented by a different type of object. Accordingly, they defined Objective-C classes such as SunGP and Cal-Comp1044.

At different times during program execution, a program variable can contain pointers to different device classes. For example, if dev refers to an instance of the class SunGP, the statement dev poly__line: coordList invokes a device-specific method in class SunGP to display a polygon on the Sun screen. If dev is later assigned a reference to a CalComp 1044, the statement dev poly__line: coordList invokes a device-specific drawing method in the class CalComp1044 to drive the pen plotter along a polygonal path. To support a new device, the the programming team can simply define a new class without modifying existing code.

Kammersgard says that where they could take advantage of special hardware features, they implemented a device-specific method in the class. For example, the method poly__line normally has to apply transformations to the coordinates supplied in its parameter list to account for the visual perspective of the viewer. To calculate these transformations involves matrix multiplications, which are time-consuming operations in a conventional computer. Because the Sun Graphics Processor implements a three-dimensional transformation pipeline in hardware, the class SunGP overrides the standard implementation of poly__line, substituting a version that is shorter and faster than transformations performed wholly in software.

Like biologists who classify life forms into species, group similar species into a genus, group related genera into a class, and so on, object-oriented programmers design hierarchies of classes according to the similarities and differences they perceive between objects. In the

Artecon system, specific output devices are the species of the graphics kingdom, and company product lines are the genera. Since different devices from the same manufacturer often have similar interface specifications, Kammersgard's team defined the class CalCompPlotter as a superclass of both CalComp1043 and CalComp1044. They moved methods common to both models up to the superclass and left model-specific methods in the subclasses. In a similar fashion they added generic classes like HPPlotter, SunDisplay, and IBM50SeriesDisplay to the class hierarchy. By sharing as much code as possible between device classes, they were able to reduce program size and development time considerably.

The hierarchy of device classes continues for two more levels. At the level above product lines, all kinds of plotters are grouped into one class, and all kinds of interactive displays into another; display classes implement methods for user input, while plotter classes do not. At the highest level is the class GKSWorkstation, which is the ancestor of all other device classes. At that level, device-independent operations are implemented—for example, the GKS primitives that change display attributes in data structures in memory without communicating to the devices.

In any graphics application, another obvious application of objects is to represent the graphical components of the drawing. For example, all ellipsoids ought to be instances of the class Ellipsoid, and all cylinders ought to be instances of the class Cylinder. In the Artecon system, all geometric modeling classes are grouped together under a superclass called GeometricObject. Geometric objects respond to messages such as draw, rotate, and store.

But a CAD system must do more than a simple drawing program. It must allow the user to indicate relationships among design components. Kammersgard's group found themselves adding "links" to geometric objects and to other objects within the system, such as instances of the class ViewPort. After a while, they realized that the various implementations of links could be combined by embodying Geometric_Object and ViewPort in a new superclass called AssociativityObject. An associativity object contains a set of links and supports operations such as add_link, remove_link, and modify_link. A member of any subclass, say, Cylinder, inherits the ability to contain links as well as the routines for manipulating them. Adding the class AssociativityObject required a modest restructuring of existing code. According to Kammersgard, it is common to restructure the class hierarchy to take advantage of newly discovered opportunities for sharing code through inheritance.

A KNOWLEDGE-BASED APPLICATION

Bill Hutchison, a behavioral psychologist living in Silver Spring, Maryland, is implementing a knowledge-based system on the IBM PC. The system organizes information in a way that allows a seemingly rational response to stimuli. After considering a number of development systems, Hutchison decided upon Methods, a Smalltalk dialect developed by Digitalk Inc. of Los Angeles, California. I spoke to Hutchison after he had been using Methods for four months. "I like the way I can think about the problem," he said. "I map out the general problem in my head and can almost extract the objects from how I write it down in English. I make an object for each physical thing, process, or activity that I am dealing with."

I asked him if Smalltalk was difficult to learn. Hutchison, who has programmed extensively in assembly language, COBOL, BASIC, PILOT, and PLANIT, said he found Smalltalk "the most natural way" to program. He admits, however, that most of his learning time went to mastering Smalltalk's extensive class library. Large libraries are typical in object-oriented systems because they are extremely easy to build and maintain using subclassing and inheritance. The library that comes with Methods includes classes that are similar in purpose to those of MacApp. That allowed him to implement the user interface of his application easily and give it fancier features than he had first thought possible.

Hutchison said he structured the application's objects in a modular way. Knowledge is stored in association networks that relate situations, conclusions, and responses. He first developed a basic Network class able to represent simple domains, and he said that doing so was not as difficult as he had expected. Later, when he decided to tackle more difficult problems, complex networks became subclasses of the basic version. The first subclass he defined was InteractionNetwork, which adds the ability for parts of networks to interact with each other. That class was itself subclassed to define MultiResponseInteractionNetwork, which permits the system to respond along multiple dimensions.

At each stage he had to restructure existing definitions a little to allow the new class to inherit as much as possible from the old classes. The modular structure of the application made it easier to change one part without affecting others. "Sometimes," Hutchison said, "a radical change that I was dreading took me only an hour or less to accomplish." But Hutchison added that to make the program that modular, he had to develop the discipline to confine knowledge of an object's internal structure to its own class—only after having done that could he make changes to an object's structure without affecting others.

OBJECT-ORIENTED FUTURE

Certainly, object-oriented programming offers a great deal to software developers who want to manage large software projects or create prototypes quickly. Now that several suitable languages are widely available, many programmers will likely invest the time necessary to acquire the skill of using them. The interviews I conducted encouraged me to believe that these languages can be applied effectively in diverse situations by people of varied technical backgrounds. Even though the learning curve is high, most programmers can easily exploit the full potential of object modularity, data abstraction, and inheritance offered by object-oriented languages. ∎

MACAPP: AN APPLICATION FRAMEWORK

BY KURT J. SCHMUCKER

This application can significantly reduce Macintosh program development time

ONE FASCINATING and potentially far-reaching use of object-oriented programming is in the design of an application framework for a personal computer or workstation. Several examples of such frameworks exist, such as the Lisa Toolkit, discussed in "Software Frameworks" by Gregg Williams (December 1984 BYTE), and more are being designed all the time. This article examines one specific application framework for the Macintosh, MacApp—The Expandable Macintosh Application from Apple.

The average end user does not generally use or even know about application frameworks. They are tools for developers who design the software for end users. In theory, an application framework can be developed for any personal computer. However, they are especially useful on those with a well-defined user-interface specification.

WHAT IS MACAPP?

The MacApp framework is basically a complete, self-contained application that implements most of the Macintosh user-interface standard. It has menus that pull down and windows that scroll and can be moved about the screen, it works correctly with desk accessories and with Switcher, and it prints on the Imagewriter and the LaserWriter. The only things missing from a complete application are the contents of the windows and the items on the menus. An application framework is only the shell of a real application—a shell that you can easily customize into a true application. This customization process differentiates an application framework from a set of merely useful subroutines.

For example, let's examine the way in which an application framework supports undoing commands. MacApp knows that after you choose a menu command, the Undo command should reverse the effect of the command. But a general application framework can't know how to undo, or do, all the commands. These operations are accomplished with the dynamic binding present in an object-oriented language. The application framework "knows" about command objects and it knows that when a command is to be performed or undone,

it should send the message DoIt or UndoIt to the current command object. The application framework defines the basic skeleton of the application, but it leaves the specifics—for example, the actual details of undoing the **Double Space** command—to the command object. To build a specific application from this framework, you need to design only the objects that perform these specific actions and then install them into the framework.

The framework knows in general what a Macintosh application is supposed to do. It knows how to make the menus work, how to give up control when a desk accessory is activated, how to scroll windows, and so on—all the things that are common to

Kurt J. Schmucker, director of educational services for Productivity Products International (Severna Park Mall, H & R Block Office, 575 Richie Highway, Severna Park, MD 21146), teaches seminars on object-oriented programming. Kurt has written three books on computer science, including the forthcoming Object-oriented Programming for the Macintosh *(Hayden, 1986).*

Macintosh applications. The framework knows that the most recent command should be undone when you choose the Undo menu item and that the current selection should be highlighted when you activate a window. However, it doesn't know how to reverse the actions of particular commands or how to highlight the current selection. The *objects* you install in your customization of the application framework determine these actions. For example, to undo the last command, the application framework sends the message UndoIt to the current command object. The dynamic binding of this UndoIt message to a method at run time invokes the routine you have designed to handle undoing this particular command. The application framework proceeds without knowing what that command, or that selection, really is.

The application framework is more than just a skeleton with a fixed number of pluggable slots for commands and selection. Using the techniques of object-oriented programming, you can override every major decision (and many minor ones). Any application on this framework can take control at any decision point in the program by overriding the preprogrammed method to perform a user-written application-specific method.

To give it this flexibility, the application framework is set up as a group of classes, or class library, that you can use and specialize while developing a new application. If you want your application to behave in some unique, specific way, you can add some new objects into the framework to provide this behavior. If you don't want anything unusual, the applica-

tion framework will handle the application correctly as is.

THE BASIC STRUCTURE OF MACAPP

The class library that is MacApp contains more than 30 different classes and over 450 methods. (Figure 1 shows the inheritance structure of these classes.) However, if you understand the operation of just three of these classes—TApplication, TDocument, and TView—and seven of their methods, you will be able to build your own application on top of the MacApp framework. The class TApplication takes care of things that are the responsibility of the application as a whole. This includes launching the application, setting up the menu bar, deciding which documents to display in the "Open Which Document?"

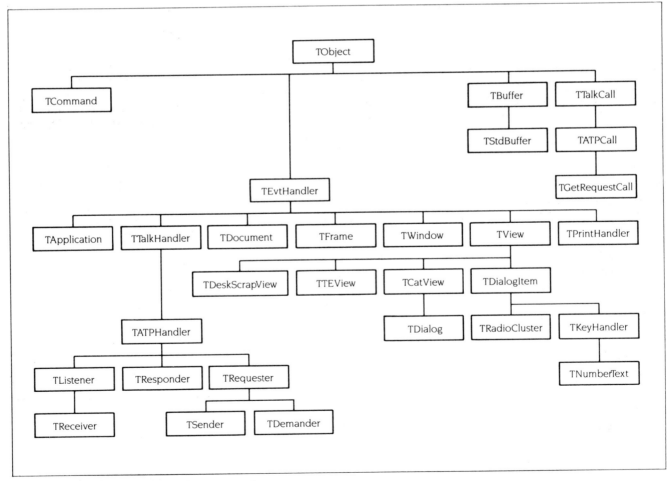

Figure 1: *The inheritance tree of the MacApp classes.*

dialog box, and so on. You design your own special subclass of TApplication, overriding whatever methods you choose in order to specialize any of these behaviors. One behavior you must always override is the type of document that holds your application's data (the method DoMake-Document).

The class TDocument processes commands like Save and Close, which are specific to each of the documents that are open at any one instant. (MacApp applications can usually deal with multiple documents being open at once.) Two behaviors that you must override in your subclasses of TDocument are the types of windows that display the data stored in the document (the method DoMakeWindows) and the contents of the windows (the method DoMake-Views). (The DoMake-something MacApp methods are the ones you *must* override.)

The class TView takes care of every-

thing inside your windows—drawing the images, highlighting the selection, handling mouse interaction with those images, and other things. TView knows when a portion of the window needs to be redrawn and when the selection should be highlighted. It doesn't know exactly how to do these things. It relies on you to override the methods that supply these behaviors in your subclasses of TView. These methods are Draw, Highlight-Selection, and DoMouseCommand.

DEVELOPING AN APPLICATION
To develop a MacApp application, you must design your own subclasses of TApplication, TDocument, and TView. It is traditional in MacApp programming to name these new subclasses so that you can easily determine their respective superclasses. Therefore, I have used the names TSmallApplication (a subclass of TApplication), TSmallDocument (a subclass of TDocument), and TSmallView (a subclass of TView). The application is called SmallApplication, and its entire source code requires only 87 lines of Object Pascal. (For a discussion of Object Pascal and other object-oriented languages, see my article "Object-oriented Languages for the Macintosh" on page 177.) Two printouts of screen shots from SmallApplication are shown in figures 2 and 3. [Editor's note: The entire source listing for SmallApplication is available in a variety of formats. See page 405 for details.] Let's look at two representative methods from this application—the DoMakeViews method of the class TSmallDocument and the Draw method of TSmallView.

DoMakeViews is one of the methods MacApp needs to access one of the classes designed specifically for SmallApplication. I call this kind of method a MacApp *hook* method. Listing 1 contains the full text of SmallApplication's DoMakeViews method. This method generates, initializes, and installs one instance of TSmallView. MacApp sends the message DoMakeViews precisely so it can obtain one of these and use it to draw inside the window. If this method seems rather short, that is a common characteristic of object-oriented programs, especially those

Figure 2: *SmallApplication—the smallest MacApp application.*

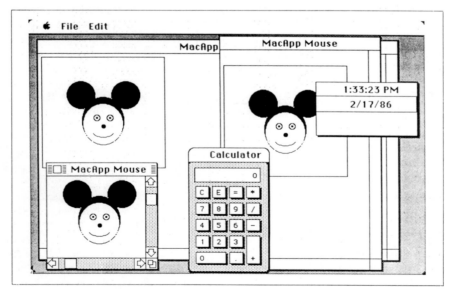

Figure 3: *MacApp applications typically work with multiple documents and always work correctly with desk accessories, even multiple ones.*

Listing 1: *The full text of* DoMakeViews.

```
PROCEDURE TSmallDocument.DoMakeViews(forPrinting: BOOLEAN); OVERRIDE;
VAR smallView: TSmallView;
BEGIN
    NEW(smallView);                    { Create a new instance of TSmallView }
    smallView.ISmallView(SELF);    { Send new view object its init message }
    SELF.fSmallView := smallView;  { Install this view object in document }
END;
```

Listing 2: *A procedure that overrides* TSmallView's Draw *method to draw a picture of a mouse.*

```
PROCEDURE TSmallView.Draw(area: Rect); OVERRIDE;

    FUNCTION MakeRect(top, left, bottom, right: INTEGER): Rect;
    VAR r: Rect;
    BEGIN
        SetRect(r, left, top, right, bottom);
        MakeRect := r;
    END;

BEGIN
    PenNormal;
    PaintOval(MakeRect(74, 72, 139, 127));       { Outline of the mouse head }
    EraseOval(MakeRect(84, 74, 138, 125));       { Outline of the mouse face }
    FrameOval(MakeRect(109, 84, 129, 115));      { Mouse mouth (part 1 of 2) }
    EraseRect(MakeRect(109, 84, 123, 115));      { Mouse mouth (part 2 of 2) }
    FrameOval(MakeRect(98, 87, 107, 96));        { Left eye }
    FrameOval(MakeRect(98, 104, 107, 113));      { Right eye }
    PaintOval(MakeRect(101, 90, 104, 93));       { Left pupil }
    PaintOval(MakeRect(101, 107, 104, 110));     { Right pupil }
    PaintOval(MakeRect(111, 97, 117, 103));      { Nose }
    PaintOval(MakeRect(53, 52, 91, 90));         { Left ear }
    PaintOval(MakeRect(53, 110, 91, 148));       { Right ear }

    FrameRect(MakeRect(20, 20, 170, 180));       { A bounding rectangle }

END;
```

designed to be overridden for many different purposes. Instead of hard coding many decisions, the designer of a class will make each such decision a method. You can change such a decision by creating subclasses and overriding the appropriate method.

The Draw method of the TSmallView class is a method for which MacApp cannot possibly provide a generic version. You can't draw anything in a window that would be useful to all Macintosh applications. In such cases, MacApp provides a stub method that does nothing, a *null* method. You don't have to override a null method like you do a hook method, but if you don't override this one, part of your application may appear to do nothing. The code in listing 2 overrides TSmallView's Draw method to draw a picture of a mouse.

If you continue this process for five other methods, you will have developed SmallApplication, an application that draws a picture of a mouse. SmallApplication is a stand-alone Mac application that works correctly on 128K-byte and 512K-byte Macs, the new Mac Plus, and the Mac XL. It works with Switcher and with any number of desk accessories, prints on the Imagewriter and the LaserWriter, supports multiple documents, and allows you to resize and move windows and use menus. As trivial as the application itself may seem, it does illustrate the flexibility of the MacApp framework.

THE BENEFITS AND COSTS OF USING MACAPP

Early studies indicate that MacApp can reduce application development time by a factor of four or five. MacApp also decreases the amount of source code you need, again by a factor of four or five. It maintains consistency with respect to the Macintosh user-interface standard and provides error handling and an interactive debugging facility, which are useful during development. It provides a conceptual framework that lets you concentrate on your application rather than on Macintosh internals.

Some feel that these gains are at the expense of performance in the finished application and of a large amount of additional memory. In fact, many MacApp programs actually run faster than their non-MacApp versions, despite the run-time overhead of messaging. MacApp applications are usually somewhat larger than their non-MacApp versions—about 10K to 15K bytes. But for most end-user applications, this is not a large penalty when weighed against the decrease in development time. ■

Intermedia: The Architecture and Construction of an Object-Oriented Hypermedia System and Applications Framework

Norman Meyrowitz

Institute for Research in Information and Scholarship (IRIS)
Brown University
Box 1946
Providence, RI 02912

ABSTRACT

This article presents a case study of the development of the Intermedia system, a large, object-oriented hypermedia system and associated applications development framework providing sophisticated document linkages. First itpresents the educational and technological objectives underlying the project. Subsequent sections capture the process of developing the Intermedia product and detail its architecture and construction, concentrating on the areas in which object-oriented technology has had a significant role. Finally, the successes and failures of the development approach are examined, and several areas of standardization and research that would enhance the process are proposed.

1. INTRODUCTION

When is an object-oriented methodology appropriate for designing a large interactive system? When is object-oriented programming the appropriate implementation vehicle for such a system? How does one coordinate the efforts of a team designing and developing an object-oriented system? What advantages does object-oriented programming provide? What disadvantages? What hardware and software exists today to serve as a base for such systems?

This paper presents a case study of the design, architecture, and construction of a large-scale, integrated set of object-oriented applications, with the objective of providing a snapshot of the object-oriented development process for those with questions such as those above.

The article is organized as a chronological tour of the design and development of Intermedia — a large-scale, object-oriented hypertext/hypermedia system. Intermedia provides the ability to create sophisticated linkages between documents from a variety of applications as well as providing a development framework for creating additional applications with that capability. The first section presents the educational and technological objectives underlying the project. Subsequent sections capture the process of developing that product and detail its architecture and construction. In particular, we cover the requirements phase, the user interface design phase,

"Intermedia: The Architecture and Construction of an Object-Oriented Hypermedia System and Applications Framework" by N. Meyrowitz from *Proceedings of the ACM Conference on Object-Oriented Programming Systems, Languages, and Applications*, 1986, pages 186-201. Copyright © 1986, Association for Computing Machinery, Inc., reprinted by permission.

the hardware and software procurement phase, the architectural design phase, and the implementation phase, concentrating on the areas in which object-oriented technology has had a significant role. Finally, we examine the successes and failures of the approach we have taken, and outline several areas of standardization and research that would enhance the process.

More detailed descriptions of Intermedia are available in [Meyr85b, Garr86, and Yank86].

2. INTERMEDIA OBJECTIVES

To determine whether an object-oriented approach to constructing systems is appropriate, one must first understand the problem to be solved. In the case of Intermedia, we focused on two major sets of objectives: 1) enhancing education through the use of innovative software and 2) enhancing the methodological and technological base on which such innovative software is built.

2.1 Background

In late 1984, as part of Brown University's campus-wide "Scholar's Workstation Project," [Meyr85a] the Institute for Research in Information and Scholarship (IRIS) undertook a research and demonstration project that involved the introduction of general-purpose scholarly software on powerful networked workstations into courses. We intended to examine the impact of *hypertext* and *hypermedia* [Nels80] — non-sequential connection of related materials — on research and teaching by integrating the same software tools into three very different courses — A Survey of English Literature, Introductory Music Theory, and Plant Cell Biology. The ideas behind such hypertext systems can be traced to work by Bush [Bush45], Engelbart [Enge68], Nelson [Nels80], van Dam [Carm69, Cata79], and others over the past several decades. [Yank86] provides a good survey of the hypertext field.

More specifically, the current Brown effort, sponsored by the Annenberg/CPB Project and IBM, attempts to: 1) build a hypermedia system on the newest generation of workstation technology, which, with its powerful graphics and networking, approaches the type of delivery vehicle necessary for a highly functional system; 2) create the system using software technology that enables new features to be added easily; and 3) test the utility of such a concept in university education and research.

2.2 Educational Objectives

In particular, our demonstration project focuses on three general educational aims:

Connectivity. First, we believe it is important to facilitate the observation and creation of connections and relationships among ideas, concepts, events and people. Our first general aim, therefore, is to provide software tools that will allow professors to create webs of information and that will allow students to follow trails of linked information, annotate text and illustrations, and communicate with other students and the professor.

Audiovisualization. Secondly, we aim to enhance "audiovisualization," the student's ability to visualize and perceive complex and/or dynamic phenomena. Such phenomena might include cell division, mathematical surfaces, the structure of ideas and information, or music notation and accompanying sound.

Exploration. Lastly, we aim to encourage exploration of an information-rich environment so that students may discover ideas, themes and facts on their own.

2.3 Technological Objectives

Besides the above educational objectives, we have several imperative technological objectives:

Extensibility. We firmly believed that a system like Intermedia, while still interesting if created as a "one-shot," closed demonstration system, would meet our educational goals only if it could be created so that individuals not intimately involved with the initial development could add additional applications without intensive training and without drastic modification to the Intermedia base.

Reusability. The software industry tolerates far too much wasteful reinvention of code. A large portion of development time for each of the thousands of software products is spent writing code that performs functions already implemented in many other packages. For example, in each of the Macintosh applications that allow users to manipulate graphic objects, the code that allows users to select, move, resize, and recolor squares, circles, and such is reimplemented essentially from scratch by each company. An important objective in our project was to provide a "lumberyard" of building blocks for developers to use to shorten the development cycle.

Consistency. An important aim of the project was to provide a consistent user interface across applications, so that selecting and moving entities, choosing commands, and creating and following links operated identically in all applications. In addition, our technical goal was to enable this consistency essentially "for free": ideally, if developers used the Intermedia system appropriately, new applications could inherit the behavior with no work on their part.

Understandability. With many applications being developed under the framework, one of the important technological requirements was a uniform way in which individual developers could understand the data structures and procedures in the system.

Modularity for Parallel Development. Similarly, if developers were simultaneously creating applications it was important to present a development environment in which they could create those applications as separate modules. The ability to create an application "stand-alone" allows developers to test their code without interfering with other developers. It was equally important that such stand-alone modules be integrated into the full Intermedia system with little effort.

2.4 Process and Product

To attempt to meet these objectives, a team of 12 individuals — one user liaison, one graphics artist, and 10 software developers — began a simultaneous requirements-gathering and development process in mid-1985. The following sections outline the 9-month effort to create Intermedia and illustrate the important role of object-oriented technology in the development process.

3. INTERMEDIA DESIGN
3.1 Initial Assumptions

Based upon past development projects and experience with end users, the first requirement we imposed on the system was that it operate entirely with a direct manipulation interface for all operations, preventing the user from being *preempted* [Swin74] from normal system operations by being locked into *modes* [Tesl81]. Furthermore, where at all possible, the system should provide "infinite undo," which would allow the user to withdraw all the operations done since the beginning of the session.

Choosing the direct manipulation's subject/verb (postfix) interaction syntax as a universal paradigm affected the remainder of the requirements and user interface design process. In the non-direct-manipulation world, most requirements documents are written as *functional* requirements, where the specifiers outline the functions that are desired, treating the entities to be represented less thoroughly.

In contrast, for direct manipulation systems, the entities and their associated behaviors are most important in understanding how a system should work. Such systems are characterized by postfix interaction syntax, where an individual first selects the target entities that he/she wants to operate upon and then chooses the desired command. Thus, in our requirements phase, we chose to develop an *object-oriented specification*. In this specification, we concentrated on understanding first what entities needed to be represented in the Intermedia system and how they were related, and concentrated secondly on what behaviors they should exhibit. That better enabled us to factor the system into components that would enable us to present a consistent, easily understood conceptual model of operations to the user. A summary of the resulting requirements and user interface design for the framework is presented below.

3.2 The Results of the Process

An assumption underlying the development of Intermedia is that users will be most likely to take advantage of the system's capabilities if they can create links as part of their regular work with spreadsheets, word processors, graphics editors or other media. Therefore, Intermedia should not be a standalone application, but rather a framework for a collection of tools that allow authors to create and links documents from a variety of applications.

Thus, the user interface should be similar to the window-based desktop environments provided on the Xerox Star or Apple Lisa, in which multiple applications run simultaneously [Smit82, Schm84]. Each application should allow the user to create material of a different type: text documents, musical scores, spreadsheets, and such. Multiple applications of the same type (e.g., multiple music editors) should be able to run simultaneously.

The material the application creates is the *document,* a part of which is viewed in the application's *window.* While the application is running, the user should be able to update the document interactively through direct manipulation techniques, with WYSIWYG (what-you-see-is-what-you-get) rendering where applicable. The user should be able to store the document in folders on disk for later retrieval. The system should provide the ability to name, open, close, move, and organize applications, windows, and documents.

In addition to the level of integration that allows the cutting and pasting of data from one document to another, Intermedia requires an additional level of integration — the *navigational link.* The process of creating links should mirror the copy/paste operation. One should be able to create a source selection, called a *block,* choose the "start link" command, pick a destination block, and choose the "end link" command. A block should be composed of any valid *selection.* For example, in text it would be an insertion point, character, or range of characters; in structured graphics, it would be a primitive or group of primitives; in music it would be a note, group of notes, measure, or group of measures. When the linking operation is finished, there should be a bidirectional tie between the source block and destination block such that whenever a user selects the a block and issues the "follow" command, the document containing the companion block is retrieved from storage, if necessary, and displayed (see Fig. 1).

Intermedia should provide *keywords* attached to blocks and links. Keywords applied to links allow the user to attach one or more attributes to a link; later users should be able to apply filters to the document so that only the link symbols meeting their filtering criteria are shown on the screen. Similarly, users should be able to filter blocks within a document according to simple or boolean search arguments. *Explainers* attached to blocks and links should allow a user to type in a small note explaining the purpose of the block and link, much as the subject line of an electronic mail message partially identifies the purpose of that mail message.

Intermedia's linking and keyword capabilities should allow individual users, groups of users, or in the extreme, an entire campus to create a shared *web* of linked materials from different applications. A web should be thought of as a database that contains both references to a set of documents and the links associated with those documents. Two webs might reference the same documents but have entirely different sets of links. For example, the English department might have a web referencing all of the Shakespearean tragedies along with links pertaining to color imagery in those plays, while the religious studies department might have a web referencing the same plays but with links pertaining to religious symbolism.

This structure implies that multiple users on different workstations should be able to access the same corpus of

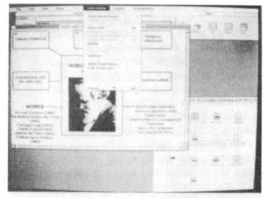

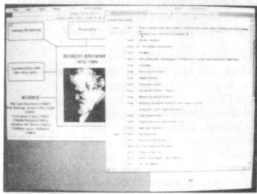

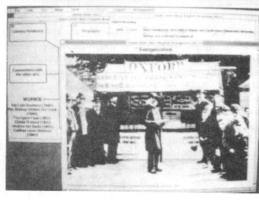

In Fig. 1a, the user selects a link marker (tiny **square** with marker in it in the graphics document and chooses the Follow command. In Fig 1b, the timeline document at the end of the link is brought up. Again, the user selects a link marker and chooses Follow, and in Fig 1c, another graphics document is opened.

documents and the same web simultaneously. Consequently, networking the workstations on which Intermedia is to be delivered, the existence of a transparent network file system through which users access documents, and *access control* that mediates the update of blocks, links, and documents to prevent concurrency problems.

Facilities for visualizing the web structures should be provided by Intermedia. The system should generate maps of the web at the global (web) level, at the document level or at the more detailed block level. In addition, the maps should indicate the user's travels through the web.

Intermedia should provide basic levels of functionality for applications to operate in the framework so that application developers can concentrate on developing those features unique to of their application. Such common features should include standard libraries for handling windows, menus, the linking and blocking functions, interactions with the desktop, and like functions.

Since many proposed applications share similar functionality (e.g., text editing, graphics editing, "spreadsheet-type" list handling), Intermedia should provide developers with *building blocks* that implement that common functionality and are useable by all applications developers with little or no modification. For first release, two building blocks are required. One is a text processing building block that provides the developer with the ability to create editable text areas anywhere on the display. This building block should support multi-font, proportionally-spaced fonts and the ability to define formatting styles that could be applied to each document entity to affect its formatting. The other necessary building block is a structured graphics building block, which provides the developer with a variety of editable graphics objects (rectangles, circles, lines, polygons) that can be placed and manipulated on a screen "canvas" whenever a developer needs to use editable graphics.

The applications that are required for first release include a direct-manipulation text processor, a direct-manipulation graphics editor, a direct-manipulation timeline editor, and a scanned image viewer/cropper (see Fig. 2).

4. BASE HARDWARE AND SOFTWARE
4.1. The Hardware
The target hardware for delivery of the Intermedia system was determined as part of Brown's campus-wide Scholar's Workstation Project. For the initial experiments of the Project, the strategic planning group chose the Sun workstation and IBM RT PC as the development vehicle and the delivery vehicle, respectively. The hope was that as the years progressed, a variety of vendors would produce machines that were in the same equivalence classes for functionality, performance, price, and software support.

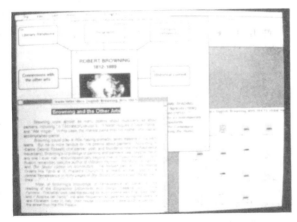

Figure 2 — Besides the graphics and timeline editors shown in Figure 1, Intermedia provides a WYSIWYG text editor and a map that provides a graphical view of the linkages between documents.

The RT PC contains a RISC microprocessor rated at over 2 MIPs and a companion memory management unit that handles a 40-bit virtual address space. The configurations we use have 3 to 4 megabytes of physical memory, a 100 x 768, 97 pixels/inch, monochrome bitmap display, an Ethernet connection to a local area network, and a 2-button mechanical mouse. The systems can each support a number of internal hard disks, though for the most part, individual workstations each have a 40 megabyte hard disk to contain only the operating system files. Each local area network has one or more central server machines that contain larger disks and more memory; the Intermedia system code, user documents and webs are typically stored on the server's hard disk.

4.2 The Operating System
Again, the base operating system was not chosen based upon specific Intermedia requirements, but rather on the features that the strategic planning group deemed necessary for the next generation of workstations. These features included virtual memory support, multitasking support, and networking support, including support of a network file system. The system chosen was Berkeley UNIX 4.2 enhanced with Sun's Network File System. This system ran on both the Suns and the RTs, meaning that development taking place on the Suns could be ported to the RTs with little or no effort.

4.3 Toolbox and Applications Framework
The next major components of the system that needed to be procured or developed were the *user interface toolbox* and a higher-level *applications framework*. The user interface toolbox needed to provide low-level keyboard and mouse handlers, a fast output graphics package, an event manager to handle the higher-level dispatching of i/o, a window manager to handle the multiplexing of the screen real estate, a menu manager, a control manager to handle scroll bars, sliders and associated input modes, and a forms/dialog manager to handle the multi-parameter input associated with style sheets and dialog boxes. The applications framework, built on top of the user interface toolbox, should provide higher-level data abstractions and a working "generic" application from which the developer can build his/her software. We understood that we would have to implement the linking/blocking paradigms of Intermedia in any applications framework, but we were hoping to be able to refine an existing framework rather than create an entirely new one.

After long deliberation, the development group decided that the Macintosh Toolbox, coupled with Apple's MacApp [Appl86, Doyl86, Schm86] on a RT/UNIX 4.2 base, provided a toolbox with the best direct manipulation interface and the best extensible applications framework on which to build. The catch: neither the Mac Toolbox nor MacApp ran on an RT PC.

First, we needed a Mac Toolbox on the RT. Cadmus Computer Systems had created the CadMac Toolbox, a Macintosh Toolbox implemented in C on a UNIX base), and under a special agreement with Cadmus, we received a license to port the CadMac code from their hardware base to the RT. The CadMac implementation ' was interesting in that, where the Mac Toolbox ran only in a single process environment, CadMac supported multiple simultaneous processes sharing the screen.

Next, we needed to move MacApp to the RT/CadMac base. MacApp is implemented using Object Pascal, an object-oriented extension of Pascal and was expressly designed to allow developers to refine the applications framework for their needs. We needed to find an object-oriented language under UNIX in order to port MacApp.

4.4 Object-Oriented Language

At that same time, we were working with Larry Tesler at Apple, trying to define an object-oriented extension to the C language that would parallel Apple's Object Pascal. The result was the specifications for a small syntactic and semantic extension to C that we called "Inheritance C" [Meyr86] In parallel, Mark Nodine of Bolt Beranek and Newman had implemented under UNIX a preprocessor for C that essentially implemented the semantics of Inheritance C with an alternative syntax. The BBN "class compiler" worked in complement with the Sumacc compiler and Mac development system, which allowed developers to cross compile and download code for the Macintosh. As well, Nodine ported parts of MacApp from its native Object Pascal to his object-oriented pre-processed version of C and got them running on the Macintosh through Sumacc.

Under special agreement with Nodine and a special experimental agreement with Apple, we began using the BBN class compiler and the partial version of C MacApp to get MacApp running natively on the RT PC with CadMac as the underlying user interface toolset.

4.5 Technology Summary

The systems integration effort proved to be successful, and by late summer 1985, we had ported CadMac and MacApp to the RT/UNIX 4.2 development base. Figure 3 depicts the foundation on which Intermedia was to rest.

5. INTERMEDIA ARCHITECTURE
5.1 MacApp

The Intermedia architecture can be understood if only one first has a broad overview of MacApp. The goal of MacApp is to handle all of the user input the content region of a window and to provide a framework for processing actions that occur insidethe content region of a window. For instance, without any new code from the application developer, MacApp will put up default menus, handle mouse events in the window's title bar to move the window, handle mouse events in the window's resize box to change the window's size, generate new windows when the "New" menu item is chosen, and save a document when the "Save" menu item is chosen. The developer can concentrate on implementing what goes on inside the content region of a window; MacApp, when receiving input for the inside of a window, will dispatch it appropriately. In fact, compiling a five line program that simply initializes the Mac Toolbox, creates and initializes the generic application object, and then tells that object to run, is all that is necessary to get a program that exhibits full Macintosh functionality — except that the insides of the windows are empty.

In its implementation, MacApp defines the major object types described below and several additional

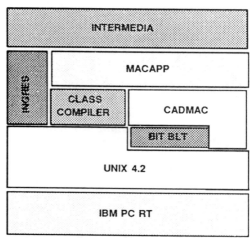

Figure 3 — Intermedia Architecture

classes to support the purposes of these major classes. (In the Apple version, class names for MacApp classes conventionally begin with the letter "T" which is removed here for readability. Additionally, Intermedia is built on version 0.2 of MacApp. The most current version (1.0) has significant changes and additions; readers are referred to [Schm86] and [Appl86], which document the newest version extremely well.)

Object. The *Object* class is the root class of all other classes defined in the system.

EvtHandler. *EvtHandler* is the superclass of most objects that want to enqueue themselves for input from the mouse, from the keyboard, and from the menus. The base classes, *Application, Doc, Pad, View,* and *Command,* are subclasses of EvtHandler, since they all need to "line up" to get input at one time or another. The EvtHandler class contains the methods *DoIdle, DoKeyCommand, DoMenuCommand, DoSetUpMenus, DoEvent, DoRead,* and *DoWrite* which are called when an appropriate event is dispatched from the application's main event loop.

Application. The *Application* class comprises the methods needed for the most general behaviors of the MacApp generic application. The methods include one to begin launch the application, one to begin running the main event loop, one to dispatch events to the target *EvtHandler,* one (which is typically overriden) to create new documents, one to close documents, and one to delete documents. A specific application that needs to intercept certain non-generic menu events would override the *DoSetUpMenus* method to indicate which menu commands it wants to intercept and would override the *DoMenuCommand* method, to indicate how to handle such a menu event. The *Application* object is typically installed at the end of the EvtHandler queue, and receives the events that no other object intercepts. The *Application* class contains no fields; rather, global variables to keep track of the windows, documents, and such that are currently open for this application replace the fields of the Application class. In a multi-tasking environment, and for the sake of modularity, it would be better to have represented those variables as fields of the Application class.

Document. The *Document* class encapsulates the fields and methods to manage the data structures of a direct manipulation tool such as a word processor, graphics editor, charting package, or timeline editor. The *Document* object is subclassed by the developer to add fields to manage the underlying data structures or *model* of such a package; in a timeline editor, for example, the *Document* subclass contains the data structures that represent the sorted events that make up the timeline. The *Document* also contains a field that points to a list of windows that hold renderings of that particular model, a field that holds the document name, and fields that manage the undoing and redoing of operations on the document. (In our case because of the availability of virtual memory, *Document* was modified to maintain an infinite undo/redo stack; the original version maintained a one level undo). Methods exist to launch new windows, initialize a new document, open a new document, and to spawn a *View* that will render a document. Again, *Document* overrides *DoSetUpMenus and DoMenuCommand* to handle menu events with which a *Document* object must be concerned.

Window. *Window* represents the rectangular area on the screen in which a user sees a document. One field of *Window* points to a Mac Toolbox window that interfaces with the Mac Window Manager, while another points to the *Document* object to which the *Window* object is associated. Methods exist to open the window, close the window, resize the window, move the window, activate/deactivate the window, and such. Again *Window* overrides the *DoXXX* methods to handle events with which a *Window* object must be concerned.

View. The *View* presents an infinite piece of paper with its own coordinate system on which the application can draw. Where the developer subclassed *Document* to maintain the data structures for a particular tool, the developer subclasses *View* to draw those document data structures in whatever fashion is desired. A portion of the *View* is rendered in a *Frame* in a *Window*. The *View* maintains fields that point directly to the*Document* that it is rendering and to the *Frame* in which the view is to be seen. The developer adds additional fields to represent the graphical information needed to perform its drawing. Most importantly, when the rendering needs to be updated, the *View's Draw* method is called to refresh the drawing appropriately.

Frame. The *Frame* class represents a rectangular subdivision of a window, with its own coordinate system. By overriding appropriate methods, the developer can divide a window into any number of *Frames*, each with its own coordinate system. As well, *Frames* can be nested in other *Frames*. Each *Frame* can have its own scroll bars and other controls. By default there is a single *Frame* in a window.

Command. It is odd at first to think of a command as an object, since it is most often thought of as a verb that operates on some object. The MacApp *Command* class represents the state of a command about to take place, and exists to have either an operation done with the *DoIt* method, undone with the *Undo* method, or redone with the *Redo* method. The *Command* object is usually subclassed to add fields that will maintain whatever state is necessary to do, undo, or redo the operation. Its representation as an object is useful, since the *Command* objects make up the undo/redo stack of the generic application.

Dialog. The *Dialog* class enables the developer to couple all the fields of a user input form with the behaviors that should control that user input. Typically, the programmer creates a subclass for each new dialog box in the system; each subclass contains specific fields that hold any special state that is necessary and overrides the *RespondToItem* method to invoke special behavior when certain dialog items are selected (i.e., inactivating some dialog fields when a particular item is activated).

MouseHand and Selection. MacApp 0.2 does not include the *MouseHand* and *Selection* classes, but because of the importance of the notion of "selection" in the direct manipulation paradigm, we added these two classes to MacApp to make the notion of selection more explicit. *MouseHand* is simply a subclass of *EvtHandler* that adds the additional method *DoMouseCommand*. The most important subclass of *MouseHand* is *Selection*. *Selection* is an abstract class which defines the *Hilite(on/off)*, *Activate*, and *Deactive* methods. *Selection* is typically subclassed for a specific application; a field of this subclass usually points to the objects that are currently in the selection. We added an *fSelection* field to *View* to point to the current selection, and implemented the methods *HaveSelection* and *HighlightSelection* to maintain the selection appropriately.

5.2 Creating Intermedia — The Constraints

One of the first architectural considerations was the tasking structure that Intermedia should take: one large integrated single process (as all applications are on the Macintosh) or a set of independent but communicating processes (as the CadMac software could support).

Intermedia could be built as a single process in which each Intermedia editor is bound together with the Intermedia framework (which manages the web, desktop, and keyword functions) to form a single executable module, similar to the Lotus Jazz product. Since all the components reside in one address space, communication between the running editors and the framework is done simply by standard method calls to appropriate objects. The advantages of this approach are 1) the elimination of difficulties associated with interprocess communications; 2) the modularity gained by having the application code completely divorced from the framework; 3) the use of a less sophisticated user interface package, i.e., one that does not support multiple independent applications accessing the screen simultaneously; 4) the reduction of the number of executable modules to one. This last advantage is particularly important under operating systems like Unix, where the libraries necessary for an executable are statically bound; each module essentially has close to .75 MBytes worth of redundant user-interface, graphics, and class libraries bound to it on top of its specific code. Several processes running simultaneously, each with 1 MByte code segments, can hinder performance, even on a machine with virtual memory. Additionally, the executables use precious disk space.

Disadvantages of the single process approach are 1) the difficulties associated with having simultaneously running tools, i.e., an animation program that can rotate an image at the same time as a terminal emulator can display long list at the same time as one can use a text processor; 2) the difficulties of integrating what are primarily independent applications into a single executable module; 3) the size of the executable when all parts are bound together.

Alternatively, the framework can be built as a separate process and each Intermedia editor can be built as a separate executable module. In this case, when the user opens a document from the framework finder, the framework must spawn a new process that executes an instance of one of the Intermedia edtior modules. In this case communications between the applications and the framework must be done through some type of interprocess communications mechanism such as remote procedure or method call. The advantages of this model are 1) the true concurrency that can be gained from multiple processes; and 2) the ease of implementing applications separate from the framework and integrating them into the framework. The disadvantages of this model are 1) the added complexity of using interprocess communications services; 2) large number of executable modules to keep up to date; 3) size of executable modules in systems with statically bound libraries; and 4) need for more sophisticated concurrent graphics support.

Because we had no remote method invocation facilities, the multiple process choice would have prevented us from using the MacApp framework as it was and/or would have caused us to undertake a large design and implementation task to implement remote method invocation and change MacApp to support it. Remote method invocation is difficult because one needs to guarantee that the inheritance hierarchy in all processes is identical if one is to obtain valid results. This is something that we have put on our research agenda, but given our time constraints, we chose to build the first release of Intermedia as a large integrated single process, while trying to maintain the modularity that would allow us to separate it into multiple processes in the future.

A second important architectural concern was the management of simultaneous access to webs of blocks and links and associated documents. This was difficult because 1) a document might appear in more than one web; 2) more than one user may acess the same webs and documents simultaneously; 3) editing the contents of a document requires careful updating of block position information for all the webs that reference the document; and 4) data integrity must be maintained not only for the contents of the documents but also for their block and link information.

The solution to this important set of concerns was to store all of the information in a single, system-wide database called the *Intermedia Database*. We needed a database management system that provided network-wide retrieval and update of such information with appropriate concurrency control. We chose Ingres as the database for reasons of availability, but our storage and retrieval scheme would work equally well with any relational database. We believe storage and retrieval would be easier with an object-oriented database, where the objects defined in the object-oriented C code could be stored and retrieved with little more than a method call, and we plan to investigate this possibility.

Our strategy was to make the existence of the database transparent to programmers, who would access the block, link, and web information through *Block, Link*, and *Web* classes that would perform the database storage and retrieval. Underneath, the Intermedia Database would maintain a relation for each web and a relation for the blocks and links in a web, and would provide the locking and concurrency management to keep the information valid.

Given the single process structure, the existence of a shared network database, and the hardware/software base described in Section 3, how would we break down the problem into parts that would leverage off of the MacApp application framework?

5.3 The Intermedia Layer

Many of the existing MacApp classes — in particular *Application, Document,* and *View* — needed to be refined and several additional classes created to factor the concepts of blocks and links into the Intermedia framework. Figure 4 depicts the inheritance structure of the layer.

5.3.1   New Intermedia Layer Classes

Block and BlockList. Recall that *blocks* are anchors to the part of a document model that is represented by a selection. The block always references the objects in that selection, regardless of where they might move in the document because of editing changes.

To represent blocks, we created the *Block* class in the Intermedia Layer. The *Block* object has as a list of *Link* objects in which that block is an end, a list of keywords that have been applied to the block, a list of objects that are members of the blocks, and several additional property fields such as the explainer, the owner of the block, and the time of last update. The *Block* has methods to show the selection the block references, to show the marker that represents the block, to display a dialog box of the links that emanate from this block, to delete links from the block, to follow a particular link, to start a link from this block, to end a link from this block, to show the properties of the block, to show the properties of the links emanating from the block, and to delete the block. Since links need to keep track of their source and destination blocks, we needed a way to identify blocks uniquely. Thus, in the Intermedia Database, a *block* relation exists for each web; each record in the relation records permanent information for one block. One of the fields of a block record holds a unique 32-bit id that identifies each block; the *Block* object maintains a copy of this as well. *BlockList*, a subclass of *HashList*, simply maintains a list of blocks hashed by the block id and a handle to the document of which it is a member.

Link and LinkList. Links are simply records that keep track of two connected block as well as link keywords, creation and modify time, author, and other link-specific data. Thus the *Link* class has fields for the source and destination block ids and doc ids, fields that keep track of the author, explainer, and keyword list as in the *Block* class, fields that contain handles to the source and destination block objects when the link is active, and a unique 32-bit link id similar to the block id described above. *Link* implements methods to complete a pending link and to remove itself from an existing block.

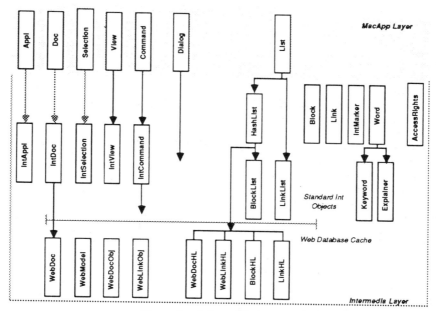

Figure 4 — Intermedia Layer

LinkList, a subclass of *List*, simply maintains an unordered list of links and a handle to the block of which that *LinkList* is a member.

WebDoc. The *WebDoc* class provides an object-oriented interface to the database that keeps the block and link information for a web. To this end, the *WebDoc* class provides accessor methods for creating a unique block id, retrieving a block list for a particular document, retrieving the properties of that block, saving a block, retrieving the explainer of a block, retrieving a unique link idea, and retrieving various link data. This set of related objects is stored as an actual partition of a relational database in Ingres. This is supplemented with a partial cache of some elements maintained in the web doc; the cache is maintained with the use of objects from the private classes *WebModel*, *WebDoc*, *WebLinkObj*, *WebDocObj*, *WebDocHashList*, *WebLinkHashList*, *BlockHashList and LinkHashList*. Yet because implementors do not access the fields directly, but only through the accessor methods, changes to the implementation of the database (of which there were three major ones during our implementation) are transparent.

AccessRights. Since shared work is so important to Intermedia, providing and mediating access to documents and webs is paramount. Such access rights are represented by instances of the *AccessRights* class. This class contains fields that indicate the rights for the owner of the document, the user's group, all other users, and the Intermedia administrator.

5.3.2   Intermedia Layer Subclasses

The Intermedia Layer subclasses refine MacApp classes by incorporating objects·from the new Intermedia classes described above and by adding additional methods. This creates an Intermedia generic application, such that a developer using this layer can compile a tiny (5-20 line) program and obtain an application that exhibits full MacApp *and* full hypertext/hypermedia functionality.

IntApplication. *IntApplication* refines *Application* in three general areas: 1) database access; 2) web creation; and 3) management of Intermedia-wide document access.

In the first area, the *IntApplication* includes methods to open the database in which the block and link information for the current web is stored. In the second area, the subclass includes methods to allow the creation of new webs in the database. In the third area, the system provides methods that enable documents to be created and immediately installed into the desktop folder system, that allow the setting of document access rights, and most importantly, that allow a document to be retrieved not only from the desktop environment, but also by the following of links. Additionally, the *IntApplication* adds a field that points to the currently pending link, a field that points to the current open web, fields that maintain the identity of the current system user, and several other fields.

IntDoc. Similarly, we created the *Document* subclass *IntDoc* to add fields and methods that would enable documents to save and retrieve blocks and links and to manage those blocks and links while the document is active. Specifically, the *Document* object maintains the *document id,* an integer that insures uniqueness of this document over the entire Intermedia Database, the *document type*, an integer that indicates the function of that document, a pathname of where the document is stored in the UNIX file system, two *AccessRights* objects that indicate what the stored rights for this document were and what the current capabilities are, and most importantly, a handle to the *BlockList* for this document. Methods like *Open* and *Close* of *Document* are overriden here to read and write block information as well as standard doc information. When a document is opened, the web database, through the current *WebDoc*, is queried to find all of the blocks in that document and returns a list of block ids and the object ids associated with each block to the *IntDoc*. Methods of the *IntDoc* and *IntView* (see below) are subsequently called to link the block ids with the actual objects that are being displayed and to post the graphical block markers that will represent the blocks on the screen.

IntView. Unlike standard Views, Intermedia views must be able to render not only the document data

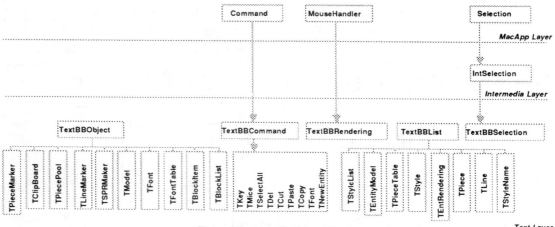

Figure 5 — Text Building Block

structures, but also the markers that must be attached to the rendered objects to indicate that they are part of a block/link. Thus the *IntView* class was created as a subclass of *View* to keep track of this additional marker rendering. Fields are added to keep track of the current markers and the state of their presentation. Methods are added to "hook" markers to their associated renderable objects, to unhook them, and to hide or show the markers. A *ViewSpecs* method enables the setting of various viewing specifications. The *DoSetUpMenus* and *DoMenuCommand* methods of *View* are overridden to enable and respond to menu commands to set the view specs, to hide and show block markers, and such.

IntSelection Class. *IntSelection* refines *Selection* by adding protocol to make the selection into a block, to start a link from the objects in the selection, to complete a link with this selection as the destination block, or to follow a link emanating from this block.

5.4 The Building Blocks

Given the MacApp Layer and the Intermedia Layer, we implemented two building blocks — the *text building block* (Fig 5) and *graphics building block* (Fig 6)— from which the remaining applications would be built.

5.4.1 Text Building Block.

In the text building block, the *TextBBRendering* class defines most of the external interface for a developer. One of the major tasks of *TextBBRendering* is to receive and perform the input requests associated with text editing such as select, scroll, insert character, set font. *TextBBRendering* is a subclass of *MouseHand* and through this inherits the ability to understand mouse hits, menu hits, and key hits. Besides these inherited methods for input, *TextBBRendering* contains methods to render the resulting text in a particular format. Methods like *Draw, Update, ScrollSection,* and well over a dozen more allow the client of the building block to control the display of the text. Most important are the methods *AddStyle, ReformatOnStyle, ApplyStyle* and *UpdateOnStyle,* which allow a client program to define named formatting macros and apply them selectively to given entities (paragraphs). A *PickCorrel* method allows the client to query where in the text the user has pointed.

A second class, *TextBBModel*, is the root of the data structure for one "instantiation" of a text building block in a client program. It essentially keeps track of the data model that is being rendered and the various renderings of that model.

The building block inherits most heavily from the Intermedia Layer in defining *TextBBSelRgn* as a subclass of *IntSelection*. Here, *TextBBSelRgn* represents the sequence of characters that is currently the focus of attention. The building block adds fields that tie the selection region to the document data structure and methods that create new paragraphs, combine new paragraphs containing the selection region, blink the cursor, draw the selection region, reformat the selection region, and such. The *TextBBSelRgn* overrides the *IntSelection* methods that determine whether a selection contains items in a block or whether a selection contains a block marker, as well as methods to perform the behaviors of activating, deactivating and highlighting the selection differently than the default.

Besides the above external classes that serve as the major client interface, the text building block is composed of a number of interrelated objects that are instances of internal classes and are unseen by the building block client; these classes are beyond the scope of this paper.

Most importantly, each class defined in the text building block implements the *LoadFrom* and *StoreOn* methods. To store a document, the client simply invokes the *StoreOn* operation of the *TextBBModel*. That method simply writes out a memory snapshot of that object to a Macintosh resource file. In writing that snapshot, if the method sees a field in that first object that is a handle to another object, it calls *StoreOn* on that second object to write itself out, replacing the handle in the first object with the resource id for the newly-written object. This recursive operation continues until all of the objects in the entire text building block chain are stored. No specialized routines are necessary to encode the text data structure into some ad hoc file format; it is stored as a hierarchical data structure with pointers replaced by resource ids. Similarly, to read a stored document back in, no specialized routines needed to be written to decode a file format. Rather, the client simply gets the resource

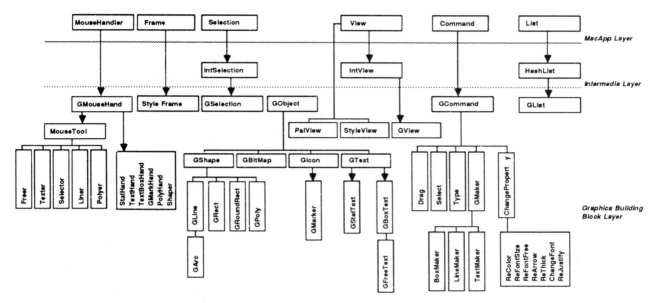

Figure 6 — Graphics Building Block

5.4.2 Graphics Building Block

id of the *TextBBModel* it is concerned with, reads it in from the resource file, and then invokes the method *LoadFrom* on that *TextBBModel*. In turn, that object goes through its data structure, and any time it sees a resource id, it reads it in from disk and recursively invokes *LoadFrom* on that newly allocated object. When the recursion is complete, the **exact** data structure that was written out when the file was stored is now back in memory.

5.4.2 Graphics Building Block

The graphics building block (see Fig. 6) provides a standard *View* in which graphics objects can be created, deleted, copied, cut, positioned, resized, and moved, by both a client program **and** an interactive user. The building block was designed to provide a programming utility that would allow an implementor to create program with functionality at least of the level of MacDraw.

The *GObject*, a subclass of *Object*, is an abstract class that is the root for all editable graphics objects. *GObjects* define methods for drawing *(Draw, Paint, Hilite, Outline, Inval, Offset, Inset, Map)*, for interacting *(IsPtIn, Select, Deselect)*, for storage and retrieval *(PutInPicture, MakeFromHandle, SaveInHandle)*, and for highlighting itself as part of an Intermedia block. Some of these behaviors are implemented at the *GObject* level, while others are expected to be implemented by subclasses. Fields of *GObject* include a rectangle indicating the primitive's bounding box, a unique id that is assigned to each object for storage and retrieval, the order in which this object should be drawn in relation to others, and a flag indicating if the object is selected.

Subclasses of *GObject* include *GShape, GText, GIcon,* and *GBitMap*. The first two of these subclasses again represent abstract subclasses that describe a particular set of behaviors (mostly behavior refined from *GObject*) that that will be refined in subclasses. *GShape* adds additional fields to keep track of fill style, pen style, and line width, since all subclasses of *GShape* are expected to use those fields. *GObject* methods *Paint, Select, Deselect,*

MakeFromHandle, and *SaveInHandle* are overridden, while a *SetPen* method is added. *GLine*, a subclass of *GShape*, adds fields that keep track of the endpoints of the line and a field that indicates whether the line has arrows on its endpoints. It adds no new methods except an initialization method, but overrides several methods of *GObject* — *Draw, Hilite, Inval, Outline, Offset, Inset,* and *Map* — to specify behavior that is specific to lines. The other *GShape* subclasses — *GRect, GRoundRect, GPoly,* and *GArc* — refine *GObject* and *GShape* to a greater or lesser extent. Similarly, *GText* has two operative subclasses, *GStaticText* and *GEditableText,* that define the specific behaviors indicated by their name. *GIcon* and *GBitMap* are typically used to created instances of the primitives they represent. Subclasses of *MouseHand* are declared to handle the interaction for each of the *GObjects*.

GView maintains the additional information needed to render a view based on the graphics building block. *GView* adds fields to keep track of the current drawing tool, to point to the current palette being used by the drawer, and most importantly, to point to the list of graphics objects that is maintained by an instance of *GList*. Since the graphics building block intends to provide capabilities to both draw **and** edit graphical primitives, it must provide facilities for adding and deleting things from the view. The *GList* is designed to maintains a list of heterogeneous objects, each an instance of some subclass of *GObject*. The *GList* implements protocol that allows a single operation to be performed on every member of the list. For example, the *Offset* method of *GList* would call the *Offset* method of every element in its list to cause it to move appropriately. The *GView* maintains one list that contains all the objects in the canvas, *GSelection*, a subclass of *IntSelection*, maintains another *GList* that contains all the objects in the current selectiion.

By virtue of being a subclass of *IntView*, *GView* inherits the ability to perform standard block/link operations and standard rendering operations. *GView* refines many of the *IntView* behaviors to reflect the

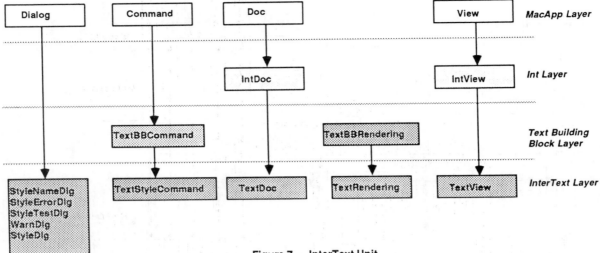

Figure 7 — InterText Unit

needs of the graphical view — *Draw*, for example, traverses the *GView's GList* to display objects. Most importantly, *GView* adds methods to enable a client to *Add* an object to the *GView*, *Delete* an object from the *GView*, perform an action on all the objects in a *GView*, and turn the entire contents of a view into a format for writing to disk.

5.5 The Units and the Test Applications

Given the Intermedia Layer and the two building blocks, we next set out to build the six major components of the Intermedia system: the folder directory system, the text processor, the graphics editor, the timeline editor, the scanned image viewer, and the web maps. Since each of these components requires a distinct data structure to represent its information and a distinct way of rendering that data structure, each component was built as an *IntDoc/IntView* pair, subclassed for its specific purpose. For each component, supplemental classes were created where necessary. We called the *IntDoc/IntView* pair plus supplemental classes a *unit*.

The most important attribute of a *unit* is that it **does not** implement a main event loop; in none of the units was an *Application* subclass defined. This was

intentional; to meet our goal of modularity and development concurrency, we wanted to be sure that each component could be tested separately before being combined into an integrated framework. We first combined a single unit with a single test *Application* to create a standalone executable, and later, when we were confident of the performance of the standalone units, we could create a *Framework* application and combine it with the five component units without even recompiling the units.

The Text Unit. The text unit (see Fig. 7), a major client of the text building block, contains the additional classes necessary to support the InterText text processor. The major text unit objects are the *TextDoc* and the *TextView*, subclasses of *IntDoc* and *IntView*, respectively. *TextDoc* adds a extra fields, the most important of which is *fCurBuildingBlock*, a handle to the instance of the text building block that this document will be using. Similarly, *TextDoc* overrides several *Doc/IntDoc* methods. *DoOpenDefault* is overridden to create and initialize the appropriate text building block objects (subclasses of *TextBBModel* and *TextBBRendering*) when a new InterText document is requested; *DoRead*, *DoWrite*, and *SaveOnFile* are

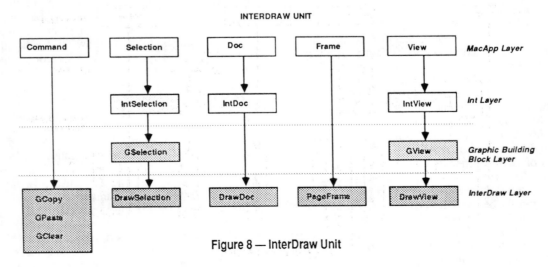

Figure 8 — InterDraw Unit

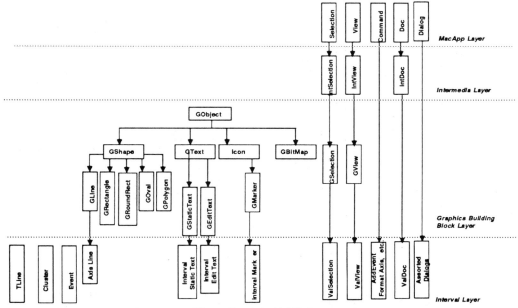

Figure 9 — InterVal Unit

overriden to initiate the recursive text storage and retrieval described above.

TextView adds no additional fields, but overrides methods such as *DoSetUpMenus*, *DoKeyCommand*, *DoMouseCommand*, *DoMenuCommand*, *Draw*, and *Activate*, in order to intercept input events appropriate for the view and either invoke an appropriate operation or pass them on to the text building block. *TextRendering*, a subclass of *TextBBRendering*, adds additional protocol to take user input from a style sheet dialog and update the rendering appropriately. The remaining classes defined in the text unit represent dialog boxes and a few additional command objects. No text processing code exists in the unit classes; all of that is done by the text building block. Rather, the text unit serves as a user interface wrapper around the building block.

To test the text unit standalone, we created *TextAppl*, a subclass of *IntApplication*. The *TextAppl* class differs from *IntApplication* in only one major way. In *IntApplication*, the *DoMakeDocument* method brings up a dialog box that allows the user to choose among several different document types to launch when the

New... menu item is chosen; in *TextAppl* the *DoMakeDocument* method is overriden so that whenever the *New...* menu item is chosen, only instances of *TextDoc/TextView* can be created. A standalone *IntApplication* subclass will be created in much the same way for each of the units described below.

The Draw Unit. The draw unit (see Fig. 8), a major client of the graphics building block, contains the additional classes necessary to create the full-fledged InterDraw interactive structured graphics editor. The major draw unit classes are *DrawDoc* and *DrawView*, subclasses of *IntDoc* and *IntView*, respectively. *DrawDoc* adds a small number of extra fields, the most important of which are *fGrafView*, a handle to the instance of the graphics building building block view that this document will be using, and *fToolView*, a handle to the drawing tool palette. *DrawDoc* overrides several *Doc/IntDoc* methods. *DoMakeView* is overridden to create and initialize the appropriate graphics building block view (*DrawView*, a subclass of *GView*) when a new graphics editing document is requested; the methods *Activate*, *DoRead*, *DoWrite*, *DoSetUpMenus*, *DoMenuCommand*,

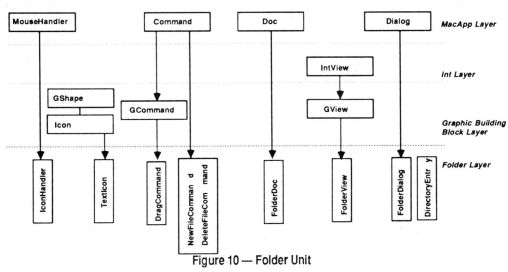

Figure 10 — Folder Unit

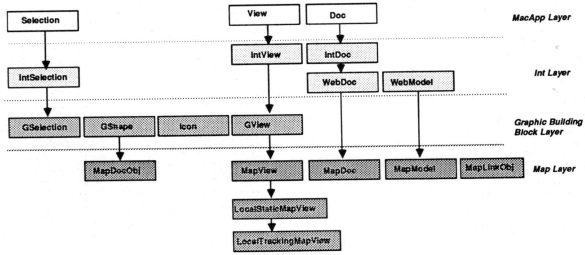

Figure 11 — Map Unit

DoKeyCommand, and *DoMouseCommand* are overriden. Additional methods are added to spawn, show, and hide the appropriate window frames.

DrawView adds no additional fields, but overrides methods such as *DoSetUpMenus*, *DoMouseCommand*, *DoMenuCommand*, and *DoMakeSelection* in order to intercept input events for this view and either invoke an appropriate operation or pass them on to the graphics building block. *DrawSelection*, an *IntSelection* subclass, overrides only the methods that cause it to enable and intercept a few specific menu commands. The remaining classes defined in the draw unit represent a few additional command objects specific to the graphics editor. No graphics editing code exists in the unit classes; all of that is done by the graphics building block. Like the text, the draw unit serves as a user interface wrapper around the building block.

The Timeline Unit. The timeline (Val) unit (see Fig. 9), which incorporates the classes for the InterVal timeline editor, is another major client of the graphics building block. Unlike the draw unit, however, the val unit uses the graphics building block not as a graphics editor, but rather as a display graphics package that provides the user limited direct editing capability.

As in the other units, *InterVal* subclasses *IntDoc* and *IntView* to create *ValDoc* and *ValView*. *ValDoc* adds fields to keep track of the timeline scaling, the number of timelines in the document, and assorted other important model data. It adds methods for adding, deleting, reading, and writing timelines, and for rescaling the timelines.

The major function of a timeline editor is to take chronological events and place them graphically on the display at the appropriate location in the scaled graph. Secondarily, the timeline editor should allow the user to edit the entries and format the timeline in a variety of ways. Rather than implementing all of the display and editing functions from scratch, the timeline editor uses *GObjects* from the graphics building block to place information on the screen and allow the user to manipulate some of it. For instance, the *TickMark* object is a subclass of *GLine*. It contains the fields it needs to keep track of its information, but inherits from *GLine* in that it knows how to draw itself at a particular

location and be resized, moved, and deleted. But since one does not want tick marks on a timeline to be arbitrarily moved around, *TickMark* overrides the standard *GLine* methods that implement such behavior and disables them. Similarly, *AxisDate* disables moving, editing, and resizing. *EventLabel* disables moving, but the editing functionality is kept intact, enabling users to alter the text of an event.

The Folder Unit. To create the graphical directory system, the graphics building block was again employed. The *FolderDoc* class, a subclass of *IntDoc*, was created to hold the data model necessary to represent one folder, i.e. one directory in a hierarchical file system. In particular, the *FolderDoc* class maintains a field that points to list of the files in a directory, as obtained from the Unix file system. Fig. 10 depicts the inheritance hierarchy.

FolderView, a subclass of *GView*, provides the "canvas" on which the graphical view of the directory is to be drawn. Like the timeline editor, the folder view needs to alter editing functionality by constraining some given features and adding others. To do this, the *TextIcon* subclass of *Icon* was created. This provides an *Icon* that has an additional label, representing a filename, appended directly below. More importantly, *TextIcon* overrides methods, in particular, the *Draw*, *Hilite*, *Select*, *Outline*, *Inval*, *Offset*, and *Free*, to allow it to differ from the standard building block. Similarly, *TextIconHandler* overrides the standard icon handling to add additional behaviors. In the standard building block, double clicking on an icon causes no default action; in the folder, double clicking on an icon should cause a document to be opened. Similarly, dragging an icon from one folder to another should cause the file to be moved from one directory to another; this behavior is added by subclassing a combination of methods of the *FolderView* and *DragCmd* classes.

The Map Unit. The map unit (see Fig. 11) represents the fourth component to be a major client of the graphics building block. The map unit operates like the folder unit, with the exception that rather than modeling a directory in a UNIX file system, the map models the connections between documents in a web. Where the folders simply put up icons representing documents, the maps must put up icons representing documents and lines representing the links between documents.

MapDoc, a subclass of *WebDoc* (which itself is a subclass of *IntDoc*) keeps track of the information to graphically render the connections for a particular web. It adds methods to manage the addition and deletion of links and associated documents to/from the map. *MapView*, a subclass of *GView*, provides the view in which to display the map. *MapView* adds additional fields to keep track of topographic information that facilitates the drawing of the map, and adds additional methods (*DrawLinks,   AddDocToView,   DeleteDocFromView, AddLinkToView,   DeleteLinkFromView*) to manage the update and drawing of the map. Where the folder unit created a *TextIcon* to manage its documents, the map unit created a *MapDocObj* as a subclass of *Icon* to manage its document depictions. The methods of *Icon* were overridden to implement the specific behavior for *MapDocObj* (e.g. *Hilite, Outline, Draw*) that differs from *Icon* and *TextIcon*.

The BitMap Unit. The last unit was literally designed and implemented in an evening. It defines a *BitMapDoc* class and an associated *BitMapView* class. The *BitMapDoc* inherits everything from *IntDoc* except *DoRead*, which it overrides to read a bitmap (scanned image) from disk. *BitMapView* inherits everything from *IntView* except *Draw*, which it overrides to display the bitmap in the view, and adds the ability crop a part of the image and place it the system clipboard. With these tiny refinements of existing classes, we were able to create a unit that had a high degree of functionality.

5.6 The Framework

To bind the units together into a coherent integrated application, we created the *FrameworkAppl* class. This class comprises a merge of all of the fields, methods, and global variables of the standalone test applications for each unit, plus a few additional fields and methods particular to the integrated world itself. Since, by design, there are very few additional fields or methods added to any *Application* class, the creation of *FrameworkAppl* consists of merging the functionality of each *DoMakeDocument* method of the standalone applications into one routine. Where each standalone method simply created a document of a specific type, the new *DoMakeDocument* contains a case statement that chooses what document to create based upon the parameter that was passed in. Creating an integrated application from a set of standalone units took only a few hours.

6.   SUMMARY AND CONCLUSION
6.1   Implementation

The final implementation consists of 219 classes, describing 624 fields and 1411 methods, distributed as follows:

Component	# Classes	# Fields	# Methods	#Overriden
MacApp Layer	21	65	167	35
Intermedia Layer	40	142	216	78
Text Bldg Blk	33	118	294	40
Graphics Bldg Blk	51	103	294	163
Text Unit	9	24	55	24
Draw Unit	13	20	52	36
Val Unit	31	108	199	74
BitMap Unit	3	4	15	9
Folder Unit	9	16	51	28
Map Unit	8	21	55	27
Framework Appl	1	3	13	10
Total	**219**	**624**	**1411**	**523**

Most of the 219 classes are internal classes; only about 25 percent are classes whose external interfaces need to be known by application developer. Similarly, about 75 percent of the methods are private methods not of concern to an application developer, but used by the building block or unit implementors. Of particular interest is the high percentage of methods that are overrides; over 1/3 of all methods fall in this category. As most of the overriden methods first invoke the inherited behavior of their superclass and then add additional code for their specific additional behavior, this implies the high-reusability of many of the method definitions.

The implementation consists of approximately 75,000

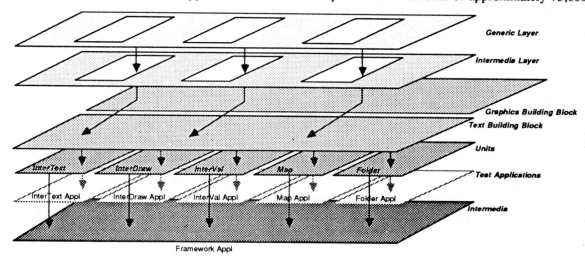

Figure 12 — Integrated Intermedia

lines of source code, spread over more than 100 files.

6.2 Meeting the Technical Objectives

Extensibility. The ability to create tools like the scanned image viewer overnight proved the extensibility of the system dramatically. The developer was able to leverage off of the existing application framework and construct a fully working document that completely conformed to the user interface specifications with little effort.

Resusbility. The graphics building block is the basis for four of the six major documents in use of the system. That a graphics editor, a timeline editor, a graphical directory system, and the web mapping system could all be built without having developers write code to draw or interact with graphical shapes was encouraging.

Consistency. All of the documents in the system behave similarly, since they all inherit from *IntDoc* and *IntView*. The ability to enforce consistency passively, by allowing users to leverage off of existing code proved to be a far superior method than trying to enforce such consistency actively, by asking developers to implement consistency by following a set of guidelines.

Understandability. Ten developers were able to understand the programmer interfaces to the system primarily because the interface was structured around well-defined classes. Even when class definitions, method definitions, or method implementations were changing, the fact that behaviors were glued to classes' method definitions, rather than scattered haphazardly around myriad files, enabled developers to discover what those changes were in a far shorter time than under conventional development. At the end of this parallel development, the class definitions files and the associated comments attached to fields and methods provided a good basis for understanding the system especially as compared to standard UNIX code.

Modularity. Because of time constrains, many of these parts were built in parallel. This parallel development was achievable partially due to the object-oriented nature of the design. For instance, in building the timeline unit, the graphics building block was not yet available. The implementors, to make sure all of their behaviors worked, implemented classes such as *TickMark* and *AxisLine* not as subclasses of graphics building block classes, but as subclasses of *Object*, quickly implementing the methods to position and draw these graphics objects by using the QuickDraw graphics package. When the graphics building block became available, they simply changed these classes to inherit from the appropriate graphics building block class and changed methods like *Draw* to inherit the standard building block behavior rather than draw its own graphics primitives.

6.3 Problems

The major problem in implementing our system was the statically-bound nature of our object-oriented language. Class hierarchy and object field layout is determined at compile time, and method references are statically bound as well — they resolve to a particular address in a structure. Thus, one could not pass method names as parameters. More importantly, this structure meant that anytime a superclass changed, all subclasses of that class needed to be recompiled, so that the method lookup would occur appropriately. This resulted in long compile times that would be eliminated in an environment with incremental compilation and with some knowledge of the object-oriented hierarchy. The hierarchy dependencies were maintained only through programmer cooperation and discipline, by adding or deleting entries to UNIX makefiles. This proved to be particularly error-prone.

Another major problem with the implementation language was the inability to pass type names as parameters or store them in fields. This meant that one had to know at compile time explicitly the type of every object one wanted to allocate, rather than priming a *type-holding* variable at run-time and generating the object based upon the contents of that variable. This situation forces developers to use global variables and hard-coded class names where local ones that could be filled in at run-time would be much more desirable. This use of globals becomes exceedingly difficult when one moves to a multi-tasking world.

6.4 Future Work

Before entering into the multi-tasking world we need techniques for using object-oriented programming in multi-tasking environments, where two tasks might have duplicate global variables, different notions of the class hierarchy, or different implementations of the same hierarchy. Similarly, remote method invocation techniques — where a call to a method could very well invoke a method on an object in another address space — are necessary to enable each document to be a separate process, but have developers still develop with the uniform abstraction that they currently have with the MacApp applications framework.

In terms of storage, an object-oriented database, in which entire objects could be written out, wholesale, with the appropriate resolution of objects pointing to other objects, would be extremely helpful in providing a uniform interface for storage.

Finally, UNIX as it stands, with its orientation towards the batch complilation of large program files into libraries that are later linked with other code fragments, does not provide the support that is necessary for object-oriented programming. It is unacceptable to require a ten minute compile and link cycle simply to change the implementation of a method and to require a one hour compile and link cycle simply to add a field to a high-level superclass! Incrementally-compiled methods and incrementally compiled and cascaded field definitions are a must for quick debugging.

6.5 Conclusion

Object-oriented techniques were vitally important to the user interface, the design, the architecture, the programmer interface, and the implementation of the *Intermedia* system. While there are numerous extensions that individuals are clamoring to make to the system, we are confident that because of such techniques, our system will not only survive those additions, but will support and encourage them.

ACKNOWLEDGEMENTS
The development of Intermedia is the culmination of a

year of intense effort by a large team which I have been fortunate enough to lead. Nicole Yankelovich coordinated the end-users of the system, developed and refined much of the Intermedia user interface and developed extensive end-user documentation. Charlie Evett developed a large part of the Intermedia architecture, the graphics building block and the InterDraw application. Ed Grossman, Matt Evett, and Tom Stambaugh developed the text building block and the InterText application. Nan Garrett and Karen Smith developed the InterVal application. Steve Drucker and Bern Haan developed the Intermedia framework. Page Elmore developed the web database and the web map capability. Helen DeAndrade created the graphics arts for the system. Mike Braca, Dave Bundy, Dan Stone, and Scott Bates provided the base operating system, the database management system, and the operating systems extensions that enabled Intermedia to run. Brian Chapin and Sam Fulcomer configured the systems countless times. Eric Wolf developed the program for decompressing scanned images. George Landow, David Cody, Glenn Everett, and Rob Sullivan produced an enormous corpus of material using Intermedia and heroically subjected themselves to the ordeal of teaching an English literature course with the system in its infancy. Suzanne Keen Morley became the first full-scale user of the system' and updated much of the documentation. Andy van Dam, Marty Michel, Bill Shipp, and Don Wolfe provided advice and support throughout the project.

This work was sponsored in part through a grant by the Annenberg/CPB Project and a joint study contract with International Business Machines Corporation. In addition, we greatly acknowledge Larry Tesler of Apple Computer, Inc., Jeff Singer and Stan Fleischman of Cadmus Computer, Inc., and Mark Nodine of Bolt Beranek and Newman for their assistance in making available key software that made Intermedia viable.

REFERENCES

[Appl84]   Apple Computer, Inc., *Lisa Toolkit,* Cupertino, CA, 1984.

[Appl85]   Apple Computer, Inc., *Inside Macintosh,* Addison-Wesley, 1985.

[Appl86]   Apple Computer, Inc., *MacApp Programmer's Manual,* Cupertino, CA, 1986.

[Bush45]   V. Bush, "As We May Think," *Atlantic Monthly,* July 1945, p. 101.

[Carm69]   S. Carmody, W. Gross, T. Nelson, D. Rice, and A. van Dam, "A Hypertext Editing System for the /360," in *Pertinent Concepts in Computer Graphics,* M Faiman and J. Nievergelt (eds.), University of Illinois Press, 1969, pp. 291-330.

[Cata79]   J. Catano, "Poetry and Computers: Experimenting with Communal Text," *Computers and the Humanities,* 13 (1979), pp. 269-275.

[Doyl86]   K. Doyle, B. Haynes, M. Lentczner, L. Rosenstein, "An Object Oriented Approach to Macintosh Application Development," *Proceedings of the 3rd Working Session on Object Oriented Languages,* Paris, France, January 8-10, 1986.

[Enge68]   D.C. Engelbart and W.K. English, "A Research Center for Augmenting Human Intellect," in *Proc. FJCC,* vol. 33, no 1, AFIPS Press, Montvale, NJ, Fall 1968, pp. 395-410.

[Garr86]   L.N. Garrett and K.E. Smith, "Building an Application from Prefab Parts," *OOPSLA '86 Conference Proceedings,* Portland, OR, Sept. 29 - Oct. 2, 1986

[Gold83]   A. Goldberg and D. Robson, *Smalltalk: The Language and Its Implementation,* Addison-Wesley, 1983.

[Hala85]   F. Halasz and R. Trigg, personal communication, April, 1985.

[Meyr85a] N. Meyrowitz, "Networks of Scholar's Workstations: End-User Computing in a University Community (Preliminary Report)," Institute for Research in Information and Scholarship, Providence, RI, May 1985.

[Meyr85b] N. Meyrowitz, et al, "The Intermedia System — A Software Framework and Applications for Education and Research: Requirements, User Interface, and Systems Design," Institute for Research in Information and Scholarship, Providence, RI, September, 1985.

[Meyr86]   N. Meyrowitz, "Inheritance C Report," Technical Report, Institute for Research in Information and Scholarship, Providence, RI, 1986.

[Nels80]   T.H. Nelson, "Replacing the Printed Word: A Complete Literary System," in *Information Processing 80,* S.H. Lavington (ed.), North-Holland Publishing Company, IFIP, 1980, pp. 1013-1023.

[Schm84]   K. J. Schmucker, *The Complete Book of Lisa,* Harper & Row, NY, 1984.

[Schm86]   K. J. Schmucker, *Object-Oriented Programming for the Macintosh,* Hayden Book Company, Hasbrouck Heights, NJ, 1986.

[Smit82]   D. Smith, C. Irby, R. Kimball, B. Verplank, and E. Harslem, "Designing the Star user interface," *BYTE* **7,** 4 (April 1982), 242-282

[Swin84]   D. Swinehart, "Copilot: A multiple process approach to interactive programming systems," Ph.D. dissertation, Stanford Artificial Intelligence Laboratory Memo. AIM-230, Stanford University, Palo Alto, CA, July 1974.

[Tesl81]   L. Tesler, "The Smalltalk Environment," *BYTE* **6,** 8 (Aug 81), 90-147.

[Yank86]   N. Yankelovich, "Intermedia User's Guide," IRIS Technical Report, Institute for Research in Information and Scholarship, Brown University, Providence, RI , January, 1986.

A Smalltalk System for Algebraic Manipulation

S. Kamal Abdali
Guy W. Cherry
Neil Soiffer

Computer Research Laboratory
Tektronix Labs

ABSTRACT

This paper describes the design of an algebra system Views implemented in Smalltalk. Views contains facilities for dynamic creation and manipulation of *computational domains*, for *viewing* these domains as various *categories* such as groups, rings, or fields, and for expressing algorithms generically at the level of categories. The design of Views has resulted in the addition of some new abstractions to Smalltalk that are quite useful in their own right. *Parameterized classes* provide a means for run-time creation of new classes that exhibit generally very similar behavior, differing only in minor ways that can be described by different instantiations of certain parameters. *Categories* allow the abstraction of the common behavior of classes that derives from the class objects and operations satisfying certain laws independently of the implementation of those objects and operations. *Views* allow the run-time association of classes with categories (and of categories with other categories), facilitating the use of code written for categories with quite different interpretations of operations. Together, categories and views provide an additional mechanism for code sharing that is richer than both single and multiple inheritance. The paper gives algebraic as well as non-algebraic examples of the above-mentioned features.

§1 Introduction

This paper describes Views — a system for performing algebraic computations designed at Tektronix Labs and written in Smalltalk. The current system allows for the manipulation of a variety of algebraic objects such as polynomials, rational functions, matrices, and elementary functions. [Abd86a]. However, the emphasis of this paper will not be on the system's algebraic capabilities but, instead, will be on the underlying design. In particular, we shall introduce some new concepts that we have added to Smalltalk: *parameterized classes*, *protocol views*, and *categories*. These mechanisms, in addition to the standard object-oriented mechanisms of Smalltalk, have provided a powerful basis for the design of a computer algebra system.

Algebraic computation systems have existed for more than two decades. The early algebra systems such as Altran [Bro77a] and SAC-1 [Col71a] were basically subroutine libraries and had limited algebraic computation capabilities. A second generation of more general systems was introduced by Macsyma [Mac83a] and Reduce [Hea83a]. These systems, which are Lisp based, have been successfully employed in a variety of application areas. However, as they have grown, they have become more difficult to extend and to maintain; they suffer all of the well-known problems of large procedure-oriented programs. In particular, expressions are not stored internally as members of specific algebraic domains.

Views is an example of a new generation of algebra system design which has been emerging since the early 1980's (Cf. [Jen81a] , [Fod83a]). A broadly stated goal of this third generation of systems is to allow for the manipulation of a large variety of algebraic objects while still maintaining system cohesion and extensibility. One strategy to achieve this goal, which we call *domain-conscious* computing, is to insist that each algebraic object be a member of a particular *computational domain*. Conceptually, a domain is a collection of some elements together with some operations defined over them. Typical examples of computational domains are 'the integers modulo 11' or 'polynomials over the rational numbers in the variable *x*'. Third generation systems also have the

"A Smalltalk System for Algebraic Manipulation" by S.K. Abdali, G.W. Cherry, and N. Soiffer from *Proceedings of the ACM Conference on Object-Oriented Programming Systems, Languages, and Applications*, 1986, pages 277-283. Copyright 1986, Association for Computing Machinery, Inc., reprinted by permission.

facilities for expressing algorithms generically for algebraic structures, such as groups, rings, or fields. The algorithms written for a ring, for example, can be used for any domain that satisfies the ring axioms. Thus, the user can write algorithms at an appropriate level of abstraction, and can more clearly document his code.

The concept of domain-conscious computing corresponds closely with the object-oriented notions of objects and classes. In fact, a computational domain in Views is essentially any Smalltalk class.[†] However, the abstractions existing in the standard object-oriented paradigm (in particular, Smalltalk) are not sufficient to completely meet our design goals. For instance, we shall require that some classes be able to spawn subclasses at run-time that differ from each other in only minor ways (e.g. 'the integers modulo 7' and 'the integers modulo 11' are subclasses of 'the integers modulo n'). To accomplish this, we introduce the notion of a parameterized class. We also allow domains to be tagged or *viewed* as specific instances of general algebraic structures such as 'ordered sets' or 'fields'. That is, we desire the possibility to express statements such as 'the domain of integers forms an ordered set' or 'the domain of integers modulo 11 forms a field'. In standard Smalltalk the only way to regard a class as being a specific instance of a more general structure is to use subclassing. For example, to regard the integers as an ordered set we could make the class Integer a subclass of a class OrderedSet. We will discuss why this is not a desirable solution and will introduce the notions of *protocol views* and *categories*. Thus, once we have constructed the domain of integers modulo 11, we can then construct a view of this domain 'as a field'. The view is an object of type 'field' and can be used anywhere in the system where a field is expected (e.g. a Gaussian elimination method inverts matrices over any field).

The remainder of this paper is organized as follows: Parameterized classes are described in §2, where we also discuss the need for creating classes using this mechanism rather than by using standard subclassing. The notion of protocol views and categories is described in §3. In both §2 and §3, non-algebraic as well as algebraic examples will be given to stress the general applicability of these concepts. Finally §4 will contain conclusions and directions for future work.

[†] More formally, we define a domain to be any class *along with all its subclasses*. Thus, 3 is in the class SmallInteger and in the domains SmallInteger, Integer, Number, Magnitude and Object.

§2 Parameterized Classes

In this section, we discuss a new kind of Smalltalk class that we call a *parameterized class*. These classes are an outgrowth of the need in Views to dynamically create domains that are identical up to the parameters used to instantiate them. A simple example of such a class is Zmodn, an implementation of the integers modulo n. Because we cannot know a priori which values of n are important, it is impossible to create standard Smalltalk classes for various values of n. The obvious alternative of making n an instance variable of Zmodn wastes space.

Parameterized classes act as templates for the *parameter subclasses* that are formed dynamically by messages sent to the parameterized class. All methods, instance variables, etc., are defined in the parameterized class and are inherited by the parameter subclasses. Parameterized classes can have any number of parameters and each parameter can be any Smalltalk object. In the case of Zmodn we have one parameter that is an integer; matrices might be defined as having two parameters (both integers) to specify the dimensions of the matrix; and the class SortedCollection might be defined with one ('comparison') parameter that is a block (or a symbol representing a method name) instead of the current practice of making the comparison function an instance variable.

Parameter subclasses are true Smalltalk subclasses in the sense that inheritance works as it normally does: any method not found locally is searched for in a superclass. However, parameter subclasses differ from normal Smalltalk classes in three important ways. First, they are created in a dynamic manner during the course of an algorithm. Hence, their creation must be efficient. Second, the scope of the parameter subclass is local to the method that created it. In this sense, a parameterized subclass is no different than any other value computed in a method. In particular, once the parameter subclass is no longer referenced, it is garbage collected. Lastly, in our current implementation, parameter subclasses cannot have subclasses themselves nor can methods be defined for them (they are defined via inheritance). We have never found a need to subclass parameter subclasses or define methods for them.

In Views, parameterized classes are used frequently. For example, polynomials are defined as a parameterized class with two parameters: a parameter describing the coefficients (this is discussed in §3) and a parameter for the variable. Again, it is impossible to state a priori what coefficient domains will be used and what variable domains will be used. For example, the modular algorithm to compute the greatest common divisor of two polynomials over the integers creates several polynomial domains dynamically. This algorithm typically reduces the polynomial coefficients modulo various primes numbers, calculates the gcd's of these modular coefficient polynomials, and then constructs the final gcd from the modular gcd's. For each prime p, the algorithm creates a new polynomial coefficient domain of integers modulo p.

We now present two simple examples of the use of parameterized classes. The first example is a more detailed look at Zmodn. First, we create the parameterized class Zmodn and write an addition method, a multiplication method, etc. for it. We also write a class method n: that takes a positive integer argument and returns a parameter subclass. Once we have done this, we can type:

> *the creation of a domain*
> Z12 ← Zmodp n: 12;
>   Zmod11
> *the creation of the object 8 mod 12*
> a ← Z12 new: 8;
>   8
> *many domains have "distinguished elements"*
>   *such as 0 or 1*
> a + (Z12 one);
>   9
> *the creation of the object 7 mod 12*
> b ← Z12 new: 7;
>   7
> a + b;
>   3   *addition modulo 12*

Parameterized classes can have normal Smalltalk subclasses. In Views for example, Zmodn has a subclass Zmodp in which it is assumed that the parameter n is prime. Under this assumption it is possible to add a method to compute the multiplicative inverse of an element. We also add the method p: to the class Zmodp. This method creates a parameter subclass of Zmodp assuming p is prime. The message n: is overridden in Zmodp to first check to make sure that n is prime.

> Z11 ← Zmodp p: 11;
>   Zmod11
> c ← Z11 with: 8;
>   8
> c inverse;
>   7   *8 * 7 = 1 (modulo 11)*

A typical scenario after a few such domains are created is depicted in the following diagram in which solid blocks represent standard Smalltalk classes and dashed blocks represent parameter subclasses.

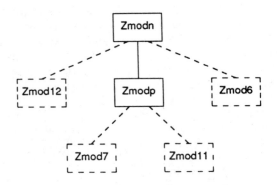

The second example involves the collection Set. A Set is a data structure in which no elements are duplicated. In order to tell if an element is already in a set, we must be able to tell if two elements are equal. In Smalltalk, the equality predicate is assumed to be named =. Set also has one subclass named IdentitySet. This class assumes that the equality predicate is named == and overrides the appropriate methods of Set. By convention, = is used to determine when two elements are equal and == is used to determine when two elements are the same object. If two elements are equal in another way, we have to subclass Set again and redefine the appropriate methods. This occurs, for instance, if we wish to build a Set consisting of strings in which upper and lower case distinctions are ignored. Creating subclasses to redefine the equality predicate is undesirable from both a code sharing point of view and because we have introduced a global change (the name of the new subclass and its equality predicate's name) for what is essentially a local property.

Parameterized classes provide a solution to the above problem. We can define Set to be a parameterized class with one parameter: a block that returns true if its two arguments are equal. Then the parameter subclass of Set that uses = as its equality predicate can be created as shown below:

> StandardSet ← Set equality: [:a :b | a = b];
>   Set[:a :b | a = b]
> StandardSet with: 1 with: 2 with: 1;
>   Set(1 2)

It is likely that = and == are used far more frequently than other equality predicates. To save the user the bother of creating StandardSet and IdentitySet each time they use it, we subclass Set in the normal manner filling in the equality: parameter appropriately.

In this example, the parameter was a block representing the equality predicate. In practice, however, we use categories as parameters instead of blocks. Categories are discussed in the next section.

To implement parameterized classes and parameter subclasses, two problems must be solved. The first is the efficient creation of parameter subclasses. In Smalltalk, this is easy. A class is just an object with several instance variables. To create a parameter subclass, we first set the superclass and name fields of the subclass. Then the method dictionary and metaclass fields are set to be those of the superclass (i.e., the parameterized class). These are just pointer copies and are fast. Normally, the subclass is then added to the subclass field of the superclass and also entered into the system dictionary. However, we want the scope of the newly created subclass to be local and so these steps are not performed.

The second problem is dealing with the parameters. As mentioned earlier, we do not want the parameters to be stored as part of each instance. Instead, we want them to be shared among all instances of a class. There are two possible ways of doing this in Smalltalk: class variables and class instance variables. Class variables are not appropriate because they are shared by every subclass. Thus, if the parameters are defined in the parameterized class as class variables, then there would be only one copy of the parameters to be shared by all parameter subclasses — clearly not what is desired. Class instance variables, however, work as desired since every subclass has its own set of instance variables.

§3 Views and Categories

In the previous section, we defined a parameterized type Set that has as its parameter an equality predicate. We saw how we could use this to create a Set of strings where the equality predicate could be = which distinguished between upper and lower case letters or the equality predicate could be sameAs: which ignored case differences. In a sense, this allows us to think of strings in two different manners. We call the different interpretation of strings *views*[†].

Views, when combined with categories, are a powerful abstraction method. A *category* is an object that represents a view of another object. To motivate categories and views, we will consider an implementation of polynomials mentioned briefly in the previous section.

Polynomials can be defined without specific knowledge of what class the coefficients come from. All that we care about is that the coefficients have the operations +, -, *, and =, along with having distinguished elements 0 and 1. To be more precise, we require that the coefficient class forms a ring. As is true with the Set example, it is *usually* the case that the coefficient operations will be named +, *, etc. — *but not always*. Hence,

to be general, we should make polynomial a parameterized class with +, *, etc., as parameters. There are many other algebraic objects (e.g., matrices) that can be defined as a parameterized class where the parameters exhibit the structure of a ring. It would be tedious and would waste time and space to constantly form all of the parameters necessary. A solution to this problem is to encapsulate all of the functions and distinguished elements into one object, an instance of class Ring. Now the polynomial parameterized class can have as its first parameter an instance of class Ring:

newDomain ← Polynomial over:
    <*some object in class* Ring> in: 'x';

Rings respond to the messages do:plus corresponding to +, do:times corresponding to *, etc. and, therefore, the code for doing polynomial arithmetic performs arithmetic on the coefficient ring by sending messages to this ring. For example, below is part of a polynomial addition routine. We assume that the coefficients of the polynomials are stored in an array named coef and that the parameter representing the coefficient ring is called coefRing.

```
+ aPoly
    ...
    newCoefs ← Array new: maxDegree.
    1 to: minDegree do:
        [:i | newCoefs at: i
            put: (coefRing do:
                (coef at: i) plus: (aPoly coef at: i))]
    ...
```

To create an instance of class Ring, we must supply it with an addition method, a multiplication method, etc. We call the methods that must be supplied *required methods*. In Views, the required methods can be either a compiled method, a block, or a symbol (the name of a method). For simplicity, the distinguished objects of a Ring (or more generally, any shared value of the viewed class) are treated as a constant functions.

We can now be more formal about what a view and a category are. A category is an abstract definition of the behavior of a domain. It consists of a set of elements and operations defined on those elements such that the operations satisfy certain axioms. A view is any mapping from an object to a category.[†] In particular, we can have views from one category to another and even from a category to itself. Categories correspond very closely to the algebraic structures used in mathematics such as group, ring, integral domain, field, etc. We have implemented these

---

† This use of the word view differs from Smalltalk's use of the word view.

† We sometimes use "view" to mean the mapping of an object to a category and sometimes we use it to mean the category element which is the result of the mapping.

categories in Views and it is easy for the user to add new categories.

As an algebraic example of how categories and views are used, we will use a very simple algebraic structure called a semigroup. A semigroup is any set with a binary operation, call it multiplication, which is associative. The domain of integers is a semigroup with the binary semigroup multiplication being either integer addition or integer multiplication, but not integer subtraction. Thus the category SemiGroup has only two required methods: do:equal and do:times. Suppose that Integer has the two messages asMultSemiGroup and asAddSemiGroup that return an instance of SemiGroup where integer multiplication and addition are the binary operations respectively.

```
multSG ← Integer asMultSemiGroup
    Integer as a SemiGroup
multSG do: 2 times: 5
    10
addSG ← Integer asAddSemiGroup
    Integer as a SemiGroup
addSG do: 2 times: 5
    7
```

Categories can form a repository for generic methods. For example, exponentiation by repeated multiplication can be written in the category SemiGroup. This method requires no knowledge of the representation of the object it manipulates:

```
do: a repeatedTimes: n
    | ans |

    n < 1 ifTrue:
        [self error '"n" must be greater than 0'].
    ans ← a.
    2 to: n do:
        [:i| ans ← self do: a times: ans].
    ↑ans
```

Thus, continuing the the above dialog we have

```
multSG do: 3 repeatedTimes: 3;
    27   3 * 3 * 3 = 27
addSG do: 3 repeatedTimes: 3;
    9    3 + 3 + 3 = 9
```

It is, of course, possible to define other exponentiation methods for SemiGroup (e.g. repeated squaring). Two other interesting examples of generic methods are the greatest common divisor and the partial fraction decomposition methods defined over the category EuclideanDomain.

In addition to many different views of the same domain (we had two views of Integer as a SemiGroup above) we can also form views from categories. For example, any Ring can be viewed as a Monoid by extracting only the additive (or multiplicative) structure of the Ring. In fact, the above messages asMultSemiGroup and asAddSemiGroup are actually a composition of two views:

```
Integer asRing asMultSemiGroup do: 2 times: 5
    10
Integer asRing asAddSemiGroup do: 2 times: 5
    7
```

This organizes the categories into a multigraph (a directed graph with multiple edges between any two nodes) and further increases the opportunities for code sharing. This form of code sharing is more general than the single inheritance tree as in Smalltalk or even the multiple inheritance lattice as in Flavors [Wei81a]. It is even possible to have circularities in the multigraph.

It is sometimes true that using domain specific knowledge, we can write more efficient versions of generic code. Consider, for example, using the repeatedTimes: method to raise a fraction to a power. The time consuming part of multiplying two fractions together is reducing the result to lowest terms (i.e., removing the gcd of the numerator and denominator). However, if we exponentiate a fraction, we can exponentiate the numerator and denominator separately and avoid any reduction because we are guaranteed the result is reduced. This is much faster. In order to allow the faster exponentiation method to be used, we augment a category's required method list with an *optional method* list. Optional methods differ from required methods in that if an optional method is not supplied when the category instance is created, a designated generic method is used in its place.

We now briefly mention how categories and views are implemented in Smalltalk. Every category consists of a domain field and a required methods field. The domain field is used to store the underlying domain of the category. This is used for accessing constants among other things. The required methods field is an array consisting of compiled methods, blocks, or symbols (representing the name of the method). For every required method, a category method is created. An example of the do:plus: method is shown below.

```
do: a plus: b
    ↑ (requiredMethod at: 5) value: a value: b
```

We have added methods to Smalltalk so that compiled methods, blocks, and symbols all respond to value:, value:value:, etc.

The implementation of views is quite simple. A view is created merely by supplying a method, block, or symbol for each required method of the category. The category is then responsible for placing these methods in the proper position in the 'required methods' array. To maintain the dynamic nature of views and still maintain speed, a dynamic evaluation scheme is used: the first time a view is taken, the mapping of methods to slots is computed and stored in a slot in the category. Future views simply reference the computed view and are very fast.

It is possible to make every category a direct subclass of the abstract class Category (the 'root' of the category hierarchy). However, we can take advantage of inheritance to share code and simplify 'viewing' in the case where the category being defined (B) is an extension of some previously defined category (A). By 'extension' we mean that the required methods of category B are a superset of the required methods of A, both notationally and axiomaticly. In this case, it is possible to simply create a larger required methods array and put the new required methods at the end of the array. This allows B to be used anywhere A can be used. It also makes B's trivial view of A a method that just returns 'self'. If B extends more than one category, then one category is singled out and treated as described above. The choice is arbitrary in regards to correctness.

We conclude this section with some less algebraic examples of views and categories. The first example involves adding 'infinity' to Integer. Sometimes it is desirable to extend the integers to include the special constant inf. For example, the shortest path algorithm [Aho74a] is defined using integers with infinity.[†] Most integer operations do not require infinity (e.g., 'for' loops). Adding infinity to integer operations requires adding checks for infinity and this would slow down all code. However, using views, we can view the integers as having infinity only when it matters, thereby allowing most integer code to still run quickly.

The second example involves Smalltalk's number hierarchy. In Smalltalk, integer division normally results in a rational number. If we want a floating point result, we can simply write another method that returns a floating point result and view the integers so that the new method is used.

The last example is an application of Views to a possible redefinition of Smalltalk's collection hierarchy. The collection hierarchy contains several abstract classes.

These abstract classes can be changed into categories and their subclasses can have views as the categories[‡]. For example, we can make Collection a category with the required methods includes: anElement (test whether a collection includes anElement), add: anElement (add anElement), remove: anElement ifAbsent: aBlock (remove anElement and perform aBlock if is is not found), and do: aBlock (perform aBlock on every element of the array). Given these required methods, it is possible to write several generic methods such remove: anElement, size, and occurancesOf: anElement. It is also possible to define several other generic methods such as select: aBlock, detect: aBlock, etc. A few of these may be made optional methods. For instance, the generic method occurancesOf: might be defined as

```
do: aCollection occurancesOf: anElement
    |tally|
    tally ← 0.
    self do: aCollection do:
        [:s | self do: anElement equal: s
            ifTrue: [tally ← tally + 1]].
    ↑ tally
```

The above method works by enumerating over all instances of the collection. For a Set, an element can occur at most once. Hence, Set can more efficiently implement occurancesOf: by stopping when anElement is found. If Set is implemented using a hashing scheme, the speedup is even more substantial.

§4 Conclusions

The ideas that we have discussed in this paper, parameterized classes, protocol views, and categories, have proven to be valuable additions for building an algebra system in Smalltalk. The ability to construct classes dynamically and to keep these classes in local environments allows the programmer to think of the environment of an algorithm not only as a collection of objects but also as a collection of active classes.

Isolating the algebraic structure from the representational information (via views) adds flexibility to Views. In Scratchpad II [Jen81a], domains are permanently attached to algebraic structures. In our system, domains are completely neutral algebraically in the sense that the operations therein can be considered as pure algorithmic computations unconstrained by any axioms. To impose any algebraic structure on the domain, a protocol view is explicitly taken. This allows a domain to take on many different algebraic structures, all of which can exist

---

[†] The shortest path problem is actually a specialization of a generic method defined over a closed semi-ring. If the real numbers are viewed as a semi-ring with (+ ← min, * ← +, 0 ← +∞, 1 ← 0), then an "edge-cost" algorithm computes the shortest path. Other views result in different computations. See [Abd86a].

[‡] Smalltalk's collection hierarchy does not map directly into categories and parameterized classes. For example, Array cannot have a view as a collection category because Array does not have the required method add:.

simultaneously.

It is interesting to contrast algebraic structures (such as ring or field) with classes in Smalltalk (equivalently, modules in Euclid [Lam77a], clusters in CLU [Lis78a], etc). A class consists of an internal representation for the elements of some set and an internal coding of operations over that set, together with an interface specifying the available operations. But in an algebraic structure, both the elements and the operations are subject only to the satisfiability of the axioms and are not confined to any particular set. That is, an algebraic structure is defined only in terms of its behavior and not in terms of its internal representation or notation. By capturing the notion of algebraic structure, categories offer an abstraction for the common behavior of classes that is a result of the objects and operations of the class satisfying certain laws independently of the implementation of those objects and operations. Thus the modularity in programming that results from the use of classes is further enhanced by the use of categories.

In standard object-oriented languages, the mechanism for sharing code among classes is inheritance, either single or multiple. In Views, the generic code residing in categories can be used from domains and other categories by taking views, with possibly quite different interpretations of the operations in the viewed categories. Thus views offer an additional mechanism for classes to share code. Furthermore, this mechanism is richer than the inheritance mechanism, since intercategory views organize the categories into a multigraph structure, rather than a tree as in the case of single inheritance, or a lattice as in the case of multiple inheritance.

In Smalltalk (and hence Views), only the class of the first argument (the receiver) is used to calculate the method used. This creates some problems. For example, it is natural to have a method 'integer * integer' for integer multiplication and another method 'integer * matrix' for multiplying an integer by a matrix. In Smalltalk, it is necessary to use two different method names. It would be interesting to see how views, etc., change in the context of languages such as CommonLoops [Bob85a] in which the types of all of the arguments are used to determine the method invoked.

Acknowledgement

We are grateful to Erich Kaltofen for his helpful critique of the design of Views, and to Alan Borning for suggesting the application of Views to Smalltalk's collection hierarchy as discussed in §3.

References

Abd86a. S. Kamal Abdali, Guy W. Cherry, and Neil Soiffer, "An Object Oriented Approach to Algebra System Design," *Symsac '86*, Waterloo, Canada, July, 1986.

Aho74a. Alfred V. Aho, John E. Hopcroft, and Jeffrey D. Ullman, *The Design and Analysis of Computer Algorithms*, Addison-Wesley, 1974.

Bob85a. D. G. Bobrow and et al., "CommonLoops: Merging Common Lisp and Object-Oriented Programming," Intelligent Systems Laborartory Series ISL-85-8, Xerox PARC, August 1985.

Bro77a. W. S. Brown, *ALTRAN User's Manual*, 4th ed, Bell Laboratories, Murray Hill, N.J., 1977.

Col71a. G. E. Collins, "The SAC-1 System: An Introduction and Survey," *Proc. 2nd ACM Symposium on Symbolic and Algebraic Manipulation*, pp. 144-152, Los Angeles, CA, March 1971.

Fod83a. John Foderaro, *Newspeak*, U. of Calfornia, Berkeley, 1983. PhD Thesis

Hea83a. Anthony C. Hearn, *Reduce User's Manual, Version 3.0*, The Rand Corporation, April, 1983.

Jen81a. R. D. Jenks and B. M. Trager, "A Language for Computational Algebra," *Proc. ACM Symposium on Symbolic and Algebraic Manipulaton*, Snowbird, Utah, 1981.

Lam77a. B. W. Lampson, J. J. Horning, R. L. London, J. G. Mitchell, and G. J. Popek, "Report on the Programming Language Euclid," *ACM SIGPLAN Notices*, vol. 12, no. 2, 1977.

Lis78a. B. Liskov, E. Moss, C. Schaffert, B. Scheifler, and A. Snyder, *CLU Reference Manual*, Computation Structure Group Memo 161, MIT, Cambridge, MA, July 1978.

Mac83a. Macsyma, *Macsyma Reference Manual, Version 10*, Laboratory for Computer Science, MIT, Cambridge, MA, January, 1983.

Wei81a. D. Weinreb and D. Moon, *Lisp Machine Manual*, Symbolics, Inc, Cambridge, MA, 1981.

OBJECTS, ICONS, AND SOFTWARE-ICS

BY BRAD COX AND BILL HUNT

Object-oriented programming can make it easier to create iconic user interfaces

MAKING COMPUTERS EASIER TO USE has been an enduring dream since the dawn of computing. This is one of the reasons for the current interest in *iconic* or *object-oriented* user interfaces—interfaces that present information as pictures instead of text and numbers. However, iconic programs can be excruciatingly difficult to build. They must not only do all that conventional programs do, but they must also present their workings as pictures instead of the usual words and numbers, and they must determine the user's needs from a graphical input device like a mouse rather than the usual commands from a keyboard. Unless tools can reduce this complexity, iconic user interfaces will remain costly and comparatively rare.

This article will demonstrate why object-oriented programming is becoming so popular, not only for building iconic programs but for programs of any kind. This popularity is the result of two language features beyond those provided by non-object-oriented languages: encapsulation and inheritance. Encapsulation means that code suppliers can build, test, and document solutions to difficult user interface problems and store them in libraries as reusable software components that depend only loosely on the applications that use them. Encapsulation lets consumers assemble generic components directly into their applications, and inheritance lets them define new application-specific components by inheriting most of the work from generic components in the library.

Building programs by reusing generic components will seem strange if you think of programming as the act of assembling the raw statements and expressions of a pro-gramming language. The integrated circuit seemed just as strange to designers who built circuits from discrete electronic components. What is truly revolutionary about object-oriented programming is that it helps programmers reuse existing code, just as the silicon chip helps circuit builders reuse the work of chip designers. To emphasize this parallel we call reusable classes Software-ICs.

Even though the examples in this article are written in Objective-C, not Smalltalk-80, you will find the graphics primitives chapter in Adele Goldberg and David Robson's book *Smalltalk-80: The Language and Its Implementation* (Addison-Wesley, 1983) helpful in understanding the portable graphics substrate on which this work is based. More information on Objective-C and the Software-IC approach to system building is contained in Lamar Ledbetter and Brad Cox's article "Software-ICs" (June 1985 BYTE) and in Cox's book *Object-oriented Programming: An Evolutionary Approach* (Addison-Wesley, 1986).

WORKBENCH

To determine how much a Software-IC library can help in building iconic applications, we developed the program whose interface is shown in the top window in figure 1.

Brad Cox, a founder and chief technical officer of Productivity Products International (27 Glen Rd., Sandy Hook, CT 06482), is the originator of Objective-C and its user interface library.

Bill Hunt currently works on user interfaces and high-speed graphics for Hewlett-Packard (P.O. Box 301, Loveland, CO 80539). He was also part of the team that developed the HP 110.

This program is called Workbench because it lets a programmer describe the files on his workbench and how they should be transformed into other files by tools like compilers and linkers. Workbench shows each file as an icon, dependencies between files as lines, and the programs that transform files as small circles. For example, the file named testOutput depends on two other files, testInput and theProgram. The file named theProgram depends on the three binary files shown as Software-IC icons, and each of these depends on its own source file. By relying on the operating system to maintain time stamps showing when each file was last changed, Workbench could be made to automatically rebuild the target files to bring them up to date when the source files they depend on change.

Since Workbench is currently only a prototype that we built to test the Software-IC library, we have not yet implemented the logic for rebuilding target files when source files change. Except for this unimplemented (but crucial)

feature, Workbench and the UNIX utility make provide radically different user interfaces for the same problem. Figure 2 shows the file a user would have to build to describe the same information described in figure 1 by Workbench.

BUILDING THE COMPONENTS

An iconic user interface is like an animated movie or cartoon. Once a cartoon has been designed through scriptwriting and storyboarding, an artist builds the components of the animation by painting gels on transparent acetate sheets, turning generic materials from an art supply store into the specialized components needed for the movie on hand. The user interface library is the programmer's art supply store. It provides generic components from which specialized ones are defined by using encapsulation and inheritance the way an artist uses paint, scissors, and glue. This section will show how a programmer builds

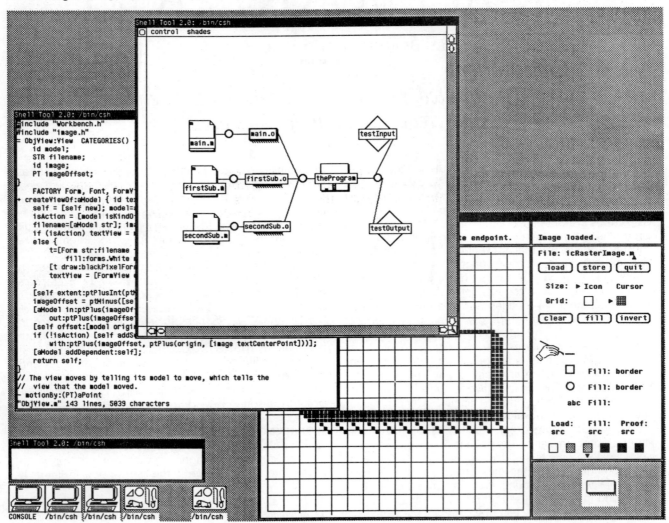

Figure 1: *Workbench as it might be seen by a programmer. The topmost window shows the iconic user interface, the window to the left shows a text editor, and the window to the right shows a bit-map editor.*

100

a stockpile of specialized components from generic components in the library. Later we will show how the components are assembled into an application and brought to life in the way that an artist assembles gels into layers and moves them with respect to each other to simulate motion.

The programmer's sheet of acetate is a generic class in the library named View. [*Editor's note*: *It is a naming convention to capitalize the first letter of class names and lowercase the first letter of the instances of these classes.*] Workbench's user interface in figure 1 was produced by many different instances of many specialized kinds of views, assembled like overlapping layers of acetate. No instances of the generic View class appear because instances of this class are transparent. But instances of specialized view classes can be seen because the programmer who defined them added "paint" to make them visible. For example, BorderedViews provide two colors of paint, one for a border of adjustable thickness and another for the region inside the border. One of these drew the white square in the upper left corner, two others drew similar squares in two other corners, and a fourth drew the tall vertical rectangle along the left edge. Several other BorderedView instances cannot be seen because they are obscured by other views lying on top of them. For example, the views in this figure are arranged on top of a large Bordered-View that serves as an opaque backing to which all the others are attached.

Having seen how views work visually, let's turn to how they are implemented. The most generic abstraction, the View class, was defined by compiling a file that contains the following class definition statement, along with a large number of methods. In this section, no methods will be shown because they would introduce far too much detail for now.

```
= View : Rectangle {
    id clipList; // list of visible regions
    id superView; // or nil
    id subViews; // OrderedCol'n of subViews
    BITS flags; // flag bits
}
```

```
testOutput: testinput theProgram
        theProgram testinput >testOutput
theProgram: main.o firstSub.o secondSub.o
        objc main.o firstSub.o secondSub.o
                            -o theProgram
main.o: main.m
        objc -c main.m
firstSub.o: firstSub.m
        objc -c firstSub.m
secondSub.o: secondSub.m
        objc -c secondSub.m
```

Figure 2: *The file a user would have to build to convey the information in figure 1 to the UNIX utility* make.

This statement defines a new class, View, as a subclass of another generic class from the library, Rectangle. This declaration is all that is needed to ensure that every view will automatically inherit the ability to behave as a rectangular region. For example, each view instance will inherit two instance variables from Rectangle, namely a point (an *x,y* pair) named extent that describes the size of the view and a point named origin that specifies its position on the screen. Finally, the declaration adds four new variables that will be used to describe how each view is attached to other views. The superView variable identifies another view that provides the background against which this view will be displayed. A view's superview also establishes its coordinate system, and it clips any graphics drawn by the subview that extend beyond the superview's margins so that they don't appear on the screen. The variable subViews identifies those views for which the current view is background. These variables will be inherited by all other views. Thus every view will be linked into an important data structure, the view hierarchy, that describes how the views are stacked into layers.

BorderedViews are a specialized kind of view that is not transparent, and their declaration states as much explicitly:

```
= BorderedView:View {
    short borderWidth; // thickness of border
    id borderPattern; // color of border
    id insidePattern; // color of inside
    id outsideRectangle; // computed rectangle
}
```

In other words, a BorderedView instance is exactly like a view but has four additional variables to describe how thick its border should be and a pattern (a "color") to display for its border and central region.

This may seem like a lot of trouble just to draw a black line around a white box, but effort spent on generic classes is seldom wasted. BorderedView actually turns up repeatedly in this and other iconic applications, both as a component that is reused directly through encapsulation and as a generic class to be specialized through inheritance. We have shown several places where unmodified BorderedViews appear, but they are also inherited by specialized subclasses that can modify their appearance in surprising ways. For example, consider MacScrollBar, the class whose instances drew the horizontal and vertical scroll bars in the topmost window of figure 1:

```
= MacScrollBar : BorderedView {
    BOOL isVertical; // NO if horizontal
    id scrollMore; // ArrowFixture
    id scrollLess; // ArrowFixture
    id elevator; // ElevatorFixture
}
```

Even though the MacScrollBar instances look very different from ordinary BorderedViews, they were imple-

Specializing from reusable generic code is what makes object-oriented programming so productive.

mented as a specialized BorderedView whose inside-Pattern variable is set to a uniform gray tone. Three instance variables are also added to refer to two instances of class ArrowFixture and one instance of class Elevator-Fixture. These too are specialized BorderedViews that have overridden the method that draws their central region with one that displays a specific iconic image rather than a plain shade of gray. They also have additional methods that make them interpret cursor events as commands to control scrolling.

This ability to define specialized new facilities from generic facilities in the library is one of the key things that makes object-oriented programming so productive. When the new classes get so specialized that they are specific to the application on hand, they are no longer stored in the generic library. Nonetheless, they are still part of the inheritance hierarchy, and they are built exactly like the generic classes shown so far. For example, the large white region in the center of the Workbench user interface was drawn by an instance of class WbView that describes the files on the Workbench, a UNIX directory area.

```
= WbView : BorderedView {
    id model; // the Wb being viewed
}
```

This class defines an instance variable, model, that identifies the instance of class Wb to be interfaced to the user. Most applications involve several kinds of application-specific views, and these are produced in exactly the same way, by defining specialized subclasses of View.

MODELS AND VIEWS
Until now we've described only how the components of this application were defined. Now let's turn to how they work together when the Workbench program first runs in a particular UNIX directory. Like most other programs, Workbench must support two very different kinds of interfaces: one between itself and the file system, and the other between itself and the user. When Workbench starts executing, it must read information from the file system and represent it in some internal form. Then it must create whatever objects it needs for its user interface, draw these objects on the screen, and accept commands from the user that then modify the internal form. Finally, Workbench must save the modified information so that it will be available the next time the program is run in that directory.

This pattern is so typical that special terms are used to distinguish the two interface levels. The word *model* refers to the internal form, that is, whatever structure is used to represent the objects to be saved between sessions. The

term *view* refers to the objects that implement the user interface. Views have been described in the previous section, and we turn now to the models.

The Workbench application uses only four kinds of model objects: Entity, Action, Obj, and Wb. Each file in the directory is represented by an instance of class Entity that holds the name of a file, its modification time, and two collections that describe those entities that depend on it and those that it depends on. When an entity's modification date is older than the date of a file that it depends on, it must be rebuilt by executing a program specified by the user. Another class, Action, holds the command string that describes how this program should be run. The Entity and Action classes have some features in common (such as where they are on the screen), and this is represented in a common superclass, Obj. A final class, Wb, represents the contents of the Workbench as a whole as a collection of entity and action instances.

When Workbench runs for the first time in a directory, it builds an instance of class Entity for each file and installs it in an empty instance of class Wb named workbenchModel. Next, the program creates a user interface so that the user can manipulate the models in the following ways: by moving them around on the screen, by describing which entities depend on which others, and by defining actions. (In the Workbench user interface, entities are presented to the user as file icons, actions are the circles, dependencies are the lines connecting the actions and entities.) The effect of this is to interconnect the models, forming a complicated web of linked objects that must somehow be saved at the end of the session so that it can be restored the next time the program runs in that directory. The code needed to do this is highly nontrivial to write, but object-oriented programming makes it seem simple. Since every class is a subclass of the most generic class in the system, Object, every object automatically inherits a method that can be used to save it in a file:

```
[workbenchModel storeOn:"workbench.io"];
```

When the application is executed again, it recreates workbenchModel by reading the file like this:

```
workbenchModel = [Wb readFrom:"workbench.io"];
if (workbenchModel == nil)
    workbenchModel = [Wb new];
[workbenchModel synchronizeWithDirectory];
```

The first statement requests the factory object for the Wb class to recreate workbenchModel from the file named workbench.io. The attempt will fail if the program has never been run in this directory, in which case the Wb factory object is requested to construct a new (empty) instance. In either event, the synchronizeWithDirectory message requests workbenchModel to examine the directory, adding or removing entities as needed to reflect files that have been created or removed since workbench.io was last written. Instance variables in the models are now updated to reflect the time at which each file was last changed.

Object-oriented programming

allows most of the work

to be developed in advance,

stored in the library,

and reused off-the-shelf

as generic Software-ICs.

Although workbenchModel is a complicated web of interconnected entity and action linked by dependency instances, the storeOn: method walks this web automatically, converting each object to a symbolic representation from which readFrom: can reconstruct the web during the next session. The developer of this application didn't have to design, code, test, document, or maintain this logic. Apart from the pair of triggering statements, this complicated data structure was saved and restored without writing any new code. The supplier of the most generic class in the system, Object, undertook this task once and for all, and every other class will inherit this work automatically.

The complete parts inventory for Workbench is shown in figure 3. Most of the classes are generic components taken directly from the user interface library. Only those in the bottom section are application-specific, and the total amount of application-specific code is 531 lines—269 lines specific to the internal representation of Workbench (model) and 262 lines used for the user interface (view). This was possible only because object-oriented programming allowed most of the work to be developed in advance, stored in the library, and reused off-the-shelf as generic Software-ICs, just as hardware designers use silicon chips to build specialized circuits.

ASSEMBLING THE USER INTERFACE COMPONENTS

We now have model objects to be interfaced to the user and a library full of components for building user interfaces. The next step is to assemble the components to to build a user interface for the model objects. First, we must build an opaque sheet of plain white acetate, on which all the others will be arranged, and attach to it another sheet painted with a standard frame of scroll bars:

```
[baseView = [BaseView new]
    addSubView:stdView = [StdSysView new]];
```

The baseView = [BaseView new] expression commands baseView, the factory object for class BaseView, to create a new instance named baseView, and baseView is immediately requested to add stdView, a newly created instance of class StdSysView, as its first subview. BaseView is a simple subclass of BorderedView that provides plain white backing on which any kind of animation can be assembled, and the StdSysView class defines a consistent

overall appearance and behavior for all applications by arranging nine subviews in three rows and three columns to cover the available space completely:

```
= StdSysView:View {
    PT topLeftExtent;
    PT botRightExtent;
}
+ new {
    self = [super new];
    topLeftExtent = pt(16,16);
    botRightExtent = pt(16,16);
    // 0 = topLeft 1 = topCenter 2 = topRight
    [self addSubView:[BorderedView new]];
    [self addSubView:[BorderedView new]];
    [self addSubView:[BorderedView new]];
    // 3 = midLeft 4 = midCenter 5 = midRight
    [self addSubView:[BorderedView new]];
    [self addSubView:[BorderedView new]];
    [self addSubView:[MacScrollBar vert]];
    // 6 = botLeft 7 = botCenter 8 = botRight
    [self addSubView:[BorderedView new]];
    [self addSubView:[MacScrollBar horz]];
    [self addSubView:[StretchFixture new]];
    return self;
}
```

This is the first example that shows how methods are defined in Objective-C. The plus sign in the fifth line assigns this method to the factory object for class StdSysView, while a minus sign in the same position signifies an instance method. Factory objects already inherit a method named new from the Object class, but it is being overridden here to create and initialize instances in a class-specific way. For example, the two instance variables (of type PT, short for Point) are given an initial value, and nine subviews are automatically installed, such as MacScrollBar instances in the center position of the bottom row and right column.

Newly created StdSysView instances contain only generic subviews initially, but they can be customized to the specific application by requesting them to replace one or more of them with application-specific views like this:

```
[stdView midCenterView:wbView =
    [WbView createViewOf:workbenchModel]];
```

WbView is an application-specific subclass of BorderedView that implements a user interface for an instance of class Wb.

```
= WbView . . .
+ createViewOf:aWorkbenchModel {
    id sequence, member;
    self = [super new];
    model = aWorkbenchModel;
    sequence = [[model entities] eachElement];
    while (member = [sequence next])
        [self addSubView:[ObjView
```

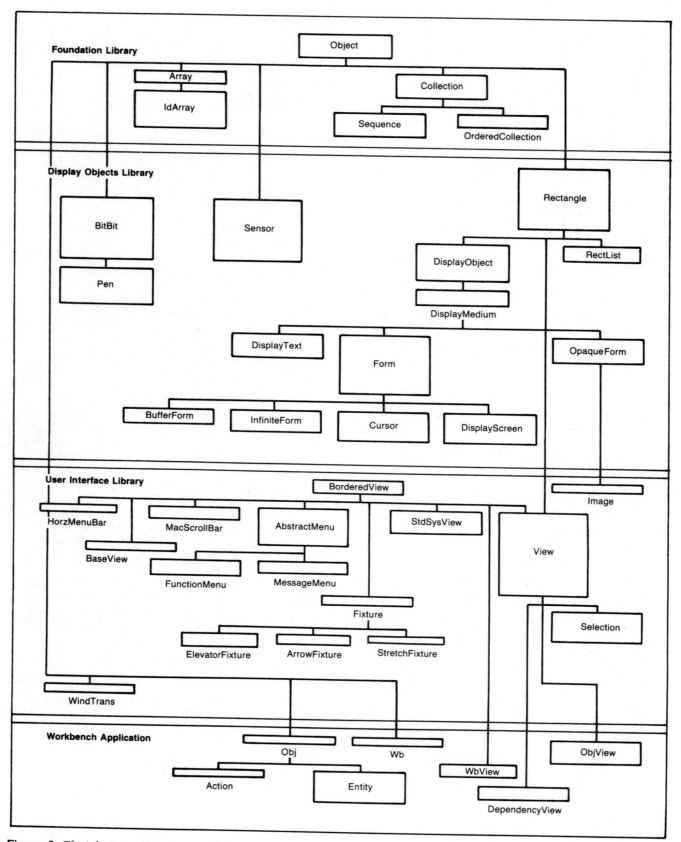

Figure 3: *The inheritance hierarchy for the Workbench classes. The source bulk in each class is represented as the height of each box.*

```
            createViewOf:member]];
    [sequence free];
    sequence = [[model actions] eachElement];
    while (member = [sequence next])
        [self addSubView:[ObjView
                createViewOf:member]];
    [sequence free];
    return self;
}
```

Application-specific views are exactly like the generic views discussed earlier, but they nearly always define an instance variable that points to the model that they are responsible for managing, plus factory methods for initializing this variable and installing any additional views that they need to implement the user interface. For example, this createViewOf: method loops over each of the entities and actions in the model and creates an instance of class ObjView for each one.

POSITIONING, SIZING, AND DISPLAYING

The application has created many different kinds of views and specified which ones lie on top of which others. But no attention has been given to how big each view should be and to where each view should be positioned on the screen. And of course, nothing has been displayed on the terminal. Since the sizing and positioning of each view may change each time the window size is changed, these functions are done separately in the course of responding to a windowChangedEvent. The event handler will automatically generate this event as soon as the application passes control to it:

[baseView controlStart];

One of BaseView's main functions is reading events from the event handler, determining which views lie under the location of the event, and sending those views messages that describe which event has occurred. Since the window-ChangedEvent affects all views, the BaseView handles it specially:

```
= BaseView . . .
- (BOOL)windowChangedEvent {
    [self rect:currentDisplay];
    [self display];
    return YES;
}
```

The global variable currentDisplay identifies an instance of class Display that manages the window in which the application is running; the rect: message sets the BaseView's position and size to that of currentDisplay. This message is eventually implemented (in class Rectangle) via two separate messages, origin: and extent:, both of which are overridden (in class View) to give views the behavior of a sheet of acetate. For example, View defines a default implementation for the origin: method that automatically repositions a view's subviews when it is repositioned, and a default extent: method that changes only the receiver (stretching a background acetate does not

stretch acetates that are attached to it). These defaults are sometimes inappropriate, so views like StdSysView override them to meet special needs, for instance, ensuring that subviews completely cover the available space. This triggers a wave of origin: and extent: messages that propagates through the view hierarchy, assigning a place and a size to every view.

Nothing appears on the screen until the window-ChangedEvent method in BaseView executes [self display], which triggers the following generic display methods into operation:

```
= View . . .
- display {
    [currentDisplay lock:self];
    [[self topView] displayExcept:nil];
    [currentDisplay unlock];
    return self;
}
- displayExcept:aCollection {
    if (aCollection && [aCollection contains:self])
        return self;
    if (!TBIT(flags, ISLOCKED))
        [self computeClipList];
    if (lockedRegion == nil
        || [self intersects:lockedRegion]) {
        [self displayView];
        SBIT(flags, ISVISIBLE);
        if (TBIT(flags, ISSELECTED))
            [self emphasizeView];
        if (subViews) [subViews
            eachElementPerform:
                @selector(displayExcept:)
            with:aCollection];
    }
    return self;
}
- displayView
    { return self; }
```

The lock: message in the display method commands currentDisplay to set its clipping region to the margins of the receiver (the lock: and unlock messages) and commands the topmost view in the hierarchy to display itself and all of its subviews. The displayExcept: method is a multipurpose method used not only for redrawing the entire view hierarchy, as here, but also for erasing views and for highlighting views when they are selected, and these extra functions obscure the fact that this method basically sends a displayView message to each view in the hierarchy. As an efficiency optimization, it avoids considering views whose graphics would be clipped by the global clipping region, lockedRegion. The argument, aCollection, is a way of using the display methods to erase views, by redisplaying everything but the views that are to be erased.

All graphics are generated by displayView messages. A default implementation is defined in the View class that displays nothing, another way of saying that the View class implements transparent acetate. The views that do draw

Conceptually, events occur at the tip of the cursor and penetrate through the views at this location.

on the screen simply override this method, like this:

```
- Fixture : BorderedView {
    id form;
}
- displayView {
    [super displayView];
    [form displayOn:display at:origin
        clipBy:clipList rule:rules.Over];
    return self;
}
```

The Fixture class is the one that draws the small iconic fixtures in the scroll bars. Its instance variable, form, identifies the fixture's image, an instance of class Form that was hand-painted with a pixel editor.

EVENT HANDLING

Once the windowChangedEvent has caused each view to draw itself on the screen, control returns to the event handler to await interrupts from the graphics substrate signaling that something has happened; perhaps a key has been struck on the keyboard, one of the mouse buttons was pressed or released, or a time-out has expired. Conceptually, events occur at the tip of the cursor and penetrate through the views at this location like a needle through a stack of acetates. Each possible event is assigned a message, for example, leftButtonDown, keyboard-Event, timeoutEvent, and the View class defines a method for each one so that, by default, all views are transparent to all events.

```
= View . . .
- (BOOL)rightButtonDown { return NO; }
- (BOOL)leftButtonDown { return NO; }
- (BOOL)middleButtonDown { return NO; }
- (BOOL)keyboardEvent { return NO; }
- (BOOL)windowChangedEvent { return NO; }
    . . .
```

When a view wants to receive an event, it just overrides the inherited method with one that works as desired and then returns YES to signify that the event has been consumed. For example, StdSysView instances attach a standard system menu to the right mouse button like this:

```
= StdSysView . . .
- (BOOL)rightButtonDown {
    static id menu = nil;
    if (menu == nil) { id tmp;
        menu = [MessageMenu str:"System Menu"];
        [menu add:[MessageMenu
            selector:@selector(exit)]];
        [menu add:[MessageMenu
```

```
            selector:@selector(refresh)]];
        [menu add:[MessageMenu
            selector:@selector(print)]];
        [menu add:tmp = [MessageMenu str:"debug"
            selector:@selector(dbgToggle)]];
        [tmp add:[MessageMenu str:"on"
            selector:@selector(dbgOn)]];
        [tmp add:[MessageMenu str:"off"
            selector:@selector(dbgOff)]];
    }
    [menu applyTo:self at:event.origin];
    return YES;
}
```

Notice that the single abstraction, views as layers of acetate, suffices to organize both directions of information transfer between the program and the user. This is a departure from the Model-View-Controller paradigm of Smalltalk-80 in which events are handled by a separate hierarchy of Controller classes.

INTERACTION

So far, we have shown how a programmer defines the components of an iconic application by defining specialized subclasses of the generic View class. When the application begins executing, instances of these classes are created and linked into a hierarchy that represents how they are arranged with respect to each other. Finally, control is passed to the event handler, at which time a position and a size are assigned to each view and they are displayed for the first time to the user. The initial frame of the animated movie has been projected onto the screen, and a data structure, the view hierarchy, has recorded where the parts of the image appear on the screen.

Very little new code is needed to get an application to this point because most has been provided by generic classes from the library. For example, the user interface for the Workbench application involved only three new classes (WbView, ObjView, and DependencyView) of two methods each, one to create a view of a specified model (createViewOf:) and another to draw a picture of the model on the screen (displayView). Now the harder part by far remains, giving life to the picture by making it respond to commands from the user. This is a huge topic that cannot be treated thoroughly here, other than to demonstrate some of the complexities and show how inheritance and encapsulation can control them by abstracting interaction scenarios into generic classes that can be reused in diverse applications. For example, in the Workbench application, the following scenario is used for selecting one or more objects for subsequent operations:

If the left button is pressed over one or more objects and released immediately, only the topmost object is selected. If it is held while the mouse is dragged, a box should outline a rectangular region. When the button is released, each of the objects inside the box should be selected. Selections are undone by selecting nothing, that is, by clicking the button over the empty background.

Items are automatically highlighted once they are selected, and the highlighting is removed when the selection is undone.

This scenario is implemented by a generic class from the library, Selection. When the left mouse button is pressed over the Workbench, WbView creates an instance of class Selection and passes control to it:

```
= WbView . . .
- (BOOL)leftButtonDown {
        [Selection fromUserIn:self];
        return YES;
}
```

The Selection class implements the fromUserIn: method like this:

```
= Selection : View {
        id selectedArea; // Rectangle
        id selectedViews; // OrderedCollection(Views)
}
+ fromUserIn:aView {
        self = [self rect:aView];
        selectedArea = [Rectangle fromUser];
        selectedViews = [OrderedCollection new];
        [aView addSubViewsIn:selectedArea
            to:selectedViews];
        if ([selectedViews isEmpty]) {
            id singleView = [aView
                subViewAt:[selectedArea center]];
            [selectedViews add:singleView];
        }
        if ([selectedViews isEmpty)
            return [self free];
        [self adjustSelectedArea];
        [selectedViews eachElementPerform:
            @selector(emphasize)];
        [aView addSubView:self];
        return self;
}
```

Once a selection has been created, it must override the usual meanings of all mouse events, so it simply behaves like a large transparent sheet of acetate that covers all of its sibling views. Since it covers them, it will receive all events before they do, and it can override the usual event meanings with new ones. For example, whereas the leftButtonDown event previously created the new selection, the selection immediately assigns it a new meaning:

```
= Selection . . .
- (BOOL)leftButtonDown {
        if ([self eventOverASelectedView]) {
            PT old = event.origin;
            [superView erase:selectedViews
                        in:selectedArea];
            [selectedViews eachElementPerform:
                @selector(motionStart)];
            while([currentSensor leftButtonDown]) {
                PT delta = ptMinus(event.origin, old);
```

```
                if (delta != 0) {
                    [selectedViews eachElementPerform:
                        @selector(motionBy:)
                        with:delta];
                    [selectedArea moveBy:delta];
                    old = event.origin;
                }
            }
            [selectedViews eachElementPerform:
                @selector(motionEnd)];
            return YES;   // consume the event
        }
        [self free];
        return NO; // not over selected view
}
```

The opening if statement tests whether the event occurred over one of the selected views, and if not, the selection is undone. Otherwise, the event signifies that the selected items should begin tracking the cursor so that the user can drag them to new screen positions.

Dragging is hardly as simple as it may seem, but the complications are handled in generic code that all views inherit from the View class. The objects to be moved must first be erased to produce a clean image of the stationary objects, and this is done by creating a clipping region around the views to be erased and redrawing the rest of the hierarchy inside this region (this is where the generality of the displayExcept: method pays off). Finally, movement is simulated by repeatedly drawing each view with exclusive-or raster operations to toggle the pixels beneath them on and off without losing information. This lets them glide across the screen without damaging their background.

SUMMARY

The design and construction of pleasant user interfaces is a remarkably deep and complicated topic, and this article has only skimmed the surface. The user interface library contains many kinds of components that have not been mentioned like menus, choice boxes, verifiers, text editors, etc., but describing these could easily take as much space as the simpler components that have been presented. We have not discussed several technical challenges in the Workbench application, such as how dependency lines between views are redrawn while views are being moved such that the lines behave like rubber bands. And we have focused only on how to build iconic interfaces and said very little about how to make them genuinely pleasant to use. This is especially important given the proliferation of poorly designed but flashy systems that are seen so often today. For a discussion of performance issues, see the text box "User Interface Performance Issues" above.

Although direct code size comparisons between Workbench and the UNIX utility make should wait until Work-

USER INTERFACE PERFORMANCE ISSUES

BY JOHN UEBBING AND CHARLES YOUNG

The human visual system has several characteristic limits that should be accounted for in building responsive iconic interfaces. For example, changes occurring in less than 20 milliseconds are perceived as instantaneous. If successive frames of a moving image are redrawn in less than 50 milliseconds, the object is perceived as moving smoothly. If feedback to user-initiated events is produced in less than 300 milliseconds, it is perceived as occurring instantaneously. These speeds represent significant qualitative thresholds past which objects move smoothly without flicker and do not interrupt the user's train of thought.

For example, Hewlett-Packard 9000-310 workstations are based on a 10-MHz Motorola 68010 chip that executes an Objective-C message in about 0.04 milliseconds. If a drawing of an animated mechanical robot consists of 100 lines, and if each line is implemented as an object and manipulated by messages, 4 of the available 20 milliseconds could be wasted just in message-passing overhead.

It would pay to avoid this overhead by implementing only the robot as an object, storing the lines as C data structures to be accessed by a high-performance polyline procedure.

On the other hand, dispatching a mouse event to one of 25 objects would spend only 1.0 of the available 300 milliseconds in messaging. Even a complex series of messages, redrawing 20 objects with 10 messages per object, would consume only 8.0 milliseconds in messaging. The lesson is to use messaging extensively for flexibility in things like menus and mouse event dispatching where messaging time is small relative to response times of the human visual system, and to avoid messaging in critical loops like displaying individual lines and characters. By judiciously combining messaging and high-performance C and assembly code, it is possible to build very flexible and powerful human interfaces with fully adequate speed using today's low-cost hardware. A general rule is to start out by using messaging, time the execution of the critical parts, and then substitute C, assembly code, or even special hardware to bring performance to the needed level.

John Uebbing and Charles Young, who have both worked extensively in electronic displays, are now involved with advanced user interface concepts. They can be contacted at Hewlett-Packard Research Laboratory, 1651 Page Mill Rd., Palo Alto, CA 94304.

bench is as mature and widely used as make is today, we find it highly encouraging that its iconic user interface could be built in only 262 lines of new code. This suggests that object-oriented programming, and its ability to capture large quantities of reusable code in generic Software-IC libraries, may actually reduce development costs to the point that iconic interfaces may become as prevalent as text-oriented interfaces are today. ■

Smalltalk-80 aids troubleshooting system development

A workstation offering object-oriented programming is used to develop an expert system that advises and assists technicians in repairing electronic equipment.

The diagnosis and repair of malfunctions in electronic equipment is a major concern for any electronics manufacturer or systems integrator. Troubleshooting equipment requires a concise understanding of its electronics and a highly developed strategy for fault isolation. Technicians must also be able to work on many types of equipment, including discontinued items. Tektronix, for example, services its equipment for nine years after it has been discontinued; therefore, thousands of products must be serviced.

Staff turnover—particularly that resulting from typical career paths of good technicians—compounds the troubleshooting problem. After gaining a few years of experience, technicians in the electronics industry tend to move on to other jobs, such as sales or engineering.

This situation makes troubleshooting an ideal application for an expert system. In its simplest form, an expert system is a repository of knowledge about a problem domain, and of procedures for applying that knowledge. Construction of such a system involves collecting knowledge on the problem-domain subject, and storing it so that it can be processed by the computer and presented to the user to enhance productivity. Because troubleshooting is such a major, problematic task, and because of its suitability for an AI solution, the authors decided to build an expert system-based tool to assist and guide technicians in repairing equipment.

An original design constraint that influenced several system-building decisions was the acceptable rate of success such a system should exhibit. The initial design decision was, therefore, made by observing how companies organize technicians to achieve this result.

In most large service firms, technicians are organized in a hierarchical fashion. Troubleshooters at the first level are expected to repair an instrument if the problem is simple. If it's not, the instrument is passed to a more experienced technician, who repairs it or passes it to an even more experienced technician. At each level, technicians are expected to detect a certain complexity of failure. The Tektronix troubleshooting expert system was designed to augment the performance of the first-level technician.

The actual expert system, the FG502 Troubleshooting Assistant System Prototype (FG502-Tasp), demonstrates the feasibility of a system that provides technicians with advice and assistance in repairing a malfunctioning Tektronix FG502 function generator. The FG502-Tasp is part of the development effort of a larger system called Detektr (Development Environment for Tektronix Troubleshooters). Detektr is an expert system-building tool to help technicians and instru-

James H. Alexander, Knowledge Engineer
Michael J. Freiling, Principal Computer Scientist
Tektronix Inc.
Artificial Intelligence Department
Computer Research Laboratory
P.O. Box 500
Beaverton, OR 97077

Reprinted with permission of the publisher from ''Smalltalk-80 Aids Troubleshooting System Development'' by J.H. Alexander and M.J. Freiling from *Systems & Software*, Volume 4, Number 4, April 1985, pages 111-118. Copyright 1985 by Elsevier Science Publishing Co., Inc.

ment designers rapidly construct troubleshooting assistant expert systems focused on the repair of a single instrument.

The building of the FG502-Tasp netted a great deal of new information about the technology of expert-system mass production. Thus, the story of the FG502-Tasp development is instructive for anyone interested in developing expert systems for his or her application.

A view of the system.

The FG502-Tasp is built in Smalltalk-80, an emerging language for expert systems and AI work. Formerly, such a system would probably have been developed using Lisp or Prolog. Smalltalk-80 was chosen because it has many of the features that make Lisp and Prolog popular languages, and because of its excellent graphics and user-interface capabilities. Electronics troubleshooting applications make extensive use of graphics. The expert system runs on the Tektronix 4404 artificial-intelligence computer, a 68010-based workstation optimized for AI development (see "What sits on your desk?" which accompanies this article).

The FG502-Tasp can play several roles in helping a technician repair a FG502. The main facilities provided by the FG502-Tasp are component cross-referencing, waveform display, and diagnostic assistance.

For component cross-referencing, the system provides a picture of the schematic (the circuit logic), a map of the parts layout on the circuit board, and a parts list with descriptions of each part (Fig. 1). Using a mouse, the user can point to a part in any of the three representations and click a mouse-button. The part will be highlighted on the diagrams, and written information about it will also be displayed. The technician can quickly locate a part without flipping through a manual, thereby maintaining train of thought.

The waveform display was developed because a technician often wants to test the signal at a given point in the circuit. The troubleshooting assistant can show the technician what the signal should look like at a specific point by presenting stored pictures. The user need only point to a location and select SHOW WAVEFORM. The stored picture of the correct wave is recalled and displayed on the screen. The user can compare this ideal waveform with what is measured on the oscilloscope.

The diagnostic assistant responds to a technician's request for assistance by asking a series of questions leading to a diagnosis of the problem. The system advisor will ask for measurements by displaying a probe icon at the appropriate location on the screen (Fig. 1). This diagnostic assistance is provided by the expert-system portion of the FG502-Tasp. These aspects of the system create an environment that augments the technician's productivity.

Building the expert system.

Four distinct stages were involved in building the FG502-Tasp. In the first stage, most of the time was spent trying to comprehend the problem. The system developers interviewed technicians to gain an understanding of the environment in which they work and problems that confront them.

In the second stage, the system developers formulated a strategy for mechanizing the troubleshooting task. This stage was marked by long discussions on the appropriate ways to represent and use troubleshooting knowledge. It was here that the theoretical foundation of the system was developed.

In the third stage, the developers built tools for displaying information to communicate with the user, and tools needed for processing knowledge while searching for a diagnosis.

The last stage involved collecting specific troubleshooting knowledge in the form of rules for the expert system to use in diagnosis. This was an iterative process in which the developers entered and tested the rules, refining them as the system-building process proceeded.

The first stage of developing an expert system is always the gathering of general information about the domain and the domain expert, not to be confused with the specific diagnostic knowledge gathered in a later stage. For the FG502-Tasp development, this involved locating people within Tektronix responsible for troubleshooting. Talking with

"What sits on your desk?"

The Tektronix 4404 artificial-intelligence machine is a dedicated, symbolic programming environment with a sophisticated graphics-user interface. It is designed to be a delivery system for AI-based software applications and a personal-development system for AI researchers. The machine, a personal computer of the AI world, costs only $14,950. This is much less than the common $30,000 to $120,000 price tag for most Lisp machines.

The 4404 boasts a 68010 32-bit cpu running at 10 MHz (with no wait states), a hardware floating-point accelerator, 1 Mbyte of RAM, 40 Mbytes of hard-disk storage, and a 640-by-480 monochrome bit-mapped graphics display packed into a compact desktop unit. A Unix-like, multitasking, virtual-memory operating system provides an 8-Mbyte address space for each running process. Interactive user input is through a three-button mouse coupled to the display, which automatically smooth-scrolls over a 1,024-by-1,024 bit-mapped window when the mouse reaches a physical display edge. The system also has a floppy disk, an RS-232 port with built-in ANSI 3.64 terminal emulation for host access, and an SCSI interface for easy peripheral expansion. Options include a 40-Mbyte disk with streaming tape backup, a second megabyte of system memory, and an Ethernet local-area network interface.

The Tektronix 4404 offers a range of AI programming environments. Smalltalk-80 comes standard with the system. Tektronix' proprietary implementation of Smalltalk-80 provides response fast enough to support on-screen animation. The Franz Lisp and MProlog programming languages, and the Emacs text editor, are available as options.

the first contacts in the training department helped the system designers understand the task at hand and the nature of potential users. To build the FG502-Tasp, it was also necessary for the system designers to visit the Tektronix factory-service facility to see how troubleshooting is done on a day-to-day basis. This step was crucial because it is essential that an expert system fit the user, as well as the domain. Such a fit allows the user to understand, and thereby trust, the system.

During the problem-formulation stage, the troubleshooting-system designers spent considerable time discussing the nature of the system to be built for the Tektronix service organization. The goal was to select one of many possible approaches for the FG502-Tasp development efforts. Decisions were made only after hours of interviewing two senior Tektronix technicians (Tim Kisor and Jim Mauck). The issues discussed were the social aspects of the troubleshooting environment, the types of problems encountered, the functional structure of the instrument and its physical organization, the electronics and strategy of troubleshooting, and some pragmatic issues.

Gradually, it was possible to iden-tify and focus on the more important aspects of troubleshooting and the types of tools to use in the system-development effort. Discussions and creation of the appropriate framework for the expert system took place between interviews with the technicians. Key features of the troubleshooting task that could be exploited were noticed. One of the features is the hierarchical structure within service organizations noted earlier.

First-level technicians provide a filtering function. They are expected to detect and repair simple failures. The more products they can fix, the more time higher-level technicians have to concentrate on complex problems requiring their expertise. Thus, bolstering the knowledge of first-level technicians can greatly enhance productivity throughout the service organization.

The interviews also netted the system designers some educational and unexpected facts on how troubleshooters use electronics knowledge. The most interesting discovery was that an exact understanding of circuits is not necessary to troubleshoot successfully; technicians do not always need an advanced understanding of electronic principles. A qualitative understanding is suffi-cient to detect and fix a large percentage of instrument failures. Furthermore, a very small proportion of the possible malfunctions in an instrument accounts for the actual failures. In the initial stages of a product's life cycle, a large percentage of failures involve active components, such as transistors and operational amplifiers.

These findings had a profound impact on the expert-system prototype design. The main result was a decision to focus on a system that helps first-level technicians detect the most simple, common failures. Thus, the system would not change the technician's job, but would just augment the quality of job performance.

Limiting design goals made the expert system-building job easier. Because the system would focus on the most common failures, it was not necessary to build in theoretical models of the FG502. Rather, it would suffice to collect ad hoc rules about circuit behavior. Thus, the FG502-Tasp troubleshooting expert system was not intended to repair any possible failure of an instrument, but to help fix most of the instruments returned to the shop.

Once the system developers' concept of the troubleshooter began

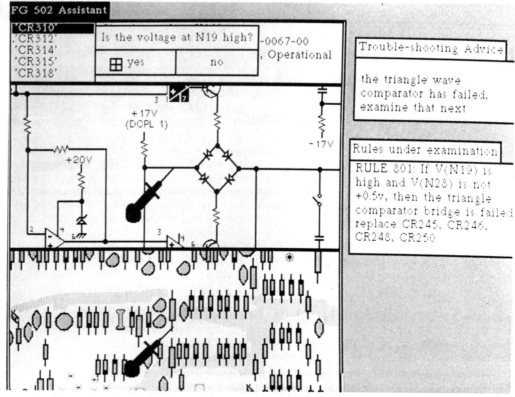

1. Panes in a repair window of the troubleshooting expert system show a picture of the schematic, a map of the parts layout on the circuit board, a list with parts descriptions, and a probe icon that points to parts that the system wants measured or has diagnosed as malfunctioning.

to gel, they launched an effort to build a prototype as rapidly as possible. Though contrary to traditional software-development practice, this is a standard procedure in expert-system development. Typically, potential expert systems have such an abstract nature that a working prototype will prove invaluable in guiding the system development. Smalltalk-80, its built-in tools, and the methods it supports for building new tools make such experimental programming simple.

What is Smalltalk-80?

Smalltalk-80 is an extendable language. When users develop an application, they extend the corpus of Smalltalk-80 code. Consequently, it is difficult to differentiate between Smalltalk-80 and the application code. In a sense, the application becomes part of Smalltalk.

The object-oriented nature of Smalltalk-80 results in a fundamental change in the way programmers think about programming. Instead of creating a procedure that controls system operation, the user creates an object (usually a data structure), and a set of methods (operations that transform, examine, and communicate with the object). Smalltalk-80 programs create objects or send messages to other objects. Once received, messages result in the execution of a method.

Programmers do not create each object and its methods individually. Instead, classes of objects are de-

The Smalltalk-80 programming environment

Tools that are part of the Smalltalk-80 environment simplify a system developer's understanding of how a program is running and where failures are occurring. Smalltalk-80 has three primary tools for assisting program development: code browsers, data inspectors, and code debuggers.

Browsers are tools for accessing all Smalltalk-80 code in the system. In the hierarchy of Smalltalk-80, classes are organized so that the user can follow the tree to find any piece of code in the system (see figure). The browser provides a series of keys to easily access the code. Different panes of the system browser window allow the user to select classes and methods for viewing. Browsers also have tools for looking at the hierarchy of the code, and for cross-referencing methods used or defined in a piece of code. The user can view any piece of code in the system including that which defines Smalltalk-80 (other than a small core stored as primitive operations).

In addition to reading the code with a browser, it is possible to modify any piece of a method and recompile it. The browser also provides assistance in the form of templates for constructing new classes. By selecting menu items in different panes of the browser, a user can look at hierarchies, instance variables, class variables, other implementors of methods, and a variety of functions useful for creating and understanding code.

Data inspectors allow the user to view the values of an object. Any object can have several different class and instance variables from which it is composed. Class variables are constants that are the same for all instances of a class. Instance variables differentiate one instance from another in a class. Using a data inspector, the user can look at and modify any of the variables that comprise the system.

Debuggers allow a person to view any interrupted process. The debugger presents the stack of methods being executed, and enables the users to select a method under execution. The system shows the code being executed, highlighting the particular interrupted message. Using inspectors, the programmer can look at variables (instance, global, class, and local) and track the changes of values. The debugger also allows execution of methods (in the context of execution), and modifications of the code being run.

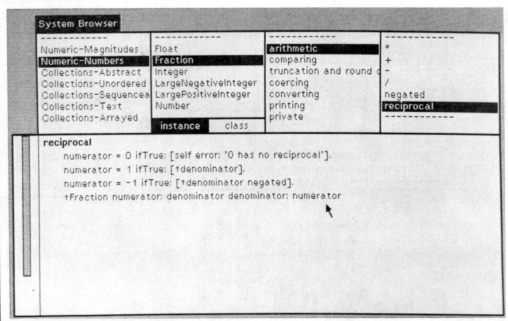

Different panes in the Smalltalk-80 system browser allow users to select classes (system objects), methods (operations on the objects), and any piece of code in the system for viewing.

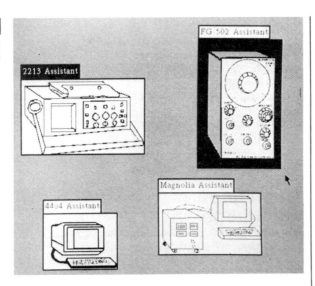

fined. A class definition describes an object and the methods that it understands. For example, numbers are objects in Smalltalk-80, and each number (1, 2, 3, . . .) is an instance for the class "number." Each number responds to messages such as plus, minus, float, and modulo. Classes are structured hierarchically, and any class automatically inherits methods from its superclass. Numbers in the class "integer" are a subclass of "number" and respond to the methods defined in "number." Likewise, "number" and its subclasses are a subclass of "object," and inherit the methods defined there. Thus, "integer" responds to any messages defined in "number" and "object."

As a result of this hierarchy and code inheritance, applications may be written by adapting previously constructed code to the task at hand. The programmer selects a class with a structure and function resembling the intended application, and creates a subclass. Much of the application code can be inherited from previously defined Smalltalk-80 code. The programmer need only redefine significant differences by overriding the inappropriate code with a customized one, using the previously written code. Programmers can also customize old pieces of code, orchestrating action as they choose.

As a further system-development aid, the Smalltalk-80 environment has several tools that facilitate debugging and modification (see "The Smalltalk-80 programming environment," which accompanies this article).

Graphic representations.

The highly graphic FG502-Tasp system involves the interaction of many parts. The system shows the instrument in several representations, each appropriate for a different purpose. It displays a group picture of various Tektronix instruments (Fig. 2). This represents a visual catalog; the user can point to the instrument needing repair and open a repair window.

A repair window contains three panes, each with a different representation of that instrument: one text and two graphic representations. The text pane presents part numbers and descriptions, while the other panes show pictures of the schematic and circuit board (Fig. 1). The user can point to a component in any representation and the same component in other representations will be highlighted.

For simplicity, a Smalltalk object that represented the entire instrument was created. In its simplest form, this object is a dictionary of all the instrument's abstract components. Every abstract component in the list has several relations associated with it, one for each representation: the numbered parts list, the schematic representation, and the circuit-board map.

The schematic and circuit-board-map representations are constructed as bit maps displayed on the screen. Neither are fully visible at any time, but the user can scroll the panes. The system keeps a list of components for both representations. These lists contain the components' location on the bit map and the icons that represent them. Thus, when the user points to an area on the screen, the appropriate list will be searched to find that component. Once found, it is then communicated to the abstract representation, which keeps track of the part being addressed.

After such a data structure was created, it was simple to apply the Smalltalk-80 tools for highlighting and component identification. Smalltalk-80 has code to track a cursor in a window and monitor mouse-button presses. This code was orchestrated so that when the mouse-button is pressed, the list is checked to identify which component is being pointed to. That component is told to reverse itself. In the process, it alerts the abstract component that it has become the active component, and the abstract component tells its various representations to highlight themselves.

In short, the pointing routine was created by building the data structure that links the parts, and then merely writing a script of actions to be taken when mouse-buttons are pressed.

The knowledge base.

The troubleshooting system contains a simple expert system composed of condition-action rules interpreted by a primitive production (rule) system. The standard Smalltalk-80 format (shown below) was used to build the FG502-Tasp expert system rules.

rule(number,condition,action,english)

The "number" is used for rule identification. The "condition" contains Smalltalk-80 code that matches patterns against those in a working memory (a section of memory in the computer). During the diagnostic process, the "if" clause ("condition" portion of a rule) is tested against this working memory. When matches are found, the "action" portion of the rule is executed. Execution might add more patterns to the working memory that match another rule, and thereby cause execution of its "action" part. When no more rules can execute or the system is ordered to stop, execution ceases. At this time, a diagnosis should have been made. The last element in the rule, "english," is a translation of the rule displayed to the user during a consultation.

Any rule interpreter is composed of four basic parts: a matcher, an indexer, a sequencer, and an executor. The matcher scans the rule base and identifies matches between the current state (patterns currently contained in working memory) and rule conditions. The indexer provides a means for accessing each of the rules and their components. The sequencer determines the order for examining and executing rules.

The executor carries out the "action" portion of the rule when the condition component matches the current state.

Smalltalk-80 has elements that made construction of the rule interpreter easy. One of its basic classes is "dictionary," which provides an associative collection of elements. Facts derived during a diagnosis are stored in a dictionary. Matching of an individual rule is accomplished by comparing its "if" clause against the facts stored in the dictionary. The methods already defined in Smalltalk support this comparison. Sequencing and indexing were accomplished by using a class "OrderedCollection," to store the rules.

Finally, the need for an executor was obviated by making the "action" portion of the rule a block of Smalltalk-80 code—a Smalltalk-80 expression that can be evaluated at any time. Because the language has these characteristics and organization, the rule interpreter required very little Smalltalk-80 code; much of it was orchestration of existing Smalltalk-80 tools.

In fact, there is more than one rule base in the system. FG502-Tasp has ten rule packets, which divide the diagnosis problem into subproblems.

A master rule base activates the action of other rule packets when appropriate. These packets correspond to the FG502 function generator's various functional blocks, any of which can fail. Thus, the rule packets can be thought of as functional-block experts. The master rule packet assigns the problem to the appropriate expert for analysis.

The knowledge base and the graphics representations work together. Each rule in the knowledge base has a set of test points for communicating with the graphics to display the required items. When measurements are required by the knowledge base, the graphics-display manager indicates on the screen where they should be taken.

Gathering knowledge.
With the understanding of the problem and the framework in place, getting the rules for the system was a simple process. Every company has at least one troubleshooter who is particularly good at his/her job. In this case, the particulars of the FG502 were discussed with Dennis Feucht, an expert troubleshooter. These discussions were the basis for producing rules in the condition-action format necessary for the system.

During the initial discussions, areas in the circuit that were key subcircuits and didn't have peculiarities in their operations were identified. The FG502-Tasp system developers started with the "average" circuit and proceeded to more difficult ones.

To help define the rules, Feucht was asked to describe possible failures, and their symptoms and detections. From his descriptions, the designers built rule packets which embodied his knowledge.

A computer was helpful during the rule-definition phase. Initially, the system designers wrote the rules on paper. Then, they discovered it was more effective to enter them directly into a computer, using a text editor and large display visible to several people at once. Direct computer entry facilitated rule definition in that the developers were more willing to change rules or define simple ones because it was easy to copy a rule and change a condition slightly. The computer thus became an indispensable tool in conducting knowledge-engineering sessions.

In this manner, rules were slowly gathered for the active components of the FG502 functional generator's major subsystem and entered into the expert system in the Smalltalk-80 format. At the end of this stage,

there were 45 to 55 rules divided into 10 rule packets. All that remained was plausibility testing of the system, which was accomplished by stepping the system through all the cases the troubleshooting experts could think of and fixing inconsistencies. The expert also was involved in the system testing to judge the accuracy of the diagnosis.

The FG502-Tasp expert system is still not complete. It has only been tested by the expert's mental simulations, not under field conditions. Yet, the prototype demonstrates the technology is feasible, and that such a system would be useful in the field-service environment. Furthermore, the FG502-Tasp is only the first step in the development of Detektr, a general tool to help build many troubleshooting assistants. For example, the developers are currently working on a broad theory of troubleshooting and a Tasp for an oscilloscope. This version will have more instrument-independent rules—knowledge that can be used in future expert systems for other Tektronix products. This Tasp will be tested under actual troubleshooting conditions.

The story of the FG502-Tasp development reveals several interesting items to anyone building an expert system. First, it was necessary to select a language (Smalltalk-80) that allowed developers to build the system quickly and easily, and to construct and modify program structures as the understanding of other requirements changed. Secondly, the greatest amount of time in the development cycle was devoted to understanding troubleshooting, and thinking about the constraints of the problem and the representation of knowledge. Once these factors were understood, construction of the system was fairly simple. It is the representation of knowledge and the careful incorporation of knowledge into the framework that will ensure an expert system's success.

Chapter 3: Implementing Object-Oriented Languages

In the beginning, at the Xerox Palo Alto Research Center, Smalltalk was implemented on the *Dorado*, a powerful, single-user, 70 ns minicomputer. Initial attempts to port Smalltalk to less expensive environments resulted in implementations that were too slow. More recent efforts, such as Smalltalk/V on the IBM PC, have been more successful but are not in a production environment. To overcome the problem, researchers have been exploring various implementation ideas, as well as modifications to the language, to make it more suitable for efficient implementation. We consider some of these ideas in this chapter.

For background information, in the first paper, "The Smalltalk-80 Virtual Machine," Glenn Krasner describes the manner in which Smalltalk-80 was implemented at Xerox PARC. The implementation uses a 10k byte "Virtual Machine" in the language of the Dorado processor and a 300k byte "Virtual Image" written in Smalltalk itself. This paper describes how the object-orientation is established in the virtual machine.

The virtual machine contains three elements, the Storage Manager, the Interpreter, and the Primitive Subroutines.

The Storage Manager manages all the free storage space and stores and retrieves objects. Each object is referenced by a special entity called an object pointer. (This is what is usually called a capability. See Chapter 5.) This pointer indirectly references the object through a table kept by the Storage Manager. This allows the Storage Manager to move objects around in memory without affecting the references to them. It also ensures that the Storage Manager is the only program concerned with the actual memory of the machine.

The Interpreter executes the machine instructions of the Smalltalk virtual machine. These machine instructions are called *bytecodes* and are similar to Pascal p-codes. The virtual machine is stack-oriented, and many of the bytecodes are concerned with stack manipulations.

The Primitive Subroutines are certain functions that are implemented in the machine code of the actual machine in order to improve performance. These include input/output, arithmetic, fetching and storing subscripted objects, screen graphics, and object allocation.

The Smalltalk Virtual Machine is a fairly small computer program that is implementable in about 1 man-year.

In the second paper, "What Price Smalltalk?," David Ungar and David Patterson describe their implementation of Smalltalk on a specially designed reduced instruction set computer. The implementation is called SOAR, for "Smalltalk on a RISC." Smalltalk runs slowly on conventional machines because it is designed to improve programmer productivity at the expense of implementation efficiency. It accomplishes this by providing the following services that are not normally found in conventional languages:

- run-time type checking instead of compile-time type declaration;
- message sending in which the method invoked depends on the type of data item;
- shortening the edit-compile-debug cycle by fast compilation to an interpreted language instead of optimizing compilation to native hardware;
- automatic dynamic storage allocation and reclamation instead of programmer-controlled dynamic structures.

In simulations, SOAR running on a 400 ns processor is able to compete with Smalltalk on a Dorado. It does this by using several new ideas in hardware and software. Three of the software ideas are:

- Compile rather than interpret.
- Once a method's address is computed, cache the address in the executable code so that the next time this instruction is executed, the lookup does not have to be performed.
- Use the generation scavenging method of storage reclamation instead of traditional garbage collection.

Two of the hardware ideas are:

- Start arithmetic and comparison operations immediately by using the hardware implementations for integers. Simultaneously check tags to see if this is the right thing to do. If it is not, trap to a software routine to perform the operation.
- Provide more registers and organize them into windows so that instead of saving and restoring registers, calls or returns can merely switch windows.

These software and hardware features reduce the penalty for using Smalltalk from a factor of 3.6 to a factor of 1.3 when compared with traditional programming systems. This does not seem to be too large of a penalty to pay for gaining the very useful object-oriented features of Smalltalk.

Charles B. Duff, in "Designing an Efficient Language," describes some ideas he used for developing *Actor*, an efficient object-oriented language.

The first idea is that of using the efficient garbage collection method of Henry Baker of MIT. Baker's idea is to split memory into two spaces and while execution proceeds in one of them, to incrementally copy the ''live'' objects into the other. When all live objects have been copied switch the roles of the two spaces.

The second idea is to replace contexts of Smalltalk with a more ordinary stack-based allocation scheme. In Smalltalk, every method activation causes the creation of a method context, which is itself an object. Each method context has its own private stack that includes its instance variables. While the Smalltalk approach makes it easier to construct a debugger, managing the potentially large number of simultaneously active stacks is a run time burden which does not seem to be worth the cost in execution time.

The third idea is to allow the programmer to decide whether to bind a generic operation name with a physical function at compile time (*early binding*) or at run time (*late binding*.) Smalltalk always uses late binding but this implies an inefficient table look-up for every method invocation. Conventional languages maintain efficiency by using early binding, but this decreases the flexibility and power of the language. Actor takes a middle ground in allowing the programmer to decide.

A final idea is to use a conventional Pascal-like syntax to reduce the learning load on new programmers.

Additional References

R.E. Johnson, ''Type-Checking Smalltalk,'' *OOPSLA '86, SIGPLAN Notices*, ACM, Inc., New York, New York, Volume 21, Number 11, November 1986, pages 211-224.

In this article, the Smalltalk language is altered by adding types in order to provide the means for an optimizing compiler to create more efficient implementations.

M.B. Ballard, D. Maier, and A. Wirfs-Brock, ''QUICK-TALK: A Smalltalk-80 Dialect for Defining Primitive Methods,'' *OOPSLA '86, SIGPLAN Notices*, ACM, Inc., New York, New York, Volume 21, Number 11, November 1986, pages 140-150.

QUICKTALK is a dialect of Smalltalk that can be compiled directly into native machine code. It includes an optional typing mechanism that programmers can use to gain efficiency in mature applications.

Y. Ishikawa and M. Tokoro, ''The Design of an Object Oriented Architecture,'' *Proceedings, The 11th Annual International Symposium on Computer Architecture*, IEEE Computer Society Press, Washington, D.C., June 1984 pages 178-187.

In this paper, a new object model suitable for a distributed computing environment is proposed and an object-oriented architecture based on the model is described.

T. Nojiri, S. Kawasaki, and K. Sakoda, ''Microprogrammable Processor for Object-Oriented Architecture,'' *Proceedings, The 13th Annual International Symposium on Computer Architecture*, IEEE Computer Society Press, Washington, D.C., June 1986, pages 74-81.

This paper describes a microprocessor that was designed for the purpose of efficiently executing programs written in an object-oriented language.

P.J. Caudill and A. Wirfs-Brock, ''A Third Generation Smalltalk-80 Implementation,'' *OOPSLA '86, SIGPLAN Notices*, ACM, Inc., New York, New York, Volume 21, Number 11, November 1986, pages 119-130.

Describes ''Tektronix Large Object Space Smalltalk,'' an interpreter-based implementation of Smalltalk-80, which incorporates a generation-based garbage collector and has no object table.

D.M. Lewis, D.R. Galloway, R.J. Francis, and B.W. Thomson, ''Swamp: A Fast Processor for Smalltalk-80,'' *OOPSLA '86, SIGPLAN Notices*, ACM, Inc., New York, New York, Volume 21, Number 11, November 1986, pages 131-139.

Describes *Swamp* (Smalltalk Without All that Much Pipelining), a processor designed for fast execution of Smalltalk-80. The processor executes an instruction set similar to bytecodes. It includes a context cache, tag checking, and a hardware method cache. It uses a simple next micro-address prediction strategy to obtain most of the performance of pipelining. Tests show that Swamp executes faster than Smalltalk on a Dorado.

R.G. Atkinson, ''Hurricane: An Optimizing Compiler for Smalltalk,'' *OOPSLA '86, SIGPLAN Notices*, ACM, Inc., New York, New York, Volume 21, Number 11, November 1986, pages 151-158.

Describes how types were added to Smalltalk in order to be able to compile to efficient native machine code.

G. Krasner, editor, *Smalltalk-80: Bits of History, Words of Advice*, Addison-Wesley, Reading, Massachusetts, 1983.

A collection of papers that discuss implementation concepts of Smalltalk-80.

Reprinted with permission from *BYTE*, Volume 6, Number 8, August 1981,
pages 300-320. Copyright © 1981 by Glenn Krasner.

The Smalltalk-80 Virtual Machine

Glenn Krasner
Learning Research Group
Xerox Palo Alto Research Center
3333 Coyote Hill Rd
Palo Alto CA 94304

The Smalltalk-80 system is a powerful system that encourages the development of large applications programs. The system contains a compiler, a debugger, a storage management system, text and picture editors, and a file system. It also contains a highly interactive user interface based on graphics that include overlapping windows.

Typically the task of bringing up such a powerful system on a new computer includes writing code to implement these pieces. The Smalltalk-80 system is different in that most of these pieces are written in Smalltalk-80 itself. The part that can be written in Smalltalk-80 is called the *Smalltalk-80 Virtual Image*, and it includes the compiler, debugger, editors, decompiler, and the file system.

The remaining part of the Smalltalk-80 system is defined in terms of an abstract machine called the *Smalltalk-80 Virtual Machine* (see figure 1). The Smalltalk-80 compiler translates source code into machine instructions for this virtual machine, rather than translating directly into machine instructions for a particular hardware machine. The task of bringing up a Smalltalk-80 system on a new "target" computer consists only of implementing (writing a program to simulate) the Smalltalk Virtual Machine on the target computer.

In this article, we will present an overview of the elements needed to implement the Smalltalk Virtual Machine. These elements are:

- the *Storage Manager*
- the *Interpreter*
- the *Primitive Subroutines*

Background

A Smalltalk-80 system is made up of *objects* that have state and exhibit behavior. Their state consists of the values of both named and indexed instance variables (which we will call *fields*), and their behavior is exhibited through sending and receiving *messages*. Objects are members of *classes*.

Classes may be *subclasses* of other classes—that is, they may inherit attributes from other classes. Programming in Smalltalk-80 is done by defining the procedures, or *methods*, that are executed when objects receive messages. Typically, messages are

sent to other objects to invoke their methods. Sometimes messages invoke *primitive* (machine-code) *subroutines* rather than Smalltalk-80 methods.

From this brief description of Smalltalk-80, we can consider the information needed to implement each of the three elements of the Smalltalk Virtual Machine:

1. To implement the storage manager, we need the information necessary to represent objects in the computer's memory. This information consists of the amount of memory that each object will occupy, which can be computed from the number of fields the object has, and the representation of fields in memory. Objects that describe classes define the number of fields their instances will have, so we also need to know how this number is represented. With this information, we can design a storage manager for objects in a Smalltalk-80 system that will:

- fetch the class of objects
- fetch and store fields of objects
- create new objects
- collect and manage free space

2. The interpreter executes the machine instructions of the Smalltalk-80 Virtual Machine. The information needed to design the interpreter is a description of these machine instructions, called bytecodes (the idea is similar to Pascal p-codes). The bytecodes are contained in methods, so we also need to know the representa-

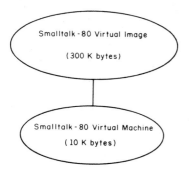

Figure 1: *The Smalltalk-80 Virtual Machine. Most of Smalltalk-80 is written in Smalltalk-80 (the Virtual Image), leaving only a small amount of code that has to be rewritten for each processor on which the language is implemented (the Virtual Machine).*

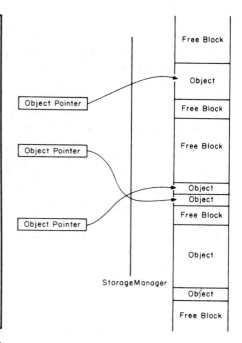

Figure 2: *Objects and memory usage in Smalltalk-80. Each Smalltalk-80 object has an object pointer that points to a block of memory that describes the object. When an object is no longer used, its memory is made available for use.*

tion of methods. From this information we can decide how the interpreter will fetch and execute bytecodes and how it will find methods to run when messages are sent.

3. The last piece of information we need to know is which messages will invoke primitive subroutines; that is, which methods we must implement in machine code to terminate the recursion of message sending and to optimize performance.

Before we go into more detail about these elements of a Smalltalk-80 Virtual Machine implementation, here are a few typical figures that will provide a little "reality" to implementors. For the systems that we have implemented at Xerox, the Smalltalk-80 Virtual Image consists of about 300 K bytes of objects. Our typical implementation of the Smalltalk-80 Virtual Machine is 6 to 12 K bytes of assembly code, or 2 K microcode instructions plus 10 K bytes of assembly code. Of this, about 40% is in the storage manager, 20% in the interpreter, and 40% in the primitive subroutines. Our average is about one person-year to implement a fully debugged version of this code.

The Storage Manager

Although the storage manager tends to be the largest and most complex of the three parts of a Small-

talk-80 implementation, the functions it provides are few and relatively simple to understand.

Everything in a Smalltalk-80 system is an object.

Everything in a Smalltalk system is an object, so from a storage point of view memory needs to be divided into blocks, one for each object, plus a pool of memory that is not yet used. Every time a new object is created, a new block of the appropriate size must be found for that object: when objects are no longer used, their memory block may be returned to the pool (see figure 2).

A special entity called an *object pointer* is assigned to each object. If an object pointer were the actual core address of the memory occupied by that object, then there would be fast access to an object given its pointer. However, in the Smalltalk-80 system the object pointer is an *indirect* pointer to the object through a table kept by the storage manager. This allows the storage manager to move an object around in memory without affecting any object that refers to it. It also insures that the storage manager is the only entity in the system concerned with (and allowed to change)

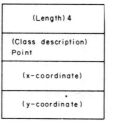

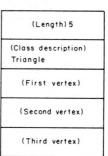

Figure 3: *Typical object representations in Smalltalk-80.*

the actual memory. In the Small-talk-80 Virtual Image, object pointers are single 16-bit words. This allows for 64 K objects in the system; these objects may take up much more than 64 K words of memory.

Since an object's class and fields are themselves objects, we can see that the block of memory corresponding to an object contains the object pointer of the object's class plus the object pointer for each of the object's fields. The storage manager also keeps the length of the block as one word of the block. This means, for example, that the block corresponding to an object that is an instance of class *Point* (see figure 3) will have:

●one word that says this block is four words long
●one word that is the object pointer of the object that describes class *Point*
●one word that is the object pointer of an object that is the *x*-coordinate field of the point
●one word that is the object pointer of an object that is the *y*-coordinate field of the point

Similarly, the block corresponding to an object that is an instance of class *Triangle* will have:

●one word saying this block is five words long
●one word that is the object pointer of the object that describes class *Triangle*
●one word that is the object pointer of an instance of class *Point*, representing one vertex field
●one word that is the object pointer of an instance of class *Point*, for the second vertex field
●one word that is the object pointer of an instance of class *Point*, for the third vertex field

For performance optimization, the values in the fields of some objects, such as instances of class *ByteArray*, will be interpreted as the numerical values themselves, rather than as object pointers. The block corresponding to the byte array containing the elements 1, 2, 3, and 4, in order, will have:

●one word saying this block is four words long
●one word pointing to the object that describes class *ByteArray*
●one byte encoding the number 1
●one byte encoding the number 2
●one byte encoding the number 3
●one byte encoding the number 4

We will represent all objects as having fields interpreted as object pointers or numerical values, not both. Objects may store numerical values as bytes or words, but not both.

As we have mentioned, the objects that describe classes also need to represent the form of instances of those classes. The essential information is the number of fields the instances will have, and whether these will be pointer or nonpointer fields. For example, the describer of class *Point* says that its instances will have two fields (*x*- and *y*-coordinates) and that these will be pointers (see figure 4). The describer of class *ByteArray* says that its instances may have a variable number of fields and that these fields will not be pointers but will be numerical values stored in bytes.

The purpose of the storage manager is to fetch and store fields of objects, to create objects, and to manage free space. A clean implementation of the storage manager would be one in which the other parts of the system had access only to the

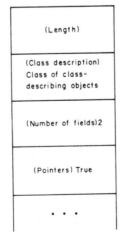

Figure 4: *Class-describing object for class Point.*

object pointers and made requests of the storage manager only through the following subroutine calls:

●*getClass(objectPointer)* returns the object pointer of the class of the given object
●*getField(objectPointer,fieldOffset)* returns the field
●*storeField(objectPointer,fieldOff-set,newValue)* replaces that field with the new value *newValue*
●*newInstance(classObjectPoint-er,numberOfFields)* returns the object pointer of a new instance of that class, and, if that class can have indexed instance variables, this instance has the given number of fields (*numberOfFields*)

Requests can be made for new storage (with the *newInstance* subroutine), but not to return used storage. In some other systems, storage that is no longer used must be explicitly returned to the free storage pool. The Smalltalk-80 philosophy is that neither the user nor any part of the system other than the storage manager need have such concerns. Therefore the storage manager must know which objects are no longer being used, so that their storage may reenter the free pool. Typically, Smalltalk-80 Virtual Machine implementations use *reference-counting* to accomplish this. For every object in the system, the storage manager keeps a count of the number of other objects that point to it. This number will change only during execution of the four storage-manager sub-routines. When this count reaches zero, the object's memory block may be reused because there are no references to that object anywhere else in the system.

The Interpreter

The interpreter is that portion of the Smalltalk-80 Virtual Machine that performs the actions described in the bytecodes of methods (ie: the machine code of the Virtual Machine). The information needed to implement the interpreter is the description of the bytecodes, the representation of methods, and the technique to find the method to run when sending a message.

The bytecodes define the Smalltalk-80 Virtual Machine as a stack-oriented machine. Each bytecode represents one of the following actions:

● push an object onto the stack
● store the top of the stack as the value for a variable
● pop the top of the stack
● branch to another bytecode
● send a message using the top few elements of the stack
● return the top of the stack as the value for this method

In the Smalltalk-80 Virtual Machine, each of these actions is realized by one or more bytecodes. Note that pushing, storing, popping, and branching are standard instruction types for any stack machine, that sending a message corresponds to calling a procedure using the top few elements of the stack as arguments, and that returning an object from a method corresponds to returning a value from a procedure. The difference between the Smalltalk-80 Virtual Machine and procedure-based stack machines is in the way the procedure is found. In most procedure-based stack machines the address of a procedure is provided in the *execute procedure* instruction; in the Smalltalk-80 system only the "name," called the *selector*, of the message is provided; the method (or procedure) to be executed is found through a strategy involving the receiver of the message and its class. We will first describe the bytecodes, then how methods are represented, and finally give a strategy for finding methods.

Stack Operations

The Smalltalk-80 Virtual Machine and corresponding bytecode set are stack oriented. Object pointers are pushed and popped from a stack, and when a message is sent, the top few elements of the stack are used as receiver and arguments of the method. These are replaced by the

Bytecode	Stack Contents After Execution (Top of Stack to Right)
-1- Push 3	(3)
-2- Push 4	(3 4)
-3- Push 5	(3 4 5)
-4- Send +	(3 9)
-5- Send *	(27)

Table 1: *Bytecodes for the Smalltalk expression 3 * (4 + 5).*

Bytecode	Stack Contents After Execution (Top of Stack to Right)
-1- Push 3	(3)
-2- Push 4	(3 4)
-3- Send +	(7)
-4- Store into a	(7)

Table 2: *Bytecodes for the Smalltalk expression a ← 3 + 4.*

Bytecode	Stack Contents After Execution (Top of Stack to Right)
-1- Push 3	(3)
-2- Store into a	(3)
-3- Pop	( )
-4- Push 4	(4)
-5- Store into b	(4)

Table 3: *Bytecodes for the Smalltalk expression a ← 3. b ← 4.*

Bytecode	Stack Contents After Execution (Top of Stack to Right)
-1- Push 3	(3)
-2- Store into a	(3)
-3- Pop	( )
-4- Push a	(3)
-5- Return top of stack	( )

Table 4: *Bytecodes for the Smalltalk expression a ← 3. ↑ a.*

object returned as the value of that method. For example, the Smalltalk-80 expression:

3 * (4 + 5)

is encoded by the bytecodes shown in table 1.

As bytecodes labeled -1-, -2-, and -3- are executed by the interpreter, the objects 3, 4, and 5 are pushed onto the stack. When bytecode -4- is executed, the message + is sent to the second object on the stack (4) with the top object of the stack as the argument (5). The 4 and 5 are popped off this stack when the message is sent, and the interpreter begins executing

the bytecodes for the method corresponding to the message + in the Smalltalk class of small integers. This method will eventually return an object, in this case 9, as its value, and the interpreter will push the 9 onto the original stack above the 3 and resume execution with bytecode -5-. Bytecode -5- will produce an effect similar to that produced by -4-, leaving the object 27 on the stack. In the same way that other stack machines push *data* onto a *stack* and use the top few data items as *arguments* for a *procedure*, replacing them with the *value* returned from that procedure, the Smalltalk-80 Virtual Machine pushes *object pointers* onto a *stack* and uses the top few as *receiver* and *arguments* of a *message*, replacing them with the *object* returned from that method.

In both machines, values from the top of the stack may be stored as the values of variables. As an example, the Smalltalk expression:

a ← 3 + 4

will be represented by the bytecodes in table 2. Here, -1-, -2- and -3- act as before and the interpreter executes bytecode -4- by storing the top of the stack 7 into the variable *a*.

Stack machines in general, and the Smalltalk-80 Virtual Machine in particular, also have the ability to pop the top element off the stack. In the statements:

a ← 3.
b ← 4

once the 3 is stored into variable *a*, it is no longer needed, so it is popped from the stack. These statements are represented by the bytecodes shown in table 3.

The top of the stack may be returned as the value for the method. The statements:

a ← 3.
↑ a

are represented by the bytecodes shown in table 4.

Branching Operations

Conditional and looping messages are used so often that they are represented not by actual messages but by bytecodes for conditional and unconditional jumps. (This is *only* for performance reasons; these branching and looping messages would work if they were actually sent like other messages.) For example:

a > 4 ifTrue: [a ← a − 1]

(which in the Smalltalk-80 system means execute the code within the brackets only if the object returned from the > message is not false) is represented in table 5 (ignoring the stack from now on).

Bytecode

-1- Push 4
-2- Push a
-3- Send >
-4- Jump to -10- if the top of the stack is false
-5- Push a
-6- Push 1
-7- Send −
-8- Store into a
-9- Pop
-10- < the next bytecode >

Table 5: *Bytecodes for the Smalltalk expression a > 4 ifTrue: [a ← a − 1].*

Bytecode

-1- Push a
-2- Push 4
-3- Send >
-4- Jump to -11- if top of stack is false
-5- Push a
-6- Push 1
-7- Send −
-8- Store into a
-9- Pop
-10- jump to -1-
-11- < the next bytecode >.

Table 6: *Bytecodes for the Smalltalk expression [a > 4] whileTrue: [a ← a − 1].*

Table 6 shows the bytecodes for the looping expression:

[a > 4] whileTrue: [a ← a − 1]

(which means execute the code in the second brackets as long as the code in the first set of brackets evaluates to something other than false).

Addressing Variables

Methods are implemented as objects whose fields contain the bytecodes plus a group of pointers to other objects called the *literal frame*. The interpreter can use the *getField* subroutine of the storage manager to fetch the next required bytecode to execute. This takes care of returns, jumps, and pops, but for the other bytecodes we need to represent more information. In particular, for the push and store bytecodes, we need to represent where to find the object pointers to push; for the send bytecodes, we need to represent where to find the selector of the message and which stack elements are the receiver and arguments.

The source code for a method contains variable names and literals, but the bytecodes of the Virtual Machine are defined only in terms of field offsets. From the Virtual Machine's point of view, there are three types of variables: variables local to the method (called *temporaries*), variables local to the receiver of the message (*instance variables*), or variables found in some dictionary that the receiver's class shares (*global variables*). Note that *class variables* are treated in the same way as other global variables. The Smalltalk-80 compiler (itself written in Smalltalk-80) translates references to these variables into bytecodes that are references to field offsets of the receiver, the temporary area, or globals. The instance variables are translated using a field of class-describing objects that associates instance variable names with field offsets. The assignment of offsets to temporaries is done when the compiler translates a method by associating names of temporaries to offsets in the temporary area. The compiler creates instances for the literals, puts their object pointers into the literal frame of the method, and produces bytecodes in terms of offsets into the literal frame. For global variables, the compiler uses system dictionaries that associate global names to indirect references to objects. Object pointers of the indirect references to the global objects are also placed in the literal frame of the method. The bytecodes for accessing globals are encoded as indirect references through field offsets of the literal frame.

This means that when the interpreter is executing a method, it has to keep a stack, a temporary area, a pointer to the receiver and arguments of the method, and a pointer to the method itself (see figure 5). It uses the storage manager's *getField* and *storeField* subroutines to push and pop pointers from the stack object, to retrieve and set values of variables in the temporary area, to retrieve and set values of variables of the receiver, and to get bytecodes and values of global variables from the method.

Finding Methods

When a message is sent, the receiver and arguments must be identified, and the appropriate method must be found by the interpreter. The technique used in Smalltalk-80 is to include in each class-describing object a dictionary, called the *method dictionary*, that associates selectors with methods. Pointers to the selectors that will be sent by any method are kept in the method (along with global variable pointers and bytecodes). The bytecodes that tell the interpreter to send a message encode a field offset in the literal frame where the selector is found, plus the number of arguments that that method needs. By convention, the top elements of the stack are the arguments and the next one down is the receiver. For example, the send bytecode for the expression:

$$3 + 4$$

will stand for "send the selector in field X of the method (which will be +), and it takes one argument." The interpreter will ask the storage manager for the X field of the method, will get the top of the stack (4) as the argument, and the next element down (3) as the receiver. It will locate the receiver's class, its method dictionary, search it for an association of the + selector with some method, and, when found, execute that method.

If no such association is found, the searching does not end. The receiver's class may be a subclass of another class, called its *superclass*. If this is the case, the method for + may be

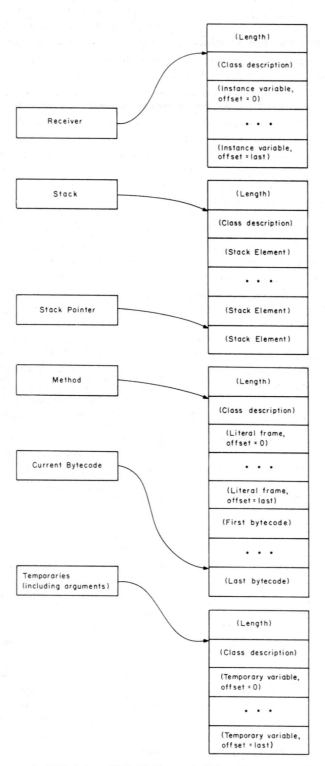

Figure 5: *Object pointers held by the interpreter.*

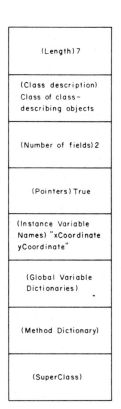

(Length) 7

(Class description)
Class of class-
describing objects

(Number of fields) 2

(Pointers) True

(Instance Variable
Names) "xCoordinate
yCoordinate"

(Global Variable
Dictionaries)

(Method Dictionary)

(SuperClass)

Figure 6: *Class-describing object for class Point, revisited.*

defined in the superclass, so the interpreter must check there. This means that each class must have a field that refers to its superclass (see figure 6). The interpreter searches the method dictionary of the superclass, its superclass, and so on, until either an appropriate method is found or it runs out of superclasses, in which case an error occurs.

To execute a method, the interpreter needs a place for temporaries and a stack for that method. In the Smalltalk-80 Virtual Machine, this is done by allocating an object that is an instance of class *MethodContext*. Objects in *MethodContext* keep track of the method, the stack for that method, a pointer to the next bytecode to be executed in that method, the temporary variables for that method, and the context from which that method was invoked, called the *caller* of that method (see figure 7). When a method returns, the value returned is pushed on the stack of the caller context, and execution continues at the next bytecode of the caller's method.

The Smalltalk-80 Virtual Machine implementation is a program running in the machine language of the target computer.

Primitive Subroutines

The Smalltalk-80 Virtual Machine implementation is a program running in the machine language of the target computer. The storage manager is the collection of subroutines in this program that deals with memory allocation and deallocation. The interpreter is the collection of subroutines in this program, one of which fetches the next bytecode from the currently running method and calls one of the others to perform the appropriate action for that bytecode. In addition to these functions, we have found that there are several other places in the Smalltalk-80 system where performance considerations make it necessary, or at least desirable, to implement certain functions as machine-code subroutines in the Smalltalk-80 Virtual Machine. These places are:

• input/output: connecting the Smalltalk-80 system to the actual hardware
• arithmetic: basic arithmetic for integers
• subscripting indexable objects: fetching and storing indexable instance variables
• screen graphics: drawing and moving areas of the screen bitmap quickly
• object allocation: connecting the Smalltalk-80 code for creating a new instance with the storage manager subroutines

We call this set of subroutines the *primitive subroutines*.

The primitive subroutines are represented in the Smalltalk Virtual Image as methods with a special flag that says to run the corresponding subroutine rather than the Smalltalk-80 bytecodes. When the interpreter is executing the code to send a message and finds one of these flags set, it calls the subroutine and uses the value returned from it as the value of the method. The number of these methods in Smalltalk-80 is small (around one hundred) in order to keep the rest of the system as flexible and extensible as possible. We will not list those methods that are primitives, but will refer the reader to *Smalltalk: the Language and Its Implementation* (Goldberg, Robson, and Ingalls, 1981) for details.

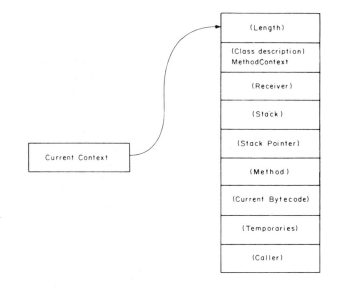

Current Context

(Length)

(Class description)
MethodContext

(Receiver)

(Stack)

(Stack Pointer)

(Method)

(Current Bytecode)

(Temporaries)

(Caller)

Figure 7: *The only object pointer used by the Smalltalk-80 interpreter is a reference to a MethodContext.*

A few of these primitive methods are executed so often that even the cost of looking them up in their classes' method dictionaries would be excessive. These methods are instead represented as special versions of the Send Message type of bytecodes. The message + , for example, is represented this way. When this bytecode is executed and the top two elements of the stack are small integers, then the primitive method is called as a subroutine. When this bytecode is executed and the top two elements of the stack are not small integers, then the + message is sent normally.

Conclusion

The Smalltalk-80 Virtual Machine is a fairly small computer program that consists of a storage manager, an interpreter, and a set of primitive subroutines. The task of implementing a Smalltalk-80 Virtual Machine for a new target computer is not large (especially when compared with the task of implementing other large programming systems) because most of the functions that must usually be implemented in machine code are already part of the Smalltalk-80 Virtual Image that runs on top of the Virtual Machine.

The Smalltalk-80 Virtual Machine could also be implemented in hardware, although this has not yet been done. Such an implementation would sacrifice some of the flexibility of software, but it would result in the performance benefits that hardware provides. Given the evolving nature of Smalltalk, it may not yet be time to implement the Virtual Machine in hardware: new Smalltalks that are more powerful would likely need at least small changes in Virtual Machine definition and implementation. However, hardware assists to Smalltalk-80 Virtual Machine software can greatly improve performance. Writable microcode stores for the pieces of code that are frequently run, hardware assists for graphics, or hardware assists for the fetching of bytecodes could all potentially improve the performance of a Smalltalk-80 Virtual Machine implementation. ■

August 1981 © BYTE Publications Inc

What Price Smalltalk?

David Ungar, Stanford University

David Patterson, University of California, Berkeley

Are reduced instruction set computers good for languages like Lisp and Smalltalk? With the addition of a few simple hardware changes and software techniques—yes.

In anticipation of the promise of tremendous hardware advances, software researchers have fashioned expansive programming environments to improve programmer productivity. Even with the march of technology, exploratory programming environments such as Smalltalk-80[1,2] require such expensive computers that few programmers can afford them. With the hope of increasing that community, a research project at the University of California created a reduced instruction set computer[3] for Smalltalk called SOAR, which stands for Smalltalk on a RISC.[4,5] Figure 1 shows SOAR, a 32-bit NMOS microprocessor.

We are now able to estimate the performance implications of the Smalltalk-80 programming environment. In the next section we list the demands that Smalltalk-80 places on traditional computer systems, then present software and hardware ideas that answer those demands.

We have learned a number of lessons from the SOAR microprocessor, including the hard lesson that we now call "the architect's trap."

The demands of Smalltalk-80

To improve programmer productivity, Smalltalk-80 removes four restrictions found in conventional programming systems. First, Smalltalk-80 programmers do not have to declare the types of variables at compile-time.

(1) Run-time data typing instead of compile-time type declarations. The Fortran statement "I = J + K" denotes integer addition and can be performed with a single Add instruction. But Smalltalk-80 has no type declarations, so J and K may hold values of any type, from Booleans to B-trees. Thus, every time a Smalltalk-80

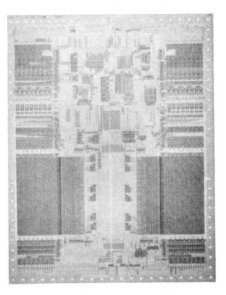

Figure 1. Microphotograph of the SOAR microprocessor. Using 4-micron line widths, Joan Pendleton led the implementation of this 32-bit microprocessor.[6,7] It is 10.7 mm by 8.0 mm, uses 35,700 transistors, dissipates about 3W, and runs about 400 ns per instruction. These chips were fabricated by MOSIS, and have performed better than expected. Xerox also volunteered to make some SOAR chips. Although they run at 330 ns per instruction, the Xerox chips do not correctly perform all tests. We are considering a fabrication attempt with 3-micron line widths to further reduce the cycle time.

system evaluates "J + K" it must first check the types and then perform the appropriate operation.

Measurements of conventional Smalltalk-80 systems show that over 90 percent of the "+" operations do the simplest possible operation, integer addition.[8] Since a type check takes at least as long as an Add instruction, most Smalltalk-80

Reprinted from *Computer*, January 1987, pages 67-74. Copyright © 1987 by The Institute of Electrical and Electronics Engineers, Inc.

Table 1. Speed of Smalltalk-80 systems.

System	Maker	Host Processor	Instruction Time in ns	Execution Model	Speed
BS	UCB	68010	400 (18%)	interpreter	11%
Tek 4404	Tektronix	68010	400 (18%)	interpreter	25%
Dorado	Xerox	Dorado	67 (100%)	microcode	100%
SOAR	UCB	SOAR	400 (18%)	compiler	107%

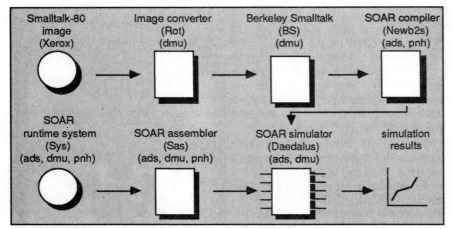

Figure 2. Steps involved in a SOAR simulation. First, Rot removes the object table from the Xerox Smalltalk-80 image. We then use BS to make any modifications necessary in the image (to eliminate some becomes). Newb2s produces a Smalltalk image for SOAR by converting the BS objects to SOAR format, and Hilfinger's Slapdash compiler translates the bytecoded programs into SOAR instructions. We have also coded the Smalltalk primitive operations and storage management software in SOAR assembly language. After this is assembled, it is fed to Daedalus, our SOAR simulator, along with the Smalltalk image. The initials below each system show its author: ads is Dain Samples, phn is Paul Hilfinger, and dmu is David Ungar.

systems waste a lot of time checking types for integer arithmetic.

(2) Dynamically bound messages instead of statically bound procedures. Smalltalk was probably the first system to be called *object oriented*, an approach to programming that associates routines with data structures to encourage programmers to think of programming as sending messages to data objects rather than as calling procedures to update shared data. Thus, the routine to be invoked depends on the type of data, and since the type of data can change at run-time, the equivalent of a simple procedure call on most systems is a comparison and table lookup in Smalltalk-80.

(3) Fast compilation to interpreter instead of optimizing compilation to native hardware. A key to improving programmer productivity is to reduce the time it takes to change a program and then test it.

To shorten the edit-compile-debug cycle, the Smalltalk programmer recompiles a routine using a simple and fast compiler that produces code for a Smalltalk interpreter. The Smalltalk interpreter provides the foundation for an excellent debugger, which further improves programmer productivity.

Like many other systems, Smalltalk supports separate compilation so that the programmer only waits for one routine to be recompiled rather than the whole system. But unlike other systems, Smalltalk further shortens this cycle by avoiding the conventional linking step: routines are linked "on the fly" as needed. To shorten program development, Smalltalk sacrifices potential compile time optimizations and static linking that lead to faster program execution.

(4) Automatic dynamic storage allocation and reclamation instead of program-

mer-controlled dynamic structures. The designers of Smalltalk believed that programmers should not be encumbered with managing dynamically varying data, so storage management was left to the system. Exploratory programming environments have the added constraint of avoiding distracting pauses while collecting garbage, since a major contributor to programmer productivity is a fast and predictable interaction with the programming environment.[9] Smalltalk is even more challenging for garbage collection, since Smalltalk programs tend to generate garbage about 10 times faster than most Lisp programs.

The costs on traditional systems

Given the demands mentioned above, the obvious question is, how well does Smalltalk-80 run on conventional computer systems? The first step in answering this question is determining a fair way to measure performance. It is always dangerous to rely on architects to supply the tests of their creations, and fortunately we were not put in that predicament. The creators of Smalltalk have a standard set of benchmarks that all Smalltalk implementors use to compare systems.[10] Xerox rates performance by taking the mean of 13 macro-benchmarks, plus the text scanning and BitBlt micro-benchmarks. Macro-benchmarks include compilation, decompilation, searching the Smalltalk program hierarchy, and so on.

Table 1 compares the performance on several Smalltalk-80 systems using five of those large benchmarks. Both the Tek 4404 and Berkeley Smalltalk (BS) use software interpreters, with BS being the experimental vehicle that we used to study Smalltalk. The Dorado is the machine used at Xerox to run Smalltalk. The SOAR chip has been placed on a board, the board has been placed in a workstation, and this package is running diagnostic programs, but we have not brought up the complete Smalltalk system, so we must use simulations to estimate performance (see Figure 2). This system was described at a recent conference.[11]

The system generally agreed to be fast enough for Smalltalk is the Dorado, a $120,000 ECL* personal computer that supports a single programmer at a time. (Think of it as a personal computer for

---

*Emitter-coupled logic is an expensive technology used in mainframes and supercomputers.

people who consider the Mercedes Benz a commuter car.) If we compare the Dorado to the Smalltalk interpreters on Motorola 68010 microprocessor-based systems, we see that the Dorado is four to eight times faster, which might be expected since the instruction time of the Dorado is about six times faster than the instruction time of the 68010. This is not the case for SOAR, which is about the same speed as the Dorado even though the instructions are six times slower. SOAR is faster than expected because it uses several innovations in software and hardware (see Table 2), as explained in the next two sections.

Reducing costs through software innovation

The first place to look for performance improvements is with software; it will be a very long time before it is as easy to build and debug hardware as it is to write and debug the equivalent program. Architects should only consider hardware implementations when there are tremendous gains to be had in total system performance, and when they are sure that function will never change. As we shall see, architects don't always follow this sound advice.

Interpretation. The Smalltalk-80 system is defined by a stack-oriented virtual machine based on the Dorado Smalltalk-80 implementation.[12] Each instruction consists of one to three bytes and generally corresponds to a token in the source program. These instructions are usually called *bytecodes*. Bytecodes have the following advantages:

• The simple correspondence between source and object code simplifies the compiler and debugger.

• Smalltalk can be transported to a new machine by writing only the virtual machine emulator.

This approach has drawbacks too:

• Decoding such dense instructions takes either substantial hardware or substantial time. For example, the instruction fetch unit consumes 20 percent of the Dorado CPU,[13] and decoding a simple bytecode takes twice as long as executing it in Berkeley Smalltalk.

• Some of the high-level instructions require many microcycles to execute. These multicycle instructions must be sequenced by a dedicated control unit.

The alternative is simply to compile to the native instruction set of the machine, hoping to gain performance with the traditional advantage of compilation over in-

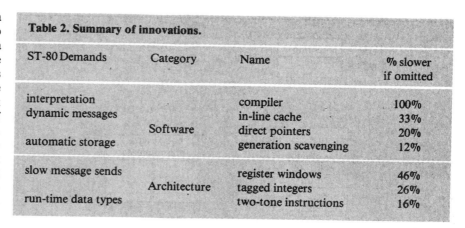

Table 2. Summary of innovations.

ST-80 Demands	Category	Name	% slower if omitted
interpretation		compiler	100%
dynamic messages		in-line cache	33%
	Software	direct pointers	20%
automatic storage		generation scavenging	12%
slow message sends		register windows	46%
	Architecture	tagged integers	26%
run-time data types		two-tone instructions	16%

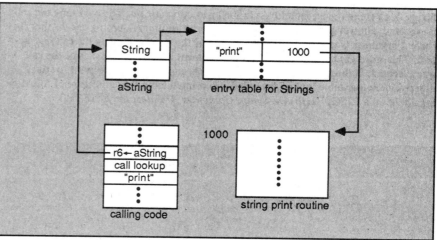

Figure 3. Caching the target address in the instruction stream. In this example, the print routine is called with an argument that is a string. (The argument is passed in r6.) The first time the call instruction is executed, the call contains the address of a lookup routine and the word after the call contains a pointer to the name "print." The lookup routine follows the pointers to the entry table for strings, and finds the entry for "print." It then overwrites the call instruction with a call to that routine and replaces the word after the call with the type of the argument (string). (Reprinted from "Architecture of SOAR: Smalltalk on a RISC," *11th An. Int'l Symp. Computer Architecture,* © IEEE.)

terpretation. We estimate compilation improves the performance of SOAR by 100 percent. A negative consequence of our decision to abandon bytecodes is that it forces us to rewrite the Smalltalk-80 debugger. Lee has designed a debugger for SOAR and has built a prototype in Berkeley Smalltalk.[14] He has exploited the hardware organization of SOAR in the design of the debugger to add a conditional breakpoint facility and increase execution speed during debugging.

SOAR may also have played a role in inspiring a compiler project at Xerox by Deutsch and Schiffman.[15] This implementation, called PS, provided the speed of compilation but maintained consistency with the interpreter so that the debug-

ger would not have to be modified. Their system runs almost twice as fast as interpreters using the same microprocessor.

Caching call targets in-line. Another way to improve Smalltalk performance is by decreasing the time taken to find the target of a call. Once computed, the target's address can be cached in the instruction stream for later use, as suggested by Schiffman and Deutsch.[15] Figures 3 and 4 illustrate this idea. This in-line caching exacts a price for its time savings: the processor must support nonreentrant code.

Although complicated, in-line caching pays handsome rewards. The conventional way for Smalltalk systems to save call

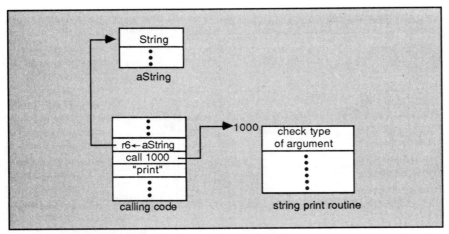

Figure 4. Caching the target address in the instruction stream. The next time the call is executed, control goes directly to the string print routine. A prolog checks that the current argument's type matches the contents of the word following the call instruction. This word contains the type that the argument had the previous time the call was executed. If the types match, control falls through to the string print routine, otherwise another table lookup is needed. (Reprinted from "Architecture of SOAR: Smalltalk on a RISC," *11th An. Symp. Computer Architecture,* © IEEE.)

Table 3. Summary of generation scavenging's performance.

	Berkeley Smalltalk	SOAR
execution model	interpreted	compiled
source of data	measurements	simulations
processor	MC68010	SOAR
cycle time	400 ns	400 ns
CPU time overhead		
mean	1.5%	0.9%
worst case	N.A.	3.3%
pause time (scavenge duration)		
mean	160 ms	19 ms
worst case	330 ms	28 ms
peak main memory usage	200 KB	200 KB

targets is a hash table. But the overhead for probing into a hash table would slow SOAR by 33 percent. The penalty for in-line caching is a software trap mechanism to synchronize process switches and cache probes. If we were forced to omit this, we could use a table containing the last addresses with an indirect in-line cache. This would slow SOAR down by 7 percent. Even with in-line caching, SOAR still spends 11 percent of its time in call-target cache probes and another 12 percent handling misses. Further research into computing the call's target might yield even more substantial savings.

Object-oriented storage management. Software is also the architect's best option for managing dynamically varying data structures, called objects in Smalltalk-80. Smalltalk-80 objects are smaller and more volatile than data structures in most other exploratory programming environments, averaging 14 words in length and living for about 500 instructions. Smalltalk-80 systems face three challenges in managing storage for objects:

• Automatic storage reclamation. On average, 12 words of data are freed and must be reclaimed per 100 Smalltalk-80 virtual machine bytecodes executed.

• Virtual memory. All objects must be in the same address space.

• Object-relative addressing. Although offsets into objects are known at compile-time, base addresses are not. Code must be compiled to address fields relative to dynamically determined base addresses.

Automatic storage reclamation. SOAR supports generation scavenging[16] to reclaim storage efficiently without requiring costly indirection or reference counting. This algorithm is based on the observation that most objects either die young or live forever. Thus, objects are placed into two generations and only new objects are reclaimed.

Storage reclamation has a strong impact on performance; most other algorithms would squander 10 percent to 15 percent of SOAR's time on automatic storage reclamation instead of generation scavenging's 3 percent (see Table 3). Hence, without generation scavenging SOAR would take 4 percent to 15 percent more cycles to run the benchmarks.

Traditional software and microcode implementations of object-oriented systems rely on an object address table (see Figure 5). Each word of an object contains an index into this table, and the table entry contains the address of each object. The indirection through the table primarily supports compaction. Generation scavenging provides compaction for free, permitting SOAR to function without an object table (see Figure 6). Without this algorithm, the extra work to follow indirect pointers through the object table would slow SOAR down by 20 percent. These results seem confirmed by a recent Smalltalk-80 interpreter that used generation scavenging with direct pointers.[17] Although we would expect it to be a factor of two slower than PS because it is interpreted rather than compiled, this implementation is close to 90 percent of the speed of PS. It may be that direct pointers and generation scavenging, not used in PS, explain the surprisingly close performance.

Reducing costs through architectural innovation

The basic theme of the SOAR architectural additions is to allow the normal case to run fast in hardware and to trap to software in the infrequent complicated case.

Tags trap bad guesses. SOAR follows the Smalltalk-80 virtual machine in supporting only two data types with tags: integers and pointers.[1] But SOAR departs from the Smalltalk-80 virtual machine by starting arithmetic and comparison operations immediately and simultaneously checking the tags. (Figure 7 shows the SOAR tag layout.) Most often both operands are integers and the correct result is available after one cycle. If not, SOAR aborts the operation and traps to routines that carry out the appropriate computation for the data types. SOAR is the only Smalltalk-80 system that overlaps these operations. Without tagging, SOAR would run 26 percent slower.

A tagged architecture that lacks microcode must include instructions that manipulate and inspect tags. Because the Smalltalk system already relies on the compiler to ensure system integrity, we can allow the compiler to mix instructions that manipulate tags with instructions constrained by tags.

Each SOAR instruction contains a bit that either enables or disables tag checking. The untagged mode turns off all tag checking and operates on raw 32-bit data. In untagged mode the tag bits are treated as data, and the complete instruction set can be used to manipulate this data. Untagged instructions also allow programs written in conventional languages such as C and Pascal to run on SOAR. Instead of providing two versions of each instruction, we could have defined a mode bit in the program status word (PSW). This would have been expensive, increasing execution time by 16 percent.

Multiple overlapping on-chip register windows. We used hardware to improve the performance of arithmetic operations, and also to improve the performance of the frequent calls and returns. SOAR, like RISC I, optimizes them by providing a large, on-chip register file. The registers are divided up into overlapping windows. Instead of saving or restoring registers, calls or returns merely switch windows (Figure 8).

When we compared Smalltalk to the C language subroutines, we found that the shorter Smalltalk subroutines pass fewer operands and use fewer local variables, and so need fewer registers. So each SOAR register window has 8 registers instead of 12 for RISC I. Figures 8 and 9 show the register organization of SOAR. In addition to 56 more registers, the inclusion of register windows results in the addition of a register to select the current window, a register to detect overflows by

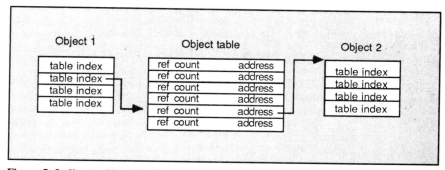

Figure 5. Indirect addressing. In traditional Smalltalk-80 systems, each pointer is really a table index. The table entry contains the target's reference count and memory address. This indirection required previous Smalltalk-80 systems to dedicate base registers to frequently accessed objects. The overhead to update these registers slowed each procedure call and return. (Reprinted from "Architecture of SOAR: Smalltalk on a RISC," *11th An. Symp. Computer Architecture*, © IEEE.)

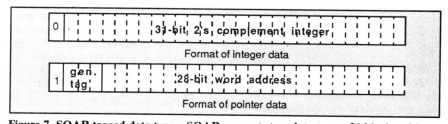

Figure 6. Direct addressing. A SOAR pointer contains the virtual address of the target object. This is the fastest way to follow pointers. (Reprinted from "Architecture of SOAR: Smalltalk on a RISC," *11th An. Symp. Computer Architecture*, © IEEE.)

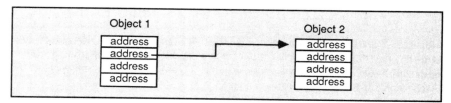

Figure 7. SOAR tagged data types. SOAR supports two data types, 31-bit signed integers and 28-bit pointers. Pointers include a generation tag. SOAR words could have contained 32 bits of data plus one bit of tag for a total of 33 bits. The scarcity of 33-bit tape drives, disk drives, and memory boards led us to shorten our words to a total of 32 bits including the tag (31 bits of data). (Reprinted from "Architecture of SOAR: Smalltalk on a RISC," *11th An. Symp. Computer Architecture*, © IEEE.)

recording the last saved window, more elaborate register decoders, and trapping logic.[7]

Despite the cost of all the added hardware, Smalltalk-80's predilection for procedure calls makes the register windows very important. The cost of saving and restoring a conventional register file would slow the machine down by 46 percent, even with Load- and Store-multiple instructions, which we discuss below.

Register windows allow many registers per procedure without making procedure calls and returns expensive.[3] Many RISC machines use optimizing compilers to cleverly allocate variables to registers and thus avoid register windows. While this may be the right way to go with conventional programming systems like C and Pascal, the extra compile time of register allocation may be inappropriate for exploratory programming environments such as Smalltalk.

Architect's trap

After the careful and clean design of the first Berkeley RISC projects, SOAR went

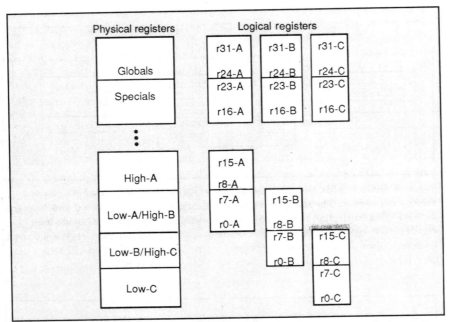

Figure 8. SOAR's register windows. Like RISC I, SOAR has many physical sets of registers that map to the logical registers seen by each subroutine. (Reprinted from "Architecture of SOAR: Smalltalk on a RISC," *11th An. Symp. Computer Architecture,* © IEEE.)

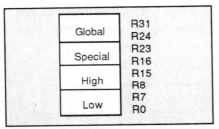

Figure 9. Logical view of the register file. The Highs hold incoming parameters and local variables. The Lows are for outgoing arguments. The Specials include the PSW and a register that always contains zero. The Globals are for system software such as trap handlers. (Reprinted from "Architecture of SOAR: Smalltalk on a RISC," *11th An. Symp. Computer Architecture,* © IEEE.)

on to try many architectural ideas. Although fully aware of the dangers, we fell into what we now call the "architect's trap" several times:

- Each idea was a clever idea;
- each idea made a particular operation much faster;
- each idea increased design and simulation time; and
- not one idea significantly improved overall performance!

Put another way, the primary impact of these clever ideas was to increase the difficulty of building SOAR and thus lengthen the development cycle.

One example is Load- and Store-multiple mentioned above. When the number of activations on the stack exceeds the on-chip register capacity, SOAR traps to a software routine that saves the contents of a set of registers in memory. Unlike RISC II, SOAR has load- and store-multiple instructions to speed register saving and restoring. These instructions can transfer eight registers in nine cycles (one instruction fetch and eight data accesses). Without them, the system would need eight individual instructions that would consume sixteen cycles (eight instruction fetches plus eight data accesses). In retrospect, these multicycle instructions added some complexity to the design, and the benefit of a three percent reduction of execution time is not worth the costs.

Another example comes from generation scavenging, which requires that a list be updated whenever a pointer to a new object is stored in an old object. While designing SOAR, we thought that stores would be frequent enough to warrant hardware support for this check. Thus, SOAR tags each pointer with its generation of the object that it points to. While computing the memory address, the store instruction compares the generation tag of the data being stored with the generation tag of the memory address. For 96 percent of the stores, list update is unnecessary and the store completes without trapping. Once again we rely on tags to confirm the normal case and trap in the unusual case. Surprisingly, tagged stores are so infrequent that hardware support saves only 1 percent of the total time. This feature does not seem worth the effort.

Alas, we have more than two examples of being caught in the architect's trap. We have put these observations to use by calculating the performance of some variations on SOAR and comparing them to some real systems (see Table 4). Our predictions of SOAR's performance are based on simulated macro-benchmark times and do not include virtual memory, operating system, and I/O overhead. However, all of the Smalltalk-80 systems we know about tend to be limited by the raw CPU speed rather than the overhead time for virtual memory, the operating system, and I/O. For a fair comparison, we assume a 400-ns cycle time for SOAR, RISC II, and MC68010.

By comparing the speeds of different systems, we can gain some insight into the reasons for SOAR's good performance.

- If we were to build a second-generation SOAR, we would implement Pendleton's reorganization of the pipeline, which would shorten SOAR's cycle time by 25 percent.[7] By combining it with the winning features from the previous table the system would run faster than SOAR, even though it lacks a half-dozen architectural innovations that SOAR has. While the overall measurements confirm that reduced instructions sets can run Smalltalk-80 efficiently, this calculation goes further; it suggests that SOAR is not RISCy enough.

- The software techniques developed for SOAR may eventually be used to construct fast, compiled Smalltalk-80 systems on general-purpose processors. The RISC II row of the table reflects the impact of removing the Smalltalk-specific architectural features of SOAR. The next row, RISC II without register windows, is representative of the commercial reduced-instruction-set microprocessors. These machines would run Smalltalk-80 twice as slow as SOAR. This may not be too high a price to pay for a simpler and more general off-the-shelf design.

Falling into architect's traps will delay your project, making it less attractive as other, competing, machines are announced. For example, the Deutsch-Schiffman Smalltalk system PS doubled performance when Motorola announced their 32-bit follow-on to the 68010, called the 68020. It includes a small on-board instruction cache, executes instructions in 180 ns, and uses about five times as many transistors as SOAR. Thus, delays in your project inevitably reduce the relative attractiveness of your machine, since it is unlikely that every other project will face the same delays.

T able 2 summarized the innovations used in SOAR to improve the performance of the exploratory programming environment Smalltalk-80. If we compare SOAR to the Motorola 68010, we have more than doubled performance while halving the number of transistors. Its features reduce the performance penalty for Smalltalk from a factor of 3.6 to a factor of 1.3, increasing the chances that programmers will use exploratory programming environments (see Table 5).

We recommend that anyone faced with the task of building a computer for an exploratory programming environment consider compilation to a reduced instruction set with register windows and one-bit tags. There are four places to look for further performance gains: compiler technology, implementation technology,[7] optimization of the run-time support primitives (which consume about two-thirds of SOAR's time), and better hardware or software algorithms to cache call-target lookups (which consume 23 percent of SOAR's time). Of these, implementation technology— circuit design and VLSI processing technology—have the most dramatic impact. Since we started this project, the standard VLSI technology available to universities has improved from four-micron line widths to three-micron. This one change could reduce our cycle time from 400 ns to 290 ns, as important a contribution as register windows.

We also warn all architects to watch their step. Be sure you evaluate your proposal in terms of benefits to the whole system and not just to one part, and remember that a software solution is better than a hardware solution in every facet except speed. The bait of the architect's trap is your own ingenuity, but the trap ensnares a whole project, not just the fool who springs it. Beware! □

Table 4. Trimming the fat from SOAR.

Assumes 400-ns cycle time for SOAR, RISC II, and 68010. Dorado and MC68010 figures are measurements. Same benchmarks as Table 1.

Configuration	Speed
Important architectural features + rearranged pipeline	103%
full SOAR	100%
Dorado	93%
important architectural features only	81%
Deutsch-Schiffman 68020	72%
RISC II	62%
RISC II without register windows	50%
full SOAR without software ideas	41%
Deutsch-Schiffman 68010	36%
full SOAR without hardware ideas	34%
Tek 68010 interpreter	24%
stripped SOAR	22%

Table 5. Cost of Smalltalk-80 features: the standard approach versus SOAR.

ST-80 Feature	Cost (% slower)	Optimization	Cost (% slower)
interpretation	100%	compiler	0%
dynamic messages	56%	in-line cache	23%
automatic storage	15%	generation scavenging	3%
object table	20%	direct pointers	0%
run-time data types	26%	tagged integers	0%
many subroutines	46%	register windows	0%
total cost of ST-80 (standard architecture)	3.6:1	(SOAR)	1.3:1

Acknowledgments

The SOAR project was sponsored by DARPA, and many students and faculty participated. We thank all of them for their hard work. We also wish to thank Walter Beach and Garth Gibson for making comments on an early draft of this article.

References

1. Adele J. Goldberg and David Robson, *Smalltalk-80: The Language and Its Implementation,* Addison-Wesley, Reading, MA, 1983.

2. Ted Kaehler and Dave Patterson, *A Taste of Smalltalk,* W. W. Norton and Company, New York, NY, 1986.

3. D. A. Patterson, "Reduced Instruction Set Computers," *Comm. ACM,* Vol. 28, No. 1, Jan. 1985, pp. 8-21. Special issue on computer architecture.

4. David Ungar et al., "Architecture of SOAR: Smalltalk on a RISC," *11th An. Int'l Symp. Computer Architecture,* Ann Arbor, MI, June 1984, pp. 188-197.

5. David M. Ungar, "The Design and Evaluation of a High Performance Smalltalk," C. S. tech. report no. UCB/CSD 86/287 (PhD dissertation), Computer Science Division (EECS), Univ. of California, Berkeley, CA, Mar. 1986. Also to be published by MIT Press as part of the ACM Doctoral Dissertation Award series.

6. J. M. Pendleton et al., "A 32b Microprocessor for Smalltalk," *IEEE J. Solid State Circuits,* Oct. 1986.

7. Joan Pendleton, "A Design Methodology for VLSI Processors," PhD dissertation, Dept. of EECS, Univ. of California, Berkeley, CA, Sept. 1985.

8. Ricki Blau, "Tags and Traps for the SOAR Architecture," *Smalltalk on a RISC: Architectural Investigation,* ed. David A. Patterson, Computer Science Div., Univ. of California, Berkeley, CA, Apr. 1983, pp. 24-41. Also *Proc. of CS292R.*

9. A. J. Thadhani, "Interactive User Productivity," *IBM Systems J.,* Vol. 20, No. 4, 1981, pp. 407-421.

10. K. McCall, "The Smalltalk-80 Benchmarks," *Smalltalk: Bits of History, Words of Advice,* ed. Glenn Krasner, Addison-Wesley, Reading, MA, 1983, pp. 151-173.

11. A. D. Samples, D. M. Ungar, and P. N. Hilfinger, "SOAR: Smalltalk Without Bytecodes,"

Proc. ACM Conf. Object-Oriented Programming Systems, Languages, and Applications, Portland, OR, Sept. 1986.

12. L. Peter Deutsch, *The Dorado Smalltalk-80 Implementation: Hardware Architecture's Impact on Software Architecture,* Addison-Wesley, Sept. 1983, pp. 113-126.

13. K. A. Pier, "A Retrospective on the Dorado, A High-Performance Personal Computer," *Proc. 10th An. Symp. Computer Architecture,* Stockholm, Sweden, June 1983, pp. 252-269.

14. Peter K. Lee, "The Design of a Debugger for SOAR," Master's thesis, Computer Science Div., Dept. of EECS, Univ. of California, Berkeley, CA, Sept. 1984.

15. L. Peter Deutsch and Allan M. Schiffman, "Efficient Implementation of the Smalltalk-80 System," *Proc. 11th An. ACM SIGACT-SIGPLAN Symp. Principles of Programming Languages,* Salt Lake City, Utah, Jan. 1984.

16. David Ungar, "Generation Scavenging: A Non-Disruptive High Performance Storage Reclamation Algorithm," *Proc. ACM SIGSOFT/SIGPLAN SE Symp. Practical Software Development Environments,* Pittsburgh, PA, Apr. 1984, pp. 157-167.

17. Patrick J. Caudill and Allen Wirfs-Brock, "A Third Generation Smalltalk-80 Implementation," *Proc. ACM Conf. Object-Oriented Programming Systems, Languages, and Applications,* Portland, OR, Sept. 1986.

David Ungar is an assistant professor in the Computer Systems Laboratory at Stanford University. His research focuses on implementation techniques and language issues relating to object-oriented exploratory programming environments and reduced-instruction-set multiprocessors.

Ungar received a PhD in computer science from the University of California, Berkeley in May 1986. Prior to his doctoral studies, he worked in the fields of operating systems and computer networks at Bell Laboratories, in New Jersey. He also holds an MS in electrical engineering and computer science, a BS in electrical engineering, and a BS in applied mathematics and computer science from Washington University, St. Louis.

David A. Patterson is a professor in the computer science division of the Department of Electrical Engineering and Computer Sciences at the University of California, Berkeley. He teaches computer architecture at the graduate and undergraduate levels, and in 1982 received the Distinguished Teaching Award from the Berkeley Division of the Academic Senate of the University of California.

Patterson received a PhD in computer science from the University of California, Los Angeles in 1976. His projects have included the design and implementation of RISC I, SOAR, and his current project, SPUR (Symbolic Processing Using RISCs. See *Computer,* Vol. 19, No. 11, Nov. 1986, pp. 8-22). SPUR investigates extending RISCs for Lisp, floating-point arithmetic, and multiprocessing. His research interests involve combining popular software, experimental architecture, and VLSI circuits to create more efficient computer systems.

Readers may write to Patterson at the Computer Science Div., 573 Evans Hall, UC Berkeley, Berkeley, CA 94720.

DESIGNING AN EFFICIENT LANGUAGE

BY CHARLES B. DUFF

*A language designer discusses the inefficiencies
of Smalltalk and suggests ways to improve upon them*

ALTHOUGH SMALLTALK is the mother of modern object-oriented languages, and is certainly the best-known, its use in the microcomputer world has been limited, primarily because of its size, relative inefficiency, and fairly long learning curve for new programmers. These problems are partially the result of a philosophy that emphasizes theoretical consistency and universal application of a few principles. By modifying this design philosophy somewhat, it is possible to develop a new language that combines the benefits of an object-oriented language and the efficiency of a popular production language such as C or Pascal.

Over the past two years, my company, The Whitewater Group, has been at work on a new language called Actor, which is targeted for artificial intelligence work on microcomputers. Our goal was to make use of the consistent object-oriented philosophy of Smalltalk but to incorporate some architectural changes that might enhance efficiency, ease of use, and accessibility for the average programmer. In this article I will discuss some

of the design details of Smalltalk and point out how we attempted to improve upon them.

The issues under discussion include garbage collection, late versus early binding, and models for the interpreter. I'll also look at the relative advantages of a token-threaded interpreter over Smalltalk's byte-code interpreter in creating a language that supports early binding and other optimizations.

GARBAGE COLLECTION

Smalltalk, like other sophisticated languages such as LISP and Prolog, includes a garbage-collection facility that automatically reclaims data structures that have been created by the programmer but are no longer needed. This is a tremendous advantage in a large, complex application because you never have to worry about memory management (unless, of course, memory becomes exhausted in spite of garbage collection).

The Smalltalk-80 specification includes a reference-counting garbage collector but does not mandate this approach. A reference-counting sys-

tem keeps track of the number of pointers to each object in the system. When the pointer count drops to 0, the object is deleted.

Unoptimized reference-counting collectors can consume up to 70 percent of total execution time because of the constant maintenance of reference counts. The University of California at Berkeley has published a number of clever optimizations that minimize the reference-counting overhead in Smalltalk. Nevertheless, reference counting has a serious chronic effect on the efficiency of the language. Anyone who attempts to create a more efficient object-oriented language would do well to consider alternate architectures for garbage collection.

THE BAKER COLLECTOR

Henry Baker at MIT developed a method of garbage collection for LISP

Charles B. Duff (The Whitewater Group, 906 University Place, Evanston, IL 60201) is a systems programmer whose last product was the language Neon for the Macintosh. His new language, Actor, should be available for the IBM PC in October.

that involves splitting memory into two spaces. As an application executes, objects that are known to be "alive" (i.e., accessible to the program) are copied from one space to a new one. Eventually all active objects are copied to the new space. The copying process is then reversed, copying back into the original space and writing over the "dead" objects.

The principal advantage of this approach is that the collection process can be performed incrementally as the program executes, allowing even real-time applications to make use of garbage collection. Also, compaction occurs naturally as a result of the copying. The efficiency of Baker's method, however, is dependent on how many objects remain alive as opposed to how many die. Highly volatile objects such as contexts (see below) may well come and go before they are copied, thereby requiring no maintenance overhead. The difficulty comes in when a large number of objects with long lifetimes are created,

resulting in much copying activity. Each application has a unique profile with respect to object lifetimes.

The best solution for this problem seems to be a variation of Baker's approach suggested by Henry Lieberman and Carl Hewitt of MIT and first applied to Smalltalk by a team at DEC. In this approach, objects that have been around for a long time are migrated to an area that is rarely checked for dead objects, thus minimizing useless copying of permanent objects and directing the energies of the collector where it can be most effective. In our design of Actor's garbage collector, we employed an approach similar to this.

CONTEXTS

Any stack-based language must have a run-time facility to create activation records for each procedure that is executed (see figure 1). This is an area at the top of the stack that contains current values of variables and parameters to be used by the procedure. As

long as a simple stack allocation discipline is used, these structures do not require any sophisticated memory management; they come and go with procedure calls and returns.

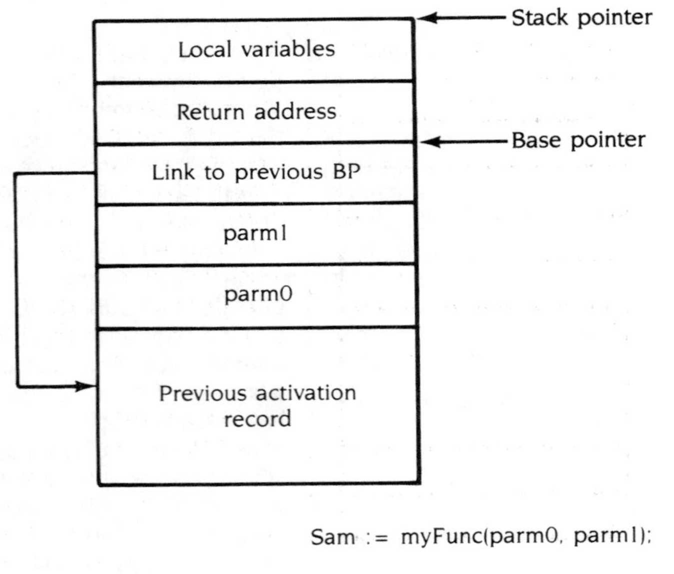

In Smalltalk, the activation record is called a context and is actually an object (see figure 2). Every time a method begins execution, a new context object must be created. The context actually combines a traditional activation record with a local work stack for use during the method's execution. Space for the stack is allocated from the context's indexed instance variables. Thus, each invocation of a method has its own private stack.

Even after a method finishes executing, its context can persist and be sent messages as a full-fledged object. A debugger can exploit this fact to reconstruct the state of a method that had a problem. On the downside, however, objects are much more expensive to allocate than stack space. Since a context is created with each method activation, it is no surprise that the Smalltalk garbage collector spends much of its time managing context objects alone. One study indicated that method contexts are responsible for 97 out of every 100 words of object space allocated.

Since the performance consequences of straying from a stack-based allocation discipline seemed too severe in relation to the benefits, we decided not to implement method contexts as objects in Actor. We did, however, implement block contexts as objects, because these contexts are used less frequently and do not conform to stack-based allocation strategies. These contexts are created only when a block is passed to another method, or function, for repetitive execution. (In this article, we will use the terms method and function interchangeably.)

As a consequence of our decision, however, the process of constructing a debugger is less elegant, requiring us to make use of assembly language primitives to access the stack. Alternatively, we could use Actor to construct an emulator that would treat contexts as objects for the sake of

Figure 1: A typical activation record in a compiled language. When a function (myFunc) is executed, the parameters passed to it by the calling routine are placed on the stack, along with the return address. The function then allocates space for its local variables. The base pointer serves as a fixed location from which to index both the passed parameters and the local variables. Below is the activation record for the function that called myFunc.

debugging. We have yet to find that step necessary, however.

EARLY AND LATE BINDING

When you call a function in a typical high-level language such as C, the compiler and linker actually generate a subroutine call to a physical address. This is very efficient, but you must be careful to associate functions with the appropriate data structures. For example, if you were to pass an array to a function that was designed to work on strings, trouble would surely result. The problem would most likely be caught at compile time by the type-checking facility of the compiler. Of course, in an untyped language such as FORTH, the problem wouldn't be caught at all until the program started behaving strangely.

Smalltalk relieves the programmer of this burden by automatically calling the appropriate method for a given data structure. The programmer uses generic names for operations, and Smalltalk uses the class of the receiving object to look up the method having the correct name. Since the lookup occurs at run time, however, it carries a rather severe efficiency penalty with respect to the previous technique.

We decided to implement a facility that combines the merits of each approach. We designed our compiler to automatically associate, or bind, a generic operation name with a physical function in the manner of Smalltalk. But, unlike Smalltalk, the programmer can choose on a case-by-case basis whether this occurs at run time (late binding) or at compile time (early binding).

ADVANTAGES OF LATE BINDING

Late binding has some notable advantages. Since all references are symbolic, a method can be recompiled without having to recompile all of its callers. More important, the same symbolic name can be used for a similar operation in several different types of objects. This is possible in Smalltalk because each object's class has, as one of its private variables, a dictionary associating names with methods. When a message is sent, the interpreter determines the class of the receiver and finds this dictionary, which it then uses to look up the method for the symbol sent.

The fact that a single message can invoke any of several methods is known as polymorphic behavior and is probably the most powerful feature of object-oriented programming. It allows code to be written that is insensitive to the type of object receiving the message. Of course, if the object doesn't happen to have a method for the name sent, an error will occur at run time. This can be disturbing to a programmer who is accustomed to such problems being resolved at compile time. But for certain types of problems, late binding greatly simplifies the code. A lot of control structure, such as if and case statements, simply vanishes, because the logic is incorporated into the distinction between classes.

Unfortunately, late binding is not very efficient. Even the best algorithms for searching the dictionary are several times slower than simply executing the method without a search. Much research, however, has been done in Smalltalk with respect to method caching, which greatly speeds message-sends. Caching uses a hash table to store the most recently used methods, avoiding the more time-consuming dictionary lookup. Caching and other optimizations have greatly improved late-binding performance, but the performance penalty remains severe.

EARLY BINDING

A sensible compromise can be made with respect to late binding. It is possible to forego the consistency of uniform polymorphic behavior in return for a good deal more efficiency. In a previous language I wrote for the Macintosh called Neon, which had object-oriented facilities and a FORTH-like syntax, I allowed the programmer to select early or late binding in each message. This has proven to be a workable and efficient solu-

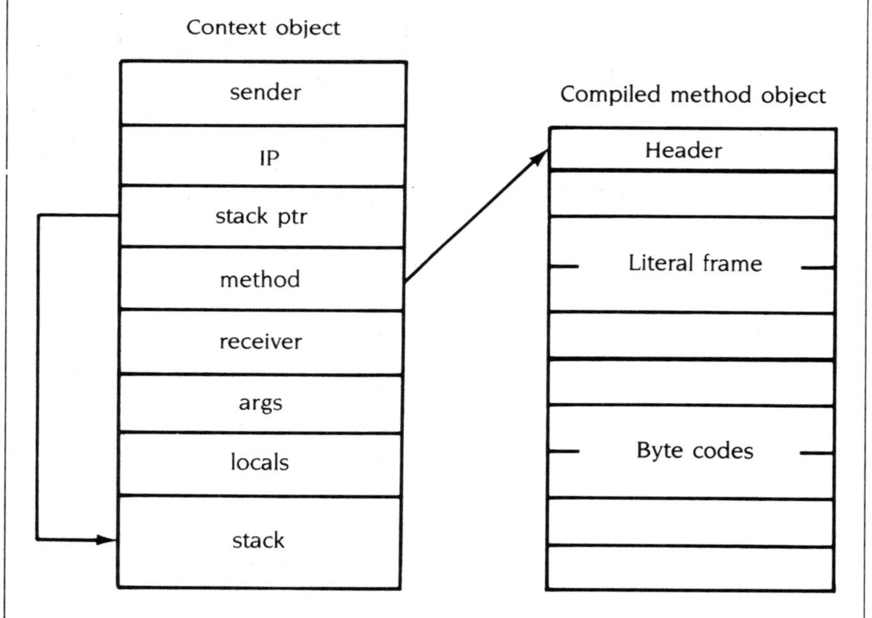

Figure 2: An activation record in Smalltalk. Instead of allocating activation records on a single continuous stack, in Smalltalk each method activation causes the creation of a method context, which is actually an object. Each method activation has its own private stack, which includes space for the instance variables designated by the Context class of objects. This arrangement, with its consequent garbage collection, is much less efficient than simple stack allocation.

tion. Neon makes no attempt, however, to ensure that the class of the receiver is appropriate at run time for the method being called. In general, the philosophy in Neon was to provide minimal protection at run time, which allows maximum efficiency. Most FORTH systems have taken this approach, but it is an unsuitable environment for complex AI work.

Even in Smalltalk, polymorphism is really used in only about 15 percent of the code. The rest of the system makes implicit assumptions about an object's class and could just as well be early-bound. Other researchers have speculated on various ways in which this fact could be exploited for more efficiency.

Our goal was to provide selective early binding with protection against class mismatches at run time. For instance, if at compile time we bound a call to a method in class Rectangle, and, at run time, an Array was actually the receiver, serious consequences could result. Either every method has to check that its arguments are of the proper class at run time, or the compiler has to ensure integrity at compile time. Run-time checking is a burden that would eat up much of the efficiency gained in early binding. And since compilation can usually be done in relatively small chunks in an object-oriented system, compilation efficiency isn't of much concern.

We decided to develop a scheme whereby the programmer can, at compile time, selectively bind "types" (classes) to variables and to the values returned by functions. This scheme is similar to type declaration in Pascal and allows the compiler to ensure the integrity of an early-bound method call at run time. We also decided to equip the compiler with a sort of miniature expert system that allows it to selectively early-bind method calls. In cases where the early binding criteria fail, it defaults to late binding.

For example, in listing 1 we have a number of list-handling method definitions, as they might be written in Actor for a class called ListCell. (Note, however, that the actual function names are different in Actor; I have used the equivalent LISP function names here to make the code more familiar to LISP programmers.)

We specified all Actor function (method) definitions to consist of the word Def followed by the name of the new function, followed by a list of formal parameters enclosed in parentheses. The first parameter is always self, because that is where the receiver appears in the method call.

The body of the function is delimited by curly braces (which are optional in the case of a single statement). A caret causes the function to return the value of the next statement.

You will notice that in the list of arguments for the append function, the formal parameters, self and arg, are followed by :ListCell. As in Pascal, this assigns a type to the formal parameters. In Actor, types are actually classes, so the definition says that at run time the formal parameter must be of class ListCell.

Listing 1: *Examples of function definitions as they might be written in Actor, illustrating how early binding may be specified. In the function* append, *the variables* self *and* arg, *along with the result of the function, have been "typed" as instances of class* ListCell.

```
/* this version of append assigns types (classes) to its
arguments.  carVal and cdrVal are the two private
variables in class ListCell.  Typing permits the compiler
to generate much more efficient code for messages
involving typed parameters.  */

Def append(self:ListCell, arg:ListCell):ListCell
{   ^cons(carVal, append(cdrVal, arg))
}

/* cons is an example of ACTOR's optimization of private
variable references.  The form cell.cdrVal is a very
efficient way of referring to the cdrVal private variable
in the local variable, cell.  If the programmer were to
assign a type to cell, an even more efficient machine
language primitive would be compiled.  */

Def cons(self, arg | cell)
{   cell := new(ListCell);
    cell.cdrVal := arg;
    cell.carVal := self;
    ^cell
}

/* The do function performs a post-order traversal of a
list by executing a passed-in block at each leaf (non-
list) node.  */

Def do(self, aBlock)
{   if  isAtom(carVal)
    then   eval(aBlock, carVal);
    else  do(carVal, aBlock);
    endif;
    if  cdrVal
    then   do(cdrVal, aBlock);
    endif
}
```

Listing 2: *Another definition for* append. *In this case neither the parameters nor the return value of the function are typed, and as a result, all messages will be late-bound.*

```
Def append(self, arg)
{   ^cons(carVal, append(cdrVal, arg))
}
```

We designed the compiler to enforce this by requiring that any early-bound call to append (i.e., a message to a typed variable) must pass a ListCell as its argument. If append is invoked as the result of a late-bound message, a type-checking routine will ensure the class integrity of its parameters. This check is performed only if a function with typed parameters is invoked in a late-bound message-send.

We can control the early binding of messages to self by typing the self formal parameter. It is usually desirable to leave self untyped, however, to allow redefinition of a function in a subclass. If typed, the message to self will be bound at compile time.

Listing 2 shows an alternative version of append whose parameters are untyped and that does not use early binding.

USING EARLY BINDING
We designed the typing facility to be most effective when used during program optimization. During initial development, the programmer can leave all variables and functions unbound. This makes the code easier to change

and debug and minimizes dependencies between the various parts of the application. After the code is debugged and has become fairly stable, the programmer can then isolate areas that are heavily executed and begin optimizing them. Variables and functions can be bound in the time-critical methods, allowing the compiler to generate more efficient early-bound references. To attempt even better performance, high-level functions might be converted to primitive functions, until performance is acceptable. The latter step is not possible in standard Smalltalk-80, which allows the user to write only high-level methods.

INTERPRETER MODELS
Smalltalk works by compiling the source code for methods into an intermediate language. This language consists of a set of basic operations, such as fetching and storing variables, fetching literal objects, sending messages, and manipulating the stack. Theoretically, users could write in this language, but then they would be working directly with the stack in the manner of FORTH and would be with-

out the protection and sophisticated features provided by the compiler.

The job of the interpreter is to scan the intermediate code and execute machine code to make the language perform. This situation is entirely analogous to a microprocessor scanning machine instructions and executing microcode. In fact, the interpreter has a register, called the interpretive pointer (IP), that is the equivalent of the instruction pointer register in a microprocessor.

THE BYTE CODE INTERPRETER
Smalltalk's intermediate language consists of byte codes—that is, a series of bytes, each of which encodes an elementary operation in the Smalltalk "virtual machine." A compiled method consists of two data areas. First there is the "literal frame," an area in which the method stores any objects that are referred to as literals in the method. (Literals are objects created without a name, such as "A string", 12000, or #aSymbol.) This is followed by the byte code area, in which the compiler places the compiled code for the method. Several byte codes are dedicated to accessing the objects in the literal frame.

Let's examine what a small piece of compiled Smalltalk code would look like. Suppose that, in the middle of a method, the compiler sees the phrase

myFile : = File new name: "users.txt"

In this phrase, myFile is the name of the zeroth local variable allocated by this method in its private stack. What gets compiled is a series of 5 byte codes and 3 words of literal data, for a total of 11 bytes, excluding the header (figure 3).

The first byte code fetches the contents of literal location 2 (the string "users.txt") and places it on the stack. This will later serve as the parameter for the name: method. The next method fetches the contents of an Association object that identifies the class File in the main dictionary, Smalltalk. This is the receiver for the new method, sent by the next byte code (several byte codes are dedicated to sending common messages like new or at:).

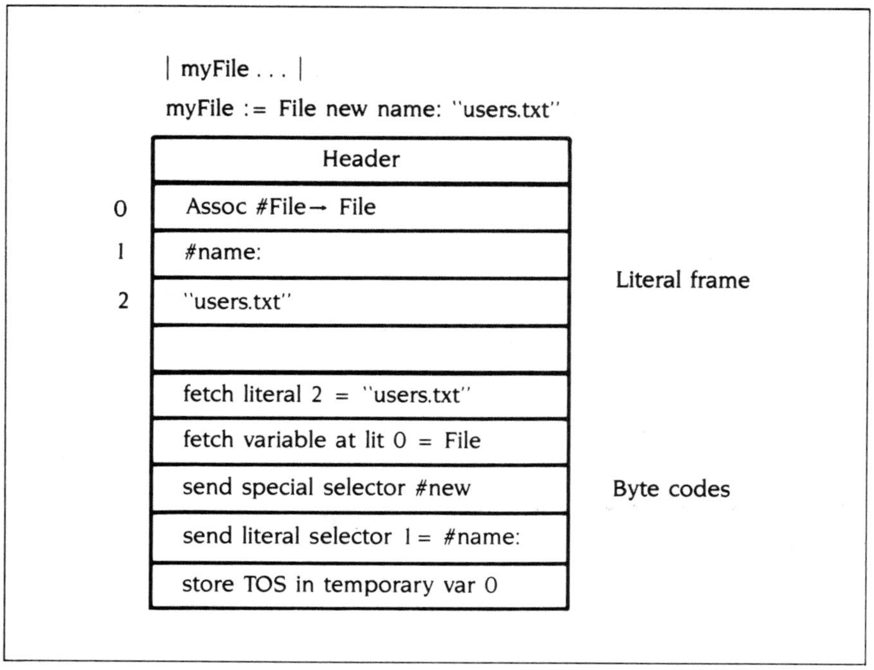

Figure 3: A sample of compiled code in Smalltalk. The compiled method consists of two data areas: the literal frame (for literal data) and a series of byte codes (1-byte instructions).

The next byte code sends the #name: selector that is stored in the literal frame at location 1. This is how any send not involving the "special" (frequently used) selectors is compiled. Finally, the result of the name: message is stored in myFile, which is temporary variable 0.

Several things are noteworthy about this arrangement. First, the literal frame is required, because only byte codes can be executed by the interpreter. Anything not a byte code (e.g., the string "users.txt") has to be stored in the literal frame and fetched by one of the access byte codes, which introduces a certain amount of overhead. Second, because the byte codes are only 1 byte in length, only 256 operations are available to the interpreter. Third, because the size of the literal frame can vary for each method, the interpreter has to calculate the address of the start of the byte code area whenever a method is executed.

THREADED INTERPRETERS
In our design of Actor, a principal goal was an efficient implementation of early binding. This led us away from the byte code interpreter to a threaded model. Early-bound function calls and literal references can be more efficiently implemented with a threaded interpreter.

There are several varieties of threaded interpreter. All models share the "threaded" aspect, which connotes building a procedure by stringing together a list of virtual or physical addresses of other procedures. At execution time, the interpreter scans through the list, picking up each thread in turn and executing it.

In a threaded environment, every object in the system, whether code or data, is assigned a "thread value." Generally, the result of executing a data object is simply the placement of its address on the stack. This works very well in an object-oriented system—a literal object simply stacks its address, which can be used as a parameter in a message.

In Smalltalk, the set of byte codes is closed and cannot be extended. In a threaded system, however, every code routine, whether primitive or

high-level, is assigned a thread value. Any high-level routine or primitive can be called (early-bound) by compiling its thread value in-line. There is a certain elegance in referring to system primitives and user routines through the same mechanism.

Another benefit that threading provides is the ability to add primitives to the system easily. In Smalltalk, a special mechanism is used for dispatching primitives, and there is no provision for users to add their own. But in FORTH users can recode certain time-critical words in machine code. Because this can be done so easily, it is an effective and powerful technique for improving performance.

TOKEN THREADING
Using physical addresses as thread values is difficult, however, in a garbage-collected system. We need to be able to move objects around very easily without having to update a lot of references to the obsolete addresses. This is the rationale for the object table in Smalltalk. An object is referred to via its object pointer (OP), which is an index into the object table. That location contains the physical address of the object and is the only place that requires updating if the object is moved.

This architecture is very reminiscent of what is called a token-threaded system in the world of threaded languages. A token table fills the same role as the object table in Smalltalk. However, in Smalltalk the object table is discrete from the byte code interpreter. For instance, you could not compile an object pointer in-line in a Smalltalk method and expect the code to execute properly. Object pointers are passive, serving only as a means of finding an object's data address. Tokens, on the other hand, are associated with executable machine code, regardless of whether they point to data or a routine.

In our design of Actor, we integrated the concepts of object table and token table, along with the byte code and primitive dispatch tables from Smalltalk (see figure 4). Every type of object, primitive, or high-level routine has an entry in the object table and

is active in the sense that its object pointer can be executed. Each object also belongs to a family that describes its behavior when interpreted. The family code is embedded within the object table entry and is used to dispatch a machine language routine in the interpreter.

This architecture makes it very easy to accomplish early binding. To bind a function call at compile time, its object pointer is simply compiled in-line. A function is then an object whose family behavior is to execute itself. When the interpreter hits the function OP, it executes code that causes the old IP to be stacked and the IP is set to the beginning of the function's data area, which may contain a series of threads to other functions and objects. By contrast, a late-bound send is compiled as the OP of a machine language primitive followed by the OP of a symbol.

Because of this difference in design, a piece of compiled code in Actor would look much different from an equivalent piece of Smalltalk code. The Actor code would lack the literal frame. This means that all functions have their code starting at the same offset. It also simplifies the construction of the interpreter and the compiler.

If early binding is used, the compiled Actor code fragment should actually be shorter than the equivalent Smalltalk code, even though each "operation" code is 2 bytes long instead of 1! The threaded model also allows more extensive optimization on the part of the compiler and allows for easy extension should the current set of primitives prove incomplete.

SYNTAX
Another aspect of efficiency relates not to the performance of a particular application, but to the time required to train a programmer how to write that application. Smalltalk's syntax can be initially confusing to the casual reader. It is sometimes difficult to sort out the relationships between identifiers in a moderately complex phrase, since the infix notation fails to make the precedence explicit.

In our design of Actor, we decided

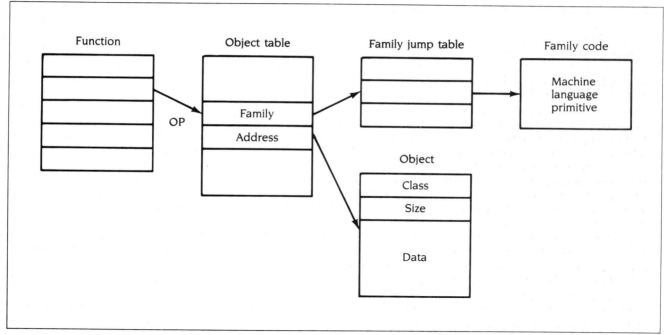

Figure 4: *An example of token threading as implemented by Actor. Here a function consists of a list of object pointers (OPs), which are offsets into the object table. The interpreter scans through the OPs and executes the code relating to the "family" for each OP. If the OP is in the Primitive family, its respective data consists of machine code, which is executed directly. If the OP is in the Function family, the current instruction pointer is placed on a stack and the interpreter begins executing the OPs within that function. For most objects, the family code simply places the OP on the stack so it can be passed as a parameter or used as a receiver of a message.*

to use a conventional, Pascal-like syntax as a means of reducing the learning load on new programmers. There is enough to absorb in learning the object-oriented paradigm itself, along with the hundreds of classes and their methods, without having to learn a completely new syntax.

CONCLUSION

There are several areas in which the basically successful model of object-oriented programming developed in Smalltalk could be made more suitable for personal computing environments. In our design of a new lan-

guage called Actor, we have implemented some of these.

Our goal was to design a threaded interpreter with an intelligent compiler that could support user primitives and optimize message passing by using early binding. We also designed an incremental garbage collector with sensitivity to object lifetimes that eliminates the long pauses and general inefficiency of other garbage-collection techniques. Finally, a syntactical model that is closer to Pascal reduces the learning load for new programmers.

There seems to be a critical mass

of interest developing in object-oriented programming. It is my belief that more efficient and accessible implementations of object-oriented languages will promote their much wider use in solving sophisticated personal computing problems.

Editor's note: Actor is scheduled to be available from the Whitewater Group (906 University Place, Evanston, IL 60201) for the IBM PC, XT, and AT in October. It will include the Microsoft Windows environment and provide interactive access to Windows system routines. It will also include a set of classes designed to support list processing and predicate logic for AI applications. ■

Chapter 4: Concepts and Issues in Object-Oriented Programming

Various concepts and isues related to object-oriented computing are gathered in this chapter. The particular ideas considered are those of

- comparing various kinds of abstraction methods;
- documentation of object-oriented programs;
- access-oriented programming, a paradigm related to object-oriented programming;
- object-oriented data base design;
- how best to learn about object-oriented computing;
- using prototypical objects rather than inheritance for implementing shared behavior in object-oriented systems.

Many other ideas are considered in the papers referenced at the end of this introduction.

The paper by Mary Shaw, "Abstraction Techniques in Modern Programming Languages," is an exploration of the kinds of abstraction mechanisms that have been and are being used in programming languages. Going to abstractions is one of the ways to attempt to solve the problem of software cost. The main problem is that of managing the intellectual complexity of computer programs. An abstraction is a simplified description of a system that emphasizes some of the system's details while suppressing others. Shaw considers early abstraction techniques, extensible languages, structured programming, program verification, and abstract data types.

The original abstraction techniques of structured programming were procedures or macros; these have evolved to abstract types and generic definitions.

An *abstract data type* is a data structure and some associated operations. Generally, current languages support abstract data types by providing an encapsulation mechanism that allows the name of the type and means to access its operations to be visible to users. But the details of the implementation of the data structure and the operations are hidden from users.

Also considered are *generic definitions* in which one abstraction is allowed to take another abstraction as a parameter. This allows the writing of one set of routines that can be shared by many data types. For example, there may be a *set* data type in which the type of element is included as a parameter. Then an insert routine could be written that would work for all different kinds of sets. This idea is similar to, but weaker than, the inheritance mechanism of Smalltalk.

The extent to which these abstractions are present in Pascal and Ada is considered by using a simple example.

The paper says little about objects per se, but the issues addressed are pertinent to object-oriented computing because the object abstraction is closely related to abstract data types and generic definitions.

The paper by David L. Parnas, Paul C. Clements, and David M. Weiss, "The Modular Structure of Complex Systems," is the only one available concerned with documentation of object-oriented programs. Parnas et al. use the term *module* to refer to an encapsulation of data and procedures (i.e., a module is an object). They found that in order to meet their goals of modular structure, hundreds of modules would be necessary in an airplane's flight software. Furthermore, with so many modules, it became impossible to find the extent of a change using inspection alone. It was found that some special kind of documentation would be needed to assist in understanding the module structure. The Module Guide was created to fill this need. It is organized around the secrets that are associated with each module. For example, hardware-hiding modules are those that might be changed if there is a change in the hardware. Portions of the paper are devoted to an extract from the Module Guide.

The paper by Mark Stefik, Daniel Bobrow, and Kenneth Kahn, "Integrating Access-Oriented Programming into a Multiparadigm Environment," describes *access-oriented programming*, a programming paradigm closely related to object-oriented programming. In fact, access-oriented programming is dual to object-oriented programming in the sense that in object-oriented programming, when an object receives a message, it may change its data; however, in access-oriented programming, when an object changes its data, it may send a message. For example, suppose part of an object's data is the shape and location of its representation on the monitor. It could be useful, if whenever this data changed, a message was sent that would cause the representation to be redrawn according to the current information. This idea can be used to create *gauges* to monitor the value of variables. The gauge is a screen representation of the variable's value, and it is updated whenever the value changes.

In Loops, access-oriented programming is implemented by attaching *active values* to variables in a way that is similar to the manner in which property lists are attached to atoms in Lisp. The active values cause methods to be automatically invoked whenever the variable is accessed from anywhere in the program.

Access-oriented programming is similar to the concept of procedural attachment that is available in certain AI programming languages. It appears to be a very useful complement to object-oriented programming.

A concept that has recently emerged and is gaining momentum is that of object-oriented databases. An object-oriented database is one in which behavioral knowledge is present along with the structure of the data. The value of this approach is similar to the virtue of object-oriented computing: A data model that contains behaviors can more closely correspond to the real-world entity it is representing.

Robert W. Peterson, in "Object-Oriented Data Base Design," presents a review of current work pertaining to object-oriented data bases. He concludes that object-oriented data base technology will in the near future take a position of importance similar to that of relational data base models.

The next paper, "Panel: The Learnability of Object-Oriented Programming Systems," presents the ideas of Tim O'Shea, Kent Beck, Dan Halbert, and Kurt Schmucker concerning how best to learn object-oriented programming. The following concensus is evident.

- The basic syntax and semantics of object-oriented systems is easy to learn.
- To be effective in object-oriented programming, one must learn the features of the reusable constructs that are available in the system library. With approximately 250 classes available in Smalltalk systems, this can be a large task.
- It is difficult to learn to be effective in creating object-oriented designs.

In the final paper, "Using Prototypical Objects to Implement Shared Behavior in Object-Oriented Systems," Henry Lieberman describes an alternative to subclassing for implementing shared behavior in object-oriented systems. In Smalltalk and most other object-oriented systems, sharing is implemented by having each class inherit the behavior of its superclass. However, sharing could be implemented in an alternative way by using prototypes. Each new object is allowed to specify a prototypical object which the new object is like. Differences from the prototype are coded in the new object. Messages for which the new object has no method are *delegated* to the prototype. In this type of system, there is no need for classes.

Lieberman shows that delegation is more powerful than inheritance in that given delegation, one can implement the functionality of inheritance, but not the other way around. He argues that various processes are easier to implement with delegation than with inheritance, for example, dribble-streams. He also argues that delegation is more flexible than inheritance for combining behavior from multiple sources.

Delegation is available in Hewitt's actor languages and in certain Lisp-based systems. On the basis of the information in this paper, delegation should be strongly considered as an alternative to inheritance by the designers of new object-oriented languages.

Additional References

Object-Oriented Databases

K. Dittrich and U. Dayal, editors, *Proceedings, 1986 International Workshop on Object-Oriented Database Systems*, IEEE Computer Society Press, Washington, D.C., 1986.

J. Diederich and J. Milton, "Oddessy: An Object-Oriented Database Design System," *Proceedings, Third International Conference on Data Engineering*, IEEE Computer Society Press, Washington, D.C., February 1987, pages 235-244.

D. Maier, J. Stein, A. Otis, and A. Purdy, "Development of an Object-Oriented DBMS," *OOPSLA '86, SIGPLAN Notices*, ACM, Inc., New York, New York, Volume 21, Number 11, November 1986, pages 472-482.

A.H. Skarra and S.B. Zdonik, "The Management of Changing Types in an Object-Oriented Database," *OOPSLA '86, SIGPLAN Notices*, ACM, Inc., New York, New York, Volume 21, Number 11, November 1986, pages 483-495.

A. Borgida, "Exceptions in Object-Oriented Languages," *Object-Oriented Programming Workshop, SIGPLAN Notices*, ACM, Inc., New York, New York, Volume 21, Number 10, October 1986, pages 107-119.

S.B. Zdonik, "Maintaining Consistency in a Database with Changing Types," *Object-Oriented Programming Workshop, SIGPLAN Notices*, ACM, Inc., New York, New York, Volume 21, Number 10, October 1986, pages 120-127.

Prototypical Objects

W.R. LaLonde, D.A. Thomas and J.R. Pugh, "An Exemplar Based Smalltalk," *OOPSLA '86, SIGPLAN Notices*, ACM, Inc., New York, New York, Volume 21, Number 11, November 1986, pages 322-330.

Inheritance

B. Meyer, "Genericity versus Inheritance," *OOPSLA '86, SIGPLAN Notices*, ACM, Inc., New York, New York, Volume 21, Number 11, November 1986, pages 391-405.

Compares the notion of generics as in Ada with inheritance as in Smalltalk.

A. Snyder, "Encapsulation and Inheritance in Object-Oriented Programming Languages," *OOPSLA '86, SIGPLAN Notices*, ACM, Inc., New York, New York, Volume 21, Number 11, November 1986, pages 38-45.

V. Nguyen and B. Hailpern, "A Generalized Object Model," *Object-Oriented Programming Workshop, SIGPLAN Notices*, ACM, Inc., New York, New York, Volume 21, Number 10, October 1986, pages 78-87.

Presents a model of objects that allows multi-dimensional inheritance.

J. Hendler, "Enhancement for Multiple-Inheritance," *Object-Oriented Programming Workshop, SIGPLAN Notices*, ACM, Inc., New York, New York, Volume 21, Number 10, October 1986, pages 98-106.

Parallel or Distributed Computing in an Object-Oriented Environment

A. Black, N. Hutchinson, E. Jul, and H. Levy, "Object Structure in the Emerald System," *OOPSLA '86, SIGPLAN Notices*, ACM, Inc., New York, New York, Volume 21, Number 11, November 1986, pages 78-86.

D.B. Anderson, "Experience with Flamingo: A Distributed, Object-Oriented User Interface System," *OOPSLA '86, SIGPLAN Notices*, ACM, Inc., New York, New York, Volume 21, Number 11, November 1986, pages 177-185.

G. Bruno and A. Balsamo, "Petri Net-Based Object-Oriented Modelling of Distributed Systems," *OOPSLA '86, SIGPLAN Notices*, ACM, Inc., New York, New York, Volume 21, Number 11, November 1986, pages 284-293.

D. Decouchant, "Design of a Distributed Object Manager for the Smalltalk-80 System," *OOPSLA '86, SIGPLAN Notices*, ACM, Inc., New York, New York, Volume 21, Number 11, November 1986, pages 444-452.

D. Wiebe, "A Distributed Repository for Immutable Persistent Objects," *OOPSLA '86, SIGPLAN Notices*, ACM, Inc., New York, New York, Volume 21, Number 11, November 1986, pages 453-465.

C.A.R. Hoare, "Monitors: An Operating System Concept," *Communications of the ACM*, Volume 17, Number 10, October 1974, pages 549-557.

The term *monitor* refers to an object used in parallel programming. Various examples of the use of monitors in programming operating system resources are presented in this paper.

A. Yonezawa, J.-P. Briot and E. Shibayama, "Object-Oriented Concurrent Programming in ABCL/1," *OOPSLA '86, SIGPLAN Notices*, ACM, Inc., New York, New York, Volume 21, Number 11, November 1986, pages 258-268.

Other Concepts:

J. Steensgaard-Madsen, "A Statement-Oriented Approach to Data Abstraction," *ACM Transactions on Programming Languages and Systems*, Volume 3, Number 1, January 1981, pages 1-10.

Introduces a way to obtain an object-orientation in language design via the use of statements, rather than types. A class of objects is defined in such a language similar to the way procedures are defined in conventional languages. In particular, parameters are allowed in the class definition. Objects can then be defined by giving values to parameters in the class definition.

P.J.L. Wallis, "External Representations of Objects of User-Defined Type," *ACM Transactions on Programming Languages and Systems*, Volume 2, Number 2, April 1980, pages 137-152.

The issue of providing I/O representations for types within the type definition is considered in this article.

S. Mittal, D.G. Bobrow, and K.M. Kahn, "Virtual Copies: At the Boundary Between Classes and Instances," *OOPSLA '86, SIGPLAN Notices*, ACM, Inc., New York, New York, Volume 21, Number 11, November 1986, pages 159-166.

D.H.H. Ingalls, "A Simple Technique for Handling Multiple Polymorphism," *OOPSLA '86, SIGPLAN Notices*, ACM, Inc., New York, New York, Volume 21, Number 11, November 1986, pages 347-349.

S.N. Khoshafian and G.P. Copeland, "Object Identity," *OOPSLA '86, SIGPLAN Notices*, ACM, Inc., New York, New York, Volume 21, Number 11, November 1986, pages 406-416.

D. McAllester and R. Zabih, "Boolean Classes," *OOPSLA '86, SIGPLAN Notices*, ACM, Inc., New York, New York, Volume 21, Number 11, November 1986, pages 417-423.

D. Sandberg, "An Alternative to Subclassing," *OOPSLA '86, SIGPLAN Notices*, ACM, Inc., New York, New York, Volume 21, Number 11, November 1986, pages 424-428.

R. Strom, "A Comparison of the Object-Oriented and Process Paradigms," *Object-Oriented Programming Workshop, SIGPLAN Notices*, ACM, Inc., New York, New York, Volume 21, Number 10, October 1986, pages 88-97.

O.L. Madsen, "Block Structure and Object Oriented Languages," *Object-Oriented Programming Workshop, SIGPLAN Notices*, ACM, Inc., New York, New York, Volume 21, Number 10, October 1986, pages 133-142.

H.L. Ossher, "A Mechanism for Specifying the Structure of Large, Layered, Object-Oriented Programs," *Object-Oriented Programming Workshop, SIGPLAN Notices*, ACM,

Inc., New York, New York, Volume 21, Number 10, October 1986, pages 143-152.

Describes a mechanism called a *grid* for representing the macro structure of large programs.

J.A. Goguen and J. Meseguer, "Extensions and Foundations of Object-Oriented Programming," *Object-Oriented Programming Workshop*, *SIGPLAN Notices*, ACM, Inc., New York, New York, Volume 21, Number 10, October 1986, pages 153-162.

Attempts to provide an algebraic foundation for object-oriented programming and to unify object-oriented programming with functional programming. The authors propose, among other things, using subsorts from order-sorted algebra for multiple inheritance and an operational semantics based on term-rewriting.

Abstraction Techniques in Modern Programming Languages

Mary Shaw

Carnegie Mellon University

Reprinted from *IEEE Software*, October 1984, pages 10-26. Copyright ©
1984 by The Institute of Electrical and Electronics Engineers, Inc.

Abstraction Techniques in Modern Programming Languages

Mary Shaw, Carnegie-Mellon University

Modern programming languages depend on abstraction: they manage complexity by emphasizing what is significant to the user and suppressing what is not.

The major issues of modern software engineering arise from the costs of software development, use, and maintenance—which are too high—and the quality of the systems—which is too low. These problems are particularly severe for today's large complex programs with long useful lifetimes. This article traces important programming language ideas back to their roots in the problems and languages of the 1970's, and it shows how modern programming languages respond to the complexity of contemporary software development. Modern programming's key concept for controlling complexity is abstraction—that is, selective emphasis on detail.

The effects of abstraction techniques and associated specification and verification issues run through the history of attempts to solve the problems of high cost and low quality. The best new developments in programming languages support and exploit abstraction techniques. These techniques emphasize engineering concerns, including design, specification, correctness, and reliability.

We begin by reviewing the ideas about program development and analysis that have heavily influenced the development of current programming language techniques. Many of these ideas are currently interesting as well as historically important. We then survey the ideas from recent research projects that are influencing modern software practice. The changes in program organization that have been stimulated by these ideas are illustrated by developing a small example in three different languages—Fortran, Pascal, and Ada. Finally, we assess the status and the potential of current abstraction techniques.

Conceptual and historical review

Controlling software development and maintenance has always involved managing the intellectual complexity of programs and systems of programs. Not only must the systems be created, they must be tested, maintained, and extended. As a result, many different people must understand and modify the systems at various times during their lifetimes. Abstraction provides a good way to manage complexity and guarantee continuity.

An abstraction is a simplified description, or specification, of a system that emphasizes some of the system's details or properties while suppressing others. A good abstraction is one that emphasizes details that are significant to the reader or user and suppresses details that are, at least for the moment, immaterial or diversionary.

"Abstraction" in programming systems corresponds closely to "analytic modeling" in many other fields. Construction of a model usually starts with observations, followed closely by formation of hypotheses about principles or axioms that explain the observations. These axioms are used to derive or construct a model of the observed

This article is an update and revision of "The Impact of Abstraction Concerns on Modern Programming Languages," which appeared in *Proceedings of the IEEE*, Vol. 68, No. 9, Sept. 1980, pp. 1119-1130.

system. The parameters or variables of the model may be derived from the axioms or they may be estimated from observation. The model is then used to make new predictions. The final step is to perform experiments in controlled or well-understood environments to determine the accuracy and robustness of the model and of the axioms. This cycle of hypothesizing and validating models is then continued with additional observations.

In software development, the requirements or intended functionality of a system play the role of the observations to be explained. The abstraction process is then very similar to the general modeling paradigm: deciding which characteristics of the system are important, what parameters should be included, which descriptive formalism to use, how the model can be validated, and so on. As in many other fields, we often define hierarchies of models in which lower level models provide more detailed explanations for the phenomena that appear in higher level models. Also, in computer science, as in other fields, the model is sufficiently different from the system it describes to require explicit validation. We refer to the abstract description provided by a model as its specification and to the next lower level model in the hierarchy as its implementation. The process of determining that the specification is consistent with the implementation is called verification. The abstractions we use for software tend to emphasize the functional properties of the software—what is computed rather than how the computation is carried out.

Abstraction techniques have evolved in step not only with our understanding of programming issues, but also with our ability to use the abstractions as formal specifications of the systems they describe. In the 1960's, for example, the important developments in methodology and languages centered on functions and procedures, which summarized a program segment in terms of a name and a parameter list. At that time, we only knew how to perform syntactic validity checks, and specification techniques reflected this:

"specification" meant little more than "procedure header" until late in the decade. By the late 1970's, developments centered on the design of data structures; specification techniques drew on quite sophisticated techniques of mathematical logic; and programming language semantics were well enough understood to permit formal verification that a program was consistent with its specification.

Early techniques. Prior to the late 1960's, the dominant programming-language issues were syntax, translation techniques, and solutions to specific implementation problems. Thus, we saw many articles on specific problems, such as parsing, storage allocation, and data representation. Procedures were well understood, and libraries of procedures were set up, but they were only partly sucessful because often the documentation (informal specification) was inadequate, or because the parameterization of the procedures did not support the cases of interest. Basic data strutures such as stacks and linked lists were just beginning to be understood, but they were sufficiently unfamiliar that it was difficult to separate the concepts from the particular implementations. Perhaps it was too early in the history of the field for generalization and synthesis to take place, but, in any event, abstraction played only a minor role.

The earliest application of abstraction to the design of programming languages may have been the symbolic assemblers of the 1950's. Instead of writing programs directly in octal codes, mnemonic names were used to stand for numeric operation codes, and the binding of variable names to specific machine locations was delegated to the assemblers.

Beginning in the late 1960's, abstraction was treated consciously as a program organization technique. Earlier languages supported built-in data types, including at least integers, real numbers, and arrays, and sometimes Booleans, high-precision reals, etc. Data structures were first treated systematically in 1968,[1] and the notion that a programmer might define data

types tailored to a particular problem first appeared in 1967. The notion that programming is an activity that should be studied and subjected to some sort of discipline dates to the NATO Software Engineering Conferences of 1968[2] and 1969.[3]

Extensible languages. The late 1960's also saw efforts to abstract from the built-in notations of programming languages in such a way that any programmer could add new notation and new data types to a base language. The objectives of this extensible language work included allowing individual programmers to extend the syntax of the programming language, to define new data structures, to add new operators (including infix operators as well as ordinary functions) for both old and new data structures, and to add new control structures to the base language.

This work on extensibility[4] died out, in part because it underestimated the difficulty of defining interesting extensions. It was difficult to keep independent extensions compatible when all of them modified the syntax of the base language, to organize definitions so that related information was grouped in common locations, and to find techniques for describing an extension accurately (other than by exhibiting the code for the extension). However, extensible languages influenced the abstract data types and generic definitions of the 1970's—abstract data types that extended the semantics, rather than the syntax of a language, and generic definitions that provided some of the operator definition facilities that extensible languages were trying to provide.

Structured programming. By the early 1970's, a methodology emerged for constructing programs by progressing from a statement of the objective through successively more precise intermediate stages to final code. Called "stepwise refinement" or "top-down programming," this methodology involved beginning program development with a version that was free to assume the existence of any

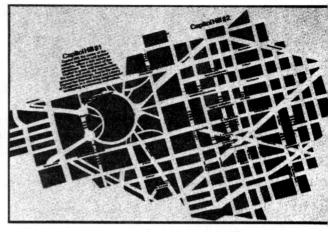

Abstraction in mapmaking

Simplification of reality is essential to good mapmaking. Like the programmer, the mapmaker must abstract available information, selectively emphasizing and suppressing detail. Picking the "right" information— features as well as scale—is a major part of his art. The effect of his intentions become especially apparent in viewing different maps of the same area—in this case, Washington, DC.

One of the earliest maps of Washington, produced in the 1790's, is the handkerchief map (p. 10) of Maj. Pierre Charles L'Enfant's plan for the city. The same area, treated in a different manner, can be seen in the four maps on these pages. The two maps on p. 12 show the considerable variation in road/street maps. One emphasizes the highway system; the other, one of a set of visitor maps by the American Institute of Architects, reduces the Capitol Hill area to a schematic block pattern. The aviation chart (p. 13, left) locates radio beacons and

---

data structures and operations that could be directly applied to the problem at hand, even if those structures and operations were quite sophisticated and difficult to implement. Thus the initial program was presumably small, clear, directly problem-related, and "obviously" correct. Although the assumed structures and operations might be specified only informally, the programmer's intuitions about them made it possible to concentrate on the overall organization of the program and defer concerns about the implementations of the assumed structures and operators. When each of the latter definitions was addressed, the same technique was applied again, and the implementations of the high-level operations were substituted for the corresponding invocations. The result was a new, more detailed program that was convincingly like the previous one, but that depended on fewer concepts or on simpler definitions. Since the translation to simpler terms eliminated problem-specific knowledge in favor of more universal operators, the new program was more nearly compilable than its predecessor. Successive steps of the program development added details more relevant to the programming language than to the problem domain until the program was completely expressed using the operations and

data types of the base language, for which a translator or interpreter was available.

This separation of concerns between the structures that were used to solve a problem and the way those structures were implemented aided in decomposing complex problems into smaller, fairly independent segments. The key to the success of the methodology was the degree of abstraction imposed by selecting high-level data structures and operations. The chief limitation of the methodology, which was not appreciated until it had been in use for some time, was that the final program did not preserve the series of abstractions through which it was created, and so the task of modifying the program after it was completed was not necessarily simpler than it would be for a program developed in any other way. Another limitation of the methodology was that informal descriptions of operations did not convey precise information. Misunderstandings about exactly what an operation was supposed to do could complicate the program development process, and informal descriptions of procedures might not have been adequate to assure true independence of modules. The development of techniques for formal program specification helped alleviate this set of problems.

At about the same time as stepwise refinement was emerging, we also began to be concerned about how people understood programs and how programs could be organized to make them easier to understand, and hence to modify. For programs written in general-purpose programming languages, this understanding was based primarily on the program state, that is, on the current values of all the variables in the program at some instant. It was of primary importance to be able to determine what assumptions about the program state were being made at any point in the program. Further, arbitrary transfers of control, especially those that spanned large amounts of program text, interfered with this goal. The control flow patterns that lent themselves to understandable programs were the ones that had a single entry point (at the beginning of the text) and, at least conceptually, a single exit point (at the end of the text). Examples of statements that satisfied this rule were the **if. . .then. . .else** form of conditional and the **for** and **while** loops. The chief violator of the rule was the **go to** statement.

The first discussion of how to make programs easier to understand appeared in 1968, and we converged on a common set of "ideal" control constructs a few years later. Although we

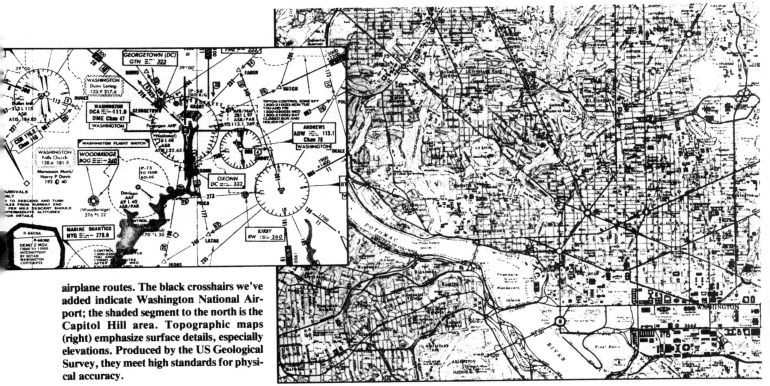

airplane routes. The black crosshairs we've added indicate Washington National Airport; the shaded segment to the north is the Capitol Hill area. Topographic maps (right) emphasize surface details, especially elevations. Produced by the US Geological Survey, they meet high standards for physical accuracy.

still have not achieved a true consensus on this set of constructs, we no longer regard the question as a major issue.

Program verification. In parallel with the development of "ideal" control constructs—in fact, as part of the motivation—computer scientists became interested in finding ways to make precise, mathematically manipulatable statements about what a program computes. The ability to make such statements was essential to the development of techniques for reasoning about programs, particularly for techniques that relied on abstract specifications of effects. New techniques were required because program text alone failed to provide adequate information for reasoning precisely about programs. Procedure headers, even accompanied by prose commentary, were imprecise. This imprecision leads to ambiguities about responsibilities for the computation and to inadequate separation between modules.

The notion that it was possible to make formal statements about the program state, and to reason rigorously about the effect on the program state of executing a statement, first appeared in the late 1960's. The formal statements were expressed as formulas in the predicate calculus, such as

$$y > x \wedge (x > 0 \supset z = x^2)$$

A programming language was described by a set of rules that defined the effect each statement had on the logical formula that described the program state. The rules for the language were applied to the program assertions to obtain theorems whose proofs assured that the program matched the specification. By the early 1970's, the basic concepts of verifying assertions about simple programs and describing the language in such a way that this was possible were well understood. Manual application of verification techniques tended to be error-prone, and formal specifications, as much as informal ones, were susceptible to errors of omission. Verification required converting a program annotated with logical assertions into logical theorems with the property that the program is correct if and only if the theorems were true. This conversion process, called verification condition generation, is now well understood, and programs have been developed to perform these steps automatically. Programs are also being developed to prove the resulting theorems, but considerable work remains to be done on this problem.

When the emphasis in programming methodology shifted to using data structures as a basis for program or-

ganization, corresponding specification and verification problems arose. Initially, the question was what information it was useful to specify. Subsequently, attention focused on making those specifications more formal and dealing with the verification problems. From this basis, work on verification for abstract data types proceeded as we describe below.

Abstract data types. In the 1970's we recognized the importance of organizing programs into modules in such a way that knowledge about implementation details was localized as much as possible. This led to language support for data types, for specifications that are organized using the same structure as data, and for generic definitions. The language facilities were based on the **class** construct of Simula, on ideas about strategies for defining modules, and on concerns over the impact of locality on program organization. The corresponding specification techniques included strong typing and verification of assertions about functional correctness.

Later in the 1970's, most research activity in abstraction techniques focused on the language and specification issues raised by these considerations; much of the work is identified with the concept of abstract data types. Like structured programming, the methodology of abstract data types emphasized locality of related collections of information. In this case, data was emphasized rather than control, and the strategy was to package each data structure and its associated operations in a single module. The resulting module contained the information necessary to treat the data structure and its operations as a type. The objective was to treat such modules in the same way as ordinary types such as integers and reals were treated; this required support for declarations, infix operators, specification of routine parameters, and so on. The result, the abstract data type, effectively extended the set of types available to a program: it explained the properties of a new group of variables by specifying the values one of these variables might have, and it explained the operations that would be permitted on the new variables by giving the effects these operations had on the values of the variables.

In a data type abstraction, we need separate specification and implementation.

In a data type abstraction, we now recognize the need for separate specification and implementation. First, we specify the functional properties of a data structure and its operations, then we implement them in terms of existing language constructs (and other data types) and show that the specification is accurate. When we subsequently use the abstraction, we deal with the new type solely in terms of its specification. This philosophy was developed in several recent language research and development projects, including Ada, Alphard, CLU, Concurrent Pascal, Euclid, Gypsy, Mesa, and Modula.

The specification techniques we use for abstract data types evolved from the predicates in simple sequential programs. Additional expressive power was incorporated to deal with the way information is packaged into modules and with the problem of abstracting from an implementation to a data type. One class of specification techniques draws on the similarity between a data type and the mathematical structure called an algebra. Another class of techniques explicitly models a newly defined type by defining its properties in terms of the properties of common, well-understood types.

In conjunction with the work on abstract data types and formal specifications, the generic definitions that originated in extensible languages have been developed to a level of expressiveness and precision far beyond the anticipation of their originators. These definitions, discussed in detail below, are parameterized not only in terms of variables that can be manipulated during program execution, but also in terms of data types. They can now describe restrictions on which types are acceptable parameters in considerable detail. [5]

Interactions. As this review has shown, programming languages and methodologies evolve in response to the perceived needs of software designers and implementors. However, these needs themselves evolve in response to experience gained with past solutions. The original abstraction techniques of structured programming and stepwise refinement were procedures or macros; these techniques have evolved to abstract types and generic definitions. (Although procedures were originally viewed as devices to save code space, they soon came to be regarded, like macros, as abstraction tools.) Methodologies for program development emerge when we find common useful patterns and try to use them as models. Languages evolve to support these methodologies when the models become so common and stable that they are regarded as standard. As abstraction techniques have become capable of addressing a wider range of program organizations, formal specification techniques have become more precise and have played a more important role in the programming process.

For an abstraction to be used effectively, its specification must express all the information needed by the programmer who uses it. Initial attempts at specification used the notation of the programming language to express things that could be checked by the compiler: the name of a routine and the number and types of its parameters. Other facts, such as what the routine computed and under what conditions it should be used, were expressed informally. [6] We have now progressed to the point that we can write precise descriptions of many important relations among routines, including their assumptions about the values of their inputs and the effects they have on the program state.

The history of programming languages shows a balance between language ideas and formal techniques; in each methodology, language constructs support the programming techniques we understand well, and the properties we specify are matched to our current ability to validate (verify) the consistency of a specification and its implementation. We can rely on formal specifications only to the extent that we are certain that they match their implementations. Thus, the development of abstraction techniques, specification techniques, and methods of verifying the consistency of a specification and an implementation must surely proceed hand in hand. In the future, we should expect to see more diversity in the programs that are used as a basis for modularization. We should also expect to see specifications that are concerned with aspects of programs other than the purely functional properties we now consider.

Abstraction facilities in modern programming languages

With this historical background, we now turn to the abstraction methodologies and specification techniques that are currently under development in the programming language research community. Some of the ideas are well enough worked out to be ready for transfer to practical languages, but others are still under development.

Although the ideas behind modern abstraction techniques can be explored independently of programming languages, the instantiation of these ideas in actual languages is also important. Programming languages are our primary notational vehicle for expressing a class of very complex ideas. The concepts we must deal with include not only the functional relations of mathematics, but also constructs that deal with relations over time, such as sequentiality and synchronization. Language designs influence the ways we think about algorithms by making some program structures easier to describe than others. In addition, programming languages are used for communication among people as well as for controlling machines. This role is particularly important in long-lived programs, because a program is in many ways the most practical medium for expressing the structure imposed by the designer—and for maintaining the accuracy of this documentation over time. Thus, even though most programming languages technically have the same expressive power, differences among languages can significantly affect their practical utility.

New ideas. Current activity in programming languages is driven by three global concerns: simplicity of design, the potential for applying precise analytic techniques to formal specifications, and the need to control costs over the entire lifetime of a long-lived program.

Simplicity of design. Simplicity has emerged as a major criterion for evaluating programming language designs. We see a certain tension between the need for "just the right construct" for a task and the need for a language small enough to understand thoroughly. This is an example of a trade-off between specialization and generality: if highly specialized constructs are provided, individual programs will be smaller, but at the expense of complexity (and feature-by feature interactions) in the system as a whole. The current trend is to provide a relatively small base language that provides ways to define special facilities in a regular way.[7]

Software development techniques

The software development methods of the early 1970's concentrated on program organization and on disciplines for programmers. As time has passed, it has become clear that software support for the programming process itself is important.

General issues of software development, including both management and implementation issues, are discussed in Brook's very readable book.[1] The philosophy of structured programming and the principles of data organization that underlie the representation issues of abstract data types have received careful technical treatment.[2-4] The proceedings of the Conference on Specifications of Reliable Software contain papers on both prose descriptions of requirements and mathematical specification of abstractions.[5]

Step-wise refinement is a method of constructing programs by progressing from a statement of the objective through successively more precise intermediate stages to final code.[3,6] Structured programming is a discipline for writing programs using control constructs that lead to easily understandable code. The first discussion of this question appeared in 1968.[7] We converged on a common set of "ideal" control constructs a few years later.[3,8] This set of control constructs has the property that each unit of control has unique entry and exit points; as a result, it's relatively easy to discover what assumptions about the program state are being made at any point. A similar argument about locality of data access[9] helped to focus the role of scope rules in constructing understandable programs.

Software environments for program development are beyond the scope of this article, but the state of the work in early 1984 is captured in the proceedings of the ACM Symposium on Practical Software Environments[10] and a recent *IEEE Software* article on the Cedar environment.[11]

References

1. F. P. Brooks, Jr., *The Mythical Man-Month: Essays on Software Engineering,* Addison-Wesley, Reading, Massachusetts, 1975.

2. O. -J. Dahl and C. A. R. Hoare, "Hierarchical Program Structures," *Structured Programming,* Academic Press, 1972, pp. 175-220.

3. E. W. Dijkstra, "Notes on Structured Programming," *Structured Programming,* Academic Press, 1972, pp. 1-82.

4. C. A. R. Hoare, "Notes on Data Structuring," *Structured Programming,* Academic Press, 1972, pp. 83-174.

5. *IEEE Proc. Conf. Spec. Reliable Software,* 1979.

6. N. Wirth, "Program Development by Stepwise Refinement," *Comm. ACM,* Vol. 14, No. 4, Apr. 1971.

7. E. W. Dijkstra, "Goto Statement Considered Harmful," *Comm. ACM,* Vol. 11, No. 3, Mar. 1968.

8. C. A. R. Hoare and N. Wirth, "An Axiomatic Definition of the Programming Language Pascal," *Acta Informatica,* Vol. 2, No. 4, 1973.

9. W. A. Wulf and M. Shaw, "Global Variables Considered Harmful," *ACM SIGPLAN Notices,* Vol. 8, Feb. 1973.

10. *Proc. ACM SIGSOFT/SIGPLAN Software Eng. Symp. Prac. Software Development Environments,* 1984.

11. Warren Teitelman, "A Tour Through Cedar," *IEEE Software,* Vol. 1, No. 2, Apr. 1984, pp. 44-73.

An emphasis on simplicity underlies a number of design criteria that are now commonly used. When programs are organized to localize information, for example, assumptions shared among program parts and module interfaces can be significantly simplified. The introduction of support for abstract data types allows programmers to design special-purpose structures and deal with them in a simple way; it does so by providing a definition facility that allows the extensions to be made in a regular, predictable fashion. The regularity introduced by using these facilities can substantially reduce maintenance problems by making it easier for a programmer who is unfamiliar with the code to understand the assumptions about the program state—that are made at a given point in the program—thereby increasing the odds that he or she can avoid introducing new errors with each change.

Formal and quantitative techniques. Our understanding of the principles underlying programming languages has improved to the point that formal and quantitative techniques are both feasible and useful. We discuss later current methods for specifying properties of abstract data types and for verifying that those specifications are consistent with the implementation. It is perhaps not surprising that there seems to be a strong correlation between the ease of writing proof rules for language constructs and the ease with which programmers can use those constructs correctly and understand programs that use them.

Lifetime costs. In the 1970's we began to appreciate that the cost of software includes the costs over the lifetime of the program, and not just the costs of initial development or of execution. For large, long-lived programs, the costs of enhancement and maintenance usually dominate design, development, and execution costs, often by large factors. These cost considerations raise two issues. [8] First, to modify a program successfully, a programmer must be able to determine what other portions of the program depend on the section about to be modified. This is simplified if the information is localized and if the design structure is retained in the structure of the program. Off-line design notes or other documents are not an adequate substitute except in the unlikely case that they are meticulously and correctly updated. Second, large programs rarely exist in only one version. On the contrary, they exist in sequential versions as improvements are added from time to time, and they may also exist in simultaneous versions for different machines or machine con-

Formal specification

One of the major themes of this article is that formal analytic methods are integral to good methodology. Formal specification techniques for software and their associated verification techniques form an important segment of the new analytic methods.

The basic verification techniques depend on making formal assertions about the computation performed by the program. Under certain circumstances it is possible to verify that these assertions are true. London surveys these ideas. [1] Manna [2] and Wulf [3] also offer introductions to the methods.

By the early 1970's the basic concepts of verifying assertions about simple programs and describing a language in such a way that this is possible were under control. [4,5] When manually applied, verification techniques tend to be error-prone, and formal specifications, like informal ones, are susceptible to errors of omission. [6] In response to this problem, systems for automatically performing the verification steps have been developed. [7]

As abstract data types emerged, so did specification and verification issues. The initial efforts addressed the question of what information is useful in a specification. [8] Subsequent attention concentrated on mak-

References

1. R. L. London, "A View of Program Verification," *Proc. IEEE Int'l Conf. Reliable Software*, Apr. 1975, pp. 534-545.

2. Z. Manna, *Mathematical Theory of Computation*, McGraw-Hill, 1974.

3. W. A. Wulf et al, *Fundamental Structures of Computer Science*, Addison-Wesley, 1981.

4. C. A. R. Hoare and N. Wirth, "An Axiomatic Definition of the Programming Language Pascal," *Acta Informatica*, Vol. 2, No. 4, 1973.

5. R. L. London et al., "Proof Rules for the Programming Language Euclid," *Acta Informatica*, Vol. 10, No. 1, 1978, pp. 1-26.

6. S. L. Gerhart and L. Yelowitz, "Observations of Fallibility in Applications of Modern Programming Methodologies," *IEEE Trans. Software Eng.*, Vol. SE-2, No. 5, Sept. 1976.

7. S. L. Gerhart and D. S. Wile, "Preliminary Report on the Delta Experiment: Specification and Verification of a Multiple-User File Updating Module," *Proc. IEEE Conf. Spec. Reliable Software*, 1979, pp. 198-211.

8. D. L. Parnas, "A Technique for Software Module Specification with Examples," *Comm. ACM*, Vol. 15, May 1972.

9. C. A. R. Hoare, "Proof of Correctness of Data Representations," *Acta Informatica*, Vol. 1, No. 4, 1972.

10. J. V. Guttag, E. Horowitz and D. R. Musser, "Abstract Data Types and Software Validation," *Comm. ACM*, Vol. 21, No. 12, Dec. 1978.

11. B. H. Liskov and S. N. Zilles, "Specification Techniques for Data Abstractions," *IEEE Trans. Software Eng.*, Vol. SE-1, Mar. 1975.

12. J. H. Morris, "Types Are Not Sets," *Proc. ACM Symp. Prin. Prog. Lang.*, 1973, pp. 120-124.

figurations. When many versions and many programmers are involved, the major issues are problems of management, not of programming. Nevertheless, software tools can significantly ease the problems, and tools for managing the interactions among many versions of a program are included in modern integrated programming environments.

Language support. As we have discussed, the major thrust of programming language research activity in the 1970's was to explore the issues related to abstract data types. The methodological concerns included the need for information hiding and locality of data access, a systematic view of data structures, a program organization strategy exemplified by the Simula **class** construct, and the notion of generic definition. The formal roots included a proposal for abstracting properties from an implementation and a debate on the philosophy of types, which finally led to the view that types share the formal characteristics of abstract algebras.

ing those specifications more formal and dealing with the verification problems.[9] A debate on the nature of types led to the view that types share the formal characteristics of abstract algebras.[10-12] Another class of techniques explicitly models a newly defined type by defining its properties in terms of the properties of common, well-understood types.[13] More recently, a specification method that draws on both viewpoints has emerged.[14] Strategies for designing data types[15] and for using specifications in the design process[16] were also explored.

A certain amount of work on formal specification and verification of properties other than computational functionality has already been done. Most of it is directed at specific properties rather than at techniques that can be applied to a variety of properties; the results are, nevertheless, interesting. The need to address a variety of requirements in practical real-time systems was vividly demonstrated at the Conference on Specifications of Reliable Software,[17] most notably by Heninger.[18] Other work includes specifications of security properties,[19,20] reliability,[21] performance,[22,23] and communication protocols.[24] The problem of showing that a specification matches an informal requirement has also been considered.[25]

Structured programming involves progressive development of a program by adding detail to its control structure. Programming with abstract data types, however, involves partitioning the program in advance into modules that correspond to the major data structures of the final system. The two methodologies are complementary, because the techniques of structured programming may be used within type definition modules, and conversely.

In most languages that provide the facility, the definition of an abstract data type consists of a program unit that includes the following information.

- *Visible outside the type definition:* the name of the type and the names and routine headers of all operations (procedures and functions) that are permitted to use the representation of the type; some languages also include formal specifications of the values that variables of this type may assume, and of the properties of the operations.

- *Not visible outside the type definition:* the representation of the type in terms of built-in data types or other defined types, the bodies of the visible routines, and hidden routines that may be called only from within the module.

An example of the externally visible portion of a module that defines an abstract data type appears in Figure 5 on page 23.

The general topic of abstract data types has been addressed in a number of research projects. These include Alphard, CLU, Gypsy, Russell, Con-

13. W. A. Wulf, R. L. London and M. Shaw, "An Introduction to the Construction and Verification of Alphard Programs," *IEEE Trans. Software Eng.*, Vol. SE-2, No. 4, Dec. 1976.

14. J. V. Guttag and J. J. Horning, "An Introduction to the Larch Shared Language," *Proc. IFIP Cong.*, Paris, 1983.

15. J. V. Guttag, "Notes on Type Abstraction (Version 2)," *IEEE Trans. Software Eng.*, Vol. SE-6, No. 1, Jan. 1980, pp. 13-23.

16. J. V. Guttag and J. J. Horning, "Formal Specification As a Design Tool," *Proc. ACM Symp. Prin. Prog. Lang.*, Jan. 1980, pp. 251-261.

17. *Proc. Conf. Spec. Reliable Software*, 1979.

18. K. L. Heninger, "Specifying Software Requirements for Complex Systems: New Techniques and Their Applications," *Proc. IEEE Conf. Spec. Reliable Software*, 1979, pp. 1-14.

19. J. K. Millen, "Security Kernel Validation in Practice," *Comm. ACM*, Vol. 19, No. 5, May 1976.

20. B. J. Walker, R. A. Kemmerer and G. J. Popek, "Specification and Verification of the UCLA Security Kernel," *Comm. ACM*, Vol. 23, No. 2, Feb. 1980.

21. J. H. Wensley et al., "SIFT: Design and Analysis of a Fault-tolerant Computer for Aircraft Control," *Proc. IEEE*, Vol. 66, No. 10, Oct. 1978, pp. 1240-1255.

22. L. H. Ramshaw, *Formalizing the Analysis of Algorithms*, PhD dissertation, Stanford University, 1979.

23. M. Shaw, "A Formal System for Specifying and Verifying Program Performance," technical report CMU-CS-79-129, Carnegie-Mellon University, June 1979.

24. D. I. Good, "Constructing Verified and Reliable Communications Processing Systems," *ACM Software Eng. Notes*, Vol. 2, No. 5, Oct. 1977.

25. A. M. Davis and T. G. Rauscher, "Formal Techniques and Automatic Processing to Ensure Correctness in Requirements Specifications," *Proc. IEEE Conf. Spec. Reliable Software*, 1979, pp. 15-35.

current Pascal, and Modula. Although they differ in detail, they share the goal of providing language support adequate to the task of abstracting from data structures to abstract data types and allowing those abstract definitions to hold the same status as built-in data types. Descriptions of the differences among these projects are best obtained by studying them in more detail than is appropriate here. As with many research projects, the impact they have is likely to take the form of influence on other languages rather than complete adoption. Indeed, the influence of several research projects on Ada and Euclid is apparent.

Programming with abstract data types requires support from the programming language, not simply managerial exhortations about program organization. Suitable language support requires solutions to a number of technical issues involving both design and implementation. These include

- *Naming.* Scope rules are needed to ensure the appropriate visibility of names. In addition, protection mechanisms[9,10] may be needed to guarantee that hidden information remains private. Further, programmers must be prevented from naming the same data in more than one way ("aliasing") if current verification technology is to be relied upon.

- *Type checking.* It is necessary to check actual parameters to routines, preferably during compilation, to be sure they will be acceptable to the routines. The problem is more complex than the type checking problem for conventional languages because new types may be added during the compilation process and the parameterization of types requires subtle decisions in the definition of a useful type checking rule.

- *Specification notation.* The formal specifications of an abstract data type should convey all information needed by the programmer. This is not yet possible, but current progress is described below. As for any specification formalism, it is also necessary to develop a method for verifying that a specification is consistent with its implementation.

- *Distributed properties.* In addition to providing operations that are called as routines or infix operators, abstract data types must often supply definitions to support type-specific interpretation of various constructs of the programming language. These constructs include storage allocation, loops that operate on the elements of a data structure without knowledge of the representation, and synchronization. Some of these have been explored, but many open questions remain.[7]

- *Separate compilation.* Abstract data types introduce two new problems to the process of separate compilation. First, type checking should be done across com-

Programming languages for abstract data types

The history of programming is marked by many programming language designs. Some have had major user communities, others have had limited use, and some have not been implemented. In addition, many of the fundamental insights into programming language design have appeared in papers that discussed individual language facilities rather than full programming languages.

The major thrust of programming language development in the 1970's was the abstract data type. This development produced languages to support programming methods based on language support for data types,[1] strategies for defining modules,[2] and concerns over the impact of locality on program organization.[3] The language facilities draw heavily on the **class** construct of Simula[4] and on the control structures of Pascal.[5] The programming language designs and implementations that explored abstract data types included Ada,[6,7] Alphard,[8] CLU,[9] Concurrent Pascal,[10] Euclid,[11] Gypsy,[12] Mesa,[13] Modula,[14] and Russell.[15]

References

1. C. A. R. Hoare, "Notes on Data Structuring," *Structured Programming*, Academic Press, 1972, pp. 83-174.

2. D. L. Parnas, "On the Criteria to be Used in Decomposing Systems into Modules," *Comm. ACM*, Vol. 15, No. 12, Dec. 1972.

3. W. A. Wulf and M. Shaw, "Global Variables Considered Harmful," *ACM SIGPLAN Notices*, Vol. 8, Feb. 1973.

4. O. J. Dahl and C.A.R. Hoare, "Hierarchical Program Structures," *Structured Programming*, Academic Press, 1972, pp. 175-220.

5. H. Ledgard, *American PASCAL Standard*, Springer-Verlag, New York, 1984.

6. US DoD, *Reference Manual for the Ada Programming Language*, Nov. 1980.

7. A. N. Habermann and D. E. Perry, *Ada for Experienced Programmers*, Addison-Wesley, 1983.

8. M. Shaw, *ALPHARD: Form and Content*, Springer-Verlag, New York, 1981.

9. B. Liskov et al., "Abstraction Mechanisms in CLU," *Comm. ACM*, Vol. 20, No. 8, Aug. 1977.

10. P. Brinch Hansen, "The Programming Language Concurrent Pascal," *IEEE Trans. Software Eng.*, Vol. SE-1, June 1975.

11. B. W. Lampson et al., "Report on the Programming Language Euclid," *ACM SIGPLAN Notices*, Vol. 12, No. 2, Feb. 1977.

12. A. L. Ambler et al., "Gypsy: A Language for Specification and Implementation of Verifiable Programs," *ACM SIGPLAN Notices*, Vol. 12, No. 3, Mar. 1977.

13. C. M. Geschke, J. H. Morris, Jr., and E. H. Satterthwaite, "Early Experience with Mesa," *Comm. ACM*, Vol. 20, No. 8, Aug. 1977.

14. N. Wirth, *Programming in MODULA-2*, Springer-Verlag, New York, 1983.

15. A. J. Demers and J. E. Donahue, "Data Types, Parameters and Type Checking," *Proc. ACM Symp. Prin. Prog. Lan.*, Jan. 1980, pp. 12-23.

pilation units as well as within units. Second, generic definitions offer significant potential for optimization (or for inefficient implementation).

Specification techniques for abstract data types are the topic of a number of current research projects. Proposed techniques include informal but precise and stylized English, models that relate the new type to previously defined types, algebraic axioms that specify new types independently of other types, and hybrids of these. Many problems remain. The emphasis to date has been on the specification of properties of the code; the correspondence of these specifications to informally understood requirements is also important. Further, the work to date has concentrated almost exclusively on the functional properties of the program without attending, for example, to its performance or reliability.

Not all the language developments include formal specifications as part of the code. For example, Alphard includes language constructs that associate a specification with the implementation of a module; Ada and Mesa expect interface definitions that contain at least enough information to support separate compilation. All of this language work, however, is based on the premise that the specification must include all information available to a user of the abstract data type. When it has been verified that the implementation performs in accordance with its public specification, the abstract specification may safely be used as the definitive source of information about how higher level programs may correctly use the module. In one sense we build up "bigger" definitions out of "smaller" ones; but because a specification alone suffices for understanding, the new definition is in another sense no bigger than the pre-existing components. It is this regimentation of detail that gives the technique its power.

Generic definitions. A particularly rich kind of abstract data type definition allows one abstraction to take another abstraction, for example, a data type, as a parameter. These generic definitions provide a dimension of modeling flexibility that conventionally parameterized definitions lack.

For example, consider the problem of defining data types for an application that uses three kinds of unordered sets: sets of integers, sets of reals, and sets of a user-defined type for points in three-dimensional space. One alternative would be to write a separate definition for each of these three types. However, that would involve a great deal of duplicated text, since both the specifications and the code will be very similar for all the definitions. In fact, the programs would probably differ only where specific references to the types of set elements are made, and the machine code would probably differ only where operations on set elements (such as the assignment used to store a new value into the data structure) are performed. The obvious drawbacks of this situation include duplicated code, redundant programming effort, and complicated maintenance (since bugs must be fixed and improvements must be made in all versions).

Another alternative would be to separate the properties of unordered sets from the properties of their elements. This is possible because the definition of the set types relies on very few specific properties of the elements —it probably assumes only that ordinary assignment and equality operations for the element type are defined. Under that assumption, it is possible to write a single definition, say

type *UnOrderedSet* (*T: type*) is . . . .

that can be used to declare sets with several different types of elements, as in

var
    Counters: UnOrderedSet (*integer*);
    Timers: UnOrderedSet (*integer*);
    Sizes: UnOrderedSet (*real*);
    Places: UnOrderedSet (*PtIn3Space*);

using a syntax appropriate to the language that supports the generic defini-

tion facility. The definition of *UnOrderedSet* would provide operations such as *Insert, TestMembership,* and so on; the declarations of the variables would instantiate versions of these operations for all relevant element types, and the compiler would determine which of the operations to use at any particular time by inspecting the parameters to the routines.

The flexibility provided by generic definitions is great enough to support a definition[5] that automatically converts any solution of one class of problems to a solution of the corresponding problem in a somewhat larger class. This generic definition is notable for the detail and precision with which the assumptions about the generic parameter can be specified.

Practical realizations

A number of programming languages provide some or all of the facilities required to support abstract data types. In addition to implementations of research projects, several language efforts have been directed primarily at providing practical implementations. These include Ada, Mesa, Pascal, and Simula. Of these, Pascal currently has the largest user community, and the objective of the Ada development has been to make available a language to support most of the modern ideas about programming. Because of the major roles they play in the programming language community, Pascal and Ada will be discussed in some detail.

The evolution of programming languages through the introduction of abstraction techniques will be illustrated with a small program. The program is presented in Fortran IV to illustrate the state of our understanding in the late 1960's. Revised versions of the program in Pascal and Ada show how abstraction techniques have evolved.

Small example program. Our example program produces the data needed to print an internal telephone list for a division of a small company. A database containing information about all employees, including their names, di-

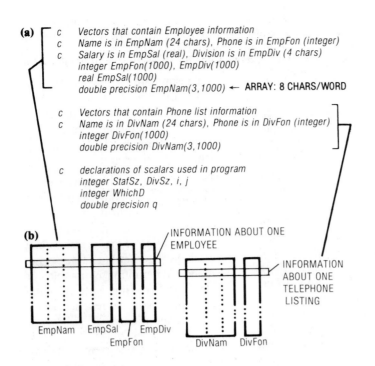

```
(a)   c   Vectors that contain Employee information
      c   Name is in EmpNam (24 chars), Phone is in EmpFon (integer)
      c   Salary is in EmpSal (real), Division is in EmpDiv (4 chars)
          integer EmpFon(1000), EmpDiv(1000)
          real EmpSal(1000)
          double precision EmpNam(3,1000)  ← ARRAY: 8 CHARS/WORD

      c   Vectors that contain Phone list information
      c   Name is in DivNam (24 chars), Phone is in DivFon (integer)
          integer DivFon(1000)
          double precision DivNam(3,1000)

      c   declarations of scalars used in program
          integer StafSz, DivSz, i, j
          integer WhichD
          double precision q
```

(b)

INFORMATION ABOUT ONE EMPLOYEE

INFORMATION ABOUT ONE TELEPHONE LISTING

EmpNam EmpSal EmpDiv
        EmpFon

DivNam DivFon

Figure 1 (above). Declarations for Fortran version of telephone list program.

Figure 2 (right). Code for Fortran version of telephone list program.

```
      c   Get data for division WhichD only

          DivSz = 0
          do 200 i = 1, StafSz
              if (EmpDiv(i) .ne. WhichD) go to 200
              DivSz = DivSz + 1
              DivNam(1,DivSz) = EmpNam(1,i)
              DivNam(2,DivSz) = EmpNam(2,i)
              DivNam(3,DivSz) = EmpNam(3,i)
              DivFon(DivSz) = EmpFon(i)
200       continue

      c   Sort telephone list

          if (DivSz .eq. 0) go to 210
          do 220 i = 1, DivSz
              do 230 j = 1 + 1, DivSz
                  if (DivNam(1,i) .gt. DivNam(1,j)) go to 240
                  if (DivNam(1,i) .lt. DivNam(1,j)) go to 230
                  if (DivNam(2,i) .gt. DivNam(2,j)) go to 240
                  if (DivNam(2,i) .lt. DivNam(2,j)) go to 230
                  if (DivNam(3,i) .gt. DivNam(3,j)) go to 240
                  go to 230
240               do 250 k = 1,3
                      q = DivNam (k,i)
                      DivNam(k, i) = DivNam(k, j)
250                   DivNam(k, j) = q
                  k = DivFon(i)
                  DivFon(1) = DivFon(j)
                  DivFon(j) = k
230           continue
220       continue
210       continue
```

visions, telephone numbers, and salaries is assumed to be available. The program must produce a data structure containing a sorted list of the employees in a selected division and their telephone extensions. Suitable declarations of the employee database and the divisional telephone list for the Fortran implementation are given in Figure 1a. Figure 1b shows how the large data structures are thought of as parallel vectors. A program fragment for constructing the telephone list is given in Figure 2.

The employee database is represented as a set of vectors, one for each unit of information about the employee. The vectors are used "in parallel" as a single data structure—that is, part of the information about the ith employee is stored in the ith element of each vector. Similarly, the telephone list is constructed in two arrays, *DivNam* for names and *DivFon* for telephone numbers.

The telephone list is constructed in two stages. First, the database is scanned for employees whose division ($EmpDiv(i)$) matches the division desired (*WhichD*). When a match is found, the name and phone number of the employee are added to the telephone list. Second, the telephone list is sorted using an insertion sort. (This selection is not an endorsement of insertion sorting in general. However, most readers will recognize the algorithm, and the topic of this article is the evolution of programming languages, not sorting techniques.)

There are several important things to notice about this program. First, the data about employees is stored in four arrays, and the relation among these arrays is shown only by the similar naming and the comment with their declarations. Second, the character string for each employee's name must be handled in eight-character segments, and there is no clear indication in either the declarations or the code that character strings are involved. (Indeed, the implementations of floating point in some versions of Fortran interfere with this type violation. Character strings are dealt with more appropriately in the Fortran 77 standard.) The six-line test that checks for

$DivNam(*, i) < DivNam(*, j)$ could be reduced to three tests if it were changed to a test for less-than-or-equal, but this would make the sort unstable. Third, all the data about employees, including salaries, is easily accessible and modifiable; this is undesirable from an administrative standpoint.

Pascal. Pascal is a simple algebraic language that was designed with three primary objectives: support modern programming development methodology; be simple enough to teach to students; and be easy to implement reliably, even on small computers. It has, in general, succeeded in all three respects.

Pascal provides a number of facilities for supporting structured programming. It provides the standard control constructs of structured programming, and a formal definition facilitates verification of Pascal programs. It also supports a set of data organization constructs that are suitable for defining abstractions. These include the ability to define a list of ar-

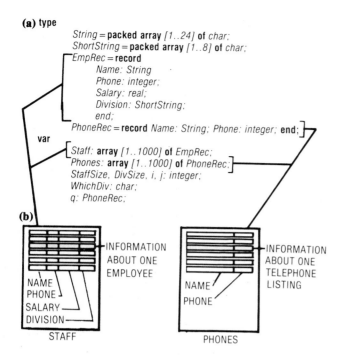

(a) type

```
String = packed array [1..24] of char;
ShortString = packed array [1..8] of char;
EmpRec = record
    Name: String
    Phone: integer;
    Salary: real;
    Division: ShortString;
    end;
PhoneRec = record Name: String; Phone: integer; end;

var
Staff: array [1..1000] of EmpRec;
Phones: array [1..1000] of PhoneRec;
StaffSize, DivSize, i, j: integer;
WhichDiv: char;
q: PhoneRec;
```

(b)

INFORMATION ABOUT ONE EMPLOYEE

NAME
PHONE
SALARY
DIVISION

STAFF

INFORMATION ABOUT ONE TELEPHONE LISTING

NAME
PHONE

PHONES

Figure 3 (left). Declarations for Pascal version of telephone list program.

Figure 4 (below). Code for Pascal version of telephone list program.

```
{Get data for division WhichDiv only}

DivSize: = 0;
for i: = 1 to StaffSize do
    if Staff [i]. Division = WhichDiv then
        begin
        DivSize: = DivSize + 1;
        Phones[DivSize]. Name: = Staff[i]. Name;
        Phones[DivSize]. Phone: = Staff[i].Phone;
        end;

{Sort telephone list}

for i: = 1 to DivSize − 1 do
    for j: = i + 1 to DivSize do
        if Phones [i]. Name > Phones[j]. Name then
            begin
            q: = Phones[i];
            Phones[i]: = Phones[j];
            Phones[j]: = q;
            end;
```

bitrary constants as an **enumerated type**, the ability to define heterogeneous **records** with individually named fields, data types that can be dynamically allocated and referred to by pointers, and the ability to name a data structure as a **type** (though not to bundle up the data structure with a set of operations).

The language has become quite widely used. In addition to serving as a teaching language for undergraduates, it is used as an implementation language for micro-computers,[11] and it has been extended to deal with parallel programming. An international standard has been established.

Pascal is not without its disadvantages. It provides limited support for large programs, for it lacks separate compilation facilities and block structure other than nested procedures. Type checking does not provide quite as much control over parameter passing as we might wish, and there is no support for the encapsulation of related definitions in such a way that they can be isolated from the remainder of the program. Many of the disadvantages are addressed in extensions, derivative languages, and the standardization effort.

We can illustrate some of Pascal's characteristics by returning to the program for creating telephone lists. Suitable data structures, including both type definitions and data declarations, are shown in Figure 3a. Figure 3b shows the view of the data structures suggested by these declarations, that is, vectors of records rather than independent vectors. A program fragment for constructing the telephone list is given in Figure 4.

The declarations open with definitions of four types that are not predefined in Pascal. Two, *String* and *ShortString,* are generally useful, and the other two, *EmpRec* and *PhoneRec,* were designed for this particular problem.

The definition of *String* and *ShortString* as types permits named variables to be treated as single units; operations are performed on an entire string variable, not on individual groups of characters. This abstraction simplifies the program, but more importantly, it allows the programmer to concentrate on the algorithm that uses the strings as names, rather than on keeping track of the individual name fragments. The difference between the complexity of the code in Figures 2 and 4 may not seem large, but when it is compounded over many individual composite structures with different representations, the difference can be large indeed. If Pascal allowed programmer-defined types to accept parameters, a single definition of strings that took the string length as a parameter could replace *String* and *ShortString.*

The type definitions for *EmpRec* and *PhoneRec* abstract from specific data items to the notions "record of information about an employee" and "record of information for a telephone list." Both the employee database and the telephone list can thus be represented as vectors whose elements are records of the appropriate types.

The declarations of *Staff* and *Phones* have the effect of indicating that all the components are related to the same information structure. In addition, the definition is organized as a collection of records, one for each employee, so the primary organization of the data structure is by employee. On the other hand, the data organization of the Fortran program was dominated by the arrays that corresponded to the fields, and the employees were secondary.

Just as in the Fortran program, the telephone list is constructed in two stages (Figure 4). Note that Pascal's ability to operate on strings and records as single units has substantially simplified the manipulation of names and the interchange step of the sort. Another notable difference between the two programs is in the use of conditional statements. In the Pascal program, the use of **if. . .then** statements emphasizes the conditions that will cause the bodies of the **if** statements to be executed. The Fortran **if** statements with **go to**'s however, describe conditions in which code is *not* to be executed, leaving the reader of the program to compute the conditions that actually correspond to the actions.

It is also worth mentioning that the Pascal program will not execute the body of the sort loop at all if no employees work in division *WhichDiv* (that is, if *DivSize* is 0.) The body of the corresponding Fortran loop would be executed once in that situation unless the loop had been protected by an explicit test for an empty list. While it would do no harm to execute this particular loop once on an empty list, in general it is necessary to guard Fortran loops against the possibility that the upper bound is less than the lower bound.

Ada. The Ada language has been developed under the auspices of the Department of Defense in an attempt to reduce the software costs of embedded computer systems. The project includes components for both a language and a programming support environment. The specific objectives of the Ada development include significantly reducing the number of programming languages that must be learned, supported, and maintained within the Department of Defense. The language design emphasizes the goals of high program reliability, low maintenance costs, support for modern programming methodology, and efficiency of compilers and object programs.

The Ada language was developed through competitive designs constrained by a set of requirements. Revisions to the language were completed in the summer of 1980 and the initial language reference manual was published in November 1980. Revisions to the manual were made in 1981 and

1982, and standardization is well underway: Ada has achieved MIL-STD and ANSI-STS status (1815A-1983). Development of the programming environment will continue over the next several years.[12] Since only a few validated compilers for the language are now available, it is too soon to evaluate how well the language meets its goals. However, it is possible to describe the way various features of the language respond to the abstraction issues raised here.

Ada programs can provide selected access to private information.

Although Ada grew out of the Pascal language philosophy, extensive syntactic changes and semantic extension make it a very different language from Pascal. The major additions include module structures and interface specifications for large-program organizations and separate compilation, encapsulation facilities and generic definitions to support abstract data types, support for parallel processing, and control over low-level implementation issues related to the architecture of object machines.

There are three major abstraction tools in Ada. The **package** is used for encapsulating a set of related definitions and isolating them from the rest of the program. The **type** determines the values a variable (or data structure) may take on and how it can be manipulated. The **generic** definition allows many similar abstractions to be generated from a single template, as we described earlier.

The incorporation of many of these ideas into Ada can be illustrated through the example we used in discussing Pascal. The data organization of the Pascal program (Figures 3 and 4) could be carried over directly to the Ada program, and the result would use Ada reasonably well. However, Ada provides additional facilities that can be applied to this problem. Recall that neither the Fortran program nor the

Pascal program can allow a programmer to access names, telephone numbers, and divisions without also allowing him to access private information, here illustrated by salaries. Ada programs can provide such selected access, and we will now extend the previous example to do so.

We organize the program in three components: a definition of the record for each employee (Figure 5), declarations of the data needed by the program (Figure 6), and code for construction of the phone list (Figure 7).

The **package** of information about employees whose specification is shown in Figure 5a illustrates one of Ada's major additions to our tool kit of abstraction facilities. This definition establishes *EmpRec* as a data type with a small set of privileged operations. Only the specification of the package is presented here, and Figure 5b suggests the view the user of this package should have, with some information hidden and only pertinent data and operations visible. Ada does not require the package body to accompany the specification (though it must be defined before the program can be executed); moreover, programmers are permitted to rely only on the specifications, not on the body of a package. The specification itself is divided into a visible part (everything from **package** to **private**) and a private part (from **private** to **end**). The private part is intended only to provide information for separate compilation.

Assume that the policy for using *EmpRec's* is that the *Name* and *Phone* fields are accessible to anyone, that it is permissible for anyone to read but not to write the *Division* field, and that access to the *Salary* field and modification of the *Division* field are supposed to be done only by authorized programs. Two characteristics of Ada make it possible to establish this policy. First, the scope rules prevent any portion of the program outside a package from accessing any names except the ones listed in the visible part of the specification. In the particular case of the *Employee* package, this means that the *Salary* and *Division* fields of an

(a)
```
package Employee is
    type PrivStuff is limited private;
    subtype ShortString is String(1..8);
    type EmpRec is
        record
            Name: string(1..24);
            Phone: integer;
            PrivPart: PrivStuff;
        end record;
    procedure SetSalary(Who: in out EmpRec; Sal: float);
    function GetSalary(Who: EmpRec) return float;
    procedure SetDiv(Who: in out EmpRec; Div: ShortString);
    function GetDiv(Who: EmpRec) return ShortString;
private
    type PrivStuff is
        record
            Salary: float;
            Division: ShortString;
        end record;
end Employee;
```

(b)

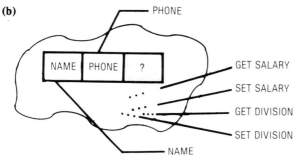

Figure 5 (above). Ada package definition for employee records.

Figure 6 (above right). Declarations for Ada version of telephone list program.

Figure 7 (right). Code for Ada version of telephone list program.

(a)
```
declare
    use Employee;

    type PhoneRec is
        record
            Name: string(1..24);
            Phone: integer;
        end record;

    Staff: array (1..1000) of EmpRec;
    Phones: array (1..1000) of PhoneRec;
    StaffSize, DivSize: integer range 1..1000;
    WhichDiv: ShortString;
    q: PhoneRec;
```

(b)

STAFF — INFORMATION ABOUT ONE EMPLOYEE

PHONES — INFORMATION ABOUT ONE TELEPHONE LISTING — NAME PHONE

—Get data for division WhichDiv only
```
    DivSize: = 0;
    for i in 1..StaffSize loop
        if GetDiv(Staff(i)) = WhichDiv then
            DivSize: = DivSize + 1;
            Phones(DivSize): = (Staff(i). Name, Staff(i). Phone);
        end if;
    end loop;
```

—Sort telephone list
```
    for i in 1..DivSize − 1 loop
        for j in i + 1..DivSize loop
            if Phones(i). Name > Phones(j). Name then
                q: = Phones(i);
                Phones(i): = Phones(j);
                Phones(j): = q;
            end if;
        end loop;
    end loop;
```

EmpRec cannot be directly read or written outside the package. Therefore the integrity of the data can be controlled by verifying that the routines that are exported from the package are correct. Presumably the routines *Set-Salary, Get Salary, SetDiv,* and *Get-Div* perform reads and writes as their names suggest; they might also keep records showing who made changes and when. Second, Ada provides ways to control the visibility of each routine and variable name.

Although the field name *PrivPart* is exported from the *Employee* package along with *Name* and *Phone,* there is no danger in doing so. An auxiliary type was defined to protect the salary and division information; the declaration

type *PrivStuff* **is limited private;**

indicates not only that the content and organization of the data structure are hidden from the user (**private**), but also that all operations on data of type *PrivStuff* are forbidden except for calls on the routines exported from the package. For **limited private** types, even assignment and comparison for equality are forbidden. Naturally, the code inside the body of the *Employee* package may manipulate these hidden fields; the purpose of the packaging is to guarantee that *only* the code inside the package body can do so.

The ability to force a data structure to be manipulated only through a known set of routines is central to the support of abstract data types. It is useful not only in examples such as the one given here, but also for cases in which the representation may change radically from time to time, and for cases in which some kind of internal consistency among fields, such as checksums, must be maintained. Support for secure computation is not among Ada's goals. It can be achieved in this case, but only through a combination of an extra level of packaging and some management control performed in the subprograms. Even without guarantees about security, however, the packaging of information about handling employee data provides a useful structure for program development and maintenance.

The declarations of Figure 6a are much like the declarations of the Pascal program. The *Employee* package is used instead of a simple record, and there are minor syntactic differences between the languages. The clause

use *Employee;*

says that all the visible names of the *Employee* package are available in the current block. Figure 6b shows that the view of the data suggested by Ada is similar to that of Figure 3b; the chief difference here is the lack of internal structure in *Employee* values.

In the code of the Ada program itself (Figure 7), visibility rules allow the non-**private** field names of *EmpRecs* and the *GetDiv* function to be used. Ada provides a way to create a complete record value and assign it with a single statement; thus the assignment

Phones(DivSize):= *(Staff(i).Name,* *Staff(i).Phone);*

sets both fields of the *PhoneRec* at once. Aside from this and minor syntactic distinctions, this program fragment is very much like the Pascal fragment of Figure 4.

Status and potential

It is clear that methodologies and analytic techniques based on the principle of abstraction have played a major role in the development of software engineering and that they will continue to do so.

Programming languages and methodologies often develop in response to new ideas about how to cope with complexity in programs and systems of programs. As languages evolve to meet these ideas, we reshape our perceptions of the problems and solutions in response to the new experiences. Our sharpened perceptions in turn generate new ideas which feed the evolutionary cycle. This article explores the routes by which these cyclic advances in methodology and specification have led to current concepts and principles of programming languages.

We can now describe the ways our current programming habits are changing to take advantage of these principles of abstraction. We also note some of the limitations of current techniques and how future work may deal with them, and we conclude with some suggestions for further reading on abstraction techniques.

Effect on programming. As techniques such as abstract data types have emerged, they have affected both the overall organization of programs and the style of writing small segments of code.

The new languages have the most sweeping effects on the techniques we use for the high-level organization of program systems, and hence on the management of design and implementation projects. Modularization features that impose controls on the distribution of variable, routine, and type names can profoundly shape the strategies for decomposing a program into modules. Project organization will also be influenced by the growing availability of support tools for managing multiple modules in multiple versions.

The availability of precise (and enforceable) specifications for module interfaces will influence management of software projects.[6] For example, the requirements document for a large avionics system has already been converted to a precise, if informal, specification. The usefulness of a formal specification is greatest when the specification can be processed or checked automatically. Automatic verification of logical assertions attached to programs is not imminent, but systems **that do partial runtime checking of assertions (given, for example, as specially-formatted comments) are already feasible.**

The organization and style of the code within modules will also be af- fected. We showed earlier in our discussion of practical realizations how the treatment of both control and data within a module changes as the same problem is solved in languages with increasingly powerful abstraction techniques.

The ideas behind the abstract data type methodology are still not entirely validated. Projects using various portions of the methodology—such as design based on data types, but without formal specification, or conversely, specification and verification without modularity—have been successful, but a complete demonstration on a large project has not yet been completed. Although complete validation experiments have not been done, some of the initial trials are encouraging. A large, interesting program using abstract data types has been written but not verified; programs using this organization in a language without encapsulation facilities have been written and largely verified; and abstract data types specified via algebraic axioms have proved useful as a design tool.

Limitations of current techniques. Efforts to use abstract data types have also revealed some limitations. In some cases problems are not comfortably cast as data types, or the necessary functionality is not readily expressed using the specification techniques now available. In other cases, the problem requires a set of definitions that are clearly very similar but cannot be expressed by systematic instantiation or invocation of a data type definition, even using generic definitions.

A number of familiar, well-structured program organizations do not fit well into precisely the abstract data type paradigm. These include, for example, filters and shells in the Unix spirit,[13] object-oriented systems,[14] production systems, table-driven interpreters, state-transition systems, and interactive programs in which the command syntax dominates the specification. These organizations are unquestionably useful and potentially as well understood as abstract data types, and there is every reason to believe that similarly precise formal models can be developed.

Although facilities for defining routines and modules whose parameters may be generic (that is, of types that cannot be manipulated in the language) have been developed over the past several years, there has been little exploration of the generality of generic definitions. Part of the problem has been lack of facilities for specifying the precise dependence of the definition on its generic parameters. A specific example of a complex generic definition, giving an algorithmic transformation that can be applied to a wide variety of problems, has been written and verified.[5]

The language investigations described above, together with other research projects, have addressed questions of functional specification in considerable detail. That is, they provide formal notations such as input-output predicates, abstract models, and algebraic axioms for making assertions about the effects that operators have on program values. In many cases, the specifications of a system cannot be reduced to formal assertions; in these cases we resort to testing in order to increase our confidence in the program.[15] In other situations, moreover, a programmer is concerned with properties other than pure functional correctness. Such properties include time and space requirements, memory access patterns, reliability, synchronization, and process independence. These have not been addressed by the data type research.

A specification methodology that addresses these properties must have two important characteristics. First, it must be possible for the programmer to make and verify assertions about the properties rather than simply analyzing the program text to derive exact values or complete specifications. This is analogous to our approach to functional specifications—we don't attempt to formally derive the mathematical function defined by a program; rather, we specify certain properties of the computation that are important and must be preserved. Further, it is important that the specifica-tion methodology avoid adding a new conceptual framework for each new class of properties. This implies that mechanisms for dealing with new properties should be compatible with the mechanisms already used for functional correctness. ∎

Acknowledgments

This research was sponsored by the National Science Foundation under Grant MCS77-03883 and by the Defense Advanced Research Project Agency, ARPA Order No. 3597, monitored by the Air Force Avionics Laboratory under contract F33615-78-C-1551. The views and conclusions contained in this document are those of the author and should not be interpreted as representing the official policies, either expressed or implied, of the National Science Foundation, DARPA, or the US government.

References

1. D. E. Knuth "Fundamental Algorithms," *The Art of Computer Programming,* 2nd ed., Vol. 1, Addison-Wesley, 1973.

2. P. Naur and B. Randell (eds.), "Software Engineering," NATO, 1969, report on conference sponsored by the NATO Science Committee, Garmisch, Germany.

3. J. N. Buxton and B. Randell (eds.), "Software Engineering Techniques," NATO, 1970, report on conference sponsored by the NATO Science Committee, Rome, Italy.

4. S. A. Schuman (ed.), "Proceeding of the International Symposium on Extensible Languages," *ACM SIGPLAN Notices,* Vol. 6, Dec. 1971.

5. J. L. Bentley and M. Shaw, "An Alphard Specification of a Correct and Efficient Transformation on Data Structures," *Proc. IEEE Conf. Spec. Reliable Software,* Apr. 1979, pp. 222-237.

6. R. T. Yeh and P. Zave, "Specifying Software Requirements," *Proc. IEEE,* Vol. 68, No. 9, Sept. 1980.

7. M. Shaw and W. A. Wulf, "Toward Relaxing Assumptions in Languages and Their Implementations," *SIGPLAN Notices,* Vol. 13, No. 3, Mar. 1980, pp. 45-61.

8. F. DeRemer and H. H. Kron, "Programming-in-the-Large vs. Programming-in-the-Small," *IEEE Trans. Software Eng.,* Vol. SE-2, No. 2, June 1976.

9. A. K. Jones and B. H. Liskov, "An Access Control Facility for Programming Languages," MIT memo 137, MIT Computation Structures Group and Carnegie-Mellon University, 1976.

10. J. H. Morris, "Protection in Programming Languages," *Comm. ACM,* Vol. 16, Jan. 1973.

11. K. L. Bowles, *Microcomputer Problem Solving Using Pascal,* Springer-Verlag, 1977.

12. Department of Defense, *Requirements for Ada Programming Support Environments: Stoneman,* 1980.

13. B. W. Kernighan and P. J. Plauger, *Software Tools,* Addison-Wesley, 1976.

14. B. J. Cox, "Message/Object Programming: An Evolutionary Change in Programming Technology," *IEEE Software,* Vol. 1, No. 1, Jan. 1984, pp. 50-61.

15. J. B. Goodenough and C. L. McGowan, "Software Quality Assurance: Testing and Validation," *Proc. IEEE,* Vol. 68, No. 9, Sept. 1980.

Mary Shaw is currently an associate professor of computer science at Carnegie-Mellon, where she has been on the faculty since 1971. Her primary research interests are in programming systems and software engineering, particularly abstraction techniques and language tools for developing and evaluating software. She received a BA in math from Rice University in 1965 and a PhD in computer science from Carnegie-Mellon University in 1972. Shaw is a senior member of the IEEE, and a member of the ACM, IEEE-CS, and the New York Academy of Sciences. Her address is Computer Science Department, Carnegie-Mellon University, Schenley Park, Pittsburgh, PA 15213.

The Modular Structure of Complex Systems

DAVID LORGE PARNAS, PAUL C. CLEMENTS, AND DAVID M. WEISS

Abstract – This paper discusses the organization of software that is inherently complex because of very many arbitrary details that must be precisely right for the software to be correct. We show how the software design technique known as information hiding, or abstraction, can be supplemented by a hierarchically structured document, which we call a module guide. The guide is intended to allow both designers and maintainers to identify easily the parts of the software that they must understand, without reading irrelevant details about other parts of the software. The paper includes an extract from a software module guide to illustrate our proposals.

Index Terms – Abstract interfaces, information hiding, modular structure of software, software engineering.

I. INTRODUCTION

MORE than five years ago, a number of people at the Naval Research Laboratory became concerned about what we preceived to be a growing gap between software engineering principles being advocated at major conferences and the practice of software engineering at many industrial and governmental laboratories. The conferences and many journals were filled with what appeared to be good ideas, illustrated using examples that were either unrealistically simple fragments or complex problems that were not worked out in much detail. When we examined actual software projects and their documentation, few showed any use of the ideas and no successful product appeared to have been designed by consistent application of the principles touted at conferences and in journals. The ideas appeared to be easier to write about than to use.

We could imagine several reasons for the gap: 1) the ideas were, as many old-style programmers claim, simply impractical for real problems; 2) responsible managers were unwilling to bet on principles that had been not been proven in practice, thus creating a startup problem; 3) the examples used in the papers were too unlike the problems of the practitioners to serve as models; 4) the ideas might need refinement or extension before they could be used as guidelines for projects with the complexity and resource constraints found in the field; and 5) the practitioners were, as some academics claim, not intellectually capable of the tasks given them. Our familiarity with both the ideas and the practitioners led us to reject 1) and 5); we decided to see what could be done about 2)-4).

Our decision was to take an undeniably realistic problem and to apply the "academic" ideas to it, so that if we succeeded, 1)

there would be evidence of the feasibility for responsible managers; 2) there would be a model for use by others with similar problems; and 3) we could refine or supplement the ideas until they would work for systems more complex than those in the literature. We chose to build an exact duplicate of an existing system so that it would be possible to compare the system built by conventional techniques to one built in accordance with the new academic principles. The project chosen was the Operational Flight Program (OFP) for the A-7E aircraft. The current program uses many dirty tricks, barely fits in its memory, and barely meets its real-time constraints. Consequently, we felt that this program, although much smaller than many programs, was a realistic test of the ideas. Because the current OFP is considered one of the best programs of its ilk, we considered the task sufficiently challenging that skeptics would not attribute our success to the poor quality of the program that we are trying to match.

Although the project is far from complete, we have already had some limited success in all three of our goals. Our ability to write a complete and precise requirements specification for the software has encouraged managers to try the same approach, and our document [9] has served as a model for those projects. We have also found useful refinements of the principles that we advocated before starting the project. For example, the concept of abstract interfaces, which we discussed in [1], has now been refined and illustrated in [2] and [3].

This paper presents another refinement of the principles that we set out to use. One of the most basic ideas in our approach was the use of the principle of information hiding [6] to decompose a project into work assignments or modules. This idea was an excellent example of the gap between academic software engineering and practice. While it has been considered self-evident by some academics, we could find no sizable product in which the idea had been consistently used. While some authors were treating the idea as "old hat," we could not persuade those charged with building real software to do something so radically different from what they had been doing.

When we tried to use the idea we found that while it was quite applicable, some additional ideas were necessary to make it work for systems with more than a dozen or so modules. This paper discusses the problems that we encountered and the additional ideas.

II. BACKGROUND AND GUIDING PRINCIPLES

A. Three Important Software Structures

A structural description of a software system shows the program's decomposition into parts and the relations between those parts. A-7E programmers must be concerned with three

Manuscript received January 31, 1984.

D. L. Parnas is with the University of Victoria, Victoria, B.C., Canada, and the Computer Science and Systems Branch, U.S. Naval Research Laboratory, Washington, DC 20375.

P. C. Clements and D. M. Weiss are with the Computer Science and Systems Branch, U.S. Naval Research Laboratory, Washington, DC 20375.

Reprinted from *IEEE Transactions on Software Engineering*, Volume SE-11, Number 3, March 1985, pages 259-266. U.S. Government work not protected by U.S. copyright.

structures: a) the module structure, b) the uses structure, and c) the process structure. This section contrasts these structures.

a) A module is a work assignment for a programmer or programmer team. Each module consists of a group of closely related programs. The module structure is the decomposition of the program into modules and the assumptions that the team responsible for each module is allowed to make about the other modules.

b) In the uses structure the components are programs, i.e., not modules but parts of modules; the relation is "requires the presence of." The uses structure determines the executable subsets of the software [5].

c) The process structure is a decomposition of the run-time activities of the system into units known as processes. Processes are not programs; there is no simple relation between modules and processes. The implementation of some modules may include one or more processes, and any process may invoke programs in several modules.

The rest of this paper discusses the module structure.

B. Design Principle

Our module structure is based on the decomposition criterion known as information hiding [6]. According to this principle, system details that are likely to change independently should be the secrets of separate modules; the only assumptions that should appear in the interfaces between modules are those that are considered unlikely to change. Each data structure is used in only one module; it may be directly accessed by one or more programs within the module but not by programs outside the module. Any other program that requires information stored in a module's data structures must obtain it by calling access programs belonging to that module.

Appying this principle is not always easy. It is an attempt to minimize the expected cost of software and requires that the designer estimate the likelihood of changes. Such estimates are based on past experience, and may require knowledge of the application area, as well as an understanding of hardware and software technology. Because a designer may not have all of the relevant experience, we have developed formal review procedures designed to take advantage of others that do have that experience. These procedures are described in [2].

C. Goals of Modular Structure

The primary goal of the decomposition into modules is reduction of overall software cost by allowing modules to be designed and revised independently. Specific goals of the module decomposition are as follows.

a) Each module's structure should be simple enough to be understood fully.

b) It should be possible to change the implementation of one module without knowledge of the implementation of other modules and without affecting the behavior of other modules.

c) The case of making a change in the design should bear a reasonable relationship to the likelihood of the change being needed. It should be possible to make likely changes without changing any module interfaces; less likely changes may involve interface changes, but only for modules that are small and not widely used. Only very unlikely changes should require changes in the interfaces of widely used modules.

d) It should be possible to make a major software change as a set of independent changes to individual modules, i.e., except for interface changes, programmers changing the individual modules should not need to communicate. If the interfaces of the modules are not revised, it should be possible to run and test any combination of old and new module versions.

As a consequence of the goals above, our software is composed of many small modules. In previous attempts to use information hiding, we had seen systems with 5-20 modules. We know now that we will have hundreds of modules. With 25 or fewer modules it would not be difficult to know which modules would be affected by a change. With hundreds of modules that is not the case. With 25 or fewer modules, careful inspection may suffice to make sure that nothing has been overlooked. With hundreds of modules we found that impossible. We realized that the use of information hiding could backfire. With most maintainers ignorant about the internal structure of most of the modules, maintainers would have to search through many module documents to find the ones they had to change. We also feared working for some time before discovering that we had left out some major modules.

We concluded that we needed some additional discipline in applying the information hiding principle, and that special documentation was needed if we were really to reduce the cost of maintaining complex software systems. We had to find a way to work with small lists of modules so that we could prepare convincing arguments that each list was complete. We needed to prepare a software module guide that would assist the maintenance programmer in finding the modules that were affected by a change or could be causing the problem.

As a result of these considerations, the modules have been organized into a tree-structured hierarchy; each nonterminal node in the tree represents a module that is composed of the modules represented by its descendents. The hierarchical structure has been documented in a module guide [9]. The hierarchy and the guide are intended to achieve the following additional goals.

e) A software engineer should be able to understand the responsibility of a module without understanding the module's internal design.

f) A reader with a well-defined concern should easily be able to identify the relevant modules without studying irrelevant modules. This implies that the reader be able to distinguish relevant modules from irrelevant modules without looking at their components.

g) The number of branches at each nonterminal module in the graph should be small enough that the designers can prepare convincing arguments that the submodules have no overlapping responsibilities, and that they cover all of the responsibilities that the module is intended to cover. This is most valuable during the initial design, but it also helps when identifying modules affected by a change.

D. Restricted and Hidden Modules

We found that it was not always possible to confine information to a single module in a real system. For example, information about hardware that could be replaced should be confined, but diagnostic information about that hardware must be communicated to modules that display information to users or hardware maintainers. Any program that uses that information is subject to change when the hardware changes. To reduce the cost of software changes, the use of modules that provide such information is restricted. Restricted interfaces are indicated by "(R)" in the Guide. Often the existence of certain smaller modules is itself a secret of a larger module. In a few cases, we have mentioned such modules in this document in order to clearly specify where certain functions are performed. Those modules are referred to as hidden modules and indicated by "(H)" in the documentation.

E. Module Description

The Module Guide shows how responsibilities are allocated among the major modules. Such a guide is intended to lead a reader to the module that implements a particular aspect of the system. It states the criteria used to assign a particular responsibility to a module and arranges the modules in such a way that a reader can find the information relevant to his purpose without searching through unrelated documentation. The guide defines the scope and contents of the individual design documents.

Three ways to describe a module structure based on information hiding are: 1) by the roles played by the individual modules in the overall system operation; 2) by the secrets associated with each module; and 3) by the facilities provided by each module. The module guide describes the module structure by characterizing each module's secrets. Where useful, a brief description of the role of the module is included. The detailed description of facilities for modules is relegated to other documents called "module specifications"; e.g., [2]. The module guide tells you which module(s) will require a change. The module specification tells you both how to use that module and what that module must do.

For some modules we find it useful to distinguish between a primary secret, which is hidden information that was specified to the software designer, and a secondary secret, which refers to implementation decisions made by the designer when implementing the module designed to hide the primary secret.

In the module guide we attempted to describe the decomposition rules as precisely as possible, but the possibility of future changes in technology makes some boundaries fuzzy. Where this occurs we note fuzzy areas and discuss additional information used to resolve ambiguities.

F. The Illustrative Example

To show how our techniques work, we give a fairly large extract from the module guide for the A-7 OFP. We discuss the way that it helps during construction and maintenance after the extract.

The design that we present is the module structure of the A-7E flight software produced by the Naval Research Laboratory. The A-7E flight software is a hard real-time program that processes flight data and controls displays for the pilot. It computes the aircraft position using an inertial navigation system, and must be highly accurate. The current operational program is best understood as one big module. It is very difficult to identify the sections of the program that must be changed when certain requirements change. Our software structure is designed to meet the goals mentioned above, but must still meet all accuracy and real-time constraints.

What follows is an extract from the module guide for NRL's version of the software [7]. A complete copy of the guide or

any of the other NRL reports can be obtained by writing to

Code 7590
Naval Research Laboratory
Washington, DC 20375

III. A-7E MODULE STRUCTURE

A. Top Level Decomposition

The software system consists of the three modules described below.

A.1 Hardware-Hiding Module

The hardware-hiding module includes the programs that need to be changed if any part of the hardware is replaced by a new unit with a different hardware–software interface but with the same general capabilities. This module implements virtual hardware that is used by the rest of the software. The primary secrets of this module are the hardware–software interfaces described in chapters 1 and 2 of the requirements document [9]. The secrets of this module are the data structures and algorithms used to implement the virtual hardware.

A.2 Behavior-Hiding Module

The behavior-hiding module includes programs that need to be changed if there are changes in the sections of the requirements document that describe the required behavior [9, ch. 3, 4]. The content of those sections is the primary secret of this module. These programs determine the values to be sent to the virtual output devices provided by the hardware-hiding module.

A.3 Software Decision Module

The software decision module hides software design decisions that are based upon mathematical theorems, physical facts, and programming considerations such as algorithmic efficiency and accuracy. The secrets of this module are *not* described in the requirements document. This module differs from the other modules in that both the secrets and the interfaces are determined by software designers. Changes in these modules are more likely to the motivated by a desire to improve performance than by externally imposed changes.

Notes on the Top-Level Decomposition

Fuzziness is present in the above classifications for the following reasons.

a) The line between requirements definition and software design has been determined in part by decisions made when the requirements documents are written; for example, weapon trajectory models may be chosen by system analysts and specified in the requirements document, or they may be left to the discretion of the software designers by stating accuracy requirements but no algorithms.

b) The line between hardware characteristics and software design may vary. Hardware can be built to perform some of the services currently performed by the software; consequently, certain modules can be viewed either as modules that hide hardware characteristics or as modules that hide software design decisions.

c) Changes in the hardware or in the bahavior of the system or its users may make a software design decision less appropriate.

d) All software modules include software design decisions;

changes in any module may be motivated by efficiency or accuracy considerations.

Such fuzziness would be unacceptable for our purposes. We can eliminate it by referring to a precise requirements document such as [9]. That document specifies the lines between behavior, hardware, and software decisions.

a) When the requirements document specifies an algorithm, we do not consider the design of the algorithm to be a software design decision. If the requirements document only states requirements that the algorithm must meet, we consider the program that implements that algorithm to be part of a software decision module.

b) The interface between the software and the hardware is specified in the software requirements document. The line between hardware characteristics and software design must be based on estimates of the likelihood of future changes. If it is reasonably likely that future hardware will implement a particular facility, the software module that implements that facility is classified as a hardware-hiding module; otherwise, the module is considered a software design module. We have consistently taken a conservative stance; the design is based on the assumption that drastic changes are less likely than evolutionary changes. If there are changes to the aspects of the hardware hiding module. If there are radical changes that provide services previously provided by software, some of the software decision modules may be eliminated or reduced in size.

c) A module is included in the software decision module only if it would remain useful, although possibly less efficient, when there are changes in the requirements document.

d) A module will be included in the software decision category only if its secrets do not include information documented in the software requirements document.

B. Second-Level Decomposition

B.1 Hardware-Hiding Module Decomposition

The hardware hiding module comprises two modules.

B.1.1 Extended Computer Module

The extended computer module hides those characteristics of the hardware-software interface of the avionics computer that we consider likely to change if the computer is modified or replaced.

Avionics computers differ greatly in their hardware-software interfaces and in the capabilities that are implemented directly in the hardware. For example, some avionics computers include a floating-point approximation of real numbers, while others perform approxiamte real number operations by a programmed sequence of fixed-point operations. Some avionics systems include a single processor; some systems provide several processors. The extended computer provides an instruction set that can be implemented efficiently on most avionics computers. This instruction set includes the operations on application-independent data types, sequence control operations, and general I/O operations.

The primary secrets of the extended computer are: the number of processors, the instruction set of the computer, and the computer's capacity for performing concurrent operations.

The structure of the extended computer module is given in Section C.1.1.

B.1.2 Device Interface Module

The device interface module hides those characteristics of the peripheral devices that are considered likely to change. Each device might be replaced by an improved device capable of accomplishing the same tasks. Replacement devices differ widely in their hardware-software interfaces. For example, all angle-of-attack sensors measure the angle between a reference line on the aircraft and the velocity of the surrounding air mass, but they differ in input format, timing, and the amount of noise in the data.

The device interface module provides virtual devices to be used by the rest of the software. The virtual devices do not necessarily correspond to physical devices, because all of the hardware providing a capability is not necessarily in one physical unit. Furthermore, there are some capabilities of a physical unit that are likely to change independently of others; it is advantageous to hide characteristics that may change independently in different modules.

The primary secrets of the device interface module are those characteristics of the present devices documented in the requirements document and not likely to be shared by replacement devices.

The structure of the device interface module is given in Section C.1.2.

Notes on the Hardware-Hiding Module Decomposition

Parts of the hardware were considered external devices by those who designed the CPU but are treated as part of the processor by other documents. Our distinction between computer and device is based on the current hardware and is described in the requirements document. Information that applies to more than one device is considered a secret of the extended computer; information that is only relevant to one device is a secret of a device interface module. For example, there is an analog-to-digital converter that is used for communicating with several devices; it is hidden by the extended computer, although it could be viewed as an external device. As another example, there are special outputs for testing the I/O channels; they are not associated with a single device. These are the responsibility of the extended computer.

If all the hardware were replaced simultaneously, there might be a significant shift in responsibilities between computer and devices. In systems like the A-7E, such changes are unusual; the replacement of individual devices or the replacement of the computer alone is more likely. Our design is based on the expectation that this pattern of replacement will continue to hold.

B.2 Behavior-Hiding Module Decomposition

The behavior hiding module consists of two modules: a function driver (FD) module supported by a shared services (SS) module.

B.2.1 Function Driver Module

The function driver module consists of a set of individual modules called function drivers; each function driver is the sole controller of a set of closely related outputs. Outputs are considered closely related if it is easier to describe their values together than individually. For example, if one output is the sine of an angle, the other the cosine of the same angle, a joint description of the two will be smaller than two separate descriptions. Note that the function driver modules deal with outputs to the virtual devices created by the hardware hiding modules, not the physical outputs. The primary secrets of the function driver module are the rules determining the values of these outputs.

The structure of the function driver module is given in Section C.2.1.

B.2.2 Shared Services Module

Because all the function drivers control systems in the same aircraft, some aspects of the behavior are common to several function drivers. We expect that if there is a change in that aspect of the behavior, it will affect all of the functions that share it. Consequently, we have identified a set of modules, each of which hides an aspect of the behavior that applies to two or more of the outputs.

The structure of the shared services module is found in Section C.2.2.

Notes on Behavior-Hiding Module Decomposition

Because users of the documentation cannot be expected to know which aspects of a function's behavior are shared, the documentation for the function driver modules will include a reference to the shared services modules that it uses. A maintenance programmer should always begin his inquiry with the appropriate function driver. He will be directed to the shared services modules when appropriate.

B.3 Software Decision Module Decomposition

The software decision module has been divided into (1) the application data type module, which hides the implementation of certain variables, 2) the physical model module, which hides algorithms that simulate physical phenomena, 3) the data banker module, which hides the data-updating policies, 4) the system generation module, which hides decisions that are postponed until system generation time, and 5) the software utility module, which hides algorithms that are used in several other modules.

B.3.1 Application Data Type Module

The application data type module supplements the data types provided by the extended computer module with data types that are useful for avionics applications and do not require a computer dependent implementation. These data types are implemented using the data types provided by the extended computer; variables of those types are used just as if the types were built into the extended computer.

The secrets of the application data type module are the data representation used in the variables and the programs used to implement operations on those variables. These variables can be used without consideration of units. Where necessary, the modules provide conversion operators, which deliver or accept real values in specified units.

Run-time efficiency considerations sometimes dictate that an implementation of an application data type be based on a secret of another module. In that case, the data type will be specified in the application data type module documentation, but the implementation will be described in the documentation, but the implementation will be described in the documentation will contain the appropriate references in such cases.

The structure of the application data type module is given in Section C.3.1.

B.3.2 Physical Model Module

The software requires estimates of quantities that cannot be measured directly but can be computed from observables using models of the physical world. The primary secrets of the physical model module are the physical models; the secondary secrets are the computer implementations of those models.

The structure of the physical model module is given in Section C.3.2.

B.3.3 Data Banker Module

Most data are produced by one module and "consumed" by another. Usually the consumers should receive a value as up-to-date as practical. The data banker module acts as a "middleman" and determines when new values for these data are computed. The data banker obtains values from producers; consumer programs obtain data from data banker access programs. The producer and consumers of a particular datum can be written without knowing whether or not the data banker stores the value or when a stored value is updated. In most cases, neither the producer nor the consumer need be modified if the updating policy changes.

The data banker is not used if consumers require specific members of the sequence of values computed by the producer, or if they require values associated with a specific time, such as the moment when an event occurs.

Some of the updating policies that can be implemented in the data banker are described in the following table, which indicates whether or not the data banker stores a copy of the item and when a new value is computed.

Name	Storage	When new value produced
on demand:	No	Whenever a consumer requests the value
periodic:	Yes	Periodically. Consumers get the most recently stored value.
event driven:	Yes	Whenever the data banker is notified, by the occurrence of an event, that the value may have changed. Consumers get the most recently stored value.
conditional:	Yes	Whenever a consumer requests the value, provided certain conditions are true. Otherwise, a previously stored value is delivered.

The choice among these and other updating policies should be based on the consumers' accuracy requirements, how often consumers require the value, the maximum wait that consumers can accept, how often the value changes, and the cost of producing a new value. Since the decision is not based on coding details of either consumer or producer, it is usually not necessary to rewrite a data banker module when producer or consumer change.

B.3.4 System Generation Module

The primary secrets of the system generation module are decisions that are postponed until system-generation time. These include the values of system generation parameters and the choice among alternative implementations of a module. The secondary secrets of the system generation module are the method used to generate a machine-executable form of the code and the representation of the postponed decisions. Most of the programs in this module do not run on the on-board computer; they run on a more powerful computer used to generate the code for the on-board system. Some of the programs are tools provided with our system; others have been developed specifically for this project.

B.3.5 Software Utility Module

The primary secrets of this module are the algorithms implementing common software functions such as resource monitor modules, and mathematical routines such as square-root and logarithm.

C. Third-Level Deocmposition

Note: For the purposes of this paper, only third-level modules whose descriptions are particularly illustrative are included. Ellipses indicate omissions.

C.1 Extended Computer Module Decomposition
C.1.1.1 Data Type Module

The data type module implements variables and operators for real numbers, time periods, and bit strings. The data representations and data manipulation instructions built into the computer hardware are the primary secrets of this module—specifically, the representation of numeric objects in terms of hardware data types; the representation of bitstrings; how to access a bit within a bitstring; and how times are represented for the hardware timers. The secondary secrets of this module are how range and resolution requirements are used to determine representation; the procedures for performing numeric operations; the procedures used to perform bitstring operations; and how to compute the memory location of an array element given the array name and the element index.

. . .

C.1.1.4 Computer State Module

The computer state module keeps track of the current state of the extended computer, which can be either operating, off, or failed, and signals relevant state changes to user programs. The primary secret is the way that the hardware detects and causes state changes. After the EC has been initialized, this module signals the event that starts the initialization for the rest of the software.

. . .

C.1.1.7 Diagnostics Module (R)

The diagnostics module provides diagnostic programs to test the interrupt hardware, the I/O hardware, and the memory. Use of this module is restricted because the information it returns reveals secrets of the extended computer, i.e., programs that use it may have to be revised if the avionics computer is replaced by another computer.

C.1.1.8 Virtual Memory Module (H)

The virtual memory module presents a uniformly addressable virtual memory for use by DATA, I/O, and SEQUENCE submodules, allowing them to use virtual addresses for both data and subprograms. The primary secrets of the virtual memory module are the hardware addressing methods for data and instructions in real memory; differences in the way that different areas of memory are addressed are hidden. The secondary secrets of the module are the policy for allocating real memory to virtual addresses and the programs that translate from virtual address references to real instruction sequences.

. . .

C.1.2 Device Interface Module Decomposition

The following table describes the device interface submodules (DIM's) and their secrets. The phrase "how to read ..." is intended to be interpreted quite liberally, e.g., it includes device-dependent corrections, filtering, and any other actions that may be necessary to determine the physical value from the device input. All of the DIM's hide the procedures for testing the device that they control.

Section	Virtual Device	Secret: How to . . .
C.1.2.1	Air data computer	read barometric altitude, true airspeed, and Mach number.
C.1.2.2	Angle of attack sensor	read angle of attack.
. . .		
C.1.2.20	Weapon release system	ascertain weapon release actions the pilot has requested; cause weapons to be prepared and released.

. . .

C.2.1 Funtion Driver Module Decomposition

The following table describes the function driver submodules and their secrets.

Section	Function Driver	Secret
. . .		
C.2.1.7	Head-up display functions	Where the movable HUD symbols should be placed. Whether a HUD symbol should be on, off, or blinking. What information should be displayed on the fixed-position displays.
C.2.1.8	Inertial measurement set functions	Rules determining the scale to be used for the IMS velocity measurements. When to initialize the velocity measurements. How much to rotate the IMS for alignment.

C.2.1.9 Panel functions — What information should be displayed on panel windows. When the enter light should be turned on.

...

C.2.2 Shared Services Module Decomposition

The shared services module comprises the following modules.

C.2.2.1 Mode Determination Module

The mode determination module determines system modes (as defined in the requirements document). It signals the occurrence of mode transitions and makes the identity of the current modes available. The primary secrets of the mode determination module are the mode transition tables in the requirements document.

C.2.2.4 System Value Module

A system value submodule computes a set of values, some of which are used by more than one function driver. The secrets of a system value submodule are the rules in the requirements that define the values that it computes. The shared rules in the requirements specify such things as 1) selection among several alternative sources, 2) applying filters to values produced by other modules, or 3) imposing limits on a value calculated elsewhere.

This module may include a value that is only used in one function driver if the rule used to calculate that value is the same as that used to calculate other shared values.

Each system value submodule is also responsible for signaling events that are defined in terms of the values it computes.

...

C.3.1 Application Data Type Module Decomposition

The application data type module is divided into two submodules.

C.3.1.1 System Data Type Module

The system data type module implements variables of the following widely used types: accelerations, angles, angular rates, character literals, densities, Mach values, distances, pressures, and speeds. These modules may be used to implement types with restricted ranges or special interpretations (e.g., angle is used to represent latitude).

C.3.1.2 State Transition Event Module

The STE module implements variables that are instances of finite state machines. Users can await the transition of a variable to/from a particular state value, cause transitions, and compare values for equality.

C.3.2 Physical Model Module Decomposition

The physical model module comprises the modules described below.

C.3.2.1 Earth Model Module

The earth model module hides models of the earth and its atmosphere. This set of models includes models of local gravity, the curvature of the earth, pressure at sea level, magnetic variation, the local terrain, and rotation of the earth, coriolis force, and atmospheric density.

C.3.2.2 Aircraft Motion Module

The Aircraft motion module hides models of the aircraft's motion. They are used to calculate aircraft position, velocity, and attitude from observable inputs.

C.3.2.3 Spatial Relations Module

The spatial relations module contains models of three-dimensional space. These models are used to perform coordinate transformations as well as angle and distance calculations.

C.3.2.4 Human Factors Module

The human factors module is based on models of pilot reaction time and perception of simulated continuous motion. The models determine the update frequency appropriate for symbols on a display.

C.3.2.5 Weapon Behavior Module

The weapon behavior module contains models used to predict weapon behavior after release.

...

IV. CONCLUSIONS

Any conclusions that we draw at this point must be considered tentative, as they have not been confirmed by the production of a running program. Nonetheless, we have been using the module guide for several years and it has proven remarkably stable. It plays a significant role in our development process; programmers and designers turn to it when they are unsure about where a certain program should reside. Numerous discussions have been resolved by this means, and relatively few and superficial changes have resulted from the discussions.

Our experience suggests that the use of information hiding in complex systems is practical, but only if the design begins with the writing of a module guide that is used to guide the design of the individual module interfaces. When we tried to work without the guide, numerous problems slipped between the cracks and responsibilities ended up either in two modules or in none. With the module guide, further progress on the design has revealed relatively few oversights. New programmers joining the project are able to get a quick grasp of the structure of our project without using much time talking to those who have been on the project longer. We feel that this will help to ameliorate Brooks' adage, "Adding more men then lengthens, not shortens, the schedule" [8].

We realize that the module guide that we are using as an illustration stops at an arbitrary point. Most of the modules mentioned in this guide are divided into submodules that are not shown in this guide. We found it more convenient to have separate module guides for the smaller modules than to keep extending this one. This module guide is the one document that all implementors must read; the others are for specialists. This one is less than 30 pages in length and we can afford to let everyone read it.

In writing this and other module guides, we have seen how important it is to focus on describing secrets rather than interfaces or roles of the modules. Where we have forgotten that (usually when we are rushing to meet a dealine), we have ended up with modules without clear responsibilities and eventually had to revise our design.

The Module Guide, like our requirements document, provides a clear illustration of the advantages of an approach that we call "design through documentation" [4]. Writing the document is our way of making progress in design. The document then serves to guide us and others in future designs.

In another paper [10], we have argued that this approach increases the likelihood that the software we produce will be reusable and reused. That paper uses the same example to argue rather different points.

ACKNOWLEDGMENT

K. Britton, now with IBM, Research Triangle Park, NC, is a coauthor of our software module guide. Parts of that guide have been included in this paper.

REFERENCES

[1] D. Parnas, "Use of abstract interfaces in the development of software for embedded computer systems," Naval Res. Lab., Washington, DC, NRL Rep. 8047, June 1977.
[2] A. Parker, K. Heninger, D. Parnas, and J. Shore, "Abstract interface specifications for the A-7E device interface module," Naval Res. Lab., Washington, DC. NRL Memo. Rep. 4385, Nov. 20, 1980.
[3] K. Britton, A. Parker, and D. Parnas, "A procedure for designing abstract interfaces for device interface modules," in *Proc. 5th Int. Conf. Software Eng.*, Mar. 1981.
[4] S. Hester, D. Parnas, and D. Utter, "Using documentation as a software design medium," *Bell Syst. Tech. J.*, vol. 60, pp. 1941–1977, Oct. 1981.
[5] D. Parnas, "Designing software for ease of extension and contraction," in *Proc. 3rd Int. Conf. Software Eng.*, May 1978; see also *IEEE Trans. Software Eng.*, vol. SE-5, Mar. 1979.
[6] ——, "On the criteria to be used in decomposing systems into modules," *Commun. ACM*, vol. 15, pp. 1053–1058, Dec. 1972.
[7] K. Britton and D. Parnas, "A-7E software module guide," Naval Res. Lab., Washinton, DC, NRL Memo. Rep. 4702, Dec. 1981.
[8] F. P. Brooks, Jr., *The Mythical Man Month—Essays on Software Engineering*. Reading, MA: Addison-Wesley, 1975.
[9] K. Heninger, J. Kallander, D. Parnas, and J. Shore, "Software requirements for the A-7E aircraft," Naval Res. Lab., Washington, DC, NRL Memo. Rep. 3876, Nov. 27, 1978.
[10] P. Clements, D. Parnas, and D. Weiss, "Enhancing reuseability with information coding," in *Proc. Workshop Reuseability in Programming*, Sept. 1983.

David Lorge Parnas was born in Plattsburgh, NY, on February 10, 1941.

He is currently Lansdowne Professor of Computer Science at the University of Victoria, Victoria, B.C., Canada, as well as Principle Investigator of the Software Cost Reduction Project at the Naval Research Laboratory, Washington, DC. He has also taught at Carnegie-Mellon University, the University of Maryland, the Technische Hochschule Darmstadt, and the University of North Carolina at Chapel Hill. He is interested in all aspects of software engineering. His special interests include program semantics, language design, program organization, process structure, process synchronization, and precise abstract specifications. He is currently leading an experimental redesign of a hard-real-time system in order to evaluate a number of software engineering principles. He is also involved in the design of a language involving new control structures and abstract data types.

Paul C. Clements received the B.S. degree in mathematical sciences in 1977 and the M.S. degree in computer science in 1980, both from the University of North Carolina at Chapel Hill.

Since 1980 he has worked in software engineering research at the Naval Research Laboratory, Washington, DC. In 1982 he became the Technical Coordinator of the Software Cost Reduction Project, whose purpose is to provide a well-engineered model of a complex real-time system. He is interested in most areas of software engineering, but most of his time is spent working on problems in modularization and specification of software designs.

David M. Weiss, for a photograph and biography, see p. 168 of the February 1985 issue of this TRANSACTIONS.

Integrating Access-Oriented Programming into a Multiparadigm Environment

Mark J. Stefik, Daniel G. Bobrow, and Kenneth M. Kahn,
Xerox Palo Alto Research Center

The Loops knowledge programming system integrates function-oriented, object-oriented, rule-oriented, and — something not found in most other systems — access-oriented programming.

Mourning bird-headed figure is a Japanese pottery of the Nara period, Tempyo era, 710-794. It is thought to have formed part of a representation of Buddha's departure from this earth. When that time came, all creatures joined with his disciples to mourn the loss. The intensity of the anguish is made more poignant by the reserved, formal kneeling posture.

Eugene Fuller
Memorial Collection,
Seattle Art Museum

The Loops knowledge programming system[1] contains a number of integrated paradigms of programming. It builds on the function-oriented programming of Interlisp-D[2] and adds the familiar paradigms of rule-oriented and object-oriented programming. Its most unusual contribution is the addition of an access-oriented programming paradigm not found in most systems.

In access-oriented programming, fetching or storing data can cause procedures to be invoked. In terms of actions and side effects, this is dual to object-oriented programming. In object-oriented programming, when one object sends a message to another, the receiving object may change its data as a side effect. In access-oriented programming, when one object changes its data, a message may be sent as a side effect.

Access-oriented programming is based on an entity called an annotated value that associates annotations with data. These annotations can be installed on object variables and can be nested recursively. In Loops there are two kinds of annotated values: property annotations and active values.

Property annotations associate arbitrary extendible property lists with data. Active values associate procedures with data so that methods are invoked when data are fetched and stored. Active values are the basic computational mechanisms of access-oriented programming.

In the access-oriented paradigm, programs are factored into two kinds of parts: parts that compute and parts that monitor the computations. Figure 1 shows this kind of factoring for a traffic simulation program. The traffic simulation program has two modules, called the simulator and the display controller. (This example was inspired by related work in Smalltalk on the partitioning of some programs into models, views, and controllers.)

The simulator represents the dynamics of traffic. It has objects for such things as automobiles, trucks, roads, and traffic lights. These objects exchange messages to simulate traffic interactions. For example, when a traffic light object turns green, it sends messages to start traffic moving.

A shorter version of this article appears in *Conf. Record HICSS-19*, Hawaii International Conference on System Sciences, January 8-10, Honolulu.

Reprinted from *IEEE Software*, January 1986, pages 10-18. Copyright © 1986 by The Institute of Electrical and Electronics Engineers, Inc.

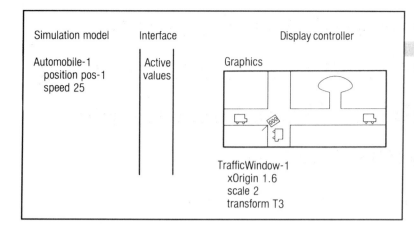

Figure 1. This traffic simulation shows an interactive graphical simulation system for city traffic. The traffic simulator's objects include automobiles, city blocks, emergency vehicles, and traffic lights that exchange messages to simulate traffic interactions. The display controller has objects for traffic icons, viewing transformations, and windows that display different parts of the city connected to the simulation objects by active values.

The display controller has objects representing images of the traffic and provides an interactive user interface for scaling and shifting the views. It has methods for presenting graphics information. The simulator and the display controller can be developed separately, provided there is agreement on the structure of the simulation objects.

Access-oriented programming provides the glue for connecting them at runtime. The process of gluing is dynamic and reversible. When a user tells the display controller to change the views, the controller can make and break connections to the simulator as needed for its monitoring.

To illustrate this example, suppose that the simulator is running and the next event is a traffic light turning green. The traffic light object could then send a go message to each of the stopped vehicles. One of the vehicles, say Car37, receives the message and computes its initial velocity and position.

When the method in Car37 updates its position instance variable, it triggers an active value that then sends an update message to the display object StreetScene13. StreetScene13 may then make a change to the computer display screen so that an image representing Car37 appears to move.

This sequence of events shows how the updating of the computer display is a side effect of running the simulator.

Basic concepts of access-oriented programing

In Loops there are two kinds of annotated values: property annotations and active values. Property annotations associate extendible sets of arbitrary properties with data. Active values associate procedures with data so that methods are invoked when data are fetched and stored.

Annotated values have several important characteristics:

Annotations are invisible to programs that are not looking for them. This is the first invariant of access-oriented programming. Adding and removing annotations are common changes to programs in this paradigm. Making these changes to programs does not cause the programs to stop working, unless the programs use the annotations. New annotations do not interfere with old programs that do not refer to them. For active values, this claim ultimately depends on the condition that the user-defined procedures have noninterfering side effects.

History of access-oriented programming

Access-oriented programming in Loops went through several stages of development. From the beginning, Loops provided one level of property values for annotating object variables. Active values were added shortly thereafter. The unification of these two ideas and their representation as objects was proposed after several years of experience and was under development at the time this article was written.

Access-oriented programming has historical roots in languages like Simula and Interlisp-D, which provide ways of converting record accesses into a computations for all records of a given type. It is also related to the virtual data idea in some computer architectures. For example in the Burroughs B5000, a tag bit associated with data caused data access to be converted into a procedure invocation.

More immediate predecessors are the ideas of procedural attachment from frame languages like KRL,[1] FRL,[2] and KL-One.[3] Attached procedures are programs that are associated with object variables and that are triggered under specific conditions.

Access-oriented programming in Loops is intended to satisfy a somewhat different set of purposes than attached procedures. This has led to a synthesis of ideas with some important differences. Although a thorough historical review is beyond the scope of this article, we occasionally return to attached procedures to show how language features in Loops diverge from that work.

References

1 . Daniel J. Bobrow and Terry Winograd, "An Overview of KRL, a Knowledge Representation Language," *Cognitive Science*, Vol. 1, No. 1, 1977.

2 . R. Bruce Roberts and Ira P. Goldstein, "The FRL Primer," Technical Report AIM-408, Artificial Intelligence Laboratory, Massachusetts Institute of Technology, Cambridge, Mass., July 1977.

3 . R.J. Brachman, "On the Epistemological Status of Semantic Networks," *Associative Networks: Representation and Use of Knowledge by Computers*, N.V. Findler, ed., Academic Press, New York, 1979.

Annotations have a low computational overhead when there are no annotations and also when there are annotations that programs do not reference (such as unreferenced properties). This characteristic takes noninterference a step further. Not only are annotations invisible to programs that ignore them, but they also do not slow things down much. Accesses can either be a function call or compiled open, and the Loops implementation reduces the overhead to a single type check which has microcode support.

Annotations are recursive; they too can be annotated. This extends the main invariant above to cover multiple annotations (that is, adding annotations to data that are already annotated). This characteristic allows the creation of descriptions of descriptions in the case of nested properties and of multiple, independent side effects in the case of nested active values.

Annotations can be efficiently accessed starting from the annotated object. This constraint demands that annotations can be accessed quickly and in a standard way. This characteristic is important for programs that reference annotations explicitly (for example, using the value of a particular property). It is also important for programs that test annotations implicitly (for example, automatic testing for and triggering of active values).

It distinguishes annotated values from ad hoc data structures for annotations that point to their data. Such annotations would have the other characteristics, but would require that programs either search for pointers to data or else provide idiosyncratic arrangements for storing and indexing the annotations.

Annotations are objects that can be specialized and used with standard protocols. This characteristic comes from the features of object-oriented programming to simplify the creation of new kinds of annotations.

Active values have their own variables for saving state. This characteristic comes for free, because active values are objects. As will be shown later, this feature removes a potential path of interaction between active values that are intended to be independent.

Active values. Active values convert a variable reference to a method invocation. They can be installed on the value of any object variable or property. When an active value has been installed, *any* part of the program that accesses the variable will trigger the computation. This is the major lever for elision in access-oriented programming.

Elision is the ability to state concisely and without redundancy what is intended. This is a hallmark of appropriate language support for a paradigm. By eliminating excess verbiage, the programmer can focus on the essentials, having both less opportunity for mistakes and more easily understood programs.

An alternative approach would be to provide a functional interface for changing *each* variable that needs to be monitored. Active values eliminate the need for functional interfaces since they can be installed on each variable as needed.

Active values appear in variables of objects. Each active value contains a localState to hold the value that should appear in that variable. Since an active value is an object, it can also contain additional information in other variables of the active value object. So users can easily view the contents of an active value, an active value is shown as

$\#[<activeValueClass> localState otherSlot1_1 Value_1 ...]$

The class of the active value < activeValueClass > determines the behavior of the active value on access. Below is an example of an active value installed in a Loops object. In this example, an active value is the interface between objects in a simulator and a display controller. The object Automobile-1 represents an automobile in a traffic simulation model. The xPosition instance variable represents the position of the car in the simulation world. The value of xPosition has been made into an active value to connect Automobile-1 with objects in the display controller.

```
Automobile-1
    speed 25
    xPosition
        #[InformDisplayController 50
           viewObjects (<DispObj1> <DispObj2>)]
```

When the simulation stores (that is, puts) a value into xPosition, the Loops access functions will recognize the active value and will send it a PutWrappedValue message. The protocol for the PutWrappedValue message is defined by the InformDisplayController class for the active value.

In this case, update messages will be sent to appropriate objects, DispOb1 and DispObj 2, in the display controller. These objects respond by updating the views in windows of the display.

InformDisplayController is an active value class that updates objects in the display controller. Its special method for storing informs all elements contained in its instance variable viewObjects.

Like other classes in Loops, classes for active values are organized in the inheritance lattice. The class ActiveValue defines a standard protocol for putting and getting values. This protocol is specialized in each kind of active value to describe the particular side effects of getting or putting a value. Most subclasses of ActiveValue either specialize the GetWrappedValue protocol to specify side effects when data are fetched or specialize the PutWrappedValue protocol to specify side effects when data are stored.

The default behavior for GetWrappedValue is to return the value in the localState. The default behavior of Put-

WrappedValue is to store the new value in the localState. As is discussed later, accessing data in the localState may trigger additional side effects if active values are nested.

Property annotations. The second kind of annotated value in Loops is property annotation. Property annotations can be installed on the value of any object variable or property. Properties are useful for describing the relationship between the value of an object variable and the object itself. They also provide a mechanism for storing derived values that can be cached locally.

The idea of property annotations in Loops was motivated by several applications to knowledge programming. Property annotations provide a way of attaching extra descriptions to data for guiding its interpretation. Instance Truck-37, shown below, contains several kinds of annotations that have been used in knowledge engineering applications.

```
Truck-37
    owner PIE          doc  (*owner of truck)
    highway I66        doc  (*Route number of the highway.)
                       prevHighway I9
    milePost 276       doc  (*location on the highway)
                       dataType Integer
    totalWeight 10     doc  (*Current weight of cargo in tons.)
                       upperLimit 12
    stoppingPlace FortWorth    reason AuditRecord12
    arrivalTime 1400   certaintyFactor .8
```

Properties can be used to keep a history of values for a variable. The variable highway has a property prevHighway to record the previous value for the variable. Properties can also be used to save data type information for dynamic checking of programs. This is illustrated by the variable milePost.

Properties can be used to save constraints on values, such as the upperLimit property of totalWeight. In some knowledge engineering applications it is important to save a record of program inferences. For example, the certaintyFactor property of arrivalTime records a measure of the confidence in the estimate of arrival time, and the reason property of stoppingPlace saves a record of the reasoning step that led to this choice of a place to stop.

These properties have no special significance to the Loops kernel. Loops just provides a way of associating the property lists with data so that application programs can find them starting with the data and interpret them appropriately.

We have also considered an implementation in which the properties are stored on an object-wide basis and are separated from the annotated value. This has the disadvantage that the collection of properties of a variable cannot be manipulated as a single entity. The advantage is that variable access is not slowed down by the presence of properties.

Like active values, the idea of extendible property lists for variables has its historical roots in frame languages. Alternative ways of annotating values have been tried in actor and constraint languages (Steele[3] is one example). The major variations in Loops are that property annotations are objects that are created on demand, can be recursively nested, and share much of the implementation of active values.

Recursive annotations. Annotated values can be nested. Nested property notations enable what we loosely call descriptions of descriptions. Nested active values allow the programming of multiple, independent side effects. Both kinds of annotated values have an instance variable, conventionally named localState, used to hold the data.

When annotated values are nested, they are arranged in a chain so the outermost annotated value points to an inner one through its localState and so the innermost annotated value contains the ultimate datum.

When active values are nested, then GetWrappedValue methods or PutWrappedValue methods are procedurally composed. Getting a value eventually causes all of the GetWrappedValue methods to be invoked. Similarly, putting a value causes all of the PutWrappedValue methods to be invoked.

The first step in this sequence is that a PutWrappedValue message is sent to the outermost active value. The outer PutWrappedValue method then performs a computation and at some point needs to store the data in its localState.

This step involves checking whether the localState contains an annotated value. If not, the data is stored directly in localState. If yes, a PutWrappedValue message is sent to the nested annotated value using the same protocol as the outermost active value.

The code for performing this test and storing the data is inherited from AnnotatedValue and is invoked using ←Super as shown below. The PutWrappedValue method invoked by the ←Super is inherited from the class ActiveValue.

```
[LAMBDA (self newValue object varName path type)
    (* This is a specialized
    PutWrappedValue method
    for. . . .)
    (* Specialized side effect code
    invoked before nesting goes here.)
    . . .
    (* This ←Super stores localState
    or invokes a nested active value.)
```

```
(←Super)
    (* Specialized side effect code
    invoked after nesting goes here.)
  . . .]
```

For multiple active values, the net effect is that all of the specialized PutWrappedValue methods for all of the nested active values will be invoked, and the data will ultimately be stored in the localState of the innermost one.

GetWrappedValue methods are based on a similar procedural template. Depending on how these procedural templates are filled out, a PutWrappedValue method or GetWrappedValue method can perform its side effects *before* accessing data in localState, *after* accessing data in localState, or in some combination of the two.

Language support for attached procedures has historically aspired to provide a discipline for controlling interactions among multiple attached procedures. To this end, two issues have been addressed: classifying the kinds of trigger conditions and specifying the order and conditions of execution for multiple procedures.

For example, FRL provided event categories for triggering such as if-needed, if-added, and if-removed. In Loops, the only triggering events are the fetching and storing of data. Specialization of fetching and storing must be programmed in the access methods of the active values.

Other events, such as object creation, are handled by methods on objects that can be specialized (thus taking advantage of the integration with the object-oriented paradigm).

Frame languages have taken various approaches to specifying the order of invocation for multiple procedures. KL-One distinguished between three types of triggers: pre, post, and after. Other frame languages have used an ordered list to specify the order, with exceptions indicated by the use of special tokens returned by the procedures as they are executed.

We have found these sublanguages unnecessary for the common case of composed procedures—and too weak for the exceptional cases of complex ordering anyhow. Loops avoids introducing a sublanguage for control by using nesting of active values for the common case of functional composition and by using the control structures of Lisp inside the methods for the complex cases.

Programming languages like Flavors[4] and Smalltalk[5] support specialized access methods for variables. However, these methods are applicable to all instances of a class. No language support is provided for dynamically attaching (and detaching) methods to individuals.

Applications of access-oriented programming

Access-oriented programming in Loops started out not as a programming paradigm, but rather as a minor varia-

Ordering of access and other operations

Loops allows programmatic control of the order of access to localState of an activeValue and other operations. Different common applications require variations in the time ordering of the side effect and accessing the localState.

For applications like checking a constraint, it is appropriate to check the constraint before the new value is stored. For applications such as computing the sum of the new localState and other data (for example, to maintain a derived value for the sum of a set of figures), one first gets data and then does the summation. A more extensive set of examples is summarized as follows:

Operation	Order of Side Effect	Side Effect for Application
Put	Side effect first	Check a constraint
Put	Side effect second	Update a gauge
Get	Side effect first	Check access privileges
Get	Side effect second	Combine with other data

tion of an implementation for attached procedures. As we have tried new applications, we have looked for ways to change Loops that would simplify our applications.

These changes and simplifications led to the development of the access-oriented paradigm. This section presents a sampling of applications that have shaped the development of the paradigm.

Gauges. When a technician fixes a broken piece of electronic equipment, he brings to the task a collection of measuring tools, such as voltmeters and oscilloscopes. These tools enable him to observe the behavior of a circuit as registered by a probe that he attaches to the circuit paths.

An analogous set of instruments is available in Loops that uses active values as probes for data. For example, one can attach a fuel-gauge active value to the contents of the fuel tank of some truck in the traffic simulator. This active value connects the truck object to a gauge object. Whenever the simulator changes the value of fuel in the truck, the gauge object updates the image on the screen.

The use of a gauge in Loops is very much like taking a meter off the shelf and attaching its probe to a circuit. One simply creates an instance of the appropriate gauge and sends it a message telling it to attach itself to the desired object variable. Figure 2 pictures the object hierarchy for the set of gauges standardly available in the Loops and the set's screen representation.

A gauge is connected to the monitored variable through an active value, an instance of the GaugeProbe class. The important features of GaugeProbe are its variable myGauge and its specialized PutWrappedValue method. Its variable myGauge is analogous to the wire that connects a physical probe to its display instrument. This arrangement also works for attaching multiple gauges on a single datum.

In an earlier implementation of gauges, the active values used fixed properties of the monitored variables to save state, such as pointers to their associated gauges. In that arrangement, special precautions were necessary to keep multiple gauges from interfering with each other.

We now recognize that multiple gauges have independent purposes and should have independent resources. By representing GaugeProbes as Loops objects and using their own state for storing state information, we eliminate an unwanted path of interaction among multiple probes.

This principle simplifies the correct implementation of independent monitoring processes. It is one of the most important differences between active values and attached procedures.

We use gauges as a tool for instrumenting programs. Although gauge-like displays have been used in computer programs for years, their special attraction in Loops is that they can be attached to data in arbitrary programs without changing the program.

To instrument data in most programming languages, it is necessary to find the all of the places in the source program that can change the data and then add code at each place to invoke a display package. Access-oriented programming makes it possible to annotate the program in only one place: the variable to be monitored.

This makes gauges considerably more practical as debugging aids. Gauges provide a more focused way of monitoring program states, with independent views of different aspects.

Traps for variables. Access traps are another application of active values that is generally useful for debugging. They are used to suspend program execution when some variable is referenced. The usual action wanted in a trap is an invocation of a debugging executive, such as the Interlisp break package. Such traps are an important tool for identifying the conditions in a large program when some data are erroneously changed.

Loops provides several kinds of traps:

- GetTraps, which detect when a program fetches a value,
- PutTraps, which detect when a program stores a value,
- AccessTraps, which detect both stores and fetches, and
- ConditionalTraps, which perform a trap operation only if an auxiliary condition is satisfied.

The example below shows the annotation of the object Truck-37 with two traps. Truck-37 has traps on the value of stoppingPlace and on the upperLimit property of total-Weight. When a program tries to change the value of stop-

pingPlace, a break will be unconditionally invoked. The ConditionalTrap on upperLimit illustrates the use of an auxiliary condition to determine when to invoke a break. In this case, the break is invoked only if the new value for the property is greater than 15.

```
Truck-37
  totalWeight #[ConditionalTrap 12
              when (GREATERP newValue
                   (@ containingObject
                        totalWeight::upperLimit))]
     upperlimit 15
  stoppingPlace #[PutTrap FortWorth]
```

Historically, access traps have been used mostly with computers that have a special built-in trap register. Active values bring this capability to a high-level language and allow multiple variables to be monitored simultaneously.

Checking data types and constraints. A generalization of the trap idea is to check new data against constraints before it is stored. An important kind of constraint is a check of the type of data being stored. This kind of specification is of central importance in strongly typed computer languages, where types are checked at compile time.

However, in a late-binding exploratory programming en-

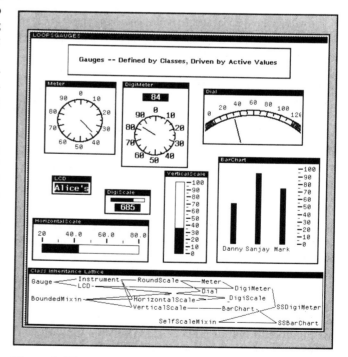

Figure 2. These gauges display the value of the variable to which they are attached. The gauges are updated when the variables are changed. Some, like the vertical scale on the left, can rescale themselves if the value exceeds the gauge limit.

vironment, type checking must be done at runtime and is easily implemented using active values. The example below illustrates some of the type checking notations in Loops.

In this example, the instance variable milePost has a property datatype with the value Integer used by various graphics programs, interpreters, and compilers. Since there is no active value on milePost, it will not be automatically checked during an arbitrary store operation. In contrast, the variable totalWeight has a CheckDataType active value.

During a store operation, this active value will detect an error (or trap) if the new value is not an integer. The case for the arrivalTime instance variable is similar, except that the property datatype has an IntegerSpecification as its value.

These specifications are special objects put on the property list of the variable. These objects have methods for checking more complicated kinds of constraints, such as numeric ranges. The stoppingPlace instance variable has a specification that checks the class lattice to verify that the value is an instance of a city in Texas. These specification objects are put on the property list (not inside the active value) because they are also used for other purposes, such as intelligent editing of the instance Truck-43.

```
Truck-43
    milePost 276 datatype Integer
    . . .
    totalWeight #[CheckDataType 10] datatype Integer
    arrivalTime #[CheckDataType 1400]
        datatype #$IntegerSpecification289
    stoppingPlace #[CheckDataType FortWorth]
        datatype #$CityInTexasSpecification
    . . .
```

Indirection. Some computers have a way of tagging a memory location as containing an indirect address. Any attempt to fetch data from such a location causes data to be fetched instead from the indirect address. Storing data works analogously.

Active values provide an implementation for this idea so that fetches and stores on data cause references to some other object. The IndirectReference class of active values provides for referencing data indirectly in another object. It stores an access path to the real storage location.

This indirection example is fundamentally different in an important way from the gauge examples cited earlier. For gauges, when there are multiple active values, the *order* of nesting doesn't matter much. Side effects are independent and it is enough to ensure that they are all carried out.

The case is different for IndirectReference. These active values do not expect other active values to be more deeply nested. Their correct operation requires that they be the most deeply nested values so they will have the last GetWrappedValue or PutWrappedValue operation.

To support this need, active values follow a protocol of informing nested active values when they are installed. This enables active values whose placement is critical to adjust the order of nesting.

Truckin' and the Track Announcer. One of the largest programs written in Loops is the Truckin' knowledge game. The Truckin' program and related programs make extensive use of access-oriented programming.

Truckin' is a board game inspired in part by Monopoly. Figure 3 shows a snapshot of a Truckin' game board. The board has road stops arranged along a highway (which implicitly loops along the edges of the board). The players in the game drive trucks around, buying and selling commodities. Their goal is to make a profit. The game is based on a relatively complicated simulation that includes such things as road hazards, perishable and fragile goods, bandits, gas stations, and weigh stations.

An unusual feature of Truckin' is that the players are actually computer programs developed by the students taking a course on knowledge programming in Loops.[6] We use the game as a rich and animated environment for teaching principles of knowledge programming.

One of the design issues in implementing Truckin' was to find a way to ensure that the picture of the game board is always up to date with the underlying simulation. Several people were involved in writing the Truckin' simulator. There are many places where the values in the road stops could be changed either by direct action of the game master or by the need to maintain some constraints.

As it was in the simulator/display controller example cited earlier, our approach was to connect the screen image of each road stop to the underlying object variables. Each road stop image in the display is a sort of gauge monitoring part of the simulator.

A related program is the Truckin' Track Announcer, written by Martin Kay. The visual display of Truckin' changes quite rapidly during a competition. One of the ideas that came up during the Loops courses was to augment the display with a sort of radio announcer, an automatic program that would generate interesting spoken commentary about the competition as it unfolded.

The design of the Track Announcer had some of the same constraints as the game display. It needed to be informed about relevant changes in the progress of the game. Furthermore, it needed to be developed separately from Truckin' at a time when Truckin' itself was still evolving. Figure 4 illustrates the basic architecture of the design. Active values were used to connect the Track Announcer to key variables in the players and road stops. These active values sent messages to a collection of objects called observers.

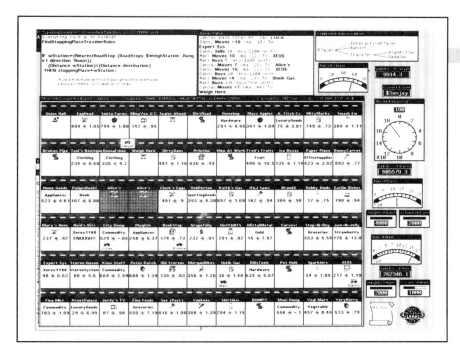

Figure 3. This is a display from the Truckin' game. Trucks are controlled by user programs. They must buy and sell goods and must avoid the bandits in black cars. The display is maintained by active value probes into the simulation.

Figure 4. Observer demons watch for interesting patterns in the Truckin' game that can be converted to utterances. A new observer can be inserted at any time using an active value probe.

Observers are responsible for detecting interesting patterns of change in the game and then generating comments about them. These comments are placed on a queue of candidate utterances. A priority scheme is then used to select the next utterance to, say, send it to a speech synthesizer device.

The observers in the Track Announcer are like demons in the Planner language.[7] Demons are programs triggered whenever specified conditions become satisfied. A key implementation consideration for demons is finding an efficient way to monitor the demon conditions.

While Loops does not currently support demons, the Track Announcer example suggests how active values could be used in their implementation. For example, a demon

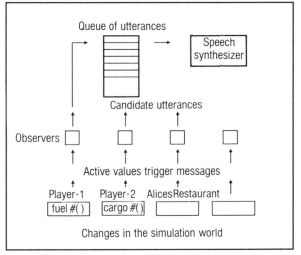

A merger of Lisp and object-oriented programming

Researchers at Xerox PARC, drawing on their experience with object-oriented languages such as Smalltalk and Loops, have proposed an object-oriented programming standard for Common Lisp. The proposed extension, CommonLoops, also allows integration of the access-oriented programming paradigm.

CommonLoops is compatible with Lisp's functional programming style. Message sending uses the same syntax as function calls. Object-oriented capabilities are simple extensions of Common Lisp structure defining operations, while object space is defined as a natural extension of the type-space in Common Lisp.

CommonLoops uses the same style of names and syntax as Common Lisp to provide a simple and direct path into object-oriented programming for those accustomed to Common Lisp. Thus programs written in Lisp can become incrementally object-oriented.

CommonLoops's small kernel is easy to integrate into Common Lisp implementations and has fewer special features than most object-oriented languages. The use of metaclasses facilitates specialized object representations and variations of multiple inheritance.

The kernel provides several extensions to object-oriented programming, including method lookup based on the class of more than one argument (a multimethod) or the identity of a particular argument.

A version of the CommonLoops proposal was aired at the August 1985 meeting of the Common Lisp Objects Committee at the International Joint Conference on Artificial Intelligence. CommonLoops and the other proposals for the standard are reviewed in "Object-Oriented Programming: Themes and Variations" by Mark J. Stefik and Daniel G. Bobrow in the winter 1986 issue of *AI Magazine*.

Xerox is building a portable implementation of CommonLoops in Common Lisp for community experimentation.

—Daniel G. Bobrow, Kenneth M. Kahn, Gregor Kiczales, Larry Masinter, and Mark J. Stefik, Xerox PARC

compiler could convert a source description of demon conditions and generate an appropriate set of active values installed on the necessary variables.

Access-oriented programming is based on annotated values that associate annotations with data. These annotations can be dynamically attached to and removed from object variables and can be nested recursively. Loops provides three language features that accommodate the dynamic addition and deletion of annotations.

The first feature is that annotated values are invisible to programs that are not looking for them. Annotations can be added to programs without causing them to stop working.

The second feature is that annotated values are recursive. They can be added to data that are already annotated. Nested properties support the notion of descriptions of descriptions. Nested active values enable multiple, independent side effects on variable access.

The third feature is that annotated values are objects and have their own independent local variables for saving state. This contrasts with the technique of using variables or properties of the monitored object to save state. This language feature removes a path of potential interference among multiple active values intended to be independent.

These language features support the access-oriented paradigm. They provide concise expression of intent and facilitate program evolution. □

Mark J. Stefik is a principal scientist in the Knowledge Systems Area in the Intelligent Systems Laboratory of the Xerox Palo Alto Research Center. His current research includes work on expert systems for design and languages for knowledge programming. He recently started the Colab project at Xerox PARC, which is exploring computer support for collaboration and problem solving in face-to-face meetings.

Stefik received his PhD from Stanford University in 1980 for his work on the Molgen program.

He is the book review editor for the journal *Artificial Intelligence*. Stefik serves as a councilor for the American Association for Artificial Intelligence.

Daniel G. Bobrow is a research fellow in the Knowledge Systems Area at Xerox PARC's Intelligent Systems Laboratory. His recent work includes design and implementation of CommonLoops, a proposed extension of Common Lisp for object-oriented programming.

He received his PhD in mathematics from the Massachusetts Institute of Technology with a dissertation on artificial intelligence.

Bobrow is editor-in-chief of the journal *Artificial Intelligence* and has been an editor of the *Communications of the ACM*. He was chair of the governing board of the Cognitive Science Society and served on the executive council of the American Association for Artificial Intelligence.

References

1. D.G. Bobrow and M. Stefik, *The Loops Manual*, Xerox Corp., Palo Alto, Calif., 1983.

2. M. Sanella, *The Interlisp-D Reference Manual*, Xerox Corp., Palo Alto, Calif., 1983.

3. G. Steele, "The Definition and Implementation of a Computer Programming Language Based on Constraints," Technical Report AI-TR-595, Artificial Intelligence Laboratory, Massachusetts Institute of Technology, Cambridge, Mass., 1980.

4. D. Weinreb and D. Moon, *Lisp Machine Manual*, Symbolics Corp., Cambridge, Mass., 1984.

5. A. Goldberg and D. Robson, *Smalltalk-80—The Language and Its Implementation,* Addison-Wesley, Reading, Mass., 1983.

6. M. Stefik et al., "Knowledge Programming in Loops: Report on an Experimental Course," *The AI Magazine*, Fall 1983.

7. C.E. Hewitt, "Planner: A Language for Proving Theorems in Robots," *Proc. First Int'l Conf. Artificial Intelligence*, Washington, DC, 1969.

Kenneth M. Kahn is a research staff member in the Knowledge Systems Area at Xerox PARC's Intelligent Systems Laboratory. His work there includes designing and implementing CommonLoops, a proposed extension of Common Lisp for object-oriented programming.

Kahn received his masters degree and PhD in computer science from the Massachusetts Institute of Technology. After a year on the staff of MIT's AI laboratory, he became a visiting professor at the University of Stockholm in Sweden.

The authors' address is Intelligent Systems Laboratory, Xerox Palo Alto Research Center, 3333 Coyote Hill Rd., Palo Alto, CA 94304.

Object-Oriented Data Base Design

Robert W. Peterson

Texas Instruments

BY ROBERT W. PETERSON

PHOTO: CLAYTON PRICE/IMAGE BANK

Object-OrientedData

Classic data management relies on a number of well-known solutions to solve business data-handling problems such as accounting and payroll. In recent years such applications as computer-aided design and computer-aided manufacturing (CAD/CAM), circuit simulation, and office automation systems have begun to stress, even overstress, classical methods of data management.

The field of object-oriented data bases is about four years old, but researchers have already organized sessions at data base conferences. Recent meetings have included the Databases session chaired by Paul McCullogh at OOPSLA '86 (Object-Oriented Programming Systems, Languages, and Applications) in Portland, Ore., and the 1986 International Workshop on Object-Oriented Database Systems in Pacific Grove, Calif. OOPSLA '86 was sponsored by the Association for Computing Machinery, while the workshop was jointly sponsored by the Association for Computing Machinery's Special Interest Group on the Management of Data (SIGMOD) and the Institute of Electronic and Electrical Engineers Computer Society.

This article discusses the idea of object-oriented data bases, contrasting this new development with classical approaches to data management. Current work in the field is outlined, followed by a discussion of some of the outstanding problems.

An understanding of data management issues will help the reader appreciate the problems and solutions discussed, but an in-depth understanding of data base management systems is not needed to see what object-oriented data bases are all about.

BaseDesign

THE PROBLEM

Data processing applications are implemented to model some real-world system. Classic accounting applications model an account's paper ledgers and journals. Electronic mail systems model the paper-based U.S. Postal Service. More obviously, a circuit-modeling program simulates the expected behavior of a real circuit.

One of the measures of a data processing tool's goodness is how easily the tool can be made to model the real world. The distance between the tool and the world is frequently referred to as the "semantic gap." Tools with a smaller gap are easier to use. For example, in coding classic business applications COBOL is easier to use than assembly language or LISP. Not only does a small semantic gap make the programmer's job easier, but it frequently results in better processing efficiency.

The classic business problems (accounting, payroll, inventory, etc.) have long relied on such data management tools as sequential and indexed files and, more recently, hierarchical, network, and relational data base management systems. The data used by these applications is for the most part very regular, which means the data items and records have well-defined formats and simple interactions. These items and records are represented by simple record declarations in programming languages such as COBOL and RPG.

Early applications that ran on computers using magnetic tape for mass storage relied on simple sequential files. Some applications still use this approach, especially for processing very large master files.

For example, an invoice or shipping rec-

> This approach provides support for more complex data applications

The relational data model is very simple but very powerful

ord might be represented in a sequential file by a header record type followed by a varying number of detail records of various types. The header record contains the data appearing in the top portion of the invoice, such as the invoice number, the name and address of the company being invoiced, and the date of the invoice. Each instance of one detail record type would correspond to one of the invoice's detail lines. One detail line type might describe an item, the item's unit price, and the number of units sold. Another might describe a back-ordered item, including the expected ship date.

As drums and disk drives became available, files began to have indexes to speed access to arbitrary records based on a record key. ISAM and, more recently, IBM's VSAM are widely used access methods.

An invoice file might also be maintained as several indexed files, one for the headers and the others for the detail record types. This organization supports the rapid retrieval required to allow interactive querying of data by a customer service person using a terminal.

A hierarchical data base management system, like early versions of IBM's IMS/DB product, organizes all data into a single, logical file. Within this file or data base, records are organized as header or parent record types with a varying number of detail or child record types. A parent record may have multiple instances of various child record types, but a child record has exactly one parent record type.

This hierarchical approach to data organization is easy to implement. However, it is not flexible and is unable to easily model the complexity of an entire business in which different hierarchies may exist (depending on one's point of view) or in which more general relationships must be represented.

Network data bases (sometimes referred to as CODASYL data bases, after the Conference on Data System Languages that described this data base model in detail in the late 1960s) relieve the major restrictions of the hierarchical data model. As a result, they reduce the semantic gap between the real world and the data processing model of that real world. Network data bases retain the idea of a header and detail records, called "owners" and "members" in network terms, but allow a member record to have multiple owners.

For example, if company A is both a supplier and customer of company B, company B's network data base might have a single record containing company A's name, address, telephone number, etc. That single name and address record might be owned by invoice header records, purchase order header records, and check records. This way of organizing the data for minimum replication is not possible in the hierarchical data model because of the single parent limitation.

All the data models discussed so far require application programs to understand how the data is logically organized. That is, processing invoices requires a program to read an invoice header record, all the detail records of that header, then the next header records, and so on. Thus if the data organization is changed, the programs referencing the data may also change. In contrast, one of the goals of the relational data model was to hide how data was organized.

The relational model is very simple but very powerful. One of its major features is its complete independence from any need to understand how data is organized. It presents data items as records, called "tuples," that are organized into simple, two-dimensional tables. A "calculus" describes how tables are combined and reorganized for processing. There are no parent or child records, only a table with rows, also called "tuples," and columns. Each column contains one field of the collection of tuples. The relational calculus describes how tables may be created, combined, divided, and queried. The relational data model provides an especially simple and elegant interface to interactive users whose queries cannot be anticipated.

Originally proposed by E.F. Codd in the early 1970s, the processing required by the relational model has been a major barrier to its widespread use. The semantic gap between these data models and classic data processing applications is relatively small. However, the gap between these models and other applications types is large.

In recent years computers have increasingly been used to support engineering and manufacturing workers. CAD/CAM, circuit simulation, architectural design support, and similar complex applications do not map well into any of the preceding data models. In addition to a rich set of data types with complex interactions, these applications are frequently interactive and demand very fast retrieval of small amounts of data.

For example, an architect using a design program to work on a house plan may wish to view the design as a floor plan, an elevation (say, a view of each side of the house), or a list of components such as doors, windows, 2x4 lumber, and bricks.

The architect may wish to switch from one view to another very quickly, making changes interactively and immediately reviewing the impact of the change from another perspective. The relationships among the data items and records that model the design are very complex compared to an invoice. In addition, the objects themselves may be very complex (for example, the circuit interconnection network to be used in a simulation, or the simulation program itself).

Even more demanding on conventional data models, the architect may wish to develop several slightly different designs, all evolving from a single, basic starting point, and then merge selected variations back into the basic design. Applications with these complexities and requirements are becoming more common, creating a need for a new data model.

OBJECT-ORIENTED DATA BASES

Object-oriented data bases are emerging to support these complex applications. Developed from the concepts of object-oriented programming, object-oriented data bases reduce the semantic gap between complex applications and the data storage supporting those applications.

The object-oriented approach to programming encapsulates into a single structure data and the procedures, also called "methods," that manage that data. The external interface of each object is defined by the object's methods. The exact form of each method, as well as any data items contained in the object, are not accessible or visible from outside the object. This object abstraction results in programs constructed of objects that interact by calling each other's methods.

While object abstraction is important, the rest of the story is inheritance. Just as Pascal types and variables are defined in terms of other types, objects are often defined in terms of other objects. Object-oriented programming extends this idea. An object may inherit attributes from more than one object definition and actually mix, match, and even substitute inherited variables and methods. This means that, for example, an object *castle* might inherit from the object *home* the notions of room, roof, window, and door but add the notions of tower and moat. The *castle* object might specialize the *door* object with methods to lock, unlock, open, and close. It might also create a *drawbridge* object by substituting raise and lower methods for open and close but retaining the *door* object's lock and unlock methods.

Well-known examples of object-oriented

Object abstraction is important, but the rest of the story is inheritance

languages include Smalltalk, LISP Flavors, and C++. There are a number of less well-known but important experiments in object-oriented systems, such as Mach, a UNIX-compatible, object-oriented operating system developed at Carnegie-Mellon University, Pittsburgh, Pa., and the Trellis/Owl system from Digital Equipment Corp.

The basic idea of an object-oriented data base is to represent an item in the real world being modeled with a corresponding item in the data base. This includes modeling the behavior of each object as well as the object's structure.

The architect's house design for the Jones family would be a single object in the data base. In addition to modeling the Jones' house structure, the design object might also model the house design's behavior in high winds or its heating and cooling requirements under varying conditions. The Jones' plan would, of course, contain many objects, each of which is also in the data base as a single addressable and sharable object. This one-to-one mapping reduces the semantic gap between the real world and the data base modeling of that world.

One result of coupling an object-oriented data base with an object-oriented programming style is the virtual elimination of the semantic gap between a program and its supporting data. In the introduction to the *Proceedings of the 1986 International Workshop on Object-Oriented Database Systems,*[1] Klaus Dittrich defines three levels of "object orientation":

(a) If the data model allows to define data structures to represent entities of any complexity, we call it *structurally object-oriented* (i.e, there are complex objects).

(b) If the data model includes (generic) operators to deal with complex objects in their entirety (in contrast to being forced to decompose the necessary operations into a series of simple object—e.g. tuple or homogeneous set of tuples—operations), we call it *operationally object-oriented*; as it is hardly meaningful without, we require that operational object-orientation includes structural object-orientation.

(c) Borrowing types from the object-

POSTGRES, GENESIS, EXODUS, and PROBE all extend relational data models

oriented programming paradigm, a data model may also incorporate features to define object types (again of any complexity) together with a set of specific operators (abstract data types); instances can then only be used by calling these operators, their internal structure may only be exploited by the operator implementations; we call systems based on this approach *behaviorally object-oriented*.

Most research efforts attempt to be either operationally object-oriented or behaviorally object-oriented.

Researchers and developers have approached object-oriented data base implementation from two directions: extending the relational model or applying the ideas of object-oriented programming to permanent storage. A reasonable case can be made for each approach, although the latter seems to be more popular. Extended relational models tend to be operationally object-oriented, while behaviorally object-oriented systems are usually extensions of object-oriented languages or environments and operating systems.

POSTGRES, a research project at the University of California at Berkeley, is a relational data base with extensions to support object management. POSTGRES extends the relational data base model with an abstract data typing mechanism and procedures as a fundamental data type. M. Stonebraker[2,3] argues that the many data models developed over the last decade exhibit widely varying concepts and that unifying these constructs into a single data model will be impossible. Stonebraker proposes developing a data model able to simulate all the various constructs. POSTGRES is an attempt to do this.

Support for abstract data types means POSTGRES allows the user to define a new data type, use that data type to define a column in a relation, and define procedures usable in a relational query that manipulate the new data type. Dates, for example, might be defined as an abstract type, along with procedures for format conversion, addition, subtraction, and comparison. A query could then ask for tuples where the date field contained any date in the range December 31, 1986, and 20 May 87.

Extending the relational model with procedures as data base objects solves three problems. First, a data base user no longer needs to access a subobject within a data base object. Procedures are the mechanism for implementing a "part of" hierarchy; for example, a wheel is part of a bicycle, and a spoke is part of a wheel.

The second problem involves the unpredictable types of subobjects. A basket on one bicycle might contain a hat, gloves, and a candy bar, while a basket on another bicycle might contain a bag of peanuts, a flashlight, and sunglasses. Using a procedure type, the contents of the various baskets can be modeled efficiently.

The third problem is that of handling subobjects shared by several objects. A circuit board is an object, and each circuit element is a subobject. Using a procedure to reference it, the circuit board object can be stored once and indirectly referenced by each circuit element.

Some efforts using unextended relational data base systems to store arbitrary objects have had performance problems. Lawrence Rowe[4] claims POSTGRES will solve the performance problem.

Other efforts to extend the relational data model with support for complex objects include the Starburst project[5] at the IBM Almaden Research Center; GENESIS[6] at the University of Texas at Austin; EXODUS[7,8] at the University of Wisconsin; and PROBE[9] at the Computer Corporation of America.

EXTENDING YOUR DATA BASE

Typical of attempts to extend the concepts of object-oriented programming to data base systems are GemStone[10] and Jasmine.[11,12]

GemStone is an object-oriented data base server being developed by Servio Logic Development Corp., and Jasmine is being developed at the University of Washington in Seattle, Wash. Efforts are under way at Tektronix Inc.,[13] the University of Grenoble, France,[14] and other places to add to the Smalltalk environment support for persistent objects.

GemStone can be classified as behaviorally object-oriented, providing the controlled shared access and permanence of data common to data base systems. Unusual for data base systems but increasingly common in object-oriented data bases, GemStone supports object identity independent of an object's physical location or contents. Thus the Jones' house plan object has a unique identity regardless of where the object is stored or what the object's fields contain (for example, the plan object retains its identity as Jones' plan even if the construction address changes or the object is made empty).

This idea of identity contrasts with indexing because indexing (also referred to as "identifier keys") depends on particular values of data items within a record. This also means an object's identity is different from and independent of the programming language symbol used to refer to it.[15]

The problems with an object-oriented approach to data bases are:

■ It lacks a coherent data model with a mathematical foundation such as relational calculus (this problem has several implications, including the difficulty of specifying queries and ensuring the data base is consistent)

■ Research into storage structures for efficient object storage is in the very early stages of development

■ Use of an object-oriented data base from a conventional data processing language such as COBOL, Pascal, or C is difficult because of the semantic gap. These langauges lack the idea of an object.

THE FUTURE

The object-oriented data model is the natural result of the union of two technologies: object-oriented programming and data base management. Significant research is going on in the areas of object-oriented data base systems and related languages. Important research areas include data models, object versions across time or through the use of "what if" to create alternative revisions, object identity, high-level language interfaces, protection and locking mechanisms for objects and subobjects, long transactions (transactions running for hours or days, a major problem for engineering applications), and data base design and administration tools.

Some of these areas are not unique to object-oriented data bases, but in the context of an object-oriented data base their importance becomes accentuated.

In the near future object-oriented data base technology will become another accepted and commonly used data model and take up a position alongside the relational model as the subject of research efforts and commercial products. **AI**

REFERENCES

1. Dittrich, Klaus R. "Object-oriented Database Systems: The Notion and The Issue." In *1986 International Workshop on Object-Oriented Database Systems*, Pacific Grove, Calif., Sept. 1986.

2. Stonebraker, Michael. "Object Management in POSTGRES Using Procedures." In *1986 International Workshop on Object-Oriented Database Systems*, Pacific Grove, Calif., Sept. 1986.

3. Stonebraker, Michael, and Lawrance A. Rowe. "The Design of POSTGRES." In *Proceedings: 1986 ACM SIGMOD International Conference on the Management of Data*, June 1986.

4. Rowe, Lawrance A. "A Shared Object Hierarchy." In *1986 International Workshop on Object-Oriented Database Systems*, Pacific Grove, Calif., Sept. 1986.

5. Schwarz, P., W. Chang, J.C. Freytag, G. Lohman, J. McPherson, C. Mohan, and H. Pirahesh. "Extensibility in the Starburst Database System." In *1986 International Workshop on Object-Oriented Database Systems*, Pacific Grove, Calif., Sept. 1986.

6. Batory, D.S., J.R. Barnett, J.F. Garza, K.P. Smith, K. Tsukuda, B.C. Twitchell, and T.E. Wise. *GENESIS: A Reconfigurable Database Management System*. Technical Report 86-07, Dept. of Computer Science, Univ.of Texas at Austin, 1986.

7. Carey, M., D. DeWitt, J. Richardson, and E. Shekita. *Technical Report*, Dept. of Computer Science, University of Wisconsin (March 1986).

8. Carey, M., D. DeWitt, D. Frank, G. Graefe, M. Muralikrishna, J. Richardson, and E. Shekita. "The Architecture of the EXODUS Extensible DBMS." In *1986 International Workshop on Object-Oriented Database Systems*, Pacific Grove, Calif., Sept. 1986.

9. Dayal, U., A. Buchmann, D. Goldhirsch, S. Heiler, F. Manola, J. Orenstein, and A. Rosenthal. *PROBE—A Research Project in Knowledge-Directed Database Management: Preliminary Analysis*, Technical Report CCA-85-03, Computer Corporation of America.

10. Maier, David, Jacob Stein, Allen Otis, and Alan Purdy, "Development of an Object-Oriented DBMS." In *ACM OOPSLA 1986 Conference Proceedings*, Sept. 1986.

11. Marczullo, K., and Wiebe, D. "Jasmine: A Software System Modeling Facility." Submitted to the 2nd ACM SIGSOFT/SIGPLAN Symposium on Practical Software Development Environments, Palo Alto, Calif., Dec. 1986.

12. Wiebe, D., "A Distributed Repository for Immutable Persistent Objects." In *ACM OOPSLA 1986 Conference Proceedings*, Sept. 1986.

13. Vegdahl, S. "Moving Structures between Smalltalk Images." In *ACM OOPSLA 1986 Conference Proceedings*, Sept. 1986.

14. Decouchant, D. "Design of a Distributed Object Manager for the Smalltalk-80 System. In *ACM OOPSLA 1986 Conference Proceedings*, Sept. 1986.

15. Khoshafian, S.N., and G.P. Copeland. "Object Identity." In *ACM OOPSLA 1986 Conference Proceedings*, Sept. 1986.

In the near future object-oriented data base technology will become commonly used

Robert Peterson is a member of the technical staff at Texas Instruments' Computer Science Center, where he is one member of a team implementing an object-oriented data base management system.

The Learnability of Object-oriented Programming Systems

Chair
Tim O'Shea, Systems Concepts Laboratory, Xerox PARC

Panelists
Tim O'Shea, Systems Concepts Laboratory, Xerox PARC
Kent Beck, Computer Research Laboratory, Tektronix, Inc.
Dan Halbert, Digital Equipment Corporation
Kurt Schmucker, Productivity Products International

There is an interesting lack of consensus on several key issues related to the learnability of object-oriented programming systems. Some experts regard these new systems as qualitatively different from procedural systems, whilst others argue that there is one general approach that can be applied to designing instruction related to any computer programming language. All the panelists have substantial relevant teaching experience and have been selected to reflect the current range of opinions. The learnability debate is an important one because its outcome should influence both the development of new curriculum materials and the overall design of new object-oriented programming systems.

In addition to the contributions from the panelists who have submitted the 4 position papers printed in the Proceedings we hope also to have a contribution from Bruce Anderson of the University of Essex who has participated (with Ralph Hodgson and Steve Cook) in a study of the views of 150 British computer users and is in the process of identifying the specific research needs of this area.

Tim O'Shea

This paper very briefly summarizes an empirical study based on five different sources of data. These sources are questionnaires issued to 31 professional programming language designers, interviews with 12 teachers, questionnaires issued to a class of 15 postgraduate students, daily learning inventories completed by 7 self-paced learners and interviews with 14 self-taught programmers. All of these subjects had a minimum of forty hours experience of an object-oriented programming system and some of the subjects have themselves successfully designed or implemented components of well known systems.

The data reveals a variety of learnability problems. Those related to syntax and the parsing of expressions are straightforward and have previously been identified as causing problems in procedural languages. The problems related to semantics are for the most part special to object-oriented programming systems. Some of the fundamental concepts (such as objects, classes and message passing) turn out to be very easy for learners to master. However some of the other concepts are very difficult and we can isolate metaclasses in particular as the single most important source of learnability problems. Another major area of difficulty is understanding the more subtle mechanisms for method inheritance. As far as the environment is concerned there turns out to be a variety of "navigation problems" that confront the learner. These are ameliorated in part by the effective use of browsers but greatly exacerbated by the horrifying size of the mature object-oriented programming systems.

The position of the learner can be eased by the development of improved curricula and by ensuring that syntactic and naming conventions that are known to be problematic are avoided. But there is also potential for improving the design of existing systems by, for example, removing metaclasses as an explicit construct, providing appropriate tracing facilities for tracking method inheritance and supporting easier navigation by adding layering to class hierarchies (moving from the "spaghetti model" to the "lasagne model").

In conclusion this empirical study provides evidence (which in the case of the learning inventories is very detailed and reliable) for learnability problems peculiar to the current generation of object-oriented programming systems.

Kent Beck

I will discuss the teaching of object-oriented programming (OOP) in the context of teaching Smalltalk-80 to Tektronix customers and new engineers.

There are five stages to mastering a complex object-oriented programming system:

1) Understanding the computational mechanism

2) Becoming facile with the environment

3) Learning about the reusable parts of the system that are already available

4) Learning to decompose problems into objects

5) Turning solutions to specific problems into generic solutions

The computational mechanism of object-oriented programming is clearly set forth in Smalltalk-80: The

Language and its Implementation [1]. Giving students an intellectual understanding of message-passing, objects, and inheritance is facilitated by just having them read the book. With practice, our students seem to internalize this knowledge effectively, leading to a comfortable understanding of objects and messages as a computational paradigm.

Similarly, Smalltalk-80: The Interactive Programming Environment [2] gives students a head start at learning the second stage, and practice solidifies this understanding.

Becoming familiar with the ~250 classes in the Smalltalk-80 image can be a daunting task to a newcomer, but after finding ready-made solutions a few times students have ample incentive to browse around and learn what is available and where it is located. Again, Smalltalk-80: The Language and its Implementation is helpful in getting them started, but experience is invaluable in reinforcing the knowledge.

The fourth stage is more difficult than the other three. System analysis in OOP is different from analysis in procedural languages because the focus is on the data rather than the functions. However, after seeing some of the examples in the image (Model-View-Controller being an exemplar), our students have been able to grasp what it means to break a problem into objects, and to go on to use OOP to solve their problems.

The last stage is much more difficult than the preceding four. Even our researchers who use Smalltalk every day do not often come up with generally useful abstractions from the code they use to solve problems. Useful abstractions are usually created by programmers with an obsession for simplicity, who are willing to rewrite code several times to produce easy-to-understand and easy-to-specialize classes.

I argue that the above five stages have exact analogues in large, complicated procedural environments. Where OOP is easy to teach, the procedural systems are easy to teach. Teaching students how to edit and compile files, how a particular procedural language works, and what subroutine libraries are available and how to use them is a straightforward if sometimes tedious task. Similarly, where OOP is hard to teach, procedural systems do not do any better. Decomposing problems into procedures is recognized as a difficult problem, and elaborate methodologies have been developed to help programmers in this process. Programmers who can go a step further and make their procedural solutions to a particular problem into a generic library are rare and valuable.

I conclude that teaching OOP is really no different than teaching procedural systems. Inertia, lack of experience, and a dearth of teaching tools and methodologies are all that keep OOP from being effectively disseminated.

[1] Goldberg, A. and Krasner, G. Smalltalk-80: The Language and Its Implementation. Addison-Wesley 1983.

[2] Goldberg, A. Smalltalk-80: The Interactive Programming Environment. Addison-Wesley 1984.

Dan Halbert

Our group, the Object-Based Systems Group at Digital, is a source of object-oriented programming expertise within the company. Though we don't teach formal courses, we are trying to introduce programmers at Digital to the concepts of object-oriented programming, mostly by giving advice and by soliciting trial users of our object-oriented programming system, Trellis.

Naturally, there have been problems, both in our own group and outside, when programmers start using object-oriented programming. Once they get the idea, programmers like object-oriented programming very much. I will skip saying why object-oriented programming is a wonderful thing; I think you know that it is. But there are hurdles to learning it. I'll cover a few of the problems and what can be done about them.

Learning object-oriented methodology

We have found that nearly all programmers have a basic, if shallow, understanding of the ideas of object-oriented programming. Most have been exposed to the concept of abstract data types, and many have an idea of what inheritance means.

But understanding these concepts is not the same as being able to apply them. For instance, many programmers are accustomed to thinking in terms of procedural abstractions, emphasizing actions and processes, rather data and state. As a result, when they first try object-oriented programming, they may map the procedural abstractions they would have created directly onto object type definitions. They have other difficulties too, such as implementing behavior in the wrong objects, or creating type hierarchies that correspond poorly to levels of abstraction.

The problem is that the programmers do not know how to apply the methodology of object-oriented programming. At present, they can learn this skill only by example, trial and error, or apprenticeship. There is plenty of material describing various object-oriented systems, but I have seen very little good material on the design of object-oriented programs.

We must spend more time in the future discovering, teaching, and writing about the general principles of object-oriented design. Right now, most good object-oriented programming practices are understood only in an intuitive way. If we can codify the methodology, we will change it from lore to principle, and can introduce it to others all the more quickly.

A good analogy to the present state of object-oriented programming is that of the early "structured programming". Despite the vagueness and misinterpretation of what this term meant, we are now better off because people wrote about and tried to follow the methodology it suggested. Today, new programmers are exposed to relatively well-written code much of the time. When they try to emulate it, they also end up with good code. I am confident the same will happen with object-oriented programming: it will become a part of ordinary programming culture. But how fast this happens will depend on how well we do in teaching the initial critical mass of object-oriented programmers.

Learning the system

Leaving methodology issues aside, it still takes programmers a relatively long time to learn to program in most object-oriented language systems. The language is not the cause. Programmers have relatively little difficulty learning the syntax and semantics of a particular object-oriented language. Each language has its idiosyncrasies, but programmers are used to learning such foibles.

Instead, much time is spent learning the large library that is an integral part of most object-oriented language systems. Many of the fundamental data types in an object-oriented system are provided by the library, rather than by the language. Large libraries are not unique to object-oriented languages (consider Lisp, for example), but the ease with which new types and behavior can be added encourages large libraries.

These libraries are actually a great advantage, because they provide functionality that would otherwise be implemented by programmers again and again. The problem is in distinguishing what in the library is essential to basic programming, and what is extra. Too often, everything seems to be interconnected. The system library should be constructed in a layered fashion, so that programmers can learn minimal subsets at first, and then gradually add to the functionality they know how to use. In the long run, standardization of parts of the library, such as the window system, will also make it easier for programmers to learn new systems.

The need for supportive programming environments

A programming system should provide tools to help the programmer in reading and writing code. Writing code in an object-oriented system with no tools but a text editor can be a frustrating experience.

As an example, consider the problem of program readability. We all know that reading ordinary paper listings of an object-oriented program is a real nuisance. The code to implement a particular type is spread out: it is in the type itself, and also in all the supertypes of that type. Following a thread of control is also not easy, and requires skipping around from type to type. When we try to read code, we spend a lot of time flipping back and forth between type definitions. Eventually we run out of fingers to use as placeholders, or else we end up with listings strewn all over the desk.

These kinds of problems can be solved by programming environment tools. For instance, tools should exist which present a complete view of a type,

including the code it has inherited. We must strive to make it more convenient to look at code using the environment than on paper.

Conclusion

There is nothing inherently difficult about object-oriented programming. But to make it accessible to and accepted by all programmers, we must, most importantly, teach the methodology, and we must also structure our systems better and provide better programming support. I think object-oriented programming will become pervasive in any case, but we can speed up the process.

Kurt J. Schmucker

During the past eighteen months I have been directly involved in teaching both the basic principles of OOP in a two-day public course entitled "The Concepts of Object-Oriented Programming" and the specifics of one object-oriented language, Objective-C®, a hybrid object-oriented extension of the C language, in a three-day, private, hands-on course. This experience has led me to the following conclusions:

- Learning the basic concepts of OOP in a language-independent setting is a better introduction to OOP than diving into the idiosyncrasies of a particular object-oriented language.

- There are some people who just can't seem to "get" the basic ideas of OOP. These individuals usually have similar difficulties understanding higher-level languages like C, Pascal, and Ada and great reservations in using such languages.

- The greatest obstacle in using a hybrid object-oriented language like Objective-C is competence in C itself. This conclusion seem to hold for other hybrid languages.

- Interactive interpreters for object-oriented languages, like the Vici® interpreter for Objective-C, are invaluable for teaching. Languages without such tools are more difficult to learn.

- Concepts like metaclasses, class messages, and class methods are only a slight complication for most people. To remove these from an object-oriented language in attempt to make the language easier to learn is probably not worth the price of lower functionality.

During the panel presentation I will defend these and other conclusions and make some recommendations concerning the teaching of OOP in the context of technical seminars for practicing programmers and software engineers.

Using Prototypical Objects
to Implement Shared Behavior
in Object Oriented Systems

Henry Lieberman

Artificial Intelligence Laboratory
Massachusetts Institute of Technology
Cambridge, Mass. 02139 USA

Electronic mail (Arpanet):
Henry@AI.AI.MIT.Edu, Henry@MIT-AI

Abstract

A traditional philosophical controversy between representing general concepts as abstract *sets* or *classes* and representing concepts as concrete *prototypes* is reflected in a controversy between two mechanisms for sharing behavior between objects in object oriented programming languages. *Inheritance* splits the object world into *classes*, which encode behavior shared among a group of *instances*, which represent individual members of these sets. The class/instance distinction is not needed if the alternative of using *prototypes* is adopted. A prototype represents the *default* behavior for a concept, and new objects can re-use part of the knowledge stored in the prototype by saying how the new object differs from the prototype. The prototype approach seems to hold some advantages for representing default knowledge, and incrementally and dynamically modifying concepts. *Delegation* is the mechanism for implementing this in object oriented languages. After checking its idiosyncratic behavior, an object can forward a message to prototypes to invoke more general knowledge. Because class objects must be created before their instances can be used, and behavior can only be associated with classes, inheritance fixes the communication patterns between objects at instance creation time. Because any object can be used as a prototype, and any messages can be forwarded at any time, delegation is the more flexible and general of the two techniques.

"Using Prototypical Objects to Implement Shared Behavior in Object-Oriented Systems" by H. Lieberman from *Proceedings of the ACM Conference on Object-Oriented Programming Systems, Languages, and Applications*, 1986, pages 214-223. Copyright 1986, Association for Computing Machinery, Inc., reprinted by permission.

1. Sets vs. prototypes: a philosophical dilemma with practical consequences

How do people represent knowledge about generalizations they make from experience with concrete situations? Philosophers concerned with the theory of knowledge have debated this question, but as we shall see, the issue is not without practical consequences for the task of representing knowledge in object oriented systems. Because much of object oriented programming involves constructing representations of objects in the real world, our mechanisms for storing and using real world knowledge get reflected in mechanisms for dealing with objects in computer languages. We'll examine how the traditional controversy between representing concepts as sets versus representing concepts as prototypes gives rise to two mechanisms, *inheritance* and *delegation*, for sharing behavior between related objects in object oriented languages.

When a person has experience in a particular situation, say concerning a particular elephant named Clyde, facts about Clyde can often prove useful when encountering another elephant, say one named Fred. If we have mental representations of a concept for Clyde, and a concept for Fred, the question then becomes: How do the representations of Clyde and Fred share knowledge? How can we answer questions, such as Fred's color, number of legs, size, etc. by reference to what we already know about Clyde? In the absence of any mechanism for sharing knowledge between related concepts, we'd have to repeat all the knowledge about Clyde in a representation of Fred.

There are two points of view we can consider adopting. The first is based on the idea of abstract sets. From learning about Clyde, we can construct a concept of the *set [or class] of elephants*, which abstracts out what we believe is true about all individual animals sufficiently similar to Clyde to be called elephants. The description of the set can enumerate all the "essential" properties of elephants. We can view Clyde as a *member* or *instance* of this class. In an object oriented system, the set approach involves creating an object to represent the set of elephants, and establishing a link representing the membership relation between the object representing Clyde and the set object. Since the description of the set represents what is true about all its members, we can answer questions about Clyde by referring to the description of the set. Establishing the same kind of membership link between Fred and the set of elephants enables Fred and Clyde to share some of the same knowledge. If Fred and Clyde share some additional properties, such as that of being Indian elephants, that are not shared by some other elephants, these can be embodied in a *subclass* object, which shares all the properties of the elephant set, adjoining the additional properties relevant to India.

But there's an alternative point of view. We can consider Clyde to represent the concept of a *prototypical elephant*. If I ask you to "think of an elephant", no doubt the mental image of some particular elephant will pop to mind, complete with the characteristics of gray color, trunk, etc. If Clyde was the elephant most familiar to you, the prototypical elephant might be an image of Clyde himself. If I ask you a question such as "How many legs does an elephant have?", a way to answer the question is to assume that the answer is the same as how many legs Clyde has, unless there's a good reason to think otherwise. The concept of Fred can have a connection marking its prototype as Clyde, as a mechanism for sharing information between the two weighty pachyderms. The description of Fred can store any information that is unique to Fred himself. If I ask "How many legs does Fred have?", you assume the answer is the same for Fred as for Clyde, in the absence of any contrary evidence. If you then learn that Fred is a three-legged elephant, that knowledge is stored with Fred and is always searched before reference to the prototype is made.

2. Prototypes have advantages for incremental learning of concepts

Thought the concept of a set has proven fruitful in mathematics, the prototype approach in some ways corresponds more closely to the way people seem to acquire knowledge from concrete situations. The difficulty with sets stems from their abstractness; people seem to be a lot better at dealing with specific examples first, then generalizing from them than they are at absorbing general abstract principles first, and later applying them in particular cases. Prototype systems allow creating individual concepts first, then generalizing them by saying what aspects of the concept are allowed to vary. Set-oriented systems require creating the abstract description of the set first, before individual instances can be installed as members.

In mathematics, sets are defined either by enumerating their members, or by describing the unifying principles that identify membership in the set. We can neither enumerate all the elephants, nor are we good at making definitive lists of the essential properties of an elephant. Yet the major impetus for creating new concepts always seems to be experience with examples. If Clyde is our only experience with elephants, our concept of an elephant can really be no different than the concept of Clyde. After meeting other elephants, the analogies we make between concepts like Fred and Clyde serve to pick out the important characteristics of elephants.

Prototypes seem to be better at expressing knowledge about defaults. If we assert grayness as one of the identifying characteristics of membership in the set of elephants, we can't say that there are exceptional white elephants without risking contradiction. Yet it is easy to say that Fred, the white elephant, is just like Clyde, except that he is white. As Wittgenstein observed, it is difficult to say, in advance, exactly what characteristics are essential for a concept. It seems that as new examples arise, people can always make new analogies to previous concepts that preserve some aspects of the "defaults" for that concept and ignore others.

3. Inheritance implements sets, delegation implements prototypes

Having set the stage with our philosophical discussion of the issues of concept representation, we turn now to how these issues affect the more mundane details of implementation of object oriented programming systems.

Implementing the set-theoretic approach to sharing knowledge in object oriented systems is traditionally done by a mechanism called *inheritance*, first pioneered by the language Simula, later adopted by Smalltalk, flavors and Loops, among others. An object called a *class* encodes common behavior for a set of objects. A class also has a description of what characteristics are allowed to vary among members of the set. Classes have the power to generate *instance* objects, which represent members of a set. All instances of a class share the same behavior, but can maintain unique values for a set of state variables predeclared by the class. To represent Clyde, you create a description for the class elephant, with an instance variable for the elephant's name, values of which can be used to distinguish Clyde and Fred. A class can give rise to *subclasses*, which add additional variables and behavior to the class.

Implementing the prototype approach to sharing knowledge in object oriented systems is an alternative mechanism called *delegation*, appearing in the actor languages, and several Lisp-based object oriented systems, such as Director [Kahn 79], T [Rees 85], Orbit [Steels 82], and others. Delegation removes the distinction between classes and instances. Any object can serve as a prototype. To create an object that shares knowledge with a prototype, you construct an *extension* object, which has a list containing its prototypes, which may be *shared* with other objects, and *personal* behavior idiosyncratic to the object itself. When an extension object receives a message, it first attempts to respond to the message using the behavior stored its personal part. If the object's personal characteristics are not relevant for answering the message, the object forwards the message on to the prototypes to see if one can respond to the message. This process of forwarding is called *delegating* the message. Fred the elephant would be an extension object that stored behavior unique to Fred in its personal part, and referenced the prototype Clyde in its shared part.

4. Tools for representing behavior and internal state are the building blocks of object oriented systems

Each object oriented system must provide some linguistic mechanisms for defining the behavior of objects. The philosophy of object oriented programming is to use the object representation to encode both the procedures and data of conventional languages. Rather than define the procedural behavior or the data content of an object all at once, it is convenient to break both aspects of an object into a set of parts that can be accessed or modified individually by name.

An object's internal state consists of *variables* or *acquaintances*, which can be accessed in most object oriented systems by sending the object a message consisting of the variable's name. An object's procedure for responding to messages [in actors, we say its *script*] can be composed of a set of procedures called *methods*, each of which is specialized for handling only a certain subset of the messages the object receives, identified by name. Breaking up an object's state into named variables means that different portions of the state can be modified incrementally, without affecting the others. Breaking up an object's behavior into named methods means that different portions of the behavior can be modified incrementally, without affecting the others. The language must then provide ways of combining groups of methods and variables to form objects, and some means of allowing an object to share behavior [implemented as methods and variables] residing in previously defined objects. We will call these composite objects *extensions*. These building blocks are represented in the illustration *"Tools for sharing knowledge"*, with "icons" to be used in further discussion.

Many object oriented languages supply primitive linguistic mechanisms for creating objects with methods, variables and extensions. An alternative approach, which is advocated in the actor formalism, is to define methods, variables and extensions as objects in their own right, with their behavior determined by a message passing protocol among them. Obviously, an object representing a method cannot itself have methods, otherwise infinite recursion would result. Using simple objects primitive to the system, a variable is defined to be an object that remembers a name and a value, and responds to access and modification messages. A method

responds only to those messages for which it is designed, rejecting others. Extension objects use delegation to forward messages from one part of the object to another to locate the appropriate response.

Everyone who is already convinced of the utility of object oriented programming shouldn't have much trouble discerning the advantages of using object oriented programming in the implementation of the knowledge sharing mechanisms. Foremost among them is the ability to define other kinds of objects which implement alternatives to the standard versions. Instead of an ordinary variable, one might like to have "active" variables that take action when changed, "read-only" variables, maybe even "write-only" variables, each of which could be defined as a different type of variable object. Alternative kinds of method objects can use differing strategies to combine behavior from contributing components, replacing the so-called "method combination" feature of the flavors system, and making "multiple inheritance" easier. Different kinds of extension objects can make different efficiency tradeoffs on the issue of copying versus sharing.

Tools for Sharing Knowledge

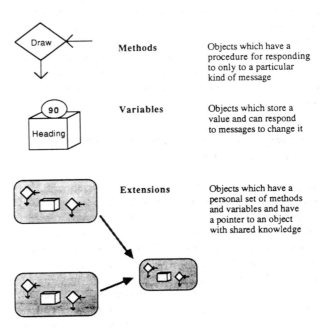

	Methods	Objects which have a procedure for responding to only to a particular kind of message
	Variables	Objects which store a value and can respond to messages to change it
	Extensions	Objects which have a personal set of methods and variables and have a pointer to an object with shared knowledge

The mechanisms for sharing knowledge in object oriented languages have now grown so complicated that it is impossible to reach universal consensus on the best mechanism. Using object oriented programming itself to implement the basic building blocks of state and behavior is the best approach for allowing experimentation and co-existence among competing formalisms.

5. A Logo example illustrates the differences between delegation and inheritance

An example from the domain of Logo turtle graphics will illustrate how the choice between delegation and inheritance affects the control and data structures in an object oriented system. The delegation approach is illustrated in the figure titled *"Sharing Knowledge with Delegation"*. The first thing we would like to do is create an object representing a pen, which remembers a location on the screen, and can be moved to a different location, drawing lines between the old and new locations.

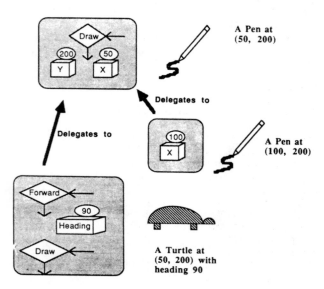

Sharing Knowledge with Delegation

We start out by creating a prototypical pen object, which has a specific location on the screen x=200, y=50, and behavior to respond to the draw message. When we would like to create a new pen object, we need only describe what's different about the new pen from the first one, in this case the x variable. Since the y is the same and behavior for the draw message is the same, these need not be repeated.

The draw method will have to use the value of the x variable, and it's important that the correct value of x is used. When the draw method is delegated from the new pen to the old pen, even though the draw method of the original pen is invoked, it should be the x of the new pen that is used.

To insure this, whenever a message is delegated, it must also pass along the object that originally received the message. This is called the SELF variable in Simula, Smalltalk and flavors, although I find the term "self" a little misleading, since a method originally defined for one kind of object often

winds up sending to a "self" of a different kind. In actor terminology, this object is called the client, since the object being delegated to can be thought of as performing a service for the original object. When a pen delegates a draw message to a prototypical pen, it is saying "I don't know how to handle the draw message. I'd like you answer it for me if you can, but if you have any further questions, like what is the value of my x variable, or need anything done, you should come back to me and ask." If the message is delegated further, all questions about the values of variables or requests to reply to messages are all referred to the object that delegated the message in the first place.

Suppose now we'd like to create a turtle at the same location as the original pen, using the original pen as a prototype. How is a turtle different from a pen? A turtle shares some of the behavior of a pen, but has additional state, namely it's heading. Remembering a heading is essential in implementing the additional behavior of being able to respond to forward and back messages by relying on the behavior of the response to the draw message. We may choose either to provide a new behavior for the turtle's draw operation, or rely on the draw operation provided by the original pen.

Let's look at the same example with the inheritance approach to sharing knowledge as found in Simula and Smalltalk, instead of delegation. This is illustrated in the figure titled *"Sharing knowledge with inheritance"*. With inheritance, it is necessary to create objects representing classes. To make a pen, it is first necessary to make a pen class object, which specifies both the behavior and the names of variables.

Individual pens are created by supplying values for all the instance variables of the pen class, creating an instance object. Values for all the variables must be specified, even if they do not have unique values in the instance. No new behavior may be attached to an individual pen. Extending behavior is accomplished by a different operation, that of creating a new subclass. The step which goes from a instance to behavior stored in its class is performed by a "hard-wired" lookup loop in systems like Simula and Smalltalk, not by message passing, as in the delegation approach.

To extend pens with new behavior, we must first create a new class object. Here a turtle class adds a new variable heading along with new behavior for the forward message. Notice that the variables from the pen class, x and y, were copied down into the turtle class. An individual turtle instance must supply values for all the variables of its class, superclass, and so on. This copying leads to larger instance objects for classes further and further down the inheritance hierarchy. The lookup of methods, performed by a primitive, unchangeable routine instead of message passing, starts a search for methods in the class of an object, and proceeds up the subclass-to-superclass chain.

How does a method inherited from the pen class to the turtle class access a method implemented in the turtle class? Since inheritance systems usually do not use message passing to communicate from subclass to superclass, they can't pass the turtle object along in the message, as we would in delegation.

Sharing Knowledge with Inheritance

Instead, most use variable binding to bind a special variable `self` to the object that originally receives a message. We shall see later on that this leads to trouble.

In addition, inheritance systems also allow the "shortcut" of binding all the variables of an instance so that they can be referenced directly by code running in methods as free variables. While this is sometimes more efficient, it short-circuits the message passing mechanism, defeating the independence of internal representation which is the hallmark of object oriented programming. Since variable references use different linguistic syntax than message sends, if we wanted to change the coordinate representation from x and y to polar coordinates using `rho` and `theta`, we'd have to change all the referencing methods. Sticking to message passing to access x and y means that even if the coordinates were changed to polar, we could still provide methods that compute the rectangular coordinates from the polar, and the change would be transparent.

I hope these diagrams leave you with the impression that the delegation approach is simpler. To create two pens and a turtle, the inheritance approach requires the additional steps

of creating pen class objects and turtle class objects. Also, we have to have two different kinds of links between objects, the subclass link and the instance link, whereas the delegation approach only requires a message passing relationship between the linked objects.

6. Are inheritance and delegation equally powerful?

An obvious question to ask about the preceding discussion of inheritance and delegation is whether the two techniques have the same expressive power. The answer is *no*.

Given delegation, it is easy to see how we could implement the functionality of inheritance. We can create special `class` objects that respond to messages to create new instances. We need only arrange that the class objects observe the copying of variables from the superclass chain when they create instances. Instance objects are given behavior that implements the lookup of variables and methods, roughly as follows.

```
If I'm an INSTANCE object
  and I receive a message
  with a SELECTOR and some ARGUMENTS:
If the SELECTOR matches
  one of the VARIABLE names
  in my CLASS [or SUPERCLASS, etc.],
I return the corresponding value,
  stored in myself.
Otherwise, I look for a METHOD
  whose NAME matches
  the SELECTOR of the message
  in the list of local METHODS
  of my CLASS.
If I find one,
  I bind the variable SELF to myself
  [the INSTANCE object].
  I bind the names of
    the variables of my CLASS,
  [and all the variables
    up the SUPERCLASS chain]
  to their values in the INSTANCE.
  Then I invoke the METHOD.
If there's no method
  in my CLASS's METHOD list,
  I try to find a method
  in the SUPERCLASS,
    and so on up the SUPERCLASS chain.
```

How about the other way? Can inheritance implement delegation? Unfortunately not. The reason is a little tricky to understand, but it has to do with the treatment of the `self` variable, which prevents a proper implementation of forwarding of messages.

Often, a method for handling a message may need to ask the object that originally received the message to perform some service. A turtle object which receives a `back` message would like to turn it into a `forward` message sent to the same object, but negating the number of steps, so that `back 100` is like `forward -100`. In delegation, when a method is delegated a message, it receives a component called the `client` in the `delegate` message, which has the object that originally received the message.

In inheritance systems, a distinguished variable named `self` is automatically bound to the recipient of a message during the execution of code for a method. When the method search proceeds from the original class to a superclass, the value of the `self` variable doesn't change, so that superclass methods can reply to the message "as if" they were methods of the original object. However, when a user sends a message, the self variable is always re-bound, so that it is generally *not* possible for the user to designate another object to reply in place of the object which originally received the message. True delegation cannot be implemented in these systems.

An example, illustrated in the figure *"The SELF Problem"* will make this clear. Suppose we would like to extend a particular `turtle` object to create a turtle which draws dashed instead of solid lines. The obvious way to do this is to have the `dashed-turtle` intercept the `forward` message and break up the interval into pieces, delegating a message to draw a series of shorter lines to a solid-line `turtle`. If, in an inheritance system, the dashed-line turtle simply sends a `forward` message to the solid-line turtle, then `self` will be bound to the solid-line turtle. Our earlier implementation of `back` in terms of `forward` will then stop working, since a message to the dashed-line turtle to go back will try to send a `forward` message to `self` and draw a solid line instead!

Be careful about confusing this example with an alternative implementation using inheritance systems, which would create a `dashed-turtle class` as a subclass of `solid-turtle class`. While such an implementation could have the correct behavior with respect to the `back` message, it still wouldn't count as an implementation of delegation. Remember, what we were trying to do was to see if an object could forward messages to some other *already existing* object. A dashed turtle instance wouldn't be forwarding any messages to an instance of solid turtle, since it would just inherit copies of the variables and methods from solid turtle.

7. What about efficiency?

The efficiency comparison between delegation and inheritance boils down to time/space tradeoffs. Some have argued that inheritance is more efficient because it requires fewer messages, but this comes at the cost of increasing the size of objects. Because variables are copied down from superclass to subclass, instances become larger and larger the farther down you get in the inheritance hierarchy. With delegation, each object need only specify what's different about it from already existing prototypes, so the size of

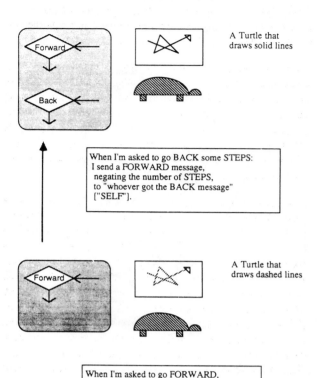

A Turtle that draws solid lines

When I'm asked to go BACK some STEPS:
I send a FORWARD message,
negating the number of STEPS,
to "whoever got the BACK message"
["SELF"].

A Turtle that draws dashed lines

When I'm asked to go FORWARD,
I ask the Turtle who draws solid lines
to go FORWARD short distances,
alternately with the pen up and down
until the distance is covered.

objects does not necessarily depend on the depth in the hierarchy of shared objects. A look at the diagram illustrating the data structures for pen and turtle objects will confirm inheritance's speed advantage and delegation's space advantage.

Smaller objects make for faster object creation times, which can be important in systems that create large numbers of small objects with short lifetimes, as opposed to small numbers of large objects with long lifetimes. Reducing the size of objects may also improve the efficiency of virtual memory, by improving locality of reference, allowing a higher density of frequently referenced objects in the primary memory. With a copying garbage collector, such as that described in [Lieberman and Hewitt 83], smaller objects can improve the efficiency of garbage collection by reducing the copying overhead.

Implementors shouldn't get scared away by the search required to find methods and variables in the delegation approach. There's a simple, effective trick for reducing the search time: *caching* the result of lookups. Caches are a way of trading space for speed, mitigating any negative effects of the speed-for-space tradeoff made by delegation. Caches make a more effective use of the extra memory than indiscriminately copying instance variables, because the memory they do use is sure to be in constant use. Caches don't restrict flexibility in interactively modifying the programming environment the way copying and compilation optimizations do.

On conventional machines, probably no implementation of delegation is going to surpass variable lookup via registers and stack indexing for raw speed. But in their zeal to speed up variable lookup, implementors have forced decisions such as large object size on object-oriented languages, which adversely affect efficiency. Parallel machines with large address spaces will make the attractiveness of such register-oriented optimizations fade.

Smalltalk [Krasner 84] reports a 93% "hit rate" for a moderately sized cache, 1000 objects. This means that any savings realized by inheritance over delegation in lookup could at best affect the remaining 7%. The best thing to do seems to be to keep a global cache, and invalidate it whenever any changes are made to the sharing hierarchy. A change will then slow the system down for the next 1000 messages, or whatever time the cache takes to fill up again. "Smarter" alternatives, such as per-object caches are probably not worth the extra trouble they would cause for incremental software modification, since the hit rate on a global cache is so high. Since both inheritance and delegation can be implemented almost equally efficiently, it seems that there's little reason to sacrifice the extra flexibility of delegation on efficiency grounds.

8. Re-directing I/O streams illustrates an important application of delegation

Many object oriented systems make good use of object oriented programming techniques to implement input-output *streams*. Such a stream is an object that receives messages to input or output a character, a line of text, an expression. Systems usually have global variables designating the "current" sources of input and output, which is by default bound to an object representing the stream of characters being displayed on the window of a screen of an interactive display.

The name "stream" suggests the continual flow of characters or pixels between the user and the system. A very useful kind of object is that which implements a "dam" to divert the stream to other destinations, or "plumbing" which connects one stream with another. A *dribble file* is a sequential file maintaining a record on disk of the history of input-output interactions, to provide a more permanent recording of interactions than the ephemeral twinkling of pixels. A dribble file can be implemented by replacing the stream which represents interactions at the terminal with one that writes them to disk also.

The dribble stream needs the ability to *masquerade* as the terminal stream. It should have the same responses to all the messages that the ordinary terminal stream, and also provide the additional behavior of writing to the disk. The streams should be considered indistinguishable from the point of view of all programs which perform input-output.

To implement the dribble stream cleanly, we'd like it to be the case that the implementation of the dribble stream shouldn't have to know the precise details of the implementation of the stream which it is replacing. We might, for example, like to use a single dribble stream with both a stream to a directly connected interactive terminal and a stream interacting over a network.

Can a dribble stream "masquerade" as a terminal stream?

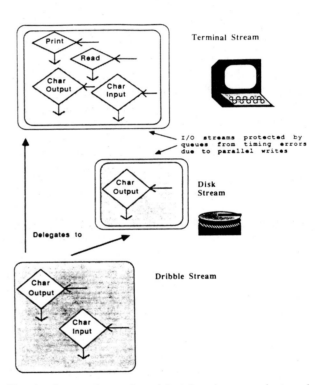

The implementation using delegation is convenient and straightforward. Messages which do character output are intercepted and the disk output is interposed.

```
A DRIBBLE-STREAM is an object
  that logs interaction on a STREAM,
  and records it on disk using a FILE-NAME

If I'm a DRIBBLE-STREAM and
  I get a message to input or output
  a CHARACTER,
  I output the CHARACTER
    to the disk stream to the FILE-NAME.
  Then I delegate the message
    to output a CHARACTER
    to the original STREAM.
```

```
If I'm a DRIBBLE-STREAM and
I get any other message,
I simply delegate the message
  to the STREAM.
```

It works to take care of only the single-character input and output messages because presumably all higher level messages like `print` of a object are ultimately implemented in terms of the single-character versions. The method which performs a higher level print operation would ultimately send a character output message to its client [send to `self`].

Surprisingly, many inheritance systems make it difficult to implement this simple extension to the behavior of streams. One villain is the insistence of systems like flavors and Smalltalk on defining separate procedures for handling each type of message. Attempting to try to implement `dribble-stream` as a subclass of `stream` in systems of this ilk, we would find that there's no easy way to say "... and send all of the irrelevant messages through to the original stream". We would be forced to define one method to intercept the character output message to write to the disk, another to intercept the `print` message, another to intercept the `print-line` message, and so on for every relevant message. Every time another message was added to the original stream, another method would have to be added to the `dribble-stream`, with tediously repetitive code. This also has the unfortunate effect of making the implementation of `dribble-stream` now sensitive to the details of exactly which messages its embedded stream accepts, inhibiting the ability to re-use the implementation with different types of streams.

Adding to the system the definition of a `dribble-stream` class or flavor would only give the ability to create *new instances* of dribble stream objects. It would not be possible to create a dribble stream which used a previously existing stream object. We'd then have to make new terminal streams, network streams, or other kind of streams, to be able to take advantage of the recording functionality. We shouldn't have to reproduce every kind of stream in the system just to have the dribble capability!

If, instead, we attempt to make a dribble stream which holds the interaction stream as one of its instance variables, we face the problem that there is no way for the dribble stream to correctly forward a message like `print` to the value of the variable. Because of the way these systems handle the `self` variable, the forwarding of messages to the original stream won't work, for the same reason as in the turtle example. Sending a `print` message to the instance variable would re-bind the `self` variable, so it would result in sending lower-level messages directly to the interaction stream and not to the dribble stream. So it seems as though any straightforward attempt to implement the dribble stream as a simple behavioral extension in many inheritance systems is doomed.

9. Parallelism causes problems in inheritance systems because of the SELF variable

There's an additional problem in the case that the stream can accept messages from more than one parallel process. Because the stream holds modifiable state [such as a screen bitmap], the stream must be protected against timing errors resulting from two processes trying to write to the stream at the same time. A technique such as `serializer` objects [Hewitt, Attardi, Lieberman 79] or monitors must be used. This means that when the stream receives a write message, it "locks", so that subsequent messages to the stream must wait in a queue for the stream to finish processing the first write message.

Now, if a message to a serialized dribble stream tries to process a `print` message by sending a `character-output` message to the `self` variable, it will find `self` bound to a serialized stream which is locked waiting for that very `print` message to complete! Deadlock!

Since delegation uses message passing, when the dribble stream delegates to a terminal stream, it can supply [as the `client` in the delegate message] an *unserialized* version of itself, which can process the message without waiting.

10. Delegation is more flexible than inheritance for combining behavior from multiple sources

Often, an object will want to utilize behavior that appears in more than one other already existing object. The behavior that a system needs to implement a particular "feature" can be packaged up as a single object, and sometimes an object will want to combine several of these features to implement its behavior. For example, window objects might have titles, borders, size adjustments, etc. A particular window object may choose some of these features and not others. Features may be independent of one another, or they may interact.

The solution in inheritance systems is to create a class object that mentions a list of other classes whose behavior it wishes to share. All the methods and variables mentioned in any of the classes are inherited by the combined object. Systems like flavors allow optionally, on a per-method basis, supplying an option for how to combine behavior when more than one component contributes a method. Typical options are to invoke all the contributing methods, impose an order on them, or return a list of the results.

The problem with this style of combining behavior from multiple sources is that it fixes the pattern of communication between objects before the time an instance object is created. This limits the extent to which behavior from previously existing objects can be used dynamically. By contrast, with delegation, the communication patterns can be determined at the time a message is received by an object.

With delegation, a method for an extension object can simply access the prototypical objects from which it derives behavior on the `shared` list. A window which wants to invoke the `draw` action of a previously defined `rectangle` object acting as its borders can simply delegate the `draw` message to the rectangle object. Thus delegation doesn't require "method combination" or an inventory of esoteric combining operations. The behavior is simply programmed in the method for the combined extension object. Should a programmer wish to build a library of common combination techniques, it is easily done by constructing variants on the standard `method` object, so delegation could be made as concise as method combination in inheritance systems. With inheritance, if a window class includes a "borders mixin", the window instance does not contain an independent object representing its borders, so it is not possible to send a message to the borders of a window independent of the window object itself. The window class merely contains a mixture of the methods and variables inherited from the borders and other contributing components.

In highly responsive interactive systems, it is often necessary to wait until a message is received to determine how behavior from component objects will be utilized. Here's a simple example in which dynamic utilization of behavior from multiple sources is required, illustrated in the figure *"Delegation allows communication patterns to be decided at run time"*.

A `bordered bitmap` can be built from a `rectangle`, which can display its borders, and a `bitmap` which can transfer an array of pixels to the screen. What should the `draw` response for the bordered bitmap be? With inheritance, you create a `bordered-bitmap class` that inherits both from `rectangle` and `bitmap`, saying that both `draw` methods are to be used. Fine.

But now suppose we'd like to give the user the option of changing dynamically which behavior is used. When the bitmap is dragged across the screen, the transfer of the entire array on every mouse movement might be too slow, so it might be preferable to give the user the option of just dragging the outline of the bitmap instead. A reasonable thing to do is to give the user an on-screen toggle switch to decide the behavior, and the user can potentially change the behavior at any time. So the behavior of the bordered bitmap cannot be decided before the object is created. With delegation, when the bordered bitmap gets a `draw` message, it can decide whether to delegate the message to the rectangle object that it contains, or to the bitmap object, or both.

Inheritance systems are also plagued by what I call the *one-instance class problem*. When systems are composed of large numbers of objects with slightly varying behavior, you wind up having to create new class objects often just to have one or a few instances. It is necessary to create ad-hoc classes such as "`window with a wide border`

`times roman font and no title`" just to combine features for a single instance.

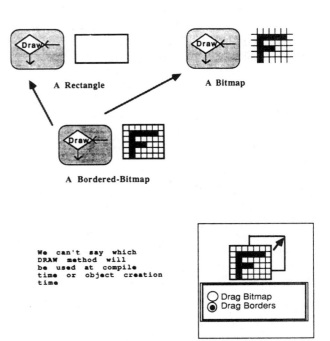

Delegation allows communication patterns to be decided at run time

A Rectangle   A Bitmap

A Bordered-Bitmap

We can't say which DRAW method will be used at compile time or object creation time

Drag Bitmap
Drag Borders

11. Delegation is advantageous for highly interactive, incremental software development

An important issue to consider when evaluating the tradeoffs between inheritance and delegation is the consequences for incremental software development. As we have seen above, inheritance tends to encourage copying of variables and methods while delegation encourages sharing. If a prototypical object changes behavior, then all objects which mention that prototype on their `shared` list will automatically "feel" the change. If changes are made to an inheritance hierarchy, such as adding a new instance variable, or changing the class structure, information copied from the old data structures may be rendered obsolete. Broadcasting the result of changes to copies puts a burden on the operations which make incremental changes in the software environment. An extreme example of this occurs in the flavors system, where simply adding a method to `vanilla-flavor`, the root of the inheritance hierarchy, results in recompilation of every flavor in the entire system! This effectively prohibits any modifications to objects near the top of the inheritance hierarchy.

Though delegation has been the minority viewpoint in object oriented languages, it is slowly becoming recognized as important for its added power and flexibility. Part of the reason for neglect of the delegation approach has been historical. Simula, one of the first object oriented languages, adopted the inheritance technique. It fixed communication patterns between objects at compile time, as was appropriate for a compiled language of the Algol family. The specific mechanisms for this were then "inherited" by Smalltalk and others, without reconsidering whether the approach was still appropriate for an interpretive language in a more highly interactive programming environment. I hope the preceding discussion has convinced you that the approach of modeling concepts using prototypes and implementing behavior in object oriented languages using delegation has distinct advantages over the alternative point of view using classes and inheritance.

12. Acknowledgments

Major support for the work described in this paper was provided by the System Development Foundation. Other related work at the MIT Artificial Intelligence Laboratory was supported in part by DARPA under ONR contract N00014-80-C-0505.

Carl Hewitt's ideas concerning actors, and especially the impact of parallelism on object-oriented programming were important influences. Kenneth Kahn and Luc Steels implemented object-oriented languages which adopted delegation mechanisms and also influenced these ideas. Alan Borning reached similar conclusions in the context of the ThingLab system implemented in Smalltalk. Koen de Smedt provided a helpful critique of a talk I gave on these issues in Nijmegen, the Netherlands.

References

[Birtwistle, Dahl, Myhrhaug, and Nygaard 73]
G. M. Birtwistle, O-J Dahl, B. Myhrhaug, K. Nygaard.
Simula Begin.
Van Nostrand Reinhold, New York, 1973.

[Bobrow 85] D. Bobrow, K. Kahn, M. Stefik, G. Kiczales.
Common Loops.
Technical Report, Xerox Palo Alto Research Center, 1985.

[Bobrow, Stefik 83]
Daniel Bobrow and Mark Stefik.
Knowledge Programming in Loops.
AI Magazine , August, 1983.

[Borning 86] Alan Borning.
Classes Versus Prototypes in Object-Oriented Languages.
In *Fall Joint Computer Conference.*
ACM/IEEE, Dallas, Texas, November, 1986.

[Goldberg, Robson 83]
Adele Goldberg and David Robson.
Smalltalk-80: The Language and its Implementation.
Addison-Wesley, Reading, MA, 1983.

[Hewitt 79] Carl Hewitt.
Viewing Control Structures as Patterns of Passing Messages.
In P. Winston and R. Brown (editors), *Artificial Intelligence, an MIT Perspective.* MIT Press, Cambridge, MA, 1979.

[Hewitt, Attardi, Lieberman 79]
Carl Hewitt, Giuseppe Attardi, and Henry Lieberman.
Security And Modularity In Message Passing.
In *First Conference on Distributed Computing.* IEEE, Huntsville, Alabama, 1979.

[Kahn 79] Kenneth Kahn.
Creation of Computer Animation from Story Descriptions.
PhD thesis, Massachusetts Institute of Technology, 1979.

[Krasner 84] Glenn Krasner, editor.
Smalltalk-80: Bits of History and Words of Advice.
Addison-Wesley, New York, 1984.

[Lieberman 86a] Henry Lieberman.
Concurrent Object Oriented Programming in Act 1.
In A. Yonezawa and Tokoro (editors), *Concurrent Object Oriented Programming.* MIT Press, Cambridge, Mass., 1986.

[Lieberman 86b] Henry Lieberman.
Delegation and Inheritance: Two Mechanisms for Sharing Knowledge in Object Oriented Systems.
In J. Bezivin, P. Cointe (editors), *3eme Journees d'Etudes Langages Orientes Objets.* AFCET, Paris, France, 1986.

[Lieberman and Hewitt 83]
Henry Lieberman and Carl Hewitt.
A Real Time Garbage Collector Based on the Lifetimes of Objects.
CACM 26(6), June, 1983.

[Moon, Weinreb 84]
David Moon, Daniel Weinreb, et. al.
Lisp Machine Manual.
Symbolics, Inc. and MIT, Cambridge, Mass., 1984.

[Rees 85] Jonathan Rees, et. al.
The T Manual.
Technical Report, Yale University, 1985.

[Steels 82] Luc Steels.
An Applicative View of Object Oriented Programming.
Technical Report AI Memo 15, Schlumberger-Doll Research, March, 1982.

Chapter 5: Principles of Object-Based Architecture

An object-based architecture is one in which the object boundaries are used in segmenting memory. That is, the basic memory element is a segment of an object rather than a bit, a byte, a word, or a page. At this level, the definition of an object as an entity containing data and a way to process the data loses its significance. Rather, one thinks of an object as a collection of memory segments that belong together. The main problem is that different segments are different in size, and, therefore, the memory management techniques become more difficult. In addition, there must be a means of unifying the various memory segments that combine to form an object. A secondary problem is that of controlling user access to the individual objects.

The paper by Ted Kaehler, "Virtual Memory for an Object-Oriented Language," is an introduction to the concepts required for an object-based architecture. He describes the reasons for virtual memory, the process of paging, and how an object-orientation may help improve the performance of a virtual memory system. An advantage of object-oriented systems is that the close connection of the various parts of an object, if maintained in memory, can make the task of memory management more meaningful. An object-oriented virtual memory management system will swap objects in and out of main memory rather than pages, because of the high probability that the different parts of an object will be executed together. If a memory reference is made to one part of an object, it is likely that the next reference will be to that object also. An object-orientation requires an environment in which virtual memory systems have been redesigned for higher performance.

Common object-oriented software systems will contain hundreds or thousands of individual objects, most of which will be smaller than a page. Systems that swap objects must keep track of where each is located in memory or on disk and effect a swap when a memory reference is made to an object that is not in main memory. This process is more complicated than that of managing pages, but the advantage of packing memory with useful objects makes up for the higher overhead in managing objects.

Kaehler describes a particular object-oriented virtual memory, OOZE, which was created to support the Smalltalk-76 system. OOZE uses a large hash table, the *Resident Object Table*, to quickly find the location of objects that are in memory. It also uses interesting memory mapping techniques to find the location of objects that are on the disk.

The relation of object-oriented programming to object-based architecture is considered in the paper by Anita K. Jones, "The Object Model: A Conceptual Tool for Structuring Software." In this paper, an object is thought of as a passive structure. However, there are certain operations that are the only means by which an object can be directly manipulated. Whether one thinks of an object as containing the procedures or not is simply a point of view. In any case, the procedures are there. The concepts of object, operation, and object type are carefully described, and some examples of their use are presented. The concepts of capability and protection rights are also considered as they relate to operating systems that support the object model. The object model is merely a structuring tool; it does not imply a particular design technique. It is amenable to use with both the "top down" and "bottom up" design techniques. The object model paradigm is a basis for designing an operating system in which different facilities are provided in different domains of privilege. If both operating system and application programs are designed by using the object model, then no artificial boundary separates the operating system from the application. The features of protection and synchronization are considered from the perspective of the object model.

Although earlier systems included addressing schemes that were similar to capabilities, the word "capability" was not introduced until 1966 in the paper, "Programming Semantics for Multiprogrammed Computations," by Jack B. Dennis and Earl C. Van Horn. This is the seminal paper about capability-based addressing.

A *capability* is a computer structure that provides access to an object and specifies the access rights to that object. The access rights allow users to perform some combination of executing, reading, or writing the object. The access rights also indicate the owner of the object and grant only to the owner the right to delete the object or to grant or deny others access to the object.

As part of its state, a process contains a list of capabilities, a C-list, for short.

From the point of view of address location, a capability for an object is a pattern of bits that must be translated into the actual address and length of the object. The capability contains a unique code associated with the object which does not change during the life of the object. Given this code, the addressing mechanism must be able to find the location of the object and does this by consulting a hash table. For each unique code entered in the table, there is a bit that tells whether or not the object is in main memory, a field giving the object's size, and a field giving its secondary storage address. All objects will not be locatable by using the hash table, however. To do so would make this internal table too large. If a reference is made to an object not locatable via the table, then the object is located by going to a much larger data structure in secondary storage which contains the location in secondary storage of all objects.

Robert H. Halstead, Jr., in "Object Management in Distributed Systems," describes a way to handle object references and garbage collection in a distributed system. He begins with the premise that the object-reference with garbage-collection approach is the best available paradigm for organizing information in a computer system. The type of system studied contains many processors, each connected to some, but not all of the others. The goal is to distribute the knowledge so that each processor knows only about the objects that it might conceivably encounter.

The processors that reference an object are listed in a connected acyclic graph called the *reference tree* for the object. There is a unique path from any processor in a reference tree to any other. The tree for an object is free to grow and shrink dynamically. There is a special, rather complex, protocol used by the processors for altering reference trees. The protocol is complex in order to avoid deadlocks and inconsistent states.

It is required that all communication concerning an object travel over links that are in the reference tree for that object. The acyclic nature of the trees ensure that a message sent from one processor can never loop back to its sender.

The garbage-collection scheme works by shrinking the reference tree for an object down to a single processor and then using traditional garbage-collection on it. The shrinking is done by processors removing themselves from the reference tree of an object when they ascertain that they are no longer needed.

This paper is included here because it presents a unique approach for obtaining object-oriented computing in a multiprocessor environment.

Additional References

H.M. Levy, *Capability-based Computer Systems*, Digital Press, Bedford, Massachusetts, 1983.

This book is an introduction, a survey, a history, and an evaluation of capability- and object-based computer systems. It discusses the object-based design methodology and the use of capabilities to support object-based systems. It describes many machines that have capability-based architectures including the MIT PDP-1, the Plessey System 250, Cambridge University's CAP computer, Hydra, StarOS, the IBM System/38, and Intel's iAPX 432. A complete bibliography on capability and object systems is included at the end of the book. This is the reference of choice for the purpose of learning about object-based architecture.

M.V. Wilkes, "Hardware Support for Memory Protection. Capability Implementations," *Proceedings of the Symposium on Architectural Support for Programming Languages and Operating Systems*, ACM, Inc., New York, New York, March-April 1982, pages 107-116.

Wilkes describes the general features of hardware supported capability systems and considers ways of reducing their inherent complexity.

E.B. Fernandez and T. Lang, "Introduction to Part IV: Object-Oriented Architectures," in *Tutorial: Software-Oriented Computer Architecture*, IEEE Computer Society Press, Washington, D.C., 1986, pages 197-204.

The authors give a short description of object-oriented architectures and illustrate the concepts by comparing the Intel 432 microprocessor with the IBM System/38 minicomputer.

J.J. Ewing, "An Object-Oriented Operating System Interface," *OOPSLA '86, SIGPLAN Notices*, ACM, Inc., New York, New York, Volume 21, Number 11, November 1986, pages 46-56.

P. Dasgupta, "A Probe-Based Monitoring Scheme for an Object-Oriented Distributed Operating System," *OOPSLA '86, SIGPLAN Notices*, ACM, Inc., New York, New York, Volume 21, Number 11, November 1986, pages 57-66.

J.M. Cotton, "Computer Design for Network Control," Infotech State of the Art Report, Pergamon Press, Elmsford, New York, 1976.

W.J. Dally and J.T. Kajiya, "An Object Oriented Architecture," *Proceedings, The 12th Annual International Symposium on Computer Architecture*, IEEE Computer Society Press, Washington, D.C., 1985, pages 154-161.

The authors describe a machine architecture whose features may help eliminate the execution overhead inherent in object-oriented systems.

A. Pashtan, "Object Oriented Operating Systems: An Emerging Design Methodology," *Proceedings, ACM Annual Conference*, ACM Inc., New York, N.Y., 1982, pages 126-131.

A comparison of eight object-oriented operating systems.

W.K. Giloi, P. Behr, and R. Gueth, "Object Addressing Architectures," *Proceedings, IEEE International Workshop on Computer Systems Organization*, IEEE Computer Society Press, Washington, D.C., 1983, pages 202-210.

A comparison of three types of object-oriented architectures.

Virtual Memory
for an
Object-Oriented Language

Ted Kaehler
Learning Research Group
Xerox Palo Alto Research Center
3333 Coyote Hill Rd
Palo Alto CA 94304

The amount of information in a person's brain is truly vast; even the amount accessed in the course of a few hours of thought is vast. This is in contrast to the amount of information in the main memory of a computer, which is minuscule by comparison. The exciting thing about computers, though, is that we can use them to extend and enhance our thought. If a computer is to serve effectively as an aid to thought, it must be able to hold enough information to be useful. However, the memory of the largest computer today is so small that it severely limits what that computer can do. There are so many orders of magnitude between the capacity of the brain and the capacity of a computer that given the question "How much memory will the computer need?" the answer should always be "As much as possible."

Software for personal computers is just crossing a threshold of usefulness and flexibility. There are tasks, such as revising a draft of a paper, which are tremendously easier to do with a computer than without. Once you have edited with a computer, it seems absurd to edit by hand. The *number* of tasks for which the computer is

essential is growing rapidly, causing a very sharp rise in the demand for storage in each personal computing system. As we design more useful aids to human thought, we will immediately want to access an amount of information closer to the amount in someone's head. Many extraordinary ideas will become software realities in the next few years. And large quantities of memory will be needed to run and store all of that wonderful software.

> **Given the question "How much memory will the computer need?" the answer should always be "As much as possible."**

The practical limit on the size of a computer's memory is cost. Every project, especially a personal computer, has cost limits. The question becomes how to get the most memory for the least cost. Roughly speaking, memory falls into two categories: fast, expensive memory and slow, in-

expensive memory. *Main memory* and *core* are common names for the fast, semiconductor memory. The slow memory, *secondary memory*, is almost always a disk. If we bought all slow memory, the processor would continually wait for the disk and would give very poor performance. If we spent all our money on fast memory, we would not get very much of it, and many of the bigger and better programs would not fit in. The game is to buy some fast memory and some slow memory and arrange things so that the processor rarely has to wait for the slow memory. This game, and specifically the mechanism which hides the slow memory from the processor, is called *virtual memory*.

If there were no way at all to predict which byte of memory the processor might want next, it would be impossible to win the game of virtual memory. However, pieces of data that are used together are often stored together, and program instructions tend to be executed and stored in a sequence. The principle of *locality of reference* states that the processor is most likely to access a memory location very near the last

Reprinted with permission from *BYTE*, Volume 6, Number 8, August 1981, pages 378-385. Copyright © 1981 by Ted Kaehler.

one it accessed (see reference 2 at the end of this article). The game of virtual memory is based on a trick: when the processor starts to ask for bytes from a block of code or data, it should move that code or data into the fast memory. If the processor continues to access that information, all of the accesses will be to fast memory. When the program moves on to a new activity, it may again be forced to get its information from the slow memory. To win the game, a virtual memory must maintain a situation where most of the processor's accesses are to the fast memory. If the strategy fails and the processor often wants data from the slow memory, the entire system will run very slowly.

The act of moving programs or data between the two kinds of memory is called *swapping* (see figure 1). The program that the user is running may or may not control the swapping explicitly. Overlays are large groups of subroutines that are moved to and from the disk under control of the user program. In an *automatic virtual memory*, however, the user program is unaware that swapping is occurring. The programmer does not specify how the program should be divided up into pieces or when swapping should occur.

In certain cases, letting the programmer control swapping directly can result in good performance. However, the virtual memory game is very complex and is played very quickly inside the computer. We believe that the programmer should not be burdened with deciding what part of the data to swap and when to do it. Asking the programmer to instruct the virtual memory is like asking a race car designer to write down, for the driver, exactly how to move the steering wheel in some future race.

In this article, we first look at a common type of automatic virtual memory called *paging*. We then introduce a new type of virtual memory that takes advantage of its knowledge of objects. We describe in detail a specific object-oriented virtual memory for the Smalltalk-76 system and explain how it plays the virtual memory game better than a paging system.

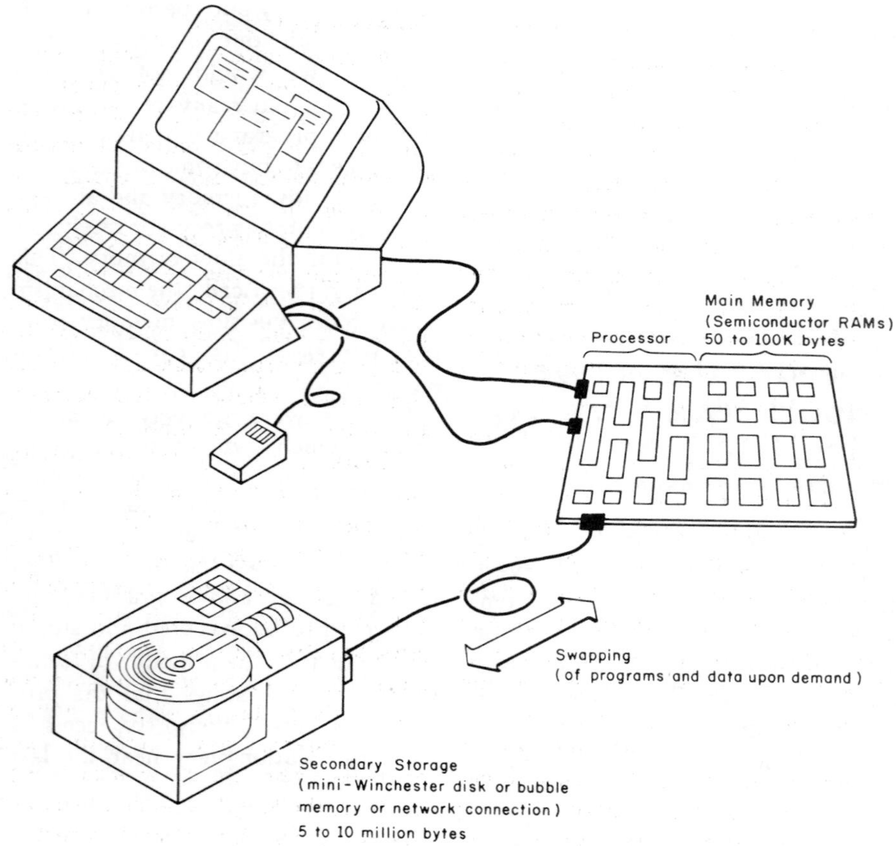

Paging

The most common kind of automatic virtual memory is called paging. In paging, the program is cut up arbitrarily into pieces. Each piece is called a *page* and contains the same number of bytes as every other page —say, 512. There are many more pages than will fit into main memory at once, so most of them stay on the disk. The processor knows only about byte addresses in one large address space called the *virtual address space*. Every time the processor accesses a byte, the address of the byte is checked. The high-order bits of the address tell which page contains that byte. (The low-order bits tell which byte within the page.) If that page is not in main memory, the user program stops. The virtual memory program starts up, finds an old page, moves it to the disk, and brings the desired page into memory in its place. (We will use the term "memory" to refer to the fast, main memory only.) The act of discovering that a page is needed from the disk and bringing it into memory is called a *page fault*.

An advantage of paging is that it works regardless of the contents of the pages. The mechanism needed to determine whether a given page is in memory is simple. Many computers have special hardware to speed up the translation between an address in the virtual space and a page in memory.

There are problems with paging, however. If the program needs a particular byte, the entire page surrounding that byte must be brought into memory. If no other bytes on that page are useful at the moment, a large amount of main memory is wasted. Since programs are cut up arbitrarily into pages in the first place, it is common that the rest of the page has nothing to do with the part currently wanted. Sometimes a significant fraction of memory is taken up by pages

Figure 1: *Main memory, secondary memory, and swapping combine to form a virtual machine that seems to have more memory.*

August 1981 © BYTE Publications Inc

from which the processor wants only a few bytes (see figure 2). These pages crowd out pages containing other parts of the program, causing many pages to be swapped to run the rest of the program. The many accesses to slow, secondary memory cause the whole system to be slow.

Another problem with paging is that every address of a byte or a word must be a long address. When an object-oriented language is built on a paging system, a pointer to an object is typically the address of the first word of the object. Every pointer must be capable of reaching any word in the entire virtual space, and each one must have enough bits to span the space. Pointers comprise a large fraction of many programs and data structures. If they could be shorter, more of the program could be packed into one page in memory and the entire program would take fewer pages of memory.

Object-Oriented Virtual Memory

Smalltalk is a system composed of *objects*. An object is a little package of functionality. It contains the values of a few variables or a small piece of program. The important thing about an object is that its parts belong together. If a program wants a part of an object, it probably wants other parts, too. Different pieces of information were packaged together in that object exactly because they will be used together. Locality of reference is strong inside an object and, in general, weak between objects.

An object-oriented virtual memor, swaps individual objects instead of entire pages between disk and main memory. Objects that are brought into memory are packed end to end with the objects already there. Memory is thus entirely filled with useful or likely-to-be-useful data. A larger percentage of memory is actually holding useful information than it would under a paging system. The result is that a larger part of the program can fit into memory at once.

There is a penalty for swapping ob-

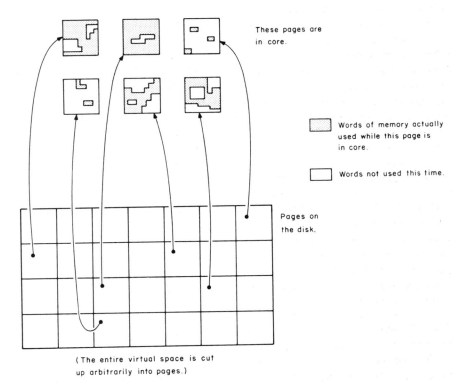

Figure 2: *Virtual memory by paging.*

jects, however. Objects are generally smaller than pages, and there are a lot of them in memory at once. The virtual memory program must keep track of which object is in which place in the memory, and it must be able to find out where each object came from on the disk. Managing individual objects is more complicated than managing pages, but the advantage of packing main memory with useful objects makes up for the time spent managing the objects.

By object-oriented virtual memory, we mean a system that swaps objects which have meaning in the high-level language and which are typically small. Segments in the B5500 (reference 4) and objects in HYDRA (reference 5), while being the units of swapping in their systems, are large. These "objects" require tens or hundreds of bytes of overhead information each. An object-oriented virtual memory, in our sense, gives an object the same swapping freedom as a segment and shrinks the overhead to a few bytes per object.

Pointers to Objects

An object consists of *fields*, which hold the values of their named and indexed instance variables. Each field contains a numeric value, which can be interpreted as itself or (usually) as a pointer to another object. This number, called the *object pointer*, is the unique identifier of the other object. Every object has an object pointer. Given an object pointer, the virtual memory must be able to locate that object, whether it is in memory or on the disk (see figure 3).

Creating, destroying, and moving objects in memory is the job of a storage manager. The virtual memory program takes the place of the storage manager (as described in Glenn Krasner's article, "The Smalltalk-80 Virtual Machine," on page 300 of this issue). It fetches and stores the fields of objects, creates new objects, and collects and manages free space. It also keeps track of the length of each object and the Smalltalk class of each object.

When the interpreter is working on

an object that is in memory, the operations of fetching a field and storing a field must run fast. Both the fetch and store operations specify an object by giving its unique object pointer. The translation from the object pointer to the object's location in memory must be fast. The virtual memory spends most of its time doing this translation. A fixed correspondence between object pointers and locations in memory does not work, since almost any combination of objects may be in memory at the same time. The translation from object pointer to memory location must be highly variable.

Once in a while, the interpreter attempts access to an object that is not in memory. The virtual memory must detect the attempt, find the object on the disk, and bring it into memory. This process is called an *object fault*. Sometimes other objects must first be removed from memory to make room for the incoming object. In order to find an object on the disk, there must

be a correspondence between an object pointer and that object's location on the disk. The data needed to hold this correspondence must be compactly represented, as there may be many objects in the system.

OOZE

In 1975 and 1976, Dan Ingalls and I designed and built a virtual memory to support the Smalltalk-74 system, called OOZE (Object-Oriented Zoned Environment). It then became the foundation for the Smalltalk-76 system (reference 3). The combination was very successful, and many interesting projects have been built in it. OOZE serves as an excellent illustration of a usable object-oriented virtual memory implemented entirely in software. At the end of this article, we discuss possible modifications of OOZE for the Smalltalk-80 system.

For OOZE to play the game of virtual memory well, we had to design it to fit the rules. Economics (of our existing hardware) dictated the size of

main memory, the size of the disk, and the ratio of their speeds. The rules also included the things that the Smalltalk interpreter expected objects to do. We considered these and decided that in OOZE an object pointer would be 16 bits long, to fit into a machine word. We wanted every combination of 16 bits to be a legal object pointer, giving a total of 64 K objects. With a mean object size of 10 to 20 words, this was a good match to the size of our disk. To guarantee good performance during a fault on an object, we specified that any object can be brought into memory by reading, at most, one place on the disk. We did not allow one disk read to look up the disk address and another disk read to get the actual object.

The design of OOZE centers around the handling of the two important object pointer translations. Finding an object's location in memory from its object pointer must be fast. This mapping must also be flexible, since the exact combination of objects in memory changes from moment to moment. The correspondence between object pointer and memory location is a large hash table, called the *Resident Object Table* (ROT). Of the 64 K objects on the disk, perhaps 4000 are in memory at once. Each of these has an entry in the ROT. To find the location of an object, the hash routine uses the object pointer to compute where to look in the ROT. If it finds an entry whose object pointer matches, that entry also contains the memory address of the object (see figure 4). If the hash routine finds no match in the few entries it searches, the object is not in memory. The magic puffs of smoke in figure 3 depict the act of hashing an object pointer into the ROT to find its memory address.

OOZE must maintain the ROT. When an object is brought in from the disk, OOZE hashes its object pointer and looks in the ROT. When it finds an empty entry among the few possibilities, it claims that entry for the new object. Conversely, when an object is removed from memory and put back on the disk, its entry in the

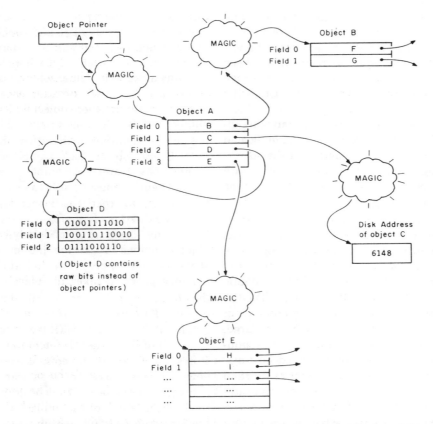

Figure 3: *Objects and object pointers (as seen by casual observers). The "magic" is the unspecified process of translating the value of the object pointer to the actual address at which the object is stored.*

August 1981 © BYTE Publications Inc

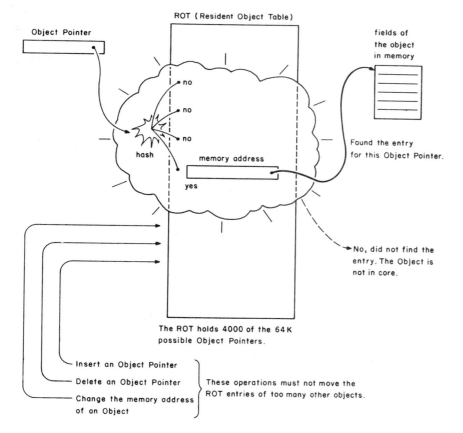

Figure 4: *Hashing an object pointer in the Resident Object Table (ROT).*

average number of entries examined to find an object in memory is only 1.8. Typically, the resident object table is 80 percent full.

Finding an Object on the Disk

The translation from an object pointer to the disk address of the object is also important. Since a list of the disk addresses of all 64 K objects would easily fill up main memory, OOZE must use a trick. Instead of object pointers being assigned randomly to objects, information is encoded in each object pointer. This is done by dividing the set of object pointers into *pseudoclasses*. The bits in the upper part of the pointer indicate to which pseudoclass that object belongs. All objects in a pseudoclass have the same Smalltalk class and have the same length. The *Pseudoclass Map* is a table that is indexed with the pseudoclass number. There OOZE finds the length of the object and its class (see figure 5). A single Smalltalk class may own as many pseudoclasses as it needs to cover all of its instances. Classes whose instances may have indexable variables, such as class *String*, own a different pseudoclass for each length or range of lengths. The pseudoclass encoding saves space because each object does not use a word to hold its class or a word to hold its length. Objects in memory in OOZE are actually two words shorter than objects in the Smalltalk-80 system.

The disk address of an object is also found by using its pseudoclass. All objects in a pseudoclass are the same length, and they are stored consecutively on the disk. By knowing which object we want within the pseudoclass, we can compute its offset from the beginning of the pseudoclass. If we know the starting disk address of the pseudoclass, we can add the offset and find the object. The Pseudoclass Map contains the starting disk address of the object's pseudoclass (see figure 5). The low bits of the object's pointer tell which object it is within the pseudoclass. This encoding allows the disk addresses of all 64 K objects to be stored in 512 words of memory.

ROT is marked empty. Sometimes an object moves in memory, and its memory address in its ROT entry must be updated (as referred to in figure 4).

Hashing object pointers into the ROT to find memory addresses is the highest bandwidth operation in OOZE. If hashing were supported by special-purpose hardware, the hashing operation would not consume much time. (Many machines provide similar hardware support for paging.) In our implementations of the Smalltalk-76 system, the best we were able to do was to write the ROT hashing algorithm in microcode. In spite of this, OOZE spends a large fraction of its time hashing into the ROT. Any hash that can be avoided saves time. We modified the Smalltalk interpreter to remember the memory addresses of certain frequently used objects. During the straight-line execution of a Smalltalk method, the interpreter holds the memory address of the currently executing method, the receiver, and the

object on the top of the stack. Smalltalk spends significantly less time in OOZE when hashes of these frequently used objects are circumvented.

Hashing into the ROT is optimized in yet another way. As mentioned before, the hash routine uses the object pointer to compute a series of places to search in the ROT. The entries examined form a chain, with different object pointers having different chains. These chains crisscross throughout the ROT. An entry on one chain is many times filled by an object pointer from a different chain that also uses this entry. The hash routine is searching for an entry that matches a certain object pointer. The search will succeed faster if the chain has all its own entries at the beginning and all other chains' entries at the end. The algorithm for deleting an entry from the ROT provides this optimization. After deleting the proper entry, it shuffles the remaining entries and moves them forward in their chains. Because of this strategy, the

(There are actually two additional levels of translation for the disk address. Tables for these take another 740 words).

By using the Pseudoclass Map, OOZE can find the disk address of any object from its object pointer. If it is in memory, OOZE also finds the object from its object pointer. *Thus the same object pointer serves to identify and find an object, no matter where the object is.* Because moving an object between disk and memory does not change its pointer, fields that point to the object need not change when the object moves. A field always contains the object pointer of the object to which it refers, regardless of the field's location and regardless of the object's location.

Storage Management

The management of the swapping space has several aspects. Objects are created and destroyed by Smalltalk upon request, and they are also moved in and out of memory. Each of these actions causes insertion or deletion in the ROT and allocation or deallocation in memory. Consider a class that wants to create a new instance: the new instance must receive an object pointer whose pseudoclass is already owned by that class. For this reason, we treat free instances of a class as legitimate objects. They "belong to the class" and can be swapped to and from the disk just like normal instances. Each class keeps a linked list of free instances. The class thinks that there are an infinite number of free instances on the disk, waiting to be swapped in. To create a new instance, the class merely pulls the first object off its "free list." If that object is not in memory, a fault brings it in from the disk. When a free list on the disk runs out, OOZE constructs new free instances on the disk as they are requested.

We have reduced the problem of managing memory and the ROT to the problem of swapping. Main memory has some free blocks between the areas being used for objects. These free blocks are linked together on free lists according to their size. The ROT also contains unused entries, which are marked as such. During an object fault, OOZE claims a free ROT entry and a proper-sized block of memory for the incoming object. Occasionally, OOZE cannot find a legal ROT entry or a free block of memory that is large enough. The fault routine stops, and OOZE starts purging objects from memory by copying them to their proper places on the disk. It then frees the memory space and ROT entries of the objects it throws out. When the purge routine finishes, the fault routine resumes its work.

The purge routine must decide which objects to throw out of memory. To play the game of virtual memory perfectly, OOZE should keep the objects which will be used soon and throw out those which will not. Since OOZE cannot see into the future, it throws out the least recently used objects. Objects that have been active recently are kept, and inactive ones are tossed out. The purge routine examines objects in memory in an order determined by their object pointers. Consider the space of all object pointers to be a circle. The purge routine tours the circle, keeping objects that have been accessed since the last time around. Objects that have remained unaccessed since the routine last visited them are purged to the disk (see figure 6). Typically, it takes several calls on the purge routine to complete a tour of the circle of object pointers.

Purging objects in order of their object pointers has a very important side effect. Since all objects in a pseudoclass are consecutive on the disk, purge sends out the objects it is purging in the same order that they appear on the disk. This minimizes the movement of the disk head and saves time.

Objects that have not been changed since they came in from the disk do not have to be rewritten. They are correct as they stand on the disk. A single bit in each object in memory tells if it is "dirty" (ie: if it has been changed since it was copied to memory). If an object about to be purged is not dirty, we do not rewrite it on the disk and thus save time. This savings can be enhanced by purging in the background. Normally the

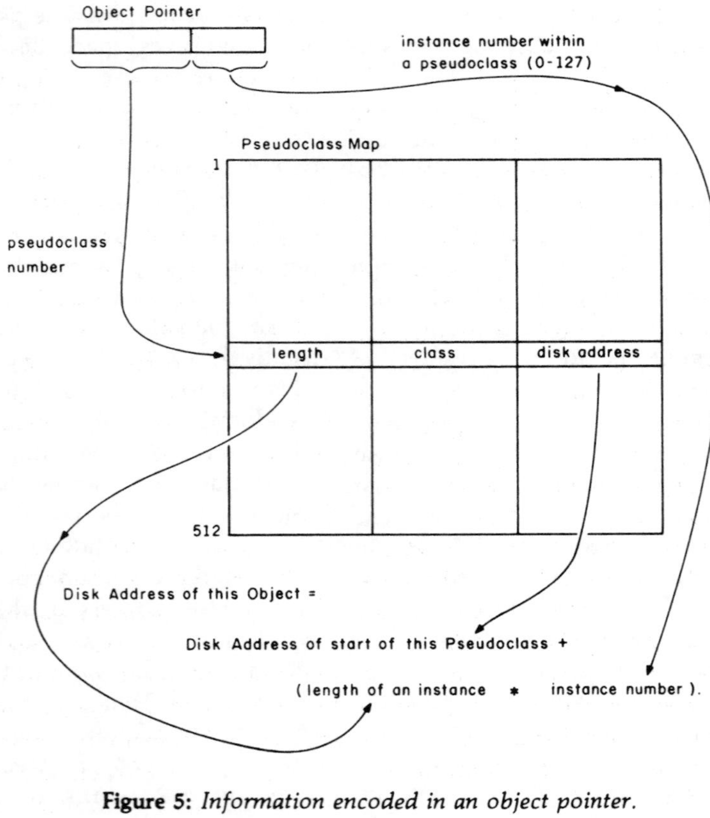

Figure 5: *Information encoded in an object pointer.*

August 1981 © BYTE Publications Inc

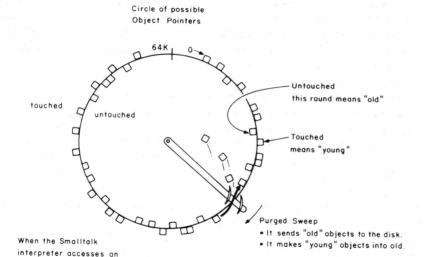

Circle of possible
Object Pointers

touched

untouched

Untouched
this round means "old"

Touched
means "young"

Purged Sweep
• It sends "old" objects to the disk.
• It makes "young" objects into old.

When the Smalltalk
interpreter accesses an
object, it is marked "touched."

Figure 6: *The order in which objects are purged from main memory.*

purge routine runs in response to an immediate demand for space in memory. A special version of the routine runs when Smalltalk is idle and looks ahead in the circle of object pointers. It writes dirty objects to the disk and marks them as being "clean." A subsequent demand call on the purge routine will run quickly because many of the objects it wants to throw out are already written on the disk.

After each round of purging, the degree of fragmentation of memory is tested. If there are too many small blocks and no big ones, we perform a *compaction*. All objects are moved to one end of memory and all free blocks are merged into a single block at the other end. Memory addresses are updated in the ROT entries of the objects that have moved. OOZE performs this operation without using additional storage in order to keep a list of which objects have moved to which place in memory.

As a storage manager, OOZE must detect when an object is no longer being used. Like the storage manager mentioned in Krasner's article, OOZE uses *reference counting*. When the reference count of an object goes to zero, its object pointer is not in any field of any other object. At this point, it is impossible for that object ever to be accessed by the interpreter. OOZE, therefore, puts the object on

its class's free list. Before doing so, however, it decreases the reference count of the object pointed to by each field of this object. In the process, more counts may go to zero, and more objects may get freed. To save space, reference counts are only fo bits wide. The few objects with fifteen or more fields pointing at them are noted in a separate overflow reference count table.

Performance

An average Smalltalk-76 system with OOZE contains 40,000 objects and occupies one megabyte of disk space. In main memory, the system uses 96 K words, including 8 K words for the ROT and 40 K words for the objects that are currently swapped in. (We sometimes run with only 64 K words of memory.) On the Alto computer (see reference 1), we implement hashing into the ROT and the allocation of common objects in microcode. Performance is equivalent to a paging system with several times the swapping space. The OOZE virtual memory has allowed the Smalltalk-76 system to grow from an experiment into a system for building large and serious applications.

OOZE was designed in 1975. Several rules of the virtual memory game have changed since then. Here are some ways in which OOZE shows its age at Xerox PARC:

• Users can afford more disk and more memory. They want to build systems that contain more than 64 K objects. OOZE cannot be easily expanded beyond this limit.

• Several extensions to the Smalltalk language encourage the user to create lots of classes. OOZE has a limit of 245 classes, and many serious users have encountered this limit.

Naturally, our minds have turned to building a virtual memory for the Smalltalk-80 system with even better performance than OOZE. In 1980, a group of us at Xerox PARC designed just such a system, the *Large Object-Oriented Memory* (LOOM). Individual objects in LOOM carry slightly more overhead than objects in OOZE. (Since users can afford more memory, this is not a problem.) Besides allowing a much larger virtual space and unlimited classes, LOOM provides some new properties:

• LOOM accesses objects that are in memory simply by indexing a table, as does the resident Smalltalk-80 system. LOOM thus saves the time that OOZE spends hashing into the ROT whenever it wants a memory address. During the table lookup which finds an object's memory address, LOOM tests for the case when the object is not actually in memory. To run faster than a hash in OOZE, the test must be very simple and fast.

• LOOM is designed with the idea in mind of grouping objects on the disk. If objects that are faulted on together can be arranged into groups on the disk, the system will run faster. LOOM will be a test bed for schemes that optimize the organization of objects on the disk.

Conclusion

The goal of the virtual memory game is to make a mixture of fast and slow memory perform almost as well as if it were all fast memory. The strategy is to guess what information the processor will need soon and move it to fast memory. In an object-oriented language such as Smalltalk, the object is an excellent unit for locality of reference. Once an object is accessed, it will most likely be accessed again soon. Recently used objects have a similar degree of locality to recently used pages, and many more objects than pages fit into a given amount of fast memory.

OOZE is the first representative of the new category of object-oriented virtual memories. These systems use a construct in the high-level language, the object, as the unit of swapping. Objects as small as one field in length are swapped individually by the same mechanism used for large strings and arrays. To be a member of this category, a virtual memory must also have automatic control of swapping and automatic creation and freeing of objects. While OOZE is implemented in software, we believe that future systems will be implemented like languages: hardware assist for a few high-bandwidth operations, some microcode, and support code in machine- or high-level language. We expect that mature object-oriented virtual memories will identify groups of objects that are used together and swap them as a unit.

As the virtual memory which supports the Smalltalk-76 system, OOZE is interesting in itself. It provides the ability to address 2^N objects with N-bit pointers. Only currently active objects occupy memory, and they are packed end to end. This provides exceedingly good use of memory. Because the class and length of an object are encoded in the object pointer, that information does not occupy space with each object in memory. Movement of the disk head is reduced because objects are purged to the disk in the order of their disk addresses. OOZE is implemented in software without any special hardware support. It runs in an amazingly sprightly fashion and performs as well as paging systems with several times the swapping space.

The fact that Smalltalk uses objects consistently and completely allows its virtual memory to be radical in design. Object-oriented virtual memories get their power from a close coupling with the high-level languages they serve. The success of OOZE and the changing rules of the virtual memory game have inspired the design of LOOM, a larger and more efficient object-oriented virtual memory.■

References

1. Bell, C G and Alan Newell. *Computer Structures: Readings and Examples*, New York: McGraw-Hill, 2nd edition, 1980.
2. Denning, P J. "Virtual Memory," *Computing Surveys*, Volume 2, Number 3, September 1970, page 153.
3. Ingalls, Daniel H H. "The Smalltalk-76 Programming System: Design and Implementation," *Conference Record, Fifth Annual ACM Symposium on Principles of Programming Languages*, 1978.
4. Shaw, Alan C. *The Logical Design of Operating Systems*, Englewood Cliffs NJ: Prentice-Hall, 1974.
5. Wulf, W A, et al. *HYDRA/C.mmp*, New York: McGraw-Hill, 1981, Chapter 11.

August 1981 © BYTE Publications Inc

THE OBJECT MODEL:

A CONCEPTUAL TOOL FOR STRUCTURING SOFTWARE

Anita K. Jones
Department of Computer Science
Carnegie-Mellon University
Pittsburgh, PA 15213 USA

Computers are programmed to simulate complex physical and abstract systems. To design, construct, and communicate these programmed systems to others, human beings need appropriate conceptual tools. The object model is both a concept and a tool. It provides guidelines for characterizing the abstract entities in terms of which we think. In particular, use of the object model can lead to clear and explicit expression of the dependency relations between these entities in a way that is conducive to rendering them as programs. An example benefit is that different programmers can be assigned different parts of a design to program, and their products can be integrated with a minimum of inconsistencies. The object model provides a framework in terms of which to think about and communicate designs for programmed systems; it is implicitly and explicitly used in other papers in this volume. Thus, it is appropriate to explore the model itself.

The notion of the object model has evolved over the past decade or so. It has roots at least as far back as the Simula language design [Dahl68]. Researchers in the area of programming methodology are investigating the object model and the kinds of abstractions it enables [Liskov76]. Some recently designed programming languages incorporate constructs to assist the programmer thinking in the framework of the object model [Wulf77, Liskov77]. In this paper I will not develop the arguments for and against use of the object model, nor will I explore its many nuances. I will explain the model generally, and consider some of its ramifications with respect to operating systems.

1. The Object Model

In the object model emphasis is placed on crisply characterizing the components of the physical or abstract system to be modeled by a programmed system. The components, that are thought of as being "passive', are called objects. Objects have a certain "integrity" which should not--in fact, cannot--be violated. An object can only change state, behave, be manipulated, or stand in relation to other objects in ways appropriate to that object. Stated differently, there exist invariant properties that characterize an object and its behavior. An elevator, for example, is characterized by invariant properties including: it only travels up and down inside its shaft; it cannot be moving and stopped at the same time; it can stop at only one floor at a time; it's maximum capacity, measured in volume and weight, cannot be exceeded. Any elevator simulation must incorporate these invariants, for they are integral to the notion of an elevator.

The object model dictates that these invariant properties are preserved by a set of operations that are the only means by which an object can be directly manipulated. To alter or even to determine the state of the object, an appropriate operation must be invoked. Thus, the set of operations for an object collectively define its behavior. In practice, the number of operations required for an object is relatively small (say, from three to twelve).

The behavior of any elevator object could be defined using three operations. The first one would be used only once to 'install' the elevator, initializing its state. For example, the Install operation would fix the relevant parameters of the building, such as the number of floors, in which the elevator exists. Once an elevator is Installed, the other two operations, Up and Down, can be invoked by passengers who wish to change floors. In a programmed simulation of the elevator, only the procedures implementing the three operations would be able to alter the state of the elevator. For example, synchronization of actions necessary to preserve elevator invariants are found in the code bodies of the procedures implementing the Up and Down operations.

Because many objects essentially have the same behavioral characteristics, it is convenient to define a single set of operations, perhaps parameterized, that are equally applicable to many objects. Two objects are said to be of the same _type_ if they share the same set of operations. The literature on programming methodology contains numerous articles explicating the notion of type. For our purposes it is not necessary to delve into the theology that surrounds the issue of precisely what constitutes a type definition. I will rely on the reader's intuitions.

In a programmed implementation of a type, the programmed operations are collected together in what is called a _type module_. Some recently designed languages provide syntactic constructs designed to permit and encourage a programmer to build his program as a set of independent type modules. Alphard [Wulf77] includes the _form_ construct; Clu [Liskov77] includes the _cluster_. Within a type module definition appears a description of the representation, if any, that is created when an object is instantiated, as well as the procedures that implement the operations of the type. Scope rules are defined so that only the code that is part of the type module can directly manipulate the representation of an object of that type. As a result, only the code in the type module implementation must be considered to determine the invariant properties that hold for objects of the type. Every type has a specification that expresses all that is known or can be assumed by programs outside the type module. Details of implementation, both of an object's representation and the exact algorithm followed in the implementation of an operation, are hidden behind the type module boundary. The intent is that from the type specifications a user can understand enough about the type to use it, but cannot make use of type module implementation details.

To express a new abstraction, a designer specifies a new type. New types are defined using existing types. First, one assumes the existence of some primitive types provided by a language or a machine. Objects may be--in fact, usually are-- represented in terms of other component objects. Operations for the new type are implemented assuming the existence of the specified operations for manipulating component objects. To implement an entire system a programmer constructs a set of type module definitions related by dependence; a second type module depends upon a first, if operations in the first are assumed for the implementation of the second.

The object model is merely a structuring tool; it does not imply a particular design technique. It is amenable to use with both the "top down" and "bottom up" design techniques. Using the "top down" technique, a programmer designs the main program in terms of whatever, as yet, nonexistent, types seem convenient, then implements the types found necessary for designing the main program. This process is repeated until all types are defined, either by the programmer or as primitives. Alternatively, a designer using the "bottom up" design technique constructs types that express low level abstractions that are deemed to be useful building blocks. He successively builds up to the higher level abstractions, and eventually to the entire system. In either case, at each step in the design process a programmer implementing a type can ignore unnecessary detail. He focuses only on the specifications and the implementation of the new type he is currently defining and on the specifications of the types he is using to construct the new type.

To illustrate the object model and the corollary notion of type modules, consider an example of a customer of a telephone service as seen by those who provide the service. Relevant operations that need to be performed for the customer include:

Lookup -- given a customer's name, determine customer's primary telephone number

ChangeService -- alter the current service provided to a customer, e.g., remove the phone, or install a new extension

Credit -- credit the customer's account by a certain amount

Debit -- debit the customer's account by a specified amount

WriteBill -- output a formatted copy of a customer's bill suitable for sending to him for payment

Each customer can be represented in the computer by an object called a telephone-service-customer. Each customer is characterized by a name and address, the kind of telephone service presently provided, as well as billing and credit information. There are various groups of people that cooperate to provide telephone service; each group has a need to reference telephone-service-customer objects. A telephone operator needs to Lookup telephone numbers upon request. Likewise, the service representatives of the company should be able to assign new numbers or otherwise alter (ChangeService) the current service that is provided to a customer. Business office employees need to be able to print bills, inspect billing and service data, and to credit and debit a user's account (WriteBill, Debit, Credit). Each of the above sees the customer from a different perspective and has available operations which support that perspective.

As part of the type definition, a customer might be represented by a record containing at least the following component objects (of types not specified here):

```
name
address
current service (an array, one entry for each installed phone number)
      assigned phone number
      location of phone
      number of extensions
      color/type of phone
billing data (an array, one entry for each installed phone number)
      rate schedule
      local call charges
      itemized long distance charges
      credit or debit carried from previous month
      billing address
```

As stated earlier, the representation of the telephone-service-customer object is not available for manipulation except by code that implements the telephone-service-customer type module, in particular the operations sketched above. Thus, details of implementation, such as record formats, are not available outside the type module.

2. The Object Model Applied to Operating Systems

An operating system provides a variety of services--address space management, i/o support, and process management including synchronization and interprocess communication. Following the object model, an operating system can be described as a set of types, each of which can be thought of as a kind of resource. Some resources have a direct physical realization, such as i/o devices. Others are further removed each time it is used (e.g., presented to the operating system as a parameter), or, if possible, restricting its use to trusted programs. It is very sad to read code in which a check of whether an address is on a double word boundary is made, as a futile attempt to determine whether a parameter is a process name or not. Such a naming scheme is inadequate.

The second technique for naming an object is to introduce a new name interpreter for each new type of object. For example, process objects may be named, say using integers that are interpreted as indices into a table of process representations. Only code in the process type module can access this table, so the interpreter of process names is part of the process type module. But this means only that the process type module maps integers to processes, not that it can determine from a submitted parameter whether that integer name designates a legitimate process, or that the caller should be able to access it in any way. This second naming scheme is also inadequate.

It would seem that a facility to name objects--not just segments--is desirable. Such a facility would make programming more convenient, and would free the programmer from the burden of mentally translating from the object to the details of that object's representation. It is unclear how such a facility should be implemented. Such naming of objects can be supported dynamically by the operating system or, applications programmers can be constrained to write programs only in languages that provide object naming syntax and a compiler to map objects to their representations.

Closely related to naming is protection, a facility provided by an operating system to constrain the way information is used and changed. Because logically separate pieces of information are encoded in different objects, it is appropriate to provide protection for each object individually. Manipulation of an object is requested by specifying an operation to be performed on that object. A straightforward technique for constraining arbitrary manipulation of an object is to constrain the ability to perform operations on that object. Rights to perform certain operations defined for an object are distributed only to those who should be able to manipulate the object. A protection mechanism permits an operation to be successfully invoked only if the invoker possesses the right to do so. Controlling the use of an object based on the operations defined for it is desirable. Certainly, it is more meaningful to users than protecting on the basis of read/write access to the memory cells used for representing objects. Such protection mechanisms enable fine distinctions between the manipulations allowed to various users. In the telephone-service-customer example the operator can be granted only the right to Lookup telephone numbers, while the telephone service office can be granted the right to perform both the Lookup and ChangeService operations, yet not be permitted to perform the billing operations. Thus, the service office can cause the customer object to be altered, but only in constrained ways related to the responsibilities of the service office.

Our conclusion is that both naming and protection can profitably be provided on the basis of objects. In an operating system in which both naming and protection are provided for all objects--not just segments, there exist implementations in which protection and naming are integrated. For now, an implementation will be sketched. It will be investigated in more detail in the paper on protection. Let the set of objects that are accessible during the execution of a program, in particular, an operation, be called the domain. A domain can be expressed as a set of descriptors, sometimes called capabilities [Dennis66]. Each descriptor is an unforgeable token

212

that identifies a particular object. The name of an object is a local name, say an integer offset into a list of descriptors. The system name interpreter locates the unique object specified by information in the descriptor. Using this naming mechanism, code is restricted to use of only those objects in its domain. For the naming mechanism and the protection mechanism to be well defined, the alteration of domains, i.e., the acquisition and dispersion of descriptors via execution in a domain must be controlled in a disciplined manner.

This naming mechanism can be extended to support protection if a domain is redefined to be not just a set of objects, but a set of rights to objects. We extend the descriptor to encode rights to an object in addition to the information needed to find a unique object. An operation can be successfully performed in a domain only if the right to do so is in that domain.

There are a number of extant systems which support the naming of objects of types besides memory segments [Burroughs61, Lampson76, Wulf74, Needham77]. It remains a research issue to determine how to provide object naming and protection cost-effectively. If the operating system supports generalized object naming, an interesting issue is what hardware support, if any, should be provided. Indeed, how inexpensive can object naming be made? Another alternative is to provide a language system as the "front end" to the operating system and have the language system support object naming. As exemplified by the Burroughs 5000 system, the compiler, and a minimal run time system would support the mapping between an object and the (virtual) memory used to represent it. The supporting operating system need only provide more modest naming and protection mechanisms. A disadvantage of this is the lack of support for individual naming and protection of objects for debugging and for runtime reliability checks.

Synchronization is yet another facility which is affected by adoption of the object model paradigm. According to the object model, each different manipulation of an object is performed by a different operation. It is frequently the case that synchronization is naturally expressed at the level of operations, i.e., that only certain sequences of operations are allowed. For example, one invariant property of a mailbox is that the number of messages removed cannot exceed the number of messages sent to that mailbox. This can be expressed by saying that the Receive operation cannot be performed more times than the Send operation. Habermann [77] has developed a notation called path expressions to express permissible operation sequences. One advantage of expressing synchronization restrictions as relations among operations is that synchronization constraints can be meaningfully stated as part of the specification of the type module. Thus, synchronization constraints are expressed to the user in natural terms--i.e., in terms of permissible operation sequences on object. One can view a path expression as a declarative statement of what synchronization constraints are to be observed. The code actually realizing that synchronization may not even be written by the author of the type module, but may be provided statically by the language system or dynamically by the operating system.

In this section I have tried to argue that three of the features that every operating system provides all have a natural expression, given the object model paradigm. In particular, each one can be phrased in terms of the objects and operations that are meaningful to the user. It is my opinion that some model, and perhaps the object model is the correct one, is needed to raise operating system designers and implementors above the level of that common denominator, the memory word, and all the extraneous, debilitating detail it forces us to think about.

3. Mechanics of Supporting Type Modules

Consider the invocation of operations defined as part of a type. The operations are implemented as procedures in hardware, firmware, and more often, in software. Provisions must be made to invoke these procedures in a well defined manner, and to provide a domain containing the objects that are to be accessible for the duration of the procedure's execution. To support the notion of a type module there must exist an invocation mechanism that, at a minimum, locates the procedure that implements the desired operation, acquires or constructs a domain to make available to the procedure those objects required for its correct execution, and causes execution of the procedure to begin at the procedure entry point.

Because objects are specified as parameters to operation invocations, a question arises: does the ability to perform operations on an object change as a result of its being passed as a parameter? If one program passes an object as a parameter to a slave program that is to perform a task that the caller could conceivably perform, the second program should not have any rights to manipulate the parameter object that the caller program does not have. In fact, the second program may have less.

In contrast, if an object is passed as a parameter to an operation defined as part of the object's type, the code implementing that operation will require the ability to manipulate the object's representation. Thus, some means for amplification, i.e., for obtaining additional rights to manipulate an object is required [Jones75]. Most extant hardware provides only an extremely primitive amplification mechanism. When a user program invokes an operation that happens to be provided by a module of the operating system, the hardware state changes so that when the operating system code is entered, it has access to all of main memory. In particular, it has all necessary access to the representation of the parameter object, but it also has much, much more.

Such a mechanism does not support the object model very well. It places an undue burden on the implementor of the operating system, because that programmer has no means to restrict the objects, or memory, that are accessible to his code, making debugging more difficult. Such mechanisms inadequately support the concept of software reliability. More selective amplification mechanisms can be designed. The Multics hardware permits domains of execution to be ordered so that segments, the nameable objects in the Multics system, that are available to one domain are available both to it and to domains lower in the ordering [Organick72]. The Multics hardware can be augmented so that each domain can be treated independently eliminating the ordering constraint [Schroeder72]. Other systems, such as Hydra, that lack hardware to perform amplification provide such support in software [Wulf74]. Programming languages that support the concept of abstract data types provide such amplification mechanisms [Jones76].

So, to support the object model requires support for the notion of a domain. Ideally, domains are small; only the rights and objects necessary to perform the task at hand are available. Domain support must include a facility for suspending execution in one domain in order to enter another, and subsequently to return to the first. Some provision for amplification is required. Domain management needs to be efficient for domain entry and exit occur often. Current operating system research and some programming language research is addressing these issues.

4. Observation

The fidelity with which a particular system adheres to the object model varies widely. Some operating systems, such as Multics, define a single type of object, the segment, and permit users to create segments at will. Other systems, such as Hydra, permit users to dynamically create new object types, as well as new objects. Hydra, in particular, provides naming and protection of objects of user defined types, as well as operating system types, as was sketched above. However, even in cases where the operating system design does not closely adhere to the object model, the model often provides a convenient vehicle for describing system components. Consequently, in the other papers in this volume authors have used the notion with greater or less fidelity, as suited their needs and their taste.

5. References

Burroughs Corporation, The Descriptor--A definition of the B5000 Information Processing System. Detroit, MI (February 1961).

Dahl, O.-J., B. Myhrhaung and K. Nygaard, The Simula 67 Common Base Language, Norwegian Computing Center, Oslo, Norway (1968).

Dennis, J. B. and Van Horn, E. C., Programming Semantics for Multiprogrammed Computations, CACM 9, 3 (March 1966) 143-155.

Habermann, A. N., On the Concurrency of Parallel Processes, Perspectives in Computer Science, A. Jones, editor, Academic Press (1977).

Jones, A. K. and W. A. Wulf, Towards the Design of Secure Systems. Software--Practice and Experience, 5, 4 (October-December 1975) 321-336.

Jones, A. K. and B. H. Liskov, A Language Extension for Controlling Access to Shared Data. IEEE Transactions on Software Engineering SE-2, 4 (December 1976) 277-284.

Lampson, B. W. and H. Sturgis, Reflections on an Operating System Design. CACM 19, 5 (May 76), 251-266.

Liskov, B. H. and S. Zilles, Specification Techniques for Data Abstractions. Proceedings of the International Conference on Reliable Software, SIGPLAN Notices 12,3 (1977).

Liskov, B. H., A. Snyder, R. Atkinson, and C. Schaffert, Abstraction Mechanisms in CLU. Proceedings of the ACM Conference on Language Design for Reliable Software, SIGPLAN Notices 10,6 (1975), 534-545.

Needham, R. and R. D. H. Walker, The Cambridge CAP Computer and its Protection System. Proceedings of the 6th ACM Symposium on Operating System Principles (November 77) 1-10.

Organick, E. I., The Multics System: iAn Examination of its Structure. MIT Press (1972).

Schroeder, M. D. and J. H. Saltzer, A Hardware Architecture for Implementing Protection Rings. CACM 15, 3 (March 1972) 157-170.

Wulf, W. A., et al, Hydra: the Kernel of a Multiprocessor Operating System. CACM 17, 6 (June 1974) 337-345.

Wulf, W. A., R. L. London and M. Shaw, Abstraction and Verification in Alphard. IEEE Transactions on Software Engineering (April 1976).

Programming Semantics for Multiprogrammed Computations

Jack B. Dennis and Earl C. Van Horn

Massachusetts Institute of Technology, Cambridge, Massachusetts

The semantics are defined for a number of meta-instructions which perform operations essential to the writing of programs in multiprogrammed computer systems. These meta-instructions relate to parallel processing, protection of separate computations, program debugging, and the sharing among users of memory segments and other computing objects, the names of which are hierarchically structured. The language sophistication contemplated is midway between an assembly language and an advanced algebraic language.

Presented at an ACM Programming Languages and Pragmatics Conference, San Dimas, California, August 1965.

Work reported herein was supported by Project MAC, an MIT research program sponsored by the Advanced Research Projects Agency, Department of Defense, under Office of Naval Research Contract Number Nonr-4102(01). Reproduction in whole or in part is permitted for any purpose of the United States Government.

Introduction

An increasing percentage of computation activity will be carried out by multiprogrammed computer systems. Such systems are characterized by the application of computation resources (processing capacity, main memory, file storage, peripheral equipment) to many separate but concurrently operating computations.

We can cite three quite different examples of multiprogrammed computer systems to illustrate their diversity of application. The American Airlines SABRE passenger record system couples ticketing agents at dispersed offices to a central data file [1]. The computer support systems of NASA provide real time control and monitoring of manned space flights [2]. The Project MAC time-sharing system permits research workers closer interaction with the powers of automatic computation [3]. Although these are all on-line systems, multiprogramming techniques have also been used successfully in systems that perform computations on an offline, job-shop basis.

We review some of the distinctive properties of a multi-programmed computer system (MCS), and then introduce some concepts and terminology that have proven useful in studying the properties of multiprogrammed computations. As we proceed, we define a number of *meta-instructions* that embody powers mostly absent from contemporary programming languages, but essential to the implementation of computation processes in an MCS. These powers relate to (1) parallel processing, (2) naming objects of computation, and (3) protection of computing entities from unauthorized access. The character of these meta-instructions is such that they might form part of a language intermediate in sophistication between an assembly language and an advanced algebraic language for an MCS. In fact, the semantics of these meta-instructions could be incorporated in the definition of an intermediate language that might be employed at some stage in the translation of a more advanced language.

We do not claim completeness for the set of meta-instructions to be described. Additional operations will prove necessary in practice for a specific MCS. In particular, no means is discussed whereby an object computation may advise the supervisor of special scheduling or allocation requirements. Also, conventions for dynamic control of segment length have been omitted.

Properties of Multiprogrammed Computer Systems

Five properties of multiprogrammed computer systems are important to the present discussion.

(1) Computation processes are in concurrent operation for more than one user. A multiprogrammed computer System is generally the creation of many individuals working in part toward a common objective and in part for private goals. A successful MCS must include mechanisms for preventing undesired interference among computations.

(2) Many computations share pools of resources in a flexible way. In consequence, the individual planner of a computation need not be concerned about efficiently using a certain fixed amount of memory and processing capacity which would otherwise go to waste. Resources not used by one computation are available to other concurrent computations.

(3) Individual computations vary widely in their demands for computing resources in the course of time.

An MCS must have mechanisms (explicit or implicit) through which a computation may request and release resources according to need. Where many computations are active, which are not closely coupled in their demands for resources, the peak demands of some computations will coincide with the slack demands of others. As the number of computations in the system is increased, the instantaneous total demand for resources will hover closer to the sum of the individual average demands. Therefore, the amount of physical resources required in such an MCS is governed by the average demand over all computations rather than by the sum of their peak demands.

(4) Reference to common information by separate computations is a frequent occurrence.

In an MCS it is advantageous to allow information to be common among computations proceeding for different users to avoid needless duplication of procedures and data. Also, communication among separately planned computations is essential to many MCS objectives. Furthermore, the sharing of a peripheral device by several computations is sometimes required.

(5) An MCS must evolve to meet changing requirements.

An MCS does not exist in a static environment. Changing objectives, increased demand for use, added functions, improved algorithms and new technologies all call for flexible evolution of the system, both as a configuration of equipment and as a collection of programs.

To meet the requirements of flexibility of capacity and of reliability, the most natural form of an MCS is as a modular multiprocessor system arranged so that processors, memory modules and file storage units may be added, removed or replaced in accordance with changing requirements [4].

Concepts and Terminology

Segments. The smallest unit of stored information that is of interest in the present discussion is called a *word*. An ordered set of words grouped together for purposes of naming is called a *segment*. A segment is created at some point in time and has a definite *length* (which may vary with time) at any instant of its existence.

Any reference by a computation to data or procedure information is specified by a *word name*, $w = [i, a]$, consisting of the *index number* i of the segment containing the desired word and a *word address* a giving the position of the word within the segment. The index number may be thought of as an abbreviation for the *name* of the segment. The correspondence between an index number and a name is established by meta-instructions which will be defined subsequently.

In the programming examples (which are written in a pseudo-ALGOL format) variable identifiers, array identifiers and labels will stand for word names. Word names are written here as $[i, a]$ only when the index number must be explicitly mentioned.

The concept of segment has influenced the design of a commercial computer (the Burroughs B5500), an experimental machine [5] and one military system (the Burroughs D825). The use of segments in software systems is discussed by Greenfield [6], Holt [7] and others. The design of addressing mechanisms for MCS's is discussed by Dennis [8]. A fuller implementation of these concepts in a machine organization has been discussed by Glaser, Couleur and Oliver [9], and interesting work in a similar direction is in progress at the MIT Lincoln Laboratory [10], IBM [11] and is continuing at Burroughs [12].

Protection. In an MCS, a computation must be denied access to memory words and other objects of computation unless access is authorized. In particular, it seems natural to implement memory protection on a segment basis. Thus, we think of a computation as proceeding within some *sphere of protection* [13] specified by a *list of capabilities* or *C-list* for short. Each capability in a *C*-list locates by means of a pointer[1] some computing object, and indicates the actions that the computation may perform with respect to that object. Among these capabilities there are usually several *segment capabilities*, which designate segments that may be referenced by the computation and also give, by means of *access indicators*, an indication of the kind of reference permitted:

X	executable as procedure including internal read references for constants.
R	readable as data but not executable.
XR	executable as procedure and readable as data.
RW	readable and writeable as data.
XRW	executable as procedure and readable and writeable as data.

Other types of capability are also permitted in the *C*-list of a computation, and are introduced in the discussion as appropriate. Every capability contains an *ownership indicator* (**O** for owned, **N** for not owned). Computations have broad powers with respect to owned computing objects, through mechanisms to be described. In the case of an owned segment, for example, a computation may delete the segment, and grant or deny other computations access to the segment.

During the execution of a computation, capabilities will frequently be added to and deleted from the *C*-list defining its sphere of protection through the use of metainstructions to be described in later sections. The linear subscript of a capability within a *C*-list is called its *index-number*. It is through the use of the index number that the capability is exercised by processes. For example, a segment is referenced by giving the index number of the segment in a word name. We assume that the allocation of these index numbers is carried out by the system (i.e., the supervisor program) during the execution of an object computation.

Processes. We consider that the system hardware comprises one or more processors, which we can identify as being distinct from the main memory, the file storage devices and the input/output devices. Each processor is capable of executing algorithms that are specified by sequences of instructions. A *process* is a locus of control within an instruction sequence. That is, a process is that abstract entity which moves through the instructions of a procedure as the procedure is executed by a processor.

In a physical computer system a process is represented by the information that must be loaded into a processor in

---

[1] The term "pointer" is used here because of its familiarity to most workers. The permanent representation of a pointer should not be a hardware address in the machine (main or auxilary storage), as it is essential that the entire naming structure be independent of physical device addresses if reallocation of storage media is to be feasible. The authors suggest the association of a unique *code* (called an effective name in [13]) with each computing entity (segment, directory, etc.), which is assigned at the time the entity is created.

order to continue execution of the successive instructions encountered by the process. We call this set of information the *state word* of the process, and note that it must not only contain the accumulator words, index words and the word name of the next instruction to be executed, but must also indicate the *C*-list applicable to the computation to which the process belongs.

A process is said to be *running* if its state word is contained in a processor which is running. A process is called *ready* if it could be placed in execution by a processor if one were free. Running and ready processes are said to be *active*. A process that is not active is *suspended* and is awaiting activation by an external event, such as the completion of an *i/o function*.

Computations. Loosely speaking, a computation may be thought of as a set of processes that are working together harmoniously on the same problem or job. More precisely, we define a *computation* to be a set of processes having a common *C*-list such that all processes using that same *C*-list are members of the same computation.

Notice that two processes having separate *C*-lists are always members of separate computations, even though these *C*-lists might describe the same set of capabilities. Notice also that there exist one-to-one correspondences among computations, spheres of protection and *C*-lists; each computation operates within the restrictions of a unique sphere of protection that is specified by a unique *C*-list. The relationship among these entities is shown schematically in Figure 1.

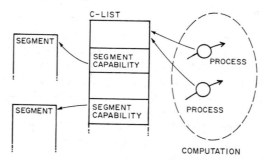

FIG. 1. A computation

Principals. The ordinary notion of a user of an MCS is of an individual who requests computing service from an MCS, or who interacts with a time-shared MCS from a console. We generalize this notion by defining the term *principal* to mean an individual or group of individuals to whom charges are made for the expenditure of system resources. In particular a principal is charged for resources consumed by computations running on his behalf. A principal is also charged for retention in the system of a set of computing entities called *retained objects*, which may be program and data segments, for example. The structure and identification of these retained objects is discussed in a later paragraph.

We can clarify our notion of a principal by giving some examples. Each individual user of the MAC time-sharing system acts as a principal, since he is able to utilize system resources to achieve any personal goal—restricted only by an accounting of his expenditure of basic resources. He may create, modify and delete segments of procedures and data solely according to his personal objectives. In the MAC system we also find principals consisting of groups of individuals. Such a group principal might be responsible for the maintenance of a system of procedures that solves a certain class of mathematical problems (e.g., matrix operations or statistical analysis). Another group principal might have cognizance over a programming language system including editing routines, compiling routines and debugging aids. Still a third principal might oversee the common procedures of an extensive design project involving the cooperative effort of many people.

In the case of an airline information processing system, the agents do not participate as principals but simply communicate with a set of procedures that enable them to perform well defined interrogations of and operations on a centrally stored data base. In such a system, a principal might consist of a team of system planners and programmers responsible for the success of a single aspect of the system's mission. Examples of such separate aspects are passenger records, aircraft scheduling and accounting.

In the case of computer support for a manned space flight, separate principals could be responsible for different aspects of the mission—guidance during propulsion, tracking while in orbit, orbital computation, medical data processing, etc.

The Supervisor

The term *supervisor* is used here to denote the combination of hardware and software elements that together implement a core of basic computer system functions around which all computations performed by the system are constructed. For present purposes we suppose that the core of functions includes mechanisms for (1) allocation and scheduling of computing resources, (2) accounting for and controlling the use of computing resources, and (3) implementing the meta-instructions.

We do not inquire in the present paper as to the internal workings of the supervisor required to perform the above functions. Instead it is our aim to point out the essential features of the interface between the supervisor and user processes which operate in lower spheres of protection. However, it is helpful to think in more concrete terms about how the supervisor accomplishes some of its functions.

The Process List. Specifically, let the *process list* be a data structure within the supervisor, with an entry for each process existing in the system. Entries are created in and removed from this list by various meta-instructions and by other mechanisms that will be described. Each entry can hold the state word of its corresponding process, as well as accounting and scheduling information.

As mentioned before, each process is either running, ready or suspended.

Allocation and Scheduling. At any time segments of information will be distributed among a hierarchy of storage devices (core, drum, disk and tape, for example) with that information most relevant to the on-going computation processes located in the more accessible media. With each computation there is associated a set of information to which it requires a high density (in time) of effective reference. The membership of this *working set* of information varies dynamically during the course of the computation. The supervisor's problem is to decide how information (segments) should be distributed in the storage hierarchy and how the queue of active processes should be disciplined to make most effective use of system resources in accomplishing the MCS mission.

Accounting and Control. We suppose the charges for the expenditure of computation resources associated with the execution of a process are assigned to the principal that was responsible for the creation of the process. We also assume that each principal is given an allotment of resources, and that appropriate action is taken by the supervisor if this allotment is exceeded.

Parallel Programming

Basic Primitive Operations. The basic primitive operation of parallel programming is implemented by the meta-instruction

fork w;

as suggested by Conway [14] where w is a word name. A **fork** meta-instruction initiates a new process at the instruction labeled w. The newly created *branch* process is part of the same computation as its creator or *main* process; that is, it is associated with the same C-list. A process that has completed a sequence of procedure steps is terminated by the meta-instruction

quit

after which the process no longer exists and its state word is discarded from the process list. A set of primitives for parallel programming must include a mechanism whereby one process may be continued just when all of a certain set of processes have completed. All that is required is a procedure step that will decrement a count and test for zero. We use the instruction

join t, w;

which is essentially Conway's join instruction. Here t is the word name of the count to be decremented and w is the word name of an instruction word to be executed if the count becomes zero as indicated in Figure 2. It is essential that the three references to the count t not be separated in time by references to t from other processes. This requirement is indicated by the dashed box in the Figure 2 and is readily achieved in practice by combining the two actions into one machine instruction that is completed with a single reference to the count word.

In describing algorithms involving parallel processes, it is convenient to declare certain quantities as *private to a process*. For this purpose the declaration

private x;

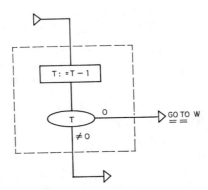

FIG. 2. The **join** procedure step

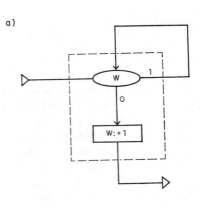

b)

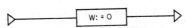

FIG. 3. **Lock** and **unlock** meta-instructions

means that the quantity named x is to exist only so long as the process executing the declaration exists; that is, private data is lost when a process quits. At a **fork** the values of any quantities declared private to the main process are assigned as values of corresponding quantities of the branch process. In practice, the state word of a process is the natural representation of private data. If there is more data declared private than can be represented in the state word, the system must create a segment for private data which is copied at each **fork** and lost upon reaching a **quit**.

Lockout. A provision whereby two processes may negotiate access to common data is a necessary feature of an MCS. Suppose a certain data object (which might be a word, an array, a list structure, a portion or all of a segment) may be updated asynchronously by several processes, which are perhaps members of different computations. Updating a data structure frequently requires a sequence of operations such that intermediate states of the data are inconsistent and would lead to erroneous computation if interpreted by another process.

The lockout feature proposed here presumes that all computations requiring access to the data object are well behaved. If it is desired to protect the data object from destructive manipulation by an untrustworthy computation, routines with protected entry points as described later in this paper must be employed.

We associate with the data object a one-bit lock indicator that is accessible to all processes requiring use of the data object. Two meta-instructions are introduced that operate on the lock indicator w.

lock w;

The effect of the **lock** meta-instruction is given in Figure 3a. The lock bit is set to one just when the data object has been found unlocked by all other processes. Again, as indicated by the dashed box, the two references to w must not be separated by references to w from other processes. The meta-instruction

unlock w;

resets the lock indicator to zero as in Figure 3b.

The use of these meta-instructions would typically be:

```
lock w;
...                 }  update sequence for data object
...                      associated with lock indicator w.
...
unlock w;
```

In practice the execution time of a typical update sequence is quite small and the chance that a process will hang up on a lock instruction will be very low. However, a process may be removed from execution if a processor is preempted by a higher priority computation. Thus, a data object could remain locked for a substantial time if such preemption occurred between a **lock**/**unlock** pair. Then hangup of other processes interrogating that lock indicator could be highly probable. A solution to this problem is to inhibit interruption of a process between execution of a **lock** and execution of the following **unlock**. Of course, this requires that a time limit be set on the separation of **lock**/**unlock** pairs.

An example. An elementary example of parallel programming that illustrates the use of these meta-instructions is the following program that evaluates that dot product of two vectors A and B.

```
begin   real array A[1:n], B[1:n];
        Boolean w;  real S;  integer t;
        private integer i;
        t := n;
        for i := 1 step 1 until n do
           fork e;
        quit;
e:              begin private real X;
substance:          X := A[i] × B[i];
                    lock w;
                    S := S + X;
                    unlock w;
                    join t, r;
                    quit;
                end;
   r:
end;
```

Obviously, this computation is too trivial for parallel programming to be of practical interest. If the algorithm expressed by the statement labeled *substance*, instead of being a simple multiplication, involved the operation of a large, complex system of procedures (e.g., the compilation of a segment of procedure), the notation of parallel processing as used above would allow several instances of that algorithm to be in simultaneous execution, thus more effectively utilizing the presence of its procedure information in main memory.

Input/Output. A basic power of computations in an MCS is the ability to communicate with peripheral (input/output) devices. Two classes of communication have evolved in terms of implementation in present day computer systems. In the simpler class a process requests the transmission of a unit of information (word or fraction of a word) to or from a peripheral device and waits in suspended status until the information is transmitted before continuing. (A *processor*, as contrasted with the *process*, may be executing other processes during the wait interval, however.) This form of implementation is appropriate for low data-rate situations, and also where a close interaction between the computation and the peripheral devices is required (e.g., quick response to brief inquiries from a remote console).

In the second form of input/output operation, a sequence of interactions between memory (i.e., a segment) and the peripheral device occurs in response to an initiation signal from a process. The process remains suspended until all interactions between memory and the peripheral device have been completed.

In either case a principal characteristic of the input/output operation is the elapse of time between initiation and completion. This *input/output wait* is generally long compared with the instruction execution time of a typical central processing unit. For present purposes we do not distinguish further between these two forms of input/output operations, and call both by the term *i/o function*.

Since peripheral devices are part of the physical resources of a computer system, the use of i/o functions must be restricted to computations authorized to do so. It is natural to consider an i/o function as representing another class of capability that may be entered in the *C*-list that defines a sphere of protection. This capability is then exercised by the meta-instruction

execute i/o function *i*;

where *i* is the index number of an i/o function capability in the *C*-list of the computation. Performance of this procedure step by a process causes initiation of the i/o function represented by the *i*th entry of the *C*-list. The process then becomes suspended and remains so until the i/o function has completed. It then becomes active again to perform subsequent procedure steps.

Particular stress has recently been placed on ability to specify computations that may compute in parallel with input/output operations. Within the scheme presented here, this goal is easily achieved through the execution of **fork** meta-instructions prior to the execution of i/o functions.

Motivation for Parallelism. The motivation for encouraging the use of parallelism in a computation is not so much to make a particular computation run more efficiently as it is to relax constraints on the order in which parts of a computation are carried out. A multiprogram scheduling algorithm should then be able to take advantage of this extra freedom to allocate system resources with greater efficiency.

Moreover, the notation of parallel programming is a natural way of expressing certain frequently occurring operations of computations running in an MCS. Suppose, for example, we wish to program a computation to receive messages from any of a number of user consoles, where the messages are to arrive in some unknown and arbitrary order, and it is not known whether some consoles will ever send messages. Let *listen*(i, j) be an **integer procedure** that waits for a message to be received from console *i* and writes the message in the segment with index number *j*. The value of *listen* is set to the number of symbols in the message. Let *analyze*(i, j, n) be a **procedure** which scans a message of *n* symbols received from console *i* and written in segment *j*, and takes whatever action is necessary in response to the content of the message. Then the message-receiving computation described above may be programmed as follows.

```
begin private integer i;
    for i := 1 step 1 until m do
        fork e;
    quit;
e:  begin integer j, n;
    j := create segment RW;
    n := listen (i, j);
    analyze (i, j, n);
    quit;
    end;
end;
```

The **create segment** meta-instruction introduces a segment capability into the *C*-list of a computation and is discussed in a following section.

Inferior Spheres of Protection

It is useful to think of a computation's sphere of protection as having been established by another computation, that is, by the action of a process operating within another sphere of protection. A major reason for taking this view concerns the debugging of programs in some programming language system (PLS). However, other uses of this concept are also possible.

In connection with program testing (debugging), suppose that the processes of a PLS are carried out, as for any object computation, within some sphere of protection *A*. These processes must have access to all of the user's computing objects pertinent to the program under test, as well as to the procedure segments of the PLS. Since the program under test is likely to be faulty, it is desirable to protect both the user's permanent objects, and any objects created by the PLS on his behalf from unintentional use or destruction by the procedure being debugged. To allow the processes under test to be operated within a sphere of protection distinct from the one effective for the PLS, we define several meta-instructions.

$i :=$ **create sphere** w; Append an owned *inferior sphere capability* to the C-list with index number i. The word name w is the return point for exceptional conditions, as explained later.

The process executing this meta-instruction operates in a sphere we call the *superior* of the created sphere. Once in possession of an inferior sphere capability (Figure 4), a process may grant some of its capabilities to the inferior sphere by the following meta-instruction.

$$i := \textbf{grant} \begin{Bmatrix} \lambda \\ \boldsymbol{O} \end{Bmatrix} \begin{Bmatrix} \lambda \\ X \\ R \\ XR \\ RW \\ XRW \end{Bmatrix} j, k;$$

Grant capability j to inferior sphere k with index number i. Here j and k are index numbers in the current C-list, and i is an index number in the inferior C-list.

The granted capability is entered in the C-list of inferior sphere k and may be a segment capability, i/o function capability, entry capability or directory capability. Entry and directory capabilities are discussed in later paragraphs. The braces mean that one of the strings within them must be selected to form part of the meta-instruction. Here λ stands for the null string. The string $\boldsymbol{O}$ indicates that the inferior sphere is to have ownership powers with respect to the granted capability. The other strings can be used only if j is the index number of a segment capability. In this case the capability is passed down with restricted access authority. For example,

$$i := \textbf{grant X } j, k;$$

grants authority to execute the segment but not to read

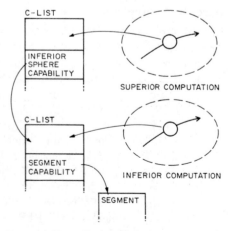

FIG. 4.   Control of an inferior computation

it, write it or exercise ownership of it. The **grant** meta-instruction cannot be used to pass a capability that is not implied by a capability present in the higher sphere.

start i, w;   Initiate a process at instruction word name w within inferior sphere i.

The new process commences with no private data, that is, a zero state word except for the instruction word name w.

Exceptional Conditions. Next we ask what should happen if a process operating in an inferior sphere encounters an *exceptional condition*, that is, a procedure step requiring intervention by a higher level before the object process may continue in a sensible manner. Some exceptional conditions call for action by the supervisor. These include the following:

(1) *Fault.* A fault is a clear indication of hardware malfunction. A memory parity error is a good example. The supervisor is responsible for correct operation of processor and memory units.

(2) *Resource excess.* A resource excess occurs if a process invokes resources in an amount exceeding the allotment to the principal responsible for its computation.

(3) *Addressing snag.* An addressing snag occurs when a process generates a valid address, but the desired information is either not in main memory or a reference mechanism has not been set up. The supervisor must move the desired information into main memory from file storage and set up the necessary linkage.

Other exceptional conditions should be acted upon by the superior computation of the process in trouble, since only the procedures which established the process know how these conditions should be interpreted. These exceptional conditions are as follows.

(1) *Sphere violation.* A sphere violation occurs if a process refers to a capability that does not exist in the C-list of its computation, or makes invalid use of a capability (attempts to write in a segment for which only the execution capability is authorized, for example). A sphere violation also takes place if a reference is made beyond the limits of a segment.

(2) *Halt instruction.* A **halt** means "terminate this process and notify superior" as contrasted with **quit** which means "terminate this process and forget it."

(3) *Breakpoint instruction.* A **breakpoint** is substituted for other instructions by a debugging program in order to conduct a breakpoint analysis of a program under test. A **breakpoint** has the same effect as **halt** except that a different indication is presented to the superior procedure.

(4) *Undefined instruction.* A processor generates this condition when it is called upon to execute an undefined operation code.

(5) *Arithmetic contingencies.* Such events as "divide check" call for action by a superior procedure when not explicitly handled by the inferior computation.

In any of these events, the process in which the exceptional condition occurred becomes suspended, and a new process is initiated in the superior sphere at the instruction word specified when the inferior sphere was created. The new process starts with two pieces of private data: a number indicating the reason for the interruption, and an index number of an owned *suspended process capability* that is appended to the C-list of the superior sphere at the time of interruption. This capability allows the superior computation to have access to the state word of the process in which the exceptional condition occurred. The following meta-instructions are defined with respect to a suspended process capability:

fetch status i, w;	Fetch the state word of suspended process i and write at word name w.
set status i, w;	Set the state word of suspended process i according to information at word name w.
continue i;	Reactivate suspended process i and delete from the C-list.

Notice that the **set status** meta-instruction must disallow a change in certain critical parts of the state word of the suspended process. For example, the superior sphere must not be able to cause the state word of the suspended process to point to a different C-list.

A debugging procedure needs primitive commands which allow it to "pick up the pieces" after a computation under test has malfunctioned. The following meta-instructions are useful under these circumstances:

stop k;	Suspend all processes operating in inferior sphere k.

Execution of this meta-instruction causes each active process in inferior sphere k to be suspended. Corresponding to each inferior process a suspended process capability is created in the C-list of the superior sphere. Also, a process in the superior sphere is initiated to correspond to each inferior process, just as though the inferior process had encountered an exceptional condition.

Capability j in the C-list of inferior sphere i can be examined by the meta-instruction

$$\textbf{examine } i, j, w;$$

The information contained in the capability is copied into several words starting at word name w.

If the inferior computation has clogged its C-list with unneeded capabilities, the superior computation can remove them with

$$\textbf{ungrant } i, j;$$

which erases capability j from the C-list of inferior sphere i.

Protected Entry Points

An important class of situations arises when a peripheral device is operated or a data object is manipulated on behalf of several concurrent computations. Examples of this situation are:

(1) A control routine for transferring messages between user computations and remote terminals of a given class. Frequently, a system of remote terminals is coupled to a central processing system through a single i/o function (rather than one per terminal device).

(2) A routine which updates a data base and may be called asynchronously by many separate user computations.

The planning of such a routine[2] requires that calling computations be protected from each other. If A and B are two computations using the routine S, it must not be possible for a malfunction of A's processes to cause incorrect execution of B's procedures. Clearly, neither A nor B should be able to modify the common data D used by S. Furthermore, A and B must be forced to initiate operation of S at a proper entry point, for erroneous transfer of control to an arbitrary instruction of S is likely to cause meaningless modification of the common data D. However, if D is to be written by S, then the processes executing S must have in their C-lists the capability to write in segment D as well as the capability to execute any instruction of S.

It follows that a modification or change of C-list must accompany transfer of control to S. A mechanism for accomplishing such restricted use of a procedure we call a *protected entry point*.

The mechanism we describe supposes that a process calling the protected procedure executes it in a distinct sphere of protection R, returning to the original sphere of protection A upon completion. The change of association of process with C-list implied here is accomplished by the **enter** meta-instruction which requires an additional capability, the *entry*. An entry capability is created by the owner of a protected procedure through the use of the meta-instruction

$$h := \textbf{create entry } w, n;$$

where h is the index number in the creator's C-list of the created capability. Here w is the word name $[i, a]$, and i must be the index number in the creator's C-list of an owned procedure segment. The entry capability thus created authorizes calls to be made to the word names $[i, a]$ through $[i, a+n]$ inclusive. Also included in the entry capability is a pointer to the C-list of the creating computation. Once created, the entry capability can be copied into the C-lists of other computations, using mechanisms to be described.

The entry to and exit from a protected procedure is depicted schematically in Figure 5. To enter a protected procedure a process gives

$$\textbf{enter } j, r, k;$$

where j is the index number of an entry capability. The calling process is suspended, and a new process is created. The C-list of this new process will be the C-list specified by the entry, with the addition of two new capabilities. One is a suspended process capability pointing to the state word of the calling process, and the other is a duplicate of the capability having index k in the caller's C-list. The index numbers of these capabilities are reported as private

---

[2] Introduced as a "protected service routine" in [4].

data in the state word of the new process. The new process is set to begin execution at word name $[i, a+r]$, where i and a are quantities specified in the entry, as mentioned above. Notice that i is an index number with respect to the new C-list, not that of the caller, and also that r must satisfy $0 \leq r \leq n$, where n is also specified in the entry. The remainder of the new state word is set equal to the corresponding parts of the caller's suspended state word. Finally the new process is made active. The protected procedure thus given control can use the **fetch status, set status** and **continue** meta-instructions to communicate with the caller and reactivate his calling process whenever this is appropriate.

The capability transmitted to the protected computation (represented by index k above) can not only be a segment capability, i/o function capability or entry capability, but can also be a *directory capability*. As described in the next section, a directory consists of a collection of capabilities. Thus the **enter** meta-instruction provides a quite general, yet reasonably efficient, facility for passing to the protected procedure the capabilities that it needs to perform its service for the caller.

Directories and Naming

Until now, the discussion has been covering those aspects of an MCS that deal with the active performance of computing tasks for the benefit of the system's users. Now consider the fact that in most MCS's, even if no active computing is taking place, each principal of the system is still represented passively in the system by a set of *retained objects*. Every retained object is either a segment, an i/o function, an entry or a directory. Here we

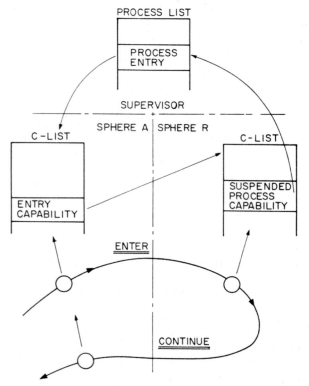

FIG. 5. Entry to and exit from a protected procedure

are letting the segment play a role which has been ascribed to something called a *file* in many MCS's, particularly in the MAC system. In the present formulation, a file is simply a long-lived segment.

Sharing of Retained Objects. The possibility of rapidly and automatically controlling the sharing among principals of retained objects, chiefly procedure and data segments, is one of the main characteristics that distinguishes the MCS from other types of computing systems [3]. The importance of sharing is testified to by the fact that the file manipulating machinery of the MAC system has recently undergone a major revision, motivated in part by a desire to facilitate such sharing [15].

Besides being useful to individual users who wish to borrow each others routines, a sharing mechanism is also useful to a group of users who wish to reference certain segments in common. Such segments might be a set of library routines or a set of procedures making up a programming language system. It is natural to think of these segments as being owned by a principal associated with the group of users as a whole. A mechanism (such as the one to be described) is required for permitting an individual user to gain access to the directory of the group principal.

Desiderata for Names. Through the capabilities in their C-lists, computations can, among other things, manipulate retained objects. In performing these manipulations, the processes of a computation must specify information that unambiguously distinguishes each object of interest from all other retained objects in the computing system. Such information constitutes the *name* of the object.

Retained objects are created and deleted arbitrarily, and any particular object may remain in existence for an arbitrarily long time. There are two reasons why the name of an object can never be changed by the system throughout the object's entire existence. First, if a name is changed, then all usages of that name that are embedded in other objects (e.g., segments) within the system must be updated. This alternative may be dismissed as being entirely impractical in a large MCS. The second reason why the system must leave all names unchanged is that every retained object is frequently referred to directly by people. People are used to thinking in terms of invariant names; to find that yesterday's "X" is suddenly today's "Y" would be disconcerting.

Another requirement which human usage places on the names of objects is that they should be alphanumeric and have mnemonic significance. Each principal should be able to choose freely the names by which he will identify the objects he retains, without regard to the choices of names made by other principals.

Ambiguous Names. If the names of two different objects have been freely chosen by two different principals, those names may possibly be identical. When this common string of characters is generated subsequently by a process, the computer system will not be able to determine which of the objects is being designated. Such a string of characters is said to form an *ambiguous name*.

The problem of ambiguous names also manifests itself in more traditional, non-multiprogrammed computing environments when groups of independently written subprograms are to be combined into one large program. One author has called for "an orderly corpus of symbology" designed to prevent name conflicts before they occur [16]. Others have offered a solution based on the loading-time definition of each subprogram's symbolic interface with its environment [17].

The most straightforward way of eliminating the possibility of name ambiguities within an MCS is to restrict each principal in his choice of names; a principal can be required to begin every one of the names of his objects with a string of caracters that constitutes his *principal name*. The remainder of the name of an object, its *chosen name*, may then be freely selected by the principal retaining the object. This method of preventing name conflicts has been employed in the MAC time-sharing system [18].

False Names. In order to conserve storage, it is reasonable to embed within a procedure segment only the chosen names of the objects being referenced, with the understanding that the computer system can supply the principal name because it knows which principal initiated the process that is executing the procedure segment. Even if a principal has a complex program consisting of many procedure segments, each containing references to the others, the above scheme still insures that when the author principal operates the program the system will always supply the correct principal name to augment the chosen names embedded within the segments.

A serious problem arises, however, if this program is shared with a second principal and this principal attempts to execute the program. Intersegment references will evoke the name of the second principal, rather than that of the author. The names thus formed will be *false names*, because they will designate objects that are very different from those intended by the author. Such names will often designate no existing object at all, but occasionally they may designate objects of the second principal that are unrelated to the borrowed program.

Preview. The problem arises of simultaneously realizing the following four goals: (1) to avoid the creation of ambiguous names, (2) to provide reasonable freedom for a principal to choose some portion of the names of his objects, (3) to allow intersegment references to consist of parts of names rather than full names, and (4) to permit sets of objects to be shared without invalidating internal references.

The solution we propose stipulates that each reference to an object be derived from a *partial name* relative to some directory of objects, together with the index number of a capability pointing to that directory. Moreover, we allow the directories of the system to be organized into a hierarchical structure, as suggested by Daley and Neuman [19].

This approach has two major advantages:

(1) A whole subhierarchy of objects can be communicated among several computations or principals by passing a single pointer to the head directory of the subhierarchy.

(2) It is easy to design the MCS so that programs can be shared without the possibility that false names will be generated by their execution.

In the following paragraphs we define the proposed naming structure and introduce the meta-instructions necessary for computing within its framework.

Directories. A *directory* is a set of items, each being an association between a *name component* and a capability which points to a segment, i/o function, entry or another directory. Recall that each capability includes an ownership indicator ($\mathbf{O}$ for owned, $\mathbf{N}$ for not owned), and that a segment capability includes an indication ($\mathbf{R}$, $\mathbf{W}$, $\mathbf{X}$ or a combination) of the type of reference permitted. Each item of a directory also contains an access indicator ($\mathbf{P}$ for private, $\mathbf{F}$, for free). The interpretation of these indicators in directories is explained below.

Associated with each principal is exactly one directory called a *root directory*, which stands at the head of a hierarchy of the principal's retained objects. We allow perhaps many items to point to the same object, and in consequence, an object may be accessible through the directory structure from different root directories.

Ownership. A principal always *owns* his root directory. Otherwise, an object is *owned* by a principal just if that principal owns a directory in which there exists an item with an $\mathbf{O}$ indicator that points to the object. Thus, a principal owns an object if and only if there is a path through the directory tree from his own root directory to the object such that each node of the path contains an $\mathbf{O}$ indicator.

When the supervisor creates a computation on behalf of a principal, it always places in the C-list of such a computation a directory capability with an $\mathbf{O}$ indicator that points to the principal's root directory. The principal is then said to *own* this computation and each of its processes. These processes are then permitted to exercise powers of ownership with respect to objects owned by the principal.

Using the Directory Structure. The powers of a computation with respect to the directory structure are embodied in meta-instructions as follows. We suppose that any process has at least one entry in its C-list giving it a directory capability.

$$j := \textbf{acquire} \begin{Bmatrix} \lambda \\ \mathbf{X} \\ \mathbf{R} \\ \mathbf{XR} \\ \mathbf{RW} \\ \mathbf{XRW} \end{Bmatrix} i, \langle \text{name component} \rangle;$$

Here i is the index number of a directory capability. This directory is searched for an association with $\langle$name component$\rangle$, the corresponding capability is entered into the C-list of the computation to which the running process belongs, and its index number is reported as j. Capability j is tagged $\mathbf{O}$ if and only if directory i is tagged $\mathbf{O}$ in the

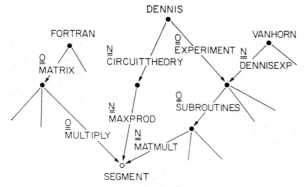

FIG. 6. A directory structure

C-list, and the capability being loaded is tagged **O** in directory *i*. A sphere violation results if the capability referenced is tagged **P** in the directory item and directory capability *i* is not owned (i.e., contains an **N** indicator). In the case of a segment, the type of reference permitted may be changed from that permitted in the directory item, but an attempt to enlarge the class of reference permitted to a nonowned segment is also deemed a sphere violation.

release *i*;

Remove the capability with index number *i* from the *C*-list of the running process.

Ownership of an object implies the ability to modify it, delete it, and grant access to the object by other principals.

$$\textbf{place} \begin{Bmatrix} \textbf{P} \\ \textbf{F} \end{Bmatrix} i, \langle \text{name component} \rangle, j;$$

Here *i* must be the index number of an owned directory capability. An item is inserted in directory *i* associating the capability having index number *j* with ⟨name component⟩.

remove *i*, ⟨name component⟩

The item associated with ⟨name component⟩ in owned directory *i* is removed from the directory.

Creation and Deletion of Retained Objects. Segments, entires and directories can come into existence upon execution of the following meta-instructions.

$$i := \textbf{create} \begin{cases} \textbf{segment} \begin{Bmatrix} \textbf{X} \\ \textbf{R} \\ \textbf{XR} \\ \textbf{RW} \\ \textbf{XRW} \end{Bmatrix}; \\ \textbf{entry } w, n; \\ \textbf{directory}; \end{cases}$$

A capability pointing to the created object is entered into the *C*-list of the process with an **O** indicator, and its index number is reported as *i*. Note that a name is not associated with the object at the time of its creation, but only when an entry is made for it in some directory by means of a **place** meta-instruction.

This illustrates the point that names are a convenience for principals. Different names may be convenient for different principals, and no name need be assigned unless a principal may need to select that object from the directory

structure at a later time. Thus for example, segments may be created by computations for temporary storage purposes without affecting the directory structure.

The owner of a segment, entry or directory can cause it to cease to exist by using the following meta-instruction:

delete *i*, ⟨name component⟩;

The owned object pointed to by the capability associated with ⟨name component⟩ in directory *i* is deleted so that it has no further existence. Any attempts to exercise capabilities pointing to a deleted object are treated as sphere violations.

The **release** and **remove** meta-instructions differ from **delete** in that the former meta-instructions simply remove capabilities from *C*-lists and items from directories, respectively, while the object itself continues its existence if there are other capabilities and items pointing to it.

We suppose then that the existence of a segment, entry or directory extends from its time of creation until either specifically **delete**'ed by its owner *or* until **release**'ed from all *C*-lists and **remove**'ed from all directories. This convention yields the possibility of having a retained object with no owner. This seems quite reasonable because the following situation may occur frequently. An obsolete subroutine segment *S* is **remove**'ed from the directories of a library principal *L* but remains in use by principals *A*, *B* and *C*. The segment was previously owned by *L*, but now has no owner. The existence of *S* continues just until *A*, *B* and *C* have abandoned use of it. Since we assume there can be no more than one owner of an object, the only alternatives are to assign ownership to one of *A*, *B* or *C* (but how do we choose?), or to generate separate copies of *S* for each sharing principal.

The Structure of Names. Since every computation initially has in its *C*-list at least one root apex directory capability, it is clear that by giving a series of **acquire**'s, a computation can make its way through the directory structure along any path, as long as it knows the correct series of name components to use. A series of name components leading from a directory to an object is called the *partial name* of the object with respect to that directory.

Because of the structure of the directories, an object can have many names, as well as many partial names with respect to any directory. For example, the directory structure in Figure 6 shows a particular segment, owned by the principal FORTRAN, which has the following names:

FORTRAN, MATRIX, MULTIPLY
DENNIS, EXPERIMENT, SUBROUTINES, MATMULT
DENNIS, CIRCUITTHEORY, MAXPROD
VANHORN, DENNISEXP, SUBROUTINES, MATMULT

Notice that the item named DENNISEXP within the root directory VANHORN points to the directory whose full name is DENNIS, EXPERIMENT.

Sharing Mechanisms. Two mechanisms to allow the sharing of retained objects are described here. One mechanism gives blanket authority to all computations within the system to **acquire** the shared object. The other mechanism allows the owner of an object to specifically authorize each instance of its sharing.

The meta-instruction

$$i := \textbf{link} \ \langle \text{principal name} \rangle;$$

inserts into the C-list at index i a nonowned directory capability pointing to the root directory named ⟨principal name⟩. Using the **acquire** meta-instruction, a computation can thus gain access to any object in the directory structure of any principal, provided that the directory items leading from the principal directory to the object all contain **F** indicators.

Any more selective sharing mechanism requires an explicit interaction between the borrower and the lender. We propose that the shared capability be passed between the C-lists of two computations that interact via the **enter** meta-instruction.

A typical interaction might proceed as follows. The lender first creates a free entry capability in one of its directories. The borrower then uses **link** and **acquire** to place this entry capability in its C-list. The borrower next creates a special entity in its C-list, called a *receiver*, by means of the meta-instruction

$$i := \textbf{receive};$$

Finally the borrower exercises the entry obtained from the lender by using **enter**. Parameters passed as private data provide to the lender the index i of the receiver in the borrower's C-list, as well as information identifying the capability desired to be borrowed.

The lender is thus given control, and proceeds to verify the right of the borrower to obtain the capability requested. In particular, the lender may wish to verify that the borrower computation is in fact owned by a certain principal. For this purpose the lender uses the meta-instruction

$$s := \textbf{owner} \ j;$$

where j is the index in the lender's C-list of the suspended process capability generated by the **enter** operation, and s is a string giving the principal name of the owner of the suspended process.

Having completed its verification, the lender then **acquire**'s into its own C-list the owned capability it wishes to transmit. If this capability has index k, the meta-instruction

$$\textbf{transmit} \ j, i, k;$$

replaces receiver i in the C-list of suspended process j with the owned capability k, giving it an **N** tag.

Having modified the borrower's C-list, the lender then returns control to the borrower with **continue**. At this point the loan is complete; the borrower may now exercise the capability and **place** it in one of his own directories.

An Example: Using a Programming System. Suppose a user wishes to use a programming system PS. The retained objects (procedure segments, directories, entries, etc.), of PS are on file in the hierarchical organization already

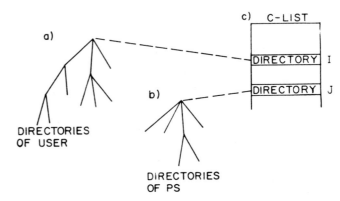

FIG. 7. Using a programming system

outlined (Figure 7b). The user has his objects organized in a private hierarchy (Figure 7a). If the use of PS is only desired for one user, then it is appropriate for an owned item in the user's directory structure to point to the directory structure of PS. If it is desired to make PS available to many or all principals at an installation, it is appropriate to place the directory hierarchy of PS under a principal of its own or as a subhierarchy within the domain of a common programming system principal. In either case, a computation for a user involving retained objects both of his own and of the PS would be carried out in the following manner:

(1) The user initiates a process which acquires access capabilities for the two hierarchies of directories—one for his own files and one for PS—by executing the necessary sequence of meta-instructions. Suppose these capabilities have index numbers i and j respectively.

(2) PS is called with i and j as parameters. PS does all addressing within the directory structure relative to the roots of their trees represented by entries i and j of the C-list (Figure 7).

Acknowledgments. We are indebted to Project MAC and the Compatible Time-Sharing System for the opportunity to make observations that have motivated much of the content of this paper. Our notion of the capability list stems from the "program reference table" idea first used in the Burroughs B5000 system. The value of duplicating private data at a **fork** was pointed out by H. Witsenhausen in an unpublished memorandum.

REFERENCES

1. DESMONDE, W. H. *Real-Time Data Processing Systems: Introductory Concepts.* Prentice-Hall, Englewood Cliffs, N. J., 1964.
2. HAMLIN, J. E. A general description of the National Aeronautics and Space Administration real time computing complex. Proc. ACM 19th Nat. Conf., Philadelphia, 1964, pp. 2–1 to 2–22.
3. FANO, R. M. The MAC system: the computer utility approach. *IEEE Spectrum 2* (Jan. 1965), 56–64.
4. DENNIS, J. B., AND GLASER, E. The structure of on-line information processing systems. Information Systems Sciences: Proc. Second Cong., Spartan Books, Baltimore, 1965, pp. 1–11.

5. Iliffe, J. K., and Jodeit, J. G. A dynamic storage allocation scheme. *Comput. J. 5* (Oct. 1962), 200–209.
6. Greenfield, M. N. FACT segmentation. AFIPS Conf. Proc. *21*, Spartan Books, Baltimore, 1962, pp. 307–315.
7. Holt, A. W. Program organization and record keeping for dynamic storage allocation. *Comm. ACM 4* (Oct. 1961), 422–431.
8. Dennis, J. B. Segmentation and the design of multiprogrammed computer systems. *J. ACM 12 (Oct.* 1965), 589–602.
9. Glaser, E., Couleur, J., and Oliver, G. System design of a computer for time-sharing applications. AFIPS Conf. Proc. *28*, Spartan Books, Baltimore, 1965, p. 197–202.
10. Forgie, J. W. A time- and memory-sharing executive program for quick-response, on-line applications. AFIPS Conf. Proc. *28*, Spartan Books, Baltimore, 1965, p. 599–609.
11. Comfort, W. T. A computing system design for user service. AFIPS Conf. Proc. *28*, Spartan Books, Baltimore, 1965, p. 619–626.
12. McCullough, J. D., Speierman, K. H., and Zurcher, F. W. A design for a multiple user multiprocessing system. AFIPS Conf. Proc. *28*, Spartan Books, Baltimore, 1965, p. 611–617.
13. Dennis, J. B. Program structure in a multi-access computer. Tech. Rep. No. MAC-TR-11, Proj. MAC, MIT, Cambridge, Mass., 1964.
14. Conway, M. A multiprocessor system design. AFIPS Conf. Proc. *24*, Spartan Books, Baltimore, 1963, pp. 139–146.
15. Crisman, P. (Ed.) *The Compatible Time-Sharing System: A Programmer's Guide.* MIT Press, Cambridge, Mass., 2d ed., 1965, sec. AD. 2.
16. Hosier, W. A. Pitfalls and safeguards in real-time digital systems with emphasis on programming. *IRE Trans. EM-8* (June 1961), 99–115.
17. McCarthy, J., Corbato, F. J., and Daggett, M. M. The linking segment subprogram language and linking loader. *Comm. ACM 6* (July 1963), 391–395.
18. MIT Computation Center. *The Compatible Time-Sharing System: A Programmer's Guide.* MIT Press, Cambridge, Mass., 1st ed. 1963.
19. Daley, R. C., and Neuman, P. G. A general purpose file system for secondary storage. AFIPS Conf. Proc. *28*, Spartan Books, Baltimore, 1965, p. 213–229.

Capability-Based Addressing

R.S. Fabry
University of California

Various addressing schemes making use of segment tables are examined. The inadequacies of these schemes when dealing with shared addresses are explained. These inadequacies are traced to the lack of an efficient absolute address for objects in these systems. The direct use of a capability as an address is shown to overcome these difficulties because it provides the needed absolute address. Implementation of capability-based addressing is discussed. It is predicted that the use of tags to identify capabilities will dominate. A hardware address translation scheme which never requires the modification of the representation of capabilities is suggested. The scheme uses a main memory hash table for obtaining a segment's location in main memory given its unique code. The hash table is avoided for recently accessed segments by means of a set of associative registers. A computer using capability-based addressing may be substantially superior to present systems on the basis of protection, simplicity of programming conventions, and efficient implementation.

Key Words and Phrases: addressing, capabilities, addressing hardware, protection, protection hardware, shared addresses, information sharing, operating systems, computer utility, segmentation, tagged architecture

CR Categories: 4.30, 4.32, 4.34, 6.21

This is a revised version of a paper presented at the Fourth ACM Symposium on Operating Systems Principles, IBM Thomas J. Watson Research Center, Yorktown Heights, New York, October 15–17, 1973, under the title "The Case for Capability-Based Computers."

Author's address: Computer Science Division, Evans Hall, University of California, Berkeley, CA 94720.

Introduction

The idea of a capability which acts like a ticket authorizing the use of some object was developed by Dennis and Van Horn [15] as a generalization of addressing and protection schemes such as the codewords of the Rice computer [28], the descriptors of the Burroughs machines [6, 7], and the segment and page tables in computers such as the GE-645 and IBM 360/67 [1, 14]. Dennis and Van Horn extended the earlier schemes to include not just memory but all systems objects—memory, processes, input/output devices, and so on—and to allow the explicit manipulation of access control by non-system programs. The idea is that a capability is a special kind of address for an object, that these addresses can be created only by the system, and that, in order to use any object, one must address it via one of these addresses.

The use of capabilities as a protection mechanism has been the subject of considerable interest [24, 29, 32, 43]. It is assumed that the reader is familiar with the use of capabilities for protection; a different aspect of capabilities is developed here.

It is argued below that there is an advantage in using capabilities as a basic component of the address of every object (except for objects associated with the processor such as its registers). In order to accomplish this, user programs must be able to store capabilities freely into various permanent user data structures (subject, of course, to some scheme for preserving the integrity of the representation of capabilities). Not all schemes which use capabilities actually allow capabilities to be used as permanent addresses in this way. For example, the original Dennis and Van Horn scheme did not because it insisted that capabilities be stored only in C-lists associated with computations.

Context-Independent Addresses

The advantage of a capability used as an address is that its interpretation is context independent. It provides an absolute address for an object. This fact is more important than it may at first appear.

Before the use of address relocation—such as base and limit registers, paging, and segmentation—jobs were allocated fixed areas of physical memory. Addresses within the jobs were relocated at load time, and a job was not moved once it had started running. The lack of the ability to dynamically relocate resulted in underutilized computers. To avoid this underutilization, address relocation was introduced. But in doing so, a new problem was also introduced. Consider two jobs which need to interact with each other. In a system without relocation, jobs share an address space and can be allowed to interact freely, sharing data structures and addresses as easily as if they were a single job. With address relocation, however, the meaning of an address becomes context dependent; each job has its own address space, or perhaps several. This fact is generally interpreted as an advantage: base and limit registers, paging, and segmentation, by virtue of their address relocation, allow users to be isolated from each other, thus providing protection of one job from another. On the other hand, the sharing of addresses becomes more difficult, and this side effect is generally ignored. This effect is particulaly ironic for those systems which stress their usefulness for cooperating users who want to work together, sharing programs and data.

Although a capability functions as an absolute address, the use of capabilities does not prevent a system from using address relocation. A capability is an absolute address for a virtual object; the system is free to relocate the virtual object so long as it maintains the correspondence between the object and its capabilities.

The Problem of Shared Segment References

Various addressing schemes making use of segment tables have been implemented in present day systems. Although the inadequacies of these schemes when dealing with shared segment addresses may be apparent to users of the systems, the inadequacies have not (with rare exception) been explained in system descriptions, nor does there exist a systematic comparison of the problems which arise with each of the schemes.

As an example of the problems encountered in these systems, consider a particular structure, a set of interacting subprograms. Figure 1 shows a process which has three segments: a data segment, a main program, and a subroutine. The segment table translates integer segment addresses into references to the appropriate segments and specifies the permitted types of access. R means reading is allowed, W means writing is allowed, and E means executing is allowed. The entries in the segment table can be thought of as descriptors, capabilities, codewords, or pointers; for our purposes these are the same. The main program in Figure 1 contains two segment references, a call on the subroutine, coded as CALL 1, and an access of the data segment, coded as ACCESS 2. The PC register associated with the process contains the segment number of the segment which the program counter addresses. In an actual system, the location of a word within a segment is also important. For simplicity, the word number components of addresses are omitted.

Figure 2 shows the case in which the program and the segment references which it contains are shared. Assume for the moment that the correspondence between integers and segments is constructed independently for each process. Then, as in the figure, a segment may be referred to by different integers in different processes. How can the segment references in the shared main program be coded? For process 1, the references should be coded CALL 1 and ACCESS 2. For process 2, however, they should be coded CALL 0 and ACCESS 1. Four different solutions to this problem of shared segment references are presented below.

Fig. 1. Segment addresses.

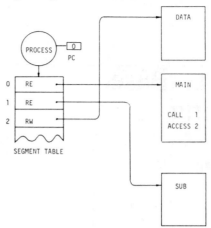

Fig. 2. Shared segment addresses.

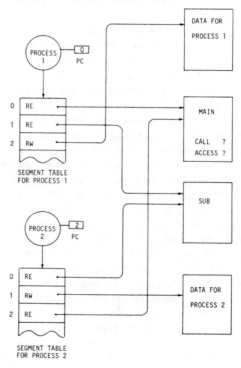

230

Communications
of
the ACM

July 1974
Volume 17
Number 7

Fig. 3. Uniform address solution.

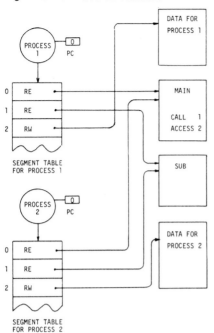

Fig. 4. Indirect evaluation solution.

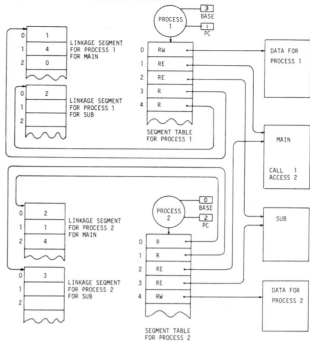

Uniform Address Solution

The uniform address solution is shown in Figure 3. This solution requires that a shared integer segment address be interpreted in a *functionally equivalent* manner for all processes sharing the address. A shared address is said to receive a functionally equivalent interpretation for a set of processes if the objects referred to by the address are used in the same way by each process. For example, in Figure 3, the segment address 2 refers to the data segment used by the process making the reference, while the segment address 1 refers to the segment containing the subroutine called by the main program in a certain instruction. Note that a functionally equivalent interpretation of a shared address sometimes causes the same object to be referenced by all processes and sometimes causes a different object to be referenced by each process.

The uniform address solution requires that the functions of the various shared integer segment addresses be defined centrally so that there will be no conflicts. This requirement rules out the possibility of a single process executing several independently constructed, shared subprograms. This is ruled out because each independent constructor would be free to choose a function for a particular index and the chosen functions would usually conflict. This is a rather serious drawback if one desires a programming environment in which a user is able to build on the work of others in a general way [13].

Generality notwithstanding, the uniform address solution is used successfully by Burroughs. The Burroughs systems require a user to compile all his program at once (except for certain standard system-wide subroutines). Thus the compiler can allocate the integer segment addresses at compile time and embed them in the code. The Program Reference Table of the B5700 functions exactly as the segment table in Figure 3 does [6, 7, 35].

Indirect Evaluation Solution

The indirect evaluation solution is shown in Figure 4. A shared integer segment address is treated as an index of a position within a linkage segment and the linkage segment contains segment table indexes. One linkage segment per independently-created subprogram per process is assumed; the linkage segment is created the first time a subprogram is executed by a process. (A slightly different scheme can be obtained if a new linkage segment is created each time the subprogram is activated.) Thus, when process 1 executes the code for ACCESS 2, word 2 of the linkage segment for process 1 for the main program is fetched. This word contains 0, which is then taken to be the segment table index of the segment to be accessed, in this case the data segment for process 1. Some processor register must be used to remember the address of the linkage segment. Base registers are indicated for this purpose in Figure 4. It is assumed that both processes are executing the main program, and thus each base register contains the segment table index of the linkage segment for the main program.

Calling independently created subprograms is more complicated with indirect evaluation of segment refer-

231

Communications
of
the ACM

July 1974
Volume 17
Number 7

ences since the base register contents must be changed. Figure 4 assumes that call instructions contain the address of the linkage segment of the subroutine to be called and that word 0 of this linkage segment contains the segment table index of the segment containing the code for the subprogram. Thus, when process 1 executes CALL 1, Word 1 of the linkage segment for process 1 for the main program is fetched. This word contains 4, which is then placed in the base register. Word 0 of the linkage segment indicated by the new contents of the base register is then fetched. This word contains 2, which is then placed in PC.

The point of linkage segments is to create independently allocated sets of integer segment addresses in order to overcome the main drawback of the uniform address solution. Thus there must be at least one linkage segment per independent allocation of addresses.

When the indirect evaluation solution is used, segment addresses passed from one subprogram to another as parameters are treated differently than addresses embedded in shared programs. Segment table indexes are passed rather than linkage segment indexes; this is because the segment table is process-wide, whereas the linkage segments are not.

The indirect evaluation solution has several disadvantages. It requires extra space to hold the indirection information, extra overhead to set up the indirection information, and extra memory references to obtain the indirection information. Most important, however, the solution is inadequate. It provides one kind of address space for addresses which are to be used by many programs but one process; it provides another kind of address space for addresses which are to be used by many processes but one program. It makes no provision for an address space for addresses which are to be used by many processes and many programs. Such addresses might be needed, for example, in a multisegment data structure which existed independently of any program or process.

Nevertheless, the indirect evaluation solution has been used successfully for Multics [3, 11, 14, 36]. The actual Multics scheme differs in details from what has been described, but it is the same in concept.

Multiple Segment Table Solution

The multiple segment table solution is shown in Figure 5. This solution can be viewed as a modification of the indirect evaluation solution in which segment table indexes in the linkage segments are replaced by capabilities and the linkage segments are renamed segment tables. The base register and the program counter which contained segment table indexes are modified to contain capabilities also. Thus, when process 1 executes the code for ACCESS 2, the evaluation of the integer segment address works in the same way as for Figure 3; the difference is that the segment table is now private to a particular program as well as to a particular process. Figure 5 assumes that the subroutine instruction con-

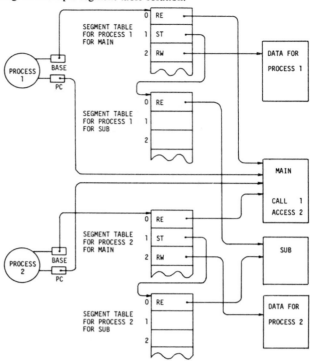

Fig. 5. Multiple segment table solution.

tains the address of the segment table for the called program, and that word 0 in the segment table points to the segment containing the called program. Thus, when process 1 executes the code for CALL 1, word 1 of the segment table for process 1 for the main program is loaded into the base register. Word 0 of this new segment table is then fetched and placed in PC.

The main disadvantage of the multiple segment table solution is that it does away with the per-process segment table and thus with the only addresses which could be shared among several programs being executed by the same process. Thus this solution compounds the problem of shared segment references.

The difference becomes apparent if one considers parameter passing during a subroutine call. For example, in the scheme of Evans and LeClerc [18, 33], which uses a multiple-segment-table-type solution, entries are made in the segment table for a subroutine each time the subroutine is called; these entries are capabilities for the various parameters passed to the subroutine. Such a scheme either disallows recursive subroutines or else requires a new version of the segment table for each level of recursion. Another solution is to store the capabilities for the parameters in a stack, much as is already done on the Burroughs machines. (The Evans and LeClerc scheme also allows a segment table to be associated with a data structure. If one reads into their scheme a mechanism for varying the contents of the segment tables associated with data structures dynamically

232

Communications
of
the ACM

July 1974
Volume 17
Number 7

Fig. 6. Capability addressing solution.

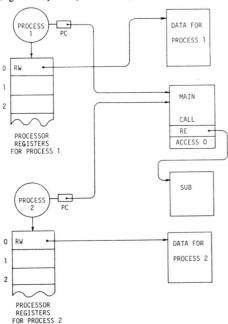

and under program control, then one would classify it as using a capability addressing solution.)

One can consider the display registers of the B6700 to define segment tables and view the B6700 as using the multiple segment table solution [8, 35].

The protection system suggested by Needham [34] uses multiple segment table addressing in which there are four simultaneously available segment tables: one for capabilities which are global to the process; one for capabilities associated with the current program and shared by all processes using the program; one for capabilities associated with the current program and private to the process; and one for the arguments for this activation of the program. As Needham points out in his paper, there are still difficulties with pointers from one segment to another which appear in some shared data structures.

Capability Addressing Solution

The capability addressing solution [21] is shown in Figure 6. In this scheme capabilities may be used wherever the integer addresses were used previously. In particular, capabilities may be stored in segments and in the registers of the processor. (There must, of course, be some scheme for preserving the integrity of the representation of capabilities. Two schemes are discussed later.) This scheme does away with segment tables and with the mandatory indirect evaluation of shared addresses. In Figure 6, when ACCESS 0 is executed, the 0 means the segment indicated by register 0 and is thus evaluated indirectly. The subroutine call instruction is assumed to be followed by a capability for the segment

containing the subroutine to be called. When the CALL is executed, this capability is placed in PC.

In comparing Figure 6 with Figure 3, a distinction is made between processor registers and the segment tables. This distinction is not related to implementation technology but rather to allocation. The allocation of processor registers is under control of the person or compiler generating even the smallest section of code; one is always free to redefine the use of these registers by saving the contents and later restoring them. Thus there is no requirement for a central mechanism to define the use of the registers, and the main problem with the uniform address solution is avoided.

Figure 6 illustrates both types of functionally equivalent interpretations for segment addresses. The access to the data segment must refer to a different segment for each process and thus specifies indirect evaluation through a processor register. The reference to the subroutine refers to the same segment for each process and is thus embedded directly in the program. (Note that this is not meant to imply that references to called programs must always be bound in advance, but that for cases in which advance binding is appropriate, it can be handled that way.)

Other Solutions

The solutions which have been compared are not the only solutions to the problem of shared segment references. They are the ones which have been most thoroughly developed and which appear to have the most promise.

Another solution is to address each segment with a unique integer which is assigned at the time the segment is created, never changed, and not reused even after the segment has disappeared from the system. Call this the unique integer solution. As is explained below in the section on implementation, a similar unique integer is the major component in a capability. In fact, aside from the access control bits which determine whether or not reading, etc., is allowed, the only difference is that in the capability addressing solution, the integers are known to refer to segments which may be accessed, while in the unique integer solution, accessing rights must be determined separately.

Comparison of Relative and Absolute Addresses

The rather lengthy example just completed is a comparatively easy one for the addressing schemes which are based on segment tables. Should we have attempted to construct a shared time-varying multisegment data structure containing internal cross-references and having an existence independent of any particular program or process, we could have done so only by using absolute addresses.

The reason for this is best understood in terms of an example. In Multics, two users can set up private indi-

Communications
of
the ACM

July 1974
Volume 17
Number 7

rection tables to translate from segment numbers contained in a shared data structure to segment table indexes for arbitrary segments. Linkage segments are, of course, an instance of such an indirection table for programs. If these two users want the segment numbers contained in the data structure to have an absolute interpretation, they need only arrange the indirection table properly. But the problem remains as to how the shared data structure can specify how the indirection table should be arranged. This specification requires some way to refer to a segment in a context-independent manner; i.e. it requires absolute addresses.

Multics, of course, provides what is, in effect, a second way of addressing all segments in order to handle this case, namely the full path names of the file system. (A different system might not provide this second way of addressing. There is no inherent reason to insist that every segment is named by the file system or that protection be provided on a per-segment basis in terms of read, write, execute, and append. The reader who doubts this is referred to systems which allow users to define new types of objects, perhaps consisting of many segments and perhaps with very different modes of access being relevant [23, 29, 32, 42, 46].)

In Multics, the use of the file system's full path name as an absolute address may be quite awkward because of its variable length. Furthermore, if the name is embedded in a data structure rather than a program, it will be necessary either to convert the name into a segment number each time it is used or else to use some ad hoc indirect evaluation. One wonders two things: What fraction of the time that a file system name is used would a simple absolute address have sufficed? and How much programmer time is spent minimizing the occurrence of absolute references in order to create programs which run efficiently? If one could measure both the direct cost of the linkage mechanisms and the indirect cost of creating programs which utilize these mechanisms in a reasonable way, it might turn out that one substantial source of inefficiency in the modern multiprogramming systems which rely on shared objects is that they have eliminated the old-fashioned idea of an absolute address for such objects.

Hardware Implementation

The problems of implementing capability addressing are now examined. There are several computers in which every explicit memory access uses an address in the form of a segment capability and word number pair and which allow capabilities to be directly manipulated by user programs in the traditional ways that addresses are used. One is the Chicago Magic Number Computer developed by the Institute for Computer Research at the University of Chicago [19, 20, 21, 41, 47]. This system was never completed. A second computer is the System 250 built by the Plessey Company in England [9, 10, 16,

17, 25, 26]. The Plessey system is available commercially.

A number of systems use capabilities as a protection mechanism at the operating system level but run on conventional machines, including the CAL-TSS system [30, 42], the BCC system [31], the SUE system [40], and the HYDRA system [46]. Since these systems interpret capabilities as addresses in software, they are somewhat less relevant to the present discussion.

Tagged machines such as the Burroughs B6700, the Rice computers [22, 23, 28], and Iliffe's Basic Machine [27] have the potential of implementing what we have described above as capability addressing. However, there appear to be no operating systems yet for these machines which allow capabilities to appear as addresses in arbitrary ways within retained data structures. Thus these systems are also somewhat less relevant to the present discussion.

Based on experience with these various implementations a number of implementation considerations have been clarified.

Integrity of Capabilities

Because of the access control properties of capabilities, it is important that no ordinary program can manufacture or modify the bit pattern with which a capability is represented. Two ways are known for maintaining the integrity of the representation of capabilities: the *tagged* approach and the *partition* approach.

The tagged approach used on the Burroughs B6700, the Rice computers, and the Basic Machine adds one or more tag bits to each word in a segment and to each processor register. This tag is used to specify whether the contents of the word or register are a capability or not. We refer to a piece of information which is not a capability as being *data;* in this sense, data includes programs. The testing and setting of the tag bits is done by the processor each time an access is made, and uses certain simple rules: when a word is copied, the copy is given the same tag as the original; arithmetic and logical instructions must be applied to words tagged as data and always produce a data tag on the result; addressing always checks that the segment address is tagged as a capability; and so on.

The partition approach is used on the Chicago Magic Number Machine and on the Plessey System 250. In the partition approach, each segment is designated at creation as containing either capabilities or data. In addition, there is one set of processor registers for data and one for capabilities. The processor instruction set satisfies rules analogous to those above: data can be copied only into data segments and registers; capabilities can be copied only into capability segments and registers; and so on.

The tagged approach and the partition approach are equivalent in the sense that a structure represented with one approach can be translated into an equivalent structure in the other approach. Which approach is better? The partition approach has several advantages. It is simple for capabilities and data words to be different lengths. This may be important, since capabilities tend to be big—at least 64 bits long and perhaps longer. (In a bit-oriented machine like the B1700 [44, 45] this argument for the partition approach may vanish, however.) The partition approach allows capabilities to be located by the operating system more easily since they are in known places. This is important for both the Chicago Magic Number Computer and the Plessey System 250 since, in both, the operating system modifies the representation of capabilities under certain conditions. An implementation is described below, however, in which such modifications are not required. Another advantage of the partition approach is that tag bits are not required in memory. A disadvantage of the partition approach is due to the fact that most objects require both data and capabilities and thus require two segments with the partition approach instead of the one required by the tagged approach. Extra capabilities are required to pair the segments as is usually desired. Various operations must then deal with two segments and become more complex. Extra secondary storage accesses may be required to move the pair of segments in and out of memory. To use Saltzer's distinction [37], the advantages of the partition approach are all technological, while some of its disadvantages are intrinsic. Thus one might expect the tagged approach to dominate in the long run.

Address Translation

From the user's point of view, a capability is simply an address for a virtual object and is specified whenever the object is to be accessed. From the implementation point of view, a capability is a bit pattern which specifies to the address translation logic where the physical object which currently represents the virtual object is located. This discussion is restricted to capabilities for segments, although analogous statements apply to other objects. Access type checking, such as checking whether or not a store operation is allowed, is well understood and will be ignored here. Furthermore, it is assumed that segments are not paged; paging may be introduced in an obvious way. Thus the situation is as follows. A user wishes to access some word in some segment. He writes an instruction which specifies a capability for the segment to be accessed and an integer which identifies the word within the segment. What does the hardware do when such an instruction is executed?

In the scheme used on the Chicago Magic Number Computer, there are two representations of segment capabilities, known as *in-form* and *out-form*. These two forms are distinguished by a bit in the capability representation. An in-form capability is used only for segments which are in primary memory. It contains the absolute address of the origin of the segment in primary memory and the length of the segment. In-form capabilities are never allowed to exist on secondary storage; a capability is converted to out-form before being moved to secondary storage. Out-form capabilities contain the

secondary storage address of the first record of the segment and a unique sequence number which serves to invalidate capabilities for segments which no longer exist. An attempt to access a segment using an in-form capability causes the hardware to compare the requested word's offset with the length of the segment and, if there is no conflict, to calculate the address of the word of primary memory to be accessed by adding the offset to the address of the origin of the segment. An attempt to access a segment using an out-form capability results in a trap to the system.

The disadvantage of the approach taken on the Chicago Magic Number Computer is that the operating system must frequently convert back and forth between in-form and out-form representations, and must occasionally update the length and address fields in all of the in-form capabilities for some segment. Various schemes are used to minimize this overhead. In retrospect, it appears that the overhead is still substantial.

The Plessey System 250 also uses a scheme of in-form and out-form capabilities. The scheme has several improvements over the Chicago Magic Number Computer, especially in the representation of in-form capabilities. In-form capabilities are evaluated indirectly. There is an indirection table stored in primary memory at a fixed location. Each segment for which capabilities are presently in primary memory has an entry in the indirection table. The in-form capability for an object contains the index of the segment's entry in the indirection table. The entry in the indirection table contains a bit which says whether or not the segment is in primary memory, and contains the segment's secondary storage address and length. If the segment is in primary memory, the entry also contains the segment's primary memory address. The indirection table entry is not fetched on every access to a segment; it is instead fetched whenever a capability is loaded into a processor register.

Using this scheme, the length and primary memory address fields for a segment appear only in one place— the segment's entry in the indirection table (assuming no process which uses the segment is running). This substantially simplifies updating this information. Furthermore, in-form capabilities appear only in primary memory, and out-form capabilities appear only in secondary storage. This convention makes it simple for the system to decide when to convert back and forth between representations. There may still be a substantial overhead in such conversion, however.

The following hardware implementation for address translation is suggested for future implementers of capability-based addressing. It would have been beyond the scope of the hardware available for the Chicago Magic Number Computer but should be reasonable for a computer being designed today. As suggested by Dennis and Van Horn, there is a *unique code* associated with each segment. The unique code is assigned at the time the segment is created and does not change during the life of the segment. It is not reused, even after the segment

235

Communications
of
the ACM

July 1974
Volume 17
Number 7

disappears from the system. There is only one representation of a capability, and it contains the segment's unique code.

The hardware must be able to find the base address and size for a segment in primary memory once it knows the unique code for the segment. It does this by consulting a hash table maintained in primary memory by the operating system which contains an entry for every segment residing in primary memory. There is a single hash table for all users. For each unique code entered in the hash table there is a presence bit which tells whether or not the segment is in primary memory; additional fields indicate the segment's size and the secondary storage address of its origin. Once an entry has been put in the hash table, the entry remains, even if the segment is written back to secondary storage. Entries age out of the hash table slowly, much as the active segment table entries are handled in Multics. The reason for keeping entries in the table after the segment has left primary memory is to speed up bringing the segment in again, should it be needed.

When a segment is accessed and the hardware looks up its unique code, there are three possible results. The segment may be in primary memory, in which case the appropriate word is accessed. The segment may be in the hash table but not present in primary memory, in which case the hardware causes a type A exception and reports the address of the hash table entry. Finally, the segment may not be in the hash table, in which case the hardware causes a type B exception and reports the unique code.

In the case of a type A exception, the operating system initiates a read using the secondary storage address and size obtained from the hash table entry and blocks the process which was making the access. When the segment has been read in, the hash table entry is updated and the process is allowed to continue. In the case of a type B exception, the operating system first obtains the segment's size and secondary storage address and places them in a newly allocated hash table entry and then proceeds as with a type A exception. Obtaining a segment's size and secondary storage address, given its unique code, is done by consulting a data structure on secondary storage which provides the mapping between the unique code and the size and secondary storage address for all segments. Such a data structure is organized as a modified hash table so as to minimize the expected number of secondary storage accesses required to find an entry.

The final feature of the suggested implementation is a small associative memory which remembers the sizes and primary memory addresses for the unique codes of the most recently accessed segments. Experience with Multics indicates that even a small associative memory can be quite effective [38].

Paging

Experience with Burroughs machines indicates that when segments are allocated in terms of "natural" units

for the problem being solved (and the compiler automatically breaks up large arrays), segment sizes are on the average smaller than typical present-day page sizes [2]. On Multics, where the cost of an additional segment is high in terms of additional linkage operations and additional system bookkeeping information, a typical user makes segments larger by combining several different objects in a single segment, thus making his program run more efficiently. This practice should be discouraged, however, since neither the protection mechanism nor the memory management mechanism allows objects thus combined to be treated individually.

Experience with the Plessey System 250 indicates segment sizes more like those of Burroughs' machines than like those of Multics. Thus a paged address translation scheme may perform worse than a nonpaged scheme. M. O'Halloran, one of the designers of the Plessey System 250, suggests that an inverse concept of paging—i.e. many segments per page rather than many pages per segment—is needed to cope with so many very small segments.

Instruction Sets

For capability-based addressing, capabilities must be able to be copied around freely. The capability functions as a basic component in addresses for every object beyond the walls of the processor. The user must be able to do anything with a capability that he would do with an ordinary address on an ordinary machine. Addresses containing capabilities may be used for parameter passing, subroutine returns, elaborate data structures, and so on. Furthermore, every instruction which addresses a word, input/output device, etc., must implicitly or explicitly specify a capability for the object to be accessed.

An *enter instruction* is needed to call a subroutine and simultaneously change the protection domain. The Chicago Magic Number Computer demonstrated that an enter instruction need be no less efficient than an ordinary call instruction. A new type of access for segments is added, called *enter access*. Enter access is weaker than read, write, or execute access and allows only the transfer of control to a fixed entry point, say word zero, using the enter instruction. The enter instruction works like the call used with Figure 6, except that the enter changes the access bits in the capability which is placed in PC to allow reading and executing the program segment. By giving the calling program a capability for the called program's segment which specifies only enter access, the called program, but not the calling program, can obtain the capabilities embedded in the called program's segment.

The Stack

When a program is organized into subroutines, each subroutine may need a temporary storage area for parameters, returns, and local storage. Such storage is often implemented as a stack frame allocated on a common stack each time there is a subroutine call. If the

Communications
of
the ACM

July 1974
Volume 17
Number 7

subroutines run in different protection domains, the stack frames cannot be allocated in a single segment. This is because a subroutine might keep a capability for its stack frame even after it returns control to its caller. It could then use this capability later to interfere with other subroutines to which the stack frame is allocated. The problem could be avoided if there was an efficient mechanism for revoking capabilities.

Assuming revocation is not possible, one solution is to allocate each stack frame in a newly-created segment which will be discarded when the stack frame is no longer needed. Such a scheme adds a substantial overhead to subroutine calling and returning. A better solution is a hardware-managed stack which is not treated as a segment for which capabilities exist, but as a stack of processor registers. The Burroughs B6700 has such a stack, although the implementation relies partly on system compilers and is complex because of its ability to cope with Algol naming. Schroeder's thesis is also relevant [39]. The design of the Chicago Magic Number Computer is quite weak in this respect.

If the stack is arranged so that the temporary storage of the calling routine is unavailable to the called routine, so that the called program cannot alter the return location, and so that parameters can be passed in an orderly way, then the simple enter instruction described above can be used for passing control to a more privileged program, to a less privileged program, or between mutually suspicious programs.

The Own Variable Problem

In addition to temporary storage allocated for a subroutine each time the subroutine is called, a routine may need storage which is allocated when a process first executes the routine and which is retained from call to call of the subroutine by that process. In Algol, such storage is provided by *own* variables. For example, a pseudo random number generator needs an own variable to remember where it is in its pseudo random sequence of numbers. Such information could be retained by the caller and passed as a parameter, but such a solution violates programming generality [13].

Linkage segments, in addition to providing for the indirect evaluation of segment addresses, provide a simple implementation for own variables. It would be unsatisfactory to remove the need for the indirection information in a linkage segment only to find that linkage segments remain so as to implement own variables.

The Algol concept of own variables is not fully general, however. It is likely that languages which provide more control over retention, such as Berry's Oregano [4], will prevail in the long run. Should this be the case, the implementation of own variables based on linkage segments will be too specialized, and one would expect to provide a stack mechanism which allows for retention of stack frames such as the scheme suggested by Bobrow and Wegbreit [5].

Conclusion

Capability-based addressing provides an efficient type of absolute address for an object. The use of such absolute addresses can simplify programming conventions when a general-purpose scheme for shared addresses is required. Recent advances eliminate the need for the modification of the representation of capabilities by the operating system and suggest how to solve the own variable problem in a general way. These advances eliminate the major implementation problems of previously designed systems. A computer using capability-based addressing may now be substantially superior to present systems on the basis of protection, simplicity of programming conventions, and efficient implementation.

References
1. Arden, B.W., Galler, B.A., O'Brien, T.C., and Westervelt, F.H. Program and addressing structure in a time-sharing environment. *J. ACM 13*, 1 (Jan. 1966), 1–16.
2. Batson, A., et al. Measurements of segment size. Proc. 3rd Symp. on Operating Systems Principles. Stanford U., Oct. 1971, 25–29.
3. Bensoussan, A., Clingen, C.T., and Daley, R.C. The MULTICS virtual memory: concepts and design. *Comm. ACM 15*, 5 (May 1972), 308–318.
4. Berry, D.M. Introduction to Oregano. In J. Tou and P. Wegner (Eds.). Sigplan Notices—Proc. Symposium on Data Structures in Programming Languages, Vol. 6., No. 2, Feb. 1971, pp. 171–190.
5. Bobrow, D.G., and Wegbreit, B. A model and stack implementation of multiple environments. *Comm. ACM 16*, 10 (Oct. 1973), 591–603.
6. Burroughs Corporation. Burroughs B5500 Information processing systems reference manual. Detroit, Mich., 1964.
7. Burroughs Corporation. The descriptor—a definition of the B5000 information processing system. Detroit, Mich., 1961.
8. Cleary, J.G. Process handling on Burroughs B6500. Proc. Fourth Australian Comp. Conf., Adelaide, South Australia, 1969, pp. 231–239.
9. Cosserat, D.C. A capability oriented multi-processor system for real-time applications. Presented at the I.C.C. Conf., Washington, D.C., Oct. 1972, 8 pp.
10. Cotton, J.M. The operational requirements for future communications control processors. Presented at Internat. Switching Symp., Cambridge, Mass., June 6–9, 1972, 5 pp.
11. Daley, R.C., and Dennis, J.B. Virtual memory, processes, and sharing in MULTICS. *Comm. ACM 11*, 5 (May 1968), 306–313.
12. Daley, R.C., and Neumann, P.G. A general purpose file system for secondary storage. Proc. AFIPS 1965 FJCC, Vol. 27, Pt. I., AFIPS Press, Montvale, N.J., pp. 213–230.
13. Dennis, J.B. Programming generality, parallelism and computer architecture. Proc. IFIP 1968, North Holland, Amsterdam, pp. C1–7.
14. Dennis, J.B. Segmentation and the design of multiprogrammed computer systems. *J. ACM 12*, 4 (Oct. 1965), 589–602.
15. Dennis, J.B., and Van Horn, E.C. Programming semantics for multiprogrammed computations. *Comm. ACM 9*, 3 (Mar. 1966), 143–155.
16. England, D.M. Architectural features of System 250. In *Infotech State of the Art Report on Operating Systems*, 1972, 12 pp.
17. England, D.M. Operating System of System 250. Presented at Internat. Switching Symp., Cambridge, Mass., June 6–9, 1972, 5 pp.
18. Evans, D.C., and LeClerc, J.Y. Address mapping and the control of access in an interactive computer. Proc. AFIPS 1967 SJCC, Vol. 30, AFIPS Press, Montvale, N.J., pp. 23–32.

19. Fabry, R.S. A user's view of capabilities. *ICR Quart. Rep. 15* (Nov. 1967), ICR, U. of Chicago, Sec. 1C.

20. Fabry, R.S. Preliminary description of a supervisor for a machine oriented around capabilities. *ICR Quart. Rep. 18* (Aug. 1968), ICR, U. of Chicago, Sec. 1B.

21. Fabry, R.S. List-structured addressing. Ph.D. Th., U. of Chicago, 1971.

22. Feustal, E.A. The Rice research computer—a tagged architecture. Proc. AFIPS 1972 SJCC, Vol. 40, AFIPS Press, Montvale, N.J. pp. 369–377.

23. Feustal, E.A. On the advantages of tagged architecture. *IEEE Trans. on Computers C-22*, 7 (July 1973), 644–656.

24. Graham, G.S., and Denning, P.J. Protection—principles and practice. Proc. AFIPS 1972 SJCC, Vol. 40, AFIPS Press, Montvale, N.J., pp. 417–429.

25. Halton, D. Hardware of the System 250 for communication control. Presented at the Internat. Switching Symp., Cambridge, Mass., June 6–9, 1972, 7 pp.

26. Hamer-Hodges, K.J. Fault resistance and recovery within System 250. Presented at I.C.C. Conf., Washington, D.C., Oct. 1972, 6 pp.

27. Iliffe, J.K. *Basic machine principles*. American Elsevier, New York, 1968.

28. Iliffe, J.K., and Jodeit, J.G. A dynamic storage allocation scheme. *Comput. J. 5* (Oct. 1962), 200–209.

29. Jones, A.K. Protection structures. Ph.D. Th., Carnegie-Mellon U., 1973.

30. Lampson, B.W. On reliable and extendable operating systems. In Techniques in Software Engineering, NATO Science Committee Workshop Material, Vol. II, Sept. 1969.

31. Lampson, B.W. Dynamic protection structures. Proc. AFIPS 1969 FJCC, Vol. 35, AFIPS Press, Montvale, N.J., pp. 27–38.

32. Lampson, B.W. Protection. Proc. 5th Ann. Princeton Conf., Princeton U., Mar. 1971, pp. 437–443.

33. LeClerc, J.Y. Memory structures for interactive computers. Project GENIE document No. 40.10.110, U. of California, Berkeley, 1966.

34. Needham, R.M. Protection systems and protection implementations. Proc. AFIPS 1972 FJCC, Vol. 41, AFIPS Press, Montvale, N.J., pp. 571–578.

35. Organick, E.I. *Computer System Organization—the B5700 B6700 Series*. Academic Press, New York, 1973.

36. Organick, E.I. *The Multics System: An Examination of Its Structure*. MIT Press, Cambridge, Mass., 1972.

37. Saltzer, J.H. Traffic control in a multiplexed computer system. MAC-TR-30, Proj. MAC, MIT, Cambridge, Mass., 1966.

38. Schroeder, M.D. Performance of the GE-645 associative memory while Multics is in operation. Proc. Workshop on System Performance Evaluation, Cambridge, Mass., 1971, pp. 227–245.

39. Schroeder, M.D. Cooperation of mutually suspicious subsystems in a computer utility. Ph.D. Th., MIT, 1972.

40. Sevick, K.C., et al. Project SUE as a learning experience. Proc. AFIPS 1972 FJCC, Vol. 41, AFIPS Press, Montvale, N. J., pp. 331–339.

41. Shepherd, J. Principal design features of the multi-computer. (The Chicago Magic Number Computer). *ICR Quart. Rep. 19* (Nov. 1968), ICR, U. of Chicago, Sec. 1-C.

42. Sturgis, H.E. A postmortem of a time sharing system. Ph.D. Th., U. of California, Berkeley, 1973.

43. Wilkes, M.V. *Time Sharing Computer Systems*. 2nd ed., American Elsevier, New York, 1972.

44. Wilner, W.T. Design of the Burroughs B1700. Proc. AFIPS 1972 FJCC, Vol. 41, AFIPS Press, Montvale, N.J., pp. 489–497.

45. Wilner, W.T. Burroughs B1700 memory utilization. Proc. AFIPS 1972 FJCC, Vol. 41, AFIPS Press, Montvale, N.J., pp. 579–586.

46. Wulf, W.A., et al. HYDRA: The kernel of a multiprocessor operating system. Carnegie Mellon U., Comput. Sci. Dep. rep., June 1973.

47. Yngve, V.H. The Chicago Magic Number Computer. *ICR Quart. Rep. 18* (Nov. 1968), ICR, U. of Chicago, Sec. 1-B.

Object Management on Distributed Systems

Robert H. Halstead, Jr.

Laboratory for Computer Science
Massachusetts Institute of Technology
Cambridge, Massachusetts 02139

Abstract

This paper describes research directed toward the construction of a distributed multiprocessor network capable of general-purpose computing. One problem to be solved in this endeavor is how to organize and manage data in the system. Object reference systems with garbage collection are chosen as the most suitable approach, and a network implementation is described.

The implementation is based on reference trees, a novel concept which allows objects to move freely through the network, with all book-keeping being done on a strictly local basis. Schemes for updating reference trees and accessing and garbage-collecting objects are outlined.

Introduction

The research described in this paper is directed toward the construction of the MuNet[13], a distributed multiprocessor network capable of general-purpose computing. Several problems need to be solved in the course of this endeavor, some of them addressed in companion papers to this one.[3,11,12] One problem that is certainly of prime importance is how best to organize and manage information in such a system. Even on single-processor computer systems, this remains the subject of some controversy. The evolution of computer science has seen the development of ever more complicated schemes for large-scale data storage in files, culminating perhaps in the MULTICS file system.[7] A parallel increase in sophistication has been observed in the storage management facilities offered by programming languages, from the simple global environment of FORTRAN,[9] through the block structure of ALGOL 60[8] to the garbage-collected heap storage of LISP 1.5[5] and its many progeny. More recently, growing support has been found for the position that "operating system" and "programming language" data management facilities should be merged into one unified scheme. With modern developments in garbage-collection techniques, an increasing consensus favors object reference systems with garbage collection.[1,2]

This concern with object reference systems is primarily motivated by a desire to create a more congenial environment for software. With software costs rising and hardware costs plummeting, gains in software productivity are worth even some loss in efficient use of hardware. In the belief that the garbage-collected object-reference approach is the best available paradigm for organizing information in a computer system, we adopt it as our goal to implement on distributed systems.

Our purpose in building a multiprocessor network rather than a single-processor system is to take advantage of the better price-performance ratios available in smaller processors. The logical extreme of this approach is achieved by constructing very large networks of microprocessors, an architecture which mandates an inexpensive interconnection technology applicable to large network sizes. We therefore abandon technologies requiring a common central medium in favor of simple bidirectional links that connect neighboring processors. Thus the network topology we are assuming is that of an undirected graph, where each processor is directly linked to some, but not necessarily (or ordinarily) all, of the other processors in the network.

Our goal of expandability is incompatible with any object management mechanism involving centralized control. Ideally, it should be possible to distribute objects to match any distribution of concurrent tasks across the processors in the network. No object should need to be known on every processor in the network. Rather, knowledge of an object should be confinable to those processors where the object might conceivably be used.

Object Structure

We now elaborate on the model of "object" to be used throughout this paper. For concreteness, some details are filled in with the design decisions actually made in the ongoing MuNet project.

Most of the information contained in an object is recorded in its text. Texts may contain both references to other objects and uninterpreted binary data. Copies of the text of an object may be stored at any of the processors where the object is known. For fast access and enhanced reliability, several redundant copies of a text may be made and moved upon demand--a protocol allows the per-

Reprinted from *Proceedings of the 7th Texas Conference on Computing Systems*, 1978, pages 7-7-7-14. Copyright 1978 by The Institute of Electrical and Electronics Engineers, Inc.

formance of side effects even upon texts which are initially stored redundantly. No permanent special responsibility for an object attaches to any particular processor, even the creator of the object; objects are free to move through the network, following the tasks that use them.

In order to facilitate the motion of objects and loci of control from one processor to another, a bound is placed on the size of object texts; thus to represent a large aggregation of data such as the Manhattan telephone book, the object-referencing capabilities of the network must be used to generate a tree-like data structure.

Objects may be referred to from other objects by means of <u>object</u> <u>references</u>. In the MuNet, object references seen by user programs are all in the form of 16-bit words. The fact that references are encoded as 16-bit words does not impose any particular bound (such as 2^{16}) on the number of objects that may exist in the network--each reference is simply a local name for an object, interpreted in the context of the processor on which the reference is used. An object's reference is the handle which the programmer can use to perform all operations on the object, such as obtaining its type, examining its text, etc.

An object text is represented within a processor as a series of words in memory. Every text is headed by format information, followed by zero or more words of object references, followed in turn by zero or more words of uninterpreted binary data. The header gives the number of words of object references and the number of words of binary data. This object structure closely resembles that used in HYDRA[14], another extant multiprocessor system. None of HYDRA's protection information has been included, but the inclusion of such information would not impact the object management mechanisms described in this paper. The hardware environment used for HYDRA is centralized in various respects, however; our desire to avoid this lack of expandability causes our implementation to be quite different.

Reference Trees

Keeping track of an object is accomplished by maintaining the processors which contain references to the object in a <u>connected</u>, <u>acyclic</u> graph called the <u>reference</u> <u>tree</u> for that object. Each reference tree consists of some subset of the nodes and arcs (processors and inter-neighbor links) of the network. The nodes which belong to the reference tree are chosen to be those processors in the network which contain references to the object, and the arcs are chosen in such a way that (1) the reference tree is <u>connected</u>, i.e., it is possible to reach any node in the tree from any other node, traveling only over arcs that are in the tree, and (2) the tree is <u>acyclic</u> in that the arcs in the tree form no closed loops. (Arcs in reference trees are undirected, hence requirement (2) means that there should be no undirected cycles.) Put another way, there is a unique path (using only arcs in the tree) from any node in a reference tree

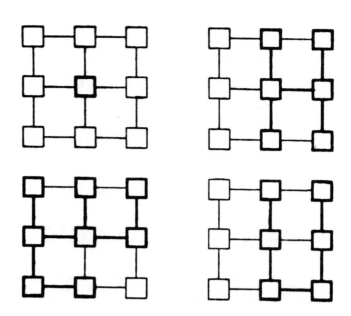

Figure 1: Examples of reference trees (in heavy lines)

to any other. Additionally, every arc in a reference tree must go between two nodes that are in the tree. Reference trees are so named because they form unrooted trees embedded in the network.

It is important to note that, in general, the reference trees for different objects need bear no relation to each other. In particular, it is not the case that there is one "reference tree" in the network, used for all objects. Central to the concept of reference trees is that they are free to grow and shrink dynamically, following changes in the roles of the corresponding objects in the operation of the system.

Also significant is the fact that reference trees can be maintained by a completely distributed mechanism in which each processor in a tree remembers only the state of its immediately adjacent links (i.e., whether each link is in the tree or not). Processors not in the tree for an object, of course, have no references to the object, and need remember no information about it. Even the cycle-free nature of the tree can be preserved on this strictly distributed basis--no central clearinghouse is needed to determine whether a cycle is being formed.

The purpose of maintaining reference trees for objects is so that any processor with a reference to an object can communicate with all other processors having references to the object. This capability is used in both object text management and garbage collection. These subjects will be dealt with below, after we see how reference trees themselves are maintained.

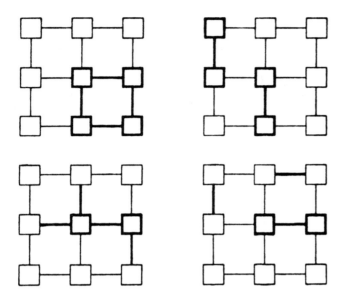

Figure 2: Examples that are not reference trees

Reference Tree Maintenance

Reference trees are maintained by means of an interprocessor communication protocol which may be used to grow and shrink reference trees while preserving the required connectedness and freedom from cycles. In order to participate in this protocol, each processor maintains, for each object it knows about, a link state for each of the processor's neighbors (there are thirteen different link states). Various flavors of messages can be sent pertaining to an object's reference tree, and a simple state transition table dictates the responses so as to keep the various link states mutually consistent. By sending appropriate messages, it is possible for a node to delete itself from a reference tree (an option only available to leaf nodes) or extend a reference tree to include a new processor. Typically, a node will attempt to delete itself if it discovers, in the course of a garbage collection, that it no longer has any accessible references to an object. The reference tree for an object will be extended if a text referencing the object is sent to a processor not previously a member of the object's reference tree.

The protocol for accomplishing this we shall call the membership protocol (because it keeps track of membership in reference trees) to distinguish it from other protocols such as that used for moving object texts. The membership protocol, a further evolution of an earlier protocol[4], is more intricate than one might at first imagine necessary, but simpler protocols failed because of deadlocks or inconsistent states reached after inopportune sequences of events. The protocol is described below in what some may find to be daunting detail; the reader who finds the going tedious can at any point skip the remainder of the section and proceed to the next without any loss of contin-

uity. The reader who perseveres, however, will hopefully be rewarded with more than merely an understanding of our particular reference tree management protocol. There is not really a reference tree protocol, rather there is a whole family of such protocols, a representative member of which is described here. The description below includes an outline of the design considerations which made the current protocol what it is. After completing this section, the reader should be equipped to design his own reference tree protocols to fit his own particular needs, or even, perhaps, improve on the one presented here. The important thing about this description is not its detail, but its illustration of the concept of using link states to maintain a global structure while keeping only local information.

The membership protocol makes no attempt to recover from damaged or lost messages, or messages arriving out of order. These problems can be solved by various well-known means[6] which may be assumed to provide the underlying protocol on each link.

The protocol requires that each object have a globally unique name. This name is needed so that when an attempt is made to extend a reference tree to a new processor, that processor can determine whether it already knows of the object via some other route. This information in turn is necessary to detect attempts to form cycles in the reference tree.

The membership protocol involves seven basic kinds of messages, whose meaning and format are as given in Table 3. Each message is specialized by identification of the object (and hence reference tree) that it pertains to. This specialization is effected in one of two ways, depending on the message type. Messages which establish new communication paths for an object (commonly by extending the object's reference tree to include another processor) include the object's global name (shown as GN in Table 3). These messages also include a shorter local name (LN) which the sender of the message will use for future references to the object sent by it over the same communication link. The other messages in the membership protocol (as well as all other messages, including, for example, text management messages) use only the local name to denote the intended object. The use of local names not only shortens messages but speeds their processing. Since the space of local names is smaller and presumably reasonably compact, conversion of an incoming local name to an internal object reference can be effected economically by means of a direct table look-up, rather than the more expensive scheme required to look up a global name.

Messages in the membership protocol may be sent either spontaneously (i.e., in response to some external stimulus, such as the need to have a local name for an object so that a text referencing it can be sent) or in response to an incoming message requesting some change in a reference tree. R+, +, and - messages are always sent spontaneously; L+, L-, A+, and A- messages are always sent as responses.

Message			Meaning
R+	GN	LN	request to add link to tree
L+	GN	LN	agreement to add link
L-	GN	LN	refusal to add link
+		LN	transfer mastery of link
-		LN	request to drop link from tree
A+		LN	positive acknowledgment
A-		LN	negative acknowledgment

Table 3: Membership protocol message types

The membership protocol operates by associating with each end of each link a state for each possible object. It is these states which actually define the extent of an object's reference tree. In terms of implementation, each processor must maintain a data base for each object it has a reference to, indicating the state (with respect to that object) of each link adjacent to the processor. It is important to realize that the two processors at the ends of a link may have different ideas of the state of the link; this may be as the result of some intentionally introduced asymmetries discussed below, or it may occur if messages regarding the object have been sent at one end of the link but not yet received at the other.

The possible states may be grossly characterized as being either stable or transient. Stable states are states which might be expected to persist over a relatively long period of time. Transient states are those in which a message has been sent across the link and a reply is expected; the reply will cause a transition to some other state, either stable or transient. Transient states exist to provide the proper sequencing so that the next pair of stable states to be established is consistent and does not result in partitioning the tree or closing a cycle. For the purposes of the discussion below, the states have been given one-to three-character mnemonic names (listed in Table 4, below). For purposes of actually manipulating object references passing over links, the most important attribute of each link state is whether a processor in that state is directly prepared to send or receive a local name for the object on that link. Processors in all states but X, N, and N?1 are directly able to send local names (i.e., such names have already been declared by R+, L+, or L- messages); processors in all states but X, N, and M? are directly able to receive them (i.e., such names have already been declared to them and recorded).

In addition to the various link states, each processor maintains for each object a processor state, either "in the reference tree" or "not in the reference tree." Certain link states are only consistent with a particular processor state. Rather than show the pair (processor state, link state) that governs a processor's response to messages arriving on a link, we encode the processor state information into the link state, adopting the convention of using state names containing the letter "X" to imply a processor state of "not in the reference tree" and other state names to imply

the opposite. Thus either all of a processor's link states for a given object will contain X's, or none will. When a link state changes between these categories, other link states in the processor must also change to preserve this consistency. Special transitions (between X and N, X? and N?), requiring neither the receipt nor the sending of messages, are provided to fulfill this need. In general, each X link state has an analogous N state, differing only in the processor state of the processor in question.

We now describe the five stable states. Perhaps the state most likely to occur is X, which indicates that not only is the link not considered part of the reference tree, the processor is not considered part of the reference tree. If a processor has no knowledge of an object, it acts as though it were in state X for that object on every link.

The state analogous to X is N. In state N, the processor is considered part of the reference tree, but still does not believe the link in question to be part of the object's reference tree. State N may come about either because the processor is the only processor to contain any references to the object, or because the processor is connected to the reference tree by some other link or links.

Another closely related state is L. State L is like state N in that the relevant link is not considered part of the reference tree, but indicates that the processor at the other end of the link does know about the object, and that local names have been established for communicating references to the object over that link. In a stable condition, the processor at the other end of the link will also be in state L with respect to the link. The reason for state L is to enable the communication of an object reference over links that cannot be allowed to join the object's reference tree because adding those links would close cycles. Such communication is not only desirable, but sometimes is necessary.

Another stable state is M, which indicates that the link in question is believed to be part of the reference tree, and furthermore that this processor is currently the master of that link (for transactions involving that object). The master of a link is the only one that can effect changes in the status of the link or send a text of the object over the link. This asymmetry seems to be necessary to prevent confusion resulting from, for instance, both ends of a link simultaneously attempting to terminate their connection with the reference tree.

In a stable condition, the state at the other end of a link from M will be S, for "slave." A processor in state S cannot directly cause a change in the status of the link; it may however request the master to commence a change (by means of a message not discussed here), and it may respond to messages sent by the master.

The transient states will not be described to the same level of detail as the stable states. For

State	R+	L+	L-	+	-	A+	A-	LN	Spontaneous Transitions
X	L+:S								:N
N	L-:L								R+:M? :X
L					A-:N?1	A+:M		:L	-:L?
M								:M	-:X? +:S
S				:M	A-:N?1			:S	
X?							A-:X	:N!	:N?
N!						A+:M?		:N!	
N?							A-:N	:N?	:X?
N?1					L+:S		:N	:N?1	R+:M?1
L?					A-:N?1	A+:M	A-:N	:L?	
M?	:L	:M	:L						
M?1						A+:S?	:M?	:M?1	
S?				:S?	:S			:S?	

The notation a:b means that under the specified circumstances, a transition to state b can occur with the emission of message a. Transitions occasioned by the receipt of a local name are shown in column LN.

Table 4: Membership protocol state transition table

the most part, they acquire their meaning from their relationship with the stable states. Instead of attempting to describe the meaning of these states, we present a complete state-transition table (Table 4), and summarize below the normal sequences for handling several situations.

The fundamental principle that motivates this protocol design (other than the need to maintain the link data base in a consistent state) is that a processor must always be able to send a reference over any link without prearrangement. For example, it is not acceptable that the sending of a reference should be the culmination of some transaction allowing the reference to be sent only upon receipt of suitable clearance from the message's target. In order to understand this requirement, the circumstances under which references may be sent must be considered.

In general, a reference will be sent as part of some text which is being communicated between processors. Sending a text involves communicating the reference to the object whose text is being sent, as well as references to other objects referred to in the text. Thus obtaining clearance to send a text may involve simultaneously obtaining clearance to send several object references. Unless every processor always has clearance to send any object reference, it is easy to see how the piecemeal aggregation of such clearance could lead to a deadlock on a link. This is especially true when, as is the case with this protocol, transactions involving different objects are completely independent--no overall master-slave relationship applies to all communication on a particular link, for example.

This need to avoid deadlock is one of the primary factors acting to complicate the protocol design, and requires that any processor always be able to send any object reference without the possibility of confusing the processor at the other side. The only exception to this requirement is state X--if a processor has no references

to an object, it has none to send! In any other state, the processor must either already have a local name to use for the object over the link, or have the option of picking a local name, declaring it to its neighbor with an R+ message, and then immediately using it in messages.

We now turn to how and why various state changes may occur. We start with a processor in state X, having no references to the object in question. The only kind of message that can be received in state X is an R+ message from some processor attempting to extend the reference tree for the object, perhaps in order to send a text mentioning the object. Upon receipt of the R+ message, our processor returns an L+ message as an indication that the link should indeed be added to the tree, and changes to state S in anticipation of the sender of the R+ message entering the M (master) state when it receives the L+ message. Simultaneously, the states of all other links to our processor change from X to N, indicating that our processor is now part of the reference tree. Also, any links in state X? change to N?.

Now that our processor is part of the reference tree, it may attempt to further extend the tree by sending a reference along one of the links just converted to state N. From state N an object reference must be preceded by an R+ message. Upon sending the R+ message, the sender's state for that link changes from N to the transient state M?; awaiting a reply. The reply to R+ depends on the condition of the processor at the other end of the link. If it was in state X, it changes to S and replies with L+, as described above. Upon receiving the L+ message, our processor changes from M? to M, and the link has been established. If the other processor is in state N, then the link cannot be added to the reference tree because it would close a cycle (since both processors are already connected by some other route in the reference tree). Consequently, the other processor responds negatively, with an L- message, and changes to state L. When the sender of the R+

243

message receives the L- message, it also enters state L. As long as both processors remain in state L, local names have been established for communicating references to the object over the link, even though the link has been agreed not to be in the object's reference tree.

Another possible scenario is that two processors, both in state N (for the same link) might simultaneously attempt to add that link to the tree by sending R+ messages to each other and entering state M?. Under these circumstances, it is clear that the link should not be added, or a cycle will be formed. Therefore, each M? will react to the R+ with a transition to state L.

Once it has been agreed that a link is part of the reference tree for an object and things have settled to a quiescent state (i.e., no messages are in transit), one processor (the master) will be in state M and the other (the slave) in state S. It is a simple matter to reverse the roles of master and slave, but the transaction must be initiated by the master. The master sends a + message and enters state S. When the slave receives the + message, it enters state M.

Having seen how a link may be established in the reference tree, we now come to the question of how a link may be deleted from the tree. Due to the connected, acyclic nature of the tree, every time a link is deleted, a node is also being removed from the tree. Thus the only reason for deleting a link is because a processor wants to remove itself from the reference tree. This in turn will be caused by that processor's discovery that it has no references to the object reachable from any active data on that processor. No node which has more than one neighbor in a reference tree can unilaterally remove itself. If it did, the tree would become partitioned, since those nodes which were originally connected by the removed node would now have no means of communicating. Only "leaf" nodes--nodes which have exactly one neighbor also in the reference tree--may disconnect themselves from it. Furthermore, no node may remove itself from a tree leaving dangling (though non-tree) links in state L. (But a link inconveniently in state L may be removed by sending a - message and changing to state L?--the reader can follow the transitions that ensue.) Thus a processor may attempt to remove itself from the tree only if all its links but one are in state N (or N?). Additionally, that one link must be in state M; if the processor is currently a slave on that link (for that object), it must first induce the master of the link to relinquish its mastery.

A master requests to remove itself from the tree by sending a - message to its slave and changing to state X? (simultaneously all N links from that processor should change to X and all N? links to X?). The slave responds with A- and changes to state N?1. Upon receiving the A-, the old master returns to state X, emitting another A-. When it receives this A-, the old slave goes to state N from N?1. The extra level of acknowledgment here is needed because a processor in state S may send out object references as local names, a capability

it must have. The old master must be prevented from returning to state X, where such references will not be accepted, until it is confirmed that the old slave is no longer in state S. In effect, the A- message sent by the old slave serves to "flush" the channel, bringing up the rear for any local names that might have been sent.

A complication for this scheme occurs precisely when a processor in state S sends such a local name to an ex-master now in state X?. In this case, the ex-master will once again be in possession of a reference to the object, and must abort its initiative to leave the reference tree. It does this by changing to state N! upon receiving the local name. In state N!, when the expected A- acknowledgment is received from the old slave, the reply will instead be an A+ message and a transition to M?, indicating a desire to remain in the reference tree after all. When the old slave, now in state N?1, receives the A+ message, it replies with L+ and returns to state S. Receipt of the L+ message by the old master will then cause it to return to state M. An L+ message is used here rather than, say, A+, because a processor in state N?1 does not have a local name it can use immediately to send references over the link. The L+ message serves to re-establish such a local name.

Other transitions in Table 4 exist to take care of other pathological occurrences. For example, the old slave, while waiting in state N?1 for either an A+ or A- reply, may discover that it needs to send out a reference to the object. Since in state N?1 it has no local name for so doing, it must declare one by sending an R+ message, which is accompanied by a transition to M?1. The reader can follow the sequence of transitions and replies triggered by this R+ message, and see some more of the entries in Table 4 come into play.

Cases like this are another source of complication in the membership protocol. Generally speaking, whenever a processor can undergo a spontaneous transition to another state, the new state must be able to respond meaningfully to any message the old state might have been expecting. When both processors at the ends of a link are susceptible to spontaneous transitions, adding one new function to the protocol may require the addition of several new transitions.

Object Text Management

Some subset of the processors having references to an object will also be custodians of a copy of the text of the object. The management of object texts has three basic goals: (1) to insure that no object text is "lost" (i.e., to insure that at least one processor has custody of an object's text at all times), (2) to keep each processor in the reference tree for an object apprised of the directions in which it may send inquiries requesting a copy of the text, and (3) to provide a mechanism for performing side effects on object texts. The primary reason for requiring reference trees to be connected is so that any processor with a reference to an object can always communicate with all custodians for that object simply by following links that are part of its reference tree. Indeed, we will require that all communication concerning an object travel strictly over links that are in the reference tree for that object.

The acyclic nature of reference trees guarantees that, once a message has been sent across a particular link, it can never "loop back" to its sender unless either (1) it leaves the reference tree, or (2) some processor returns the message back along the same link over which it was received. Thus when a processor wants to send a message to a custodian of a text, all it needs to know locally is "which way" to send the message initially; i.e., which of its neighbors in the reference tree lies along the unique path from it to the desired custodian. It does not even need to know the identity of the custodian, since the message can be forwarded from node to node using only the local information telling which way the desired custodian lies. Consequently, the only information processors need to record concerning the location of custodians is which ways (through the reference tree) they may be found. This in turn means that local changes in custody need only cause data base updates in the processors directly involved--the remainder of the reference tree need not be affected.

If a processor without a copy of some text needs to access that text, it must send an inquiry message to some custodian of the text. In response to the inquiry, the custodian will send back a copy of the desired text. The strategy for initiating or forwarding an inquiry is simply to pick some link over which a custodian can be reached, and send the inquiry in that direction. In addition, any processor forwarding an inquiry will need to remember the direction from which the inquiry came, so that the reply can be routed back along the same route. The same state information can be used when a processor is attempting to obtain non-shared access to an object text, for example, in order to perform a side effect on it: if there is no direction in which another custodian can be reached from a processor, the processor itself must have the only copy of the text. If such other directions exist, those are the directions in which messages must be sent inducing processors to delete their copies of the text. Such requests must be time-stamped with globally unique time stamps to prevent deadlocks between different processors trying to obtain nonshared access to the same objects.

Garbage Collection

A reference tree network includes garbage-collected storage as a standard part of the programming environment it supports. Garbage collection on such a network entails the identification and disposal of objects that will never be used again. When an object becomes inaccessible, it may have become known on several processors. None of these processors can take the initiative to delete the object outright because, in general, none knows whether accessible references to the object exist on other processors. Therefore, it seems that it might be very difficult to ever

reclaim the object. If the object is only known on one processor, the story is different. In this case, it is obvious that no references to the object exist on other processors (else the reference tree would be larger) and therefore the object can be deleted if it is not accessible on the one processor where it is known.

Our garbage-collection scheme works by shrinking the reference tree of an object to be collected until only one processor knows about it, at which point the object can be collected by traditional means. In order for a reference tree to shrink, nodes must remove themselves from it. As we have seen, only "leaf" nodes of a tree may do this. Fortunately, since reference trees are acyclic, every reference tree has leaf nodes. (An additional consideration is that no leaf node which is a custodian of a text for an object may remove itself from that object's reference tree without first preserving the text by passing it on to its neighbor.)

This garbage-collection scheme depends on the fact that a garbage-collectable object will not be used anywhere once it becomes garbage-collectable. Thus, after some interval, processors with references to such an object may guess that it can be collected by the fact that they have not seen it used recently. Even if an object is still potentially accessible, it is inefficient to keep it on processors where it is not needed. Therefore, it is economical for a processor in the reference tree for such an object to remove itself if it can. If that strategy is applied consistently, the reference tree of any garbage-collectable object should slowly shrink to a point (a single node), whereupon the object can be disposed of.

There is one unfortunate problem with this scheme, involving the collection of objects which are part of certain cyclic data structures. The problem, described more thoroughly elsewhere[4], is similar to the problem of cyclic restart in some transaction-based data management systems[10] and involves the existence of infinitely long sequences of reference tree "contractions" which may occur in trying to collect such objects. A garbage collector will not inevitably fall into one of these traps, even where it exists, but it may. Perhaps there are solutions to this garbage-collection problem which are analogous to solutions to the cyclic restart problem. For a practical system, it may be quite safe to rely on random timing differences caused by changing loads to prevent any such continuing pattern from persisting forever.

Drawbacks of Reference Trees

The reference tree approach has two principal liabilities. Both are suggested by the reference tree depicted in Figure 5. One liability is that reference trees may not always grow in the most desirable shapes. In Figure 5, the shaded processor's inquiry and the solid processor's response will both have to travel the entire length of the reference tree, when in fact the processors are adjacent. The other liability, which can also occur in more "stretched-out" reference trees, is

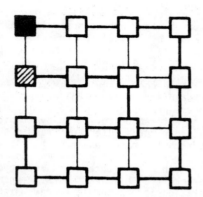

The solid box represents a processor with a
copy of the object's text; the shaded box
represents a processor inquiring for the text.

Figure 5: A non-optimal reference tree

the overhead involved in keeping reference trees
connected. Even if the two end processors in Figure 5 are the only two which continue to have any
interest in the object, all the intermediate processors must still stay in the object's reference
tree to keep it connected. In a large system with
many objects, such extended reference trees could
impose significant overhead on each processor.

There are various ways of attacking these
problems, should they prove serious[4]. No experimentation has yet been conducted, however, to
determine whether these theoretical problems are
also practical problems.

Conclusion

In the spectrum of ideas about how to use distributed systems, the concept of reference trees
certainly occupies a position on the far left. As
such, it is more likely to be spectacular in either
its failure or its success. The scheme presented
here has been shown to at least function in various
toy situations, but its testing in more demanding
circumstances awaits the further maturation of the
MuNet project. Only then will it be seen how much
the generality of the reference tree scheme really
costs, and how serious the difficulties discussed
above really prove to be. It is anticipated, however, that the reference tree approach will survive
the test, if not in the "pure" form described here,
then as the basis of some more finely optimized
scheme.

References

1. Baker, H., _Actor Systems for Real-Time Computa-
   tion_, LCS TR-197, Laboratory for Computer Science, M.I.T., March 1978.

2. Bishop, P., _Computer Systems with a Very Large
   Address Space and Garbage Collection_, LCS
   TR-178, Laboratory for Computer Science, M.I.T.,
   May 1977.

3. Gula, J., "Operating System Considerations for
   Multiprocessor Architectures," _Proc. Seventh
   Texas Conf. on Computing Systems_, October 1978.

4. Halstead, R., _Multiple-Processor Implementa-
   tions of Message-Passing Systems_, LCS TR-198,
   Laboratory for Computer Science, M.I.T.,
   February 1978.

5. McCarthy, J., _et al._, _The LISP 1.5 Programming
   Manual_, M.I.T. Press, 1965.

6. Metcalfe, R., _Packet Communication_, MAC TR-114,
   Project MAC, M.I.T., December 1973.

7. _Multics Programmers' Manual_, Honeywell Information Systems, Inc., 1976.

8. Naur, P. (Ed.), "Revised Report on the Algorithmic Language ALGOL 60," _Comm. ACM_, January
   1963.

9. Rabinowitz, I.N., "Report on the Algorithmic
   Language FORTRAN II," _Comm. ACM_, June 1962.

10. Stearns, R.E., Lewis, P.M., and Rosenkrantz, D.,
    "Concurrency Control for Database Systems,"
    _IEEE Symposium on Foundations of Computer Sci-
    ence CH1133-8C_, October 1976.

11. Strovink, E., "Compilation Strategies for
    Multiprocessor Message-Passing Systems," _Proc.
    Seventh Texas Conf. on Computing Systems_,
    October 1978.

12. Ward, S., "The MuNet: A Multiprocessor Message-
    Passing System Architecture," _Proc. Seventh
    Texas Conf. on Computing Systems_, October 1978.

13. Ward, S., Halstead, R., Gula, J., Strovink, E.,
    and Baker, C., "MuNet Implementation Notes,"
    internal memoranda, M.I.T. Laboratory for Com-
    puter Science, 1978.

14. Wulf, W., _et al._, "HYDRA: The Kernel of a
    Multiprocessor Operating System," _Comm. ACM_,
    June 1974.

Chapter 6: Examples of Object-Based Architecture

In this chapter, examples of machines that use or used an object-oriented architecture are presented. These examples include:

- Hydra, an object-based operating system (1974, Carnegie Mellon), and Cola, an object-based command language for Hydra (1981).
- the IBM System/38, a commercial machine with an object-oriented architecture (1980).
- the Intel iAPX 432, an object-based micro processor (1981).
- LOOM, a virtual memory that supports the Xerox implementation of Smalltalk-80 (1979-1985).

Hydra (see Additional References, Wulf et al., 1981 and 1974) was an object-based operating system built for the C.mmp (Carnegie-Mellon Multi-Mini Processor) hardware. In Hydra, all physical and logical resources available to programs are viewed as objects. Examples are procedures, processes, disks, files, and message ports. The Hydra kernel supports the creation and maintenance of new object types, instances of those types, and capabilities. Each Hydra object is described by a name that uniquely identifies the object, a type that determines the operations that can be performed on the object, and a representation of the current state of the object.

When procedures are invoked, Hydra creates a local name space (LNS) object for that invocation. The LNS represents the dynamic state of the procedure's execution. Several LNS's can simultaneously exist to represent different activations of a procedure. This allows procedures to be reentrant and recursive. Hydra was the first system to present the philosophy that every resource is an object. This philosophy is now part of Smalltalk and is being incorporated in other languages.

The first paper, "An Object-Oriented Command Language," by Richard Snodgrass, describes the command language Cola, a user interface for Hydra. Cola is an object-based language naturally built on the capability-based operating system Hydra. Cola is compared with the previous, nonobject-oriented, command language for Hydra, and is judged superior in many respects. Cola contains all the major features of Smalltalk including classes, messages, instances, a class hierarchy, and automatic inheritance. It is interesting that these features can be incorporated into an operating system command language.

Frank G. Soltis and Roy L. Hoffman, in "Design Considerations for the IBM System/38," describe the IBM System/38, an example of a modern commercial machine with

an object-oriented architecture. It was announced in 1978 and first delivered in 1980. The architecture uses capabilities called pointers. The system uses hashing with linked list collision resolution for finding an object when given its pointer. The paper describes the particular hashing scheme used in some detail.

Unfortunately, the System/38 product is limited to commercial languages that do not reveal or emphasize the machine architecture. However, it is the object-based machine that most people are likely to be aware of or come in contact with.

The next three papers describe the Intel iAPX 432 processor and iMAX, its multiprocessor operating system. Whereas Smalltalk is the ultimate (so far) object-oriented language, the 432 is the ultimate object-oriented processor. In both Smalltalk and the 432, everything is an object. The 432 naturally creates a multiprocessor environment out of the object orientation. The Intel 432 was introduced in 1981 and is the first object-based microprocessor. The design of the chip set was based on the Hydra operating system and took more than 100 man-years. Unfortunately, the 432 has not been a commercial success. This was probably due to premature marketing of an underdeveloped product. However, it is an impressive microprocessor in comparison to others and has ushered in a new era of microprocessor design.

The paper, "iMax: A Multiprocessor Operating System for an Object-Based Computer," by Kevin C. Kahn, William M. Corwin, T. Don Dennis, Herman D'Hooge, David E. Hubka, Linda A. Hutchins, John T. Montague, Fred J. Pollack, and Michael R. Gifkins describes iMAX, a commercially available object-based operating system for the 432. A major goal of the 432 system is conceptual uniformity of architecture, operating system, and language, each using an object-oriented approach. The architecture is capability-based, the language is Ada, and the operating system interfaces between the two. Issues involved in operating system design, such as the user's view of the system, process management, memory management, hardware type enforcement, garbage collection, and object finalization are considered.

In the paper, "The iMax-432 Object Filing System," by Fred J. Pollack, Kevin C. Kahn, and Roy M. Wilkinson, the object filing system in iMAX is described. It is capability-based, with a capability being referred to as an "access-descriptor." The paper describes the structure of the object space, active and passive forms of access-descriptors, a way to reduce overhead by using composite objects, and object space management using an ownership scheme of garbage collection.

The 432 object filing system utilizes both an active and a passive space. This is in contradistinction to Hydra and System/38, which utilize a one-space model. The two-space model helps to preserve system consistency in the presence of a system crash.

To improve the performance of the filing system, objects are gathered into collections called composite objects. The elements of a composite object should be semantically related to each other. A composite object is stored in a manner similar to that of storing a single large object.

The garbage collection scheme for the active object space is based on reference counts (i.e., a count is kept of the number of references to an object, and when there are none left, the object is deleted). However, the garbage collection scheme for the passive object space is ownership based (i.e., the owner of an object decides when it is to be deleted).

The paper by Stephen Zeigler, Nicole Allegre, David Coar, Robert Johnson, James Morris, and Greg Burns, "The Intel 432 Ada Programming Environment," describes how the object-oriented architecture of the iAPX-432 enables the support of Ada packages and tasks. Some object-oriented extensions to Ada that are supportive of developing "dynamic systems" (as opposed to embedded systems) are considered.

Ada was chosen as the primary implementation language for the 432 because several language features are supported directly by or are easily implementable in the hardware. In particular, the 432 provides a set of instructions and special objects that assist the development of tasking. The 432 provides transparent multitasking. That is, any program that executes correctly on n processors requires no modification to execute correctly on $n+1$ processors.

The 432 systems implementation language is a superset of Ada. It adds facilities to Ada that allow it to be more conveniently used to model dynamic systems. These facilities include the ability to write a procedure that has an arbitrary function as a parameter.

In the final paper, "Virtual Memory on a Narrow Machine for an Object-Oriented Language," Ted Kaehler describes LOOM (Large Object-Oriented Memory), a virtual memory that supports the Xerox Dorado implementation of Smalltalk-80. LOOM is specifically designed to run on computers with a narrow, 16-bit, word size. The major design goals and constraints are as follows:

- Provide to Smalltalk the illusion that memory is a large space of objects.
- Utilize only the hardware available on the Dorado, (i.e., 16-bit words and no double-word registers).
- Provide a virtual memory space that can grow without conceptual limit.

- Retain the best possible execution speed as compared to a nonvirtual memory Smalltalk-80 system.

To provide for a large virtual space, pointers into secondary memory have 32 bits. To provide for the interpreter to be fast on the 16-bit machine, pointers into primary memory have 16 bits. The use of these separate address spaces in primary and secondary memory is the primary design decision of LOOM. The bulk of the paper describes how various other problems were solved by using an interesting question and answer format. Along the way Kaehler, explains why LOOM is faster than paging, even though the Dorado hardware supports paging.

Additional References

A.K. Jones, R. Chansler, Jr., I. Durham, K. Schwans, and S. Vegdahl, "StarOS: A Multiprocessor Operating System for the Support of Task Forces," *Proceedings of the 7th Symposiusm on Operating System Principles*, ACM, Inc., New York, New York, December 1979, pages 117-127.

StarOS is an example of an object-oriented multiprocessor operating system. It is specifically designed to support task forces, that is, large collections of concurrently executing processes that cooperate to accomplish a single purpose. All information is encoded and stored in objects which may be between 2 and 4096 bytes in size. Capability-based addressing is used, and each object contains both data and a capability list. The paper describes the object-based nature of StarOS and many of its other features.

E.I. Organick, *A Programmer's View of the Intel 432 System*, McGraw-Hill, New York, New York, 1983.

This is the book to get if you really want an in-depth understanding of the details of the Intel 432 processor. The nature of object-oriented computing is discussed, including object-oriented programming, object-based operating systems, object-based computer architecture, and object filing systems. The relation of these object-based concepts to the details of the 432 are discussed in the body of the book. The various standard objects used by the 432 are described in detail, as is the interface to the iMAX operating system and the Ada programming language. The use of the 432 for multiprocessing is also considered.

M.E. Houdek, F.G. Soltis, and R.L. Hoffman, "IBM System/38 Support for Capability-Based Addressing," *Proceedings, The 8th Annual Symposium on Computer Architecture*, IEEE Computer Society Press, Washington, D.C., May 1981, pages 341-348.

iAPX-432 Object Primer, Intel Corporation, *Manual Order Number 171858-001*, Santa Clara, Calif., 1981.

An interesting discussion of the object philosophy and how it relates to the Intel 432 architecture.

Introduction to the iAPX-432 Architecture, Intel Corporation, *Manual Order Number 171821-001*, Santa Clara, Calif., 1981.

K.C. Kahn and F.J. Pollack, "An Extensible Operating System for the Intel 432," *Digest of Papers: COMPCON Spring 81*, IEEE Computer Society Press, Washington, D.C., February 1981, pages 398-404.

F.G. Soltis, "Design of a Small Business Data Processing System," *Computer*, Volume 14, Number 9, September 1981, pages 77-93.

In this paper, Soltis explains the reasons for using an object-oriented architecture in the IBM System/38.

W.A. Wulf, R. Levin, and S.P. Harbison, *C.mmp/Hydra: An Experimental Computer System*, McGraw-Hill, New York, New York, 1981.

W. Wulf, E. Cohen, W. Corwin, A. Jones, R. Levin, C. Pierson, and F. Pollack, "HYDRA: The Kernel of a Multiprocessor Operating System," *Communications of the ACM*, Volume 17, Number 6, June 1974, pages 337-345.

E.F. Gehringer and R.P. Colwell, "Fast Object-Oriented Procedure Calls: Lessons from the Intel 432," *Proceedings, The 13th Annual International Symposium on Computer Architecture*, IEEE Computer Society Press, Washington, D.C., June 1986, pages 92-101.

The reasons for slow execution of procedure calls on Intel's 432 processor are examined and used to derive ways of improving procedure-call performance in object-oriented systems.

D.M. England, "Architectural Features of System 250," in *Infotech State of the Art Report on Operating Systems*, Volume 1, Pergamon Press, Elmsford, New York, 1972.

D.M. England, "Capability Concept Mechanism and Structure in System 250," *Proceedings, IRIA International Workshop on Protection in Operating Systems*, 1974, pages 241-259.

D.M. England, "Operating System of System 250," *International Switching Symposiusm*, Cambridge, Massachusetts, June 6-9, 1972.

The previous three papers describe the features of the Plessey 250, the first commercial machine to incorporate capabilities and object-oriented techniques in both hardware and software.

M.B. Jones and R.F. Rashid, "Mach and Matchmaker: Kernel and Language Support for Object-Oriented Distributed Systems," *OOPSLA'86, SIGPLAN Notices*, ACM, Inc., New York, New York, Volume 21, Number 11, November 1986, pages 67-77.

An Object-Oriented Command Language

RICHARD SNODGRASS, MEMBER, IEEE

Abstract—This paper describes Cola, an object-oriented command language for Hydra; Hydra is a capability-based operating system that runs on C.mmp, a tightly coupled multiprocessor. The two primary aspects of Cola, that it is a command language for Hydra, and that it is based on the object paradigm, are examined. Cola was designed to effect a correspondence between capabilities in Hydra and objects that are supported by the language. Cola is based on Smalltalk in that it uses message-passing as a control structure to allow syntactic freedom in the expression of commands to the system. Cola objects are arranged in a hierarchy, and the message-passing mechanism was designed to exploit this structure by automatically forwarding an unanswered message up the hierarchy. Two ramifications of this mechanism, automatic inheritance and shadowing, are discussed. An evaluation of the design decisions is also given.

Index Terms—Capabilities, command language, knowledge representation languages, message-passing, multiprocessors, object-based languages, object hierarchies, Simula, Smalltalk.

I. INTRODUCTION

COLA is an object-oriented command language which grew out of a need for a comfortable user interface for Hydra [51], a capability-based operating system that runs on C.mmp [48], a tightly coupled multiprocessor. Hydra provides a comprehensive set of facilities to the user, yet the previous command language for Hydra (called the CL[1]) presented these facilities as an unrelated collection of procedures. The overall character of the operating system was not reflected in the way that the user interacted with the command language. In the design of Cola, much effort was expended to mirror the philosophy of the operating system in the command language. The incorporation of *objects*, similar to Simula classes, in the command language was a result of this objective.

That the concept of class might be a valuable addition to command languages is suggested by an analogy between the development of command languages and general purpose languages. When the hardware is first introduced, one programs in assembly language, due in part to a lack of higher level software, an inadequate understanding of what structuring concepts are useful, and a desire to make the most of a scarce resource. Assembly language programs can be characterized by their utilization of the full power of the hardware by building on only the basic facilities available. One command language analog to assembly languages is the OS/360 Job Control Language [31], which shares these same properties. As with assembly language, anything is possible in JCL, and almost everything is difficult. The first step toward making the machine easier to program was Fortran, which provides a few basic control structures, such as DO-loops and subroutines, as well as a few data structures, such as arrays and COMMON storage. The George 3 Command Language [33], which includes conditional and looping statements, as well as user-defined macros, embodies some of the advances found in Fortran.

Algol was the next major development in programming languages; concepts such as data types, block structure, and recursive procedures first appeared in this language. Similar ideas can be found in the Burrough's Work Flow Language [9], IBM's CMS language [18], OSL/2 [2], SCL [6], and the CL, although they have been adapted for a command language domain.[2] For example, SCL uses the block structure of a control program to limit both the scope of variables (as in Algol) and the scope of operating system resources, and the CL interprets certain names to refer to objects in the file system rather than in main memory. The next major step in programming languages (one that is currently still in progress) is the introduction of abstract data types [39]. The concept of class first appeared in Simula [3], with Euclid [25], Alphard [50], and CLU [30] continuing the emphasis on abstraction and modularization. Despite the advantages inherent in these developments, the concept of abstract data types has not yet appeared in command languages.

A similar analogy between general purpose languages and operating systems also suggests incorporating classes into the command language. In one sense, an operating system is merely a large, complex runtime system for the user's program. This was true before multiprocessing, and applies even more with the advent of operating systems for personal computers, which are usually single language machines [26], [35]. The concepts introduced in programming languages tend to be transfered to the runtime systems, as well as the operating systems, which support them [20]. Thus, there has been a flurry of activity in recent years concerning object-based operating systems [21], [34], [46]. In systems such as these

Manuscript received April 13, 1981. This work was supported by the Defense Advanced Research Projects Agency (DOD), ARPA Order 3597, monitored by the Air Force Avionics Laboratory under Contract F33615-78-C-1551. The author was supported by a National Science Foundation Fellowship.

The author was with the Department of Computer Science, Carnegie-Mellon University, Pittsburgh, PA 15213. He is now with the Department of Computer Science, University of North Carolina, Chapel Hill, NC 27514.

[1] The CL [37] is a general expression-oriented block structured programming language. The syntax resembles Bliss [49], the system implementation language Hydra itself was written in. Some features have been added (such as a capability data type) or altered (such as a more versatile assignment statement) to allow access to specific Hydra facilities.

[2] Lisp has also been taken as a starting point in the design of a command language [10], [29].

Reprinted from *IEEE Transactions on Software Engineering*, Volume SE-9, Number 1, January 1983, pages 1-8. Copyright © 1983 by The Institute of Electrical and Electronics Engineers, Inc.

where the concept of object pervades the programming language, its runtime system, and the operating system itself, the command language should provide consistency by also supporting objects.

This paper describes an object-oriented command language (Cola) for an object-based operating system (Hydra). The first part examines the correspondence between objects in Hydra and objects in Cola. The second part considers structuring objects in ways that have been found to be useful in structuring knowledge. Hence, this paper investigates the two main aspects of Cola: that it is a command language for Hydra and that it is based on the object paradigm.

II. COLA AS A COMMAND LANGUAGE

As indicated above, much progress has been made in providing more powerful command languages. There are, however, arguments for eliminating the command language completely, and instead embedding the functionality previously provided by the command language in the programming system, resulting in a programming *environment* with a uniform syntax and semantics [12], [16], [28], [38], [42], [43]. These arguments include not having to learn a different command language, being able to utilize the control and data structures present in the existing language when writing job control programs, and aiding the standardization task for command languages.

Despite these advantages, such an approach is not always appropriate. Each programming environment must be developed separately for each language that is desired. Also, it is very difficult to write a system in several different languages if each is supported by its own environment. Due to these reasons, plus the lack of existing systems that provide operating system primitives within the language, it is necessary to provide some kind of user-level interface that can interact with all these language systems. Since the operating system is the one entity shared by the users of the various languages, and it is the operating system that is providing the services that the command language refers to, it is appropriate to align the command language as closely as possible with the operating system [44].

A. Overview of Hydra

Cola is a command language that was designed for Hydra [51], a capability-based operating system that runs on C.mmp [48], a tightly coupled multiprocessor consisting of 16 DEC PDP-11's. The two most important attributes of Hydra—supporting a multiprocessor and implementing an object-based protection scheme—are relatively orthogonal. In Hydra, capabilities are protected pointers that refer to resources, both physical and virtual, called *objects*. Each object consists of an array of capabilities (a *clist*) and an array of integers (a *datapart*). A particular capability is referred to by specifying the index into a clist; similarly, data are referenced by indexing into the datapart. Since every resource in Hydra is associated with an object, all resources can contain data and capabilities. For instance, the datapart of a procedure object contains information relevant for execution and debugging (such as its trap and interrupt addresses, saved registers, etc.); the clist contains capabilities used by that procedure, including capabilities for *page objects*, which contain the code for the procedure.

In addition to using capabilities to support a very flexible protection scheme [7], Hydra provides powerful abstraction mechanisms. Objects are typed, and associated with each type is a set of procedures that can manipulate the representation of objects of that type. The user can define new types by specifying the representation of objects of that type in terms of types that are already defined, and by providing procedures that can perform operations on objects of the new type. In this way, Hydra types are analogous to the abstract data types of Simula or Alphard. Cola was designed to support this notion in a uniform manner.

Although capabilities and Hydra objects are quite different entities, the two terms are often used interchangeably. Hence, instead of refering to 'the length of the datapart of the object pointed at by the capability called "ACapa," ' one would refer to 'the length of the datapart of "ACapa." ' Also, the names of capabilities (and Cola instances, defined later) will be enclosed in double quotation marks, strings in single quotation marks, and the names of Cola classes will be in small capitals. These conventions will be followed in the remainder of this paper.

B. Objects and Message Passing

Cola is also based on the concept of objects. A *Cola object* is a potentially active piece of knowledge that communicates by sending messages composed of objects [17]. Cola is modeled closely after Smalltalk [13], [40]. Although it shares many characteristics with conventional languages incorporating abstract data types, Cola is unusual in that it uses message passing as a control structure to allow syntactic freedom in the expression of commands to the system, an important consideration in the design of an interactive language.

As an example of message passing, evaluating <object> + 4 means the message ' + 4 ' is sent to <object>, which interprets the message, and returns another object as a reply. In the procedural view, ' + ' would be an infix operator defined in the types within which the plus operator was valid. In Cola, the message ' + 4 ' is interpreted by the <object> itself. For instance, if the <object> were the integer 3, then the ' + ' in the message interpreted as ordinary addition, with the integer 7 returned; for the <object> 'a string,' the plus sign is interpreted as string concatenation, with the string 'a string4' returned. Each object can interpret a message in any way it sees fit. Message passing is entirely consistent with, and indeed, supports, the information hiding aspects inherent in abstract data types [19].

Every object in Cola belongs to a *class*, which is analogous to a type in other languages. The class, also an object, defines the messages that all its members can accept, as well as the semantics for each of the messages. It also defines the data structures that can reside in each member. The code that is associated with a class is shared by all the members of that class. Hence, the object 4 is a member of the class INTEGER; the object 'a string' is a member of the class STRING. The class structure is actually much richer than described here; more will be said when the object hierarchy is discussed in Section III.

C. The Cola/Hydra Correspondence

Cola was designed to effect a correspondence between objects (actually, capabilities) in Hydra and objects that are supported by the language: every object (capability) in the user's environment in Hydra is associated with an object in the user's environment in Cola. A system call embedded in a program can cause Hydra to perform an operation on an object referred to by capability mentioned in the system call. In the same way, a message can be sent to the Cola object associated with that capability to perform the operation. In responding to the message, the Cola object, as a side effect, executes the system call on that capability. Thus, there is no distinction between Hydra objects (capabilities) and Cola objects, resulting in an isomorphism between the two entities.[3]

To illustrate the Cola/Hydra correspondence, it is useful to examine the Cola equivalents of several object types defined in Hydra. The (Cola) class CAPA includes the operations which apply to all (Hydra) capabilities. The syntax for these operations is similar to record accessing in Pascal (corresponding to the conceptual view of an object as a record consisting of an array of capabilities (the clist) and an array of integers (the datapart), both indexed by integers). In the examples below, A and C denote instances of the class CAPA, S is a STRING, and x and y are INTEGERS. In accessing the datapart,

C . data [x to y]

returns a vector of INTEGERS, and

C . data length

returns an INTEGER specifying the length of the datapart. Similar operations apply to the clist. The operation

C . clist [x to y] vacate

removes the CAPAS in the selected slots of the clist.

A Hydra *catalogue* [1] is conceptually an array of capabilities indexed by strings (since it is still a Hydra object, it is implemented as a datapart and a clist). The Cola class CATALOGUE supports this conceptual view by interpreting a record access as a lookup operation on the CATALOGUE. So the operation

C [S]

looks up the entry S in CATALOGUE C and returns a CAPA. To remove an entry, execute

C [S] vacate

This correspondence is qualitatively different from the view of Hydra presented by the CL. The CL appears to the user as a set of predefined procedures which can operate on capabili-

[3]This is not strictly true, since there are Cola objects such as INTEGER which do not have a Hydra analog. (Ideally, Hydra would handle integers as objects, but the implementation makes small objects inefficient.)

ties. These procedures correspond directly to the system calls available to Bliss programs running on Hydra [8]. Hence the CL is effectively an interpreted Bliss (indeed, if Bliss were an interactive language, then the CL as implemented would have added little functionality.)

Although the use of Bliss as a base for the command language resulted in a rather powerful user interface, it suffered from the restriction that communication with the operating system can occur only via system calls. For example, the conceptual view of objects as records consisting of arrays is not supported in the CL. Instead, one retrieves the data of an object by executing a system call (actually, in this case an ad hoc extension was made to the CL to allow array accessing to be done on Hydra capabilities). Thus the CL does not provide an adequate conceptualization of the objects defined in the operating system. In addition, the CL lacks the ability to *dynamically* define new types at the command level, and to define operations associated with these types which are reflected via system calls to the Hydra objects that are referred to by the command objects.

Cola provides this functionality and, as a result, presents to the user a different perspective on the operating system. Cola integrates the objects supported by the operating system into the language itself (due to the Cola-Hydra object isomorphism), eliminating the cumbersome system call interface. Note that the implementation still uses system calls, but this detail is hidden from the user. Instead, the user interacts with the command language using the abstractions with which he or she is familiar, namely those supported by the operating system.

D. Nonobject-Based Operating Systems

The object concept in Cola can be usefully incorporated into command languages for operating systems that are not themselves based on the object model. The function of an operating system is to provide resources for user jobs that can be manipulated by the job by executing system calls. These resources are essentially typed objects (such as files, directories, I/O ports, memory) with operations defined on them (such as print, add entry, send a character, reserve), although they are not always implemented as such in the operating system. It is this thinking that has motivated research in object-based operation system, and the use of objects in the command language is merely an extension of this concept, independent of the use of objects in the underlying system.

III. THE OBJECT HIERARCHY

Although the main impetus for this research was the design of a command language for Hydra, the language that evolved out of this effort is interesting in its own right. Cola objects are useful not only as command language surrogates for objects (capabilities), but also have many properties that make them useful in models of computation [15] and in personal computer languages [14], [22], [45]. Since an object is an active piece of knowledge, one aspect of this research considered structuring objects in ways that have been found to be useful in structuring knowledge [32]. Although this aspect does not concern user interfaces directly, the mechanisms which evolved were useful in a command language domain. Cola uses a hierarchical ordering of classes coupled with an execution semantics and binding mechanism to represent static and dynamic knowledge within the class structure.

A. Simula Subclassing

Simula, the first language to incorporate classes, used a *subclassing* mechanism to structure objects. A *subclass* is a refinement of a class: it inherits all of the procedures and data structures of its parent class, and augments these with its own procedures and data structures. Subclasses can also be refined further by their own subclasses, resulting in a tree structure. An *instance* of a class contains the values of all the data structures defined in all of its defining classes. The subclassing mechanism of Simula is a static, compile-time structure that almost completely disappears in the runnable version of the program. Smalltalk-76 has a similar mechanism that is partially interpreted at runtime [19].

There are several advantages inherent in such a scheme. Since the subclass inherits all of the traits of its defining class (its *superclass*), the code for the superclass need not be duplicated. Instead, the subclass uses all of the code it needs from its superclass, and adds traits of its own. Thus the mechanism provides a powerful structuring capability to the language. Other advantages, due to the message passing mechanism, will be discussed shortly.

The disadvantages of subclasses stem from the decision to place all of the data structures in the instance. Information associated with a superclass is replicated in all of the instances of that class. This arrangement complicates the modification of data associated with a class located several levels above the instance, and invokes the traditional consistency problems associated with redundant data (such as how does one make sure that *all* the instances of replicated data have been updated). There is thus an asymmetry in the distribution of data structures and procedures in Simula: procedures are shared by all subclasses of the class containing the procedure; data structures are not shared at all, but exist separately in every instance (note, however, that the *names* of the data structures are shared in the same manner as procedures). The Cola subclassing mechanism has been designed to allow the sharing of data structures while retaining the advantages mentioned above.

The Cola subclassing mechanism orders all objects in a hierarchical fashion. At the top of the hierarchy is the class (or object, since all classes are objects) called OBJECT. OBJECT is associated with a set of classes (called *subclasses* of OBJECT) through the relation *subclass*. Similarly, each of these classes is associated with OBJECT through the relation *superclass*. Subclass is a many-to-one relation—a class can (and usually does) have many subclasses. Superclass is a one-to-many relation—a class is restricted to having a unique superclass, but several classes can have the same superclass. Thus the subclass-superclass relation produces a tree structure of classes, as in Simula, with the class OBJECT being the root node.

B. Naming

Associated with every class are three kinds of variables, permitting flexibility in the placement of the values of the variables within the object hierarchy. These variables are class variables, instance variables, and temporary variables. *Class variables* are named in the class and are associated with values that reside in the class. They correspond to **Own** variables, in that their value is shared by all instantiations of the class. (In Fig. 1, "B" is a class variable of "Three," with value "0.05".) *Instance variables*, on the other hand, are named in a class, but are associated with values that reside in the *immediate subclasses* of the class. They correspond to the data structures defined in Simula classes, except that the values are stored in the next lower level, rather than in the leaves (i.e., the instances) as in Simula. ("C" and "D" are instance variables of "Three," with values in "Four" and "Five.") Values for *temporary variables* are created on every invocation of the object they are associated with using the traditional stack discipline, and are destroyed when the object returns. They correspond to variables designated as **Local**, **Var**, or **Recursive** in other languages. ("E" and "ThisTemp" are temporary variables.) When a class is defined, the names of these three types of variables are declared. The name of the superclass must also be declared when the class is defined.

C. Instances

Instances are objects that differ from classes in only one way: there is no code associated with instances, whereas there must be code associated with classes. This distinction is not necessitated by the logical framework developed so far, but occurs because of the way that classes are defined. The restriction that results is that instances cannot create subclasses or subinstances. Therefore, instances appear as leaf nodes in the hierarchy produced by the subclass-superclass relation. (In Fig. 1, "Six" and "Seven" are instances, each containing values for the instance variables declared in "Five.")

Instances correspond to values of variables, where the type of the variable is the superclass of the instance. Hence the instance 3 has as a superclass the class INTEGER. The name associated with the instance corresponds to the variable itself.

Since instances do not have any code associated with them, they also do not have either class variables or temporary variables associated with them. Instances contain only the values of instance variables declared in the superclass of the instance.

Most of the statements expressed in the remainder of this section apply to all objects; where there exists differences for classes and instances, the differences will be noted.

D. Execution Semantics and the Binding Mechanism

The control flow is tied to the object hierarchy and allows procedures contained in a class to be shared by its subclasses (the sharing mechanism will be detailed in the next section). When an object is sent a message, the code for that object is invoked. If there is no code associated with the object (i.e., the object is an instance), or if the class does not recognize the message, then the superclass of the object is sent the same message (called *forwarding* the message). This process continues until some class recognizes the message, or the class OBJECT is invoked (OBJECT recognizes every message and responds with some default reply). A class recognizes a message by *returning* a reply. As an example, if the instance "Seven" (in Fig. 1) were sent a message, that message would be forwarded to the class "Five." If "Five" did not recognize the message, it would be forwarded again.

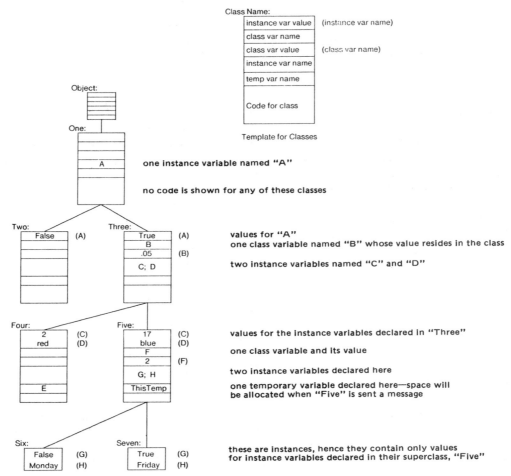

Fig. 1. A class hierarchy with the data structures shown (the arcs represent the subclass–superclass relation).

The binding mechanism is also tied to the object hierarchy and allows data structures to be distributed. The binding mechanism is a combination of static binding (for class and temporary variables) and dynamic binding (for instance variables). When a class is defined, the names of the class, instance, and temporary variables are given, as well as the code to be associated with the class. The binding mechanism for class variables appearing in the class code simply binds the name to the value that resides in the class. Temporary variables are bound to the storage allocated at the time of invocation. The binding of temporary variables remains in effect until the object returns a reply, at that time the storage is recovered and the binding broken.

The binding mechanism for instance variables is more complicated due to the possible forwarding of a message. If a message is being forwarded from a subclass or instance, then the instance variables are bound to the values which reside in that subclass or instance. If the class was the class that was originally sent the message, then there are no values to bind to the instance variables, and an error occurs if they are referenced. For example, if "Seven" (in Fig. 1) were sent a message which was forwarded to "Five," then "Five" would have access to the instance variable "G" bound to the value residing in "Seven." However, if "Five" is sent a message directly, there is no value to bind to "G." Cola provides ways to determine if the current class was the one originally sent the message, and

to name the class that *was* sent the original message. It is thus possible to associate different procedures with messages sent to a class and messages sent to a subclass of the class (analogous to *triggers* and *traps*, respectively, in KRL [4].)

The binding mechanism restricts the set of variables that may be referenced by the code in any given class. Since definitions must proceed in a top-down fashion (the superclass must be specified in the definition of a class), it makes no sense for a class to refer to a variable declared in one of its subclasses. Similarly, variables declared in a separate branch of the hierarchy are also inaccessible. To access a variable that is defined in a superclass, the class must send a message to its superclass requesting the value of the variable; this message is forwarded up to the appropriate superclass, which responds with the value of the desired variable. This process also applies to information contained in classes that are above the object originally sent the message, yet below the class currently dealing with the message, since a request for that information can be sent by a class to the class that was originally sent the message.

E. Automatic Inheritance and Shadowing

One of the ramifications of the execution semantics and the data structuring is the *automatic inheritance* by a class of the ability to respond to all the messages that the successive superclasses of the class can respond to.

As an example, the class CAPA responds to the message 'is ?'

by returning the STRING 'capability.' When the subclass CATALOGUE is defined, it automatically inherits the ability to respond to the message 'is ?' by simply forwarding the message up the CAPA. The subclasses FILE and TERMINAL also inherit this ability, as well as all the other operations defined in CAPA (and in the superclasses of CAPA, including OBJECT).

The mechanism of automatic inheritance is very useful. Simula [3] applied a form of automatic inheritance to build up an entire sublanguage suited to the construction of simulation programs. Most knowledge representation systems incorporate the concepts of *prototypes* (i.e., classes), *entities* (subclasses and instances), and *property inheritance* [47]. KRL [4], for example, includes a subclassing mechanism with automatic inheritance through the use of *perspectives*. However, sometimes this mechanism is not desired, as in the case of a subclass that needs to respond differently to a message than its superclass. In Cola, one can override automatic inheritance through the use of *shadowing*.

To illustrate shadowing, suppose that CATALOGUES were to respond to the message 'is ?' with the STRING 'catalogue' rather than 'capability' (the latter is correct, but the former is more precise). One way to do this is to have CATALOGUE *itself* respond to 'is ?' *without* forwarding the message up to CAPA. This enables CAPA to contain the commonality of its subclasses, and enables any subclass to respond differently to any particular message if it sees fit to do so. A second example of shadowing is the handling of messages containing 'vacate'. Most subclasses of CAPA do not recognize such messages, resulting in these messages being forwarded up to CAPA. However, CATALOGUE responds to 'vacate' *itself*, effecting a separate system call, since a different semantics is associated with this message when it is sent to a CATALOGUE.

The general mechanism can be summarized as follows: each class represents static knowledge (in the form of class and instance variables) and dynamic knowledge (in the form of the ability to reply to certain messages). Subclasses and instances automatically inherit the knowledge that is found higher in the hierarchical tree, and augment this knowledge with further knowledge. Through the use of shadowing, it is possible for a subclass to respond differently to a particular message than its superclass would have, thus making possible the expression of exceptions without nullifying the knowledge that exists higher in the tree.

IV. CONCLUSIONS

Essentially all of Cola has been implemented. The interpreter is written in Bliss/11 [49], with Cola code augmenting the low level objects. The static and dynamic structures are very similar to Smalltalk-76 [19], even though they were designed independently. It should be emphasized that Cola is an experimental system and very little effort has gone into tuning the implementation for efficiency.

There are several conclusions to be drawn from this effort. A useful correspondence between the entities supported by the command language (Cola objects) and those supplied by the operating system (Hydra capabilities) has been achieved. This correspondence is indeed "natural," in that there exist facilities in the language that support typed objects and the notion of operations (messages) that may be performed on

these objects just as the operating system does. It is argued that the Cola paradigm can be successfully incorporated into a command language for a conventional operating system, although this premise has not been demonstrated concretely with an implementation.

Arguments for the message passing (versus procedure call) mechanism are less conclusive. At a basic level, this issue does not apply, since a duality exists between message-oriented languages and procedure-oriented languages just as it does in operating systems [29], [36]. As an example, the command

A print

in Cola (which sends the object "A" the message *print*, causing "A" to print a representation of itself on the terminal) is equivalent to the statement

print(A)

in the CL, with the instance (in this case, "A") passed as a parameter. The entire message forwarding mechanism can be simulated in Simula, although it must be done explicitly using additional procedure calls.

The primary advantage of message passing is that it is simple and does not impose a strict grammar on the language. The latter is usually considered to be a disadvantage in general purpose languages, but is convenient for a casual user interacting with a system at a terminal instead of carefully composing his or her programs before typing them in. A secondary advantage of message passing is that the mechanism lends itself naturally to multiprocess(or) systems [52]. Although C.mmp, on which Cola runs, is a multiprocessor, this aspect was not dealt with in the design.

The primary disadvantage of message passing is that it is inefficient when implemented in the obvious fashion. This drawback is not as worrisome as might first be expected, for several reasons. In a command language, efficiency is not a primary concern, since, on the average, a relatively small number of statements are executed as a result of a command typed by the user [24]. It can be argued that a command language procedure that is unacceptably slow should be rewritten in one of the languages supported by the operating system [5]. In addition, the general message passing mechanism can be avoided most of the time in the interpreter (the semantics of the language would, of course, still be defined in terms of message-passing) by applying a few relatively simple transformations to the source before it is interpreted and by designing the interpreter so that it uses the local state to circumvent the message assembly mechanism except for special cases, primarily when an error occurs [23].

The object hierarchy, coupled with the message-passing and -forwarding mechanism, has been shown to have several useful attributes concerning the structuring of objects. Static knowledge, in the form of class and instance variables, is stored as high in the hierarchy as possible, eliminating redundancy at lower levels. Similarly, dynamic knowledge, encoded in the ability to respond to certain messages, is shared among many classes and instances. The mechanism allows flexibility in the placement of both procedures and data structures within the hierarchy.

One disadvantage is the restriction that the values of instance variables declared in a class must reside in each subclass of the class. This restriction can be removed by allowing more flexibility in the sharing of *names* of data structures within the object hierarchy. The names of class variables, for instance, are not shared at all, since both the names and the values reside in the class they were declared in. In Cola, the names (but not the values) of instance variables are shared by the immediate subclasses of the class they were declared in. In Simula, the names of instance variables are shared by *all* the subclasses. However, the optimal placement of the value (and the name) of an instance variable depends to a large extent on the semantics desired for the information contained in that variable (and the sharing of the name of the variable), and mechanisms for allowing more variability for the binding and storage of instance variables need to be developed.

There are several other ·areas where additional research is needed. It is not clear how one would incorporate multiple process(or) concepts into the language. Several possible alternatives seem likely, including utilizing the message-passing mechanism and/or allowing multiple objects to execute concurrently, but the ramifications these various schemes have on the language have not been investigated at all. More work is necessary to make the paradigm of objects communicating via messages a viable one in terms of efficiency (although much has been done in this area by the Learning Research Group at Xerox PARC [19]). Lastly, the techniques used to mirror the abstractions provided by Hydra in the command language should be applied to other operating systems, including more conventional ones, in order to assess the applicability of these concepts.

ACKNOWLEDGMENT

The CL [37] provided valuable insight into some of the inherent advantages and disadvantages of a command language under Hydra. Most of the underlying language concepts can be traced directly back to Smalltalk-72 [13]. The concept of classes and instances originated with Simula [3], and some of the concepts of the class hierarchy (especially the concept of shadowing) were developed independently by S. Fahlman [11] and were hinted at in the Pygmalion system [41].

REFERENCES

[1] G. Almes and G. Robertson, "An extensible file system for Hydra," Dep. Comput. Sci., Carnegie-Mellon Univ., Feb. 1978, available as CMU-CS-78-102.

[2] P. Alsberg, "OSL/2: An operating system language," Ph.D. dissertation, Cen. for Advanced Comput., Univ. Illinois, Urbana-Champaign, 1971.

[3] G. M. Birtwistle, O.-J. Dahl, B. Myhrtag, and K. Nygaard, *Simula Begin*. Philadelphia, PA: Auerbach, 1973.

[4] D. G. Bobrow and T. Winograd, "An overview of KRL: A knowledge representation language," Xerox PARC, July 1976, available as CSL-76-4.

[5] S. R. Bourne, "The Unix shell," *Bell Syst. Tech. J.*, vol. 57, part 2, pp. 1971–1990, July-Aug. 1978.

[6] R. F. Brunt and D. E. Tuffs, "A user-oriented approach to control languages," *Software–Practice and Experience*, vol. 6, pp. 93–108, 1976.

[7] E. Cohen and D. Jefferson, "Protection in the Hydra Operating System," in *Proc. 5th Symp. Operating Syst. Principles*, ACM, Austin, TX, Nov. 1975, pp. 141–160.

[8] E. Cohen et al., "Hydra kernel reference manual," Dep. Comput. Sci., Carnegie-Mellon Univ., Nov. 1976.

[9] R. M. Cowan, "Burroughs B6700/B7700 work flow language," in *Command Languages*, C. Unger, Ed. North-Holland, 1975, pp. 153–171.

[10] J. R. Ellis, "A LISP shell," *SIGPlan Notices*, vol. 15, pp. 24–34, May 1980.

[11] S. E. Fahlman, *Netl: A System for Representing and Using Real-World Knowledge*. Cambridge, MA: M.I.T. Press, 1979.

[12] P. H. Feiler and R. Medina-Mora, "An incremental programming environment," Dep. Comput. Sci., Carnegie-Mellon Univ., Apr. 1980, available as CMU-CS-80-126.

[13] A. Goldberg and A. C. Kay, Eds., *Smalltalk-72 Instruction Manual*. Palo Alto, CA: Xerox PARC, 1978.

[14] A. Goldberg and D. Robson, "A metaphor for user interface design," in *Proc. 12th Hawaii Int. Conf. Syst. Sci.*, 1979, pp. 148–157.

[15] I. Grief and C. Hewitt, "Actor semantics of PLANNER-73," in *Proc. 2nd Conf. Principle of Programming Languages*, Jan. 1975.

[16] A. N. Habermann, "An overview of the Gandalf project," Dep. Comput. Sci., Carnegie-Mellon Univ., CMU Comput. Sci. Res. Rev. 1978-1979, 1980.

[17] C. Hewitt, "Viewing control structures as patterns of passing messages," *Artificial Intell.*, vol. 8, pp.323–364, 1977.

[18] *IBM Virtual Machine Facility/370: CMS Command and Macro Reference Manual*, 1980. Order GC20-1818.

[19] D. Ingalls, "The Smalltalk-76 programming system: Design and implementation," in *Proc. 5th Conf. Principles of Programming Languages*, ACM, Jan. 1978, pp. 9–16.

[20] A. K. Jones, "The narrowing gap between language systems and operating systems," in *Proc. IFIP Conf.*, 1977.

[21] A. K. Jones, R. Chansler, Jr., I. Durham, K. Schwans and S. Vegdahl, "StarOS: A multiprocessor operating system for the support of task forces," in *Proc. 7th Symp. Oper. Syst. Principles*, Pacific Grove, CA, Dec. 1979, pp. 117–127.

[22] A. C. Kay and A. Goldberg, "Personal dynamic media," *IEEE Computer*, vol. 10, pp. 31–41, Mar. 1977.

[23] A. C. Kay, personal communication.

[24] B. W. Kernighan and J. R. Mashey, "The Unix programming environment," *Sofware–Practice and Experience*, vol. 9, pp. 1–15, 1979.

[25] B. W. Lampson, J. J. Horning, R. L. Lampson, J. G. Mitchell, and G. L. Popek, "Report on the programming language Euclid," *SIGPLAN Notices*, vol. 12, Feb. 1977.

[26] B. W. Lampson and R. Sproull, "An open operating system for a single-user machine," in *Proc. 7th Symp. Operating Syst. Principles*, ACM, Pacific Grove, CA, Dec. 1979, pp. 98–105.

[27] H. C. Lauer and R. M. Needham, "On the duality of operating system structures," in *Proc. 2nd Int. Symp. Operating Sys.*, IRIA, Oct. 1979, reprinted in *Oper. Syst. Rev.*, vol. 13, pp. 3–19, Apr. 1979.

[28] S. Lauesen, "Program control of operating systems," *BIT*, vol. 13, pp. 323–337, 1973.

[29] J. Levine, "Why a Lisp-based command language?," *SIGPLAN Notices*, vol. 15, pp. 49–53, May 1980.

[30] B. Liskov, A. Snyder, R. Atkinson, and C. Schaffert, "Abstraction mechanisms in CLU," *Commun. Ass. Comput. Mach.*, vol. 8, pp. 564–576, Aug. 1977.

[31] G. H. Mealy, "The functional structure of OS/360," *IBM Syst. J.*, vol. 5, no. 2, 1966.

[32] M. Minsky, "A framework for representing knowledge," in *The Psychology of Computer Vision*, P. Winston, Ed. New York: McGraw-Hill, 1975, pp. 211–277.

[33] M. D. Ostreicher, M. J. Bailey, and J. I. Strauss, "GEORGE 3–A general purpose timesharing and operating system," *Commun. Ass. Comput. Mach.*, vol. 10, pp. 685–693, Nov. 1967.

[34] J. Ousterhout, D. Scelza, and P. Sindu. "Medusa: An experiment in distributed operating system structure," *Commun. Ass. Comput. Mach.*, vol. 23, pp. 92–104, Feb. 1980.

[35] D. Redell, Y. Dalal, T. Horsley, H. Lauer, W. Lynch, P. McJones, H. Murray, and S. Purcell. "Pilot: An operating system for a personal computer," *Commun. Ass. Comput. Mach.*, vol. 23, pp. 80–91, Feb. 1980.

[36] L. G. Reid, "Control and communication in programmed systems," Ph.D., dessertation, Carnegie-Mellon Univ., Sept. 1980, available as CMU-CS-80-142.

[37] A. Reiner and J. Newcomer, Eds. *The Hydra Users Manual*. Carnegie-Mellon Univ., Dep. Comput. Sci., 1977.

[38] E. Sandewall, "Programming in the interactive environment: The LISP experience." *Comput. Surveys*, vol. 10, pp. 35–72, Mar. 1978.

[39] M. Shaw, "The impact of abstraction concerns on modern pro-

gramming languages," *Proc. IEEE* vol. 68, Sept. 1980.

[40] J. F. Shoch, "An overview of the programming language Small-talk-72," *SIGPLAN Notices*, vol. 14, pp. 64–73, Sept. 1979.

[41] D. Smith, "Pygmalion: A creative programming environment," Ph.D. dissertation, Stanford Artificial Intell. Lab., Stanford Dep. Comput. Sci., Stanford, CA, June 1975, available as STAN-CS-75-499.

[42] T. Teitelbaum, "The Cornell program synthesizer: A microcomputer inplementation of PL/CS," Cornell Univ., July, 1979, available as TR 79-370.

[43] W. Teitelman, *INTERLISP Reference Manual.* Xerox PARC, 1978.

[44] S. Treu, "Interactive command language design based on required mental work," *Int. J. Man–Machine Studies*, vol. 7, pp. 135–149, 1975,

[45] S. Warren and D. Abbe, "Rosetta Smalltalk: A conversational, extensible microcomputer language," in *Proc. 2nd Symp. Small Syst.*, ACM SIGPC, Dallas, TX, Oct. 1979.

[46] M. V. Wilkes and R. M. Needham, *The Cambridge CAP Computer and Its Operating System.* New York: Elsevier North-Holland, 1979.

[47] T. Winograd, "Breaking the complexity barrier (again)," *SIGPLAN Notices*, vol. 10, pp. 13–30, Jan. 1975.

[48] W. A. Wulf and C. G. Bell, "C.mmp–A multi-mini-processor," in *Proc. 1972 Fall Joint Comput. Conf.*, pp. 765–777.

[49] W. A. Wulf, R. K. Johnsson, C. B. Weinstock, S. D. Hobbs, and C. M. Geschke, *The Design of an Optimizing Compiler.* New York: Elsevier North-Holland, 1975.

[50] W. A. Wulf, R. London, and M. Shaw, "Abstraction and verification in Alphard: Introduction to language and methodology," Dep. Comput. Sci., Carnegie-Mellon Univ., June, 1976.

[51] W. A. Wulf, R. Levin, and S. P. Harbison, *C.mmp/Hydra: An Experimental Computer System.* New York: McGraw-Hill, 1981.

[52] A. Yonezawa and C. Hewitt, "Modeling distributed systems," in *Proc. 5th Int. Joint Conf. Artificial Intell.*, ACM, MIT, Aug. 1977, pp. 370–376.

Richard Snodgrass (M'81) received the B.A. degree in physics from Carleton College, Northfield, MN, in 1977 and the Ph.D. degree in computer science from Carnegie-Mellon University, Pittsburgh, PA, in 1982.

He is currently an Assistant Professor at the Department of Computer Science, University of North Carolina, Chapel Hill. His research interests include user interfaces and the application of database and artificial intelligence concepts to programming environments.

Mr. Snodgrass is a member of the IEEE Computer Society, the Association for Computing Machinery, and Sigma Xi.

DESIGN CONSIDERATIONS FOR THE IBM SYSTEM/38

Frank G. Soltis and Roy L. Hoffman

IBM General Systems Division,
Rochester, Minnesota

Abstract

The IBM System/38 is the product of advances in hardware and programming technology and brings to the small business computer market more function and ease-of-use than previous IBM systems in its price range. It features a layered design and a new high-level machine interface, which is discussed in this paper. Implementation of high-level functions in hardware and microcode is described.

Introduction

The IBM System/38, a family of small business computing systems, was announced in October 1978. Two processors, the 5381 Models 3 and 5, a complement of peripherals and programming support is offered. Systems/3, 32, and 34 established that a small business system offering simplified installation, operation, and maintenance appeals to a wide range of users. An overall design objective of the System/38 project was to bring to the small system user computing facilities once available only on large systems and continue to provide ease-of-use.

System/38 designers were challenged to provide a simplified system including advanced hardware and programming technology with enhanced system integrity. The answer, they found, was a layered design and implementation with each layer providing an interface highly independent of the implementation details of the other layers[1]. The top layer provides to the application programmer traditional high-level languages and utilities. The next layer, Control Program Facility (CPF), provides system control language and data base/device file definition language facilities. The most significant consequence of the System/38 layered structure is the third layer: a new high-level machine interface which makes programming more independent of hardware implementation configuration details than ever before. The System/38 machine interface differs from conventional machine interfaces because, in addition to basic computation, data manipulation, and branching operators, it provides system management functions which have been enhanced from the primitive level of most conventional machines to that traditionally found in supervisory programs.

The decision to provide high-level functions in the System/38 machine interface was based on several factors: the system management functions included have been successfully applied in previous systems, they exhibit design stability, and redundancy is reduced by standardizing and sharing common functions. Microcode implementation enhances the performance and/or operational characteristics of many of these functions. Technology is available which makes a high-level machine interface practical from a cost-performance viewpoint.

Dwelling on technology for a moment, consider what has happened to storage and logic since System/3 was introduced in 1969. Purchase price for an additional 16KB of 1500 ns/byte main storage for the System/3 5410 (Model 10) processor was, at the time of announcement, over $20000 (today the price has been reduced to $9100). Today the System/38 5381 Model 3 offers an additional 256KB of 1100 ns/4 bytes main storage for $5000, more than 64 times improvement in cost per byte and over 5 times performance improvement. Control Storage has also experienced cost-performance gains.

Packaging density has improved for both memory and logic. System/3 Model 10 logic chips typically contain an average of 6 circuits with a nominal circuit delay of about 7 ns. The System/38 processor logic chips contain up to 704 circuits with a nominal delay of about 3 ns, over 100 times improvement in density and 2 times improvement in performance. These advances in storage and logic technology allow the increases in storage for microcode and the additional logic circuits to efficiently execute the microcode that is necessary to implement the System/38 high-level machine interface at a competitive system cost.

Overview

The System/38 machine interface, like the programming support above it, is implemented in layers (Figure 1). The first layer is implemented as microcode executed in main storage. In addition to computation and branching operators, main store microcode includes routines which provide system management and system control function support. These include management processes of resources, addresses, objects, indexes, the data base, and source/sink devices. Facilities for handling authorization, events and exceptions, and machine performance observation are offered. Also provided are program translation and management functions.

Reprinted from *Digest of Papers, COMPCON S'79*, 1979, pages 132-137.

SYSTEM/38 MACHINE INTERFACE

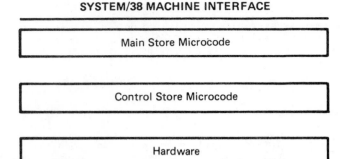

Figure 1   Machine structure

Main store microinstructions, whose operator-operand formats are similar to conventional level machine instructions, are executed by an interpreter which is one function of the control store microcode. In addition, control store microcode provides extensive task (process) management, I/O device management, virtual address translation, queue and stack manipulation, and object sharing facilities. Control store microcode, as the name implies, executes in control storage. Highly used routines are locked in control store while less critical routines are loaded as needed from main store to a control store overlay area. Each

overlay load contains up to 64 control words. Multiple overlay areas are provided and managed by a control store resident overlay supervisor.

System/38 hardware, shown in Figure 2, consists of a processing unit communicating over a high-speed channel to independently functioning I/O units. The processor and the I/O units have access to the main storage array. The processor, which is implemented in a new bipolar LSI technology, fetches 32-bit microinstructions from the RAM control store. There are 4K words of control store for the 5381 Model 3 and 8K words for the 5381 Model 5. One control store microinstruction is executed for each processor cycle. The processor cycle times are 400 or 500 ns for the 5381 Model 3 (200 or 300 ns for the 5381 Model 5) depending on the microinstruction operation. In a single cycle either one or two-byte arithmetic operations may be performed on signed binary, unsigned binary, or packed format decimal data.

High density MOSFET technology main storage is available at two performance levels: 64K bit chips offering a 1100 ns fetch cycle time for the 5381 Model 3 and 32K bit chips offering a 600 ns fetch cycle for the 5381 Model 5. Data path width is four bytes to either memory. Available memory capacities are 512K, 768K, 1024K for the Model 3 and 512K, 768K, 1024K, 1280K, and 1536K bytes for the Model 5. Error Correction Coding (ECC) is used in both models to provide single-bit error correction and double-bit error detection.

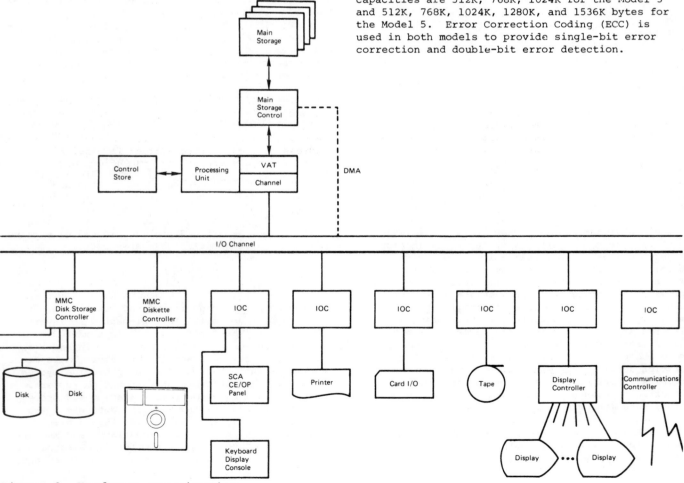

Figure 2   Hardware organization

Direct memory access for I/O units, as well as the processor, is provided by the Virtual Address Translation (VAT) hardware which converts virtual addresses to main storage addresses. Virtual addresses are used in I/O operations, and page faults are allowed during data transmissions with low-speed devices. Each I/O device is attached to a controller which is attached to the channel. Magnetic Media Controllers (MMC), implemented using high-density programmable logic array (PLA) technology, are used for high data-rate devices such as disks, while microprogrammed I/O Controllers (IOC) handle a multiplicity of lower data-rate devices.

Each system also includes a System Control Adapter (SCA) which together with the keyboard/display console share an IOC. The SCA performs the system maintenance functions including the ability to test the hardware logic circuitry.

Support for the High-Level Instruction Interface

During the design and implementation of the System/38, trade-offs between the various implementation layers of the machine were made considering system-wide cost and performance. Support for new architectural features of the machine interface is provided at each level of the hardware and microcode. In the following sections some of the features of the machine interface are described along with the unique hardware and microcode support functions. In addition, the reasons for implementing a function at a given level are discussed.

Addressing

To provide a high degree of system integrity the System/38 uses an object-oriented addressing structure. Some objects are similar to programs and data files of conventional systems while others are unique to the System/38.

The internal format of an object is not visible to the user. Since this internal structure is only accessible to the machine, object integrity can be assured. In addition, the space required for an object is managed by the machine, freeing the user from concerns about storage.

System/38 instructions are also object-oriented rather than byte-oriented. This allows the use of generic instructions, where a single instruction can be applied to many types of objects. For example, only one numeric ADD instruction is needed to operate on data of various types and lengths. In those situations where bit and byte-oriented operations are required, a special object, called a space, can be created. Within a space object the user can reference and operate on individual bytes.

Addressing to all objects and to bytes within space objects is provided through the use of pointers. A pointer is a 16-byte area contained in a space object. Pointers identify objects and can contain information about the status of the object, authorization characteristics, and even attributes of the object.

Pointers are used only for addressing. Because pointers are contained in space objects, their format is visible. In order to detect misuse or accidental modification of pointers, a protection mechanism is provided by the hardware.

Special tag bits are contained in storage to identify pointers. The main store for both the Models 3 and 5 is configured 40 bits wide: 32 data bits, 7 ECC bits, and 1 tag bit. The tag bit is set on to indicate that the four bytes of data are a part of a pointer. Four tag bits in consecutive storage locations must be set for a full 16-byte pointer. The tag bits are set and reset by the hardware and are not accessible through the instruction interface. Special instructions are provided to set or manipulate pointers in a controlled manner. The use of standard byte-oriented instructions causes the tag bits to be reset, making the pointer unusable for addressing purposes. These same tag bits are also maintained with the data on auxilary storage.

Single-Level Store

Object-oriented addressing is supported in the machine by a single-level storage management implementation. All main and secondary storage is treated as a single, uniformly addressable space. To provide such a large address space, the hardware implements a 48-bit virtual address. This yields a 281-trillion-byte virtual address space, large enough to contain all programs and data required by the system.

The functions required to support the single-level store are distributed among the two levels of microcode and the hardware. The management of the secondary storage and the movement of data between main and secondary storage is accomplished by the main store microcode. The translation of a virtual address to a main store address is handled by the control store microcode and the hardware.

Virtual address space is divided into 512-byte pages. Pages are stored on secondary storage in 512-byte units with an 8-byte header which contains the virtual page address and other information used for recovery/system integrity. Pages are moved to main storage when needed and are stored in 512-byte units called page frames.

A novel feature of System/38 is the address translation mechanism. Its job is to convert the page address portion (39 bits) of the virtual address into the page frame identifier. The 48-bit virtual address precludes using any conventional translation scheme having directly-indexed page tables since there are 2^{39} page addresses. Rather, an indirect scheme using a form of address compression known as hashing[2] is used.

The page address is translated to a frame identifier using the hash generation hardware and the two main storage tables shown in Figure 3. Each page directory describes a page frame in main storage. The index of a particular entry into the page directory is identical to the page frame identifier for that entry. The first entry of the page directory corresponds to the first frame of main storage and so on.

VIRTUAL ADDRESS

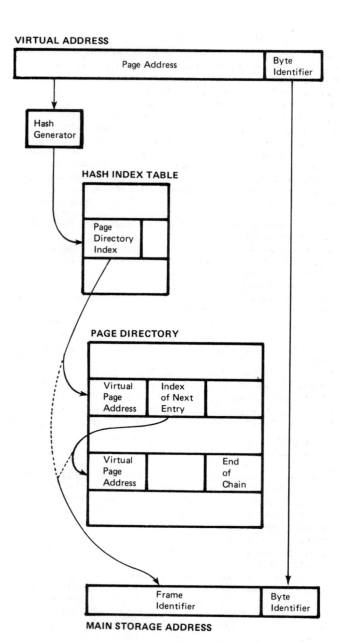

Figure 3   Virtual address translation

The page directory contains the translation information. One field of each page directory entry contains the page address of the virtually addressed page located in the corresponding frame of main storage. When this field matches the page address of the virtual address to be translated, the index of that page directory entry becomes the frame identifier for that virtually addressed page.

The hash generator and hash table are used only to select an entry from the page directory. Specific bits from the virtual address are combined by the hash generator to select an entry in the hash index table which contains an index into the page directory. Many virtual addresses can have the same hash value. A field in each page directory entry is used as a pointer or index to indicate

where additional entries with the same hash value, if any, are to be found. In this way all entries with the same hash value are chained together in the page directory.

To minimize the number of accesses to the page directory for each translation, it is necessary to have a large number of short page chains. To accomplish this the hash generator must provide a uniform distribution of hash index table entries. The actual hashing algorithm used takes advantage of the way addresses are assigned and used.

During any translation only one chain of page directory entries has to be searched. If a match of the virtual page address is found, the index of that page directory entry is the frame identifier for that virtual page. If no match is found, the desired page is not located in the main storage and must be brought in from secondary storage.

With both the hash index table and the page directory contained in main storage, an average of 2.25 main store accesses are required to perform the translation. This is comparable to other virtual storage systems which use conventional translation techniques. To improve the performance of the translation process, a 64x2-way set associative lookaside buffer is implemented in the hardware for both the Model 3 and the Model 5. This buffer contains the most recently translated addresses.

Object Sharing

An important part of resource management is the control of object sharing. How processes are allowed to acquire objects for their use is determined by the system strategy for prevention of deadlock and by the rules for object shareability. For example, the rules applicable to data files permit many processes to read a file but only one can update the file at any given time.

An elegant means for resource sharing is the access matrix[3]. The rows of the matrix correspond to processes, the columns correspond to objects. At the intersection is found either the access rights of a process to an object or, in the case of resource control, the current status of any hold or acquisition rights the process now has on the object.

A direct implementation of the access matrix for resource control is not storage efficient. There are many processes and many objects; the access matrix is a large array. Typically each process acquires only a few objects at any given time and thus, the matrix is sparse.

The System/38 implementation of the access matrix takes advantage of sparseness and uses hashing technology similar to that for virtual address translation to achieve a compact representation. Each element in a "hold" table contains an object identifier (its virtual address), a process identifier, and an indicator of the hold placed on the object by the process. Elements are chained together and accessed by hashing the virtual address of the object. An intermediate hash table is used. Special main store microinstructions are provided to access and update elements in the hold table. Example operations include adding or deleting a hold placed on an object by a process and finding all holds on an object. These operations require only a single chain be searched. Freeing all holds a process may have outstanding is used less frequently. This operation requires searching the chains for all objects on which the process has placed a hold.

Program Execution

The System/38 instruction interface is not directly executed in either the Model 3 or 5. A special instruction, called CREATE PROGRAM, is used to convert a program into an internal form, called a program object. A program object contains, among other things, an instruction stream with instructions having the same format as the main store microinstructions. With this implementation the interpreter contained in the control store microcode is used to execute a program object.

Instructions at the machine interface can be grouped into two major classes: simple computation and branching instructions, and more complex system control instructions. Most computational instructions are converted into computation-type microinstructions. These microinstructions were designed to support the operations performed by the instruction interface. They are heavily oriented towards storage-to-storage operations and perform such functions as adding two operands of different lengths together. In general, the simple instructions are converted into in-line microinstructions.

More complex instructions are converted into a special microinstruction called a Supervisor Linkage (SVL). An SVL causes a "call" at execution time to a routine in the main store microcode which performs the desired operation. The particular routine called is determined by parameters associated with the SVL. Another special microinstruction, Supervisor Exit (SVX), performs the return function from the routine.

Support for the call/return functions is provided in the control store microcode by using chained lists of save elements in storage. For an SVL an available element is obtained and the status of the processor, including register contents, is automatically stored in the element. Nested calls cause multiple elements, one for each call, to be chained together in storage. An SVX causes the state of the processor to be restored from the last element. This same call/return mechanism is also used by the processor to report numerous types of exceptions, such as page faults, to the appropriate main store microcode routines.

For those routines which require more temporary storage than is provided by a call/return element, another set of main store microinstructions can be used. Called STACK and UNSTACK, these microinstructions obtain and release variable sized blocks of storage from any number of push-down storage stacks. It is important to note that stacks in this system are used primarily for temporary storage rather than for transfer of control. The transfer of control functions use the call/return elements.

Tasking and Intertask Communications

One of the most unique aspects of the System/38 implementation is the processor control structure. All computer systems need to control execution and, in multiprogrammed systems like System/38, switch between units of execution called tasks. A traditional approach to implement this function is to build, on the hardware, an interrupt structure with a fixed number of levels or classes, and then use a software supervisor to transform this hardware into a multiprogramming structure which controls program execution. The System/38 replaces this interrupt structure with a single tasking mechanism to control all processing in the system.

A multilevel, queue-driven task control structure is implemented in control store microcode and hardware on the System/38. A task dispatcher implemented in control store microcode allocates processor resources to prioritized tasks. I/O and program processing tasks are integrated in a common dispatching structure with their priorities adjusted for system balance. I/O processing runs when system resources are available, not when an I/O interrupt occurs. I/O and program processing requests are stacked in main storage on a chained list called the Task Dispatching Queue (TDQ). The task dispatcher selects the highest priority request from the TDQ and gives it control of the processor. Instructions associated with this function, known as the active task, are executed until control is passed to another task.

The method used to synchronize the execution of tasks, as well as to communicate between tasks, is based on the work of Dijkstra[4]. A set of main store microinstructions (SEND and RECEIVE) is used to communicate between tasks and to pass control between tasks via the task dispatcher. If the active task is to communicate with another task, it does so by sending a message to a queue in main storage known to both tasks. If the active task is to obtain a message from a queue, it executes a RECEIVE operation. If the message is available on the queue, the message is passed to the active task and processing continues. If the message is not available (that is, if it has not yet been sent), the active task is made inactive and the task waits for the message. The task dispatcher is then invoked to select the new active task from the TDQ. The task dispatcher also is invoked on a SEND operation if a task of higher priority than the active task is waiting for the sent message. If the waiting task is of lower priority than the active task, the task dispatcher is not invoked, but the processing request for the waiting task is placed on the TDQ.

Another set of main store microinstructions called SEND COUNT and RECEIVE COUNT, use binary counters instead of messages to communicate between tasks. A SEND COUNT causes a counter to be incremented by one and compared to a limit.value associated with the counter. If the count equals or exceeds the limit value, the processing request for any task waiting for the counter is placed on the TDQ. A RECEIVE COUNT causes the counter to be decremented by the limit value if the count equals or exceeds the limit; if the count is less than the limit, the task executing the RECEIVE COUNT waits.

I/O Processing

I/O on System/38 is implemented with a queue-driven command structure using the same SEND/RECEIVE mechanism to pass information across the I/O interface. To a task, a device looks like another task. Commands to devices and responses from devices are exchanged in the same way that messages are communicated between any two tasks in the system. The messages sent to the devices are specially formatted and contain the device commands. In addition to individual commands, a complete channel program can be sent as a single message. Because a queue structure is used, command stacking is automatic. In a similar manner the device sends response and status information back to a task via a main storage queue. Note that only commands and responses use the queuing structure; data transfers between devices and main storage are direct.

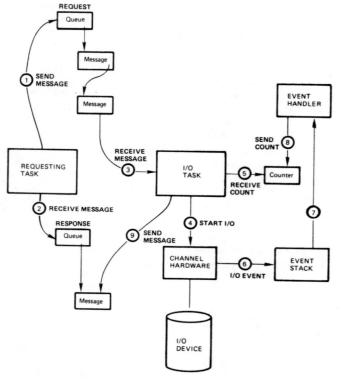

Figure 4 I/O structure

Figure 4 illustrates an I/O operation in the System/38. The task requesting an I/O operation sends a message containing the device commands to the request queue associated with the particular device. When the device response is required by the requesting task, it executes a RECEIVE from the response queue. If the response is not yet available, the task waits for I/O completion. The

I/O task obtains the message with a RECEIVE operation from the request queue. I/O tasks execute control store microinstructions, and one I/O task exists for each device on the system. The I/O task starts the device by issuing a command to the channel. The I/O task then waits for device completion by executing a RECEIVE COUNT operation to a counter with an initial count of zero and a limit of one.

The channel signals device completion by recording an entry on a special stack, called the event stack, and notifies the processor. A control store microcode routine, the event handler, removes the event from the stack and executes a SEND COUNT operation to the counter associated with the device which has posted the event. The waiting I/O task gets control of the processor and determines if the operation is complete or if additional commands to the device are required. If the operation is complete, the I/O task sends a message to the requesting task via the response queue.

Summary

The primary design objective for the System/38 was to provide the small user with a system which incorporates advanced hardware and programming technologies, and at the same time maintains and extends our commitment to ease-of-use. A further objective was to make the instruction interface independent of implementation and hardware configuration details.

The objectives have been met through the use of a new high-level machine architecture. The internal microcode and hardware layers absorb much of the complexity and shield the user from dependencies on specific low-level implementation details. This design allows future implementations to take advantage of new technologies and new hardware configurations without impacting the programming support or user applications.

References

1   A. S. Tanenbaum, Structured Computer Organization, Prentice-Hall, 1976

2   R. Morris, "Scatter Storage Techniques," Communications of the ACM, Volume 11, Number 1, January 1968, pp. 38-44

3   P. J. Denning, "Third Generation Computing Systems," Computing Surveys, Volume 3, Number 4, December 1971, pp. 175-216

4   E. W. Dijkstra, "The Strucure of the 'THE'-Multiprogramming System," Communications of the ACM, Volume 11, Number 5, May 1968, pp. 341-346

iMAX: A Multiprocessor Operating System for an Object-Based Computer

Kevin C. Kahn, William M. Corwin, T. Don Dennis, Herman D'Hooge,
David E. Hubka, Linda A. Hutchins, John T. Montague,
and Fred J. Pollack

Intel Corporation, Aloha, Oregon

Michael R. Gifkins

Standard Telecommunications Laboratory, Harlow, U.K.

ABSTRACT

The Intel iAPX 432 is an object-based microcomputer which, together with its operating system iMAX, provides a multiprocessor computer system designed around the ideas of data abstraction. iMAX is implemented in Ada and provides, through its interface and facilities, an Ada view of the 432 system. Of paramount concern in this system is the uniformity of approach among the architecture, the operating system, and the language. Some interesting aspects of both the external and internal views of iMAX are discussed to illustrate this uniform approach.

1. Introduction

The Intel iAPX 432 is an object-based microcomputer system with a unified approach to the design of its architecture, operating system, and systems programming language. Its underlying addressing structure is capability-based.[1] It incorporates support for data abstraction, typing, and program structuring, using Ada as its system programming language. The 432 also uses its object orientation as a basis for moving a number of critical software operations into the hardware.

A major goal of the 432 and therefore of iMAX has been to uniformly structure the hardware and software of the system around a single set of concepts based on objects. In addition to providing a common framework for the design of the system, this approach leads to an economy of concepts that eases learning and using the system. Once the notion of object-oriented design is understood, it can be applied equally well to all aspects of the system from the underlying VLSI hardware to the programmer's language interface. This property contrasts sharply with conventional systems that use quite different structures in their base hardware, central operating system, file stores, languages, etc. The major goal of this paper is to demonstrate the uniformity achieved in iMAX via the integration of concepts in the underlying architecture, Ada, and the operating system itself.

This paper presents an overall view of the 432 as seen through iMAX, its operating system.[2] As an object-oriented operating system, iMAX has its roots in the academic research embodied in systems like Hydra,[3,4] CAP,[5,6] StarOS,[7] and the CAL timesharing system.[8] After a brief overview of the 432 hardware, some of the most important external attributes of iMAX are described, then interesting aspects of the internal structure of iMAX and various issues that arise in designing an object-oriented computer system are discussed.

2. The 432 Architecture

Because the 432 blurs the distinction between hardware and software, it is worth distinguishing some important aspects of the conceptual architecture that are actually implemented in the two chip VLSI processor. The 432 addressing structure is capability-based. **Access descriptors** or capabilities* name entries in a global **object descriptor table.**

* The term access descriptor was chosen over capability due to its close correspondence to an Ada *access*.

"iMAX: A Multiprocessor Operating System for an Object-Based Computer" by K.C. Kahn, W.M. Corwin, T.D. Dennis, H. D'Hooge, D.E. Hubka, L.A. Hutchins, J.T. Montague, and F.J. Pollack from *Proceedings of the 8th Symposium on Operating System Principles,* Volume 15, Number 5, December 1981, pages 127-136. Copyright 1981, Association for Computing Machinery, Inc., reprinted by permission.

Each **object descriptor** in this table describes a segment of from 1 byte to 128K bytes in length. An object consists of two parts, one containing data and the other containing access descriptors. Each part may be up to 64K bytes in length. The one object descriptor for a given segment provides the physical base address and length of the segment, indicates whether the segment contains data or accesses, indicates what type of object it represents, and includes information needed for virtual memory management and parallel garbage collection. Each access descriptor (there may be many) for a given object contains rights flags that control the access available via that access descriptor.

The simplest type of object is generic for which no additional semantics exist. Other types of objects are recognized by the processor and are used to control its operation. Examples of these are processor, process, storage resource, and port objects. These objects are used by the 432 processor as a basis for providing a number of high level implicit operations and instructions. For example, ready processes are dispatched on processors automatically by the hardware via algorithms that involve processor, process, and dispatching port objects. Interprocess communication is provided by **send** and **receive** instructions that pass any access descriptor as a message via a communication port object. Likewise, memory allocation, user-defined types, and processor control are accomplished via instructions that involve other system objects.

Finally, the 432 supports small protection domains with **domain** objects. [9,10,11] These correspond to the package construct in Ada, namely, they are a structure for grouping and restricting accesses to the implementation of a module. The 432 subprogram **call** instruction performs the dynamic transition between domains, providing the proper addressing environment for any invoked subprogram via **a context** object. Much has been made of the cost of domain switching in a domain structured architecture. For comparison with other architectures, a domain switch on the 432 takes about 65 microseconds for an 8 megahertz processor with no wait state memory. This compares reasonably with the cost of procedure activation on other contemporary processors. Full details of the 432 architecture can be found in the 432 Architecture Reference Manual. [12]

3. iMAX Design Philosophy

For Intel, the 432 and iMAX are products primarily intended to be used by original equipment manufacturers in the construction of their products, rather than by than end-users. This means that support for minimum systems, range of application, and configurability are the most important iMAX goals. This is in marked contrast to a typical end-user system for which a particular application is defined (such as general purpose time-sharing) and whose facilities are targetted to that application. For such a system facilities needed to implement the application would be paramount. iMAX emphasizes breadth of support over depth.

iMAX is fundamentally a multiprocessor operating system, providing a tightly coupled environment in which all processors see a single homogeneous memory. The 432 hardware is designed to support multiprocessing in the standard configuration, and in fact makes the existence of multiple general data processors transparent to virtually all of the system software. With the bussing schemes designed for the 432, a factor of 10 in total processing power of a single 432 system is realizable. Multiple independent I/O subsystems provide a similar expansion for the I/O bandwidth of a single system. To support multiprocessing, therefore, it is merely necessary that the design of iMAX never assume that only a single processor is running. That is, all synchronization within the system must be explicit, never assuming that process priority or other scheduling artifact is sufficient to guarantee exclusion. Since this is a design principle that should be followed in a multiprogramming environment in any case, we will not comment further in this paper on the multiprocessing aspects of iMAX.

Given the 432 architecture, the relationship between iMAX and the 432 hardware is more preordained than that of most systems and their host hardware. iMAX is obligated to complete the model of computation supported in the hardware. Operations are provided in the 432 hardware for one of three reasons: they are time critical, thus benefitting from hardware implementation; they are security sensitive, thus requiring hardware enforcement; or they are complex in a way that benefits from special hardware structures on chip. iMAX is responsible for cooperating with the hardware to provide such remaining operations as initialization of complex objects, object maintenance, and object disposal. iMAX also extends the semantics of the hardware to provide a more convenient view of those abstractions that are built into the hardware.

Although some of the facilities provided by iMAX are actually realized as hardware primitives, iMAX provides a uniform external view of the 432 system through an interface that is expressed as a set of Ada specifications. Its users can be unaware of which operations have been implemented in hardware and which have been left to software.

Ada has been chosen as the systems implementation language of the 432 because its facilities complement the 432 architecture well. Packages in Ada provide a natural representation of type managers and map exactly the protected domain structure of the architecture. The specification/body distinction agrees with our desire to blur the hardware/software boundary and with the natural implementation hiding of the domain structure. The only area in which Ada falls short of our needs is that its design focus is a static, embedded environment. Since the 432 is intended for these as well as other, more dynamic applications, a few extensions[13] have been made to Ada to permit runtime type checking and dynamic package creation.

From an internal point of view, iMAX exploits the architecture to provide a more robust and flexible system than might otherwise be possible. The small protection domains supported by the language and the hardware are used to improve reliability. The uniform approach allows us to take full advantage of the duality between the language notions of data abstractions and the operating system notion of domains.

4. iMAX and Ada

The applications interface to iMAX is a set of Ada package specifications, each of which corresponds to a particular service provided by the system. This interface provides a uniform Ada view of both the underlying hardware and the iMAX extensions to it. Heavy use is made of generic Ada packages and in-line subprograms to provide an efficient but fully Ada typed view of the hardware. Unlike many systems for which calls to the operating system are very different from calls to other subprograms, the iMAX user sees no difference whatsoever between calling an operating system subprogram and calling some user-defined subprogram. This is particularly attractive for at least two distinct reasons. Compilers do not need any special mechanism for interfacing to the system. The standard calling sequences work for both system and user defined subprograms. Perhaps more importantly, any system interface can be mimicked by a user package. This makes it straightfor-

ward for a user to extend the system interface, trap certain system calls, or otherwise alter iMAX services.

As an example of how powerful this technique can be, we will consider the example of interprocess communication via the 432 port mechanism. This mechanism is more flexible than the Ada intertask communication model. It is used by the Ada compiler to implement the Ada model but is also available to the user who wishes the more general mechanism via a set of iMAX packages. The hardware defines a **communications port** object which functions as a queueing structure for interprocess communications. There are machine instructions available for sending and receiving messages via these objects. Full details of this model are provided in a companion paper. [14]

The simplest view of this mechanism is via the iMAX package specification Untyped_Ports, a fragment of which is shown in figure 1. The type *any_access* is predefined in the standard environment for the 432 and corresponds to an otherwise untyped access descriptor. Any Ada access type can be converted to this type but unchecked conversions are needed to do anything else with it. The type *port* is an Ada access to a hardware port object. Of the three subprograms specified in figure 1, Send and Receive will correspond to single instructions, while Create is software implemented. The Ada inline pragma provides efficient implementations of the first two.

The Ada code insertion facilities are used in the package body of Untyped_Ports to implement Send and Receive as the corresponding single instructions. This means that the compiler does not need any extraordinary knowledge of the 432 high-level instructions in order to permit the most efficient implementation. The Create procedure is implemented conventionally to provide proper construction of port objects. The 432 protection structures guarantee that only this package has the necessary access environment to create port objects. To the user of Untyped_Ports none of these details are important and a uniform view is provided to both the software and hardware parts of the port abstraction.

Since it is undesirable to force the user to escape from the Ada type system, another view of ports is provided via the generic package Typed_Ports, a fragment of whose specification is shown in figure 2. The user may create an instance of this package for any access type, thus creating a new Ada level type *user_port* that can be type checked at compile time to ensure that only objects of the specified *user_message* type can be sent.

```
package Untyped_Ports is

    function Create_port(
        message_count:    short_ordinal range 1 .. max_msg_cnt;
        port_discipline: q_discipline := FIFO)
      return port;
      -- Create a port with the given size and queueing
      -- discipline.
    procedure Send(
        prt:   port;                 -- port to which a message is
                                     -- to be sent
        msg:   any_access);  -- message that is sent
      -- The calling process will send the message to the
      -- specified port.  If the message queue of the port
      -- is full then the calling process will block until
      -- a message slot becomes available.
    procedure Receive(
        prt:   port;                 -- port from which to receive
                                     -- message
        msg:   out any_access); -- received message
      -- The calling process will receive a message from the
      -- specified port.  If no message is available the
      -- process will block until a message becomes available.
      -- The received message is returned to the caller.
    . . .
private
    pragma inline (Send, Receive);
end Untyped_Ports;
```

Figure 1: Package specification for hardware level ports.

The user of Typed_Ports thus maintains the advantage of strong compile time typing. The implementation of this package is in terms of Untyped_Ports and an unchecked_conversion from any_access to the user_message type. The inline facility allows the code generated for any instance of this package to be *identical* to that generated for the untyped port package. Thus the user of typed ports suffers no penalty relative to even a hypothetical assembly language programmer.

An important observation is that this approach is very general, needing no special compiler support. It is possible to take the idea of typed ports one step further in the 432 to provide the type checking dynamically at runtime. The implementation would require a few more generated instructions making use of user-defined types but would otherwise be the same as above. It should be apparent in this example that the consistency of the architecture, system, and language contribute greatly to reducing the set of things a user need learn about process communication. A similar effect is seen throughout the 432 system.

5. The Process-Memory Model of iMAX

A good example of the manner in which iMAX provides a smooth bridge between the base architecture implemented directly in the hardware and the set of user-visible operating system facilities can be seen in the process and memory model provided by iMAX. The 432 hardware provides the essential support for both processes and memory management. For process management, the hardware defines a process object which contains the necessary information for scheduling processes, dispatching them on any one of several potentially available processors, and sending them back to software when various fault or scheduling conditions arise. All hardware operations involving a process object occur implicitly, as the result of such events as time-slice end and successful message communications. For memory management, the hardware defines a storage resource object (SRO) which describes free areas of memory and provides the information necessary to allocate both physical and logical address space. Hardware operations involving memory management occur as a result of instructions such as *create object* which explicitly request a memory allocation. For example, assuming that sufficient free storage is available, it takes 80 microseconds

268

```
with Untyped_Ports;
generic
    type user_message is private;
                    -- Ada "private" indicates that no internal
                    -- details of this type are availble within
                    -- this generic package.
package Typed_Ports is
    --  This package enables the user to create ports and do
    --  simple operations on those ports involving only
    --  messages of type "user_message".

    use Untyped_Ports;

    type user_port is private;

    function Create(
        message_count:   short_ordinal range 1 .. max_msg_cnt;
        port_discipline: q_discipline := FIFO;
      return user_port;
        -- A user_port with the specified message_count and the
        -- specified message queue discipline is created.
    procedure Send(
        prt: user_port;        -- port to which to send message
        msg: user_message);  -- message that is to be sent
    procedure Receive(
        prt: user_port;             -- port from which to receive
        msg: out user_message);  -- received message
  private
    pragma inline (Send, Receive);
    type user_port is new port;
end Typed_Ports;
```

Figure 2: Typed access to the hardware mechanism.

at 8 megahertz to allocate a segment from an SRO via the creation instruction. It is important that this function be relatively fast since storage allocation plays an important role in an object oriented system. Actually a number of other system objects are involved in providing process and memory services, but these two suffice for this discussion.

iMAX provides operations to create and maintain both SRO's and process objects. It also extends the base architecture to further support the semantics of languages such as Ada.

To understand the latter role, consider the scoping and lifetime rules of objects in Ada. If a type is declared at the Ada library level then it exists forever. As a result, the lifetime of any object of that type is potentially infinite. Such objects may cease to exist only when they become inaccessible to any agent in the system. Proper implementation of these semantics require either an infinite capacity storage system or garbage collection. Types declared at deeper nesting levels than the library level come into existence anew whenever the scope of their declaration is entered and exist only as long as this scope. The lifetime of an object of such a type is constrained to be no longer than that of its type. This constraint is due to Ada's choice of name equivalence and is not applicable to languages that support structural equivalence of types. An object of such a type may never become accessible above the tree of dynamic environments rooted in the scope defining the type. A consequence of these conditions is that any object of such a type may safely be destroyed whenever the scope of its type is exited. Nevertheless, garbage collection may be necessary for objects of such a type if the lifetime of its scope is very long.

The 432 hardware and iMAX together provide exactly this model. Each object in the 432 has associated with it a level number which indicates the dynamic depth at which it is logically defined. Each context object (i.e., activation record) within a process has a level one greater than that of its caller. Each SRO creates objects with a fixed level number. The hardware ensures that an access for an object may never be stored into an object with a lower (more global) level number. The level numbers may be viewed as an indication of relative lifetime, where objects at level 0 are called *global* and exist forever while objects with higher level numbers are called *local* and have progressively shorter lifetimes. These rules are actually sufficient to ensure that the lifetime rules expressed above for Ada are maintained even though the same level number may appear in the execution of independent processes.

iMAX uses these hardware facilities to provide a uniform tree structure encompassing both processes and storage resource objects. An SRO that creates objects at level 0 is called a *global heap* and is always available to a process. A process may create an SRO with a level number corresponding to its current depth called a *local heap* and then create objects from it. Since access to these objects will not escape their proper environment, objects may be destroyed whenever their ancestral SRO is destroyed, without leaving dangling references. This SRO will be destroyed automatically when the process returns above the call depth to which it corresponds. A more detailed explanation of this model can be found in [15].

Processes themselves are each created from an SRO and have their lifetimes constrained just as described for all objects. This corresponds exactly to the Ada task model. Likewise, the 432 model of interprocess communication corresponds to the lifetime constraints on processes, ports, and messages. A group of tasks communicate with each other via ports defined in a scope common to all tasks in the group. Objects passed through these ports are of a type whose scope is no less global than the scope of the port. The ports and messages will exist at least as long as the processes which are depending on them for communication.

Once again the coherence of the architecture model with those of the operating system and the language should be noted. iMAX uses the primitive 432 objects to build a structure which corresponds directly to a model of a typed, statically scoped language with pointers. At the same time, a user is free to use global SRO's exclusively, or other combinations of local SRO's, to build models with differing lifetime properties. All objects are subject to garbage collection; those allocated from local SRO's will be collected more efficiently whenever their ancestral SRO is destroyed.

6. System Configurability

As indicated above, configurability is an important design goal for a system like iMAX. For the main function of the system, iMAX uses two complementary approaches: selection of needed packages and alternate imple-

mentations of standard specifications. Once again, both the 432 hardware and Ada aid in achieving the goal. The domain structure also provides a convenient mechanism for supporting various levels of device independent I/O.

6.1. Process Management Via Selection of Packages

As an example of the first approach, consider the case of process management. The basic process manager of iMAX completes the model of processes embedded in the hardware by providing the functions briefly described above. It does not arbitrate conflicting requests on the processor resource, however. It makes directly available to the user the dispatching parameters of the hardware and users are free to over-commit or otherwise misuse these parameters. The basic process manager's control primitives were chosen so that process schedulers can manage the physical processing resources of the system without being aware of the logical structure of process trees described in the previous section. For example, it supports nested stopping and starting of processes. Each process has a count of the number of stops or starts outstanding against it which determines if it is currently runnable.

Since starts and stops apply to entire trees, a user wishing to control a computation need not be aware of the internal structure of that process, i.e., whether it is implemented in terms of other processes. These counts are maintained by the basic process manager. Control requests can be passed through a process scheduler based on the basic process manager without being tracked, even though they will ultimately have an effect on the set of processes ready to consume system resources. Whenever an individual process would enter or leave the dispatching mix as the result of start or stop requests, it will be sent to its process scheduler. The scheduler can then make resource decisions by regarding it as an individual process without concern for the logical structure of a computation of which it is a part. Of course this structure may be examined by the scheduler if desired.

Using this basic process manager, many resource control policies are possible. For example, the null policy simply passes through the dispatching parameters of the hardware and permits its users to commit them in any way they wish. This is completely acceptable for simple embedded systems in which the system load can be preevaluated.

On the other hand, it is clearly unacceptable in a multi-user environment where the processing resource must be allocated fairly. For this and other more complex applications a user-process manager may build much more complex policies on the basic process manager to provide a safer or more tailored application interface. The protection structures guarantee that only this second manager would then have access to the basic process management facility. The system is configured by selecting those packages that provide the facilities needed in a particular application: just the basic process manager, it plus some simple scheduler, or an arbitrarily complex resource controller.

6.2. Memory Management Via Alternate Implementations

As an example of the second approach to configurability, consider the case of memory management. Virtually all processes make use of memory management facilities via a standard interface that permits allocation of new objects. Few processes depend upon whether the underlying implementation includes swapping or not. A single Ada specification defines the common interface. This interface defines mechanisms corresponding to the stack allocation, global heap allocation, and local heap allocation described earlier. Both a swapping and a non-swapping implementation meet this specification but are optimized internally to the level of function they provide. Each may provide an additional management interface that can be used by resource managers or others that need information specific to the implementation. The system is configured by selecting one of the alternate implementations; most applications will not be affected by this selection. We have implemented the non-swapping version for the first release of the system, and are currently building a swapping version for the second release.

6.3. I/O Device Independence

iMAX is implemented entirely in a superset of Ada. The extensions are defined to permit full use of the more dynamic environment afforded by the 432 as compared to the very static one assumed by pure Ada. The major extension is the raising of packages to the status of types. This allows multiple instances of a module to be dynamically created and multiple implementations of a single package specification to coexist within a single system.

The clearest example of the use of this facility occurs in I/O. A single specification is defined for device independent input and another for device independent output. Each instance of an I/O device may have a distinct implementation. The user interacts with each device identically but the code is specific to the device. This is really a different approach from conventional device independent I/O because it avoids any centralized I/O control or interface. Any user can create a new device implementation which will behave identically to existing ones without in any way altering system code, say to update a master I/O device list or to add a new element to a *case* construct in the system I/O controller. We actually go one step further with this approach by requiring only that a device implementation provide the common device independent interface as a subset. Thus device dependent I/O fits smoothly into the scheme. Any device interface will consist of a domain in which the first set of operations are the device independent ones and any additional operations are more device specific. In fact, classes of devices may share a specification which includes more than the minimum set of device independent operations, thus providing class dependent but device independent interfaces.

7. The Internal View of iMAX

7.1. Hardware Type Enforcement

One interesting aspect of the implementation is the hardware enforcement of protection both at the operating system interface and within the operating system itself. This attribute of any hardware-implemented capability-based system has several ramifications within iMAX. First, a module's access is routinely limited to the objects which it manages. Thus, for example, the process management module has no access to memory management structures. Second, the object orientation of the system implies that at any given time, a package will generally have access to only a single instance of the type that it manages. For example, there is no central table of all processes in the system. Rather, the manager acquires an access for a given process object, either from the hardware dispatching mechanism or from a user, whenever it is asked to perform an operation upon it. Damage due to a machine error or latent program bug is limited to the particular object with which the module is dealing at a given moment.

This second property has an interesting side effect. Global system inquiries which are easily answered in most systems by consulting some central table become difficult to answer in this style of system. For example, the process manager does not know what all the processes in the system are. While it would be possible to link together all processes, this would be problematic for garbage collection since all processes would then always be accessible. It is an interesting philosophical question whether such inquiries should be permitted; it is a convenient tenet of the capability approach to protection that they should not.

7.2. Hardware Type Enforcement

Another interesting aspect of the implementation is that the hardware type enforcement dictates that even objects that originate in applications coded in a language other than Ada are fully protected from misuse. Just as important for Ada programs is that objects are fully protected even when they pass through channels which might cause them to lose their compile-time type identity. An example of such a channel is any storage system. By the definition of Ada, if a storage system exists before the compilation of a package, then it cannot know of and therefore cannot preserve the type of some object that it is asked to store. In general, unchecked conversions need to be used to store and later retrieve objects, thus compromising type security. No matter what path a system object follows within the 432, its hardware-recognized type identity is guaranteed to be preserved and checked, either by the hardware or by object filing. [16] Moreover, via the user type definition facilities of the 432 such a guarantee is available to any user defined object type as well as to those object types recognized by the hardware.

7.3. Levels and Abstractions in iMAX

The strong adherence to notions of data abstraction in the design of iMAX provide a very clear example of the difference between levels and abstractions discussed by Habermann *et al.* [17] Internally, the system is constructed as a set of Ada packages each of which provides a well defined abstraction. Even within the system the inter-package interfaces are rigidly enforced. Only the well-defined operations defined in the package specifications are available to the other parts of the system.

It is quite reasonable that a set of abstractions be mutually dependent at the module level. For example, there are interdependencies between parts of memory and process management. On the other hand, it is important that the design of the system not include any circular dependencies among functions that might cause deadlocks to occur. Additionally, the clean virtual environment provided at the user interface level of the system

must be built up in stages. For example, processes at the user level should be unaware of the possibility that a segment might be being moved and therefore be inaccessible for some period of time. Processes deep within the system, on the other hand, may depend on the fact that such a situation will not arise.

To solve these problems, the implementation of iMAX defines a set of levels which dictate what operations are permitted to processes at that level. Processes below level 3 of the system, for example, are in general not permitted to fault. Processes at level 2 are actually permitted a limited set of timeout faults while those at level 1 are not permitted even these. To avoid dependency couplings, all communications between levels 2 and 3 of the system must be asynchronous and upward communication must never depend upon a reply. The implementation of a given abstraction may span several levels. These design guidelines span all abstractions and thus represent an orthogonal way of viewing the internal structure of the system. From one view each function is a part of the abstraction to which it relates regardless of the constraints under which it operates. From the other view, each function operates at the level in the system determined by those constraints.

8. Issues in the Design of an Object-Oriented System

In this section two issues are discussed that arise in the design of a system such as iMAX: garbage collection and object finalization. These will in fact be issues for any system that ruthlessly follows the approach to design implied by Ada. A third issue, object filing, is discussed at length in a companion paper. [16]

8.1. Garbage Collection

The first issue is garbage collection. The general provision of global heap allocation in most modern languages demonstrates the desirability of removing questions of memory allocation from the programmer's concern. Unfortunately, explicit deletion of heap objects is prone to dangling reference problems. Furthermore, when an object is part of a complex data base of information, it is often difficult or impossible to know when the object should be deleted. The 432 approach to this issue is to remove questions of memory deallocation as well as questions of memory allocation from the programmer's concern. We noted above that objects whose types are defined at the library level may only be reclaimed via garbage collection. iMAX provides a system-wide parallel garbage collector based upon the algorithm of Dijkstra *et*

272

al.[18] To support this, the 432 hardware implements the *gray* bit of that algorithm, setting it whenever access descriptors are moved. When there is a natural expression within the programming language of a constraint upon the lifetime of an object, iMAX can take advantage of this to optimize deallocation via the local heap memory allocation strategy mentioned above.

The iMAX garbage collector is implemented as a daemon process that globally scans the system. It requires only minimal synchronization with the rest of the operating system. The local heap and level mechanisms effectively partition the system into nested sets of objects based on lifetime. Since object references can never escape from the level of the nest at which they were created, a local garbage collection strategy could be added to our global one. It would be possible to perform garbage collection on a local basis, either asynchronously or synchronously, but we have not chosen to do this until we have data that suggests that it would be worthwhile.

It is perhaps worth noting that the Ada literature is curiously ambivalent about facing up to the issue of garbage collection. This has been noted in a different context when Ada was evaluated as a language for the implementation of AI applications.[19] Avoidance of the problem will likely lead to either contorted programming styles or to the continued presence of dangling pointer problems in complex systems.

8.2. Object Finalization

Another interesting issue in the design of an object-oriented system is object finalization and lost objects. While most languages provide some form of initialization for structures, they do not address finalization of those same objects. So long as the objects in question do not have any dual in the real world, this may be an acceptable position. When an object represents a physical resource of some sort, however, it becomes very important that its type manager be able to describe how that object is destroyed as well as how it is created. Consider for example an implementation of a tape drive in which each drive is represented by an object of type **tape_drive**. In Ada terms, this would be a private type. A user requests from the managing package a tape_drive instance, calls operations in that package to use it and eventually to close or return it. If, however, the user loses access to the object through accident or intent, it will be garbage collected and the system will be short one tape drive. This is what we mean by a lost object.

While narrow solutions may be available for individual cases, they often will pervert a natural implementation design in undesirable ways. A general solution would permit a type manager to guarantee that an object is properly disassembled when it becomes garbage. iMAX provides the notion of a destruction filter for exactly this purpose. Since all objects may be typed, the garbage collector can recognize when an object of a particular type has been found. A type manager can specify to the system via a type definition object that it wishes to have an opportunity to see any of its objects as they become garbage. The garbage collector will manufacture an access descriptor for such objects and send them to a port defined by the type manager. The first release of iMAX uses this facility only to recover lost process objects. The next release will make the facility generally available in the context of object filing.

9. Project Status

The first release of iMAX is now undergoing field test and will be shipped for general customer use in early 1982. Portions of this version have been running in our laboratory since late spring of this year. Since a fairly rigorous methodology of design and code review was followed in its implementation, most of the problems that we encountered during debugging have been the result of compiler or hardware problems. As with most new computer development efforts, the operating system has been the first major test for all other system components. The first release of the system is non-swapping and concentrates on providing a development and debugging base for customer applications. Most of the detailed design of the second major release of the system is complete and implementation is now underway. This release includes swapping support and object filing.

10. Conclusions

A paramount concern in the design of the 432 system has been the conceptual uniformity of the architecture, operating system, and language. In addition to the aesthetics of this uniformity, it has a number of practical benefits. These include a more flexible and safer programming environment. Extensibility is enhanced because the system software is not fundamentally different from user software. Once the object paradigm is learned, the user can apply it to all aspects of the system. Special treatment is not required when crossing boundaries in the system between hardware and software, language and system, virtual storage and files. The overall learning burden is reduced.

By providing the notion of domains and capability/object-oriented addressing in the architecture, proper support has been given to such language issues as garbage collection and dangling pointers. By reflecting the module structure of the language in the system, configurability has been enhanced. Overall, the 432 represents an entire system constructed around the single notion of supporting an object oriented approach to program design. iMAX plays a key role by completing the architecture within an Ada framework to provide a comprehensive base for the design of advanced computer applications.

Acknowledgements

This work has benefited greatly from the creative environment generated by all of the members of Intel's Special Systems Operation. Particular note should be paid to Justin Rattner and George Cox, principal architects, to Konrad Lai and Dan Hammerstrom, who were responsible for the microcode of the processor, and to Gary Raetz, for his work on an earlier prototype of iMAX. Special thanks should also go to the Ada compiler implementors, Steve Zeigler, Bob Johnson, Jim Morris, and Greg Burns, for their outstanding work in bringing up a very comprehensive Ada compiler in an amazingly short period of time.

References

1. R. S. Fabry, "Capability Based Addressing," *Communications ACM* **17**(7) pp. 403-412 (July, 1974).

2. K. C. Kahn and F. J. Pollack, "An Extensible Operating System for the Intel 432," *Proceedings Compcon Spring 1981*, pp. 398-404 (February, 1981).

3. W. Wulf, E. Cohen, W. Corwin, A. Jones, R. Levin, and F. Pollack, "HYDRA: The Kernel of a Multiprocessor Operating System," *Communications ACM* **17**(6) pp. 337-345 (June, 1974).

4. W. Wulf, R. Levin, and S. Harbison, *Hydra: C.mmp: An Experimental Computer System*, McGraw—Hill Book Company (1981).

5. R. M. Needham and R. D. H. Walker, "The Cambridge CAP Computer and its Protection System," *Proceedings of the 6th Symposium on Operating System Principles*, (November, 1977).

6. M. V. Wilkes and R. M. Needham, *The Cambridge CAP Computer and its Operating System*, Elsevier North Holland (1979).

7. A. K. Jones, R. J. Chansler, I. D. Durham, K. Schwans, and S. R. Vegdahl, "StarOS, a Multiprocessor Operating System for the Support of Task Forces," *Proceedings of the 7th Symposium on Operating System Principles*, pp. 117-127 (December, 1979).

8. B. Lampson and H. Sturgis, "Reflections on an Operating System Design," *Communications of the ACM* **19**(5) pp. 251-265 (May, 1976).

9. D. Cook, "In Support of Domain Structure for Operating Systems," *Proceedings of the 7th Symposium on Operating System Principles*, pp. 128-130 (December, 1979).

10. P. J. Denning, "Fault—Tolerant Operating Systems," *Computing Surveys* **8**(4) pp. 359-389 (December, 1976).

11. T. A. Linden, "Operating System Structures to Support Security and Reliable Software," *Computing Surveys* **8**(4) pp. 409-445 (December, 1976).

12. Intel 432 GDP Architecture Reference Manual, Intel Corporation 1981.

13. S. Zeigler, N. Allegre, D. Coar, R. Johnson, J. Morris, and G. Burns, "The Intel 432 Ada Programming Environment," *Proceedings Compcon Spring 1981*, pp. 405-410 (February, 1981).

14. G. W. Cox, W. M. Corwin, K. Lai, and F. J. Pollack, "A Unified Model and Implementation for Interprocess Communication in a Multiprocessor Environment," *Proceedings of the 8th Symposium on Operating System Principles*, (December, 1981).

15. F. J. Pollack, G. W. Cox, D. W. Hammerstrom, K. C. Kahn, K. K. Lai, and J. R. Rattner, "Supporting Ada Memory Management in the iAPX-432," *Symposium on Architectural Support for Programming Languages and Operating Systems*, (March, 1982). Submitted

16. F. J. Pollack, K. C. Kahn, and R. M. Wilkinson, "The iMAX-432 Object Filing System," *Proceedings of the 8th Symposium on Operating System Principles*, (December, 1981).

17. A. N. Habermann, L. Flon, and L. Cooprider, "Modularization and Hierarchy in a Family of Operating Systems," *Communications ACM* **19**(5) pp. 266-272 (May, 1976).

18. E. W. Dijkstra, L. Lamport, A. J. Martin, C. S. Scholten, and E. M. F. Steffens, "On-the-Fly Garbage Collection: An Exercise in Cooperation," *Communications ACM* **21**(11) pp. 966-975 (November, 1978).

19. R. L. Schwartz and P. M. Melliar-Smith, "On the Suitability of Ada for Artificial Intelligence Applications," SRI Technical Report (July, 1980).

The iMAX-432 Object Filing System

Fred J. Pollack, Kevin C. Kahn, and Roy M. Wilkinson

Intel Corporation, Aloha, Oregon

ABSTRACT

iMAX is the operating system for Intel's iAPX-432 computer system. The iAPX-432[1] is an object-oriented multiprocessor architecture that supports capability-based addressing. The object filing system is that part of iMAX that implements a permanent reliable object store.

In this paper we describe the key elements of the iMAX object filing system design. We first contrast the concept of an object filing system with that of a conventional file system. We then describe the iMAX design paying particular attention to five problems that other object filing designs have either solved inadequately or failed to address. Finally, we discuss an effect of object filing on the programming semantics of Ada.

1. Introduction

The object filing system of iMAX is responsible for supporting the permanent storage of 432 objects in a manner that is consistent with the access control mechanisms of the hardware. It is a store permitting the storage and retrieval of any 432 object, simple or complex, while safeguarding all essential characteristics of the object including, most significantly, its identity, type, and structure.

The iMAX object filing system differs from conventional file systems. In such systems, the filing store is organized as a tree-structured hierarchy where the interior nodes are directories and the leaf nodes are files. Most files are used to store unstructured data streams. Since programs in such systems map into relatively flat and static addressing structures, they may also be stored in files as an unconnected collection of pages or segments.

In contrast, the iMAX object filing system is responsible for the 432 **object space**, the collection of all objects in the system. Although simple unstructured data is contained in this space, it in general has much more structure. It can be viewed as a network in which a node is an object and a directed arc from node A to node B is an access descriptor contained in object A which references object B. Any object may contain access descriptors for other objects. Such references may be circular and may cross device boundaries. Because the 432 supports a more dynamic and structured addressing environment, a 432 program consists of a network of objects connected by access descriptors. Object filing stores such a network on a permanent memory device (e.g. disk) in a manner consistent with the 432 architecture. In addition to programs, the object filing system can also be used to store structured data. This is accomplished by extending the protection and addressing mechanisms of the architecture from volatile memory to permanent memory. The result is a computer system in which all facets of protection are based on a single mechanism. In contrast, conventional computer systems implement several protection mechanisms, one for memory, a different one for files, a third for directories, a fourth for privileged programs or users, and so forth. Without doubt, the use of multiple mechanisms creates difficulties where the

"The iMAX-432 Object Filing System" by F.J. Pollack, K.C. Kahn, and R.M. Wilkinson from *Proceedings of the 8th Symposium on Operating System Principles*, Volume 15, Number 5, December 1981, pages 137-147. Copyright 1981, Association for Computing Machinery, Inc., reprinted by permission.

different mechanisms must interface, e.g. a particular file protection indicates a particular memory protection if the file contains a runnable program. The difficulty in defining the interfaces between protection mechanisms also leads to a lack of security. For example, on most systems it is impossible for a user to run a program and limit that program's access to the user's files.

2. Overview

Object filing systems have been implemented in two commercial systems, IBM System/38[2] and the Plessey/250. [3] There have also been two research implementations, for the Hydra[4,5] and CAP[6,7,8] operating systems. In addition, MIT has done significant research in this area. [9,10,11] In this paper, we give special emphasis to five problems. These are problems that previous designs have either solved inadequately or failed to address. While we will describe these problems in more detail as we present the iMAX design, we begin with a brief description of them.

The first problem is assuring the uniqueness of object names across system boundaries. An access descriptor in the object store contains a name for the object which it references. If uniqueness of object names were not assured, the movement of an object from one system to another (e.g. moving a disk pack containing objects) could result in a loss of protection; i.e., a moved object's access descriptor could reference an object with the same name as the one referenced on the originating system.

The second problem is providing an object-oriented, logical naming mechanism. Unlike conventional systems in which absolute object identification is difficult but indirect naming is easy, capability-based systems have the problem that names may be too tightly bound to their referants. For example, a user program normally should contain a logical name for a utility program in order to get the most recent version, as opposed to the version of the utility that existed when the user program was compiled and linked. If the user program holds an absolute access descriptor to the utility, this will not occur.

The third problem is maintaining the consistency of a collection of objects across updates, i.e. supporting atomic actions. This involves the ability to make a group of changes, called a transaction, to a collection of objects such that if the system crashes, either all the changes or none of the changes that make up the transaction will be reflected in the collection. While this problem is addressed by most data base systems, it is considered by very few operating systems.

The fourth problem is the efficient management of the object space. The major aspect of this problem is the reclamation of space that is no longer needed. Because of the network organization of the object space, it is difficult to know when the space for an object can be reclaimed.

The fifth and final problem to receive special consideration in this paper is the inefficiecy, both in space and time, of dealing with small objects. In Hydra measurements, [12] the average size of an object in the filing store (i.e. the Hydra passive GST) was 222 bytes. In the active system, the average was 326 bytes. In Batson's study of the B5500 MCP, [13] the average size of Overlayable Data Segments was 59 48-bit words. Both studies emphasize a preponderance of small objects. Our initial data indicate that the average size of an object on the 432 will be slightly less than these figures. The space overhead for storing such small objects could be large. Also, if small objects had to be accessed individually, the performance of the system would suffer. For example, since a large 432 program will typically consist of hundreds of objects, the loading of such a program would be grossly inefficient if each object had to be loaded individually. Consequently, grouping objects is essential to providing acceptable performance and space utilization.

In the next section, we discuss the role of type managers in the overall design of iMAX. Following that, we describe the structure of the object space. We then present the object filing extensions to the protection and addressing mechanisms of the 432 architecture. Then we describe an example of object filing on programming semantics. Finally, we review how the iMAX object filing design has addressed the problems we stated above.

3. Types And Their Managers

The major goal of iMAX[14,15] is to provide Intel customers, principally original equipment manufacturers, with an extensible operating system. This is made possible by the 432's uniform approach in the design of its hardware, operating system, and language. The key element in this approach is support for data abstraction. The architecture provides efficient hardware operations that enable a user to define a new object type and a type manager that operates on objects of that type. The iMAX object filing system provides the software operations that give type managers the ability to store their objects in a permanent file store in a manner consistent with the architecture's protection and representation mechanisms.

Through the operations it provides, a **type manager** is the exclusive agent for changing the state of an object. An object, however, can enter some states that only the operating system (in our case, iMAX), and not the type manager, is aware of. For example, the iMAX garbage collector[15, 16] finds objects that are no longer accessible. When such an object is found, iMAX manufactures an access descriptor for it and sends it to its type manager.

A **type definition object** forms the basis of the mechanism that enables iMAX to communicate with a type manager. Every object has an access descriptor for the type definition object that represents its type. A type manager can store access descriptors in its type definition object for ports[15] and subprograms. In the above example, iMAX selects the appropriate port access descriptor from the object's type definition object and sends an access descriptor for the object to this port.

4. Structure of the Object Space

The **object space** (i.e. the collection of all objects in the system) is decomposed into two distinct spaces, **active** and **passive**. The passive space supports the permanent storage of objects. While stored in the passive space, the representation of an object can only be manipulated by invoking the operations of the object filing system. For a programmer to address the object's representation directly (e.g. as the operand of a hardware instruction), the object must first be mapped into the active space. This action will create a 432 object descriptor for the object. Hence, the active space consists of those objects for which hardware-recognized object descriptors exist.

A consequence of the two-space approach is that it is possible for the active version of an object to be different than its passive version. The updating of a passive object, based on its active version, is under the control of the object's type manager. For this reason, the passive space should not be viewed as a virtual store.

It is, in fact, the active space that is implemented in virtual memory. An object in the active space is not necessarily in primary memory; i.e., the object could be swapped. Such an object is still considered to be in the active space since it is still in hardware-recognized form. For example, a swapped object can contain hardware-recognized access descriptors. The object descriptor for the swapped object would indicate that the object was swapped; so that a reference to its representation would result in a swap-in request.

One important property of the two-space approach is that a typical system crash (e.g., a power failure), while destroying the active space, will not destroy the passive space. Such a crash should not have catastrophic effects since users can periodically update their objects in the passive space.

In addition to accessing a passive object by activating it, it is convenient for a type manager to be able to manipulate its objects' passive definitions. Directory objects are a case in point. A typical directory operation is to retrieve an access descriptor from a directory. The activation of the entire directory object would result in needless overhead. All access descriptors in the directory would have to be transformed from passive to active form even if only one was actually being accessed. Subsequent passivation would perform the reverse operation. The directory manager can avoid this overhead by invoking software operations provided by the object filing system. These operations will access the passive definition of the directory without causing an activation.

4.1. The One-Space Alternative

Other object filing systems, e.g., Hydra and System/38, have chosen to implement a one-space model as opposed to our two-space model. We rejected the one-space model because of the difficulty in maintaining object consistency in the presence of system crashes. In the one-space model, the operating system chooses when to update the passive version of an object with its active version. Since an object may go through several intermediate transitions between consistent states, the operating system may choose to update the object in a transitional state. If an active space crash occurs, the passive object would not be in a consistent state. Since it is not possible for the operating system to know when an object or a collection of objects is in a consistent state, there is no convenient solution to this problem for one-space systems.

In our two-space model, a type manager has control of storing its objects in the passive store. This control can be used to guarantee the consistency of a passive object. A request for the passivation of an object can be triggered explicitly by a user with an access descriptor for it or implicitly by the operating system. An explicit request occurs when a user program calls the object filing subprogram, Update, passing an access descriptor for an object. Update will call the type-specific update subprogram for the passed object. This subprogram is found in the type definition object that is referenced by the passed object. The type-specific update program, part of the type manager, can choose to update the object's passive definition, or simply refuse the update request. iMAX will generate an implicit passivation request when an active object, which has a passive version, becomes inaccessible in the active space. An access descriptor for the inaccessible object will be sent to the port object referenced by the object's type definition object. The type management process that is receiving messages from this port has the same options as the update procedure.

If a type manager chooses not to supply a type specific update subprogram or port object, iMAX will supply reasonable defaults. For update, it will change the passive version so that its value is the same as the active version. For an inaccessible object it will do the same, and also delete it from the active space.

Although iMAX implements the two-space model, most users, namely, those who do not write their own type managers, actually see a one-space model. This is best illustrated by example. When a user accesses the representation of an object, the object will be activated. It will remain in the active space as long as active access descriptors for it exist. When the object is no longer accessible via active access descriptors, the object will usually be stored in the passive space. The actual storing is under the control of the object's type manager. Hence, the two-level nature of the store is more visible to type managers than it is to casual users.

4.2. Active and Passive Forms

An access descriptor consists of an object name and rights which determine the operations permitted on the object using the access descriptor. The active and passive forms of an access descriptor differ in the format of the object names. The active form of a name is a 24-bit address, mapped by hardware, for an object descriptor. In the passive form of an access descriptor, the name is a unique identifier, **UID**. The first time an access descriptor for an object is stored in the passive space, the object is assigned a UID.

When an access descriptor is made active, the active space must first be checked to see if the referenced object has already been activated. The **active object directory** (AOD) contains this information. An AOD entry contains a UID object name and an active access descriptor for the object. (Note: This reference is not considered by the garbage collector; if it were, the active object would never be considered inaccessible.) If a UID is not found in the AOD, a new entry is made and an object descriptor is allocated. The object itself is not activated until an attempt is made to access the representation of the object.

In the passive space, the mapping of a UID to an object is accomplished using the passive **object directory** (POD). An object's POD entry consists of its UID and its physical location, e.g. a disk address. Part of a UID contains an index into the POD. Hence, given a UID it is simple to find the corresponding POD entry. Since the POD is typically too large to keep in primary memory, a directory of the POD is kept in memory, and a software implemented cache scheme is used to keep the most recently used POD blocks in primary memory.

4.3. The Uniqueness of UIDs

Since a passive object on one device may contain a passive access descriptor (UID) for an object on another device, and devices may be moved from one system to another, the uniqueness of UIDs must be assured in order to prevent protection violations. To see how this is done in iMAX, we will examine the format of a UID in detail.

A UID is 80-bits in length and consists of four parts: (1) a logical-device name, (2) an index into the POD of the device, (3) a generation number, and, (4) a 16-bit checksum of the first three fields. The purpose of the checksum is to prevent the transformation of a data error into a protection violation and to differentiate between a corrupted access descriptor and the case of an object that has been destroyed before all access descriptors for it have been deleted.

Two objects that have non-intersecting life-times may be assigned the same POD index. However, the two objects will have different UIDs since their generation number will be different. When an object is assigned a UID, the object filing system guarantees that the UID's generation number will be different from all UIDs, past and present, that share the same POD entry. The size of the POD index field is 24 bits. The size of the generation field is also 24 bits. The size of these fields is sufficient to assure the uniqueness of a UID within a device over a reasonable lifetime (100 years).

The name of a logical-device consists of two parts, an ASCII name chosen by a system administrator and an 8-byte random number chosen by the system when the device is created. The object filing system presumes that this is sufficient to guarantee the uniqueness of device names within an acceptable probability. The uniqueness of device names and the large number of identifiers within a device assures the uniqueness of a UID.

Since the logical-device name part of a UID is long, a UID actually contains a short 16-bit device ID. This ID is an index into a device name table, one per logical-device. Since different logical-devices will have different device name tables, the object filing system maintains a set of tables to efficiently translate between device-relative UIDs and system-relative UIDs.

5. Extensions to the Hardware Mechanism

The object filing system extends the object-oriented addressing and protection mechanisms of the 432 hardware. The extensions are made to deal with the problems of supporting a passive object space and do not change the active space semantics.

5.1. Composite Objects

To improve the performance and reduce the overhead associated with an object filing system, we introduce the notion of a composite object. A **composite** object consists of one or more objects. A composite object has a single root object. The other objects of a composite are called **components**. Each component of a composite is reachable from the root via an access path contained within the composite. Only the root object has a UID and can therefore be referenced by passive access descriptors contained in other composite objects. Hence, an object should not be made a component of a composite unless it is semantically part of the composite.

Since a composite object is stored in a manner comparable to storing a single large object, The activation (or passivation) of a composite object is more efficient than would be the separate activation of each object contained in the composite. Also, a composite object can be stored more efficiently than storing each element of the composite individually. Since a composite object is assigned only one UID, the overhead of the POD and, more importantly, the AOD is less.

Composite objects solve the small object problem in the passive space. The bulk of a 432 program, i.e. the non-sharable part, can exist as a single composite object, sometimes consisting of hundreds of objects. Hence, the loading of a such a program is one or two orders of magnitude faster than if each object of the program had to be loaded individually.

5.2. Object Space Management

The major space management issue in both the active and passive spaces is knowing when to destroy an object so that its space can be reclaimed. Other designs have used either a **reference-based** approach or an **ownership** approach. In the former, an object is destroyed only if it can no longer be referenced. Reference counts, a parallel garbage collector, or both are used to locate objects to be destroyed. Since reference circularities can exist, reference counts can not form the sole basis of object reclamation. In the ownership approach, the owner of the object can explicitly destroy the object. The major disadvantage of this scheme is that explicit deletion of objects is prone to dangling reference problems. Also, ownership schemes are difficult to implement in a dynamic environment.

Based on the disadvantages of the ownership scheme, we chose the reference-based scheme to manage the active object space, i.e. iMAX implements a parallel garbage collector. However, we chose an ownership scheme for the passive space, because we found garbage collection to be inappropriate for this space for three reasons.

First, object space is reclaimed only at the end of a garbage collection pass. On large devices, a garbage collector may not be able to keep up with the rate at which garbage is being created.

Second, since we allow inter-device references and transportable devices, garbage collection becomes more complex, if not undoable. For example, the only references for an object on one device may exist on a device that currently resides on a different system. Although it may be possible to deal with such situations, [10] some objects may exist, if not forever, then much longer than they should.

Last, with no concept of ownership, it is difficult to determine the cause of a full disk condition. This is due to the spreading of access descriptors, an inherent problem in capability systems. Since it is difficult to track down all the access descriptors for unneeded objects and delete them, unneeded objects will not always be reclaimed.

For these reasons, we chose a scheme based on ownership. In this scheme, an **owner** right is defined in passive access descriptors. An object will be deleted from the passive space when there are no outstanding access descriptors for the object with owner rights. Since we expect that the number of passive access descriptors with owner rights for a given object will be small (almost always 1), they will be handled in a special way to facilitate object reclamation. Specifically, the representation of a passive object, say P, will have a list of other objects which contain passive access descriptors with owner rights for P. When this list becomes empty, P will be destroyed.

Since circularities can occur, waiting for the list to become empty is not sufficient, i.e. a garbage collector is still needed. The garbage collector is responsible for detecting passive objects that are unreachable through an access path consisting of "owner" access descriptors. Since only owner access descriptors are considered, the garbage collector involves less overhead than one that would look at all access descriptors. Also, since the generation of such unreachable objects is likely to be rare, garbage collection can be run infrequently.

An implicit assumption in the above discussion is that a passive access descriptor with owner rights cannot reference an object contained on a different logical-device. If this were allowed, this garbage collection scheme would not be any less difficult or costly than the one without owner access descriptors.

5.3. Linkage
As so far described, an access descriptor contains an absolute name for an object. That is, no provision is made for an access descriptor that logically names an object such that at different times it might reference different objects. Lacking this provision has two consequences which we will describe by two examples.

First suppose that a user program has an access descriptor for a system program (e.g. a data base manager). When a new version of this system program supplants the old version, we would want the user's program to reference the new one without causing the user to recompile or relink.

Second, consider the effects of transporting the above user program to a different system, e.g. moving a disk pack between two systems. The program would not run correctly, because it would try to invoke the system program (i.e. the data base manager) on the originating system.

Provision for logical naming could be made by interposing a **link** object between a passive access descriptor and the object it references. On activation the link object would be evaluated, so that the program would have an active access descriptor for the object.

Provision for dynamic linking at activation time is not a sufficient solution. When the above described user program is passivated, the passivated program will have an absolute access descriptor for the system program unless a link object is inserted at passivation. We refer to this as **dynamic unlinking**.

We will first describe our preferred solution, which was not implementable due to hardware constraints. We will then describe our actual solution.

5.3.1. The Preferred Linkage Solution
A solution to both the dynamic linking and unlinking problem is to insert a more permanent link object between an access descriptor and the underlying object. This could be provided by a "link" object descriptor. Such a descriptor would contain two access descriptors, one for the link object and one for the underlying object when the link object was evaluated. When a link object descriptor is valid, it would be invisible; i.e., access to the representation of an object would result in the automatic traversal of any intervening link object descriptors.

Figure 1 depicts the usage of a link object descriptor to implement link objects. In figure 1a, a program has an access descriptor for a link object (which contains the name of

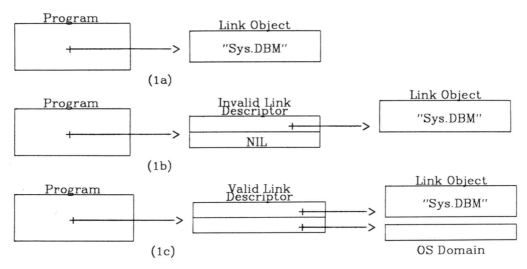

Linkage Using Link Object Descriptors

Figure 1

a system program). Figure 1b is a picture of the program when it is activated, i.e. a link object descriptor is created -- the link object is not yet evaluated. When the program tries to call the system program, a process-level fault will occur. This will cause the evaluation of the link object and make the link object descriptor valid. This results in figure 1c. Hardware will automatically traverse the link object descriptor. When the program is passivated, the link is undone, resulting again in figure 1a. The functionality described allows multiple links for the same object to co-exist even through independent activations and passivations.

5.3.2. The Actual Linkage Solution

Unfortunately, link object descriptors are not implementable with the present 432 hardware implementation. Hence, a less functional but compatible link design is implemented.

When an access descriptor for a link object is activated, the link will be evaluated. This will result in an absolute access descriptor to the object, i.e. no indirection through a link object descriptor. This implies that when an access descriptor for an object is passivated, the link object used in the activation cannot be recovered. To deal with this problem, we permit the owner of an object to assign a link object to his object. When an access descriptor without owner rights is passivated, the link object is copied into the composite object containing the passivated access descriptor. It is quite possible that this link object is not the same one that was used for activation.

5.3.3. Link Objects

We have been using the term "link object" quite loosely, we will now be more precise. A **link** object is an object whose type definition object has the "link" attribute. This attribute can be assigned programatically to any type definition object. This attribute has significance at activation; i.e. when an access descriptor for a link object is activated, the link is evaluated. Hence, link objects themselves are never activated.

This linkage mechanism solves the naming problems described above except for the problem of references to type definition objects. Every typed object, including link objects, contains an access descriptor to its type definition object. When a composite object is activated, the component link objects are evaluated. That is, an access descriptor for a link object is sent to a port for evaluation. An access descriptor for this port is found by examining the type definition object referenced by the link object. However, if the composite object being activated originated from another system, the referenced type definition object would be in the originating system and not accessible. Consequently, the port could not be found and the link object could not be evaluated.

This problem is solved in iMAX by recognizing a distinguished set of type definition objects. These are assigned UIDs that are recognized by iMAX and these are the same on all iMAX-based systems. The linkage types that are supported by iMAX are part of this set.

5.4. Synchronization

Several applications that will use object filing require primitives to synchronize access to shared objects. These primitives could be built on top of object filing or as part of object filing. We have chosen to do the latter because the concepts of consistency and synchronization are related and treating them independently would likely result in a non-uniform user interface.

Our synchronization strategy is based on the notion of Reed's atomic actions. [18, 19] Atomic actions allow a user to update a collection of composite objects in a consistent manner. Specifically, the changes made to such a collection is not visible until the atomic action is committed. When this happens all changes appear to happen simultaneously. If an atomic action is aborted, no changes are made to the objects that are part of the atomic action.

Reed describes the basic philosophy of his scheme as follows: "Updating an object will be thought of as creating a new version, while reading an object will be thought of as selecting the proper version and obtaining a value." Thus, the implementation of atomic actions involves creating, maintaining, and providing access to the collection of object versions.

A literal implementation of Reed's scheme would be rather inefficient. [20] Consequently, we have made a number of modifications that improve performance and storage space utilization, and reduce the complexity of implementation. On the other hand, in making these modifications we also give up some flexibility and functionality. A description of our scheme follows.

5.4.1. Implementation Strategy

As in Reed's scheme, timestamping is used for synchronization. Each version of an object has two associated times, when the version was written, and, when the version was most recently read. At the beginning of an atomic action, a **pseudo-temporal environment** (PTE) object is created. A PTE has an associated timestamp. A PTE is specified in all operations on an object and it is the PTE's timestamp that is reflected in the two timestamps of an object version. When a PTE is created, a timeout for the transaction is specified. If the transaction fails to be committed in the allotted time, it will be aborted. An atomic action is committed by calling the Commit operation and passing an access descriptor for a PTE. An atomic action can be aborted by calling the Abort operation.

Our first modification is to allow only one write operation to be in progress for an object at a time. With this simplification, only the most recently committed version of an object needs an associated read time. The read time of an older version is implicitly assigned to be one time unit less than the write time of the subsequent version. The read time of the most recent committed version is kept in the object's POD entry. Hence, updating the read time of an object version does not affect the version's immutability.

Our second modification is to make Open operations the primitive operations instead of individual reads and writes. An Open operation specifies a PTE, an object to be accessed, and an intent (read, write, or update). An Open for reading will select the most recent version of those whose write time is less than the timestamp of the PTE specified in the Open. If a new version for the object is being written and its write time is earlier than the PTE timestamp of the Open for reading, the Open will block until the new version is committed or aborted.

An Open for writing will produce a new version of an object. The timestamp of the PTE specified in the Open must be later than the read time of the most recently comitted version. If it is not, the Open will be refused. Otherwise, the Open will be allowed, but will wait until the uncommitted version is either aborted or committed. Open operations that block will be enqueued in order of the timestamps of their associated PTEs.

Our third modification is to delete committed versions when they are replaced by a newer commited version and when they are no longer being actively accessed (i.e., there are no outstanding Opens). For example, when version J of an object is committed, version I of the object will be destroyed if it is not being accessed. Thus, version deletion times are well-defined. This has the disadvantage of reducing potential parallelism and causing transactions to abort. For instance, if an Open for reading is done using an old PTE, the requested object version might have already been deleted. This would cause the Open to fail, and typically, the transaction to be aborted.

Our fourth, and final, modification is to implement sharing between versions of the same object. That is, we exploit the immutability of versions by allowing them to share storage, e.g. disk sectors. When a version is to be deleted, its list of disk addresses can be compared with the subsequent version to determine which disk areas can be freed.

5.4.2. Commit

Committing of object versions in iMAX is simpler than the general scheme of Reed's. In our first release of object filing we are only concerned with atomic actions within a single processing node. In a commit of a transaction that involves a single object, i.e. the typical case, only the POD entry of the object needs to be changed. To make this change atomically and to increase POD reliability, the POD is implemented in **stable storage**.[21] To handle multiple object commits, the value of the POD entries to be changed are first written as a single commit record to stable storage. After this completes, the appropriate POD entries are updated. When this completes, the commit record is deleted. Once the commit record is successfully written, the transaction is committed. If a system crash occurs, the commit records will be processed in order of timestamps as part of the system start-up procedure.

5.5. Data Files

The object filing system incorporates support for simple data files. iMAX supplies a type manager for objects of type **data-file**. Data-file objects exist only in the passive space and do not have the 128K byte limitation as do other 432 objects. Since the data-file type manager is integrated into object filing, a more efficient implementation is possible than if a separate type manager implemented this type.

The opening of a data file is implemented as the opening of the data-file object's passive definition. Such a file open will return a stream-like I/O interface package.[15] File synchronization and consistency are accomplished by atomic actions.

6. An Example of Object Filing on Programming

Object filing provides new programming semantics that can be easily exploited by users through high-level languages such as Ada.[22,23] One example of this is object filing's ability to save the state of a collection of objects, e.g. a computation. This facility can provide a programming workspace construct similar to that supplied by APL and LISP programming systems.

An Ada programmer on the 432 can choose a workspace environment for a data abstraction by properly structuring his Ada program. This is best illustrated by an example. Suppose a user program consists of a package P which contains variable declarations and sub-

programs, and a procedure Main (the main program). We will examine two possibilities: both P and Main are defined as library units; and, P is defined within Main, i.e. only Main is a library unit.

First suppose that both are library units, Main is invoked, and Main calls subprograms within P which change the variables declared in P. The use of Main and P cause their activation. Sometime after Main completes, Main and P will be passivated. The passivation of Main is a no-op since a procedure does not have any state. P does have state, namely, the variables declared in P. Changes made to these will be reflected in the passive definition of P when passivation occurs. When Main is invoked again, causing a reactivation of Main and P, the state of P will not be the same as when Main was first invoked. This is the workspace form of a data abstraction.

In the second case, package P is defined within the procedure Main. When Main is invoked, a new package P will be created. This package will be deleted when Main is exited. That is, a different instance of P is tied to each invocation of Main. If two processes call Main, each will have a different package P, i.e. they will not access the same variables within P. This does not preclude sharing; i.e. the compiler supports the sharing of constant objects, specifically, the instruction objects that make up instances of P. This form of program structuring provides the programming semantics supplied by traditional systems.

In this example, we showed that the data state of an abstraction can be saved in the object filing store. Object filing is also able to save the control state of an abstraction, i.e. save a process object. This facility is provided by the iMAX process manager, the type manager for process objects.

7. Summary

We have described the key elements of the iMAX object filing system. In this section, we review how these provide solutions to the problems that we stated at the top of this paper.

The first problem was assuring the uniqueness of UIDs. This was solved by guaranteeing the uniqueness of a UID within an object filing device and by reducing the probability to an acceptable level, of any two object filing devices having the same name.

The second problem was providing an object-oriented, logical naming mechanism. We described a link object mechanism that provided for dynamic linking at activation and dynamic unlinking at passivation.

The third problem was maintaining the consistency of a collection of objects. This was solved by: (1) decomposing the object space into two spaces, active and passive, and giving type managers control of the movement of their objects between the two spaces; (2) providing the facility of composite objects which allows a type manager to treat a complex object as a single entity; and, (3) supplying atomic actions to deal with a collection of composite objects.

The fourth problem was the management of the object space. Although other designs have relied solely on a parallel garbage collector to reclaim object filing space, we argued against this approach. In its place, we described an ownership scheme that is more efficient in reclaiming object space.

The last problem we posed dealt with the implicit overhead of an object filing system. To address this problem we introduced the notion of composite objects. The use of composite objects reduces the space requirements for the AOD and POD. It also speeds up activation and passivation by involving more objects in each physical I/O operation.

To summarize, we undertook the implementation of an object filing system for iMAX in order to meet our objective of providing to our customers (mainly original equipment manufacturers) an extensible operating system. This is made possible by the architecture of the 432 and by the choice of Ada as our systems implemenation language. Extensibility is achieved by the addition of new object types and their managers. The 432 architecture provides for these in an efficient manner. The iMAX object filing system complements the other parts of the 432 system by providing for the permanent storage of objects and giving each type manager exclusive control over the creation, preservation, and ultimate destruction of the objects it manages.

Acknowledgements

The iMAX design has benefited from the first author's involvement in the design and implementation of the Hydra object filing system. Conversations with Bill Wulf, Guy Almes, and Roy Levin were useful in determining the weaknesses of the Hydra design and in identifying the difficult problems to be solved in the design of an object filing system.

This work has also benefited from the creative and cooperative environment generated by all of the members of Intel's Special Systems Operation. Particular note should be paid to Bill Corwin who provided detailed criticisms of two earlier designs and challenged us to find better solutions. Justin Rattner, George Cox, and Steve Zeigler have supplied motivational support. Steve Tolopka and Karl Deiretsbacher have recently joined us in our implementation efforts.

We would also like to thank Anita Jones, whose many comments and suggestions helped to enhance the clarity of this paper.

References

1. Intel 432 GDP Architecture Reference Manual, Intel Corporation 1981.

2. IBM System/38 Technical Developments, International Business Machines Corporation 1978.

3. D. M. England, "Architectural Features of System 250," pp. 395-428 in *Infotech State of the Art Report 14: Operating Systems*, Infotech International Ltd., Maidenhead, Berkshire, England (1972).

4. W. Wulf, E. Cohen, W. Corwin, A. Jones, R. Levin, and F. Pollack, "HYDRA: The Kernel of a Multiprocessor Operating System," *Communications ACM* **17**(6) pp. 337-345 (June, 1974).

5. W. Wulf, R. Levin, and S. Harbison, *Hydra: C.mmp: An Experimental Computer System*, McGraw—Hill Book Company (1981).

6. M. V. Wilkes and R. M. Needham, *The Cambridge CAP Computer and its Operating System*, Elsevier North Holland (1979).

7. C. Dellar, "Removing Backing Store Administration from the CAP Operating System," *Operating Systems Review* **14**(4) pp. 41-49 (October, 1980).

8. J. Dion, "The Cambridge File Server," *Operating Systems Review* **14**(4) pp. 26-35 (October, 1980).

9. P. Bishop, "Computer Systems with a Very Large Address Space and Garbage Collection," M.I.T. Laboratory for Computer Science Technical Report TR-178 (May, 1977).

10. R. Halstead, "Object Management on Distributed Systems," *Proceedings of the 7th Texas Conference on Computing Systems*, pp. 7-7:7:14 (October, 1978).

11. J. L. Gula, "Operating System Considerations for Multiprocessor Architectures," *Proceedings of the 7th Texas Conference on Computer Systems*, pp. 7-1:7-6 (October, 1978).

12. G. T. Almes, "Garbage Collection in an Object-Oriented System," Ph.D. Thesis, Department of Computer Science, Carnegie-Mellon University (June, 1980).

13. A. P. Batson and A. W. Madison, "Characteristics of Program Localities," *Communications of the ACM* 19(5) pp. 285-294 (May, 1976).

14. K. C. Kahn and F. J. Pollack, "An Extensible Operating System for the Intel 432," *Proceedings Compcon Spring 1981*, pp. 398-404 (February, 1981).

15. K. C. Kahn, W. M. Corwin, T. D. Dennis, H. D'Hooge, D. E. Hubka, L. A. Hutchins, J. T. Montague, F. J. Pollack, and M. R. Gifkins, "iMAX: A Multiprocessor Operating System for an Object-Based Computer," *Proceedings of the 8th Symposium on Operating System Principles*, ().

16. E. W. Dijkstra, L. Lamport, A. J. Martin, C. S. Scholten, and E. M. F. Steffens, "On-the-Fly Garbage Collection: An Exercise in Cooperation," *Communications ACM* 21(11) pp. 966-975 (November, 1978).

17. G. W. Cox, W. M. Corwin, K. Lai, and F. J. Pollack, "A Unified Model and Implementation for Interprocess Communication in a Multiprocessor Environment," *Proceedings of the 8th Symposium on Operating System Principles*, (December, 1981).

18. D. P. Reed, "Naming and Synchronization in a Decentralized Computer System," Ph.D. Thesis, M.I.T. Department of Electrical Engineering and Computer Science (September, 1978). Also available as M.I.T. Laboratory for Computer Science Technical Report TR-205

19. D. P. Reed, "Implementing Atomic Actions on Decentralized Data," *Preprints of Proceedings of the 7th Symposium on Operating System Principles*, pp. 66-74 (December, 1979).

20. D. P. Reed and L. Svobodova, *SWALLOW: A Distributed Data Storage System for a Local Network*, Submitted to the International Workshop on Local Networks in Zurich, Switzerland August, 1980.

21. H. E. Sturgis, J. G. Mitchell, and J. Israel, "Issues in the Design and Use of a Distributed File System," *Operating Systems Review* 14(3) pp. 55-69 (July, 1980).

22. S. Zeigler, N. Allegre, R. Johnson, J. Morris, and G. Burns, "Ada for the Intel 432 Microcomputer," *Computer* 14(6) pp. 47-56 (June, 1981).

23. Reference Manual for the Ada Programming Language, U.S. Department of Defense Proposed Standard July, 1980.

The Intel ^{R} 432 Ada Programming Environment

Stephen Zeigler
Nicole Allegre
David Coar
Robert Johnson
James Morris

Intel Corporation*

Greg Burns

Standard Telecommunication Laboratories+

Abstract

Intel Corporation has recently introduced a new VLSI Micromainframe computer, the iAPX 432, that supports many of the features of the Ada Programming Language directly in the architecture. The relationship between Ada and the iAPX 432 is discussed; in particular, the direct architectural support of Ada's packages, activation records, procedures and tasks is examined. New language features suggested by the special characteristics of the architecture are analyzed. An environment for iAPX 432 program development is also discussed.

Introduction

In 1977 the United States Department of Defense (DoD) embarked on one of the most ambitious software related projects in its history. A major goal of the project is to produce a new, general-purpose programming language that embodies the latest concepts in language design. The new language is targeted ultimately to replace hundreds of locally developed languages historically used by DoD contractors for scientific and systems software development. The language standard that results from this commonality of usage should increase the effective transportability of software developed at different sites, producing a significant overall reduction in the cost of DoD sponsored software development. The design of the language was completed in August, 1980, and is named *Ada*, after one of the world's first programmers: Ada Augusta, Countess of Lovelace.

* 3585 SW 198th Avenue, Aloha, Ok 97007.

+ Harlow, Essex, United Kingdom.

Ada [1] is destined to be a significant programming language for scientific and sytems related software development. It will undoubtedly find favor among programmers other than those specifically associated with DoD projects; its use is sure to spread beyond its original intent. The driving force behind Ada's popularity will not only be its attraction as a programming language *per se*, but also the language standard that it will represent. Intel Corporation intends to establish itself as an early center of Ada technology by using the language (with minor extensions) as the systems implementation language for its new iAPX 432 (henceforth simply called "the 432") architecture [2]. An important motivation behind Intel's selection of Ada as the primary language for the 432 is the relationship of the language to the underlying 432 architecture: several Ada language features either are supported directly by or are more easily implemented because of the 432 architecture. Important Ada features supported by the architecture include access protection for packages, automatic maintenance of activation record stacks, and multiprocessor support mechanisms that significantly ease the burden of implementing concurrent multitasking. In several following sections we discuss specific support of Ada language features by the 432.

Although Ada represents a modern model of computation, the 432 is somewhat more advanced in several significant areas. These include user-defined, small protection domains and execution-time type checking by means of extended-type objects. These features illustrate 432 architectural concepts that are not directly supported by the Ada programming language. In order to expose these 432 features at the outer language level, we have

Reprinted from *Digest of Papers, COMPCON S'81*, 1981, pages 405-410.
Copyright © 1981 by The Institute of Electrical and Electronics Engineers, Inc.

chosen to extend Ada slightly because of those aspects of the 432's model of computation that are lacking in Ada. However, Ada is a proper subset of the 432 systems implementation language.

Initial 432 software systems will rely on established host computers as the primary vehicle for program development. The compiler for the 432 systems implementation language and the companion linker (link editor) will execute on a host computer. Linked modules are downloaded to an Intellec Series III system that is bus-coupled to a 432, on which eventual execution will occur. The final section of this paper relates the specific details of the 432 cross-development programming environment.

Object Oriented Architectures

It is important for the reader to understand that the 432 is an *object oriented architecture* [2,3]. The total address space visible to a 432-resident process cannot be accessed as a single, contiguous block of memory as in most classical computers. Rather, the memory must be considered as a collection of address spaces called *objects*. The advantages of using a memory structured in this manner [2,3] are outside the scope of this paper. Here it is only necessary to understand that a 432 process perceives its memory as a collection of objects rather than as a single, contiguous block of memory units.

Each 432 object is classified as to its intended use. For example, *procedure objects* contain bit strings that represent instructions for some algorithmic procedure while *data objects* contain bit strings that are intended to be used as numbers or some other form of data. The 432 architecture can determine the classification of an object and therefore can ensure that instruction objects are never interpreted as data while data objects are never interpreted as procedures (i.e., executed). Later in this paper we will introduce other classifications of objects as they are needed.

Every 432 object is not only classified according to its intended use, but also according to its structure. Earlier we stated that the memory of a 432 should be thought of as a collection of objects. Every object residing in a 432 memory is classified either as an *access object* or as a *simple object*. Access objects are composed of *access descriptors* (similar to capabilities [3]) that allow access to other objects. Simple objects contain data informa-

tion. A fundamental characteristic of the 432 architecture is that access objects contain *only* access descriptors (no data) while simple objects contain *only* data (no access descriptors).

An object can physically exist as a subpart of another object even though the two objects are "logically" different. An object that is physically contained within a parent object is said to be a *refinement* of the parent object. Although refinements are physical subparts of other objects, they still enjoy the full privileges of being objects, just as if they had been physically distinct.

Packages and Procedures

A feature of Ada that will aid in the development of large programs is the *package*. Largely an organizational aid, a package provides a convenient method for grouping a set of data objects with a set of procedures (operators) that operate on the objects. A package representing a portion of a larger system of programs (packages) may be developed by programmers working independently and may be compiled separately from other packages in the system. The separately compilable package defined by Ada should help to stimulate the software industry's movement toward more modular program development styles.

The Ada package is attractive primarily because it enables a programmer to group related ideas together as a unit that can remain as a separate entity until needed. The corresponding 432 concept is the *domain object*, an object that, like the Ada package, is a collection of *data objects* and *procedure objects* (instruction objects). There are several advantages in designating certain objects as domain objects. Just as the Ada package provides an organizational methodology for collecting related Ada procedures and data, the domain object provides a recognizable unit in which previously compiled procedures and associated data are collected. The domain object provides a unit that can be constructed by the separate compilation of an Ada package and stored in an object filing system as a compiled unit, awaiting later access as required. The domain object can never be mistaken as, for example, a data object or a procedure object. The 432 architecture guarantees that a domain object is used only as a domain object.

Another form of object that exhibits a direct correspondence to an Ada construct is the *procedure object* (instruction object), corresponding to the Ada procedure or function. A procedure object consists of a set of executable 432 instructions along with some control information required to form the *context object* (activation record), representing the procedure's local storage at the time it is activated.

In Ada, a procedure in package P may call a procedure in a different package Q. This form of inter-package procedure call in Ada corresponds to an inter-domain procedure object activation in the 432 that is invoked by a special procedure call instruction. This instruction requires three parameters in order to activate a procedure object. The first parameter designates the domain object in which the called procedure object resides; the second parameter gives the offset of a particular procedure object within the domain object. The third parameter designates the object containing the actual parameters for the called procedure object.

Domain objects have also been called extended-type objects [4]. As mentioned in the introduction, the 432 is somewhat more advanced than Ada in its approach to extended-type objects. More detailed discussion of this subject can be found in [2,4,5]. In the next section we will investigate the result of a series of 432 procedure object activations.

Activation Records

Since the introduction of the Algol 60 programming language, the dynamically created *activation record* has been the primary execution-time mechanism for implementing block structured programming languages. An activation record represents the local variable storage associated with the activation of a procedure, along with some control information that allows a procedure to access global variables and to return to the procedure from which it was called. A basic tenet of this approach is that there exist distinct, dynamically allocated activation records for each execution-time activation of a procedure. Since most modern programming languages (including Ada) enforce the semantic requirements that (1) return from a procedure P cannot occur until all procedures called from P have returned and (2) references (pointers) to data stored in activation records are not allowed, a simple LIFO stack is sufficient (in the absence of tasking) for the storage management of activation records.

The management of a LIFO stack to implement an activation record stack for block structured languages is quite efficient and has been used effectively by compiler writers for years. Recursion is made possible by an activation record stack implementation of a block structured language. Unfortunately, many programmers have avoided programming languages that support recursion because of myths that pronounce the inherent inefficiency of the activation record stack implementation technique.

The designers of the 432 recognized the superiority of the activation record stack as the foundation for the execution-time environment of block structured languages, such as Ada. Consequently the 432 architecture provides support for this implementation technique. Central to this support is an object called a *context object* that represents an activation record. Two special instructions are used to create new context objects and destroy context objects that are no longer required: the *procedure call* and *procedure return* instructions, respectively.

Tasks

An important relationship between Ada and the 432 is the support provided by the 432 for Ada's tasking model. The 432 can optionally be configured as a multiprocessor system. The architecture provides a useful set of instructions and special objects that assist systems developers in achieving efficient multiprocessing. These special objects include *communication port* objects and *dispatching port* objects. Communication ports are message queues that act as buffers between processes that may be executing concurrently. If process A wishes to send a message to process B then process A builds an object containing the message and sends it to a communication port by a special "send message" instruction. Process B, using the same communication port, may already be waiting on the message or may receive the message later, in either case effecting the message reception by a special "receive message" instruction. A dispatching port is a special form of message queue in which a process waits for an available processor or in which a processor waits for the arrival of a process. Overhead associated with the implementation of communication ports and dispatching ports is low, since the 432 architecture directly implements operations such as "send message" and "receive message" in microcode. By directly implementing task communication operations and other operations critical to the support of multiprocessing, the 432 is able to implement the Ada tasking model very efficiently.

Unlike most early multiprocessing architectures, the 432 provides *transparent multiprocessing*. This means that any software module that executes correctly on a 432 configured with n >= 1 processors requires no modification to execute correctly on a system with n+1 processors. Of particular importance to 432 Ada programmers is the fact that the use of Ada's tasking facilities will result in concurrent multiprocessing of Ada tasks on a 432 processor configured with multiple processors. If an Ada program is correctly written to use tasks, it will execute properly on a 432 that is configured with a single processor as well as on one configured with, for example, five processors. The only noticeable difference will be in the real time required to complete the program.

Extensions to Ada

Ada forms an ideal basis for a 432 systems implementation language primarily because the design goals for Ada so closely match those of the 432, as discussed in earlier sections. However, Ada is designed primarily to support the development of "embedded systems" whereas the 432 also supports the development of "dynamic systems". Embedded systems are characterized as static; new users, programs and devices do not arise during user program execution. Thus, embedded systems have no need to deal with the spontaneous appearance of new entities and their new demands. Dynamic systems, on the other hand, are characterized by the appearance of new users, new programs, new devices and new demands during program execution. Programs executing in dynamic systems require the ability to describe and manipulate spontaneously appearing entities. The following situations are typical of dynamic systems:

Implementation of a procedure to be selected at execution time. A user wishes to define several alternative implementations of a package, desiring to programmatically select a specific implementation based on the execution-time needs of the system, e.g., a specific sorting algorithm is chosen based on the number of items to be sorted.

Implementation to be altered at execution time. A user wishes to suspend his program and replace a subprogram with a new implementation, e.g., terminal output is replaced with file output to limit information displayed to the console during a particular execution.

Implementation unknown. A user wishes to write programs that deal with other user programs or subprograms having unknown implementations, e.g., a program to graph functions is designed to accept arbitrary functions from other users.

Data structures partially unknown: A user wishes to supply a procedure that depends only on some aspects of the objects it manipulates, allowing other aspects to remain unknown, e.g., a sort requires only that an integer be the key that it sorts, leaving unspecified any other parts of the objects to be sorted.

Data structures entirely unknown: A user wishes to write procedures that manipulate objects of arbitrary structure, either performing very general operations or investigating the object's type at execution time, e.g., garbage collection algorithms are required to manipulate arbitrary objects.

Ada supports applications such as those described above only if the user recompiles those parts of his system that are unknown or changing and then restarts his program. The 432 architecture supports these dynamic applications directly. However, in order to use these features, a systems implementation language must effectively describe such manipulations without recompilation. The 432 systems implementation language extends Ada to enable effective description of dynamic operations such as those described above, while still allowing both compile-time and execution-time type checking.

The extensions to Ada required by the 432 architecture are simple enough to be easily grasped by users knowing Ada. No "unlearning" is required since Ada remains a proper subset of the 432 systems implementation language. The extensions are aimed at increasing the power of the language in dealing with dynamically defined entities. They allow users to manipulate entities whose definitions were compiled *after* some parts of the user program began their execution. Yet the extensions still allow complete type protection because of the underlying type protection facility of the 432. They allow users to manipulate entities whose implementations may change dynamically. They allow users to dynamically specify the rights of other users and programs to use operations on specific data structures.

While the extensions are lexically small, they are semantically powerful, expanding the application of Ada as a program development tool in dynamic environments. Although a full discussion of the extensions is outside the scope of this paper, the following summary is provided to indicate the flavor of the extensions.

(1) Types (e.g., INTEGER) have representations as values at execution time.

(2) A type called DYNAMIC_TYPED is introduced that can be thought of as a generalization of variant records in which discriminant tags are type values rather than scalar values. Note that the use of DYNAMIC_TYPED essentially removes the restriction in Ada that a program specify all possible variants at compile time.

(3) The **suchthat** operator allows a type to be constrained by any boolean expression, as in the following example that defines odd integer values:

subtype ODD **is** INTEGER
suchthat instance **rem** 2 /= 0;

The predefined identifier *instance* designates the constrainee type value in question.

(4) Packages have representations as values at execution time. This extension introduces the concept of a package type.

The 432 Program Development Environment

The 432 program development environment is a *cross-development* environment. The compiler for the 432 systems implementation language is resident on an established host machine, producing object code for the 432. The object code is translated to a loadable object code image by a linker, also resident on the host machine. The loadable object code image is transferred by means of a link from the host machine to an Intellec Series III/432 development system. Using the Intellec system, the user can load his program into the 432 memory for execution under control of a debugger that is operational on the Intellec. The Intellec console serves as an "intelligent" console interface to the 432. The subsystems of interest are listed below, along with the machine on which each is resident in the cross-development environment.

Subsystem	Computer Of Residence
Compiler	Host Computer
Linker	Host Computer
Debugger (including loader)	Intellec Series III
Executable Program Image	iAPX 432

The initial host computer for the 432 cross-development system will be the VAX 11/780 or 11/750 (VMS Operating System). The compiler and the linker can easily be rehosted to other machines.

The standard mode of program development consists of program construction, compilation, and linking on the host computer. This is followed by downloading to the Intellec System, after which a memory image for the 432 is produced on the Intellec system. The memory image is transferred to the 432 memory where it begins execution, under control of the debugger.

In order to reduce host computer to Intellec traffic, it is possible to preserve 432 memory images on local Intellec mass storage. Later, a programmer may choose to recompile and relink only a small portion of a larger program on the host machine. After downloading the small, relinked program portion to the Intellec, the relinked portion can be merged with an earlier, complete memory image on the Intellec to provide a new memory image ready for execution on the 432. The diagram given below illustrates the 432 program development environment.

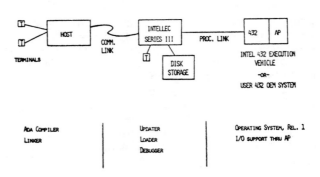

Summary

The 432 Micromainframe computer provides direct architectural support for many of the execution-time requirements of Ada programs. Besides this, the 432 offers such advanced features as dynamic typing and dynamic package values to go beyond the requirements of the Ada language in the support of dynamic software systems. The 432 provides a functionality normally considered the dominion of computer systems in the midrange and above. 432 programs will be initially developed in a cross-development environment although larger 432 systems have the capability to support a fully resident Ada compiler that executes directly on the 432.

REFERENCES

1. *Reference Manual for the Ada Programming Language,* United States Department of Defense, July, 1980.

2. Colley, S., Cox, G., Lai, K., Rattner, J., and Swanson, R. The Object-Based Architecture of the Intel 432. Proceedings of the IEEE CompCon, February, 1981.

3. Fabry, R. S. Capability Based Addressing. *Comm. ACM* **17**, 7 (July, 1974), 403-412.

4. Linden, T.A. Operating Systems Structures to Support Security and Reliable Software. *Computing Surveys* **8**,4(Dec 1976), 409-445.

5. Zeigler, S., Allegre, N., Burns, G., Johnson, R. and Morris, J. Ada for the Intel 432 Microcomputer. To be published in IEEE Computer Magazine.

Virtual Memory on a Narrow Machine for an Object-Oriented Language

Ted Kaehler

Apple Computer, 20525 Mariani Ave. ms 22/Y, Cupertino, CA 95014

The work described here was done when the author was at the
Xerox Palo Alto Research Center, 3333 Coyote Hill Road, Palo Alto, CA 94304

Abstract: LOOM (Large Object-Oriented Memory) is a virtual memory implemented in software that supports the Smalltalk-80(TM) programming language and environment on the Xerox Dorado computer. LOOM provides 8 billion bytes of secondary memory address space and is specifically designed to run on computers with a narrow word size (16-bit wide words). All storage is viewed as objects that contain fields. Objects may have an average size as small as 10 fields. LOOM swaps objects between primary and secondary memory, and addresses each of the two memories with a different sized object pointer. When objects are cached in primary memory, they are known only by their short pointers. On a narrow word size machine, the narrow object pointers in primary memory allow a program such as the Smalltalk-80 interpreter to enjoy a substantial speed advantage. Interesting design problems and solutions arise from the mapping between the two address spaces and the temporary nature of an object's short address. The paper explains why the unusual design choices in LOOM were made, and provides an interesting example of the process of designing an integrated virtual memory and storage management system.

Introduction

LOOM (Large Object-Oriented Memory) is a virtual memory that supports the Smalltalk-80 programming language and environment [Gold83] on the Xerox Dorado computer [Lamp81]. Since Smalltalk uses objects to represent absolutely everything in the system, the LOOM virtual memory makes all storage look like Smalltalk objects. An object is referred to by a unique **object pointer** (also called its **address** or OOP). As far as the virtual memory is concerned, an object is an object pointer that has an array of fields associated with it. Typically, a field contains a pointer to another object, but some fields contain passive bytes of raw data. An object has between one and 64K fields, but so many objects are small that the median size is only 10 fields [Stam82]. Once an object has been created, its size does not change (with certain exceptions). The unit of storage that LOOM swaps between primary and secondary memory is the individual object. LOOM is also in charge of memory management in main memory, storage reclamation, and the creation and destruction of objects [Kaeh83].

The design of a virtual memory is governed by a series of constraints. LOOM is an unusual virtual memory because it has unusual constraints. The first part of Loom's design constraints come from the Smalltalk-80 language itself. In accordance with the specifications in Chapter 30 of *Smalltalk-80: The Language and its Implementation* [Gold83], LOOM provides the illusion of objects to the Smalltalk interpreter. The second set of constraints comes from the hardware on which the virtual memory must run. The Xerox Dorado is a machine with 16-bit wide words and no double-word registers. The fact that a machine word is not wide enough to hold a virtual address is the single largest influence on the design decisions for LOOM. The third set of constraints is what one normally thinks of as design goals; how big the virtual space will be and how fast the resulting system will run. The ambitious goal here is a virtual space that can grow without conceptual limit, yet retain the best

Smalltalk-80 is a registered trademark of the Xerox Corporation.

"Virtual Memory on a Narrow Machine for an Object-Oriented Language" by T. Kaehler from *Proceedings of the ACM Conference on Object-Oriented Programming Systems, Languages and Applications,* 1986, pages 87-106. Copyright 1986, Association for Computing Machinery, Inc., reprinted by permission.

possible execution speed compared to a non-virtual memory Smalltalk-80 system.

It is important to note which problems the design of LOOM is not trying to solve. LOOM is intended to run on a computer with only one central processing unit. Multiple concurrent tasks are allowed, but multiple CPUs each running Smalltalk independently cannot live in the same virtual space. LOOM is intended to store parts of its secondary storage on server machines over a local network, but LOOM does not attack the problem of arbitrating between several users trying to write into the same object at once. Transactions to preserve the consistency of the virtual memory are not supported. The only way to make sure the virtual space will survive a machine crash is to make a copy of it, which is fast but still takes scores of seconds. Journaling could be added. LOOM does not explicitly deal with the problem of long term stable storage. In the design of LOOM we were not allowed to ask for changes to the hardware of the Dorado. Thus LOOM is a virtual memory executed entirely in software, without the benefit of address look-aside buffers or other special hardware.

The Major Guiding Constraints

The Smalltalk-80 language interpreter can be thought of as a program that obtains access to a series of objects, reads the fields of those objects, copies pointers out of some fields, and writes pointers into other fields. When all objects needed for a computation are already present in primary memory (and without LOOM knowing they are), a Smalltalk using LOOM should perform as close as possible to its speed in a non-virtual memory system. The basic strategy for speed is to bring into primary memory the objects that the interpreter needs, and then allow the interpreter to execute quickly, without interference from the virtual memory code. We must find out which operations the interpreter does most often, and make sure that LOOM does not slow those operations. When all objects needed by the interpreter are already in primary memory, the only Loom-related code that should be executing are tests to determine that the needed objects are indeed still present in primary memory.

The nucleus of the design of LOOM is presented here in a problem-solution format. This format emphasizes the reasons behind each of the major components of the design.

Problem: Providing a large virtual space

Solution: Use long addresses in secondary memory
Pointers into secondary memory are 32-bit pointers.

Problem: Allowing the interpreter to be fast on a narrow machine
The most frequent operations performed by the interpreter on an object (loading a field, storing a field, and sending a Smalltalk message) must execute as quickly as possible.

Solution: Use short addresses in primary memory
On a narrow machine, narrow addresses are significantly faster to handle than wide addresses. Fields in primary memory contain 16-bit object pointers. Since the Smalltalk interpreter is a program written in microcode, and the machine has 16-bit words and no double-word registers, 16-bit pointers are much faster to handle than 32-bit wide pointers.

Since every field in every object in main memory contains a short address, the language interpreter believes the fiction that object pointers are only 16-bits wide. The permanent address of an object is its long secondary memory address, and a short address is the object's temporary name while it is cached in main memory. The use of two separate address spaces for objects in primary and secondary memories is the central design decision of the LOOM virtual memory. The two different address spaces require a mapping between them.

Problem: Mapping from short to long pointers
We need a simple mapping between the two address spaces that does not take too much room in primary memory nor too much time to compute.

Solution: Each object stores its own long address
Each object in primary memory holds its own long address. The 32-bit long address is stored with the object, but is only used by the virtual memory code.

Problem: Objects in primary space must point at objects in secondary space
A tree of interpointing objects must be allowed to straddle the boundary so that some of them are in primary memory and some are not. A field in an object in primary memory contains a 16-bit pointer. How can that pointer denote an arbitrary object in the 32-bit secondary memory address space?

Solution: Use leaves (stubs of objects)
A field pointing to an object that is absent from primary memory contains the short address of an object called a leaf. A

leaf is similar to an object in primary memory, except that it is only a stub. It stores its own long address, but has no fields.

Problem: Mapping from long to short pointers
While bringing the fields of an object from secondary to primary memory, we want to know if a long pointer in a field denotes an object that is already cached in primary memory. If so, we want to know its short address. (As usual, we need to minimize space and time required for the mapping.)

Solution: A short address is the hash of a long address
The short address of an object is chosen to be a location in the hash table corresponding to its long address. The entire short address space indexes a hash table that can be probed with a given long address to see if any target object has a matching long address (to see if the object is already cached in primary memory).

To review the scheme so far: Figure 1 shows secondary memory as the true home of objects. They have 32-bit identifiers and fields that contain 32-bit pointers to other objects. Primary memory is a cache for objects temporarily involved in computation. Objects are identified there by 16-bit pointers and contain 16-bit values in fields. The interpreter, all

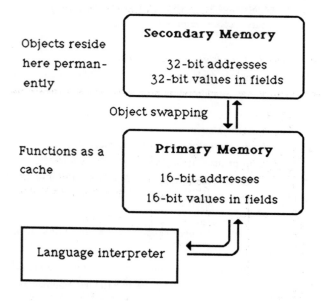

Figure 1   An Overview of LOOM

programs in Smalltalk, and all utility programs see only 16-bit pointers. Figure 2 shows a diagram of the different states of the cached representation of an object. In the left frame, the objects A and B exist only in secondary memory and are unknown in primary memory. In the next frame to the right,

object A is a leaf in primary memory. Moving right again, LOOM has expanded object A into a whole object with fields. LOOM looked at A's representation in secondary memory and found B's long address in one of the fields. LOOM created a leaf for B. The only thing known about B at this time is its long address. In the final frame, B is expanded into a full object. The interpreter can now manipulate object B. After the interpreter is finished with an object, it slowly works its way back to secondary storage. Objects move leftward in the diagram when LOOM needs their memory space or short addresses to use with other objects.

Objects live permanently in secondary memory and cycle into primary as they are needed in computation. To find the long address of an object given its address in primary memory, LOOM goes to the object in primary memory and loads its long address. Going in the other direction, LOOM hashes the long address into the primary memory space and reprobes to find an object with a matching long address. If none is found during the reprobe sequence, the object is not currently cached in primary memory. Hence, the entire bidirectional mapping between objects in the two spaces costs exactly 32-bits of memory for each object in the primary space.

Practical Constraints

We have sketched the broad outline of LOOM: objects that live in a large secondary spaces are swapped into primary memory where they are known by short addresses. This section adds some constraints of speed, space, and features that are required to make LOOM a usable virtual memory.

Problem: Testing for a leaf quickly
Minimize the time the interpreter spends checking objects to see if they are leaves.

Solution: Check one bit when an object is first touched
The interpreter can manipulate an object only when it has all of its fields in primary memory. Each object contains a bit which is on when the object is a leaf. Before the interpreter loads the real address of any object into a base register, it checks the leaf bit. If the bit is on, the interpreter calls LOOM to get the object expanded. In analogy to a page fault, this is called an **object fault**. Once the interpreter has the object's starting address in a base register, it usually performs several loads or stores on fields. The leaf check costs a fraction of a bit-test per load or store of an object field.

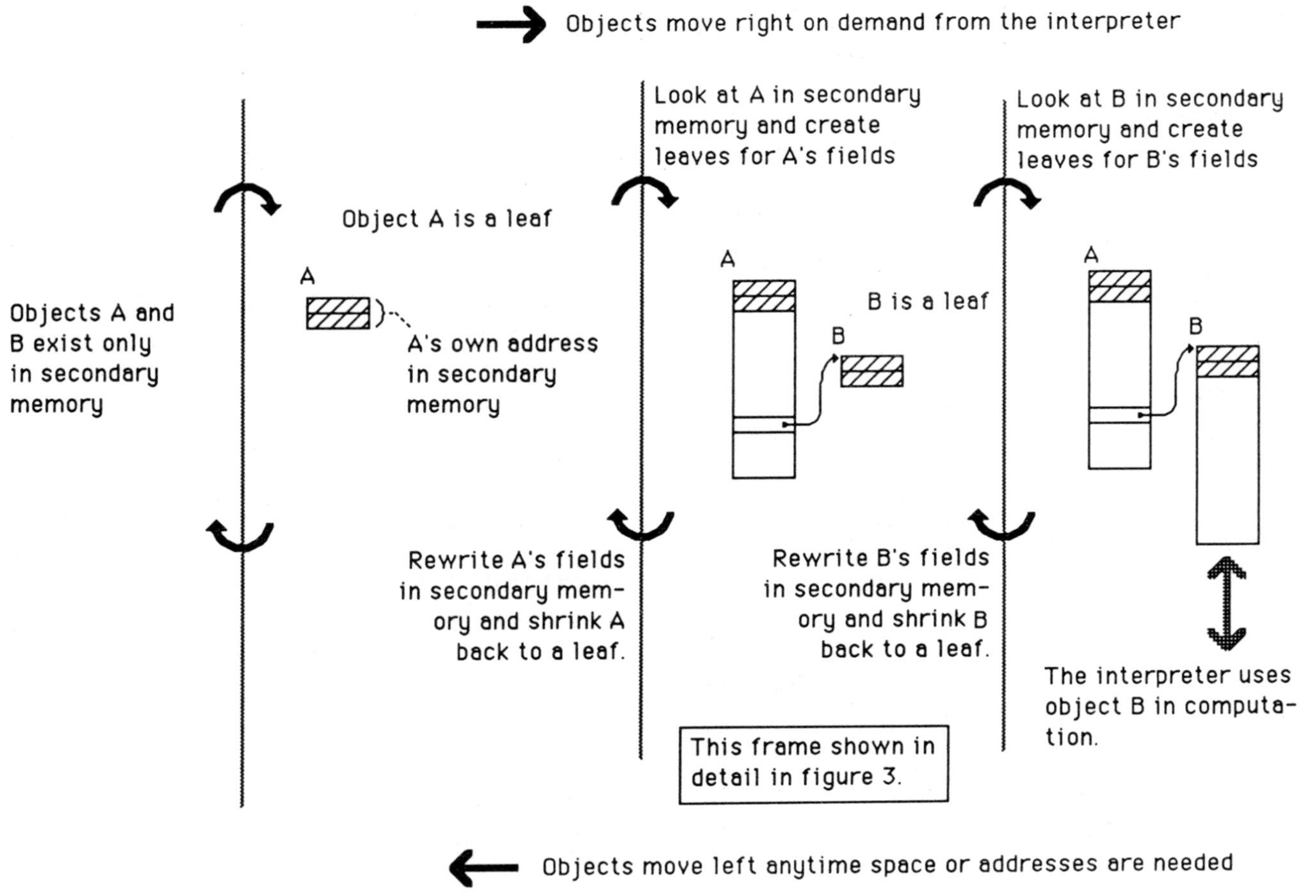

Objects move right on demand from the interpreter

Objects A and
B exist only
in secondary
memory

Object A is a leaf

A

A's own address
in secondary
memory

Look at A in secondary
memory and create
leaves for A's fields

A

B is a leaf

B

Rewrite A's fields
in secondary mem-
ory and shrink A
back to a leaf.

Look at B in secondary
memory and create
leaves for B's fields

A

B

Rewrite B's fields
in secondary mem-
ory and shrink B
back to a leaf.

This frame shown in
detail in figure 3.

The interpreter uses
object B in computa-
tion.

Objects move left anytime space or addresses are needed

Figure 2. A history of the states of object B in primary memory

Problem: Compacting primary memory

LOOM needs to be able to compact main memory when that
memory gets fragmented.

Solution: An object table gives indirection

The memory-resident Smalltalk-80 system described in the
Smalltalk books [Gold83][Inga83][Wirf83] puts a level of
indirection between object pointers and main memory. The
16-bit object pointers are indexes into an **object table** (OT)
which in turn contains the 20-bit real address of the object in
main memory. Figure 3 shows the middle part of Figure 2
expanded to include the object table entries for objects A and B.
The speed penalty for the indirection is offset by allowing
objects with 16-bit names to occupy 1024K words (2048K
bytes) instead of just 64K words and by allowing objects to be
moved. The data part of each object (the part that contains the
object's fields) is stored in a heap that occupies the rest of main
memory. When the heap becomes fragmented, it can be
compacted easily by moving objects and fixing up their

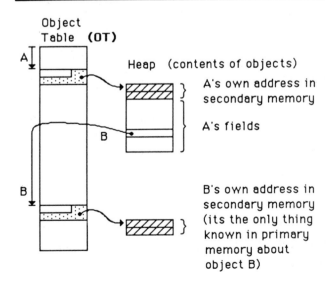

Object
Table **(OT)**

A

Heap (contents of objects)

A's own address in
secondary memory

A's fields

B

B

B's own address in
secondary memory
(its the only thing
known in primary
memory about
object B)

Figure 3. Object B is a leaf and is referenced
by a field in object A. The object table contains
20-bit pointers into the heap.

295

addresses in the OT. Memory fragmentation is more common in LOOM than in a resident system, since objects not only leave holes when they die, but also when they are swapped out. The OT also contains some status bits and a reference count for each object. The indirection provided by the OT is almost completely orthogonal to the rest of the issues surrounding LOOM, so now that we have noticed it, we will ignore it and think of short addresses (16-bit object names) as pointing directly to objects in main memory.

Problem: Reclaiming storage automatically

The overhead of storage reclamation should be no worse than in a non-virtual memory system for objects already in primary memory. Specifically, we want to avoid any access to secondary memory during storage reclamation of objects in primary memory, except after it has been determined that a given object should be reclaimed.

Solution: Reference counts for short and long pointers are kept separately

LOOM on the Dorado uses reference counting in both primary and secondary memory. A **primary reference count** holds the number of short pointers to an object in primary space. A **secondary reference count** holds the number of long pointers to an object. A given pointer is only counted once; if the pointer resides in a field of an object cached in primary memory, it contributes only to the short count of its target, and not to the target's long count. The interpreter does not need to know about secondary reference counts because every object it operates on is in the primary memory. The primary counts are raised and lowered by the interpreter exactly as they are in the memory-resident system. (At this point in the paper, we have only sketched the reference counting scheme; we will examine it in detail later.) If garbage collection is preferred, the garbage-collection program sweeps primary memory, and then keeps a summary of what should happen to objects in secondary memory. (If garbage collection is used on the disk, the summary is a list of objects represented in primary memory; if reference counting is used on the disk, the summary is the net change in the counts on long pointers.)

Problem: Minimizing disk head movement

Total disk head movement must not be too great. Schemes that involve upwards of one disk seek per object fault or object writeback are too slow.

Solution: Direct pointers into secondary memory, objects are grouped together

Objects are assembled into groups on disk pages, so that objects that are used together are brought into primary memory together. Close placement of related objects in secondary memory and cached disk pages from a pool of buffers in primary memory lower the seek rate enough so that LOOM does not need a complex mechanism for grouping. Depth first grouping of objects is used, and the static grouping strategy can easily be changed at the time the system is generated. In addition, pointers in secondary memory are direct pointers. LOOM uses direct pointers in the secondary space so that there will not be more than one disk access per object fault. (There is an exceptional case when an object has changed size. It has been moved and has left behind a forwarding block in secondary storage. In this case, a fault causes two disk accesses.)

Trying out different static or dynamic grouping strategies is very easy in virtual memories that swap objects. OOZE, the virtual memory for Smalltalk-74 and Smalltalk-76, grouped objects by their class [Kaeh81]. Stamos has compared different object grouping strategies for LOOM [Stam82].

A Brief Contrast with Paging Virtual Memories

Two independent address spaces for primary and secondary memory constitute a fairly drastic design solution. The code must be quite complex in order to handle the conversion of objects from 16-bit to 32-bit formats, the two-level reference-counting scheme, and forwarding blocks in both primary and secondary memory. The question naturally comes up -- why not build a 32-bit paging system and use two words in primary memory to hold each object pointer?

One configuration for a paging system would be exactly like the resident Smalltalk-80 system, except paged. A whole disk page, possibly containing many objects, is brought into primary memory whenever any object stored on that page is needed. A pointer to an object would be the 32-bit virtual address of an OT entry and the entry itself would contain the virtual address of the rest of the object. The object table could be quite large, allowing more than 64K objects. Stoney Ballard at Digital Equipment Corporation built such a system and discovered that it thrashed badly. He then departed from straight paging and built an interesting hybrid system that mixes paging and object swapping [Ball83]. Dave Ungar's Smalltalk-80 implementation called *Berkeley Smalltalk* uses paging combined with direct objects pointers (no object table) [Unga84]. He uses an efficient storage management scheme called **generation scavanging** that is very similar to an earlier scheme we called **name composting** [Kaeh77]. Both of these paging schemes are intended for machines with 32-bit wide words.

There are two kinds of arguments about the merits of LOOM versus paging. The first centers around the number of disk accesses needed to do a given computation with a given amount of primary memory. LOOM packs main memory tightly with objects, each of which is needed in the computation. Paging brings in whole pages, even if only one small object on a page is needed. Since objects tend to be small (30 bytes average for this comparison), and Smalltalk uses lots of them, primary memory can become clogged with under-utilized pages. LOOM can arrange just the right working set in main memory, and add and subtract individual objects from it. A penalty that LOOM pays for this high utilization of main memory is that it must fault separately for each additional object that the interpeter wants. A paging system automatically brings all the objects on a single page into main memory whenever one is needed. The rest of the objects on the page are available instantly if they are needed. LOOM can simulate the locality of objects on a page by using page buffers to keep the recently used pages in main memory. Jim Stamos did an extensive simulation comparing LOOM with a corresponding paging system [Stam82], [Stam84], [Stam85]. The result is that, if objects that are used together can be grouped together in secondary memory, both paging and LOOM do well. When objects are not grouped and the size of primary memory is small and close to the working set size, both paging and LOOM tend to thrash. The success of grouping schemes and the size of primary memory are more important than the differences between the schemes.

The second point of comparison between LOOM and paging is the speed of execution of Smalltalk when all required objects are already in primary memory. On a narrow machine, LOOM has a clear advantage over a 32-bit paging system. The Dorado is a microcoded machine with a large instruction and data cache between the processor and main memory. The microcode can do a memory reference in one microcycle if the data is already in the cache. There is 4K of user-writable horizontal microcode that contains the Smalltalk-80 interpreter and other code. The microstore is full and microcode space is a scarce resource. Changing the Smalltalk interpreter to use double-word object pointers would slow down execution. Since a pointer occupies two words, and memory operations are single-word only, it takes about twice as many microinstructions to load, store, or compare pointers (see left

side of Figure 4). Besides taking longer, these instructions consume space in the microstore, forcing other routines out of microcode and into slower-running machine code. The interpreter uses machine registers to hold object pointers for various reasons. 32-bit pointers consume twice as many registers and can cause a shortage. Since the registers are addressed in banks, the additional instructions for bank switches will be needed and these take time and microstore (see middle of Figure 4). Finally, fewer pointers and thus fewer objects fit into the main memory cache and into main memory itself. This effectively reduces the working set of the computer. (This reduction in the number of objects in main memory was included in Stamos' simulations.) The high-speed tests that LOOM needs to make add very little time to the execution. The extra microcode needed by LOOM (mostly to enter and leave the LOOM code around an object fault) takes space, but this is 261 instructions versus substantially more than 470 to upgrade the interpreter to double word pointers.

Because handling double words is so slow, LOOM provides faster execution for an interpreter using memory-resident objects despite the fact that the Dorado hardware supports paging. The Dorado has a hardware page map, hardware interrupts for page faults, and microcode in which to write fast

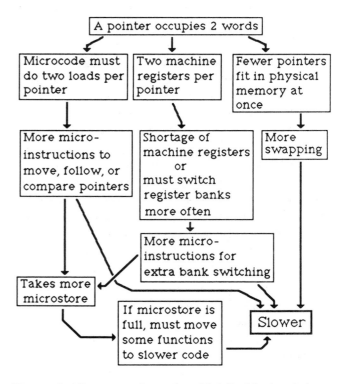

Figure 4   Reasons why using 32-bit object pointers on a 16-bit machine slows the language interpreter

page fault handlers. LOOM ignores this hardware and is implemented entirely in microcode and machine code. Even if unlimited microcode space were available, LOOM would have a speed advantage over a system that used two words for each pointer.

Purging Objects From Primary Memory

Objects are brought into primary memory because the interpreter needs them. An object fault is a straightforward algorithm, and is called on demand. Removing (**purging**) objects from primary memory, however, is less straightforward and has more latitude as to when it may occur.

Problem: Purging objects from primary memory
Objects must be moved from main memory to secondary memory in order to recover and reuse their memory space and/or short addresses.

Solution: Turn old objects into leaves and wait for other leaves to be dereferenced
We would like LOOM to be able to simply pick an arbitrary object, rewrite it in secondary memory, and take possession of its short address and space in primary memory. This will not work because some other object may still hold the short address of that object in one of its fields. If LOOM uses that short address for a new object, the field will point to the wrong object. Purging objects, the act of removing them from primary memory, must be done indirectly. LOOM may pick any object in primary memory and convert it to a leaf. To do this, LOOM uses the object's long address to bring the object's page in from secondary memory. The short pointer in each field in the object is converted to a long pointer, and that pointer is written into the proper place in the object's image in the page buffer. LOOM **contracts** the object's image in primary memory into a leaf. The leaf, and thus the object's short address, can only be recovered when all of the fields pointing to it in primary memory disappear.

When an object shrinks to a leaf, it may release some leaves by destroying the last short pointers to them. If a pointer from the object we contracted was the last pointer to a leaf, LOOM converts the pointer to a long pointer and destroys the leaf. Thus, the way that LOOM recovers short addresses is to contract arbitrary objects into leaves and collect those other short addresses that lose their last reference.

Problem: Choosing the objects to be purged

LOOM must identify which object to purge. The objects chosen should be unlikely to be needed by the interpreter in the near future and a minimum amount of time should be spent making the choice.

Solution: A sweep looks at the touched bit to give approximately LRU ordering
LOOM sweeps the space of short addresses by using a clock algorithm to advance a pointer in the object table. A single bit per object provides aging by recording whether the object was touched by the interpreter since the last time the sweep went by. The interpreter sets the touched bit when it begins to load or store fields in an object. The purge sweep marks a touched object untouched. When the sweep finds an object that has remained untouched for an entire cycle, it contracts the object to a leaf.

Problem: Quickly purging objects that have not changed
If we can distinguish between **clean** and **dirty** objects in primary memory, the purge can be more efficient. Objects that have not been altered while they were cached in primary memory (clean objects) do not have to be rewritten in secondary memory when they are purged.

Solution: Mark objects dirty that are changed
Each object has a clean bit that is set when the object is newly created or newly swapped in. The bit is cleared whenever a field of the object is overwritten. Changes to the object's reference count are not reflected in the clean bit, and only when LOOM has guessed the object's final reference count correctly can an access to secondary memory actually be avoided (we will discuss this later).

A Special Case for Short-lived Objects

Problem: Reducing the overhead for short-lived objects
Smalltalk creates and destroys new objects at a furious rate. Ungar determined that an object was created an average of once every 7.7 bytecodes ([Unga83] page 199), and Stamos measured a rate of once every 17 bytecodes ([Stam82] Appendix D). Even when stack frames (MethodContexts) are taken out of the object space, Ungar records an object being created every 48 bytecodes and Stamos every 105 bytecodes. At the most conservative rate measured, the Smalltalk-80 interpreter on the Dorado creates and destroys 2400 objects per second. We need to avoid the overhead of putting these short-lived objects into secondary memory, or even assigning

them addresses in the secondary space.

Solution: Immature objects have no long pointer
New objects are created in the primary space, and have a flag value in place of their own long address. They can be created and reclaimed without looking in secondary memory, as shown in Figure 5. A new object must be made **mature** (assigned a location in secondary memory) when some object that holds a

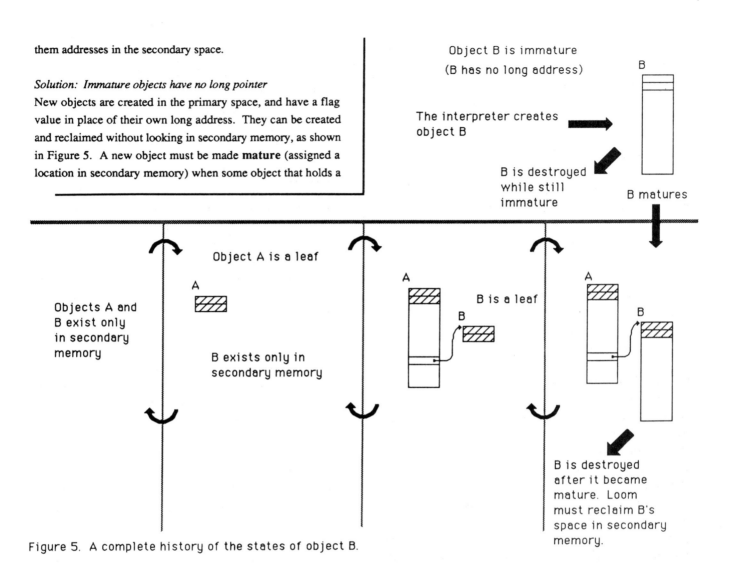

Figure 5. A complete history of the states of object B.

pointer to it has its fields written out into secondary memory. The fields written out must be long pointers, so LOOM must assign a long pointer for any immature object it discovers in an object it is rewriting or contracting.

Problem: Immature objects have the wrong hash when matured
When LOOM matures an object, that object's address in the secondary space is assigned. The actual long address is determined by the free space available in secondary memory. The new long pointer to the object will, in general, not hash correctly to its current short address (see Figure 6). It is essential that LOOM be able to "connect up" a new object owning a random short address to the long address that is assigned later as its final location in secondary memory.

Solution: Forwarding blocks in primary memory

Our solution is to rename the object in the primary space, so it hashes correctly, and to build a forwarding block at its former address, as shown in Figure 7. A forwarding block merely contains a flag and a pointer to its new short address. A forwarding block may be reclaimed when all fields pointing to it have been updated to the new address, or destroyed. If reference counting is used, the forwarding block retains the original count of the object to which it points, and it contributes a single count to the reference count of the object in its new location. When the reference count of a forwarding block falls to zero, it is reclaimed, and its target object's count is decremented. The interpreter checks for a forwarding block every time it begins to load fields from an object. The check is combined with the leaf check.

Ideally, the interpreter would "fix up" the original pointer every time it discovers a forwarding block. That is, it would store

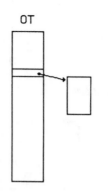

Figure 6a. A temporary object is created at the first available short address.

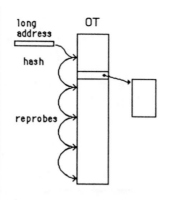

Figure 6b. The temporary object turns out to be long-lived and is assigned a long address that does not hash correctly to its old address.

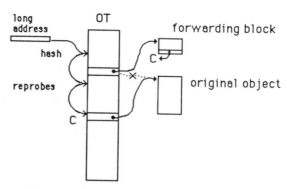

Figure 7. Short address C, which hashes correctly becomes the object's name, and the old short address becomes a forwarding block.

the short pointer of the target of the forwarding block into the place where it first found the pointer to the forwarding block. When the Smalltalk interpreter begins to load fields from an object, that object is usually on the stack. Knowledge of how it arrived on the stack has been lost. It could have been pushed on the stack from any of the five different kinds of variables, it could have been passed down through several messages as an argument, or it could be a result returned by an earlier message. Rather than search for the original location of the pointer, LOOM only fixes up a forwarding block when it finds one in a field it is converting from a short to a long pointer. Objects that are purged and then faulted back into primary memory have no pointers to forwarding blocks in their fields.

Storage and Address Space Management in Primary Memory

The conflicting demands of various parts of LOOM seem to meet in the storage allocation routines. Every object that enters primary memory needs a short address and an exact-sized piece of storage. Most objects are small, can be assigned any short address, and need to be allocated quickly. Other objects need to be created with a specific short address (in order to hash correctly), may be large in size, and, of course, need to be allocated quickly. The purge routine recovers space and short addresses when the allocator runs out, which is usually at the "worst possible time." Paradoxically, the purge routine may consume some space and short addresses before it can free any.

Problem: Allocating new objects quickly

There needs to be a way of holding onto unused short addresses and free space in primary memory that allows fast allocation and deallocation of objects. We need this because of the high traffic in short-lived objects.

Solution: Lists of free objects
Free objects are kept on freelists. A free object is a short address, an OT entry, and a block of memory of a certain size. The forty smallest sizes of free blocks are segregated on forty freelists, each containing only one size of block. All larger blocks reside together on a single large freelist. Free objects on a list are linked; each block holds the short address of the next block. Allocation and deallocation of small objects is fast because the OT entry already points to a block of memory of the proper size.

LOOM maintains a supply of **surplus** short addresses (and associated OT entries). These are used when the allocator splits a large free block to create a small block for a new object. Both the remaining large block and the new object need short addresses, so a surplus one must be found. The surplus OT entries are not linked, but are found by linearly searching the OT. If the search routine fails to turn up a surplus short address after 1024 tries, it starts a purge of primary memory.

Problem: Allocating objects that have a specific hash
The storage allocator must respond to two different kinds of requests. When a new object is created, the interpreter wants a short address, and wants a free block of the proper size to be attached. This is the conventional type of storage allocation explained above. When LOOM is creating a leaf or assigning a secondary memory address to an immature object, it wants a short address that can be reached by hashing a particular long address. The free OT entry singled out by the hashing routine

may have no memory block attached, or may already be part of a free object that is on a freelist. If it is a free object, it must be removed from the middle of its freelist.

Solution: Remove a free object from the middle of its freelist
If the short address found by the hash routine is surplus, the allocator goes to the freelist of the proper size, removes the front free object, and swaps the contents of the two OT entries. The OT entry of the free block becomes surplus, and the original short address now points to the proper sized block. On the other hand, if the short address chosen by the hash routine already points to a free object, the allocator must remove the free block from the middle of its freelist. After it is removed, it still has the wrong sized block attached. The allocator selects a new block of the proper size, swaps pointers in the OT entries, and puts the block of the wrong size back on an appropriate freelist.

Problem: Quickly removing a free object from the middle of its list
Removing a free block from the middle of a freelist requires a search of the freelist if the list is only singly linked. (The block before the one that is being removed needs to have its link fixed-up.) The freelists are only singly linked to make the high bandwidth allocation and deallocation go fast for new objects. We would like the freelists to be doubly linked when the second type of allocation is happening.

Solution: Lazy doubly-linked lists
The routines that ask the allocator for a free object with a specific short address are the same routines that do faulting and purging. Faults and purges tend to come in clumps, so it is advantageous to convert the freelists temporarily to a doubly-linked format.

Every free block has a flag that tells if it is singly- or doubly-linked. When the allocator tries to remove a block from the middle of a freelist and the block's flag indicates single linking, the allocator doubly links the list (i.e. it starts at the head of the list inserting backlinks and setting the flags).

When the allocator tries to remove a block from the middle, and both the block and its predecessor say they are doubly linked, it simply unlinks the block. When the allocator is creating and destroying new objects at high bandwidth, it removes and adds blocks from the front of the list. It always marks them singly linked (which is quick to do). Thus the usual state of a freelist is that the front part is singly linked, and the rear part is doubly

linked as shown in Figure 8. Often a block that must be removed from the middle is already in the doubly linked part and it can be unlinked immediately. If it is not, the routine that does the double linking must only traverse up to the beginning of the doubly-linked part. This structure might be called "lazy doubly-linked lists." The net effect is that double linking is only done when it is absolutely needed, and having been done, it persists until high-bandwidth allocation erases it.

The reason to search for surplus OT entries, rather than keeping them on a linked list, is that the "lazy doubly-linked list" trick does not work for OT entries. An OT entry only has 20 bits of pointer in it, which is not enough space for both a forward link and a backward link.

Problem: Producing surpus OT entries during a purge
LOOM sometimes calls the purge routine in order to get more surplus OT entries. Any time that the distribution of sizes of objects is changing, and big blocks of memory in the heap are being split, surplus OT entries are needed. In systems with enough real primary memory, the allocator runs out of short addresses before it runs out of memory space.

Solution: Create a bubble of free space, coalesce adjacent free objects
The purge routine passes over the objects in the primary space and decides which ones to contract from a full object to a leaf. The fields of the objects being contracted are converted from short to long pointers. Whenever a field was the last short pointer to an object (usually a leaf), that short address with its

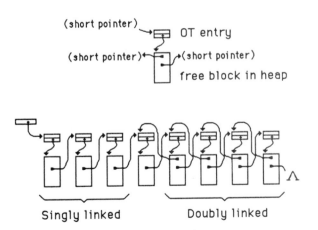

Figure 8. Lazy doubly-linked freelist. Stack-like traffic caused front to be singly-linked. Doubly-linked portion is left over from the last time the entire list was doubly-linked.

memory space attached is freed. Leaves and objects that are liberated in this way wind up on freelists, but do not raise the number of surplus short addresses. Unattached short addresses can only be recovered when free blocks are merged.

Free blocks can be merged in two ways. One way is during the compaction of main memory. A bubble of free space is pushed through the heap in primary memory and merged with any free blocks found. Besides merging into one big free block all space freed by contracting full objects, the sweep also discovers the space and short pointers of leaves freed at some earlier time. Because so many newly created objects are short-lived, there is a second way to merge free blocks. Adjacent free blocks are merged together whenever they are noticed. Using the length of a free block, it is possible to find the next object in the heap, derive its short address, and test if it is also free. If a purge is called and many free blocks already exist, a fraction of them are tested to see if another free block follows. If enough space and short addresses are recovered by coalescing adjacent ones, the purge routine returns without contracting any objects. (When a storage request can be satisfied by coalescing adjacent blocks, it is much faster than an average memory compaction).

Problem: Ensuring forward progress during a purge
It is very important that the purge routine be guaranteed to make forward progress when it is collecting free space and short addresses. A purge may lose ground momentarily when it finds an object that points to many immature objects and turns it into a leaf. LOOM must mature the immature objects, creating forwarding blocks that consume short addresses and free space.

Solution: Back out of messes, reserve space
The act of contracting an object causes its fields to be converted to long pointers. If any object pointed at by a field has never been assigned a long pointer, one must be assigned. Indeed, if the original object is being sent to the disk for the first time, it must be given a long address. When an object is assigned a long pointer, the long pointer almost never hashes to the the object's old location in the OT, and the object gets a new OT entry and short address. A forwarding block is created at the object's old short address. All of this consumes a short address and space in the heap (for the forwarding block). The middle of a purge is not the ideal time to be allocating memory and short addresses, and sometimes the request cannot be met. If LOOM cannot supply the space or a short address needed to contract a given object, it backs off, passes over that object,

and tries to contract another. Since trying to contract an object and backing off wastes time, we lower the chance of failure by providing buffers of space and short addresses. The OT is maintained at 85% full. The other 15% forms a pool of short addresses that can be used when a forwarding block is needed. In addition, the allocator holds a large block of space in reserve and releases it before every purge.

While a purge may lose ground momentarily when maturing a bunch of objects, it will gain everything back when all the objects that point to the new forwarding blocks are contracted. Then the forwarding blocks and the leaves of the original objects will be collected. It is theoretically possible for LOOM to deadlock if every object points at at least one immature object and either the heap space or the short addresses are entirely used up. We have chosen the reserves at the beginning of a purge so that a deadlock is extremely unlikely.

Problem: Maximum size of an object
LOOM swaps whole objects between primary and secondary spaces. Either there must be a limit on the size of an individual object, or the swapping of incomplete parts of objects must be supported. (Paging systems impose no maximum size on their objects because they can swap pieces of objects.)

Solution: Limits on the size of an object
LOOM places a limit on the size of an object, determined by the width of the field that holds an object's size. If the user wants to create a very large object, he or she should make a separate object for each logical part of the object and install these as instance variables of the original object. In a large object, any logical parts of the object should be separated out into objects in their own right. Trouble arises when the object has no logical parts or when it is required by an I/O device to be contiguous. Applications programs that use several large bit-maps at once may cause thrashing because each bit-map must be swapped whole. We considered the possibility of allowing LOOM to swap in only part of a large object, so that parts of many of them could be in primary memory at once. If LOOM swaps incomplete objects and attempts to hide this knowledge from the interpreter, the present mechanism for detecting faults will not work. We have not thought of another way of detecting a "miss" in a partial object that is as fast or clean as the current method of testing the leaf bit.

The Hashing Algorithm

The hash algorithm establishes the connection between long

and short addresses. An object's long address is hashed into the object table to see if it is already cached in primary memory. The most important requirement is that almost any arbitrary group of 30,000 objects (out of the $2\uparrow31$ potential long addresses in secondary memory) be able to be cached in primary memory at the same time. Any set of objects that cannot fit into the hash table at the same time must be examined closely to make sure it is extremely unlikely. Hashing a long pointer and getting a hit (discovering that it is indeed cached in primary memory) must be fast. Insertion and deletion must not change the location in the table of any other objects, because the location of an object in the table is the object's short address and is stored in many fields. The hash function must allow high occupancy of the short address space. Hashing a long address and discovering that it is not there is allowed to take longer than detecting a hit, because a hashing miss in the OT will be followed by the creation of a leaf.

Problem: Choosing the proper hashing algorithm
We must choose a hashing function that is fast to compute, fast to detect a hit in the short address space, and places only insignificant restrictions on which objects can be in primary memory at the same time.

Solution: Xor with quadratic reprobes. Limits on certain unusual working sets.
The hashing scheme works like this: The two halves of the 31-bit long address are Xor-ed together to give a 15-bit short address. A reprobe sequence begins with this initial short address and probes at short addresses found by adding squares of integers to the initial address. (To avoid multiplies, successive odd numbers are used as the intervals between probes.) For each probe, LOOM tests the long address of the object at that location in the OT to see if it matches the original long address. Ideally, any arbitrary set of 32K objects from the secondary space could be accommodated in primary memory at once. Because we need to detect quickly that a long address is not in the hash table, we accepted the limitation that certain sets of objects cannot reside together in primary memory. The reprobe chain is 64 tries long. The limit of 64 reprobes means that there exist sets of 65 objects which cannot be in primary memory at the same time. If a loop in a program were ever to access 65 objects which happen to have the same initial hash, LOOM would thrash badly. However, this conflict is not even possible until $2\uparrow21$ long addresses have been used. In a LOOM virtual memory which is full, the chance of a given set of 32K objects containing more than 64 with an identical initial hash is less than $10\uparrow-124$. Congestion from other reprobe chains

clearly dominates collisions within a chain.

Problem: Hash entries may not be moved
Entries in the table must be deleted when an object is no longer needed in primary memory. However, entries may not be moved because the location of an object in the table is its short address (and this is held in the fields of other objects in primary memory). Interspersed in the table are non-hashed entries for immature objects, and these are inserted and removed more rapidly than any other hash table operation. The short address space needs to be maintained at a fixed percent of fullness. The occupancy should be as large as possible (because short addresses are a scarce resource), but not large enough to drive up the average reprobe chain length.

Solution: Must test entire reprobe chain to detect a miss
Since objects cannot be easily moved in the short address space, no other objects are moved when an object is deleted. (The reprobe chains are not fixed up upon deletion.) Thus, the entire chain must be searched to ascertain that a target long address is not in primary memory. Insertion and deletion occur with equal frequency. If a test for presence of a key fails, that key is always inserted. (It is inserted without having to test the reprobe chain again, because the initial probe remembered the first free entry it found.) The probability of success when testing for the presence of a key varies from 0.1 to 1.0 depending on the structure of the objects being faulted in from secondary memory. Some insertions of long addresses are made with the knowledge that the long address is new and not in the primary memory. These insertions are made without searching the entire reprobe chain. Object table entries for newly created immature objects are interspersed with hashed entries. Entries for immature objects come and go without effecting the hashing of mature objects. The occupancy should be as large as possible. The short address space is maintained at 85 percent full, and the chance of a given insertion finding its reprobe chain full is $(.85)\uparrow64$ or $3\times10\uparrow-5$. Since a purge occurs on the average of once every 100 insertions simply to prevent the table from getting too full, purges because of full reprobe chains do not dominate. A large maximum number of reprobes slows the hash routine when it is detecting a "miss," but it also reduces the chances that an object will arrive in primary memory and not be able to find an empty OT entry.

Problem: Imbedding the values of small integers in their pointers
In the standard resident Smalltalk-80 system, SmallIntegers are represented differently from other objects. Part of the address

space of objects is reserved for the integers from -16K to +16K. The value of the integer is held in the pointer itself, so these objects have no fields or OT entries. Encoding the value of a SmallInteger in its pointer enables the interpreter to execute +, -, *, /, and the comparison operators by doing arithmetic directly on the object pointers. SmallInteger arithmetic occurs often and using literal integer pointers saves time. Since SmallIntegers are common, the encoding also saves space.

Solution: Reserve part of the primary space for literal integers
Smalltalk already knows not to try to load fields from SmallIntegers, so LOOM will never be asked to fault on one. LOOM reserves the same set of short addresses for integers as the resident system did. LOOM must store pointers to SmallIntegers in fields of objects in secondary storage. A special flag value in the high-order 16 bits of a long address means that the low 16 bits represent the short pointer of a SmallInteger. The literal representation of integer values does not cause any trouble for LOOM.

Reference Counting

Here we provide the details of the dual level reference counting scheme sketched earlier. The major goal is to make the common operations of increasing and decreasing a refernece count go as fast as in a non-virtual memory system.

Problem: Two purposes for reference counts
Reference counting keeps track of the number of pointers to each object and actually serves two separate purposes. One purpose is to detect when the total count of any object goes to zero. The other is to detect when the last short pointer to any object disappears so that the short pointer may be reused. Both purposes must be served with a minimum number of accesses to secondary storage.

Solution: Two counts, immature object uses only one. Delta reference count
The primary reference count holds the number of short pointers to an object and the secondary count holds the number of long pointers. We have chosen the definitions of the counts so that both goals are easy to accomplish. When the primary count goes to zero, the short address has no pointers to it and may be reused. At that time, the secondary count must be checked. If it is also zero, the object has no references from secondary memory either, and may be reclaimed. All of the complication that follows is directed at minimizing accesses to secondary storage.

Immature objects have no representation in secondary storage and it is important that they can be reclaimed without checking there. These short-lived objects are created at a high rate, so it is important that their reference counting and reclamation not use secondary storage. When the primary count of an object goes to zero and the object has no long address, it is reclaimed immediately.

Suppose a field of an object is being brought from secondary to primary memory. The pointer in that field must be converted to a short pointer. The short pointer points to either a representation of the target object that already existed in primary memory, or to a new leaf created for this purpose. The pre-existing object or the leaf is now losing a reference from a long pointer and gaining one from a short pointer. LOOM records this by raising the primary count of the object and lowering its secondary count. Normally the act of lowering the object's secondary count would require fetching the object from secondary storage, an act not required just to make a pointer to the object. LOOM avoids the access by keeping the net change of the object's secondary count with the object in primary memory. This **delta reference count** is shown in the center of Figure 9. Path A in the figure shows the act of moving one count from the delta count to the primary count when a long pointer to the object is converted to a short pointer. Path B moves a count the other way when a short pointer is converted to a long pointer (because the field that holds the pointer is being purged from primary memory). Only when the object's image in secondary memory is fetched for other purposes does LOOM correct the object's secondary count by adding delta to it. Path C shows the secondary count being updated, after which delta becomes zero. Delta may be either positive or negative.

We can squeeze in one other savings by using the delta count. Eventually the object's primary reference count will go to zero, and it will be time to rewrite the object in secondary memory and remove it from primary memory. If it is known to be clean (it was only read and not changed), LOOM could avoid actually fetching and modifying the object in secondary storage. On first glance it appears that the write can't be avoided because even clean objects must have their reference counts updated. However, if delta happens to be zero, the secondary count is already correct and no access to secondary memory is needed. The trick is to choose the right value for delta when the object is originally fetched from secondary memory. We set delta on the assumption that in the long term, the number of pointers to the object will show no net change. When this turns out to be true, LOOM saves a trip to secondary memory. (Exception: If delta is zero, and the secondary reference count is also zero, failing to look in secondary memory is incorrect. We should go there to free the object's space. To avoid this bad case, we require that when secondary counts are cached in the delta count, the remaining reference count in secondary memory is always positive.)

Problem: *Reference counts must be fast*

The act of storing one pointer over another in the interpreter must not be slower than in simple, single-level reference counting schemes.

Solution: *Overflow is an exception condition*

As mentioned before, all pointers in all fields that the interpreter sees are short pointers. When the interpreter stores one pointer over another, it raises the primary count of the new pointer and lowers the primary count of the old pointer. There are two exceptional conditions that take longer than normal to handle. When the primary count goes to zero, the object may have a total count of zero and may need to be reclaimed. In addition, LOOM keeps a table of objects whose primary counts have overflowed and sets the overflow bit in any object whose count is large. Whenever a count overflows or goes to zero, the bit must be checked and counts may need to be moved, as shown in paths D and E in Figure 9. Reclaiming an object or looking in the overflow table is an exceptional operation, so, as will be discussed later, LOOM delays acting on primary count overflow or underflow until the current bytecode has finished. Changing primary counts is as fast as any reference counting scheme can go, and is compatible with various schemes for deferring the reference counting of objects on the Smalltalk stack [Wirf83][Deut76].

Resuming After a Virtual Memory Operation

Problem: *How does the interpreter resume computation after a LOOM operation?*

As with any virtual memory system, there are two strategies for resuming computation after a virtual memory operation, such as an object fault. One is to keep absolutely all of the state of the user's computation, and continue from the exact point where the fault occurred. The other strategy is to restart at some convienient unit of computation. Saving all state can be complicated and costly. On the other hand, backing up to a standard place puts restrictions on the order of state-altering operations.

Solution: *Restart the current bytecode*

Many computers restart instructions after taking a page fault. In LOOM, we restart the current Smalltalk bytecode after any virtual memory intervention. To restart successfully, the bytecode must do all operations that may trigger virtual memory activity first, before changing any permanent state. State changes occur when fields of objects are stored into, or when new objects are allocated. For example, the primitive that does floating point addition examines the contents of two objects of class Float, computes the sum, and creates an instance of class Float to hold the answer. Under LOOM, the primitive cannot create the new empty instance of Float first, before it examines the arguments. If either addend were a leaf, and caused an object fault, another instance of Float would be allocated when the primitive restarted, causing the first one to get lost. All objects involved in a bytecode or primitive are touched before any allocation or permanent state change occurs. This allows restarting after a virtual memory operation.

The two kinds of unexpected virtual memory operations are object faults and a failure to allocate a new object. (Allocation fails if the allocator cannot find enough primary memory space or a new short address.) In addition, virtual memory activity needed to service a reference count overflow or underflow is a potentially large source of restarts. Since the bytecode can complete its work without having to wait for the reference count change to actually occur, we place any overflow or underflow of reference counts on a queue and delay their effects until after the bytecode is finished.

Problem: *Multiple state changes in the same bytecode*

There are three situations that have two or more state changes are intermixed with possible LOOM calls. These cannot simply

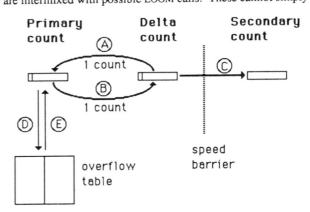

Figure 9. Two level reference counting scheme. The delta count is a cache of the change in the object's secondary count.

be restarted and must remember their intermediate state when a virtual memory operation occurs.

Solution: A special state -- and make some objects unpurgable
Two of the situations have just two permanent state changes. For these, the interpreter remembers when it is between state changes, and LOOM resumes that special state if a virtual memory operation interrupts the bytecode. When Smalltalk sends a message and the code for the message cannot be found, it sends the message *doesNotUnderstand:* instead. *doesNotUnderstand:* needs an argument that is an array of all the arguments to the message that failed. After a storage allocation for the array to store the arguments, and after removing the arguments from the stack, the interpreter sends *doesNotUnderstand:*, which can cause arbitrarily many object faults. The primitive message *perform:with:with:* has exactly the same problem. It must package its arguments and then launch a "send" of a different message. The interpreter must create a special state by marking a register when it is about to execute one of these cases, and clear it after the operation succeeds.

The third intractable state change is so complicated that we forbid virtual memory operations while it is in progress. The primitives in the Smalltalk-80 virtual machine that implement process switching can cause a large number of faults while modifying a substantial amount of state (the lists of active processes). The bytecode restarting mechanism assumes that a single process is currently executing and some specific bytecode is next to be executed. Rather than define many new states for the virtual memory to return to (the variations of being between processes), we forbid virtual memory activity in the middle of a process switch. This means that instances of class Process, Semaphore, and LinkedList are not allowed to cause faults. Instances of these classes are **unpurgable** (permanently immature). Unpurgable objects have a special flag in their long address field and are not allowed to leave primary memory. If the restriction of instances of these classes from secondary memory ever becomes a problem, they can be made purgable at the cost of some microcode space and complication in the process switching primitives.

Surprising Constraints on the Design

One of the surprising things about the design of a virtual memory is the large impact of relatively minor aspects of the system specifications. We spent a large part of the design time for LOOM accommodating necessary but little-known features

of the Smalltalk-80 langauge. All of these requirements were associated with one or other of the Smalltalk primitives.

Problem: Testing if two pointers point to the same object
The equivalence message in Smalltalk (==) tells whether two objects are the same object. Under LOOM, an object has either a short pointer, or a long pointer, or both, and one or more forwarding blocks may stand between a pointer and the actual object it represents. Which two pointers should LOOM compare to determine if they point to the same actual object?

Solution: Fetch a field from each, then compare short pointers
We solve this by loading a field from each of the objects being compared. This causes both of them to enter primary memory, become full objects (as opposed to leaves), and trace through any forwarding blocks they may have. A simple comparison of their short pointers then determines if they are equivalent.

Problem: Smalltalk hash must be constant for the lifetime of an object
In Smalltalk, each object responds to the *hash* message. The hash is a number used to decide where to put the object in hash tables or dictionaries. It should not be confused with the hash that LOOM uses to associate short pointers with long pointers. The only important property of the Smalltalk hash is that it must remain constant during the lifetime of an object. In the resident Smalltalk-80 system, the hash was simply the short address of the object, returned as an integer. In LOOM, the short address is different every time an object is in primary memory. An object begins life with no long address, so neither of these addresses is constant over the lifetime of the object.

Solution: Each object holds its Smalltalk hash in a field
One solution is to assign the long address when the object is created, and use a number derived from it as the hash. However, because of the *become:* primitive, explained below, even the long address may change during the life of an object. As a result, we were forced to add an extra field to every object in the system to hold an arbitrarily assigned number to be the hash. The number installed in the hash field is the short address of the object when it was first created and it stays constant over the life of the object.

Problem: become: swaps the contents of two objects
The *become:* primitive swaps two objects. It does this in the resident Smalltalk-80 system by changing the OT entry of the first object to point at the body of the second, and vice-versa.

The effect is to make all pointers to the first object now point to the second object, without having to locate the fields that point to the objects. (The short address of the first object becomes the short address of the second object.) The *become:* primitive is used to grow Arrays in place and to add fields to existing instances of a class. In LOOM, objects are packed tightly in secondary memory, and pointed at without indirection, so growing an object and allowing it to keep the same long address is impossible.

Solution: Use forwarding blocks in secondary memory
We introduce forwarding blocks in secondary memory so that an object can be relocated when it grows. Only objects that have participated in a *become:* that changed their size need a forwarding block. In LOOM, the *become:* primitive is a mess, as shown in Figure 10. All forwarding blocks are followed during a fault, and are circumvented when the fields pointing at them are rewritten to secondary memory.

Hash, ==, and *become:* have forced us to seal off Loom's internal identifiers for objects from the Smalltalk-80 language and system code. Since Loom's identification number for an object is not available to the clients of the virtual memory, there should be no more problems associated with Loom's changing the identifier of an object. This is not true, however! The enumeration primitives, *someInstance* and *nextInstance* are sensitive to an object's identifier changing, even though those identifiers are completely inaccessible at the Smalltalk level.

Problem: Enumerating the members of a class requires an ordering of objects
someInstance returns a specific already-existing instance of a class of objects. Subsequent calls on *nextInstance* return in turn all other instances of the class, with no repetition. During the enumeration, between calls on *nextInstance*, an arbitrary amount of computation may go on, including full or partial enumerations of other classes. As long as the user does not create new instances of the class, the enumeration must not skip any instances or return any twice. If the user is enumerating instances for the purpose of executing *become:* on each one, the user must collect all instances first, then *become:* them afterwards. (This restriction is part of the official specification of the *become:* primitive.) The user may abandon the enumeration in the middle without informing the system. In systems with fixed object names, these requirements can be met as follows: *someInstance* returns the instance with the lowest address, and *nextInstance* delivers the one whose address in next in ascending order. In LOOM, the instances of

a class must be forced into an ordering that will be preserved in spite of an arbitrary amount of virtual memory activity caused by intervening computation. Extra data structures to hold the state of the search are not useful, because they can be overwhelmed by the existence of a large number of partially completed or abandoned searches.

Solution: Scan secondary memory after forcing objects to go there
Our solution is to force all instances of the target class to mature and claim an address in secondary memory, and then to use long addresses as an ordering. During *someInstance*, we scan primary memory, mature any immature instances of the class, and look for any instances that are unpurgable. Unpurgable instances are returned first, and then secondary memory is scanned in ascending order.

Scanning the entire virtual space takes a long time when the space is large. When the speed of enumeration becomes a problem we advise users to create data structures, such as inversions and linked lists of instances, to hold the objects they wish to search often. We have made several changes to Smalltalk kernel classes to reduce the number of searches invoked by system code. Assuming that some searches are unavoidable, we have proposed but not implemented a scheme to reduce the fraction of secondary space that must be searched. Each class would keep a bit-vector with a bit representing a portion of secondary address space, and the mature routine would turn on bits for those portions actually containing an instance of the class. Most classes will have instances sparsely distributed in secondary memory. For this minimal overhead, LOOM can avoid searching large parts of the secondary space.

Meeting the criteria of these little-known primitives adds a lot of complication and machine code to LOOM, but does not effect its average performance.

Threats to the Speed of the Interpreter

Problem: Interpreter needs to handle certain objects quickly
The Smalltalk-80 interpreter knows the names of certain objects, mostly classes whose instances must be treated specially. The object that represents the class SmallInteger is one such object. The conservative way for the interpreter to hold onto these objects, is to require them to be mature, and to reference them by their long addresses. Every time the special object is needed, the interpreter must hash the long address into the OT to find the object's current short address. This

Object Table   Primary Memory   Secondary Memory

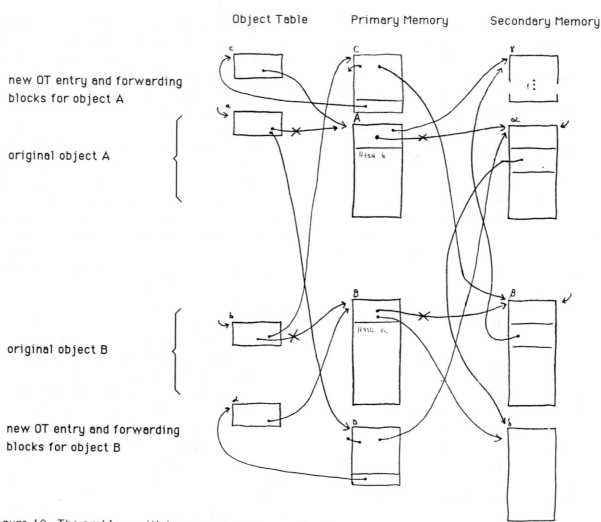

new OT entry and forwarding
blocks for object A

original object A

original object B

new OT entry and forwarding
blocks for object B

Figure 10. The problem with become:. In this example, We executed A become: B when A and B were mature.

approach slows high bandwidth operations like arithmetic and message lookup, complicates the interpreter, and wastes microcode space.

Solution: Make special objects unpurgable and use short addresses

It is much simpler to hold the short addresses of these special objects, and forbid them from leaving primary memory so that the short addresses will not change. Unpurgable objects have a special flag in their long address field and are not allowed to leave primary memory. Keeping the 27 objects that are known to the interpreter in primary memory, along with all instances of Process, Semaphore, and LinkedList, decreases the available working set by only a small number of objects.

Problem: Message lookup cannot use short addresses

The Smalltalk-80 interpreter hashes the name of a message into

a message dictionary in order to find the code that the receiving object should execute. The name of the message is an instance of class Symbol, and the non-Loom interpreter uses the Symbol's short address as its Smalltalk hash (see the previous section *Smalltalk hash must be constant for the lifetime of an object*). How can message lookup continue to work when an object's short address is just a temporary name?

One solution is to make all instances of class Symbol unpurgable. If they are forced to stay in primary memory, they will always have the same short address and the existing message lookup code in the interpreter will work. Making Symbols unpurgable, however, consumes too many short addresses. As many as 21% of all objects in the entire *virtual* space are Symbols. A large LOOM system may have more Symbols than short addresses.

Solution: Message lookup uses an object's Smalltalk hash

As discussed above, every object has a special "hash" field that contains a number which does not change. We modify the interpreter to use the Smalltalk hash of each Symbol (instead of its short address) as the key for message lookup. This is slower than using the short address, but a cache for previously successful message lookups shields the interpreter from this slight slowdown. The purpose of an instance of· class Symbol is to be a unique name for a Smalltalk message. If the Symbol at a location in a dictionary and the Symbol being looked up are the same object, the message has been found. At each probe in the message dictionary, the Symbol there is compared with the Symbol being looked up.

Problem: Message lookup should work on leaves

We would like the Symbols in a message dictionary to be allowed to be leaves, instead of full objects. The issue here is not the space occupied by the full Symbols, but the time needed to fault on a message dictionary. A leaf can be created for a long address without looking in secondary memory. Bringing in the message dictionary object and creating leaves for all of its Symbols requires just one access to secondary memory. However, expanding twenty leaves into the Symbols they represent would require twenty reads in secondary memory. Clearly the interpeter should be able to look messages up while the Symbols in the dictionary are leaves. The normal comparison for two objects, the == primitive, fetches a field from each object and them compares the objects' short pointers. Fetching a field from a leaf expands it. How can the interpreter compare two Symbols if they are leaves?

Solution: Compare short addresses and forbid forwarding blocks to Symbols

The interpeter could compare the long addresses of the two Symbols to see if they are the same object. For this to work, a leaf in a message dictionary must not represent a forwarding block in secondary memory. We can enforce this by forbidding Symbols to participate in the become: operation, which creates forwarding blocks on the disk. Symbols are not suppose to change in any case, so this is not a restriction. It would be faster to compare short addresses instead of long addresses. To make this work, we must forbid Symbols from having forwarding blocks in primary memory. A Symbol gets a forwarding block in primary memory when it matures. Not allowing Symbols to go through the maturation process means that newly created Symbols must stay immature and thus be unpurgable.

The final rules for looking up a message in LOOM are these: Symbols present at system generation time are mature and cannot participate in a *become:*. Newer Symbols are marked unpurgable by the routine that matures objects. The interpreter probes a message dictionary according to the hash field of the Symbol being looked up, and compares the Symbol's short address with short addresses (of leaves) it finds in the dictionary. We know that the performance of message lookup is shielded by the massage cache (we once did linear lookup in message dictionaries and only lost 5% of performance), so this change will not effect speed.

Summary of high bandwidth operations

Several of the algorithms used by LOOM require tests during common interpreter operations. Here is the list of high-bandwidth interpreter operations annotated with the additional work that LOOM causes.

> *Load a field from an object.*

Before the first field is loaded from an object, it must be tested to see if it is a leaf, if it is untouched, or if it is a forwarding block. The bits for these exceptional conditions are in the object's OT entry, and they can all be tested at the same time by masking out the other bits and testing for zero. This only costs one extra microinstruction in speed. If the test fails, the interpreter has inline code to mark an untouched object touched and to follow a forwarding block. For each additional field loaded from the object, no checks are necessary.

> *Store a new pointer in a field.*

Clear the clean bit in the object. Reference counting is completely unchanged by LOOM. Overflow and underflow are detected by the ALU during the reference counting arithmetic. When an exception is detected, the actual work is done between bytecodes. An interrupt in the instruction fetch unit of the Dorado stops the interpreter between bytecodes to handle exceptions. There is no speed penalty between bytecodes when no reference count has overflowed or underflowed.

> *Send a Smalltalk message.*

Mark a register to flag that a message send is in progress. If the message is not understood and an object fault occurs, the flag tells how to resume the instruction. Before the send, also set an interrupt in the instruction fetch unit. In the normal case when the send succeeds, the interrupt will wake up between bytecodes and clear the flag register. (Using the message's hash field instead of its short address as a hash key takes no measurable extra time, because it is shielded by the message lookup cache.)

> *Create a new object or destroy an old one.*

No speed penalty when a free object of the proper size is available. When splitting a large block, search for a surplus short address and check for running low on short addresses. When an object is freed, check to make sure it was immature (that is, it has no long address and thus is not allocated in secondary storage). If the object is mature, LOOM must test the object's delta count and free the object in secondary memory.

The net effect is that the LOOM Smalltalk-80 system, running with the working set already in primary memory, performs at a speed close to the speed of a non-Loom system. The largest speed difference comes from the shortage of microcode memory space. The microstore of the Dorado was full before LOOM was added to the resident Smalltalk-80 system. A number of optimizations had to be removed from microcode to make room for the microcode that LOOM need. We removed the storage compactor, shortened the microcode primitive dispatch table, and moved 10 Smalltalk primitives from microcode to machine code. LOOM runs the Smalltalk compiler benchmark (a reasonable representative test [McCa83]) .76 times as fast as the equivalent resident Smalltalk-80 system. Only a small part of this slowdown is the result of tests that LOOM makes. Our removal of optimizations in the Smalltalk interpreter account for the rest.

We can only mention in passing two major optimizations which could be added to LOOM. Leaves are created as place holders for objects in fields of an objects brought into primary memory. Many of these stubs of objects are never expanded into whole objects. To save the time now used creating and destroying leaves, we can allow a field in an object in primary may contain a special flag called **lambda**. A lambda in a field means that LOOM has delayed assigning a short address (building a leaf) to the object pointed to by the field. If a short address for that object (pointed to by the field) is ever needed, the object's long address must be found again. LOOM must go the image of the parent object in secondary memory, look in the corresponding field, retrieve the long address of the object from the field, and then create a leaf in primary space. This "lazy leaf creation" saves time and short addresses if most lazy

leaves are never expanded while the parent is cached in primary space.

Glenn Krasner has suggested a scheme that gets most of the benefits of lambdas for little of their cost. About 78% of the pointer fields in objects in primary memory are indexed fields, as opposed to named fields. Indexed fields are the fields in variable length objects like Arrays or Dictionaries. There are exactly seven places in the interpreter that load from indexed fields and one place that stores into them. The extra execution time and number of microinstructions required to detect and handle lambdas in indexed fields is very modest. Besides the *at:* and a*t:put:* primitives and the message sending code, the LOOM code that reclaims mature objects must be modified to test for lambda. By allowing lambdas in indexed fields, but not in named fields, we can permit a large fraction of all leaves to be candidates for replacement by lambdas. (For lambdas to be effective in MethodDictionaries, we must make the dictionary entries sparse, so that miss in the dictionary lookup will be detected without encountering too many lambdas. We are looking for effective ways to use memory space, so this is no problem.) Lambdas reduce the number of leaves needed in primary memory. More objects can fit into the primary address space, and more real memory can be useful.

Conclusion

The LOOM virtual memory provides the illusion of a large virtual space of objects on a machine with a narrow word width. The user enjoys a fast execution speed because the language interpeter sees only short object pointers, and on a narrow machine short pointers are faster to handle than long pointers. The disadvantages of LOOM are that it is a complex system with complicated object translation code, and that beyond a certain limit, adding real memory to the system will not increase its performance.

Acknowledgements

LOOM was designed in the Fall of 1979 and the Spring of 1980. Implementation and improvement spanned a period of five years and included simulations of LOOM from within the Smalltalk-76 and Smalltalk-80 systems, implementation on the Alto and the Dorado, and implementation of the swapping code in Smalltalk and BCPL. The author was responsible for the project and did most of the implementation. Glenn Krasner and Diana Merry helped with the implementation, along with Ricki

Blau, Dan Ingalls, Steve Putz, and Dave Robson. The author is indebted to the following people for suggestions they made on the initial design of LOOM: Dan Ingalls, Peter Deutsch, Glenn Krasner, Danny Bobrow, and Larry Tesler. These same people also offered valuable improvements to LOOM later. Jim Stamos and Ricki Blau did important analysis and measurement work. Adele Goldberg provided support and guidance and Bob Flegal reviewed the manuscript and made valuable suggestions.

References

[Ball83] Ballard, Stoney, and Stephen Shirron, "The Design and Implementation of VAX/Smalltalk-80", in *Smalltalk-80: Bits of History, Words of Advice*, Glenn Krasner, ed., Addison-Wesley, Reading, Mass., 1983.

[Deut76] Deutsch, L. P. and D. G. Bobrow, "An Efficient Incremental Realtime Garbage Collector", *CACM*, October 1976.

[Gold83] Goldberg, Adele, and Dave Robson, *Smalltalk-80: The Language and its Implementation*, Addison-Wesley, Reading, Mass., 1983.

[Inga83] Ingalls, Dan "The Evolution of the Smalltalk Virtual Machine", in *Smalltalk-80: Bits of History, Words of Advice*, Glenn Krasner, ed., Addison-Wesley, Reading, Mass., 1983.

[Kaeh77] Kaehler, Ted, "Name Composting", Xerox internal memo, 29 April 1977.

[Kaeh81] Kaehler, Ted, "Virtual Memory for an Object-Oriented Language", *Byte* vol. 6, no. 8, August 1981.

[Kaeh83] Kaehler, Ted, and Glenn Krasner, "LOOM - Large Object Oriented Memory for Smalltalk-80 Systems", in *Smalltalk-80: Bits of History, Words of Advice*, Glenn Krasner, ed., Addison-Wesley, Reading, Mass., 1983.

[Lamp81] Lampson, Butler W., and Kenneth A. Pier, "A Processor for a High-performance Personal Computer", Seventh International Symposium on Computer Architecture, SIGARCH/IEEE, La Baule, France, May 1980; (also in Xerox PARC report CSL-81-1, January 1981).

[McCa83] McCall, Kim, "The Smalltalk-80 Benchmarks", in *Smalltalk-80: Bits of History, Words of Advice*, Glenn Krasner, ed., Addison-Wesley, Reading, Mass., 1983.

[Stam82] Stamos, James W., "A Large Object-Oriented Virtual Memory: Grouping Strategies, Measurements, and Performance", Xerox PARC report SCG-82-2, May 1982. (His undergraduate thesis at MIT.)

[Stam84] Stamos, James W., "Grouping Objects to Enhance Performance of a Paged Virtual Memory", *ACM Transactions on Computer Systems*, May 1984.

[Stam85] Stamos, James W., "A Large Object-Oriented Virtual Memory: Simulated Performance and Evaluation", to be published (check this).

[Unga84] Ungar, David, "Generation Scavenging: A Non-disruptive High Performance Storage Reclamation Algorithm", ACM SIGSOFT/SIGPLAN Software Engieering Symposium on Practical Software Development Environments, Pittsburgh, Pa., April 1984.

[Wirf83] Wirfs-Brock, Allen, "Design Decisions for Smalltalk-80 Implementors", in *Smalltalk-80: Bits of History, Words of Advice*, Glenn Krasner, ed., Addison-Wesley, Reading, Mass., 1983, p54.

Author Biography

Gerald E. Peterson is currently a Principal Investigator in Automated Reasoning for McDonnell Douglas Aerospace Information Services Company, St. Louis, Missouri. He holds B.S. (1961), M.A. (1963), and Ph.D. (1965) degress in mathematics from the University of Utah. He taught at the University of Utah, Brigham Young University, the University of Missouri at St. Louis, and Southern Illinois University at Edwardsville prior to joining McDonnell Douglas on a full-time basis. From 1981 to 1986 he worked part-time in software engineering methodology for McDonnell Douglas Astronautics Company. During this time he developed an interest in object-oriented computing. He is the author or coauthor of several research papers in mathematics and computer science.

Other IEEE Computer Society Press Titles

MONOGRAPHS

Analyzing Computer Architectures
Written by J.C. Huck and M.J. Flynn
(ISBN 0-8186-8857-2); 206 pages

Desktop Publishing for the Writer:
Designing, Writing, and Developing
Written by Richard Ziegfeld and John Tarp
(ISBN 0-8186-8840-8); 380 pages

Digital Image Warping
Written by George Wolberg
(ISBN 0-8186-8944-7); 340 pages

Integrating Design and Test—CAE Tools for ATE Programming
Written by K.P. Parker
(ISBN 0-8186-8788-6); 160 pages

JSP and JSD—The Jackson Approach to Software Development
(Second Edition)
Written by J.R. Cameron
(ISBN 0-8186-8858-0); 560 pages

National Computer Policies
Written by Ben G. Matley and Thomas A. McDannold
(ISBN 0-8186-8784-3); 192 pages

Physical Level Interfaces and Protocols
Written by Uyless Black
(ISBN 0-8186-8824-2); 240 pages

Protecting Your Proprietary Rights in Computer
and High-Technology Industries
Written by Tobey B. Marzouk, Esq.
(ISBN 0-8186-8754-1); 224 pages

TUTORIALS

Advanced Computer Architecture
Edited by D.P. Agrawal
(ISBN 0-8186-0667-3); 400 pages

Advances in Distributed System Reliability
Edited by Suresh Rai and Dharma P. Agrawal
(ISBN 0-8186-8907-2); 352 pages

Computer and Network Security
Edited by M.D. Abrams and H.J. Podell
(ISBN 0-8186-0756-4); 448 pages

Computer Architecture
Edited by D.D. Gajski, V.M. Milutinovic, H. Siegel, and B.P. Furht
(ISBN 0-8186-0704-1); 602 pages

Computer Arithmetic I
Edited by Earl E. Swartzlander, Jr.
(ISBN 0-8186-8931-5); 398 pages

Computer Arithmetic II
Edited by Earl E. Swartzlander, Jr.
(ISBN 0-8186-8945-5); 412 pages

Computer Communications: Architectures,
Protocols and Standards (Second Edition)
Edited by William Stallings
(ISBN 0-8186-0790-4); 448 pages

Computer Graphics Hardware: Image Generation and Display
Edited by H.K. Reghbati and A.Y.C. Lee
(ISBN 0-8186-0753-X); 384 pages

Computer Graphics: Image Synthesis
Edited by Kenneth Joy, Nelson Max, Charles Grant,
and Lansing Hatfield
(ISBN 0-8186-8854-8); 380 pages

Computer Networks (Fourth Edition)
Edited by M.D. Abrams and I.W. Cotton
(ISBN 0-8186-0568-5); 512 pages

Computers for Artificial Intelligence Applications
Edited by B. Wah and G.J. Li
(ISBN 0-8186-0706-8); 656 pages

Database Management
Edited by J.A. Larson
(ISBN 0-8186-0714-9); 448 pages

Digital Image Processing and Analysis:
Volume 1—Digital Image Processing
Edited by R. Chellappa and A.A. Sawchuk
(ISBN 0-8186-0665-7); 736 pages

Digital Image Processing and Analysis:
Volume 2—Digital Image Analysis
Edited by R. Chellappa and A.A. Sawchuk
(ISBN 0-8186-0666-5); 680 pages

Digital Private Branch Exchanges (PBXs)
by Edwin Coover
(ISBN 0-8186-0829-3); 394 pages

Distributed Computing Network Reliability
Edited by Suresh Rai and Dharma Agrawal
(ISBN 0-8186-8908-0); 357 pages

Distributed Software Engineering
Edited by Sol Shatz and Jia-Ping Wang
(ISBN 0-8186-8856-4); 294 pages

DSP-Based Testing of Analog and
Mixed Signal Circuits
Edited by Matthew Mahoney
(ISBN 0-8186-0785-8); 272 pages

Fault Tolerant Computing
Edited by V. Nelson and B. Carroll
(ISBN 0-8186-8677-4); 428 pages

Formal Verification of Hardware Design
Edited by Michael Yoeli
(ISBN 0-8186-9017-8); 340 pages

Hard Real-Time Systems
Edited by J.A. Stankovic and K. Ramamritham
(ISBN 0-8186-0819-6); 624 pages

Human Factors in Software Development
(Second Edition)
Edited by Bill Curtis
(ISBN 0-8186-0577-4); 736 pages

Integrated Services Digital Networks (ISDN)
(Second Edition)
Edited by William Stallings
(ISBN 0-8186-0823-4); 406 pages

Local Network Technology (Third Edition)
Edited by William Stallings
(ISBN 0-8186-0825-0); 512 pages

Microprogramming and Firmware Engineering
Edited by V. Milutinovic
(ISBN 0-8186-0839-0); 416 pages

Modeling and Control of Automated Manufacturing Systems
Edited by A. A. Desrochers
(ISBN 0-8186-8916-1); 384 pages

Nearest Neighbor Pattern Classification Techniques
Edited by Belur V. Dasarathy
(ISBN 0-8186-8930-7); 464 pages

For Further Information Call 1-800-CS-BOOKS or Write:

IEEE Computer Society Press, 10662 Los Vaqueros Circle, PO Box 3014,
Los Alamitos, California 90720-1264, USA

IEEE Computer Society, 13, avenue de l'Aquilon,
B-1200 Brussels, BELGIUM

IEEE Computer Society, Ooshima Building, 2-19-1 Minami-Aoyama,
Minato-ku, Tokyo 107, JAPAN

DATE DUE